Development and Underdevelopment

Development and Underdevelopment

SECOND EDITION

Development and Underdevelopment

• • • • • • • • • •

The Political Economy of Global Inequality

edited by

Mitchell A. Seligson
John T Passé-Smith

LYNNE
RIENNER
PUBLISHERS

BOULDER
LONDON

For
Susan Berk-Seligson
and
Mary Sue Passé-Smith

Published in the United States of America in 1998 by
Lynne Rienner Publishers, Inc.
1800 30th Street, Boulder, Colorado 80301

and in the United Kingdom by
Lynne Rienner Publishers, Inc.
3 Henrietta Street, Covent Garden, London WC2E 8LU

© 1998 by Lynne Rienner Publishers, Inc. All rights reserved

Library of Congress Cataloging-in-Publication Data
Development and underdevelopment : the political economy of global
  inequality / edited by Mitchell A. Seligson and John T Passé-Smith.
  —2nd ed.
      p. cm.
  Includes bibliographical references (p.) and index.
  ISBN 1-55587-794-X (pbk. : alk. paper)
    1. Developing countries—Economic conditions. 2. Economic
  development. 3. Income distribution. 4. Capitalism. 5. Economic
  history—1945– 6. Social history—1945– I. Seligson, Mitchell A.
  II. Passé-Smith, John T
  HC59.7.D4453   1998
  338.9—dc21   98-14864
                                                                    CIP

British Cataloguing in Publication Data
A Cataloguing in Publication record for this book
is available from the British Library.

Printed and bound in the United States of America

⊗   The paper used in this publication meets the requirements
     of the American National Standard for Permanence of
     Paper for Printed Library Materials Z39.48-1984.

5 4 3 2 1

Contents

PART 7   CONCLUSION

Preface

Few residents of industrialized nations are not forcibly struck by the vast gap in wealth separating them from those who reside in the world's poor countries. Whether they travel to those countries or visit them vicariously through television and film, the gap is probably the single most vivid impression that remains in their minds. A second gap, one that exists within the poor countries themselves, is found between the tiny affluent minority and the vast majority of the poor. This dichotomy can be observed in urban areas as well as in rural villages.

Two questions concern most social scientists who conduct research in the Third World, where they experience these gaps firsthand. First, what causes the gaps? Second, are the gaps narrowing or widening? This book attempts to provide the clearest answers that these same social scientists have been able to offer to date.

This book is a substantially revised version of its two predecessors, *The Gap Between Rich and Poor* (1984) and *Development and Underdevelopment: The Political Economy of Inequality* (1993). The original volume grew out of a seminar taught by Mitchell Seligson at the University of Arizona. In preparing for the seminar, he recognized that much research addressed the two questions posed here, and he attempted to organize that material for his students. Although a number of collections examined political and economic development, none directly addressed the questions he sought to answer. In addition, the then most recent theoretical and empirical research on dependency and world systems was generally absent from those volumes.

When the seminar was first taught, the students attending helped to refine the thinking that went into its preparation. One of those students, John Passé-Smith, was so stimulated by the subject matter that he wrote his doctoral dissertation on it. When Seligson was about to begin a sabbatical,

Passé-Smith suggested that a new edition of the volume be produced, incorporating the latest scholarship on the dual gaps between rich and poor. Hence, this collaborative effort emerged, with Seligson and Passé-Smith serving as coeditors.

We have sought to retain the classics included in the first version, but much new material has emerged since the early 1980s when the original volume was prepared, and more has emerged since the 1993 edition was published. As a result, of the thirty-five selections in this volume, fifteen are new. We now have better, more extensive databases on which to judge the magnitude and direction of the gaps between rich and poor. Economic historians have pushed back in time the data on national wealth statistics, and new measures of the contemporary wealth of nations are available based on purchasing power rather than exchange rate comparisons. As a result, new literature is available on the prospects of "convergence" among the world economies, a theme we treat in Part 3 of this new edition.

There has been a recent and impressive revival of cultural explanations of development, some of which have been supported by large cross-national data sets. Part 4 contains some of the classic pieces, as well as more recent contributions to this approach. Dependency and world-system thinking have prospered less well, however, perhaps because of the fall of socialist systems throughout the world. Yet many of the concepts of those theories have been incorporated into our thinking, and therefore we have devoted Part 5 to what we consider the best material on the subject.

The newest and most dynamic area emerges in Part 6, in which the focus of the causes of the gap moves back from the international system and lands squarely at the door of national governments. Some research seems to show convincingly that it is misdirected state policies that slow growth and increase the gap between rich and poor people. This research has grown into a school of thought called *rent-seeking* and another known as *urban bias*. Some scholars have rejected this thesis, arguing instead that the great successes of the East Asian newly industrializing countries (NICs) are the result of historical factors that will not be repeated. Others have suggested that it is not government policies per se but the form of government that exacerbates the gaps. Thus, in Part 6 we examine the impact of democracy on growth and inequality. Part 6 also includes some of the most recent research on the importance of investment in human capital, as well as the negative impact of environmental degradation on economic growth.

We have organized the volume so it will be of maximum utility in the classroom. The seven parts of the book enable the instructor to assign any part as a self-contained unit. We find, however, that the order in which the seven parts are presented creates a logical path the student can easily follow. Parts 1 and 2 provide the basic "facts" of the gap: the size of the gaps between rich and poor countries and between rich and poor people. Part 3 deals with the dynamics question: Is the gap widening or narrowing? Part 4 presents cultural explanations for the gaps. Part 5 covers dependency and world-system theories, with much empirical evidence and case study data supporting both sides of the debate. Part 6 covers the role of the state in stimulating or inhibiting growth and inequality. Finally, we offer some conclusions and directions for future research in Part 7.

We are indebted to numerous people for helping us prepare the revised manuscript. In particular, we thank Mariana Collins for her help with many administrative chores. Also, Mary Sue Passé-Smith worked relentlessly and offered invaluable advice; the book would not have been completed without her help. At the University of Pittsburgh, Mitchell Seligson's graduate and undergraduate assistants, José René Argueta and Katherine Good, ably assisted in the process. Finally, we thank the many authors and publishers who so kindly granted permission for their works to appear here.

Mitchell A. Seligson
John T Passé-Smith

PART 1

· · · · · · · · · · · · · · ·

The Classic Thesis and the Contradictory Evidence: Will the Whole World Eventually Grow Rich?

· · · · · · · · · · · · · · ·

1

· · · · · · ·

The Dual Gaps:
An Updated Overview
of Theory and Research

· · · · · · ·

MITCHELL A. SELIGSON

Classical economic theory tells us that in the end we will all be rich, but this volume contains a great deal of evidence that contradicts that theory. According to W. W. Rostow's thesis (see Chapter 2), underdevelopment is only a stage nations pass through on their way to becoming developed. But the data we have at hand tell a different story. The income gap between rich and poor countries has grown dramatically since World War II. In 1950, the average per capita income (in 1980 U.S. dollars) of low-income countries was $164, whereas the per capita income of the industrialized countries averaged $3,841, yielding an absolute income gap of $3,677. Thirty years later, in 1980, incomes in the poor countries had risen to an average of only $245, whereas those in the industrialized countries had soared to $9,648; the absolute gap stood at $9,403.

For this period, then, clear evidence supports the old adage that "the rich get richer." It is not true, however, that the poor get poorer—not literally, anyway—but that would be a perverse way of looking at these data. A more realistic view of the increases in "wealth" in the poor countries would show that in this thirty-year period their citizens' incomes increased by an average of only $2.70 a year, about what a North American might spend for lunch at a fast-food stand. And in terms of relative wealth, the poor countries certainly did get poorer; the total income (gross national product; GNP) of the low-income countries declined from 4.3 percent of that earned by the industrialized countries in 1950 to a mere 2.5 percent in 1980.[1]

The growth in that gap has continued into the 1990s. By 1995 the gap was wider than ever: the high-income countries had a per capita average of $24,930 versus $430 in the low-income countries, for an absolute gap of $24,500 (1995 U.S. dollars). The relative gap had become even greater, with the income of low-income countries equal to only 1.7 percent that of

3

the industrialized countries. Hence, between 1950 and 1995, the relative gap between rich and poor countries widened by 60 percent.[2]

One might suspect that these data do not reflect the general pattern of growth found throughout the world but may be excessively influenced by the disappointing performance of a few "basket case" nations. That suspicion is unfounded. The low-income countries contain over half of the world's population; 3.2 billion of the world's 5.7 billion people live in countries with per capita incomes that average $430 a year. It is also incorrect to speculate that because the growth rates of some poor countries have recently outperformed those of industrialized countries, the gap will soon narrow. In Chapter 4, John Passé-Smith tells us that it could take Pakistan's 134 million people 495 years to close the gap. Even in the "miracle countries" such as South Korea and Taiwan, where growth rates have been twice as high as those in the industrialized countries, the gap has doubled.

Another gap separates rich from poor: Many developing nations have long experienced a growing gap between their own rich and poor citizens, as the chapters in Part 2 of this volume demonstrate. Many poor people who live in poor countries, therefore, are falling further behind not only the world's rich but also their more affluent countrymen. Moreover, precisely the opposite phenomenon has taken place in the richer countries, where the gap between rich and poor is far narrower. The world's poor, therefore, find themselves in a situation of double jeopardy.

The consequences of these yawning gaps can be witnessed on many levels. In the international arena, tensions between the "haves" and the "have-nots" dominate debates in the United Nations and other international fora. The poor countries demand a New International Economic Order (NIEO), which they hope will result in the transfer of wealth away from the rich countries or at least stem the hemorrhage of the loss of their own wealth. The industrialized countries have responded with foreign aid programs that, by all accounts, have at best made only a small dent in the problem. Indeed, some argue that foreign aid exacerbates the gap.[3] Within the developing countries, domestic stability is frequently tenuous at best, as victims of the gap between rich and poor (along with their sympathizers) seek redress through violent means. The guerrilla fighting that spotted the globe during the Cold War may have been fueled by international conflict, but as Edward N. Muller and Mitchell A. Seligson show in Chapter 8, its root cause can invariably be traced to domestic inequality and deprivation, whether relative or absolute. This remains true in the post–Cold War era.

Thinking and research on the international and domestic gaps between rich and poor have been going through a protracted period of debate that can be traced back to the end of World War II. The war elevated the United States to the position of world leader, and the nation found itself confronted with a Western Europe in ruins. The motivations behind the Marshall Plan to rebuild Europe are debated to this day, but two things remain evident:

Unprecedented amounts of aid were given, and the expected results were rapidly achieved. War-torn industries were rebuilt, new ones were begun, and economic growth quickly resumed.

The successful rebuilding of Europe encouraged many to believe similar success would meet efforts to stimulate growth in the developing world. More often than not, however, such efforts have failed or fallen far below expectations. Even when programs have been effective and nations have seemed well on the way to rapid growth, they nonetheless continued to fall further and further behind the wealthy countries. Moreover, growth seemed almost inevitably to be accompanied by a widening income gap within developing countries. Only in Asia have we seen some reversal of this worldwide trend; poor nations have grown rapidly, whereas income inequality has not worsened and in some cases has even improved. The lessons of Asia, therefore, are important ones.

By the mid-1990s, an impressive collection of research on the "gap" issue had been generated, and we have attempted to include some of the very best of it in this collection. The authors represented here present a comprehensive treatment of the thinking that is evolving on the international and domestic gaps between rich and poor. The studies are not confined to a single academic discipline or geographic area; rather, they reflect a variety of fields, including anthropology, economics, history, political science, psychology, and sociology. Further, the authors have examined the problem from the viewpoint of a single country or region, as well as with a microanalytic approach.

The volume is organized to first give the reader a broad picture that defines the international and domestic gaps between the rich and the poor; that picture is contained in Parts 1 and 2. Part 3 challenges the conventional wisdom on the existence of the international gap. The rest of the volume, Parts 4 through 6, attempts to explain the existence of the gaps.

In Part 1 we present what we call the *classic thesis*, which suggests that the gaps will disappear as development proceeds. A number of economists, most notably W. W. Rostow (Chapter 2), have made this case. But Angus Maddison (Chapter 3) and John T Passé-Smith (Chapter 4) show that the gaps are long lasting and have been growing worse since perhaps the sixteenth century. Part 2 examines domestic inequality. Simon Kuznets (Chapter 5) sees widening domestic income inequality as an almost inevitable by-product of development. Kuznets traces a path that seems to have been followed rather closely by nations that have become industrialized. The process begins with relative domestic equality in the distribution of income. The onset of industrialization produces a significant shift in the direction of inequality and creates a widening gap. Once the industrialization process matures, however, the gap is again reduced. This view is held by those who still regard the Marshall Plan as the model for the resolution of world poverty. The chapters by Montek Ahluwalia (Chapter 6) and Klaus

Deininger and Lyn Squire (Chapter 7) show that the cross-national data on income distribution support the Kuznets perspective.

Whereas Parts 1 and 2 present the basic argument on the extent and duration of the international and domestic gaps, Part 3 examines the evidence for the so-called convergence thesis. This thesis argues that even though Kuznets may have been right, in the long run the rich and the poor are converging (see Moses Abramovitz, Chapter 9). Several authors in Part 3 show, however, that such convergence is in fact an ever-receding dream.

Explanations for the gaps have often focused on different aspects of national culture. We have heard the expression "Germans are so industrious; that is why they are rich," or "the Japanese work so hard; it is no wonder they are so wealthy." Part 4 of this volume presents evidence pro and con on the role of culture in development. Specifically, the cultural values associated with industrialization are seen as foreign to many developing nations, which are deeply attached to more traditional cultural values. According to the cultural thesis, punctuality, hard work, achievement, and other "industrial" values are the keys to unlocking the economic potential of poor countries. Most adherents of this perspective believe such values can be inculcated through deliberate effort; others argue that they will emerge naturally as the result of a worldwide process of diffusion of values functional for development. This perspective has been incorporated into a more general school of thought focusing on the process called *modernization*. Development occurs and the international gap is narrowed when a broad set of modern values *and* institutions is present. The recent success of the Asian economies has led some to speculate that cultural values are found there that foster growth. This view, a variant on Max Weber's old notion of the value of the Protestant ethic, is termed the *Confucian ethic*.

In marked contrast to these two perspectives, which suggest that the phenomena of the disparity are transitory, a third, more recent, school of thought comes to rather different conclusions (see Part 5). The scholars who support this approach—known as *dependentistas*—observe that the economies of developing nations have been shaped in response to forces and conditions established by the industrialized nations and that their development has been both delayed and dependent as a result. The *dependentistas* conclude that poor countries have failed because of the distorted development brought on by dependency relations. A further elaboration on this thinking has emerged in recent years in the form of the world-system perspective developed by Immanuel Wallerstein and his followers. According to this group, since the sixteenth century a world capitalist economy has existed, divided geographically (rather than occupationally, as in the earlier system of empires) into three primary zones: core, semiperiphery, and periphery. The core dominates the system and drains the semiperiphery and periphery of their economic surpluses. Both of these perspectives contend that the gaps will be perpetuated by the nature of the international system and cannot be narrowed unless a major restructuring of that system is undertaken. In Part 5, the dependency and world-system perspectives are presented by the major writers in the field and refuted by others based on careful studies of large data sets.

Part 6 presents the most recent explanation of the gaps, focusing attention on the role of states within the Third World. As socialist economies throughout the world proved incapable of keeping up with the capitalist industrialized countries, international development agencies focused their attention on the need for policy reforms within the Third World. This attention brought a host of neoliberal policy prescriptions, including privatization, trade liberalization, and the termination of import substitution industrialization (ISI) policies. The collapse of the Soviet Union and the socialist states of Eastern Europe, along with increasingly capitalist economics in China, has reinforced this tendency.

According to the perspective that focuses on the state, errors of state policy are largely responsible for the gaps. The growth of parastatal marketing boards in Africa is shown by Robert Bates (Chapter 28) to be a significant factor in slowing growth in countries there. These boards distort the prices paid to producers, ostensibly to provide them with income stabil ity But the primary purpose is actually to curry support among urban dwellers by guaranteeing low consumer prices for agricultural goods. In fact, the prices paid are so low that producers have no incentive to continue to grow their crops, and production falls, thus impoverishing the nation. The Bates perspective is generalized by Erich Weede (Chapter 29) into what is called rent seeking, a situation in which government policy allows favored groups to charge prices above those that would have been set by the market. According to Weede, it is not dependency as imposed from abroad but domestic policies within the Third World that allow and in fact encourage rent-seeking behavior, which in turn explains the slow growth and inequality in those countries. Another related manifestation of rent-seeking distortions is that of urban bias, suggested by Michael Lipton (Chapter 30). From this perspective, numerous policies in the Third World favor cities over the countryside, with the result that growth is slowed and the gap between rich and poor nations widens.

Because of the dramatic increase in the number of democratic governments in recent years, the focus on states has raised concerns over the connection between democracy on the one hand and growth and inequality on the other. Some have argued that democratic political systems are less capable than their authoritarian counterparts of setting a clear economic agenda, whereas others have argued that democracies are not only good for growth but are also inherently egalitarian in nature and hence help to reduce the domestic gap between rich and poor. Adam Przeworski and Fernando Limongi (Chapter 31) present the evidence in this debate.

Finally, the dramatic successes in both growth and equality in the so-called miracle economies of Asia, the "gang of four" and the "little tigers," have led to a careful examination of state policy in those countries. Those economies have shown consistent growth that far exceeds that of the Third World and that of industrialized countries. Moreover, this growth has been achieved in countries such as Taiwan, South Korea, and Japan at the same time income inequality has been *reduced*. Some observers, such as Herman Kahn (Chapter 18), believe the success can be explained largely by cultural factors, especially the Confucian ethic. But others believe state policies have driven those successes. The evidence is ably summarized by Michael Sarel (Chapter 32). According to the most recent thinking on the subject, the key to the Asian successes has been investment in human capital, specifically health and education. Nancy Birdsall and Richard Sabot (Chapter 33) show how the failure to invest in human capital in Latin America has been responsible for slowed growth and high inequality, compared with Asia. Yet, Asia has shown particular disregard for the environment, and Vinod Thomas and Tamara Belt (Chapter 34) show that environmental destruction can have a very negative impact on growth rates.

Readers will come away from this volume with a clear sense of the causes of the gaps between the rich and the poor. It is hoped that some of those readers might someday help in implementing the "cure."

NOTES

1. These figures are based on the World Bank, *World Development Report 1980* (New York: Oxford University Press, 1980), 34.

2. Data from World Bank, *World Development Report 1997* (New York: Oxford University Press, 1997), 214–215.

3. See Volker Bornschier, Christopher Chase-Dunn, and Richard Rubinson, "Cross-National Evidence of the Effects of Foreign Investment and Aid on Economic Growth and Inequality: A Survey of the Findings," *American Sociological Review*, 84 (November 1978), 651–685.

2

. . . .

The Five Stages of Growth

. . . .

W. W. ROSTOW

Early research on economic underdevelopment suggested that the problem was only short-term and that in the end all countries would become rich. In this excerpt from W. W. Rostow's classic work, The Stages of Economic Growth, Rostow outlines this optimistic scenario by positing five stages of economic development all societies eventually experience as they mature into industrialized developed countries: tradition, the preconditions for takeoff, the takeoff, the drive to maturity, and the age of high mass consumption. Although this tremendously influential publication did not focus specifically on the causes of the gaps, the author suggests the reason they arise and their potential resolution. As a country moves out of the traditional stage and prepares for economic takeoff, its economy begins to grow much faster than the economies of countries that remain in the first stage. The gap between rich and poor would then be explained by the fact that not all countries enter the development process at the same time. Thus the gap between rich and poor countries would be expected to disappear as the countries progress into the later stages of growth. As a country progresses through the stages of development, those who adopt the new economic rules and succeed accumulate the profits of their success and internal inequality arises. As more people join the monied economy and play by the new rules, the extent of the inequality should diminish.

Reprinted with permission of Cambridge University Press from *The Stages of Economic Growth* by W. W. Rostow, pp. 4–12. New York: Cambridge University Press, 1990.

9

It is possible to identify all societies, in their economic dimensions, as lying within one of five categories: the traditional society, the preconditions for take-off, the take-off, the drive to maturity, and the age of high mass-consumption.

THE TRADITIONAL SOCIETY

First, the traditional society. A traditional society is one whose structure is developed within limited production functions, based on pre-Newtonian science and technology, and on pre-Newtonian attitudes towards the physical world. Newton is here used as a symbol for that watershed in history when men came widely to believe that the external world was subject to a few knowable laws, and was systematically capable of productive manipulation.

The conception of the traditional society is, however, in no sense static; and it would not exclude increases in output. Acreage could be expanded; some *ad hoc* technical innovations, often highly productive innovations, could be introduced in trade, industry and agriculture; productivity could rise with, for example, the improvement of irrigation works or the discovery and diffusion of a new crop. But the central fact about the traditional society was that a ceiling existed on the level of attainable output per head. This ceiling resulted from the fact that the potentialities which flow from modern science and technology were either not available or not regularly and systematically applied.

Both in the longer past and in recent times the story of traditional societies was thus a story of endless change. The area and volume of trade within them and between them fluctuated, for example, with the degree of political and social turbulence, the efficiency of central rule, the upkeep of the roads. Population—and, within limits, the level of life—rose and fell not only with the sequence of the harvests, but with the incidence of war and of plague. Varying degrees of manufacture developed; but, as in agriculture, the level of productivity was limited by the inaccessibility of modern science, its applications, and its frame of mind.

Generally speaking, these societies, because of the limitation on productivity, had to devote a very high proportion of their resources to agriculture; and flowing from the agricultural system there was an hierarchical social structure, with relatively narrow scope—but some scope—for vertical mobility. Family and clan connexions played a large role in social organization. The value system of these societies was generally geared to what might be called a long-run fatalism; that is, the assumption that the range of possibilities open to one's grandchildren would be just about what it had been for one's grandparents. But this long-run fatalism by no means excluded the short-run option that, within a considerable range, it was possible and legitimate for the individual to strive to improve his lot, within his lifetime. In Chinese villages, for example, there was an endless struggle to acquire or to avoid losing land, yielding a situation where land rarely remained within the same family for a century.

Although central political rule—in one form or another—often existed in traditional societies, transcending the relatively self-sufficient regions, the centre of gravity of political power generally lay in the regions, in the hands of those who owned or controlled the land. The landowner maintained fluctuating but usually profound influence over such central political power as existed, backed by its entourage of civil servants and soldiers, imbued with attitudes and controlled by interests transcending the regions.

In terms of history then, with the phrase 'traditional society' we are grouping the whole pre-Newtonian world: the dynasties in China; the civilization of the Middle East and the Mediterranean; the world of medieval Europe. And to them we add the post-Newtonian societies which, for a time, remained untouched or unmoved by man's new capability for regularly manipulating his environment to his economic advantage.

To place these infinitely various, changing societies in a single category, on the ground that they all shared a ceiling on the productivity of their economic techniques, is to say very little indeed. But we are, after all, merely clearing the way in order to get at the subject of this book; that is, the post-traditional societies, in which each of the major characteristics of the traditional society was altered in such ways as to permit regular growth: its politics, social structure, and (to a degree) its values, as well as its economy.

THE PRECONDITIONS FOR TAKE-OFF

The second stage of growth embraces societies in the process of transition; that is, the period when the preconditions for take-off are developed; for it takes time to transform a traditional society in the ways necessary for it to exploit the fruits of modern science, to fend off diminishing returns, and thus to enjoy the blessings and choices opened up by the march of compound interest.

The preconditions for take-off were initially developed, in a clearly marked way, in Western Europe of the late seventeenth and early eighteenth centuries as the insights of modern science began to be translated into new production functions in both agriculture and industry, in a setting given dynamism by the lateral expansion of world markets and the international competition for them. But all that lies behind the break-up of the Middle Ages is relevant to the creation of the preconditions for take-off in Western Europe. Among the Western European states, Britain, favoured by geography, natural resources, trading possibilities, social and political structure, was the first to develop fully the preconditions for take-off.

The more general case in modern history, however, saw the stage of preconditions arise not endogenously but from some external intrusion by more advanced societies. These invasions—literal or figurative—shocked the traditional society and began or hastened its undoing; but they also set in motion ideas and sentiments which initiated the process by which a modern alternative to the traditional society was constructed out of the old culture.

The idea spreads not merely that economic progress is possible, but that economic progress is a necessary condition for some other purpose, judged to be good: be it national dignity, private profit, the general welfare, or a better life for the children. Education, for some at least, broadens and changes to suit the needs of modern economic activity. New types of enterprising men come forward—in the private economy, in government, or both—willing to mobilize savings and to take risks in pursuit of profit or modernization. Banks and other institutions for mobilizing capital appear. Investment increases, notably in transport, communications, and in raw materials in which other nations may have an economic interest. The scope of commerce, internal and external, widens. And, here and there, modern manufacturing enterprise appears, using the new methods. But all this activity proceeds at a limited pace within an economy and a society still mainly characterized by traditional low-productivity methods, by the old social structure and values, and by the regionally based political institutions that developed in conjunction with them.

In many recent cases, for example, the traditional society persisted side by side with modern economic activities, conducted for limited economic purposes by a colonial or quasi-colonial power.

Although the period of transition—between the traditional society and the take-off—saw major changes in both the economy itself and in the balance of social values, a decisive feature was often political. Politically, the building of an effective centralized national state—on the basis of coalitions touched with a new nationalism, in opposition to the traditional landed regional interests, the colonial power, or both, was a decisive aspect of the preconditions period; and it was, almost universally, a necessary condition for take-off. . . .

THE TAKE-OFF

We come now to the great watershed in the life of modern societies: the third stage in this sequence, the take-off. The take-off is the interval when the old blocks and resistances to steady growth are finally overcome. The forces making for economic progress, which yielded limited bursts and enclaves of modern activity, expand and come to dominate the society. Growth becomes its normal condition. Compound interest becomes built, as it were, into its habits and institutional structure.

In Britain and the well-endowed parts of the world populated substantially from Britain (the United States, Canada, etc.) the proximate stimulus for take-off was mainly (but not wholly) technological. In the more general case, the take-off awaited not only the build-up of social overhead capital and a surge of technological development in industry and agriculture, but also the emergence to political power of a group prepared to regard the modernization of the economy as serious, high-order political business.

During the take-off, the rate of effective investment and savings may rise from say, 5 percent of the national income to 10 percent or more; although where heavy social overhead capital investment was required to create the technical preconditions for take-off the investment rate in the preconditions period could be higher than 5 percent, as, for example, in Canada before the 1890s and Argentina before 1914. In such cases capital imports usually formed a high proportion of total investment in the preconditions period and sometimes even during the take-off itself, as in Russia and Canada during their pre-1914 railway booms.

During the take-off new industries expand rapidly, yielding profits a large proportion of which are reinvested in new plants; and these new industries, in turn, stimulate, through their rapidly expanding requirement for factory workers, the services to support them, and for other manufactured goods, a further expansion in urban areas and in other modern industrial plants. The whole process of expansion in the modern sector yields an increase of income in the hands of those who not only save at high rates but place their savings at the disposal of those engaged in modern sector activities. The new class of entrepreneurs expands; and it directs the enlarging flows of investment in the private sector. The economy exploits hitherto unused natural resources and methods of production.

New techniques spread in agriculture as well as industry, as agriculture is commercialized, and increasing numbers of farmers are prepared to accept the new methods and the deep changes they bring to ways of life. The revolutionary changes in agricultural productivity are an essential condition for successful take-off; for modernization of a society increases radically its bill for agricultural products. In a decade or two both the basic structure of the economy and the social and political structure of the society are transformed in such a way that a steady rate of growth can be, thereafter, regularly sustained.

. . . One can approximately allocate the take-off of Britain to the two decades after 1783; France and the United States to the several decades preceding 1860; Germany, the third quarter of the nineteenth century; Japan, the fourth quarter of the nineteenth century; Russia and China the quarter-century or so preceding 1914; while during the 1950s India and China have, in quite different ways, launched their respective take-offs.

THE DRIVE TO MATURITY

After take-off there follows a long interval of sustained if fluctuating progress, as the now regularly growing economy drives to extend modern technology over the whole front of its economic activity. Some 10–20 percent of the national income is steadily invested, permitting output regularly to outstrip the increase in population. The make-up of the economy changes unceasingly as technique improves, new industries accelerate, older industries level off. The economy finds its place in the international economy: goods formerly imported are produced at home; new import requirements develop, and new export commodities to match them. The society makes such terms as it will with the requirements of modern efficient production, balancing off the new against the older values and institutions, or revising the latter in such ways as to support rather than to retard the growth process.

Some sixty years after take-off begins (say, forty years after the end of take-off) what may be called maturity is generally attained. The economy, focused during the take-off around a relatively narrow complex of industry and technology, has extended its range into more refined and technologically often more complex processes; for example, there may be a shift in focus from the coal, iron, and heavy engineering industries of the railway phase to machine-tools, chemicals, and electrical equipment. This, for example, was the transition through which Germany, Britain, France, and the United States had passed by the end of the nineteenth century or shortly thereafter. But there are other sectoral patterns which have been followed in the sequence from take-off to maturity. . . .

Formally, we can define maturity as the stage in which an economy demonstrates the capacity to move beyond the original industries which powered its take-off and to absorb and to apply efficiently over a very wide range of its resources—if not the whole range—the most advanced fruits of (then) modern technology. This is the stage in which an economy demonstrates that it has the technological and entrepreneurial skills to produce not everything, but anything that it chooses to produce. It may lack (like contemporary Sweden and Switzerland, for example) the raw materials or other supply conditions required to produce a given type of output economically; but its dependence is a matter of economic choice or political priority rather than a technological or institutional necessity.

Historically, it would appear that something like sixty years was required to move a society from the beginning of take-off to maturity. Analytically the explanation for some such interval may lie in the powerful arithmetic of compound interest applied to the capital stock, combined with the broader consequences for a society's ability to absorb modern technology of three successive generations living under a regime where growth is the normal condition. But, clearly, no dogmatism is justified about the exact length of the interval from take-off to maturity.

THE AGE OF HIGH MASS-CONSUMPTION

We come now to the age of high mass-consumption, where, in time, the leading sectors shift towards durable consumers' goods and services: a phase from which Americans are beginning to emerge; whose not unequivocal joys Western Europe and Japan are beginning energetically to probe; and with which Soviet society is engaged in an uneasy flirtation.

As societies achieved maturity in the twentieth century two things happened: real income per head rose to a point where a large number of persons gained a command over consumption which transcended basic food, shelter, and clothing; and the structure of the working force changed in ways which increased not only the proportion of urban to total population, but also the proportion of the population working in offices or in skilled factory jobs—aware of and anxious to acquire the consumption fruits of a mature economy.

In addition to these economic changes, the society ceased to accept the further extension of modern technology as an overriding objective. It is in this post-maturity stage, for example, that, through the political process, Western societies have chosen to allocate increased resources to social welfare and security. The emergence of the welfare state is one manifestation of a society's moving beyond technical maturity; but it is also at this stage that resources tend increasingly to be directed to the production of consumers' durables and to the diffusion of services on a mass basis, if consumers' sovereignty reigns. The sewing-machine, the bicycle, and then the various electric-powered household gadgets were gradually diffused. Historically, however, the decisive element has been the cheap mass automobile with its quite revolutionary effects—social as well as economic—on the life and expectations of society.

For the United States, the turning point was, perhaps, Henry Ford's moving assembly line of 1913–14; but it was in the 1920s, and again in the post-war decade, 1946–56, that this stage of growth was pressed to, virtually, its logical conclusion. In the 1950s Western Europe and Japan appeared to have fully entered this phase, accounting substantially for a momentum in their economies quite unexpected in the immediate post-war years. The Soviet Union is technically ready for this stage, and, by every sign, its citizens hunger for it; but Communist leaders face difficult political and social problems of adjustment if this stage is launched.

BEYOND CONSUMPTION

Beyond, it is impossible to predict, except perhaps to observe that Americans, at least, have behaved in the past decade as if diminishing relative marginal utility sets in, after a point, for durable consumers' goods; and they have chosen, at the margin, larger families—behavior in the pattern of Buddenbrooks dynamics.[1] Americans have behaved as if, having been born into a system that provided economic security and high mass-consumption, they placed a lower valuation on acquiring additional increments of real income in the conventional form as opposed to the advantages and values of an enlarged family. But even in this adventure in generalization it is a shade too soon to create—on the basis of one case—a new stage-of-growth, based on babies, in succession to the age of consumers' durables: as economists might say, the income-elasticity of demand for babies may well vary from society to society. But it is true that the implications of the baby boom along with the not wholly unrelated deficit in social overhead capital are likely to dominate the American economy over the next decade rather than the further diffusion of consumers' durables.

Here then, in an impressionistic rather than an analytic way, are the stages-of-growth which can be distinguished once a traditional society begins its modernization: the transitional period when the preconditions for take-off are created generally in response to the forces making for modernization; the take-off itself; the sweep into maturity generally taking up the life of about two further generations; and then, finally, if the rise of income has matched the spread of technological virtuosity (which, as we shall see, it need not immediately do) the diversion of the fully mature economy to the provision of durable consumers' goods and services (as well as the welfare state) for its increasingly urban—and then suburban—populations. Beyond lies the question of whether or not secular spiritual stagnation will arise, and, if it does, how man might fend it off. . . .

NOTES

1. In Thomas Mann's novel of three generations, the first sought money; the second, born to money, sought social and civic position; the third, born to comfort and family prestige, looked to the life of music. The phrase is designed to suggest, then, the changing aspirations of generations, as they place a low value on what they take for granted and seek new forms of satisfaction.

3

· · · · · · ·

Income Growth,
Income Gaps, and
the Ranking of Nations

· · · · · · ·

ANGUS MADDISON

Angus Maddison has long been one of the most prominent economic historians, providing development scholars with some of the most reliable historical data with which to judge long-term economic growth patterns. In this chapter Maddison discusses world economic growth over the past five centuries. Only after 1820 did the world begin to experience the type of rapid growth that people have grown used to in recent years. Prior to 1820, according to Maddison, the world's average per capita income was probably only a thirtieth of that achieved since 1820. In Part 3 of this book, we turn to convergence theory, which proposes that over the long run, per capita incomes will converge. Maddison's conclusions suggest that the long-term pattern is one of marked divergence rather than convergence. Converging per capita incomes are found among the already rich countries, and some evidence is found for the Asian economies, but according to Maddison, that is not a global trend.

Three main features emerge from our quantitative evidence:

a) Economic growth was extraordinarily fast from 1820–1992, World population increased five-fold, per capita product eight-fold, world GDP forty-fold, and world trade 540-fold;

b) The rise in per capita income differed widely between countries and regions, so intercountry and interregional spreads became very much wider;

c) The momentum of growth varied significantly. The best performance was in the post-war golden age 1950–1973 when per capita income improved dramatically in all regions, the second best was 1871–1913, the third best 1973–92.

THE POST-1820
ACCELERATION IN LONG-TERM PERSPECTIVE

Growth performance since 1820 has been dramatically superior to that in earlier history. Table 3.1 gives a very rough summary picture of the situation over the past five centuries.

Before our present "capitalist" epoch,[1] economies were predominantly agrarian, and economic advance was largely extensive. In response to demographic pressure, economic activity was successful over the long-term in sustaining living standards, but technology was virtually stagnant and evidence of advances in economic well-being is very meager.

There were some stirrings of economic growth after 1500 when the European "discovery" of the Americas and Australasia opened up new horizons, and different parts of the world became increasingly interactive, but over three centuries performance was extremely modest. From 1500 to 1820, the average growth of world per capita income was probably only a thirtieth of that achieved since 1820. There were some advances in technology, living standards and productivity in Western Europe and its offshoots, and more limited progress in the European periphery. But the rest of the world was economically stagnant, and by 1820 the West had established a substantial leadership margin.[2]

THE HIERARCHY OF REGIONS

For analytical convenience, I have divided the world into seven groups of countries, ranking them in order of their developmental promise as it might

Table 3.1   Rates of World Economic Growth, 1500–1992 (annual average compound growth rates)

	1500–1820	1820–1992
World Population	0.29	0.95
GDP per Capita	0.04	1.21
World GDP	0.33	2.17
World Exports	n.a.	3.73

Source: Figures calculated by author from multiple sources. See Table 1-1 [of the original work] for a listing of the various sources.

have been assessed by a well informed observer at the beginning of the capitalist epoch. My hierarchy is very similar to that in Adam Smith's *Inquiry into the Nature and Causes of the Wealth of Nations*. This was published in 1776 but his criteria for ranking nations were close to mine.

The main considerations I had in mind in allocating countries to these regions were: (a) their initial level (or assumed range) of per capita income in 1820; (b) their initial resource endowment in relation to population; (c) institutional or societal characteristics likely to influence economic performance.

The intra-regional congruence of countries and the regional groupings themselves may legitimately be challenged by some readers, but the basic evidence for the 56 sample countries is presented transparently, and it is quite easy for the reader to construct alternative groupings.

Table 3.2 shows the performance of the seven different regions since 1820. They are ranked in order of their initial levels of per capita income. This ranking has not changed much over the very long run. The most prosperous have retained their privileged position, and the poorest have remained relatively poor.

Table 3.2   The Performance of Major Regions, 1820-1992

	Population (millions)		GDP per Head (1990 $)		GDP (billions 1990 $)	
	1820	1992	1820	1992	1820	1992
Absolute Levels						
Western Europe	103	303	1,292	17,387	133	5,255
Western Offshoots	11	305	1,205	20,850	14	6,359
Southern Europe	34	123	804	8,287	27	1,016
Eastern Europe	90	431	772	4,665	69	2,011
Latin America	20	462	679	4,820	14	2,225
Asia & Oceania	736	3,163	550	3,252	405	10,287
Africa	73	656	450	1,284	33	842
World Total	1,068	5,441	651	5,145	695	27,995
Coefficients of Multiplication (1820–1992)						
Western Europe	3		13		40	
Western Offshoots	27		17		464	
Southern Europe	4		10		38	
Eastern Europe	5		6		29	
Latin America	23		7		161	
Asia & Oceania	4		6		25	
Africa	9		3		26	
World Average	5		8		40	

Source: Derived from Appendix G [in the original work]. The figures for GDP per head are weighted averages for 199 countries.

PER CAPITA GDP PERFORMANCE

Per capita growth since 1820 has been fastest in countries which were already the most prosperous in the initial year, with a 13-fold increase in Western Europe and a 17-fold increase in the Western Offshoots. The next fastest growth—a ten-fold increase—occurred in Southern Europe, which was the third most prosperous region in 1820. The fourth ranking region in 1820 was Eastern Europe. It had the fourth fastest per capita growth up to the 1980s, but with the large drop since the collapse of communism it ranks fifth in long-run per capita income gains. Latin America, the fifth most prosperous region in 1820 had a seven-fold increase in real income by 1992. Asia which had sixth rank in income in 1820, had the same ranking in 1992 with a six-fold increase in real product. Africa had the lowest per capita level in 1820. It was in the same position in 1992 with very modest gains to show. After 17 decades, its average per capita income in 1992 was about the same as Western Europe had achieved in 1820! However, . . . the regional growth paths have not been regular and have criss-crossed over time. Western Europe lost ground to the Western Offshoots, most of which it has now recouped. Southern Europe fell behind both Eastern Europe and Latin America, but has now forged well ahead of both. Asia fell below Africa but is now far ahead.

The overall long-run pattern of income spreads has been strikingly divergent. The interregional spread was less than 3:1 in 1820 and grew steadily larger at each successive benchmark. In 1870, it was 5:1, 1913 9:1, 1950 11:1, 1973 12:1, 1992 16:1. If we turn from regional spreads to look at the range between individual countries, the long-term divergence is even more marked. In 1820 the intercountry range (i.e., the distance between the lead country and the worst performer) was over 3:1, in 1870 7:1, in 1913 11:1, in 1950 35:1, in 1973 40:1, in 1992 72:1 (see Table 3.3).

Although the global long-term picture is one of divergence, there has been a substantial degree of catch-up since 1950. In that year, the US economy had a commanding lead over the Western and Southern European economies. Its per capita GDP was 1.7 times as big as the West European average in 1950 and four times the average for Southern Europe. By 1992, these gaps were substantially narrowed. For Western Europe the spread was 1.2:1; in Southern Europe 2:1. In Asia too, after 130 years when growth was feeble and gaps widened greatly there was a sharp narrowing after 1950. The average spread between U.S. and Asian incomes dropped from 11:1 in 1950 to 4:1 in 1992.

Within Asia, there have been some striking success stories. Japanese per capita income is now in third place, very close to the USA and Switzerland. Between 1820 and 1992 it rose nearly 28-fold—the world record. Since 1950, the most rapid growth in our Asian sample has been in South Korea, Taiwan and Thailand. All three countries are now within the

Table 3.3   GDP per Capita in 1990 International Dollars in the 56 Country Sample

	1820	1870	1900	1913	1950	1973	1992
12 Western European Countries							
Austria	1,295	1,875	2,901	3,488	3,731	11,308	17,160
Belgium	1,291	2,640	3,652	4,130	5,346	11,905	17,165
Denmark	1,225	1,927	2,902	3,764	6,683	13,416	18,293
Finland	759	1,107	1,620	2,050	4,131	10,768	14,464
France	1,218	1,858	2,849	3,452	5,221	12,940	17,959
Germany	1,112	1,913	3,134	3,833	4,281	13,152	19,351
Italy	1,092	1,467	1,746	2,507	3,425	10,409	16,229
Netherlands	1,561	2,640	3,533	3,950	5,850	12,763	16,898
Norway	1,004	1,303	1,762	2,275	4,969	10,229	17,543
Sweden	1,198	1,664	2,561	3,096	6,738	13,494	16,927
Switzerland	—	2,172	3,531	4,207	8,939	17,953	21,036
UK	1,756	3,263	4,593	5,032	6,847	11,992	15,738
Arith. Average	1,228	1,986	2,899	3,482	5,513	11,694	17,412
4 Western Offshoots							
Australia	1,528	3,801	4,299	5,505	7,218	12,485	16,237
Canada	893	1,620	2,758	4,213	7,047	13,644	18,159
New Zealand	—	3,115	4,320	5,178	8,495	12,575	13,947
USA	1,287	2,457	4,096	5,307	9,573	16,607	21,558
Arith. Average	1,236	2,748	3,868	5,051	8,083	13,828	17,475
5 South European Countries							
Greece	—	—	—	1,621	1,951	7,779	1,0314
Ireland	954	1,773	2,495	2,733	3,518	7,023	11,711
Portugal	—	1,085	1,408	1,354	2,132	7,568	11,130
Spain	1,063	1,376	2,040	2,255	2,397	8,739	12,498
Turkey	—	—	—	979	1,299	2,739	4,422
Arith. Average	—	1,194[a]	1,676[a]	1,788	2,259	6,770	10,015
7 East European Countries							
Bulgaria	—	—	—	1,498	1,651	5,284	4,054
Czechoslovakia	849	1,164	1,729	2,096	3,501	7,036	6,845
Hungary	—	1,269	1,682	2,098	2,480	5,596	5,638
Poland	—	—	—	—	2,447	5,334	4,726
Romania	—	—	—	—	1,182	3,477	2,565
USSR	751	1,023	1,218	1,488	2,834	6,058	4,671
Yugoslavia	—	—	—	1,029	1,546	4,237	3,887
Arith. Average	—	876[a]	1,174[a]	1,527[a]	2,235	5,289	4,627
7 Latin American Countries							
Argentina	—	1,311	2,756	3,797	4,987	7,970	7,616
Brazil	670	740	704	839	1,673	3,913	4,637
Chile	—	—	1,949	2,653	3,827	5,028	7,238
Colombia	—	—	973	1,236	2,089	3,539	5,025
Mexico	760	710	1,157	1,467	2,085	4,189	5,112
Peru	—	—	817	1,037	2,263	3,953	2,854
Venezuela	—	—	821	1,104	7,424	10,717	9,163
Arith. Average	—	783[a]	1,311	1,733	3,478	5,017	5,949
11 Asian Countries							
Bangladesh	531	—	581	617	551	478	720
Burma	—	—	647[b]	635	393	589	748
China	523	523	652	688	614	1,186	3,098
India	531	558	625	663	597	853	1,348

(continues)

Table 3.3 *(continued)*

	1820	1870	1900	1913	1950	1973	1992
11 Asian Countries (continued)							
Indonesia	614	657	745	917	874	1,538	2,749
Japan	704	741	1,135	1,334	1,873	11,017	19,425
Pakistan	531	—	687	729	650	981	1,642
Philippines	—	—	1,033	1,418	1,293	1,956	2,213
South Korea	—	—	850	948	876	2,840	10,010
Taiwan	—	—	759	794	922	3,669	11,590
Thailand	—	717	812	846	848	1,750	4,694
Arith. Average	609[a]	638[a]	775	872	863	2,442	5,294
10 African Countries							
Cote d'Ivoire	—	—	—	—	859	1,727	1,134
Egypt	—	—	509	508	517	947	1,927
Ethiopia	—	—	—	—	277	412	300
Ghana	—	—	462	648	1,193	1,260	1,007
Kenya	—	—	—	—	609	947	1,055
Morocco	—	—	—	—	1,611	1,651	2,327
Nigeria	—	—	—	—	547	1,120	1,152
South Africa	—	—	—	1,451	2,251	3,844	3,451
Tanzania	—	—	—	—	427	655	601
Zaire	—	—	—	—	636	757	353
Arith. Average	—	—	—	—	893	1,332	1,331

a. Hypothetical average, assumes that average movement of GDP per capita in countries of the group with data-gaps, was the same as the average for the countries remaining in the sample.

b. 1901.

Source: Appendix D [of the original work]. All figures in this table are adjusted to exclude the impact of frontier changes.

South European range. There are other (non-sample) Asian countries which have also reached relatively high income levels—Bahrain, Hong Kong, Israel, Qatar, Saudi Arabia, Singapore and the United Arab Emirates.

Thus there is clear evidence within Asia that substantial catch-up is achievable, and that falling behind in per capita incomes is not inexorable. In other areas, the picture is less encouraging. In Africa, the income gaps *vis-à-vis* the USA rose in 9 of the 10 sample countries from 1950 to 1992, they rose in 4 of the 7 East European countries and 4 of the 7 Latin American countries. In the 7 countries in these three areas where there was some catch-up on the USA, the margin of advance was generally small.

CHANGES IN THE SHARE OF CONSUMPTION

It should be remembered that changes in per capita GDP are not the same as changes in per capita private consumption.

Over time, there have been substantial increases in the proportion of expenditure going to investment, and to government consumption. Table 3.4 gives some idea of the situation in 1992, when private consumption was well below 60 per cent of GDP in Western Europe, Eastern Europe and Asia, and below three-quarters elsewhere.

Around 1820, the share of private consumption was around 84 per cent in France and 88 per cent in the UK. If the price movement had been the same for consumption and for GDP, this would mean that French private consumption levels in 1992 were about ten-and-a-half times as high as in 1820, compared with a per capita GDP about fourteen-and-a-half times as high. For the UK it would mean a rise in per capita consumption of six-and-a-half times compared with the nine-fold rise in per capita GDP. For the world as a whole, the average level of private consumption in 1992 was probably around five-and-a-half times higher than in 1820 compared with the eight-fold increase in per capita GDP.

The increase in the non-consumption share is a reflection of the effort required to sustain growth. A good deal of collective consumption goes to improve human capital (health and education), and a substantial savings effort was needed to finance the massive increase in physical capital.

PRODUCTIVITY LEVELS

The ranking of countries in per capita GDP is not necessarily the same as their standing in terms of productivity. In 1992, for example, Japanese per capita income was nearly 15 per cent higher than that in the Netherlands, but labour productivity was little more than two-thirds of Dutch levels. . . .

Table 3.4   Private Consumption as a Share of GDP at Market Prices, 1992 (percentages)

France	60.5	Argentina	80.5
Germany	54.0	Brazil	64.7
Netherlands	60.3	Mexico	73.9
Sweden	53.9	Average	73.0
UK	64.1		
Average	58.6	China	52.4
		India	67.1
USA	67.4	Indonesia	53.0
		Japan	57.0
Portugal	62.9	Korea	52.7
Spain	63.2	Average	56.4
Czechoslovakia	51.1	Egypt	79.5
USSR	55.1	Ghana	84.9
Average	53.1	Morocco	67.0
		Nigeria	70.9
		South Africa	64.9
		Average	73.4

France and the Netherlands have attained virtually the same labour productivity levels as the USA, even though they have lower inputs of physical capital, human capital, and natural resources. This means that their level of total factor productivity is even better relative to the USA than their labour productivity. It is clear from this kind of confrontation that one cannot judge the economic performance of nations only by the yardstick of per capita GDP.

DEMOGRAPHIC EXPERIENCE IN THE MAJOR REGIONS

In demographic terms, the most rapid long-term growth has been in places which were relatively empty in 1820 and attracted large-scale immigration from Europe. Thus the "Western Offshoots" increased their population 27-fold and Latin America 23-fold. The other relatively empty region, Africa, increased its population nine-fold. Demographic expansion was below the long-term world average in Western and Southern Europe and Asia.

Population growth in Western Europe has been modest over the long run. In the nineteenth and twentieth centuries there was a gradual but substantial increase in life expectation from about 37 to 77 years. The long decline of mortality was matched by gradual reductions in fertility, and there was significant migration to the Western Offshoots and Latin America. Since 1973, the widespread availability of contraceptive techniques and changing attitudes to family size have reduced population growth to historically low levels. In Eastern Europe there have also been drops in fertility, increased emigration, and in some cases higher death rates because of worsening economic conditions. In Bulgaria and Hungary there were declines in population, a phenomenon with little historical precedent in the modern era, except in Ireland.

In the nineteenth century, population growth was very fast in the Western Offshoots because of unusually high fertility and immigration.

In Latin America, population growth was rapid by world standards from 1820 to 1950, because of rapid immigration and high fertility. The transition to lower fertility was slow when death rates began to fall. Population increase accelerated substantially to an average of 2.8 per cent a year in 1950–73. After 1973 it slowed somewhat, but was still very much faster than in Europe or North America.

Asian countries had an overall population growth rate similar to that of Europe in 1820–1950. When economic progress accelerated after 1950, mortality fell and population grew at an average rate of 2.3 per cent a year to 1973. Thereafter voluntaristic controls on fertility increased and population growth rates declined.

In Africa, evidence on long-term demographic trends is poor. Until the 1950s, fertility and mortality were probably a good deal higher than in

Europe. Since then, cheap modern methods of disease control have reduced death rates quite sharply, and by 1992, life expectation was about 55 years. However, fertility remains very high and population growth accelerated to an average of 3 per cent a year in 1973–92, i.e., ten times the European rate. . . .

NOTES

1. Simon Kuznets (1966) put the turning point for "modern economic growth" at 1750, but in the light of recent evidence suggesting that growth in the eighteenth century was slower than previously thought (Crafts 1985). I prefer to use 1820 as a starting point. Recent evidence has also falsified the earlier view, espoused most strongly by Rostow (1960) and Gerschenkron (1962), that there was a long drawn-out sequence of staggered "takeoffs" in West European countries throughout the nineteenth century. It now seems clear that growth was generally much faster after 1820 than it was in the "protocapitalist" period from 1500 to 1820, when Western Europe was slowly pulling ahead of the rest of the world.

2. Paul Bairoch (1981) published estimates showing a much narrower gap between his "developed" and "third world" groups at the beginning of the nineteenth century, but it is not clear how he derived his estimate for the "third" world. See Maddison (1983) for a comment.

BIBLIOGRAPHY

Bairoch, Paul. 1981. "The Main Trends in National Economic Disparities Since the Industrial Revolution." In Paul Bairoch and Maurice Lévy-Leboyer, eds. *Disparities in Economic Development Since the Industrial Revolution.* London: Macmillan Press Ltd.

Crafts, N.F.R. 1985. *British Economic Growth During the Industrial Revolution.* Oxford: Oxford University Press.

Gerschenkron, A. 1965. *Economic Backwardness in Historical Perspective.* New York: Praeger.

Kuznets, Simon. 1966. *Modern Economic Growth.* New Haven: Yale University Press.

Maddison, Angus. 1983. "A Comparison of Levels of GDP per Capita in Developed and Developing Countries, 1700–1980." *Journal of Economic History.* 43 (March):27–41.

Rostwo, W. W. 1960. *The Stages of Economic Growth.* Cambridge: Cambridge University Press.

4

· · · · · · ·

The Persistence of the Gap Between Rich and Poor Countries: Taking Stock of World Economic Growth, 1960–1993

· · · · · · ·

JOHN T PASSÉ-SMITH

One of the primary goals of this book is to trace the debate over the causes of the gap between rich and poor countries, referred to as the external gap. Before the causes of that gap can be fruitfully discussed, however, the student of development should understand the extent of the gap and the characteristics of worldwide economic growth. In Chapter 3, Angus Maddison reached back into the nineteenth century and provided a valuable picture of historical patterns of growth. This chapter focuses on a more recent period, 1960 to 1993. In examining trends in and characteristics of economic growth, I have divided the chapter into four sections: rates of growth, the absolute gap, the relative gap, and country mobility.

RATES OF ECONOMIC GROWTH, 1960–1993

Following Western Europe's fast recovery after World War II, the governments of the industrialized countries turned their attention to aiding Third World nations in their development efforts. In the 1950s and early 1960s, economic growth became the centerpiece of economists' development plans. To that end, the United Nations declared the 1960s the Development Decade and set a goal of 6 percent annual growth as necessary to raise the poverty-stricken to a decent standard of living (Dube 1988:2–3). Almost two decades later, David Morawetz (1977) was commissioned by the World Bank to take stock of what had been accomplished in the area of development. Morawetz evaluated the world's growth between 1950 and 1975, concluding that although the entire world had experienced relatively rapid growth, the gap between the rich and poor countries in terms of per capita gross national product (GNP/pc) was growing wider.

For the period under investigation in this chapter, 1960 to 1993, data

27

were obtained from *World Data 1995* (World Bank 1995) and *International Financial Statistics: Supplement on Output Statistics,* no. 8 (IMF 1984). Figures on GNP/pc are presented in constant 1987 U.S. dollars, and growth rates were computed from the constant per capita GNPs using the regression method described in the *World Development Report* (World Bank 1988:288–289).[1] Income groups are defined as follows: Those countries with a GNP/pc of $4,000 or greater are considered rich, middle-income countries have a GNP/pc of $500 to $3,999, and the poor countries are those with a GNP/pc of less than $500.

Over the thirty-four-year period 1960–1993, the annual average rate of GNP/pc growth for the world was about 2.0 percent (see Table 4.1). To put this achievement in perspective, we must realize that modern growth among the countries considered developed today began in the mid-nineteenth century. During the hundred years prior to 1950, according to Simon Kuznets (1972:19), those countries experienced a century of unprecedented rates of growth (1.6 percent annually). Since 1960, the entire world—not just the fastest-growing countries—has surpassed the 1.6 percent mark; in fact, in the 1960s, worldwide GNP/pc grew at almost 3 percent per annum. A more sobering observation is that every decade since the 1960s has witnessed a decelerating growth rate (Table 4.1). The largest drop came between the 1970s' 2.5 percent and the 1980s' 0.9 percent rate of growth. By the early 1990s, the rate of economic growth had dropped to less than one half of one percent. Data from more recent years should help to cushion that decline and perhaps even reverse it.

For the period as a whole, the richer countries had the highest growth rates. The mean growth rate of rich countries between 1960 and 1993 was 2.5 percent, whereas the middle-income countries grew at an average annual rate of 1.8 percent; the poor countries grew the slowest at 1.7 percent (Table 4.1). This fact is contrary to the expectations of convergence theorists who assert that over the long run nonrich countries will have the highest growth potential (see convergence theorists' possible explanations for these growth rates in Chapter 9 by Moses Abramovitz and Chapter 10 by William Baumol).

Table 4.1   Growth Rates by Income Grouping

	1960–1993	1960–1969	1970–1979	1980–1989	1990–1993
World	2.0	2.8	2.5	0.9	0.4
Rich	2.5	3.8	2.4	1.4	1.1
Middle	1.8	3.3	2.5	0.5	0.3
Poor	1.7	1.8	2.1	0.2	–.7

Source: Computed from *World Data 1995* (World Bank).

If convergence in its purest form were occurring today, the growth rates of the poorest countries would be the highest, followed by the middle-income countries; the rich would have the lowest growth rates. In his 1982 study of world growth between 1960 and 1978, Robert Jackman[2] found that whereas middle-income countries were growing faster than the rich, the poor countries suffered the lowest growth rates. Jackman labeled this phenomenon the "modified Matthew effect" (1982:175). In the Bible, the Book of Matthew contains a reference to the continued accumulation of wealth by the rich and the further impoverishment of the poor. By the modified Matthew effect, Jackman meant both the rich and middle-income countries were growing richer; in fact, the middle-income countries were growing faster than the rich ones (converging). Alas, the poor were falling further behind.

Looking at Table 4.1, the annual average rates of growth for rich, middle-income, and poor countries are broken down by decades. The modified Matthew effect is found only during the 1970s, when the middle-income countries grew at an annual average rate of 2.5 percent and the rich achieved a rate of 2.4 percent. Although the poor countries grew the slowest, at 2.1 percent, this was their most prosperous decade during the period under study. Whatever forces were modifying the Matthew effect during the 1970s were no longer dominant. Middle-income countries may have the highest potential for growth when global economic expansion is taking place but may be less able than rich countries to protect themselves during economically difficult times. As for the rich, the oil shock in the early 1970s quadrupled the cost of imported oil and slowed the growth of their oil-consuming, industrialized economies. Awash in petrodollar wealth generated by the rising cost of oil, bankers in the First World made more money available to developing countries.

In many regions of the world, the 1980s are referred to as "the lost decade," in which development plans contrived during the 1970s period of easy money gave way to a debt crisis. Table 4.1 shows the collapse of growth. The rich countries slowed to an annual rate of expansion of 1.4 percent; both middle-income and poor countries' rates of economic growth dropped below 1 percent. Unfortunately, the economic slump continued into the 1990s. In fact, the first four years of the 1990s represented the slowest period of growth for all three income groups during the period under study.

Regional categories were constructed using the classifications devised by the World Bank and the International Monetary Fund (IMF).[2] Economic growth rates by the world's regions are shown in Table 4.2. The World Bank extracted developed countries from their geographic regions and displayed them as a group. The regions listed in the first column are ranked according to their growth rates for the period 1960 to 1993. Table 4.2

Table 4.2   World Economic Growth Rates by Region, 1960–1993 (%)

	1960–1993	1960–1969	1970–1979	1980–1989	1990–1993
Developed	2.5	3.9	2.3	2.1	0.5
East Asia/Pacific	4.5	3.8	4.7	3.3	5.2
Middle East	3.7	6.4	3.9	1.2	1.2
Europe	3.5	5.5	3.9	2.2	0.2
Asia	2.2	2.4	2.7	1.8	−2.1
Western Hemisphere	0.9	2.6	1.9	−1.3	1.5
Africa	0.9	1.4	1.7	−0.4	−1.2
Countries with less than 1 million people	3.0	3.1	3.1	2.9	1.7

Source: Computed from World Data 1995 (World Bank).

shows that East Asia, containing the so-called Asian newly industrializing countries (NICs), was the fastest-growing region with an annual growth rate of 4.5 between 1960 and 1993. During the 1960s, East Asia was the third-fastest-growing region, but during the 1970s, 1980s, and 1990s it had the highest growth rates. During the 1980s two of the regions experienced economic contraction: the Western Hemisphere (−1.3 percent) and Africa (−0.4 percent). Countries in the Western Hemisphere had restored growth rates in the 1990s, averaging 1.5 percent expansion, but Asia and Africa experienced negative economic growth at −2.1 percent and −1.2 percent, respectively.

Analysis of income groups and regions makes it difficult to judge the performance of individual states. Table 4.3 remedies that problem by high-lighting the world's ten fastest- and slowest-growing countries between 1960 and 1993. The fastest-growing countries grew at an annual average rate ranging from 4.7 percent (Japan and Thailand) to 9.5 percent (South Korea). One of the most striking features is that five of the ten fastest-growing countries during that era—Botswana, China, South Korea, Suriname, and Thailand—started the period with GNP/pcs of less than $500. As can be expected, Asia is well represented on the list. Botswana, Africa's sole representative among the fastest-growing countries, achieved the second-fastest average annual growth rate (7.5 percent) in the world over the thirty-four-year period. Japan is the only developed country among the ten fastest growers.

Unfortunately, one region of the world dominates the list of the slow-est-growing countries. Of the ten slowest-growing countries in the world between 1960 and 1993, eight are African. The only non-African coun-tries—Guyana and Nicaragua—are both in the Western Hemisphere. The slowest-growing countries all experienced negative growth ranging from −0.005 percent (Somalia) to −3.1 percent (Niger).

Table 4.3   World's Fastest- and Slowest-Growing Countries, 1960–1993

Rank	Country	Economic Growth Rate (1960–1993) (%)	Income Group
		The Ten Fastest-Growing Countries	
1	South Korea	9.5	Poor
2	Botswana	7.5	Poor
3	Singapore	6.7	Middle income
4	Malta	6.5	<1 million/middle income
5	Oman	6.4	Middle income
6	Suriname	6.0	<1 million/poor
7	China	5.9	Poor
8	Belarus	5.4	Middle income
9	Thailand	4.7	Poor
10	Japan	4.7	Rich
		The Ten Slowest-Growing Countries	
1	Niger	−3.1	Middle income
2	Nicaragua	−2.1	Middle income
3	Zaire	−1.8	Poor
4	Madagascar	−1.5	Poor
5	Zambia	−1.4	Poor
6	Ghana	−1.2	Poor
7	Guyana	−1.0	<1 million/poor
8	Chad	−0.007	Poor
9	Central African Republic	−0.006	Poor
10	Somalia	−0.005	Poor

Source: Computed from World Data 1995 (World Bank).

THE ABSOLUTE GAP

In 1965 Simon Kuznets reported that rich countries' mean per capita GNP was $1,900, whereas that of poor countries was $120.[3] One of the major trends over the previous 100 to 125 years, Kuznets argued, was that the absolute gap had widened very slowly until World War II and then began to accelerate. Kuznets stated, "A reasonable conjecture is that, in comparison with the quintupling of the per capita product of developed countries over the last century, the per capita product of the 'poor' LDCs rose two-thirds at most" (Kuznets 1972:19).

The absolute gap, as defined by David Morawetz (1977), is the difference between the mean GNP/pc of a set of rich countries and that of poorer countries or groups of countries. Morawetz found that between 1950 and 1975, the absolute gap between the Organization for Economic Cooperation and Development (OECD) and developing countries more than doubled (from $2,191 in 1950 to $4,839 in 1975 in U.S. dollars). Neither the developing countries as a group nor any of the geographic regions reported by Morawetz were able to narrow the absolute gap.

Comparable results were obtained for the 1960 to 1993 period. The data presented in Table 4.4 show that the dollar amount (as measured by GNP/pc) separating the rich and middle-income countries grew from $6,452 to $12,201 (in U.S. dollars) and that the gap between rich and poor countries grew from $7,477 to $13,454 for the 1960–1993 period. The right-hand column of Table 4.4 lists the annual average increase in the absolute gap. On average, the gap between the rich and middle-income countries increased $169 per year, and the distance between the rich and the poor widened by $176 per year.

If, over the thirty-four years covered in this chapter, the percentage of people who lived in poor countries had dropped to a relatively small number or if they lived in only a few countries, interest in the gap would probably wane. But poverty has remained a persistent problem for more than half the world's population. Table 4.5 provides the percentages of the world's population living in rich, middle-income, and poor countries during the 1960–1993 period. The data indicate that in 1993, 57 percent of the world's population lived in countries with per capita GNPs of less than $500 (1987

Table 4.4   Absolute Gap, 1960–1993 (1987 U.S. dollars)

Income Group	1960	1980	1993	Annual Average Increase in the Gap
Middle income (Rich GNP/pc–Middle income GNP/pc)	6,452	10,112	12,201	+169
Poor	7,477	11,322	13,454	+176
Region				
Africa	7,180	10,783	12,881	+168
Asia	7,327	10,807	12,944	+165
East Asia/Pacific	7,109	9,957	10,591	+102
Europe	6,657	8,444	9,620	+87
Middle East	5,857	6,431	8,378	+74
Western Hemisphere	6,389	9,494	11,555	+154
Less than 1 million	5,262	6,516	7,377	+62

Countries That Have Closed the Absolute Gap		
	1960	1993
Israel	$4,255	$3,960
Singapore	$6,205	$1,674

Source: Computed from *World Data 1995* (World Bank).

U.S. dollars). This statistic is grim. Table 4.5 also shows, however, that a larger percentage of people lived in middle-income countries in 1993 than in 1960, whereas both the rich and the poor groups shrank in size. Unfortunately, the population distribution means the gap among rich, middle-income, and poor countries is affecting more than a small percentage of the world's population.

The data set out thus far demonstrate that the gap between the rich and the other two groups is growing. But does this prove the adage that "the rich get richer while the poor get poorer?" Figure 4.1 shows that although

Table 4.5   World Population Living in Rich, Middle-Income, and Poor Countries, 1960–1993 (%)

Income Group	1960	1980	1993
Rich	22.33	19.93	18.62
Middle income	16.23	20.68	24.25
Poor	61.32	59.29	57.00

Note: Countries with less than one million people were not included.
Source: Computed from *World Data 1995* (World Bank).

Figure 4.1   GNP/pc of Rich, Middle-Income, and Poor Countries, 1960–1993

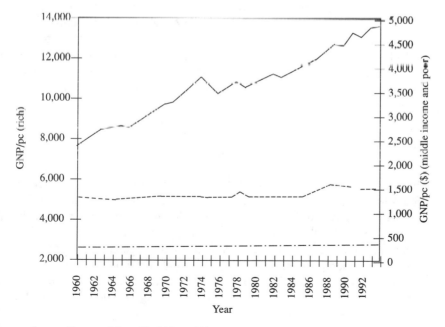

Source: Computed from *World Data 1995* (World Bank).

the gap has opened, the middle-income and poor countries as groups are not getting poorer. Does this raise the hope that some countries can catch up to the GNP/pc of the rich? Table 4.4 shows that only two countries, Israel and Singapore, were able to close the absolute gap between 1960 and 1993.

To eventually catch up with the rich countries' GNP/pc, nonrich countries must simply grow faster than the rich. But catching up could take hundreds if not thousands of years if the nonrich countries are relatively poor and they grow only slightly faster than the rich. Indeed, in such a case the absolute gap will continue to widen for years before it begins to shrink because of what Morawetz called the "simple algebra of the gap." The gap between rich and poor countries will not close until the ratio of their GNP/pcs is equal to the inverse ratio of their growth rates.

A relatively simple way to determine whether a nonrich country can close the absolute gap is to divide the rich country's growth rate by the ratio of the nonrich country's GNP/pc to the rich country's GNP/pc. This equation yields the growth rate the nonrich country must exceed to begin closing the absolute gap immediately. If, for example, the rich country has a mean GNP/pc of $8,000 and a growth rate of 2 percent, a nonrich country with a GNP/pc of $1,000 must exceed a growth rate of 16 percent to begin closing the absolute gap that year. Few countries can achieve or maintain such a rate of economic expansion for very long.

Can any country close the absolute gap? Replicating Morawetz's projections, I have attempted to find out if any country is capable of catching up to the rich. The results presented in Table 4.6 assume that countries will maintain the same growth rates they achieved during the base period 1960–1993. Given that assumption, the majority of countries cannot hope to close the gap. Only Belarus, Botswana, and Suriname have any chance to catch up to the rich within a century. Five more countries could catch up in the following century.

THE RELATIVE GAP

The relative gap measures the GNP/pc of the poor or middle-income groups as a percentage of that of the developed countries. Morawetz (1977) reported that between 1950 and 1975, developing countries narrowed the relative gap by about one half of a percentage point. He added that it might be easier for nonrich countries to narrow the relative gap than to narrow the absolute gap, thereby making it a more accessible development goal.

My results as shown in Table 4.7, however, indicate that the middle-income countries' GNP/pc expressed as a percentage of the GNP/pc of the rich has grown smaller over time. The middle-income countries' percentage

Table 4.6 Closing the Absolute Gap, 1960–1993

Country	GNP/pc (1987 U.S. dollars)	Annual Average Growth Rate, 1960–1993 (%)	Number of Years (until the gap is closed)
Rich[a]	13,736	2.500	—
Botswana	1,747	7.475	44
Suriname	2,049	5.977	58
Belarus	2,125	5.351	69
Thailand	1,544	4.737	102
Malaysia	2,606	4.061	110
China	367	5.894	112
Lesotho	460	4.472	179
Hungary	2,125	3.489	195
Egypt	709	3.939	213
Indonesia	557	3.947	229
Turkey	1,762	3.388	238
Ukraine	1,482	3.442	244
Belize	2,087	3.105	321
Brazil	1,885	3.096	343
Tunisia	1,357	3.090	404
Pakistan	374	3.249	495
Mauritius	2,308	2.867	500
Swaziland	745	2.808	971
Congo	914	2.764	1,054
St. Vincent/Grenadines	1,717	2.610	1,932
Sri Lanka	486	2.812	2,000

a. Those countries with a GNP/pc of over $4,000 in 1993.
Source: Computed from *World Data 1995* (World Bank).

Table 4.7 Relative Gap, 1960–1993 (percentage of the GDP/pc of rich countries)

	1960	1980	1993
Income Group			
Middle Income	16.7	13.0	11.2
Poor	3.4	2.6	2.1
Region			
Africa	6.9	6.6	5.3
Asia	5.4	6.9[a]	5.8
East Asia/Pacific	7.4	14.1[a]	24.2[a]
Europe	14.0	24.4[a]	25.4[a]
Middle East	24.3	44.7[a]	39.1
Western Hemisphere	16.2	16.2	13.0
Less than 1 million	32.0	43.9[a]	46.3[a]

a. Denotes an improvement in the relative gap over the previous period reported.
Source: Computed from *World Data 1995* (World Bank).

declined such that by 1993 their GNP/pc as a percentage of that of the rich had dropped below the 1960 level of 16.7 percent. By 1993, the middle-income countries had a relative gap score of only 11.2 percent. The relative gap score of poor countries fell from 3.4 percent to 2.1 percent over the thirty-four-year period. In other words, the relative gaps between rich and middle-income countries and rich and poor countries widened between 1960 and 1993.

MOBILITY

Can countries move from one income group to another or substantially improve their ranking within a grouping? In terms of upward mobility across income groups, the record has been unimpressive. Table 4.8 summarizes the movement of countries from one income group to another between 1960 and 1993. Of the 112 countries, 88 remained in the same category in 1993 that they had occupied in 1960. Even though the number of upwardly mobile countries was relatively small, only one country—Niger—moved down an income group, dropping from middle income to poor. Eleven countries moved up from the middle-income group to the rich, and one—South Korea—moved from the poor to the rich. Eleven that were in the poor group in 1960 had become middle-income countries by 1993.

Although 79 percent of the countries in this sample remained within the same income group, Table 4.9 shows that quite a bit of movement occurred within the ranks. Table 4.9 offers the ten countries that moved the most between 1960 and 1993, up or down, in terms of GNP/pc rank. South Korea (+53) and Botswana (+40) made the most impressive jumps. Among the top ten movers, China ranked the lowest in 1960, at 112, but moved up twenty-one places. Other than Suriname (+34), Latin American (Western Hemisphere) countries failed to move up significantly in the rankings; in fact, four countries from the Western Hemisphere—Nicaragua, Peru, Jamaica, and Haiti—were among the ten that *dropped* the most in the GNP/pc ranking. The remaining six countries that fell the most precipitously were from Africa.

CONCLUSION

If scholars such as Simon Kuznets (1972) and Michael Lipton (1977) are correct, the worldwide economic growth experienced since World War II is unprecedented. Between 1850 and 1950, the countries considered rich in 1950 experienced economic growth averaging 1.6 percent. Between 1960 and 1993, the entire world grew at an annual average rate of 2.0 percent, and between 1960 and 1969, the growth rate hovered at 2.8 percent. Post–

Table 4.8   Mobility Across Income Groups, 1960 and 1993

Rich

Rich in 1960 and 1993 (N = 21)
Australia, Austria, Bahamas,[a] Belgium, Canada, Denmark, Finland, France, Germany,
Iceland,[a] Ireland, Italy, Japan, Luxembourg,[a] Netherlands, New Zealand, Norway,
Sweden, Switzerland, United Kingdom, United States

Joined Rich from the Middle-Income Category (N = 11)
Barbados,[a] Greece, Israel, Malta,[a] Oman, Portugal, Puerto Rico, Saudi Arabia,
Seychelles,[a] Singapore, Spain

Joined Rich from the Poor Category (N = 1)
South Korea

Middle Income

Middle Income in 1960 and 1993 (N = 39)
Algeria, Argentina, Belarus, Belize,[a] Bolivia, Brazil, Cameroon, Chile, Colombia, Costa
Rica, Dominica,[a] El Salvador, Fiji,[a] Gabon, Guatemala, Honduras, Hungary, Jamaica,
Kazakhstan, Malaysia, Mauritius, Mexico, Nicaragua, Panama, Papua New Guinea,
Paraguay, Peru, Senegal, South Africa, St. Vincent/Grenadines, Sudan, Syria, Trinidad and
Tobago, Tunisia, Turkey, Turkmenistan, Ukraine, Uruguay, Venezuela

Joined Middle Income from the Poor Category (N = 11)
Botswana, Congo, Côte d'Ivoire, Dominican Republic, Egypt, Indonesia, Morocco,
Philippines, Suriname,[a] Swaziland,[a] Thailand

Poor

Poor in 1960 and 1993 (N = 28)
Bangladesh, Benin, Burkina Faso, Burundi, Central African Republic, Chad, China,
Gambia, Ghana, Guyana,[a] Haiti, India, Kenya, Lesotho, Madagascar, Malawi, Mauritania,
Myanmar, Nepal, Nigeria, Pakistan, Rwanda, Somalia, Sri Lanka, Tanzania, Togo, Zaire,
Zambia

Joined Poor from the Middle-Income Category (N = 1)
Niger

a. Less than 1 million population throughout the entire period.
Source: Computed from *World Data 1995* (World Bank).

World War II generations have grown accustomed to rapid economic
growth, leading many people to believe such growth will continue. The
research of Kuznets and others suggests that over time, however, countries
have likely experienced long periods of stagnation or periods of economic
expansion followed by periods of contraction.

Second, the data here indicate that not everyone has shared in the
growth. The absolute gaps between rich and middle-income countries and
between rich and poor countries have grown steadily since 1960. For middle-income countries the absolute gap grew from $6,452 in 1960 to
$12,201 in 1993, and the poor fell from a deficit of $7,477 to a deficit of

Table 4.9   Mobility in GNP/pc Rankings (differences in rankings from 1960 to 1993)

	Upwardly Mobile				Downwardly Mobile		
	GNP/pc Rank				GNP/pc Rank		
Country	1960	1993	Diff.	Country	1960	1993	Diff.
South Korea	86	33	+53	Nicaragua	39	78	−39
Botswana	95	55	+40	Niger	63	99	−36
Suriname	82	48	+34	Sudan	49	76	−27
Thailand	89	57	+32	Peru	46	68	−22
Belarus	72	45	+27	Senegal	60	82	−22
Oman	56	31	+25	Jamaica	38	59	−21
Malaysia	61	38	+23	Haiti	80	101	−21
Lesotho	108	85	+23	Madagascar	85	105	−20
China	112	91	+21	Zambia	84	102	−18
Indonesia	103	83	+20	Zaire	91	109	−18

Source: Computed from World Data 1995 (World Bank).

$13,454 during that period. On average, each year the absolute gap widened $169 for middle-income countries and $176 for the poor countries. The mean annual expansion of the absolute gap for African countries was $1,682. In addition, neither the middle-income nor the poor group made significant improvements in the relative gap. Two regions increased their GNP/pc as a percentage of that of the rich: East Asia/Pacific and those European countries that were not in the rich category. East Asia/Pacific increased its GNP/pc as a percentage of the GNP/pc of the rich from 7.4 percent in 1960 to 24.2 percent in 1993, whereas European countries' percentage increased from 14.0 to 25.4 percent during the period.

Third, this analysis of income groups would have proven irrelevant if the percentage of the world's population in the lowest income group had fallen significantly. Unfortunately, that was not the case. The percentage of the world's population living in countries with GNP/pcs of less than $500 was 57 percent, or more than 2.5 billion people, in 1993. This figure does represent a decline from 61 percent in 1960, but the number of people living in poor countries increased during the period.

Fourth, the number of countries with GNP/pcs greater than $4,000 (1987 U.S. dollars) increased from eighteen (plus three rich countries with populations under 1 million) in 1960 to twenty-seven (plus six rich countries with populations under 1 million) in 1993. Twelve countries joined the rich during the thirty-four-year period, and eleven moved up into the middle-income category. In all, twenty-four countries became mobile and crossed from one income category to another; only one of those countries moved down.

Finally, it appears that only three countries can close the gap with the rich within the next century: Belarus, Botswana, and Suriname. If growth rates remain similar to those of the thirty-four-year period or even to those between 1960 and 1993, Botswana will be the first African country to surpass the $4,000 per capita level and join the rich.

NOTES

1. The least squares method finds the growth rate by fitting a least squares trend line to the log of the gross national product per capita. This takes the equation form of $X_t = a+bt+e_t$, where x equals the log of the GNP/pc, a is the intercept, b is the parameter to be estimated, t is time, and e is the error term. The growth rate, r, is the [antilog (b)]−1. For further information, see World Bank (1988: pp. 288–289). For a discussion of different methods of computing growth rates, see Jackman (1980).

2. The regional categories were drawn from distinctions made by the International Monetary Fund (see IMF 1984) and the World Bank (World Data 1995 [CD-ROM]) except for the East Asian/Pacific category, which was drawn from World Bank (1992).

3. Kuznets (1972) defined the rich countries as those with a GNP/pc greater than $1,000 (1965 U.S. dollars). A "narrow" definition of the poor countries set the GNP/pc cutoff point at $120 or less. For his more broadly defined poor category, Kuznets raised the cutoff point to $300. The middle-income group varied according to Kuznets's choice of a narrowly or broadly defined poor group in any particular example. Kuwait and Qatar were excluded because their growth had been dependent on a single commodity and did not reflect diversity. Puerto Rico was excluded because its GNP/pc was so tightly connected to the United States. Japan was included in the rich group even though its GNP/pc was below the cutoff point because it had managed tremendous growth with very few natural resources; thus, its growth was achieved through diversified development of the economy. For further information on how Kuznets defined income groups, see Kuznets 1972.

REFERENCES

Dube, S. C. 1988. *Modernization and Development: The Search for Alternative Paradigms*. London: Zed.

International Monetary Fund (IMF). 1984. *International Financial Statistics: Supplement on Output Statistics*, no. 8. Washington, D.C.: IMF.

Jackman, R. W. 1980. "A Note on the Measurement of Growth Rates in Cross-National Research." *American Journal of Sociology* 86:604–610.

———. 1982. "Dependence on Foreign Investment and Economic Growth in the Third World." *World Politics* 34:175–197.

Kuznets, S. 1972. "The Gap: Concept, Measurement, Trends." In G. Ranis, ed., *The Gap Between Rich and Poor Nations*. London: Macmillan.

Lipton, M. 1977. *Why the Poor People Stay Poor: A Study of Urban Bias in World Development*. London: Temple Smith.

Morawetz, D. 1977. *Twenty-Five Years of Economic Development: 1950–1975.* Washington, D.C.: World Bank.

World Bank. 1988, 1990. *World Development Report.* Oxford: Oxford University Press.

———. 1992. *The World Tables 1992.* Washington, D.C.: World Bank.

———. 1995. *World Data 1995: World Bank Indicators on CD-Rom.* Washington, D.C.: The International Bank for Reconstruction and Development.

PART 2

· · · · · · · · · · · · · · ·

Domestic Income Inequality: The Rich Get Richer

· · · · · · · · · · · · · · · ·

5

. . . .

Economic Growth and
Income Inequality

. . . .

SIMON KUZNETS

Most debate on the internal gap between rich and poor people in
developing nations begins with this seminal presidential address deliv
ered by Simon Kuznets to the American Economic Association in
1954. The address, portions of which are reprinted here, uses limited
data from Germany, the United Kingdom, and the United States to
show that since the 1920s, and perhaps even earlier, there has been
a trend toward equalization in the distribution of income. Kuznets discusses in some detail the possible causes for this trend, examining
those factors in the process of industrialization that tend to counteract the concentration of savings in the hands of the wealthy. That
particular discussion is not included here, but the interested reader
can consult the original piece. Our interest lies in Kuznets's conclusion
that the central factor in equalizing income must have been the rising
incomes of the poorer sectors outside of the traditional agricultural
economy. Kuznets introduces the critically important notion of the
"inverted U-curve" (although he does not label it as such in the
address), arguing that there seems to be increasing inequality in the
early phases of industrialization, followed by declines in the later
phases only. Finally, Kuznets opens the debate over the relevance of
these findings for the developing nations by examining data from
India, Ceylon (Sri Lanka), and Puerto Rico. The findings that income
inequality in the developing countries is greater than that in the
advanced countries and that such inequality may be growing form
the basis of virtually all subsequent research and debate on this subject.

Reprinted with permission from the *American Economic Review*, vol. 45 (March
1955):1, 3–6, 17–26.

The central theme of this chapter is the character and causes of long-term changes in the personal distribution of income. Does inequality in the distribution of income increase or decrease in the course of a country's economic growth? What factors determine the secular level and trends of income inequalities?

These are broad questions in a field of study that has been plagued by looseness in definitions, unusual scarcity of data, and pressures of strongly held opinions. . . .

TRENDS IN INCOME INEQUALITY

Forewarned of the difficulties, we turn now to the available data. These data, even when relating to complete populations, invariably classify units by income for a given year. From our standpoint, this is their major limitation. Because the data often do not permit many size groupings, and because the difference between annual income incidence and longer-term income status has less effect if the number of classes is small and the limits of each class are wide, we use a few wide classes. This does not resolve the difficulty; and there are others due to the scantiness of data for long periods, inadequacy of the unit used—which is, at best, a family and very often a reporting unit—errors in the data, and so on through a long list. Consequently, the trends in the income structure can be discerned but dimly, and the results considered as preliminary informed guesses.

The data are for the United States, England, and Germany—a scant sample, but at least a starting point for some inferences concerning long-term changes in the presently developed countries. The general conclusion suggested is that the relative distribution of income, as measured by annual income incidence in rather broad classes, has been moving toward equality—with these trends particularly noticeable since the 1920s but beginning perhaps in the period before the first world war.

Let me cite some figures, all for income before direct taxes, in support of this impression. In the United States, in the distribution of income among families (excluding single individuals), the shares of the two lowest quintiles rise from 13.5 percent in 1929 to 18 percent in the years after the second world war (average of 1944, 1946, 1947, and 1950); whereas the share of the top quintile declines from 55 to 44 percent, and that of the top 5 percent from 31 to 20 percent. In the United Kingdom, the share of the top 5 percent of units declines from 46 percent in 1880 to 43 percent in 1910 or 1913, to 33 percent in 1929, to 31 percent in 1938, and to 24 percent in 1947; the share of the lower 85 percent remains fairly constant between 1880 and 1913, between 41 and 43 percent, but then rises to 46 percent in 1929 and 55 percent in 1947. In Prussia, income inequality increases slightly between 1875 and 1913—the shares of the top quintile rising from 48 to 50 percent, of the top 5 percent from 26 to 30 percent; the share of the lower 60 percent, however, remains about the same. In Saxony, the change between 1880 and 1913 is minor: the share of the two lowest quintiles declines from 15 to 14.5 percent; that of the third quintile rises from 12 to 13 percent, of the fourth quintile from 16.5 to about 18 percent; that of the top quintile declines from 56.5 to 54.5 percent, and of the top 5 percent from 34 to 33 percent. In Germany as a whole, relative income inequality drops fairly sharply from 1913 to the 1920s, apparently due to decimation of large fortunes and property incomes during the war and inflation, but then begins to return to prewar levels during the depression of the 1930s.[1]

Even for what they are assumed to represent, let alone as approximations to shares in distribution by secular income levels, the data are such that differences of two or three percentage points cannot be assigned significance. One must judge by the general weight and consensus of the evidence—which unfortunately is limited to a few countries. It justifies a tentative impression of constancy in the relative distribution of income before taxes, followed by some narrowing of relative income inequality after the first world war—or earlier.

Three aspects of this finding should be stressed. First, the data are for income before direct taxes and exclude contributions by government (e.g., relief and free assistance). It is fair to argue that both the proportion and progressivity of direct taxes and the proportion of total income of individuals accounted for by government assistance to the less privileged economic groups have grown during recent decades. This is certainly true of the United States and the United Kingdom, but in the case of Germany is subject to further examination. It follows that the distribution of income after direct taxes and including free contributions by government would show an even greater narrowing of inequality in developed countries with size distributions of pretax, ex-government-benefits income similar to those for the United States and the United Kingdom.

Second, such stability or reduction in the inequality of the percentage shares was accompanied by significant rises in real income per capita. The countries now classified as developed have enjoyed rising per capita incomes except during catastrophic periods such as years of active world conflict. Hence, if the shares of groups classified by their annual income position can be viewed as approximations to shares of groups classified by their secular income levels, a constant percentage share of a given group means that its per capita real income is rising at the same rate as the average for all units in the country; and a reduction in inequality of the shares means that the per capita income of the lower-income groups is rising at a more rapid rate than the per capita income of the upper-income groups.

The third point can be put in the form of a question. Do the distributions by annual incomes properly reflect trends in distribution by secular incomes? As technology and economic performance rise to higher levels, incomes are less subject to transient disturbances, not necessarily of the cyclical order that can be recognized and allowed for by reference to business cycle chronology, but of a more irregular type. If in the earlier years the economic fortunes of units were subject to greater vicissitudes—poor crops for some farmers, natural calamity losses for some nonfarm business units—if the over-all proportion of individual entrepreneurs whose incomes were subject to such calamities, more yesterday but some even today, was larger in earlier decades, these earlier distributions of income would be more affected by transient disturbances. In these earlier distributions the temporarily unfortunate might crowd the lower quintiles and depress their shares unduly, and the temporarily fortunate might dominate the top quintile and raise its share unduly—proportionately more than in the distributions for later years. If so, distributions by longer-term average incomes might show less reduction in inequality than do the distributions by annual incomes; they might even show an opposite trend.

One may doubt whether this qualification would upset a narrowing of inequality as marked as that for the United States, and in as short a period as twenty-five years. Nor is it likely to affect the persistent downward drift in the spread of the distributions in the United Kingdom. But I must admit a strong element of judgment in deciding how far this qualification modifies the finding of long-term stability followed by reduction in income inequality in the few developed countries for which it is observed or is likely to be revealed by existing data. The important point is that the qualification is relevant; it suggests need for further study if we are to learn much from the available data concerning the secular income structure; and such study is likely to yield results of interest in themselves in their bearing upon the problem of trends in temporal instability of income flows to individual units or to economically significant groups of units in different sectors of the national economy. . . .

Hence we may conclude that the major offset to the widening of income inequality associated with the shift from agriculture and the countryside to industry and the city must have been a rise in the income share of the lower groups within the nonagricultural sector of the population. This provides a lead for exploration in what seems to me a most promising direction: consideration of the pace and character of the economic growth of the urban population, with particular reference to the relative position of lower-income groups. Much is to be said for the notion that once the early turbulent phases of industrialization and urbanization had passed, a variety of forces converged to bolster the economic position of the lower-income groups within the urban population. The very fact that, after a while, an increasing proportion of the urban population was "native," i.e., born in cities rather than in the rural areas, and hence more able to take advantage of the possibilities of city life in preparation for the economic struggle, meant a better chance for organization and adaptation, a better basis for securing greater income shares than was possible for the newly "immi-grant" population coming from the countryside or from abroad. The increasing efficiency of the older, established urban population should also be taken into account. Furthermore, in democratic societies the growing political power of the urban lower-income groups led to a variety of protec-tive and supporting legislation, much of it aimed to counteract the worst effects of rapid industrialization and urbanization and to support the claims of the broad masses for more adequate shares of the growing income of the country. Space does not permit the discussion of demographic, political, and social considerations that could be brought to bear to explain the off-sets to any declines in the shares of the lower groups, declines otherwise deducible from the trends suggested in the numerical illustration.

OTHER TRENDS RELATED
TO THOSE IN INCOME INEQUALITY

One aspect of the conjectural conclusion just reached deserves emphasis because of its possible interrelation with other important elements in the process and theory of economic growth. The scanty empirical evidence suggests that the narrowing of income inequality in the developed countries is relatively recent and probably did not characterize the earlier stages of their growth. Likewise, the various factors that have been suggested above would explain stability and narrowing in income inequality in the later rather than in the earlier phases of industrialization and urbanization. Indeed, they would suggest widening inequality in these early phases of economic growth, especially in the older countries where the emergence of the new industrial system had shattering effects on long-established pre-industrial economic and social institutions. This timing characteristic is particularly applicable to factors bearing upon the lower-income groups: the dislocating effects of the agricultural and industrial revolutions, com-bined with the "swarming" of population incident upon a rapid decline in death rates and the maintenance or even rise of birth rates, would be unfa-vorable to the relative economic position of lower-income groups. Further-more, there may also have been a preponderance in the earlier periods of factors favoring maintenance or increase in the shares of top-income groups: in so far as their position was bolstered by gains arising out of new industries, by an unusually rapid rate of creation of new fortunes, we would expect these forces to be relatively stronger in the early phases of industrialization than in the later when the pace of industrial growth slack-ens.

One might thus assume a long swing in the inequality characterizing the secular income structure: widening in the early phases of economic growth when the transition from the pre-industrial to the industrial civiliza-tion was most rapid; becoming stabilized for a while; and then narrowing in the later phases. This long secular swing would be most pronounced for older countries where the dislocation effects of the earlier phases of modern economic growth were most conspicuous; but it might be found also in the "younger" countries like the United States if the period preceding marked industrialization could be compared with the early phases of industrialization, and if the latter could be compared with the subsequent phases of greater maturity.

If there is some evidence for assuming this long swing in relative inequality in the distribution of income before direct taxes and excluding free benefits from government, there is surely a stronger case for assuming a long swing in inequality of income net of direct taxes and including government benefits. Progressivity of income taxes and, indeed, their very importance characterize only the more recent phases of development of the presently developed countries; in narrowing income inequality they must have accentuated the downward phase of the long swing, contributing to the reversal of trend in the secular widening and narrowing of income inequality.

No adequate empirical evidence is available for checking this conjecture of a long secular swing in income inequality;[2] nor can the phases be dated precisely. However, to make it more specific, I would place the early phase in which income inequality might have been widening from about 1780 to 1850 in England; from about 1840 to 1890, and particularly from 1870 on in the United States; and from the 1840s to the 1890s in Germany. I would put the phase of narrowing income inequality somewhat later in the United States and Germany than in England—perhaps beginning with the first world war in the former and the last quarter of the nineteenth century in the latter.

Is there a possible relation between this secular swing in income inequality and the long swing in other important components of the growth process? For the older countries a long swing is observed in the rate of growth of population—the upward phase represented by acceleration in the rate of growth reflecting the early reduction in the death rate which was not offset by a decline in the birth rate (and in some cases was accompanied by a rise in the birth rate); and the downward phase represented by a shrinking in the rate of growth reflecting the more pronounced downward trend in the birth rate. Again, in the older countries, and also perhaps in the younger, there may have been a secular swing in the rate of urbanization, in the sense that the proportional additions to urban population and the measures of internal migration that produced this shift of population probably increased for a while—from the earlier much lower levels; but then tended to diminish as urban population came to dominate the country and as the rural reservoirs of migration became proportionally much smaller. For old, and perhaps for young countries also, there must have been a secular swing in the proportions of savings or capital formation to total economic product. Per capita product in pre-industrial times was not large enough to permit as high a nationwide rate of saving or capital formation as was attained in the course of industrial development: this is suggested by present comparisons between net capital formation rates of 3 to 5 percent of national product in underdeveloped countries and rates of 10 to 15 percent in developed countries. If then, at least in the older countries, and perhaps even in the younger ones—prior to initiation of the process of modern development—we begin with low secular levels in the savings proportions, there would be a rise in the early phases to appreciably higher levels. We also know that during recent periods the net capital formation proportion, and even the gross, failed to rise and perhaps even declined.

Other trends might be suggested that would possibly trace long swings similar to those for inequality in income structure, rate of growth of population, rate of urbanization and internal migration, and the proportion of savings or capital formation to national product. For example, such swings might be found in the ratio of foreign trade to domestic activities; in the aspects, if we could only measure them properly, of government activity that bear upon market forces (there must have been a phase of increasing freedom of market forces, giving way to greater intervention by government). But the suggestions already made suffice to indicate that the long swing in income inequality must be viewed as part of a wider process of economic growth, and interrelated with similar movements in other elements. The long alternation in the rate of growth of population can be seen partly as a cause, partly as an effect of the long swing in income inequality which was associated with a secular rise in real per capital income levels. The long swing in income inequality is also probably closely associated with the swing in capital formation proportions—in so far as wider inequality makes for higher, and narrower inequality for lower, countrywide savings proportions.

COMPARISON OF DEVELOPED
AND UNDERDEVELOPED COUNTRIES

What is the bearing of the experience of the developed countries upon the economic growth of underdeveloped countries? Let us examine briefly the data on income distribution in the latter, and speculate upon some of the implications.

As might have been expected, such data for underdeveloped countries are scanty. For the present purpose, distributions of family income for India in 1949–50, for Ceylon in 1950, and for Puerto Rico in 1948 were used. While the coverage is narrow and the margin of error wide, the data show that income distribution in these underdeveloped countries is somewhat *more* unequal than in the developed countries during the period after the second world war. Thus the shares of the lower 3 quintiles are 28 percent in India, 30 percent in Ceylon, and 24 percent in Puerto Rico—compared with 34 percent in the United States and 36 percent in the United Kingdom. The shares of the top quintile are 55 percent in India, 50 percent in Ceylon, and 56 percent in Puerto Rico, compared with 44 percent in the United States and 45 percent in the United Kingdom.[3]

This comparison is for income before direct taxes and excluding free benefits from governments. Since the burden and progressivity of direct taxes are much greater in developed countries, and since it is in the latter that substantial volumes of free economic assistance are extended to the lower-income groups, a comparison in terms of income net of direct taxes and including government benefits would only accentuate the wider inequality of income distributions in the underdeveloped countries. Is this difference a reliable reflection of wider inequality also in the distribution of *secular* income levels in underdeveloped countries? Even disregarding the margins of error in the data, the possibility raised earlier in this chapter that transient disturbances in income levels may be more conspicuous under conditions of primitive material and economic technology would affect the comparison just made. Since the distributions cited reflect the annual income levels, a greater allowance should perhaps be made for transient disturbances in the distributions for the underdeveloped than in those for the developed countries. Whether such a correction would obliterate the difference is a matter on which I have no relevant evidence.

Another consideration might tend to support this qualification. Underdeveloped countries are characterized by low average levels of income per capita, low enough to raise the question of how the populations manage to survive. Let us assume that these countries represent fairly unified population groups, and exclude, for the moment, areas that combine large native populations with small enclaves of nonnative, privileged minorities, e.g., Kenya and Rhodesia, where income inequality, because of the excessively high income shares of the privileged minority, is appreciably wider than even in the underdeveloped countries cited above.[4] On this assumption, one may infer that in countries with low average income, the secular level of income in the lower brackets could not be below a fairly sizable proportion of average income—otherwise, the groups could not survive. This means, to use a purely hypothetical figure, that the secular level of the share of the lowest decile could not fall far short of 6 or 7 percent, i.e., the lowest decile could not have a per capita income less than six- or seven-tenths of the countrywide average. In more advanced countries, with higher average per capita incomes, even the *secular* share of the lowest bracket could easily be a smaller fraction of the countrywide average, say as small as 2 or 3 percent for the lowest decile, i.e., from a fifth to a third of the countrywide average—without implying a materially impossible economic position for that group. To be sure, there is in all countries continuous pressure to raise the relative position of the bottom-income groups; but the fact remains that the lower limit of the proportional share in the secular income structure is higher when the real countrywide per capita income is low than when it is high.

If the long-term share of the lower-income groups is larger in the underdeveloped than in the average countries, income inequality in the former should be narrower, not wider as we have found. However, if the lower brackets receive larger shares, and at the same time the very top brackets also receive larger shares—which would mean that the intermediate income classes would not show as great a progression from the bottom—the net effect may well be wider inequality. To illustrate, let us compare the distributions for India and the United States. The first quintile in India receives 8 percent of total income, more than the 6 percent share of the first quintile in the United States. But the second quintile in India receives only 9 percent, the third 11, and the fourth 16; whereas in the United States, the shares of these quintiles are 12, 16, and 22 respectively. This is a rough statistical reflection of a fairly common observation relating to income distributions in underdeveloped compared with developed countries. The former have no "middle" classes: there is a sharp contrast between the preponderant proportion of population whose average income is well below the generally low countrywide average, and a small top group with a very large relative income excess. The developed countries, on the other hand, are characterized by a much more gradual rise from low to high shares, with substantial groups receiving more than the high countrywide income average, and the top groups securing smaller shares than the comparable ordinal groups in underdeveloped countries.

It is, therefore, possible that even the distributions of secular income levels would be more unequal in underdeveloped than in developed countries—not in the sense that the shares of the lower brackets would be lower in the former than in the latter, but in the sense that the shares of the very top groups would be higher and that those of the groups below the top would all be significantly lower than a low countrywide income average. This is even more likely to be true of the distribution of income net of direct taxes and inclusive of free government benefits. But whether a high probability weight can be attached to this conjecture is a matter for further study.

In the absence of evidence to the contrary, I assume that it is true: that the secular income structure is somewhat more unequal in underdeveloped countries than in the more advanced—particularly in those of Western and Northern Europe and their economically developed descendants in the New World (the United States, Canada, Australia, and New Zealand). This conclusion has a variety of important implications and leads to some pregnant questions, of which only a few can be stated here.

In the first place, the wider inequality in the secular income structure of underdeveloped countries is associated with a much lower level of average income per capita. Two corollaries follow—and they would follow even if the income inequalities were of the same relative range in the two groups of countries. First, the impact is far sharper in the underdeveloped countries, where the failure to reach an already low countrywide average spells much greater material and psychological misery than similar proportional deviations from the average in the richer, more advanced countries. Second, positive savings are obviously possible only at much higher relative income levels in the underdeveloped countries: if in the more advanced countries some savings are possible in the fourth quintile, in the underdeveloped countries savings could be realized only at the very peak of the income pyramid, say by the top 5 or 3 percent. If so, the concentration of savings and of assets is even more pronounced than in the developed countries; and the effects of such concentration in the past may serve to explain the peculiar characteristics of the secular income structure in underdeveloped countries today.

The second implication is that this unequal income structure presumably coexisted with a low rate of growth of income per capita. The underdeveloped countries today have not always lagged behind the presently developed areas in level of economic performance; indeed, some of the former may have been the economic leaders of the world in the centuries preceding the last two. The countries of Latin America, Africa, and particularly those of Asia, are underdeveloped today because in the last two centuries, and even in recent decades, their rate of economic growth has been far lower than that in the Western World—and low indeed, if any growth there was, on a per capita basis. The underlying shifts in industrial structure, the opportunities for internal mobility and for economic improvement, were far more limited than in the more rapidly growing countries now in the developed category. There was no hope, within the lifetime of a generation, of a significantly perceptible rise in the level of real income, or even that the next generation might fare much better. It was this hope that served as an important and realistic compensation for the wide inequality in income distribution that characterized the presently developed countries during the earlier phases of their growth.

The third implication follows from the preceding two. It is quite possible that income inequality has not narrowed in the underdeveloped countries within recent decades. There is no empirical evidence to check this conjectural implication, but it is suggested by the absence, in these areas, of the dynamic forces associated with rapid growth that in the developed countries checked the upward trend of the upper-income shares that was due to the cumulative effect of continuous concentration of past savings; and it is also indicated by the failure of the political and social systems of underdeveloped countries to initiate the governmental or political practices that effectively bolster the weak positions of the lower-income classes.

Indeed, there is a possibility that inequality in the secular income structure of underdeveloped countries may have widened in recent decades—the only qualification being that where there has been a recent shift from colonial to independent status, a privileged, *nonnative* minority may have been eliminated. But the implication, in terms of the income distribution among the *native* population proper, still remains plausible.

The somber picture just presented may be an oversimplified one. But I believe that it is sufficiently realistic to lend weight to the questions it poses—questions as to the bearing of the recent levels and trends in income inequality, and the factors that determine them, upon the future prospect of underdeveloped countries within the orbit of the free world.

The questions are difficult, but they must be faced unless we are willing completely to disregard past experience or to extrapolate mechanically oversimplified impressions of past development. The first question is: Is the pattern of the older developed countries likely to be repeated in the sense that in the early phases of industrialization in the underdeveloped countries income inequalities will tend to widen before the leveling forces become strong enough first to stabilize and then reduce income inequalities? While the future cannot be an exact repetition of the past, there are already certain elements in the present conditions of underdeveloped societies, e.g., "swarming" of population due to sharp cuts in death rates unaccompanied by declines in birth rates, that threaten to widen inequality by depressing the relative position of lower-income groups even further. Furthermore, if and when industrialization begins, the dislocating effects on these societies, in which there is often an old hardened crust of economic and social institutions, are likely to be quite sharp—so sharp as to destroy the positions of some of the lower groups more rapidly than opportunities elsewhere in the economy may be created for them.

The next question follows from an affirmative answer to the first. Can the political framework of the underdeveloped societies withstand the strain which further widening of income inequality is likely to generate? This query is pertinent if it is realized that the real per capita income level of many underdeveloped societies today is lower than the per capita income level of the presently developed societies before *their* initial phases of industrialization. And yet the stresses of the dislocations incident to early phases of industrialization in the developed countries were sufficiently acute to strain the political and social fabric of society, force major political reforms, and sometimes result in civil war.

The answer to the second question may be negative, even granted that industrialization may be accompanied by a rise in real per capita product. If, for many groups in society, the rise is even partly offset by a decline in their proportional share in total product; if, consequently, it is accompanied by widening of income inequality, the resulting pressures and conflicts may necessitate drastic changes in social and political organization. This gives rise to the next and crucial question: How can either the institutional and political framework of the underdeveloped societies or the processes of economic growth and industrialization be modified to favor a sustained rise to higher levels of economic performance and yet avoid the fatally simple remedy of an authoritarian regime that would use the population as cannon-fodder in the fight for economic achievement? How to minimize the cost of transition and avoid paying the heavy price—in internal tensions, in long-run inefficiency in providing means for satisfying wants of human beings as individuals—which the inflation of political power represented by authoritarian regimes requires?

Facing these acute problems, one is cognizant of the dangers of taking an extreme position. One extreme—particularly tempting to us—is to favor repetition of past patterns of the now developed countries, patterns that, under the markedly different conditions of the presently underdeveloped countries, are almost bound to put a strain on the existing social and economic institutions and eventuate in revolutionary explosions and authoritarian regimes. There is danger in simple analogies; in arguing that because an unequal income distribution in Western Europe in the past led to accumulation of savings and financing of basic capital formation, the preservation or accentuation of present income inequalities in the underdeveloped countries is necessary to secure the same result. Even disregarding the implications for the lower-income groups, we may find that in at least some of these countries today the consumption propensities of upper-income groups are far higher and savings propensities far lower than were those of the more puritanical upper-income groups of the presently developed countries. Because they may have proved favorable in the past, it is dangerous to argue that completely free markets, lack of penalties implicit in progressive taxation, and the like are indispensable for the economic growth of the now underdeveloped countries. Under present conditions the results may be quite the opposite—withdrawal of accumulated assets to relatively "safe" channels, either by flight abroad or into real estate; and the inability of governments to serve as basic agents in the kind of capital formation that is indispensable to economic growth. It is dangerous to argue that, because in the past foreign investment provided capital resources to spark satisfactory economic growth in some of the smaller European countries or in Europe's descendants across the seas, similar effects can be expected today if only the underdeveloped countries can be convinced of the need of a "favorable climate." Yet, it is equally dangerous to take the opposite position and claim that the present problems are entirely new and that we must devise solutions that are the product of imagination unrestrained by knowledge of the past, and therefore full of romantic violence. What we need, and I am afraid it is but a truism, is a clear perception of past trends and of conditions under which they occurred, as well as knowledge of the conditions that characterize the underdeveloped countries today. With this as a beginning, we can then attempt to translate the elements of a properly understood past into the conditions of an adequately understood present.

NOTES

1. The following sources were used in calculating the figures cited: *United States*. For recent years we used *Income Distribution by Size, 1944–1950* (Washington, 1953) and Selma Goldsmith and others, "Size Distribution of Income Since the Mid-Thirties," *Rev. Econ. Stat.*, Feb. 1954, XXXVI, 1–32; for 1929, the Brookings Institution data as adjusted in Simon Kuznets, *Shares of Upper Groups in Income and Savings* (New York, 1953), p. 220.

United Kingdom. For 1938 and 1947, Dudley Seers, *The Levelling of Income Since 1938* (Oxford, 1951), p. 39; for 1929, Colin Clark, *National Income and Outlay* (London, 1937) Table 47, p. 109; for 1880, 1910, and 1913, A. Bowley, *The Change in the Distribution of the National Income, 1880–1913* (Oxford, 1920).

Germany. For the constituent areas (Prussia, Saxony and others) for years before the first world war, based on S. Prokopovich, *National Income of Western European Countries* (published in Moscow in the 1920s). Some summary results are given in Prokopovich, "The Distribution of National Income," *Econ. Jour.*, March 1926, XXXVI, 69–82. See also, "Das Deutsche Volkseinkommen vor und nach dem Kriege," *Einzelschrift zur Stat. des Deutschen Reichs*, no. 24 (Berlin, 1932), and W. S. and E. S. Woytinsky, *World Population and Production* (New York, 1953) Table 192, p. 709.

2. Prokopovich's data on Prussia, from the source cited in footnote 1, indicate a substantial widening in income inequality in the early period. The share of the lower 90 percent of the population declines from 73 percent in 1854 to 65 percent in 1875; the share of the top 5 percent rises from 21 to 25 percent. But I do not know enough about the data for the early years to evaluate the reliability of the finding.

3. For sources of these data see "Regional Economic Trends and Levels of Living," submitted at the Norman Waite Harris Foundation Institute of the University of Chicago in November 1954 (in press in the volume of proceedings). This paper, and an earlier one, "Underdeveloped Countries and the Pre-industrial Phases in the Advanced Countries: An Attempt at Comparison," prepared for the World Population Meetings in Rome held in September 1954 (in press) discuss issues raised in this section.

4. In one year since the second world war, the non-African group in Southern Rhodesia, which accounted for only 5 percent of total population, received 57 percent of total income; in Kenya, the minority of only 2.9 percent of total population, received 51 percent of total income; in Northern Rhodesia, the minority of only 1.4 percent of total population, received 45 percent of total income. See United Nations, *National Income and Its Distribution in Underdeveloped Countries*, Statistical Paper, Ser. E, no. 3, 1951, Table 12, p. 19.

6

. . . .

Cross-National Evidence
of the Domestic Gap

. . . .

MONTEK S. AHLUWALIA

This frequently cited study presents the data that have been used by many analysts to show that the gap between rich and poor is considerably wider within the developing economies than within the developed ones. The study notes a number of major limitations of the data upon which this conclusion is based but goes on to argue that these are "the only data we have" and that the conclusions drawn from such data can do more good than harm. Some critics of this view believe, however, that because large sums of development assistance funds are spent based upon the findings of studies such as this, faulty conclusions can do considerable harm—such funds will neither produce the desired result nor be available to projects that might truly benefit from them. Moreover, entire national development plans could fail if such conclusions were found to be unsupported by better data or better analysis.

Recent discussions of economic development reflect an increasing concern with widespread poverty in underdeveloped countries. The fact of poverty is not new: it was always self-evident to those familiar with economic realities. What *is* new is the suspicion that economic growth by itself may not solve or even alleviate the problem within any "reasonable" time period. Indeed it is often argued that the mechanisms which promote economic growth also promote economic concentration, and a worsening of

Reprinted by permission of Oxford University Press, Inc., from *Redistribution with Growth* by Hollis Chenery, Montek S. Ahluwalia, C. L. G. Bell, John H. Duloy, and Richard Jolly, pp. 3–10. Copyright © 1974 by the International Bank for Reconstruction and Development/The World Bank.

the relative and perhaps even absolute position of the lower-income groups. This pessimistic view has led to some questioning of growth-oriented development strategies which assume that the poverty problem would be solved without much difficulty if growth could be accelerated.

The empirical evidence underlying the new pessimism is limited but persuasive. Detailed studies of the nature and extent of poverty in particular countries show that the problem is of truly gigantic proportions. A study of poverty in India estimated that, in 1960, about 38 percent of the rural population and 50 percent of the urban population lived below a poverty level defined by consumption yielding 2,250 calories.[1] A recent study of Brazil showed that, also in 1960, about 30 percent of the total population lived below a poverty level defined by the minimum wage in northeast Brazil (the poorest region).[2] More importantly, both studies argued that the situation had worsened over the sixties, at least in terms of relative equality. Similarly pessimistic results on changes in relative equality over time were reported in a study of Argentina, Mexico, and Puerto Rico.[3] In addition to these case studies there is some evidence from cross-country analysis of distribution patterns which can be interpreted as showing that economic growth is associated with a worsening in the distribution of income, at least in the initial stages of development.

These studies raise important questions relevant to policy formulation. What is the extent of relative and absolute poverty in underdeveloped countries and does it vary systematically with the level of development? What evidence is there on the relationship between growth and inequality and how far can this relationship be affected by policy? What are the economic characteristics of the poor and what do they imply for distributional strategies? In this chapter we will attempt to sift the available evidence to provide qualitative answers to some of these questions. But first a general caveat is necessary. Analysis of income distribution problems is severely limited by the quality and reliability of the available data and a brief digression on this subject is desirable.

LIMITATIONS OF THE DATA

The primary sources of information on patterns of income distribution are sample surveys which provide data on income (and in some cases only consumption) and other socio-economic characteristics of the units sampled. Until recently, data of this type were available for only a few underdeveloped countries and generalizations about patterns of distribution were therefore based on very limited information. For example, Kuznets's (1963) study of cross-country patterns of income distribution included only eleven underdeveloped countries. The situation has changed considerably since then. A large number of surveys have been carried out in underdeveloped countries and results from these surveys are increasingly being used in analyses of income distribution problems.

Unfortunately, the increase in data availability has not been accompanied by an adequate improvement in statistical quality. In many cases the growing interest in the subject has simply led to the proliferation of crude estimates of income distribution for various countries, based on data sources which may be "the best available" but are simply not good enough. An exhaustive review of these problems is beyond the scope of this chapter, but some indication of their importance can be obtained by considering three major sources of error in this field.

First, the income concept used in many surveys falls far short of the comprehensive definition needed. For purposes of welfare measurement, the income concept should refer to "permanent income" and should include income from all sources whether accruing in the form of money income or income in kind (including production for own consumption and investment).[4] Furthermore, if it is to be a measure of welfare, the income concept should be adjusted for tax incidence and transfer payments. In practice, available surveys measure income over a short period usually a month or at most a year. Frequently they cover only money income, and sometimes only wage income, giving a distorted picture of the true distribution of income in the economy.

Second, even if the income concept is properly defined, it may be difficult to measure in practice. Very different problems arise at the two ends of the income scale. In the highest income groups there is the ever present likelihood of deliberate understatement of income for fear of incurring a tax liability. At the other end of the income scale there is a genuine difficulty in valuing production for own consumption or investment in the subsistence sectors of the economy.[5] Closely related to the measurement problem is the difficulty in using relative money incomes as a measure of relative real incomes, given the wide variation in prices facing different consumers. Rural prices of some goods are typically much lower than urban prices, so that comparisons of urban-rural money incomes typically understate rural real income levels.

Third, there is the problem of accuracy in estimating the distribution of income in the population from the observed distribution in sample surveys. The accuracy of sample estimates depends upon a number of factors relating to the size of the sample and its representativeness. Many available estimates of income distribution are derived from samples that are statistically inadequate in these respects, with the result that sample estimates are both biased and have a large variance. In several cases the samples from which data are available were never originally intended to be representative of the population as a whole.[6] In other cases, despite an attempt at ensuring representativeness, the difficulties of sample design or implementation may have proved overwhelming. For example, no adequate sampling frame may exist from which to select a sample ensuring proportional coverage of different income groups. The existence of nomadic populations or inaccessible regions presents the most extreme form of this problem.

Because of these problems, available estimates of income distribution in most underdeveloped countries are, at best, approximations of the underlying distribution we wish to measure. Inaccuracy of measurement is not, of course, unique to income distribution; national accounts data are also subject to such errors. But the data limitations for income distribution are usually regarded as more serious. National accounts data are at least collected on a systematic basis and are therefore much more comparable over time and (although to a lesser extent) between countries. No such comparability can be claimed for data on income distribution. Estimates for different countries, and even for the same country at different points of time, are typically based on noncomparable data sources, making intercountry and intertemporal comparisons very hazardous.

These limitations present a familiar dilemma in empirical analysis. The data are very weak, but they are also the only data we have. An extreme response to the problem is to reject any use of most of the available data for analytical purposes. The approach adopted in this chapter is less puristic. We assume that until better data become available, cautious use of existing data—with all its limitations—provides some perspective on the nature of the problem. In common with Kuznets (1955), our excuse "for building an elaborate structure on such a shaky foundation" is the view that "speculation is an effective way of presenting a broad view of the field and . . . so long as it is recognized as a collection of hunches calling for further investigation, rather than a set of fully tested conclusions, little harm and much good may result."

THE EXTENT OF INEQUALITY

The first step in defining the dimensions of the problem with which this volume is concerned is to consider the extent of inequality in developed and underdeveloped countries. Cross-section data are particularly useful for this purpose because they reveal possible "uniform patterns" which characterize the problem in different countries. Identifying such uniformities helps to establish "averages" with which levels of inequality observed in particular countries can be compared. They also serve to determine reasonable "benchmarks" in terms of which targets and prospects for improvement can be defined. . . .

The conventional approach to income inequality is to define the problem in purely relative terms. A familiar technique for this purpose is to measure inequality by the extent to which the income share of groups of individuals or households differs from their population share. In this section, we will examine the problem in terms of income shares of the lowest 40 percent, the middle 40 percent, and the top 20 percent of households ordinally ranked by income.[7] For some countries, distribution estimates are available only for individuals in the workforce. We have included these estimates in our data set as the best available approximation to household income distribution.

The choice of income shares instead of one of the various conventional indexes of inequality calls for some explanation.[8] The conventional indexes are designed to provide summary measures of inequality over the entire range of the population and as such may be insensitive to the degree of inequality in particular ranges. Our treatment in terms of the income shares of ordinally ranked income groups enables us to concentrate on inequality at the lower end of the income range, which may be of special interest for policy.

Table 6.1 presents income share data for sixty-six countries cross-classified according to different levels of overall inequality and per capita income levels.[9] The table distinguishes between three inequality levels defined as high, moderate, and low (according to specified ranges of the share of the lowest 40 percent) and three income groupings defined as high, middle, and low (according to specified ranges of per capita GNP). The extent of inequality varies widely among countries but the following broad patterns can be identified.

The *socialist countries* have the highest degree of overall equality in the distribution of income. This is as we would expect, since income from the ownership of capital does not accrue as income to individuals.[10] The observed inequality in these countries is due mainly to inequality in wages between sectors and skill classes. Since the structural factors operating toward equality are the strongest in these countries, their average income share of the lowest 40 percent—amounting to about 25 percent of total income—may be taken as an upper limit for the target income share to which policymakers in underdeveloped countries can aspire.

The *developed countries* are evenly distributed between the categories of low and moderate inequality. The average income share of the bottom 40 percent amounts to about 16 percent, which is lower than the average for socialist countries but better than most of the underdeveloped countries. A major problem in comparing income distribution data between developed and underdeveloped countries is that pretax data do not reflect the equalizing impact of progressive taxes combined with welfare-oriented public transfer mechanisms. These fiscal corrections are generally more substantial and more egalitarian in developed countries. If this factor is taken into account, developed countries may be somewhat more egalitarian than appears from Table 6.1.

Most of the *underdeveloped countries* show markedly greater relative

Table 6.1 Cross-Classification of Countries by Income Level and Equality

High Inequality — Share of Lowest 40 Percent Less than 12 Percent

Country (Year)	GNP/pc US$	Low 40%	Middle 40%	Top 20%
Income up to U.S. $300				
Kenya (69)	136	10.0	22.0	68.0
Sierra Leone (68)	159	9.6	22.4	68.0
Philippines (71)	239	11.6	34.6	53.8
Iraq (56)	200	6.8	25.2	68.0
Senegal (60)	245	10.0	26.0	64.0
Ivory Coast (70)	247	10.8	32.1	57.1
Rhodesia (68)	252	8.2	22.8	69.0
Tunisia (70)	255	11.4	33.6	55.0
Honduras (68)	265	6.5	28.5	65.0
Ecuador (70)	277	6.5	20.0	73.5
Income U.S. $300–$750				
Malaysia (70)	330	11.6	32.4	56.0
Colombia (70)	358	9.0	30.0	61.0
Brazil (70)	390	10.0	28.4	61.5
Peru (71)	480	6.5	33.5	60.0
Gabon (68)	497	8.8	23.7	67.5
Jamaica (58)	510	8.2	30.3	61.5
Costa Rica (71)	521	11.5	30.0	58.5
Mexico (69)	645	10.5	25.5	64.0
South Africa (65)	669	6.2	35.8	58.0
Panama (69)	692	9.4	31.2	59.4

Moderate Inequality — Share of Lowest 40 Percent Between 12 Percent and 17 Percent

Country (Year)	GNP/pc US$	Low 40%	Middle 40%	Top 20%
Income up to U.S. $300				
Salvador (69)	295	11.2	36.4	52.4
Turkey (68)	282	9.3	29.9	60.8
Burma (58)	82	16.5	38.7	44.8
Dahomey (59)	87	15.5	34.5	50.0
Tanzania (67)	89	13.0	26.0	61.0
India (64)	99	16.0	32.0	52.0
Madagascar (60)	120	13.5	25.5	61.0
Zambia (59)	230	14.5	28.5	57.0
Income U.S. $300–$750				
Dominican Republic (69)	323	12.2	30.3	57.5
Iran (68)	332	12.5	33.0	54.5
Guyana (56)	550	14.0	40.3	45.7
Lebanon (60)	508	13.0	26.0	61.0
Uruguay (68)	618	16.5	35.5	48.0
Chile (68)	744	13.0	30.2	56.8

Low Inequality — Share of Lowest 40 Percent and Above 17 Percent and Above

Country (Year)	GNP/pc US$	Low 40%	Middle 40%	Top 20%
Income up to U.S. $300				
Chad (58)	78	18.0	39.0	43.0
Sri Lanka (69)	95	17.0	37.0	46.0
Niger (60)	97	18.0	40.0	42.0
Pakistan (64)	100	17.5	37.5	30.0
Uganda (70)	126	17.1	35.8	47.1
Thailand (70)	180	17.0	37.5	45.5
Korea (70)	235	18.0	37.0	45.0
Taiwan (64)	241	20.4	39.5	40.1
Income U.S. $300–$750				
Surinam (62)	394	21.7	35.7	42.6
Greece (57)	500	21.0	29.5	49.5
Yugoslavia (68)	529	18.5	40.0	41.5
Bulgaria (62)	530	26.8	40.0	33.2
Spain (65)	750	17.6	36.7	45.7

Income Above U.S. $750

Country	GNP			
Venezuela (70)	1004	7.9	27.1	65.5
Finland (62)	1599	11.1	35.6	49.3
France (62)	1913	9.5	36.8	53.7
Argentina (70)	1079	16.5	36.1	47.4
Puerto Rico (58)	1100	13.7	35.7	50.6
Netherlands (67)	1990	13.6	37.9	48.5
Norway (68)	2010	16.6	42.9	40.5
Germany (64)	2144	15.4	31.7	52.9
Denmark (68)	2563	13.6	38.8	47.6
New Zealand (69)	2859	15.5	42.5	42.0
Sweden (63)	2949	14.0	42.0	44.0
Poland (64)	850	23.4	40.6	36.0
Japan (63)	950	20.7	39.3	40.0
U.K. (68)	2015	18.8	42.2	39.0
Hungary (69)	1140	24.0	42.5	33.5
Czechoslovakia (64)	1150	27.6	41.4	31.0
Australia (65)	2509	20.0	41.2	38.8
Canada (65)	2920	20.0	39.8	40.2
United States (70)	4850	19.7	41.5	38.8

Note: Sources for these data are listed in the Appendix [of the original article—*Eds.*]. The income shares of each percentile group were read off a free-hand Lorenz curve fitted to observe points in the cumulative distribution. The distributions are for pretax income. Per capita GNP figures are taken from the World Bank data files and refer to GNP at factor cost for the year indicated in constant 1971 U.S. dollars.

inequality than the developed countries. About half of the underdeveloped countries fall in the high inequality range with another third displaying moderate inequality. The average income share for the lowest 40 percent in all underdeveloped countries as a group amounts to about 12.5 percent, but there is considerable variation around this average. Those of the underdeveloped countries classified in the low inequality category have income shares for the lowest 40 percent averaging 18 percent, as is the case with the most egalitarian of the developed countries. Against this, however, half the underdeveloped countries show income shares of the lowest 40 percent, averaging only 9 percent.

It is worth noting that overall income inequality in the underdeveloped countries is not particularly associated with relatively low income shares for the middle-income group rather than the poorest group. This view was originally put forward by Kuznets (1963) on the basis of data for eighteen countries in which it was observed that the shares of the lowest-income groups in underdeveloped countries were comparable with those in developed countries but the shares of upper-income groups were markedly larger. Kuznets suggested that higher income inequality in underdeveloped countries may be due to greater inequality between the top and middle group and speculated that the equalizing impact of development was perhaps based on a rising share of the middle. Table 6.1 suggests that this generalization is not valid when the sample is widened to include other countries. There are many underdeveloped countries which show high inequality in terms of low income shares for both the middle and the poorest groups.

NOTES

1. Dandekar and Rath (1971). See also Bardhan (1970) and (1973).
2. Fishlow (1972).
3. Weisskoff (1970).
4. Permanent income takes account of variations over the lifetime of the individual arising from both the age profile of income and random fluctuations around this profile. Income differences due to age are an important element of observed inequality in most samples of individuals at different stages in their working life.
5. Even if the consumption items can be quantified in physical terms, there is the problem of determining the appropriate prices to use in obtaining a "money value" for this consumption. Producer prices (farm gate prices) differ from retail prices, especially in different seasons. The problem of valuing production for direct investment (i.e., various types of labor using farm improvements) is even more complex since there is typically no market for the capital good produced.
6. This is true, for example, of labor force surveys directed at determining the structure of wages, urban household surveys aimed at constructing cost-of-living indexes for particular socio-economic sections of the population and, of course, tax data which cover only a very small percentage of the population.
7. The choice of households rather than individuals as the basic income unit reflects the assumption that income within a household is equally distributed. Even

so there are problems arising from variations in household size and age structure. An alternative is to rank the population according to household per capita income, but data on this basis are available only for a few countries.

8. The best known of the various indexes is the Gini coefficient, which is based on the Lorenz curve. Others include the variance of income, the variance of logarithms of income, the coefficient of variation, and also entropy measures borrowed from information theory such as the index developed by Theil (1967). Atkinson (1970) proposes a new measure of inequality which is explicitly related to an underlying social welfare function and therefore provides a more meaningful basis for comparing or ranking alternative distributions.

9. The data are taken from Jain and Tiemann (1974). The original sources for each country as reported in that document are listed in the Appendix to Chapter 1 [in the original work—Eds.].

10. Income distribution data for these countries may overstate income equality since they frequently refer to "workers," which may exclude workers outside the state system who are usually in the lower income ranges.

REFERENCES

Atkinson, A. B. 1970. "On the Measurement of Inequality." *Journal of Economic Theory*, 2(September):244–263.

Bardhan, P. K. 1970. "On the Minimum Level of Living and the Rural Poor." *Indian Economic Review*, 5(April):129–136.

———. 1973. "On the Incidence of Poverty in Rural India in the Sixties." *Economic and Political Weekly*, 8 (February special number):245–254.

Dandekar, V. M. and N. R. Rath. 1971. "Poverty in India." *Economic and Political Weekly*, 6(January 2):25–48; (January 9):106–146.

Fishlow, A. 1972. "Brazilian Size Distribution of Income." Papers and Proceedings of the American Economic Association, 62(May):391–402.

Jain, S. and Tiemann, A. 1974. "Size Distribution of Income: A Compilation of Data." Development Research Center Discussion Paper no. 4, mimeographed. Washington, D.C.: World Bank.

Kuznets, S. 1955. "Economic Growth and Income Inequality." *American Economic Review*, 45(March):1–28.

———. 1963. "Quantitative Aspects of Economic Growth of Nations: III, Distribution of Income by Size." *Economic Development and Cultural Change*, 11(January):1–80.

Theil, H. 1967. *Economics and Information Theory.* Amsterdam: North-Holland.

Weisskoff, R. 1970. "Income Distribution and Economic Growth in Puerto Rico, Argentina and Mexico." *Review of Income and Wealth*, 16(December):303–332.

7

. . . .

A New Data Set
Measuring Income Inequality

. . . .

Klaus Deininger & Lyn Squire

In Chapter 5, Simon Kuznets suggests that income inequality worsens with economic growth until a threshold is achieved, and then increasing levels of per capita income mean a lessening of inequality. This phenomenon has been referred to as the inverted U-curve. In this chapter Klaus Deininger and Lyn Squire present the results of analysis based on a new data set on inequality in the distribution of income. The authors dispute Kuznets's assertion of the relationship between growth and changes in aggregate inequality. They do find a positive relationship, however, between growth and the reduction of poverty.

Following a long-standing recognition of potentially important relationships between economic growth and inequality, the profession has recently rediscovered the topic, emphasizing, in particular, the potential endogeneity of growth and interactions between the economic and political systems. Earlier discussions, such as the famous Kuznets Hypothesis, were framed mainly in terms of an exogenous growth process and its implications for inequality. In contrast, the recent literature has focused on the potential effects of inequality on growth in a wide variety of circumstances. Although attention has focused on both political and economic explanations for such a relationship, the underlying processes are still imperfectly understood. Indeed, theoretical models arrive at widely different conclusions, depending on the underlying assumptions. Which of these assumptions is more accurate is an empirical question that can only be

---

Excerpts reprinted with permission by the World Bank from *The World Bank Economic Review*, vol. 10, no. 3.

decided by confronting the hypotheses emerging from such models with actual data.

Empirical work using cross-country data to draw inferences regarding the relationship between growth and inequality has a long tradition and has led to a number of fruitful (or controversial) hypotheses, including Kuznets's conjecture that inequality would increase with rising incomes at early stages of development and decrease at higher levels of per capita income. The lack of time series that are sufficiently long has prevented appropriate testing of these hypotheses. Furthermore, problems in the quality of data and the fact that existing measures are often based on different definitions hamper comparability between countries—and often even within the same country over time—thus affecting empirical results in unpredictable ways. These concerns become more important as the complexity of theories about inequality and growth increases beyond the often simplistic mechanisms that characterized early models. . . .

SOME DESCRIPTIVE EVIDENCE

Our data set can be used to revisit many of the relationships among growth, inequality, and poverty that have been studied in the literature. We undertake such an analysis in a separate paper (Deininger and Squire 1996). Here we use our data set to illustrate intertemporal and interregional differences in inequality and to provide an exploratory descriptive assessment of the relationship between growth, inequality, and poverty defined on the basis of income received by the bottom quintile. We highlight, among other points, how share data can usefully complement the one-dimensional Gini index of income inequality. We also explore the relationship between aggregate growth and changes in real income received by different quintile groups in the population. A similar exercise has been undertaken by Ravallion and Chen (1995), who focus on poverty defined as percentage of the population receiving less than a certain percentage of the mean. Ravallion and Chen concentrate on growth spells observed during the 1980s for forty-two developing countries. Given the large number of observations from Eastern European countries included, together with the relatively atypical performance of this group during the period concerned, the results of the study depend heavily on sample composition but, in general, do not contradict the findings reported here.

Regional Differences in Inequality

Decadal averages of inequality indexes across regions are presented in Table 7.1. The regional averages are unweighted means of country averages during the period under concern. We have used raw data (that is, unadjusted data) and note that the composition of each regional sample can change

Table 7.1   Decadal Averages of Inequality Indexes, by Region (Gini coefficients)

Region	Overall Average	1960s	1970s	1980s	1990s
Latin America and the Caribbean	49.78	53.24	49.06	49.75	49.31
Sub-Saharan Africa	46.05	49.90	48.19	43.46	46.95
Middle East and North Africa	40.49	41.39	41.93	40.45	38.03
East Asia and the Pacific	38.75	37.43	39.88	38.70	38.09
South Asia	35.08	36.23	33.95	35.01	31.88
Industrial countries and high-income developing countries	34.31	35.03	34.76	33.23	33.75
Eastern Europe	26.57	25.09	24.63	25.01	28.94

Note: Figures reported are unweighted averages of Gini coefficients of economies in each region. The sample includes 108 economies. Changes within regions may be caused by the fact that not all economies have observations for all decades.

Source: Authors' calculations based on various sources as described in the text.

over the four decades. The measures are relatively stable through time, but they differ substantially across regions, a result that emerges for individual countries as well (Li, Squire, and Zou 1996). The average standard deviation within countries (in a sample of countries for which at least four observations are available) is 2.79, compared with a standard deviation for the country-specific means of 9.15. We distinguish between three groups of regions, with considerable variation of Gini coefficients within regions:

- Latin America and the Caribbean and Sub-Saharan Africa. Inequality is highest in Latin America and Sub-Saharan Africa, where the simple average of country-level Gini coefficients is almost 50, ranging from 57 in Brazil to 42 in Bolivia. None of the Latin American countries has an average Gini coefficient below 40, in contrast to Sub-Saharan Africa, where the range is from 28.9 in Rwanda to 62.3 in South Africa. Gini coefficients for the countries in the Middle East and North Africa region are in the 40s, although the fact that most of the coefficients are based on expenditure rather than income may imply that they somewhat understate actual income inequality.
- *East Asia and South Asia.* East Asia and South Asia are characterized by average Gini coefficients in the middle to upper 30s that range from a high of about 50 in Malaysia and the Philippines to less than 30 in Taiwan (China). Gini coefficients are based on income for all economies except India.
- *Industrial and high-income developing countries.* Gini coefficients in the low 30s characterize the industrial and high-income developing economies. Although inequality in several industrial countries (including the United Kingdom and the United States) increased during the 1990s, this increase was compensated for by a decrease

in inequality in countries such as Canada and Finland and by a relatively constant distribution of income in the Netherlands and Sweden. The historically low levels of Eastern Europe, a region that, with Gini coefficients in the mid-20s, is much more egalitarian than the rest of the world, show a considerable increase in the 1990s. For many of these countries (including the Russian Federation), Gini coefficients now stand in the lower 30s, comparable to those of some of the industrial countries.

Shares of total income received by different quintiles, possibly a more tangible indicator of inequality, are given in Table 7.2. Although the aggregate picture is similar to the one conveyed by Gini coefficients, the share of income received by specific quintiles is not always completely congruent with the Gini coefficient, even at the regional level. For example, despite

Table 7.2   Income Shares of Different Quintiles, by Decade and Region

Quintile and Region	Overall Average	1960s	1970s	1980s	1990s
Lowest quintile					
Sub-Saharan Africa	5.26	2.76	5.10	5.70	5.15
East Asia and the Pacific	6.34	6.44	6.00	6.27	6.84
South Asia	7.74	7.39	7.84	7.91	8.76
Eastern Europe	9.34	9.67	9.76	9.81	8.83
Middle East and North Africa	6.66	5.70	—	6.64	6.90
Latin America and the Caribbean	3.86	3.42	3.69	3.67	4.52
Industrial countries and high-income developing countries	6.42	6.42	6.31	6.68	6.26
Middle class (third and fourth quintiles)					
Sub-Saharan Africa	34.06	32.72	32.15	35.40	33.54
East Asia and the Pacific	37.02	36.29	36.88	37.18	37.53
South Asia	37.25	37.05	37.89	37.17	38.42
Eastern Europe	40.65	39.69	41.59	41.25	40.01
Middle East and North Africa	36.28	35.30	—	35.88	36.84
Latin America and the Caribbean	33.21	28.13	34.59	33.58	33.84
Industrial countries and high-income developing countries	40.99	39.89	40.61	41.21	41.80
Top quintile					
Sub-Saharan Africa	51.79	61.97	55.82	48.86	52.37
East Asia and the Pacific	45.73	45.90	46.50	45.51	44.33
South Asia	43.01	44.05	42.19	42.57	39.91
Eastern Europe	36.11	36.30	34.51	34.64	37.80
Middle East and North Africa	46.32	49.00	—	46.72	45.35
Latin America and the Caribbean	55.12	61.62	54.18	54.86	52.94
Industrial countries and high-income developing countries	40.42	41.22	41.11	39.89	39.79

— Not Available

Source: Authors' calculations based on various sources described in the text.

similar Gini coefficients in both regions, the top and bottom quintiles receive a higher share of total income in South Asia than in industrial countries. Despite a lower Gini coefficient than in Eastern Europe, the middle class in industrial countries receives a greater share and the top quintile a lower share than in Eastern Europe.

It has long been known that, in the presence of intersecting Lorenz curves, movements of the Gini coefficient may not accurately indicate changes in the welfare of individual groups in a population. Our data suggest that intersecting Lorenz curves are indeed observed in most cases (55 percent of the countries). This observation would imply that, within countries, there may be considerable changes in the income shares received by individual quintile groups of the population, despite the apparent stability of the Gini coefficient. By contrast, large differences in the Gini coefficient across countries need not necessarily be accompanied by an equally large variation in the shares of individual income groups.

Within countries, we do indeed find that changes in the aggregate Gini index and changes in the income shares of individual income groups are not very highly correlated, especially for the subsample of countries with intersecting Lorenz curves. Simple correlation coefficients for this subsample range from –0.3 for changes in the share of the bottom 20 and 40 percent to 0.2 for the top 20 percent. The correlation is insignificant for changes in the shares of the third and fourth quintiles. The corresponding correlation coefficients for the complete sample are –0.53 between the change in the Gini coefficient and income growth for the bottom 20 and 40 percent, –0.26 between changes in the Gini and changes in the shares of the third and fourth quintiles, and 0.48 between changes in the Gini and changes in the share of the top quintile of income receivers.

Changes of similar magnitude in the income share of any given quintile could be associated with quite significantly different changes in the aggregate Gini coefficient. To illustrate, we compare two cases in which the share of the bottom quintile declined by about 4 percentage points. In Indonesia the decline occurred between 1978 and 1980 and was accompanied by a significant increase in the shares of the second to fourth quintiles and a decrease in the share of the top quintile, resulting in a net decrease of the Gini coefficient by about 3 points. In Hong Kong, a similar decline occurred between 1986 and 1991, but in this case the shares of both the third and the fourth quintiles increased, resulting in an increase in the Gini coefficient of 1.4 points.

Across countries, the intersection of Lorenz curves in pairwise comparisons is a frequent occurrence. As a consequence, large differences in Gini coefficients can be associated with income shares for individual population groups that are remarkably similar. Countries in which Gini coefficients differ by as much as 10 or more points may have almost identical shares of income for the bottom quintile. For example, the Gini coefficient in Korea in 1985 was 35.5, compared with 50 in Colombia in 1970. The bottom quintile received almost 7 percent of total income in both cases.

We conclude that, because Lorenz curves are observed to cross frequently, Gini coefficients and income shares can usefully complement each other in many types of analysis. . . .

Growth, Inequality, and Poverty

The question of whether, or under what conditions, growth is associated with changes in inequality has intrigued economists for a long time. For all but a few countries for which long-enough time series have been available, for example, India, a satisfactory treatment of this issue has been precluded by a lack of sufficient country-level data and the fact that cross-sectional studies might pick up unobservable country-specific effects. Our data can be used to eliminate time-invariant country effects and to investigate the relationship between growth rates of aggregate income and inequality as measured by the Gini index. In addition, we can use the information on changes in individual quintiles' shares of total income together with information on aggregate growth to investigate changes in the real income received by different quintile groups and in particular the bottom 20 percent in the population. Real income is obtained by multiplying the share of each quintile with real national per capita income (purchasing-power parity estimates, obtained from the Summers-Heston 1991 data set). Here we provide a descriptive analysis of these relationships.

We focus on the relation between changes in overall income and inequality during decadal growth episodes that are defined by the availability of distributional data that span at least one decade. The results illustrate two points (see Table 7.3). First, there appears to be little systematic relationship between growth and changes in aggregate inequality. Periods of aggregate growth were associated with an increase in inequality almost as often (forty-three cases) as with a decrease in inequality (forty-five cases). Similarly, periods of economic decline were associated with increased

Table 7.3   Growth, Inequality, and Poverty

Indicator	Periods of Growth (88)		Periods of Decline (7)	
	Improved	Worsened	Improved	Worsened
Inequality	45	43	2	5
Income of the poor[a]	77	11	2	5

Note: "Improved" in the income distribution implies a decrease of the Gini coefficient; "worsened" implies an increase. The sample includes ninety-five economies.
    a. The income of the lowest quintile.
Source: Authors' calculations based on various sources as described in the text.

inequality in five cases and with a more equitable distribution of income in two cases. The simple correlation between contemporaneous as well as lagged income growth and the change in the Gini coefficient is insignificant for the whole sample as well as for subsamples defined in terms of country characteristics (rich or poor, equal or unequal, fast-growing or slow-growing economies), suggesting no strong relationship between growth and changes in aggregate inequality.

The main reason for the lack of relationship appears to be that, whether average incomes are increasing or declining, changes in the Gini coefficient of inequality tend to be small (see Li, Squire, and Zou 1996). Thus, the average annual percentage change in the Gini coefficients in our sample was only 0.28 points, compared with an average growth rate in per capita income of 2.16 percent. Some examples illustrate the quantitative significance of this point. In Taiwan (China), real income per capita increased fivefold, from US$1,540 in 1964 to US$8,063 in 1990, whereas the Gini index barely changed, declining from 32.2 to 30.1. Similar outcomes can be observed in other economics: In the United States, real income increased from US$8,772 in 1950 to US$17,594 in 1991, yet the Gini index changed hardly at all, moving from 36.0 to 37.9. Brazil saw real income increase from US$1,784 in 1960 to US$4,271 in 1989 while the Gini index moved from 53.0 to 59.6. Even where inequality changed considerably, as in Thailand, where the Gini index moved from 41.3 in 1962 to 51.5 in 1991, the change in the index seems small compared with the fourfold increase in real income. This lack of change suggests that efforts to find systematic links between inequality and aggregate growth may have to be rethought (see Deininger and Squire 1996).

The second point is that changes in the absolute income received by different quintiles reveal additional information that is not captured in our aggregate measure of inequality. In particular, although we do not find significant correlations between aggregate growth and changes in inequality, there is a strong correlation between aggregate growth and changes in the income of all quintiles except the top one. Changes in absolute income enable us to investigate to what degree growth would be impoverishing, that is, to what degree increases in mean income would be associated with a fall in the income of the poor. We find that for most of the growth episodes in our sample, growth of average income, even if accompanied by increases in inequality, led to an increase in incomes for the members of the lowest quintile (see Table 7.3). Aggregate growth was associated with an increase in the incomes of the poorest quintile in more than 85 percent of the ninety-one cases.

Nonconforming growth episodes are ones in which either the economy grew and the income of the poor decreased or the economy declined and the poor benefited. A case-by-case review of the thirteen nonconforming growth episodes confirms the strong association between aggregate growth and improvements in income for all groups of the population. In nine of the thirteen cases, the association can be shown to be caused by the use of ten-year growth spells; the association disappears when longer periods are considered. In three of the remaining four cases, aggregate growth was low—below 2 percentage points. This leaves only one case, Colombia from 1970 to 1980, where a growth rate of slightly more than 2 percent was associated with a slight decrease (0.9 percent) in the income of the poor. Thus, there is not a very strong basis on which to question the generally positive association between growth and the welfare of the bottom quintile.

To sum up, our data suggest no systematic relationship between growth of aggregate income and changes in inequality as measured by the Gini coefficient. The data do, however, suggest that a mere focus on distribution that neglects the large cross-country differences in overall growth may lead to flawed conclusions. Especially because changes in inequality tend to be relatively modest, we find a strong link between overall growth and a reduction in poverty. This link supports the hypothesis that economic growth benefits the poor in the large majority of cases, whereas economic decline generally hurts the poor.

CONCLUSION

This article originated in an attempt to provide a data set on inequality that could narrow the gap between the far-reaching implications of the theoretical literature on inequality and the much more limited empirical evidence available to actually support and test such theories. To that end, we have expanded the available information on inequality. In our view, we have been more successful in improving the within-country, time-series dimension of the data, a significant improvement given that the evolution of inequality is inherently an intertemporal issue. At the same time, we have identified a number of factors that are likely to affect cross-country research. We therefore caution researchers who use these data to interpret results carefully in light of the issues discussed here, to subject them to sensitivity analysis and tests for robustness, and to complement analysis based on summary statistics (such as the Gini coefficient) with data on income shares.

NOTES

Klaus Deininger and Lyn Squire are with the Policy Research Department at the World Bank. The authors are grateful to Roland Benabou, Shaohua Chen, Gaurav Datt, Hamid Davoodi, Bill Easterly, Gary Fields, Emmanuel Jimenez, Peter Lanjouw, Branko Milanovic, Lant Pritchett, and Yvonne Ying for their advice and/or data, and to participants in seminars at the World Bank, Cornell University, the Harvard Growth Conference, and the Institute of Developing Economies (Tokyo) for their comments. The authors thank Hongyi Li and Tao Zhang for very able research assistance.

REFERENCES

The word "processed" describes informally reproduced works that may not be commonly available through library systems.

Alesina, Alberto, and Dani Rodrik. 1994. "Distributive Politics and Economic Growth." *Quarterly Journal of Economics* 109(2, May):465–90.

Anand, Sudhir, and R. S. M. Kanbur. 1993. "Inequality and Development: A Critique." *Journal of Development Economics* 41(1):19–43.

Chen, Shao-hua, Gaurav Datt, and Martin Ravallion. 1995. "Is Poverty Increasing in the Developing World?" Data Appendix, updated version. World Bank, Policy Research Department, Washington, D.C. Processed.

Cromwell, Jerry. 1977. "The Size Distribution of Income: An International Comparison." *Review of Income and Wealth* 23(3, September):291–308.

Deininger, Klaus, and Lyn Squire. 1996. "New Ways of Looking at Old Issues: Inequality and Growth." World Bank, Policy Research Department, Washington, D.C. Processed.

Fields, Gary S. 1989a. "Changes in Poverty and Inequality in Developing Countries." *The World Bank Research Observer* 4(2):167–85.

———. 1989b. "A Compendium of Data on Inequality and Poverty for the Developing World." Cornell University, Department of Economics, Ithaca, N.Y. Processed.

Jain, Shail. 1975. *Size Distribution of Income: A Compilation of Data.* Washington, D.C.: World Bank.

Jenkins, Stephen P. 1991. "The Measurement of Income Inequality." In Lars Osbert, ed., *Economic Inequality and Poverty: International Perspectives.* Armonk, N.Y.: Sharpe, pp. 3–38.

Lecaillon, Jacques, Felix Paukert, Christian Morrisson, and Dimitri Germidis. 1984. *Income Distribution and Economic Development: An Analytical Survey.* Geneva: International Labour Office.

Li, Hongyi, Lyn Squire, and Heng-fu Zou. 1996. "Explaining International and Intertemporal Income Inequality." World Bank, Policy Research Department, Washington, D.C. Processed.

Persson, Torsten, and Guido Tabellini. 1995. "Is Inequality Harmful for Growth?" *American Economic Review* 84(3, June):600–21.

Ravallion, Martin, and Shaohua Chen. 1995. "What Can New Survey Data Tell Us about Recent Changes in Living Standards in Developing and Transitional Economies?" World Bank, Policy Research Department, Washington, D.C. Processed.

Summers, Robert, and Alan Heston. 1991. "The Penn World Table (Mark 5): An Expanded Set of International Comparisons, 1950-1988." *Quarterly Journal of Economics* 106(2, May):327–68.

World Bank. 1995. *World Development Report 1995: Workers in an Integrating World.* New York: Oxford University Press.

8

· · · · · · ·

Inequality and Insurgency

· · · · · · ·

Edward N. Muller
& Mitchell A. Seligson

What are the consequences of the widespread domestic income inequality that have been noted in Part 2 of this volume? In this chapter Muller and Seligson conduct a cross-national test using a large database. They find that when income inequality is high, the probability of domestic political violence increases substantially. This finding suggests that income inequality can lead to uprisings, guerrilla movements, and civil wars, as have occurred in Vietnam, Central America, and elsewhere. Since the violence invariably causes considerable destruction of property, not to speak of the lives lost, economic growth is adversely affected. Thus, in addition to creating normative problems, income inequality also seems to be responsible for violence and, in turn, slowed economic growth. The inescapable conclusion is that income inequality matters a great deal, for when it is high, a vicious circle of violence and slowed growth is the result.

Many students of domestic political conflict consider inequality in the distribution of land and/or lack of land ownership (landlessness) to be among the more fundamental economic preconditions of insurgency and revolution (e.g., Huntington 1968; Midlarsky 1981, 1982; Midlarsky and Roberts 1985; Paige 1975; Prosterman 1976; Prosterman and Riedinger 1982; Russett 1964; Tanter and Midlarsky 1967). Huntington (1968, 375), whose writing on the subject has been particularly influential, advanced a strong version of the land maldistribution hypothesis as follows: "Where the conditions of land-ownership are equitable and provide a viable living for the

Reprinted with permission by the American Political Science Association from *American Political Science Review*, vol. 81, no. 2 (1987):425–450.

peasant, revolution is unlikely. Where they are inequitable and where the peasant lives in poverty and suffering, revolution is likely, if not inevitable, unless the government takes prompt measures to remedy these conditions." However, because mass revolutions are rare events, it is more plausible to relax the postulate that revolution is an inevitable consequence of land maldistribution and to restate the hypothesis: the greater the maldistribution of land, the greater the probability of mass-based political insurgency and, consequently, the greater the *vulnerability* of a country to revolution from below. This weaker, necessary-but-not-sufficient version of the land-maldistribution-leads-to-revolution hypothesis directs attention to the relationship between land distribution and mass political violence.

The land maldistribution hypothesis is based on the assumption that discontent resulting from a highly concentrated distribution of land and/or lack of land ownership (landlessness) in agrarian societies is an important direct cause of mass political violence. Advocates of what has come to be called the "resource mobilization" approach to the explanation of collective protest and violence (e.g., Gamson 1975; Oberschall 1973; Tilly 1978) reject such discontent hypotheses for the reason that inequality and discontent are more or less always present in virtually all societies and that consequently the most direct and influential explanatory factor must not be discontent per se but rather the *organization* of discontent. Thus Skocpol (1979, 112–57), who is skeptical of discontent theories of revolution, argues that the peasant revolts that were a crucial insurrectionary ingredient in the French, Russian, and Chinese revolutions occurred not because of the maldistribution of landholdings but rather because communities of French, Russian, and Chinese peasants had sufficient autonomy from local landlords to enable them to mobilize collectively. By contrast, Midlarsky (1982, 15–20), a proponent of discontent theory, explains the peasant revolts in each of these cases by the fact that rapid population growth severely exacerbated land inequality until a level of deprivation was reached that no longer could be tolerated.

Two contemporary cases cited by Midlarsky and Roberts (1985) in support of the land maldistribution hypothesis are El Salvador and Nicaragua.[1] Compared with other middle-income developing countries, population growth in El Salvador and Nicaragua was above average during the 1960s and 1970s (see World Bank 1981, tbl. 17). Maldistribution of land also was a serious problem, as the Gini coefficient of land concentration was .80 for Nicaragua and .81 for El Salvador (values well above the global mean of .60) and agricultural households without land (i.e., tenants, sharecroppers, and agricultural laborers) amounted to 40% of the total labor force in El Salvador circa 1970, which was the highest level of landlessness in the world at that time (data are not available for Nicaragua).[2] Each country subsequently experienced a relatively high rate of mass political violence, which in the Nicaraguan case culminated in revolution.

But the seemingly obvious conclusion that land maldistribution must have been a primary cause of political violence in El Salvador and Nicaragua ignores the fact that, during the same period of time, two other Central American states, Costa Rica and Panama, remained quite peaceful despite the presence of exactly the same preconditions supposed to have caused the insurgency in El Salvador and Nicaragua. Costa Rica and Panama experienced above-average population growth (in fact, Costa Rica's 3.4% annual population-growth rate during 1960–70 not only exceeded the 2.9% rate registered by El Salvador and Nicaragua but was also among the highest in the entire world); land was concentrated in the hands of the few to about the same degree in Costa Rica (the Gini coefficient was .82) and Panama (Gini coefficient of .78) as in El Salvador and Nicaragua; and the amount of landlessness in Costa Rica (24%) and in Panama (36.2%) ranked ninth and third highest in the world, respectively. Nevertheless, during 1970–77 Panama registered only a single death from political violence, and there were no instances of deadly political violence in Costa Rica (see Taylor and Jodice 1983, vol. 2, tbl. 2.7).

Comparison of Costa Rica and Panama with El Salvador and Nicaragua thus raises the issue of the general validity of the land maldistribution hypothesis: Are Costa Rica and Panama merely exceptions to the rule, or is maldistribution of land in reality a minor or even irrelevant factor in the process that generates insurgency and revolution? That question is significant not only because inequality is frequently assumed in academic writing to be an important determinant of political instability; it also has profound policy implications because land reform has traditionally been a cornerstone of U.S. efforts to promote political stability in developing countries.

INEQUALITY, RESOURCE MOBILIZATION, AND THE STRUCTURE OF THE STATE

We argue that theories emphasizing land maldistribution as a fundamental precondition of insurgency and revolution are misspecified. They attribute direct causal significance to an inequality variable that plays only a relatively small, indirect part in the generation of mass political violence. We hypothesize that the more important direct cause of variation in rates of political violence cross-nationally is inequality in the distribution of income rather than maldistribution of land. This hypothesis is predicated on the following assumptions:

1. Inequality in the contemporary world generates discontent;
2. Although inequality is present to some degree in all societies, some societies are significantly more inegalitarian than others;

3. Inequality in the distribution of land and inequality in the distribution of income are not necessarily tightly connected; in particular, they are sufficiently independent of each other that an effect of one on a response variable such as the rate of political violence does not necessarily imply that the other will have a similar effect;

4. Given the existence of inequality-based discontent, it is more difficult to mobilize peasant communities than urban populations for political protest; peasants normally become the foot soldiers of insurgent movements only if they are effectively organized by a "vanguard" of urban professional revolutionaries.

From these assumptions we derive the following postulates:

1. A high level of income inequality nationwide significantly raises the probability that at least some dissident groups will be able to organize for aggressive collective action. This is because, first, the pool of discontented persons from which members can be drawn will include the more easily mobilized urban areas; and, second, it may be possible for urban revolutionaries to establish cross-cutting alliances with groups in the countryside.

2. A high level of agrarian inequality does not necessarily raise the probability that dissident groups will be able to organize for aggressive collective action; this is because the pool of discontented persons from which members can be drawn may be restricted to the countryside, which is difficult to mobilize; consequently, we predict that if income inequality is relatively low, the rate of political violence will tend to be relatively low, even if agrarian inequality is relatively high; whereas if income inequality is relatively high, the rate of political violence will tend to be relatively high, even if agrarian inequality is relatively low.

Our inequality hypothesis, which is based on an integration of discontent (or relative deprivation) arguments (e.g., Gurr 1970) with the resource mobilization approach, can be illustrated by the cases of Costa Rica and Venezuela, where egalitarian redistribution of income occurred despite persisting high agrarian inequality; and the case of Iran, where income inequality worsened, especially in urban areas, despite an egalitarian land reform.

Costa Rica circa 1960 had a relatively inegalitarian distribution of land (the 1963 Gini coefficient was .78) and an extremely inegalitarian distribution of income (the richest 20% of families received 61% of total personal income in 1961). During the decade of the 1960s the distribution of land in Costa Rica became slightly more concentrated (the 1973 Gini coefficient was .82). The distribution of income, however, was substantially altered in an egalitarian direction by democratically elected reformist administrations who pursued welfare-state policies similar to those of European social democratic governments. By 1970 the share of national income accruing to the richest quintile of Costa Rican households had been reduced to 50%.[3] As mentioned above, violent conflict was absent from Costa Rican politics during the 1970s.

Venezuela was a similarly inegalitarian society circa 1960, when a democratic regime was inaugurated. The 1956 Gini index of land concentration was .91—the second highest in the world next to Peru—and the richest quintile of Venezuelan households received 59% of total personal income in 1962. During the 1960s the distribution of land in Venezuela remained highly concentrated (the 1971 Gini coefficient was .91), but the distribution of income became more egalitarian—although not as dramatically so as in Costa Rica—due to a combination of reformist administrations and an expanding petroleum-based economic pie (by 1970 the income share of the richest quintile of households had been reduced to 54%). Deaths from political violence in Venezuela registered a sharp decline over this period (according to Taylor and Jodice 1983, vol. 2, tbl. 2.7, they amounted to 1,392 during the years 1958–62; 155 during 1963–67; 53 during 1968–72; and 9 during 1973–77). . . .

Of course, income inequality is not the only cause of mass political violence. In Panama, for example, income was distributed very unequally circa 1970, as the richest 20% of households earned 62% of total national income. But by the early 1970s, General Omar Torrijos Herrera, who had led a successful coup d'etat by officers of the national guard in 1968, had crushed all opposition, established firm censorship of the media, and taken control of the judiciary. Ratings of political rights and civil liberties in Panama during the mid-1970s on a scale of one to seven (most free to least free) averaged 6.5.[4] During this period (1973–77) the Torrijos regime in Panama was the most repressive in the Western Hemisphere next to Cuba, where the rating of political rights and civil liberties averaged 6.9. Inequality-induced discontent presumably existed in Panama, and it probably was relatively widespread, but there was little or no opportunity to organize it.

By contrast, Panama's next-door neighbor to the northwest, Costa Rica, enjoyed the distinction in the mid-1970s of being the oldest democracy in Latin America. Since 1949 Costa Rica had held regularly scheduled free and fair elections, the media were uncensored, unions were free to organize, the judiciary was independent of the executive and legislative branches of government, and citizens were not subject to arbitrary arrest. Costa Rica's political and civil rights ratings averaged a maximum score of 1.0 during 1973–77.

The "open" and "closed" political systems of Costa Rica and Panama exemplify polar extremes of regime repressiveness. Differences in regime structure are relevant to the explanation of cross-national variation in mass political violence because they can be assumed to affect three important variables emphasized in some versions of resource mobilization theory (e.g., McAdam 1982): (1) the extent to which dissident groups are able to develop strong organizations, (2) their belief in the likelihood of success of collective action, and (3) the range of political opportunities available to them for achieving their goals.

In the context of an extremely repressive regime, dissident groups are severely restricted in their ability to organize; their belief in the likelihood of success of collective action will probably be low; and opportunities to engage in collective action of any kind will be quite limited. Consequently, under the condition of a high level of regime repressiveness, rational actors most likely will attach a relatively low utility to violent collective action, and the rate of mass political violence therefore should be relatively low.

In the context of a nonrepressive or "democratic" regime, dissident groups will not face significant restrictions on their ability to organize for collective action, and their belief in the likelihood of achieving at least some success from collective action will probably be relatively high. Moreover, a democratic regime structure will afford a variety of opportunities for dissident groups to participate legally and peacefully in the political process. Because the costs of peaceful collective action will be lower than those of violent collective action and because the likelihood of success of peaceful collective action will be reasonably high, rational actors under the condition of a nonrepressive regime structure presumably will usually attach a much higher utility to peaceful as opposed to violent collective action, and, therefore, the rate of mass political violence here too should be relatively low.

In the context of a semirepressive regime, it is possible for dissident groups to develop relatively strong organizations. However, opportunities to engage in nonviolent forms of collective action that effectively exert influence on the political process are limited. Semirepressive regimes allow only for, in Green's (1984, 154) apt terminology, "pseudoparticipation . . . an elaborate charade of the participatory process." Polities with pseudoparticipation typically have elections that are not free and fair, legislatures that are little more than debating societies, and a judiciary that is not independent of the will of the executive; the media are subject to censorship at the whim of the executive; and citizens are subject to arbitrary arrest and detention by security forces, which are under the exclusive control of the executive. In short, semirepressive regimes erect a facade of participatory institutions but do not permit popular input to significantly influence governmental output. Because opportunities for genuine participation are restricted, many politically activated citizens may come to perceive civil disobedience and violence as being more efficacious than legal means of pseudoparticipation; and since the expected costs of insurgency may not be perceived to be prohibitive, rational actors may well attach a relatively high utility to aggressive political behavior. Therefore, it is plausible to expect that the rate of mass political violence cross-nationally will be highest under semirepressive authoritarian regimes.

The analysis of the causes of the Iranian revolution by Green (1982, 1984) documents in detail how the Shah vacillated between fully restricting mass participation and allowing pseudoparticipation and concludes that "the effects of such tactics served to increase popular hostility among those socially mobilized Iranians eager to have a measure of influence over the manner in which their society was ruled" (Green, 1984, 155). Green's case study description is corroborated by global comparative measures of regime repressiveness, which show that Iran in the late 1950s was classified as having a "semi-competitive" regime (Coleman 1960), was scored for 1960 and 1965 as intermediate (34.9 and 45.0, respectively) on a 0–100 scale of extent of political democracy (Bollen 1980); was ranked circa 1969 at an intermediate level on a scale of opportunity for political opposition (Dahl 1971); received a mean rating of 5.7 on political and civil rights for 1973–77; and had shifted in 1978 to a mean rating of 5.0 on political and civil rights. Thus, while pursuing a strategy of economic development that had the short-term consequence of increasing inequality in the distribution of income, the Pahlavi government would appear to have added fuel to the fire by following a semirepressive political development strategy that allowed opposition groups to organize but did not enable them to participate effectively.

If one takes income inequality and the repressiveness of the regime into account simultaneously, it might be argued that each variable could have an independent causal impact on the likelihood of mass political violence. An equally plausible specification of the joint relationship is that discontent resulting from income inequality will affect political violence only (or most strongly) in countries with semirepressive regime structures; whereas in countries with nonrepressive regime structures, inequality-induced discontent will tend to be channeled into peaceful participation; and in countries with repressive regime structures, it will be borne apathetically or else perhaps lead to various kinds of nonpolitical deviant behavior. . . .

A CROSS-NATIONAL TEST OF THE CAUSAL MODEL

There have been no studies reported to date that compare the causal importance of land maldistribution versus income inequality as determinants of mass political violence cross-nationally.[5] Until the 1970s, reasonably reliable information on the distribution of land and income was available for only a limited number of countries. Thus in Hibbs's (1973) comprehensive cross-national study of determinants of mass political violence during the 1948–67 period, inequality variables had to be excluded because of insufficient data. We now have been able to compile a relatively comprehensive data set on inequality circa 1970 [appendix in original—Eds.]. Information on land inequality is available for approximately three-quarters of the population of independent political units in 1970, while information on landlessness and income inequality is available for approximately one-half of the population. Regionally, these data are quite comprehensive for Europe and the Americas. In regard to landlessness and, especially, income distribution, coverage is poor for states in the Middle East and North Africa, and it is somewhat limited for the states of sub-Saharan Africa. Since it is unlikely that much new data on inequality circa 1970 will emerge in the future, results using the current data set can probably be regarded as being about as definitive as possible for this time period.

Measurement of the Dependent Variable

Political violence is measured by the natural logarithm of the death rate from domestic conflict per one million population.[6] Annual death counts are from Table 2.7 of Taylor and Jodice (1983, vol. 2). Current political violence is the logged sum of annual deaths from domestic political conflict during 1973–77 divided by midinterval population; lagged political violence is the logged sum of annual deaths from domestic political conflict during 1968–72 divided by midinterval population. Countries where domestic political conflict overlaps with major interstate wars are excluded: Kampuchea, Laos, and South Vietnam for the 1968–77 period; and Pakistan for the 1968–72 period (where an extremely high death rate reflects the conflict between India and Pakistan in 1971 over the secession of Bangladesh). Ireland also is excluded for the 1973–77 period because the relatively high death rate there reflects a spillover from the Northern Ireland conflict.

In the vast majority of countries, the death rate from political violence per one million population is less than 50. A few countries register very extreme scores, however; for example, Zimbabwe's 1973–77 death rate from political violence was 544 per million and Argentina's death rate was 177 per million. Even after logging, countries with political violence death rates of 50 or more almost always show up as outliers in regression equations (i.e., they usually have extremely high standardized residuals). Consequently, in order to reduce the problem of extreme scores on the dependent variable, it is desirable to set a ceiling on the death rate. The upper limit that we have selected is 50 deaths per million. The adjusted death rate variables thus range from a minimum value of 0 to a maximum value of 50 or more; and the range of the logged death rate variables is from 0 to 3.93.

Measurement of the Independent Variables

The data on land inequality circa 1970 encompass 85 states in which agriculture was not collectivized. Land inequality is measured by the Gini coefficient of land concentration. A weighted index of land inequality is the geometric mean of the Gini coefficient (expressed as a percentage) and the percentage of the labor force employed in agriculture in 1970 (see Taylor and Jodice 1983, vol. 1). Apart from measurement of the extent to which land is concentrated in the hands of the few, we also take into account a second aspect of land maldistribution, landlessness, as measured by agricultural households without land as a proportion of the total labor force. These data are derived from estimates by Prosterman and Riedinger (1982) of the proportion in 64 countries of agricultural households without land.

Income inequality is measured by the size of the share of personal income accruing to the richest quintile of recipients, based on information about the nationwide distribution of income in 63 countries compiled principally from publications of the World Bank. Although some previous studies have used Gini coefficients of income concentration, this measure tends to be unduly sensitive to inequality in the middle of the distribution, whereas inequality in reference to the top of the distribution probably is more relevant to political violence. In any event, income shares also have a more direct meaning than Gini coefficients and are currently more frequently used in research on income inequality.

Regime repressiveness is measured by a country's 1973–77 average annual combined rating on 7-point rank-order scales of political rights and civil liberties that have been reported by Raymond D. Gastil since 1973 (the data are from Taylor and Jodice 1983). A semirepressive regime structure is defined operationally as a mean political rights and civil liberties rank in the range of 2.6–5.5. These cutpoints are identical to those used by Gastil for classifying political systems as "free" (1.0–2.5), "partly free" (2.6–5.5), and "not free" (5.6–7.0).

The indicator of governmental acts of coercion is the negative sanctions variable (imposition of sanctions) from Taylor and Jodice 1983 (vol. 2, tbl. 3.1). Current negative sanctions is the frequency of negative sanctions summed over the years 1973–77 and divided by midinterval total population in millions; lagged negative sanctions are the 1968–72 frequency per one million midinterval population. The negative sanctions variables are expressed as natural logarithms (after adding an increment of one).

The indicator of intensity of separatism is an ordinal scale developed by Ted and Erika Gurr. The data for circa 1975 are from Taylor and Jodice 1983, 55–57 and tbl. 2.5. We express intensity of separatism as a dummy variable, scored 1 (i.e., high intensity) if groups or regions actively advocating greater autonomy were forcibly incorporated into the state (codes 3 and 4) and 0 (i.e., low intensity) otherwise (codes 0, 1, and 2).[7]

Level of economic development is measured by energy consumption per capita in 1970 (from Taylor and Jodice 1983, vol. 1). Values of this variable are expressed as natural logarithms.

Land Maldistribution, Income Inequality, and Political Violence

According to what is generally considered to be the most appropriate specification of the land inequality hypothesis (e.g., Huntington 1968; Nagel 1976; Prosterman 1976), the strongest effect on political violence should be observed when inequality in the distribution of land is weighted by the proportion of the labor force employed in the agricultural sector of the economy. This specification implies a multiplicative interaction between land inequality and the size of the agricultural labor force, which we call *agrarian inequality*, defined operationally as the geometric mean of Gini land concentration and the percentage of the labor force employed in agriculture (i.e., the square root of the product of these variables). . . .

RESULTS

The results of testing the inequality hypotheses in the context of a multivariate model of determinants of political violence are summarized in Figure 8.1. All of the evidence that we have considered points to the presence of a robust, positive monotonic (positively accelerated) relationship between income inequality and political violence that is independent of the other variables in the model. The effect of income inequality on political violence may be enhanced by the presence of a semirepressive regime, but the evidence is not conclusive in that regard, so we represent the possibility of an interaction between income inequality and semirepressiveness by dashed arrows. The other solid arrows linking explanatory variables to political violence also denote relationships that hold for change as well as level of violence and seem to be robust. We have tested the regime-repressiveness hypothesis with a dummy variable in this study (in order to take into account the possibility of an interaction with income inequality). It should be noted, however, that the same kind of effect appears if regime repressiveness is expressed as a continuous quantitative variable—that is, if the semirepressive-regime dummy variable is replaced by regime repressiveness and its square, a statistically significant nonmonotonic-inverted-U-curve relationship between regime repressiveness and political violence is consistently observed in multivariate equations that include income inequality and the other explanatory variables. We have not tested for the possibility of an instantaneous reciprocal relationship between political violence and governmental acts of coercion (see Hibbs 1973) because that

Figure 8.1   Observed Causal Paths in the Multivariate Causal Model

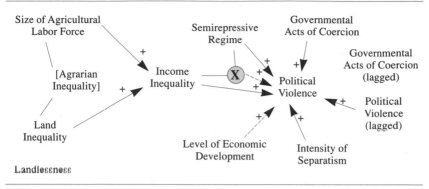

is a complex topic requiring a separate paper. From preliminary work, however, we are confident that it is valid to infer the presence of a positive effect of current governmental acts of coercion on current political violence. . . .

The only completely irrelevant variable in the model is landlessness, a finding that runs counter to the strong claim of causal importance for this variable made by Prosterman (1976). Moreover, at least as a general determinant of mass political violence, the condition of high agrarian inequality also fails to warrant the strong causal claims made for it by many scholars. The components of agrarian inequality, land inequality and size of the agricultural labor force, affect income inequality and, therefore, are indirectly relevant to political violence, but neither the weighted index of agrarian inequality nor land inequality per se has any direct effect on political violence.

DISCUSSION

The finding that agrarian inequality is relevant only to the extent that it is associated with inequality in the nationwide distribution of income has important policy implications. Land reform in third world countries all too often is considered to be a panacea for problems of inequality. However, as Huntington (1968, 385) points out, redistribution of land is the most difficult of reforms for modernizing governments because it almost always entails some degree of outright confiscation. And our study indicates that land redistribution is also not necessarily the most meaningful of reforms. If land redistribution is carried through to the point of actually effecting an egalitarian redistribution of income, as seems to have been the case in countries as diverse as Taiwan and Egypt, and/or if other economic development policies do not exacerbate income inequality, then land reform can make a contribution to the promotion of political stability. However, there are cases such as Bolivia and Mexico in which land reform has not been associated with egalitarian income redistribution. Land reform without income redistribution is probably at best merely a temporary palliative; and at worst, as the case of Iran demonstrates, it can be quite counterproductive by alienating powerful conservative groups such as the nobility and the clergy. Indeed, by simultaneously encouraging both land reform and a policy of rapid economic growth that ignored inegalitarian distributional consequences, U.S. advisors to the Shah would appear unwittingly to have exacerbated the economic preconditions of revolution in Iran.

If the effect of income inequality on change in political violence and its level, observed for 60 and 62 cases, is reliable and more or less generalizable across time in the contemporary world (at least for nontraditional societies where modern values like equality can be assumed to have become salient), it follows that redistribution of income must be ranked as one of the more meaningful reforms that a modernizing government can undertake in the interest of achieving political stability. Unfortunately, redistribution of income may conflict not only with the class interests of many third world governments but also with their predilection for rapid industrialization. The Shah's great dream of surpassing Sweden by the year 2000 was dashed in part by his single-minded concern with economic growth and the raising of per capita income. As Green (1982, 70–71) points out, "the premise of the Pahlavi development ethos rested on the assumption that economic development was more important than political rights or justice." Iran in the years immediately preceding the revolution indeed registered an extraordinary growth of per capita gross national product, which averaged an increase of 13.3% annually during 1970–78, the highest rate of growth of GNP per capita in the world (see Taylor and Jodice 1983, vol. 1, tbl. 3.6); but at the same time that per capita income was increasing phenomenally, the distribution of that income was apparently becoming more concentrated at the top, presumably heightening perceptions of economic injustice. It is important to emphasize, however, that there is no necessary trade-off between rapid economic growth and income inequality. Taiwan's average annual growth of GNP per capita during 1960–78 was 6.6% (see World Bank 1980, tbl. 1), a rate that, although surpassed by Iran (the world leader excluding Romania), was nevertheless almost twice as high as the average rate (3.7%) for all middle-income countries. At the same time (1964–78), the income share of the richest 20% of households in Taiwan declined from 41.1% to 37.2% (see Tsiang 1984, tbl. 9). Thus, by following a different set of economic policies than the Shah, the government of Taiwan achieved growth with equity. And the death rate from political violence in Taiwan during 1973–77 was .06, as compared with Iran's rate of .91. . . .

NOTES

A version of this paper was presented at the 1985 Midwest Political Science Association meeting in Chicago, April 18–21. Support for this research was provided by National Science Foundation Grant SES83-2021.

1. Midlarsky and Roberts distinguish between these cases in regard to the dynamics of coalition formation leading to different kinds of revolutionary movements. Although both countries had inegalitarian distributions of land, creating a potential for insurgency in each case, the revolutionary movement in El Salvador was more narrowly class-based than in Nicaragua, due to differences in population density that produced greater land scarcity in El Salvador than in Nicaragua. This difference is thought to have enhanced the likelihood of a successful revolution in Nicaragua.

2. Unless otherwise noted, data on land and income distribution referred to in the text are either from Table A-1 [see original work] or, for years other than those in Table A-1, from the sources cited therein.

3. Based on a study reported by Céspedes (1979). Trejos (1983) reports the income share of the richest 20% of households in Costa Rica as 51.1% in 1971, 52.1% in 1974, and 53% in 1977.

4. These and all subsequent data on civil and political liberties referred to in the text are calculated from the data file of the *World Handbook of Political and Social Indicators*. For a description of the ratings, see Taylor and Jodice 1983 (1:58–65).

5. The only previous research on this topic is reported in Midlarsky 1981, where income distribution is measured by an index of intersectoral inequality. As Sigelman and Simpson (1977, 111) have pointed out, however, this index "is at best a second-rate measurement proxy for personal income, lacking theoretical interest of its own."

6. Deaths from political violence are an attribute of political-protest events like riots, armed attacks, and assassinations. Deaths are thus a summary measure of the intensity of political-protest events. Deaths are used in preference to a composite index for the following reasons: (1) a single-variable indicator is more easily interpretable than a composite measure; (2) deaths will necessarily correlate very strongly with a composite measure such as that constructed by Hibbs (1973), which includes deaths, armed attacks, and assassinations; and (3) there is probably less reporting bias for deaths than for indicators such as armed attacks (see Weede 1981). Death *rate* is preferred over raw counts because the former is an indicator of the extent to which the regime is threatened by insurgency, which depends not on the absolute frequency of political violence but rather on its frequency relative to size of population (for further discussion of this issue see Linehan 1976; Muller 1985; and Weede 1981). The logarithmic transformation is theoretically appropriate because death rate from political violence is expected to vary as a positively accelerated function of inequality; it is also necessary because of the presence of extreme values—although the problem of extreme values still exists after logging. An increment of one is added to each death score before logging because the log of zero is undefined.

7. In testing the multivariate model across 62 cases, the following countries are missing data on intensity of separatism: Barbados, Gabon, Honduras, Ivory Coast, Malawi, Nepal, Sierra Leone, and Trinidad and Tobago. Based on country descriptions from Banks 1976, these countries were scored zero on intensity of separatism.

REFERENCES

Ahluwalia, Montak S. 1976. Inequality, Poverty, and Development. *Journal of Development Economics* 3:307–42.

Bandura, Albert. 1973. *Aggression: A Social Learning Analysis.* Englewood Cliffs, NJ: Prentice-Hall.

Banks, Arthur S., ed. 1976. *Political Handbook of the World: 1976.* New York: McGraw-Hill.

Bharier, Julian. 1971. *Economic Development in Iran 1900–1970.* New York: Oxford University Press.

Bollen, Kenneth A. 1980. Issues in the Comparative Measurement of Political Democracy. *American Sociological Review* 45:370–90.

Bornschier Volker, and Peter Heintz, eds. 1979. *Compendium of Data for World System Analysis.* Zurich: Soziologisches Institut der Universität.

Buss, Arnold H. 1961. *A Psychology of Aggression.* New York: Wiley.

Céspedes, Victor H. 1979. *Evolución de la distribución del ingreso en Costa Rica.* Serie divulgación económica, No. 18. Costa Rica: Ciudad Universitaria Rodrigo Facio.

Coleman, James S. 1960. Conclusion: The Political Systems of the Developing Areas. In *The Politics of the Developing Areas,* ed. Gabriel A. Almond and James S. Coleman. Princeton: Princeton University Press.

Dahl, Robert A. 1971. *Polyarchy.* New Haven: Yale University Press.

Fei, John C. H., Gustav Ranis, and Shirley W. Y. Kuo. 1979. *Growth with Equity: The Taiwan Case.* New York: Oxford University Press.

Food and Agriculture Organization of the United States. 1981. *Nineteen Seventy World Census of Agriculture: Analysis and International Comparison of the Results.* Rome: author.

Gamson, William A. 1975. *The Strategy of Social Protest.* Homewood, IL: Dorsey.

Green, Jerrold D. 1982. *Revolution in Iran.* New York: Praeger.

Green, Jerrold D. 1984. Countermobilization as a Revolutionary Form. *Comparative Politics* 16:153–69.

Gurr, Ted Robert. 1970. *Why Men Rebel.* Princeton: Princeton University Press.

Hardy, Melissa A. 1979. Economic Growth, Distributional Inequality, and Political Conflict in Industrial Societies. *Journal of Political and Military Sociology* 5:209–27.

Hibbs, Douglas A. 1973. *Mass Political Violence.* New York: Wiley.

Huntington, Samuel P. 1968. *Political Order in Changing Societies.* New Haven: Yale University Press.

Jabbari, Ahmad. 1981. Economic Factors in Iran's Revolution: Poverty, Inequality, and Inflation. In *Iran: Essays on a Revolution in the Making,* ed. Ahmad Jabbari and Robert Olson. Lexington, KY: Mazda.

Jain, Shail. 1975. *Size Distribution of Income.* Washington, DC: World Bank.

Keddie, Nikki R. 1968. The Iranian Village before and after Land Reform. *Journal of Contemporary History* 3:69–91.

Leal, Maria Angela. 1983. Heritage of Hunger: Population, Land, and Survival. In *Revolution in Central America,* ed. Stanford Central America Action Network. Boulder, CO: Westview.

Linehan, William J. 1976. Models for the Measurement of Political Instability. *Political Methodology* 3:441–86.

McAdam, Doug. 1982. *Political Process and the Development of Black Insurgency.* Chicago: University of Chicago Press.

Midlarsky, Manus I. 1981. The Revolutionary Transformation of Foreign Policy:

Agrarianism and Its International Impact. In *The Political Economy of Foreign Policy Behavior*, ed. Charles W. Kegley and Patrick J. McGowan. Beverly Hills, CA: Sage.

Midlarsky, Manus I. 1982. Scarcity and Inequality. *Journal of Conflict Resolution* 26:3–38.

Midlarsky, Manus I., and Kenneth Roberts. 1985. Class, State, and Revolution in Central America: Nicaragua and El Salvador Compared. *Journal of Conflict Resolution* 29:163–93.

Muller, Edward N. 1985. Income Inequality, Regime Repressiveness, and Political Violence. *American Sociological Review* 50:47–61.

Muller, Edward N. 1986. Income Inequality and Political Violence: The Effect of Influential Cases. *American Sociological Review* 51:441–45.

Nagel, Jack. 1976. Erratum. *World Politics* 28:315.

Norusis, Marija J. 1986. *SPSS/PC+*. Chicago: SPSS.

Oberschall, Anthony. 1973. *Social Conflict and Social Movements*. Englewood Cliffs, NJ: Prentice-Hall.

Paige, Jeffery M. 1975. *Agrarian Revolution*. New York: Free Press.

Paukert, Felix. 1973. Income Distribution at Different Levels of Development: A Survey of Evidence. *International Labour Review* 108:97 125.

Prosterman, Roy L. 1976. IRI: A Simplified Predictive Index of Rural Instability. *Comparative Politics* 8:339–54.

Prosterman, Roy L., and Jeffrey M. Riedinger. 1982. Toward an Index of Democratic Development. In *Freedom in the World: Political Rights and Civil Liberties 1982*, ed. Raymond D. Gastil. Westport, CT: Greenwood Press.

Roberti, Paolo. 1974. Income Distribution: A Time-Series and a Cross-Section Survey. *Economic Journal* 84:629–38.

Russett, Bruce M. 1964. Inequality and Instability: The Relation of Land Tenure to Politics. *World Politics* 16:442–54.

Sawyer, Malcolm. 1976. Income Distribution in OECD Countries. *OECD Economic Outlook*, Occasional Studies, July, 3–36.

Seligson, Mitchell A., Richard Hough, John Kelley, Stephen Miller, Russell Derossier, and Fred L. Mann. 1983. *Land and Labor in Guatemala: An Assessment*. Washington, DC: Agency for International Development and Development Associates.

Sigelman, Lee, and Miles Simpson. 1977. A Cross-National Test of the Linkage between Economic Inequality and Political Violence. *Journal of Conflict Resolution* 21:105–28.

Skocpol, Theda. 1979. *States and Social Revolutions*. New York: Cambridge University Press.

Tanter, Raymond, and Manus I. Midlarsky. 1967. A Theory of Revolution. *Journal of Conflict Resolution* 11:264–80.

Taylor, Charles L., and Michael C. Hudson. 1972. *World Handbook of Political and Social Indicators*. 2d ed. New Haven: Yale University Press.

Taylor, Charles L., and David A. Jodice. 1983. *World Handbook of Political and Social Indicators*. 3d ed. Vols. 1 and 2. New Haven: Yale University Press.

Tilly, Charles. 1969. Collective Violence in European Perspective. In *Violence in America: Historical and Comparative Perspectives*, ed. Hugh Davis Graham and Ted Robert Gurr. New York: Signet Books.

Tilly, Charles. 1978. *From Mobilization to Revolution*. Reading, MA: Addison-Wesley.

Trejos, Juan Diego. 1983. *La distribución del ingreso de las familias Costarricenses: Algunas características en 1977*. San Jose: Instituto investigaciones en ciencias económicas, Universidad de Costa Rica, No. 50.

Tsiang, S. C. 1984. Taiwan's Economic Miracle: Lessons in Economic Development. In *World Economic Growth*, ed. Arnold C. Harberger. San Francisco: Institute for Contemporary Studies.

United States Agency for International Development. 1983. *Country Development Strategy Statement: Jamaica, FY 1985*. Washington, DC: Government Printing Office.

Webb, Richard C. 1976. The Distribution of Income in Peru. In *Income Distribution in Latin America*, ed. Alejandro Foxley. New York: Cambridge University Press.

Weede, Erich. 1981. Income Inequality, Average Income, and Domestic Violence. *Journal of Conflict Resolution* 25:639–53.

Weede, Erich. 1986. Income Inequality and Political Violence Reconsidered. *American Sociological Review* 51:438–41.

World Bank. 1979, 1980, 1981, 1982, 1983, 1984, 1985. *World Development Report*. New York: Oxford University Press.

PART 3

· · · · · · · · · · · · · ·

The Classic Thesis Revisited: Limits to Convergence

· · · · · · · · · · · · · ·

9

· · · · · · ·

Catching Up, Forging Ahead, and Falling Behind

· · · · · · ·

MOSES ABRAMOVITZ

In this chapter Moses Abramovitz explains convergence theory, the idea that there is an inverse relationship between the level and rate of productivity growth: Labor productivity in poor countries is thought to have a higher potential for rapid growth than in rich countries. The expectation is that over time the GNP/pc growth rates of poor countries will be more rapid than those of the rich, and thus the gap between rich and poor countries will close. However, not all poor countries have higher labor productivity rates than rich countries, according to Abramovitz, because they lack the "social capacity" to utilize modern technology. Recently there has been considerable discussion of how developed countries can remain "competitive" with developing countries, where labor costs are often a fraction of those in the developed countries. Abramovitz suggests that this is as much a political as an economic question.

Among the many explanations of the surge of productivity growth during the quarter century following World War II, the most prominent is the hypothesis that the countries of the industrialized "West" were able to bring into production a large backlog of unexploited technology. The principal part of this backlog is deemed to have consisted of methods of production and of industrial and commercial organization already in use in the United States at the end of the war, but not yet employed in the other countries of the West. In this hypothesis, the United States is viewed as the "leader," the other countries as "followers" who had the opportunity to "catch up." In

Reprinted with permission of Cambridge University Press from *Journal of Economic History*, vol. 46, no. 2 (June 1986): 386–405. Copyright © 1986 The Economic History Association.

conformity with this view, a waning of the opportunity for catching up is frequently advanced as an explanation of the retardation in productivity growth suffered by the same group of followers since 1973. Needless to say, the size of the initial backlog and its subsequent reduction are rarely offered as sole explanations of the speedup and slowdown, but they stand as important parts of the story.

These views about postwar following and catching up suggest a more general hypothesis that the productivity levels of countries tend to converge. And this in turn brings to mind old questions about the emergence of new leaders and the historical and theoretical puzzles that shifts in leadership and relative standing present—matters that in some respects fit only awkwardly with the convergence hypothesis. . . .

I. THE CATCH-UP HYPOTHESIS

The hypothesis asserts that being backward in level of productivity carries a *potential* for rapid advance. Stated more definitely the proposition is that in comparisons across countries the growth rates of productivity in any long period tend to be inversely related to the initial levels of productivity.

The central idea is simple enough. It has to do with the level of technology embodied in a country's capital stock. Imagine that the level of labor productivity were governed entirely by the level of technology embodied in capital stock. In a "leading country," to state things sharply, one may suppose that the technology embodied in each vintage of its stock was at the very frontier of technology at the time of investment. The *technological* age of the stock is, so to speak, the same as its *chronological* age. In an otherwise similar follower whose productivity level is lower, the technological age of the stock is high relative to its chronological age. The stock is obsolete even for its age. When a leader discards old stock and replaces it, the accompanying productivity increase is governed and limited by the advance of knowledge between the time when the old capital was installed and the time it is replaced. Those who are behind, however, have the potential to make a larger leap. New capital can embody the frontier of knowledge, but the capital it replaces was technologically superannuated. So—the larger the technological and, therefore, the productivity gap between leader and follower, the stronger the follower's potential for growth in productivity; and, other things being equal, the faster one expects the follower's growth rate to be. Followers tend to catch up faster if they are initially more backward.

Viewed in the same simple way, the catch-up process would be self-limiting because as a follower catches up, the possibility of making large leaps by replacing superannuated with best-practice technology becomes smaller and smaller. A follower's potential for growth weakens as its productivity level converges towards that of the leader.

This is the simple central idea. It needs extension and qualification. There are at least four extensions:

(1) The same technological opportunity that permits rapid progress by modernization encourages rapid growth of the capital stock partly because of the returns to modernization itself, and partly because technological progress reduces the price of capital goods relative to the price of labor. So—besides a reduction of technological age towards chronological age, the rate of rise of the capital-labor ratio tends to be higher. Productivity growth benefits on both counts. And if circumstances make for an acceleration in the growth of the capital stock its chronological age also falls.[1]

(2) Growth of productivity also makes for increase in aggregate output. A broader horizon of scale-dependent technological progress then comes into view.

(3) Backwardness carries an opportunity for modernization in disembodied, as well as in embodied, technology.

(4) If countries at relatively low levels of industrialization contain large numbers of redundant workers in farming and petty trade, as is normally the case, there is also an opportunity for productivity growth by improving the allocation of labor.

Besides extension, the simple hypothesis also needs qualification.

First, technological backwardness is not usually a mere accident. Tenacious societal characteristics normally account for a portion, perhaps a substantial portion, of a country's past failure to achieve as high a level of productivity as economically more advanced countries. The same deficiencies, perhaps in attenuated form, normally remain to keep a backward country from making the full technological leap envisaged by the simple hypothesis. I have a name for these characteristics. Following Kazushi Ohkawa and Henry Rosovsky, I call them "social capability."[2] One can summarize the matter in this way. Having regard to technological backwardness alone leads to the simple hypothesis about catch-up and convergence already advanced. Having regard to social capability, however, we expect that the developments anticipated by that hypothesis will be clearly displayed in cross-country comparisons only if countries' social capabilities are about the same. One should say, therefore, that a country's potential for rapid growth is strong not when it is backward without qualification, but rather when it is technologically backward but socially advanced.

The trouble with absorbing social capability into the catch-up hypothesis is that no one knows just what it means or how to measure it. In past work I identified a country's social capability with technical competence, for which—at least among Western countries—years of education may be a rough proxy, and with its political, commercial, industrial, and financial institutions, which I characterized in more qualitative ways.[3] I had in mind mainly experience with the organization and management of large-scale enterprise and with financial institutions and markets capable of mobilizing capital for individual firms on a similarly large scale. On some occasions the situation for a selection of countries may be sufficiently clear. In explaining postwar growth in Europe and Japan, for example, one may be able to say with some confidence that these countries were competent to absorb and exploit then existing best-practice technology. More generally, however, judgments about social capability remain highly problematic. A few comments may serve to suggest some of the considerations involved as well as the speculative nature of the subject.

One concerns the familiar notion of a trade-off between specialization and adaptability. The content of education in a country and the character of its industrial, commercial, and financial organizations may be well de-signed to exploit fully the power of an existing technology; they may be less well fitted to adapt to the requirements of change. Presumably, some capacity to adapt is present everywhere, but countries may differ from one another in this respect, and their capacities to adapt may change over time.

Next, the notion of adaptability suggests that there is an interaction between social capability and technological opportunity. The state of education embodied in a nation's population and its existing institutional arrangements constrains it in its choice of technology. But technological opportunity presses for change. So countries learn to modify their institutional arrangements and then to improve them as they gain experience. The constraints imposed by social capability on the successful adoption of a more advanced technology gradually weaken and permit its fuller exploitation. . . .

Social capability, finally, depends on more than the content of education and the organization of firms. Other aspects of economic systems count as well—their openness to competition, to the establishment and operation of new firms, and to the sale and purchase of new goods and services. Viewed from the other side, it is a question of the obstacles to change raised by vested interests, established positions, and customary relations among firms and between employers and employees. The view from this side is what led Mancur Olson to identify defeat in war and accompanying political convulsion as a radical ground-clearing experience opening the way for new men, new organizations, and new modes of operation and trade better fitted to technological potential.[4]

These considerations have a bearing on the notion that a follower's potential for rapid growth weakens as its technological level converges on the leader's. This is not necessarily the case if social capability is itself endogenous, becoming stronger—or perhaps weaker—as technological gaps close. In the one case, the evolution of social capability connected with catching up itself raises the possibility that followers may forge ahead of even progressive leaders. In the other, a leader may fall back or a follower's pursuit may be slowed.

There is a somewhat technical point that has a similar bearing. This is the fact, noticed by Kravis and Denison, that as followers' levels of per capita income converge on the leader's, so do their structures of consumption and prices. R.C.O.[5] Matthews then observed that the convergence of consumption and production patterns should make it easier, rather than more difficult, for followers to borrow technology with advantage as productivity gaps close.[6] This, therefore, stands as still another qualification to the idea that the catch-up process is steadily self-limiting.

The combination of technological gap and social capability defines a country's *potentiality* for productivity advance by way of catch-up. This, however, should be regarded as a potentiality in the long run. The pace at which the potentiality is realized depends on still another set of causes that are largely independent of those governing the potentiality itself. There is a long story to tell about the factors controlling the rate of realization of potential.[7] Its general plot, however, can be suggested by noting three principal chapter headings:

(1) The facilities for the diffusion of knowledge—for example, channels of international technical communication, multinational corporations, the state of international trade and of direct capital investment.

(2) Conditions facilitating or hindering structural change in the composition of output, in the occupational and industrial distribution of the workforce, and in the geographical location of industry and population. Among other factors, this is where conditions of labor supply, the existence of labor reserves in agriculture, and the factors controlling internal and international migration come in.

(3) Macroeconomic and monetary conditions encouraging and sustaining capital investment and the level and growth of effective demand.

Having considered the technological catch up idea, with its several extensions and qualifications, I can summarize by proposing a restatement of the hypothesis as follows:

Countries that are technologically backward have a potentiality for generating growth more rapid than that of more advanced countries, provided their social capabilities are sufficiently developed to permit successful exploitation of technologies already employed by the technological leaders. The pace at which potential for catch-up is actually realized in a particular period depends on factors limiting the diffusion of knowledge, the rate of structural change, the accumulation of capital, and the expansion of demand. The process of catching up tends to be self-limiting, but the strength of the tendency may be weakened or overcome, at least for limited periods, by advantages connected with the convergence of production patterns as followers advance towards leaders or by an endogenous enlargement of social capabilities.

II. HISTORICAL EXPERIENCE WITH CATCHING UP

I go on now to review some evidence bearing on the catch-up process. The survey I make is limited to the 16 countries covered by the new Maddison estimates of product per worker-hour for nine key years from 1870 to 1979.[8] The estimates are consistently derived as regards gross domestic product and worker hours and are adjusted as regards levels of product per worker hour by the Kravis estimates of purchasing power parities for postwar years. I have compressed the message of these data into three measures (See Tables 9.1 and 9.2):

(1) Averages of the productivity levels of the various countries relative to that of the United States, which was the leading country for most of the period. (For 1870 and 1890, I have also calculated averages of relatives based on the United Kingdom.) I calculate these averages for each of the nine key years and use them to indicate whether productivity levels of followers, *as a group,* were tending to converge on that of the leader.[9]

(2) Measures of relative variance around the mean levels of relative

Table 9.1   Comparative Levels of Productivity, 1870–1979: Means and Relative Variance of the Relatives of 15 Countries Compared with the United States (U.S. GDP per manhour = 100)[a]

	(1) Mean	(2) Coefficient of Variance[b]
1870	77 (66)	.51 (.51)
1890	68 (68)	.48 (.48)
1913	61	.33
1929	57	.29
1938	61	.22
1950	46	.36
1960	52	.29
1973	69	.14
1979	75	.15

a. 1870 and 1890. Figures in parentheses are based on relatives with the United Kingdom = 100.

b. Standard deviation divided by mean.

Source: Calculated from Angus Maddison, *Phases of Capitalist Development* (New York, 1982), Tables 5.2 and C.10.

Table 9.2   **The Association (Rank Correlation) Between Initial Levels and Subsequent Growth Rates of Labor Productivity (GDP per manhour in 16 countries, 1870–1979)**

Shorter Periods			Lengthening Periods Since 1870	
	(1)	(2)		(3)
1870–1913	–.59		1870–1890	–.32
1870–1890		–.32	–1913	–.59
1890–1913		–.56	–1929	–.72
			–1938	–.83
1913–1938	–.70		–1950	–.16
1913–29		–.35	–1960	–.66
1929–38		–.57	–1973	–.95
			–1979	–.97
1938–1950	+.48			
1950–1979	–.92			
1950–60		–.81		
1960–73		–.90		
1973–79		–.13		

Source of underlying data: Maddison, *Phases*, Tables 5.1, 5.2, and C.10.

productivity. These provide one sort of answer to the question of whether the countries that started at relatively low level of productivity tended to advance faster than those with initially higher levels.

(3) Rank correlations between initial levels of productivity and subsequent growth rates. If the potential supposedly inherent in technological backwardness is being realized, there is likely to be some inverse correlation; and if it works with enough strength to dominate other forces the coefficients will be high.

The data I use and the measures I make have a number of drawbacks. The data, of course, have the weaknesses that are inherent in any set of estimates of GDP and manhours, however ably contrived, that stretch back far into the nineteenth century. Beyond that, however, simple calculations such as I have made fail, in a number of respects, to isolate the influence of the catch-up hypothesis proper.

To begin with, my measures do not allow for variation in the richness of countries' natural resources in relation to their populations. Labor productivity levels, therefore, are not pure reflections of levels of technology. In the same way, these levels will also reflect past accumulations of reproducible capital, both physical and human, and these may also be independent of technological levels in one degree or another. Further, the measured growth rates of labor of productivity will be influenced by the pace of capital accumulation. As already said, differences in rates of accumulation may reflect countries' opportunities to make advances in technology, but rates of capital formation may also be independent, to some degree, of countries' potentials for technological advance. Finally, my measures make no allowance for countries' variant abilities to employ current best-practice technology for reasons other than the differences in social capability already discussed. Their access to economies of scale is perhaps the most important matter. If advanced technology at any time is heavily scale-dependent and if obstacles to trade across national frontiers, political or otherwise, are important, large countries will have a stronger potential for growth than smaller ones.

There are many reasons, therefore, why one cannot suppose that the expectations implied by the catch-up hypothesis will display themselves clearly in the measures I present. It will be something if the data show some systematic evidence of development consistent with the hypothesis. And it will be useful if this provides a chance to speculate about the reasons why the connections between productivity levels and growth rates appear to have been strong in some periods and weak in others.

Other countries, on the average, made no net gain on the United States in a period longer than a century (Table 9.1, col. 1). The indication of very limited, or even zero, convergence is really stronger than the figures suggest. This is because the productivity measures reflect more than gaps in technology and in reproducible capital intensity, with respect to which catch-up is presumably possible. As already said, they also reflect differences in natural resource availabilities which, of course, are generally favorable to America and were far more important to America and to all the other countries in 1870 than they are today. In 1870, the agricultural share of United States employment was 50 percent; in 1979, 3.5 percent. For the other 15 countries, the corresponding figures are 48 and 8 percent on the average. The declines were large in all the countries.[10] So the American advantage in 1870 depended much more on our favorable land-man ratio than it did in 1979. Putting it the other way, other countries on the average must have fallen back over the century in respect to the productivity determinants in respect to which catch-up is possible.

In other respects, however, one can see the influence of the potential for catching up clearly. The variance among the productivity levels of the 15 "follower" countries declines drastically over the century—from a coefficient of variation of 0.5 in 1870 to 0.15 in 1979. Not only that: the decline in variance was continuous from one key year to the next, with only one reversal—in the period across World War II. In the same way, the inverse rank correlation between the initial productivity levels in 1870 and subsequent growth rates over increasingly long periods becomes stronger and stronger, until we reach the correlation coefficient of −.97 across the entire 109 years.[11] (Again there was the single reversal across World War II when the association was actually—and presumably accidentally—positive.)

I believe the steadily declining variance measures and the steadily rising correlation coefficients should be interpreted to mean that initial productivity gaps did indeed constitute a potentiality for fast growth that had its effect later if not sooner. The effect of the potentiality became visible in a very limited degree very early. But if a country was incapable of, or prevented from, exploiting that opportunity promptly, the technological growth potential became strong, and the country's later rate of advance was all the faster. Though it may have taken a century for obstacles or inhibitions to be fully overcome, the net outcome was that levels of productivity tended steadily to even out—at least within the group of presently advanced countries in my sample.

This last phrase is important. Mine is a biased sample in that its members consist of countries all of whom have successfully entered into the process of modern economic growth. This implies that they have acquired the educational and institutional characteristics needed to make use of modern technologies to some advanced degree. It is by no means assured—indeed, it is unlikely—that a more comprehensive sample of countries would show the same tendency for levels of productivity to even out over the same period of time.[17]

This is the big picture. How do things look if we consider shorter periods? There are two matters to keep in mind: the tendency to converge *within* the group of followers; and the convergence—or lack of it—of the group of followers vis-à-vis the United States. I take up the second matter in Section III. As to the convergence *within* the follower group, the figures suggest that the process varied in strength markedly from period to period. The main difference was that before World War II it operated weakly or at best with moderate strength. For almost a quarter-century following the war it apparently worked with very great strength. Why?

Before World War II, it is useful to consider two periods, roughly the decades before 1913, and those that followed. In the years of relative peace before 1913 I suggest that the process left a weak mark on the record for two reasons, both connected with the still early state of industrialization in many of the countries. First, the impress of the process was masked because farming was still so very important; measured levels of productivity, therefore, depended heavily on the amount and quality of farmland in relation to population. Productivity levels, in consequence, were erratic indicators of gaps between existing and best-practice technology. Secondly, social competence for exploiting the then most advanced methods was still limited, particularly in the earlier years and in the more recent latecomers. As the pre–World War I decades wore on, however, both these qualifying circumstances became less important. One might therefore have expected a much stronger tendency to convergence after 1913. But this was frustrated by the irregular effects of the Great War and of the years of disturbed political and financial conditions that followed, by the uneven impacts of the Great Depression itself and of the restrictions on international trade.

The unfulfilled potential of the years 1913–1938 was then enormously enlarged by the effects of World War II. The average productivity gap behind the United States increased by 39 percent between 1938 and 1950; the poorer countries were hit harder than the richer. These were years of dispersion, not convergence.

The post–World War II decades then proved to be the period when—exceptionally—the three elements required for rapid growth by catching up came together.[13] The elements are large technological gaps; enlarged social competence, reflecting higher levels of education and greater experience with large-scale production, distribution, and finance; and conditions favoring rapid realization of potential. This last element refers to several matters. There was *on this occasion* (it was otherwise after World War I) a strong reaction to the experience of defeat in war, and a chance for political reconstruction. The postwar political and economic reorganization and reform weakened the power of monopolistic groupings, brought new men to the fore, and focused the attention of governments on the tasks of recovery and growth, as Mancur Olson has argued.[14] The facilities for the diffusion of technology improved. International markets were opened. Large labor reserves in home agriculture and immigration from Southern and Eastern Europe provided a flexible and mobile labor supply. Government support, technological opportunity, and an environment of stable international money favored heavy and sustained capital investment. The outcome was the great speed and strength of the postwar catch-up process.[15]

Looking back now on the record of more than a century, we can see that catching up was a powerful continuing element in the growth experience of the presently advanced industrial countries. The strength of the process varied from period to period. For decades it operated only erratically and with weakened force. The trouble at first lay in deficient social capability, a sluggish adaptation of education and of industrial and financial organization to the requirements of modern large-scale technology. Later, the process was checked and made irregular by the effects of the two world wars and the ensuing political and financial troubles and by the impact of the Great Depression. It was at last released after World War II. The results were the rapid growth rates of the postwar period, the close cross-country association between initial productivity levels and growth rates, and a marked reduction of differences in productivity levels, among the follower countries, and between them and the United States.

Looking to the future, it seems likely that this very success will have weakened the potentiality for growth by catching up among the group of presently advanced countries. The great opportunities carried by that potential now pass to the less developed countries of Latin America and Asia.

III. FORGING AHEAD AND FALLING BEHIND

The catch-up hypothesis in its simple form does not anticipate changes in leadership nor, indeed, any changes in the ranks of countries in their relative levels of productivity. It contemplates only a reduction among countries in productivity differentials. Yet there have been many changes in ranks since 1870 and, of course, the notable shift of leadership from Britain to America towards the end of the last century.[16] This was followed by the continuing decline of Britain's standing in the productivity scale. Today there is a widely held opinion that America is about to fall behind a new candidate for leadership, Japan, and that both Europe and America must contemplate serious injury from the rise of both Japan and a group of still newer industrializing countries. . . .

The Congruity of Technology and Resources: United States as Leader

Why did the gap between the United States and the average of other countries resist reduction so long? Indeed, why did it even appear to become larger between 1870 and 1929—before the impact of World War II made it larger still? I offer three reasons:

(1) The path of technological change which in those years offered the greatest opportunities for advance was at once heavily scale-dependent and biased in a labor-saving but capital- and resource-using direction. In both respects America enjoyed great advantages compared with Europe or Japan. Large-scale production was favored by a large, rapidly growing, and increasingly prosperous population. It was supported also by a striking homogeneity of tastes. This reflected the country's comparative youth, its rapid settlement by migration from a common base on the Atlantic, and the weakness and fluidity of its class divisions. . . .

(2) By comparison with America and Britain, many, though not all, of the "followers" were also latecomers in respect to social capability. In the decades following 1870, they lacked experience with large-scale production and commerce, and in one degree or another they needed to advance in levels of general and technical education.

(3) World War I was a serious setback for many countries but a stimulus to growth in the United States. European recovery and growth in the following years were delayed and slowed by financial disturbances and by the impact of territorial and political change. Protection, not unification, was the response to the new political map. The rise of social democratic electoral strength in Europe favored the expansion of union power, but failed to curb the development and activities of industrial cartels. Britain's ability to support and enforce stable monetary conditions had been

weakened, but the United States was not yet able or, indeed, willing to assume the role of leadership that Britain was losing. In all these ways, the response to the challenge of war losses and defeat after the First World War stands in contrast to that after the Second.

Points (2) and (3) were anticipated in earlier argument, but Point (1) constitutes a qualification to the simple catch-up hypothesis. In that view, different countries, subject only to their social capability, are equally competent to exploit a leader's path of technological progress. That is not so, however, if that path is biased in resource intensity or if it is scale-dependent. Resource-rich countries will be favored in the first instance, large countries in the second. If the historical argument of this section is correct, the United States was favored on both counts for a long time; it may not be so favored in the future. Whether or not this interpretation of American experience is correct, the general proposition remains: countries have unequal abilities to pursue paths of progress that are resource-biased or scale-dependent.

Interaction Between Followers and Leaders

The catch-up hypothesis in its simple form is concerned with only one aspect of the economic relations among countries: technological borrowing by followers. In this view, a one-way stream of benefits flows from leaders to followers. A moment's reflection, however, exposes the inadequacy of that idea. The rise of British factory-made cotton textiles in the first industrial revolution ruined the Irish linen industry. The attractions of British and American jobs denuded the Irish population of its young men. The beginnings of modern growth in Ireland suffered a protracted delay. This is an example of the negative effects of leadership on the economies of those who are behind. Besides technological borrowing, there are interactions by way of trade and its rivalries, capital flows, and population movements. Moreover, the knowledge flows are not solely from leader to followers. A satisfactory account of the catch-up process must take account of these multiple forms of interaction. Again, there is space only for brief comment.

Trade and Its Rivalries. I have referred to the sometimes negative effects of leading-country exports on the economies of less developed countries. Countries in the course of catching up, however, exploit the possibilities of advanced scale-dependent technologies by import substitution and expansion of exports. When they are successful there are possible negative effects on the economies of leaders. This is an old historical theme. The successful competition of Germany, America, and other European countries is supposed to have retarded British growth from 1870 to 1913 and perhaps longer.[17] Analogous questions arise today. The expansion of exports from Japan and the newer industrializing countries has had a serious impact on the older industries of America and Europe, as well as some of the newer industries.

Is there a generalized effect on the productivity growth of the leaders? The effect is less than it may seem to be because some of the trade shifts are a reflection of overall productivity growth in the leader countries themselves. As the average level of productivity rises, so does the level of wages across industries generally. There are then relative increases in the product prices of those industries—usually older industries—in which productivity growth is lagging and relative declines in the product prices of those industries enjoying rapid productivity growth. The former must suffer a loss of comparative advantage, the latter a gain. One must keep an eye on both.

Other causes of trade shifts that are connected with the catch-up process itself may, however, carry real generalized productivity effects. There are changes that stem from the evolution of "product cycles," such as Raymond Vernon has made familiar. And perhaps most important, there is the achievement of higher levels of social capability. This permits followers to extend their borrowing and adaptation of more advanced methods, and enables them to compete in markets they could not contest earlier.

What difference does it make to the general prospects for the productivity growth of the leading industrial countries if they are losing markets to followers who are catching up?

There is an employment effect. Demand for the products of export- and import-competing industries is depressed. Failing a high degree of flexibility in exchange rates and wages and of occupational and geographical mobility, aggregate demand tends to be reduced. Unless macroeconomic policy is successful, there is general unemployment and underutilization of resources. Profits and the inducements to invest and innovate are reduced. And if this condition causes economies to succumb to protectionism, particularly to competitive protectionism, the difficulty is aggravated.

International trade theory assures us that these effects are transitory. Autonomous capital movements aside, trade must, in the end, balance. But the macroeconomic effects of the balancing process may be long drawn out, and while it is in progress, countries can suffer the repressive effects of restricted demand on investment and innovation.

There is also a Verdoorn effect. It is harder for an industry to push the technological frontier forward, or even to keep up with it, if its own rate of expansion slows down—and still harder if it is contracting. This is unavoidable but tolerable when the growth of old industries is restricted by the rise of newer, more progressive home industries. But when retardation of older home industries is due to the rise of competing industries abroad, a tendency to generalized slowdown may be present.

Interactions via Population Movements. Nineteenth-century migration ran in good part from the farms of Western and Southern Europe to the farms and cities of the New World and Australia. In the early twentieth century, Eastern Europe joined in. These migrations responded in part to the impact on world markets of the cheap grains and animal products produced by the regions of recent settlement. Insofar they represent an additional but special effect of development in some members of the Atlantic community of industrializing countries on the economies of other members.

Productivity growth in the countries of destination was aided by migration in two respects. It helped them exploit scale economies; and by making labor supply more responsive to increase in demand, it helped sustain periods of rapid growth. Countries of origin were relieved of the presence of partly redundant and desperately poor people. On the other hand, the loss of population brought such scale disadvantages as accompany slower population growth, and it made labor supply less responsive to industrial demand.

Migration in the postwar growth boom presents a picture of largely similar design and significance. In this period the movement was from the poorer, more slowly growing countries of Southern Europe and North Africa to the richer and more rapidly growing countries of Western and Northern Europe.[18] There is, however, this difference: The movement in more recent decades was induced by actual and expected income differences that were largely independent of the market connections of countries of origin and destination. There is no evidence that the growth boom of the West itself contributed to the low incomes of the South.

Needless to say, migrations are influenced by considerations other than relative levels of income and changing comparative advantage. I stress these matters, however, because they help us understand the complexities of the process of catch-up and convergence within a group of connected countries.

Interaction via Capital Flows. A familiar generalization is that capital tends to flow from countries of high income and slow growth to those with opposite characteristics or, roughly speaking, from leaders to followers. One remembers, however, that that description applies to gross new investments. There are also reverse flows that reflect the maturing of past investments. So in the early stages of a great wave of investment, followers' rates of investment and productivity growth are supported by capital movement while those of leaders are retarded. Later however, this effect may become smaller or be reversed, as we see today in relations between Western leaders and Latin American followers.

Once more, I add that the true picture is far more complicated than this idealized summary. It will hardly accommodate such extraordinary developments as the huge American capital import of recent years, to say nothing of the Arabian-European flows of the 1970s and their reversal now under way.

Interactions via Flows of Applied Knowledge. The flow of knowledge from leader to followers is, of course, the very essence of the catch-up hypothesis. As the technological gaps narrow, however, the direction changes. Countries that are still a distance behind the leader in average productivity may move into the lead in particular branches and become sources of new knowledge for older leaders. As they are surpassed in particular fields, old leaders can make gains by borrowing as well as by generating new knowledge. In this respect the growth potential of old leaders is enhanced as the pursuit draws closer. Moreover, competitive pressure can be a stimulus to research and innovation as well as an excuse for protection. It remains to be seen whether the newly rising economies will seek to guard a working knowledge of their operations more closely than American companies have done, and still more whether American and European firms will be as quick to discover, acquire, and adapt foreign methods as Japanese firms have been in the past.

Development as a Constraint on Change:
Tangible Capital

The rise of followers in the course of catching up brings old leaders a mixed bag of injuries and potential benefits. Old leaders, however, or followers who have enjoyed a period of successful development, may come to suffer disabilities other than those caused by the burgeoning competitive power of new rivals. When Britain suffered her growth climacteric nearly a century ago, observers thought that her slowdown was itself due in part to her early lead. Thorstein Veblen was a pioneer proponent of this suggestion, and Charles Kindleberger and others have picked it up again.[19] One basis for this view is the idea that the capital stock of a country consists of an intricate web of interlocking elements. They are built to fit together, and it is difficult to replace one part of the complex with more modern and efficient elements without a costly rebuilding of other components. This may be handled efficiently if all the costs and benefits are internal to a firm. When they are divided among different firms and industries and between the private and public sectors, the adaptation of old capital structures to new technologies may be a difficult and halting process.

What this may have meant for Britain's climacteric is still unsettled. Whatever that may be, however, the problem needs study on a wider scale as it arises both historically and in a contemporaneous setting. After World War II, France undertook a great extension and modernization of its public transportation and power systems to provide a basis for later development of private industry and agriculture. Were the technological advances embodied in that investment program easier for France to carry out because its infrastructure was technically older, battered, and badly maintained? Or was it simply a heavy burden more in need of being borne? There is a widespread complaint today that the public capital structure of the United States stands in need of modernization and extension. Is this true, and, if it is, does it militate seriously against the installation of improved capital by private industry? One cannot now assume that such problems are the exclusive concern of a topmost productivity leader. All advanced industrial countries have large accumulations of capital, interdependent in use but divided in ownership among many firms and between private and public authorities. One may assume, however, that the problem so raised differs in its impact over time and among countries and, depending on its importance, might have some influence on the changes that occur in the productivity rankings of countries.

Development as a Constraint on Change: Intangible Capital and Political Institutions

Attention now returns to matters akin to social capability. In the simple catch-up hypothesis, that capability is viewed as either exogenously determined or else as adjusting steadily to the requirements of technological opportunity. The educational and institutional commitments induced by past development may, however, stand as an obstacle. That is a question that calls for study. The comments that follow are no more than brief indications of prominent possibilities.

The United States was the pioneer of mass production as embodied in the huge plant, the complex and rigid assembly line, the standardized product, and the long production run. It is also the pioneer and developer of the mammoth diversified conglomerate corporation. The vision of business carried on within such organizations, their highly indirect, statistical, and bureaucratic methods of consultation, planning and decision, the inevitable distractions of trading in assets rather than production of goods—these mental biases have sunk deep into the American business outlook and into the doctrine and training of young American managers. The necessary decentralization of operations into multiple profit centers directs the attention of managers and their superiors to the quarterly profit report and draws their energies away from the development of improved products and processes that require years of attention.[20] One may well ask how well this older vision of management and enterprise and the organizational scheme in which it is embodied will accommodate the problems and potentialities of the emerging computer and communications revolution. Or will that occur more easily in countries where educational systems, forms of corporate organization, and managerial outlook can better make a fresh start?

The long period of leadership and development enjoyed by the United

States and the entire North Atlantic community meant, of course, a great increase of incomes. The rise of incomes, in turn, afforded a chance to satisfy latent desires for all sorts of non-market goods ranging from maintenance in old age to a safe-guarded natural environment. Satisfying these demands, largely by public action, has also afforded an ample opportunity for special interest groups to obtain privileges and protection in a process that Mancur Olson and others have generalized.

The outcome of this conjuncture of circumstances and forces is the Mixed Economy of the West, the complex system of transfers, taxes, regulations, and public activity, as well as organizations of union and business power, that had its roots long before the War, that expanded rapidly during the growth boom of the fifties and sixties, and that reached very high levels in the seventies. This trend is very broadly consistent with the suggestion that the elaboration of the mixed economy is a function of economic growth itself. To this one has to add the widely held idea advanced by Olson and many others that the system operates to reduce enterprise, work, saving, investment, and mobility and, therefore, to constrict the processes of innovation and change that productivity growth involves.

How much is there in all this? The answer turns only partly on a calculation of the direct effects of the system on economic incentives. These have proved difficult to pin down, and attempts to measure them have generally not yielded large numbers, at least for the United States.[21] The answer requires an equally difficult evaluation of the positive roles of government activity. These include not only the government's support of education, research, and information, and its provision of physical overhead capital and of the host of local functions required for urban life. We must remember also that the occupational and geographical adjustments needed to absorb new technology impose heavy costs on individuals. The accompanying changes alter the positions, prospects, and power of established groups, and they transform the structure of families and their roles in caring for children, the sick, and the old. Technical advance, therefore, engenders conflict and resistance; and the Welfare State with its transfers and regulations constitutes a mode of conflict resolution and a means of mitigating the costs of change that would otherwise induce resistance to growth. The existing empirical studies that bear on the economic responses to government intervention are, therefore, far from meeting the problem fully.

If the growth-inhibiting forces embodied in the Welfare State and in private expressions of market power were straightforward, positive functions of income levels, uniform across countries, that would be another reason for supposing that the catch-up process was self-limiting. The productivity levels of followers would, on this account, converge towards but not exceed the leader's. But these forces are clearly not simple, uniform functions of income. The institutions of the Welfare State have reached a higher degree of elaboration in Europe than in the United States. The objects of expenditure, the structures of transfers and taxes, and people's responses to both differ from country to country. These institutional developments, therefore, besides having some influence on growth rates generally, may constitute a wide card in the deck of growth forces. They will tend to produce changes in the ranks of countries in the productivity scale and these may include the top rank itself.

A sense that forces of institutional change are now acting to limit the growth of Western countries pervades the writings of many economists—and, of course, other observers. Olson, Fellner, Scitovsky, Kindleberger, Lindbeck, and Giersch are only a partial list of those who see these economies as afflicted by institutional arthritis or sclerosis or other metaphorical malady associated with age and wealth.

These are the suggestions of serious scholars, and they need to be taken seriously. One may ask, however, whether these views take account of still other, rejuvenating forces which, though they act slowly, may yet work effectively to limit and counter those of decay—at least for the calculable future. In the United States, interregional competition, supported by free movement of goods, people, and capital, is such a force. It limits the power of unions and checks the expansion of taxation, transfers, and regulation.[22] International competition, so long as it is permitted to operate, works in a similar direction for the United States and other countries as well, and it is strengthened by the development in recent years of a more highly integrated world capital market and by more vigorous international movements of corporate enterprise. . . .

Finally, it is widely recognized that the process of institutional aging, whatever its significance, is not one without limits. Powerful forces continue to push that way, and they are surely strong in resisting reversal. Yet it is also apparent that there is a drift of public opinion that works for modification both in Europe and North America. There is a fine balance to be struck between productivity growth and the material incomes it brings and the other dimensions of social welfare. Countries are now in the course of readjusting that balance in favor of productivity growth. How far they can go and, indeed, how far they should go are both still in question. . . .

NOTES

1. W.E.G. Salter, *Productivity and Technical Change* (Cambridge, 1960) provides a rigorous theoretical exposition of the factors determining rates of turnover and those governing the relation between productivity with capital embodying best-practice and average (economically efficient) technology.

2. *Japanese Economic Growth: Trend Acceleration in the Twentieth Century* (Stanford, 1973), especially chap. 9.

3. Moses Abramovitz, "Rapid Growth Potential and Its Realization: The Experience of Capitalist Economies in the Postwar Period," in Edmond Malinvaud,

ed., *Economic Growth and Resources,* Proceedings of the Fifth World Congress of the International Economic Association, vol. 1 (London, 1979), pp. 1–30.

4. Mancur Olson, *The Rise and Fall of Nations: Economic Growth, Stagflation and Social Rigidities* (New Haven, 1982).

5. Kravis et al., *International Comparisons;* Edward F. Denison, assisted by Jean-Pierre Poullier, *Why Growth Rates Differ, Postwar Experience of Nine Western Countries* (Washington, D.C., 1967), pp. 239–45.

6. R.C.O. Matthews, Review of Denison (1967), *Economic Journal* (June 1969), pp. 261–68.

7. My paper cited earlier describes the operation of these factors in the 1950s and 1960s and tries to show how they worked to permit productivity growth to rise in so many countries rapidly, in concert and for such an extended period ("Rapid Growth Potential and Its Realization," pp. 18–30).

8. The countries are Australia, Austria, Belgium, Canada, Denmark, Finland, France, Germany, Italy, Japan, Netherlands, Norway, Sweden, Switzerland, United Kingdom, and United States.

9. In these calculations I have treated either the United States or the United Kingdom as the productivity leader from 1870 to 1913. Literal acceptance of Maddison's estimates, however, make Australia the leader from 1870–1913. Moreover, Belgium and the Netherlands stand slightly higher than the United States in 1870. Here are Maddison's relatives for those years (from *Phases,* Table 5.2):

	1870	1890	1913
Australia	186	153	102
Belgium	106	96	75
Netherlands	106	92	74
United Kingdom	114	100	81
United States	100	100	100

Since Australia's high standing in this period mainly reflected an outstandingly favorable situation of natural resources relative to population, it would be misleading to regard that country as the technological leader or to treat the productivity changes in other countries relative to Australia's as indicators of the catch-up process. Similarly, the small size and specialized character of the Belgian and Dutch economies make them inappropriate benchmarks.

10. Maddison, *Phases,* Table C5.

11. Since growth rates are calculated as rates of change between standings at the terminal dates of periods, errors in the estimates of such standings will generate errors in the derived growth rates. If errors at both terminal dates were random, and if those at the end-year were independent of those at the initial year, there would be a tendency on that account for growth rates to be inversely correlated with initial-year standings. The inverse correlation coefficients would be biased upwards. Note, however, that if errors at terminal years were random and independent and of equal magnitude, there would be no tendency *on that account* for the variance of standings about the mean to decline between initial and end-year dates. The error bias would run against the marked decline in variance that we observe. Errors in late-year data, however, are unlikely to be so large, so an error bias is present.

12. See also William J. Baumol, "Productivity Growth, Convergence and Welfare: What the Long-run Data Show." C. V. Starr Center for Applied Economics, New York University, Research Report No. 85–27, August 1985.

13. See Abramovitz, "Rapid Growth Potential and Its Realization."

14. Olson, *Rise and Fall.*

15. Some comments on the catch-up process after 1973 may be found in Abramovitz, "Catching Up and Falling Behind" (Stockholm, 1986), pp. 33–39.

16. If one follows Maddison's estimates (*Phases,* Table C.19), the long period from 1870 to 1979 saw Australia fall by 8 places in the ranking of his 16 countries, Italy by 2.5, Switzerland by 8, and the United Kingdom by 10. Meanwhile the United States rose by 4, Germany by 4.5, Norway by 5, Sweden by 7, and France by 8.

17. See also R.C.O. Matthews, Charles Feinstein, and John Odling-Smee, *British Economic Growth, 1856–1973* (Stanford, 1983), chaps, 14, 15, 17. Their analysis does not find a large effect on British productivity growth from 1870 to 1913.

18. The migration from East to West Germany in the 1950s was a special case. It brought to West Germany educated and skilled countrymen strongly motivated to rebuild their lives and restore their fortunes.

19. Charles P. Kindleberger, "Obsolescence and Technical Change." *Oxford Institute of Statistics Bulletin* (Aug. 1961), pp. 281–97.

20. These and similar questions are raised by experienced observers of American business. They are well summarized by Edward Denison, *Trends in American Economic Growth, 1929–1982* (Washington, D.C., 1985), chap. 3.

21. Representative arguments supporting the idea that social capability has suffered, together with some quantitative evidence, may be found in Olson, *Rise and Fall;* William Fellner, "The Declining Growth of American Productivity: An Introductory Note," in W. Fellner, ed., *Contemporary Economic Problems, 1979* (Washington, D.C., 1979); and Assar Lindbeck, "Limits to the Welfare State," *Challenge* (Dec. 1985). For argument and evidence on the other side, see Sheldon Danzigar, Robert Haveman, and Robert Plotnick, "How Income Transfers Affect Work, Savings and Income Distribution," *Journal of Economic Literature* 19 (Sept. 1982), pp. 975–1028; and Edw. F. Denison, *Accounting for Slower Economic Growth* (Washington, D.C., 1979), pp. 127–38.

22. See R. D. Norton, "Regional Life Cycles and US Industrial Rejuvenation," in Herbert Giersch, ed., "Industrial Policy and American Renewal," *Journal of Economic Literature,* 24 (March 1986).

10

· · · · · · ·

Productivity Growth, Convergence, and Welfare: What the Long-Run Data Show

· · · · · · ·

WILLIAM J. BAUMOL

William Baumol provides empirical analysis of convergence theory and finds that for a sample of sixteen countries between 1870 and 1979 labor productivity and its growth are inversely related. In Chapter 9, Moses Abramovitz explained that not all countries will experience convergence because they lack the social capacity to utilize technology to achieve rapid growth. Baumol turns to the post–World War II era (1950–1980) to see if this relationship can be found for all countries. Using RGDP/pcs and growth rates as proxies for labor productivity, Baumol finds that the poorest countries have the slowest RCDP/pc growth, thus failing to converge with the rich. The rest of the countries belong to what Baumol calls a "convergence club." Hence, if Baumol is correct, convergence will take place but the poorest countries will be excluded from the process, meaning that the gap will widen between them and the rest of the world.

> No matter how refined and how elaborate the analysis, if it rests solely on the short view it will still be . . . a structure built on shifting sands.
> —Jacob Viner (1958, pp. 112–131)

Recent years have witnessed a reemergence of interest on the part of economists and the general public in issues relating to long-run economic growth. There has been a recurrence of doubts and fears for the future— aroused in this case by the protracted slowdown in productivity growth

---

Reprinted with permission from the *American Economic Review*, vol. 76 (December 1986): 1072–1084.

since the late 1960s, the seeming erosion of the competitiveness of U.S. industries in world markets, and the spectre of "deindustrialization" and massive structural unemployment. These anxieties have succeeded in redirecting attention to long-run supply-side phenomena that formerly were a central preoccupation of economists in the industrializing West, before being pushed aside in the crisis of the Great Depression and the ensuing triumph of Keynesian ideas.

Anxiety may compel attention, but it is not necessarily an aid to clear thinking. For all the interest now expressed in the subject of long-run economic growth and policies ostensibly directed to its stimulation, it does not seem to be widely recognized that adequate economic analysis of such issues calls for the careful study of economic history—if only because it is there that the pertinent evidence is to be found. Economic historians have provided the necessary materials, in the form of brilliant insights, powerful analysis as well as a surprising profusion of long-period data. Yet none of these has received the full measure of attention they deserve from members of the economics profession at large.

To dramatize the sort of reorientation long-term information can suggest, imagine a convincing prediction that over the next century, U.S. productivity growth will permit a trebling of per capita GNP while cutting nearly by half the number of hours in the average work year, and that this will be accompanied by a sevenfold increase in exports. One might well consider this a very rosy forecast. But none of these figures is fictitious. For these developments in fact lay before the United Kingdom in 1870, just as its economic leadership began to erode.

This chapter outlines some implications of the available long-period data on productivity and related variables—some tentative, some previously noted by economic historians, and some throwing a somewhat surprising light on developments among industrialized nations since World War II. Among the main observations that will emerge here is the remarkable convergence of output per labor hour among industrialized nations. Almost all of the leading free enterprise economies have moved closer to the leader, and there is a strong inverse correlation between a country's productivity standing in 1870 and its average rate of productivity growth since then. Postwar data suggest that the convergence phenomenon also extends to both "intermediate" and centrally planned economies. Only the poorer less developed countries show no such trend.

It will also emerge that over the century, the U.S. productivity growth rate has been surprisingly steady, and despite frequently expressed fears, there is no sign recently of any *long-term* slowdown in growth of either total factor productivity or labor productivity in the United States. And while, except in wartime, *for the better part of a century,* U.S. productivity growth rates have been low relative to those of Germany, Japan, and a number of other countries, this may be no more than a manifestation of the convergence phenomenon which requires countries that were previously behind to grow more rapidly. Thus, the chapter will seek to dispel these and a number of other misapprehensions apparently widespread among those who have not studied economic history.

Nonspecialists may well be surprised at the remarkably long periods spanned in time-series contributed by Beveridge, Deane, Kuznets, Gallman, Kendrick, Abramovitz, David, and others. The Phelps Brown-Hopkins indices of prices and real wages extend over seven centuries. Maddison, Feinstein (and his colleagues), and Kendrick cover productivity, investment, and a number of other crucial variables for more than 100 years. Obviously, the magnitudes of the earlier figures are more than a little questionable, as their compilers never cease to warn us. Yet the general qualitative character of the time paths is persuasive, given the broad consistency of the statistics, their apparent internal logic and the care exercised in collecting them. In this chapter, the period used will vary with topic and data availability. In most cases, something near a century will be examined, using primarily data provided by Angus Maddison (1982) and R.C.O. Matthews, C. H. Feinstein, and J. C. Odling-Smee (1982—henceforth, M-F-O).

MAGNITUDE OF THE ACCOMPLISHMENT

The magnitude of the productivity achievement of the past 150 years resists intuitive grasp, and contrasts sharply with the preceding centuries. As the *Communist Manifesto* put the matter in 1848, with remarkable foresight, "The bourgeoisie, during its rule of scarce one hundred years, has created more massive and more colossal productive forces than have all preceding generations together." There obviously are no reliable measures of productivity in antiquity, but available descriptions of living standards in Ancient Rome suggest that they were in many respects higher than in eighteenth-century England (see Colin Clark, 1957, p. 677). This is probably true even for the lower classes—certainly for the free urban proletariat, and perhaps even with the inclusion of slaves. An upper-class household was served by sophisticated devices for heating and bathing not found in eighteenth-century homes of the rich. A wealthy Roman magically transported into an eighteenth-century English home would probably have been puzzled by the technology of only a few products—clocks, window panes, printed books and newspapers, and the musket over the fireplace.

It is true that even during the Middle Ages (see, for example, Carlo Cipolla, 1976), there was substantial technological change in the workplace and elsewhere. Ship design improved greatly. Lenses and, with them, the telescope and microscope appeared in the sixteenth century, and the eighteenth century brought the ship's chronometer which revolutionized water transport by permitting calculation of longitude. Yet, none of this led to rates of productivity growth anywhere near those of the nineteenth and twentieth centuries.

Nonhistorians do not usually recognize that initially the Industrial Revolution was a fairly minor affair for the economy as a whole. At first, much of the new equipment was confined to textile production (though some progress in fields such as iron making had also occurred). And, as David Landes (1969) indicates, an entrepreneur could undertake the new types of textile operations with little capital, perhaps only a few hundred pounds, which (using the Phelps Brown-Hopkins data) translates into some 100,000 1980 dollars. Jeffrey Williamson (1983) tells us that in England during the first half-century of the Industrial Revolution, real per capita income grew only about 0.3 percent per annum,[1] in contrast with the nearly 3 percent achieved in the Third World in the 1970s (despite the decade's economic crises).

Table 10.1 shows the remarkable contrast of developments since 1870 for Maddison's 16 countries. We see (col. 1) that growth in output per work-hour ranged for the next 110 years from approximately 400 percent for Australia all the way to 2500 percent (in the case of Japan). The 1100 percent increase of labor productivity in the United States placed it somewhat below the middle of the group, and even the United Kingdom managed a 600 percent rise. Thus, after not manifesting any substantial long-period increase for at least 15 centuries, in the course of 11 decades the median increase in productivity among the 16 industrialized leaders in

Table 10.1   Total Growth from 1870 to 1979[a]: Productivity, GDP per Capita, and Exports, Sixteen Industrialized Countries[b]

	Real GDP per Work-Hour	Real GDP per Capita	Volume of Exports
Australia	398	221	—
United Kingdom	585	310	930
Switzerland	830	471	4,400
Belgium	887	439	6,250
Netherlands	910	429	8,040
Canada	1,050	766	9,860
United States	1,080	693	9,240
Denmark	1,098	684	6,750
Italy	1,225	503	6,210
Austria	1,270	643	4,740
Germany	1,510	824	3,730
Norway	1,560	873	7,740
France	1,590	694	4,140
Finland	1,710	1,016	6,240
Sweden	2,060	1,083	5,070
Japan	2,480	1,661	293,060

a. In 1970 U.S. dollars.
b. Shown in percent.
Source: Angus Maddison (1982, pp. 8, 212, 248–53).

Maddison's sample was about 1150 percent. The rise in productivity was sufficient to permit output per capita (col. 2) to increase more than 300 percent in the United Kingdom, 800 percent in West Germany, 1700 percent in Japan, and nearly 700 percent in France and the United States. Using Robert Summers and Alan Heston's sophisticated international comparison data (1984), this implies that in 1870, U.S. output per capita was comparable to 1980 output per capita in Honduras and the Philippines, and slightly below that of China, Bolivia, and Egypt!

The growth rates of other pertinent variables were also remarkable. One more example will suffice to show this. Table 10.1, which also shows the rise in volume of exports from 1870 to 1979 (col. 3), indicates that the median increase was over 6,000 percent.

THE CONVERGENCE OF
NATIONAL PRODUCTIVITY LEVELS

There is a long and reasonably illustrious tradition among economic historians centered on the phenomenon of convergence. While the literature devoted to the subject is complex and multifaceted, as revealed by the recent reconsideration of these ideas by Moses Abramovitz (1985), one central theme is that forces accelerating the growth of nations who were latecomers to industrialization and economic development give rise to a long-run tendency towards convergence of levels of per capita product or, alternatively, of per worker product. Such ideas found expression in the works of Alexander Gerschenkron (see, for example, 1952), who saw his own views on the advantages of "relative backwardness" as having been anticipated in important respects by Thorstein Veblen's writings on the penalties of being the industrial leader (1915). Although such propositions also have been challenged and qualified (for example, Edward Ames and Nathan Rosenberg, 1963), it is difficult to dismiss the idea of convergence on the basis of the historical experience of the industrialized world. (For more recent discussions, see also the paper by Robin Marris, with comments by Feinstein and Matthews in Matthews, 1982, pp. 12–13, 128–147, as well as Dennis Mueller, 1983.)

Using 1870–1973 data on gross domestic product (GDP) per work-year for 7 industrialized countries, M-F-O have shown graphically that those nations' productivity levels have tended to approach ever closer to one another. . . .[2]

The convergence toward the vanguard (led in the first decades by Australia—see Richard Caves and Laurence Krause, 1984—and the United Kingdom and, approximately since World War I, by the United States) is sharper than it may appear to the naked eye. In 1870, the ratio of output per work-hour in Australia, then the leader in Maddison's sample, was about eight times as great as Japan's (the laggard). By 1979, that ratio for the leader (the United States) to the laggard (still Japan) had fallen to about 2. The ratio of the standard deviation from the mean of GDP per work-hour for the 16 countries has also fallen quite steadily, except for a brief but sharp rise during World War II.

The convergence phenomenon and its pervasiveness are confirmed by Figure 10.1, on which my discussion will focus. The horizontal axis indicates each Maddison country's absolute level of GDP per work-hour in 1870. The vertical axis represents the growth rate of GDP per work-hour in the 110 years since 1870. The high inverse correlation between the two is evident. Indeed, we obtain an equation (subject to all sorts of statistical reservations)[3]

$$Growth\ Rate\ (1870–1979) = 5.25 – 0.75 \ln\ (GDP\ per\ WorkHr,\ 1870),$$
$$R^2 = 0.88.$$

That is, with a very high correlation coefficient, the higher a country's productivity level in 1870 the more slowly that level grew in the following century.

Figure 10.1   Productivity Growth Rate, 1870–1979 vs. 1870 Level (in percent)

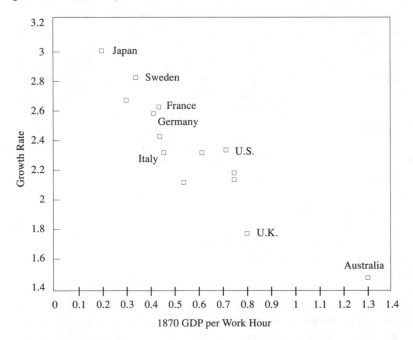

Source: Maddison (p. 212).

IMPLICATIONS OF THE INVERSE CORRELATION: PUBLIC GOODS PROPERTY OF PRODUCTIVITY POLICY

The strong inverse correlation between the 1870 productivity levels of the 16 nations and their subsequent productivity growth record seems to have a startling implication. Of course, hindsight always permits "forecasts" of great accuracy—that itself is not surprising. Rather, what is striking is the apparent implication that *only one variable,* a country's 1870 GDP per work-hour, or its relation to that of the productivity leader matters to any substantial degree, and that other variables have only a peripheral influence. It seems not to have mattered much whether or not a particular country had free markets, a high propensity to invest, or used policy to stimulate growth. Whatever its behavior, that nation was apparently fated to land close to its predestined position in Figure 10.1.

However, a plausible alternative interpretation is that while national policies and behavior patterns do substantially affect productivity growth, the spillovers from leader economies to followers are large—at least among the group of industrial nations. If country A's extraordinary investment level and superior record of innovation enhance its own productivity, they will almost automatically do the same in the long run for industrialized country B, though perhaps to a somewhat more limited extent. In other words, for such nations a successful productivity-enhancing measure has the nature of a public good. And because the fruits of each industrialized country's productivity-enhancement efforts are ultimately shared by others, each country remains in what appears to be its predestined *relative* place along the growth curve of Figure 10.1. I will note later some considerations which might lead one to doubt that the less developed countries will benefit comparably from this sharing process.

This sharing of productivity growth benefits by industrialized countries involves both innovation and investment. The innovation-sharing process is straightforward. If industry in country A benefits from a significant innovation, those industries in other countries which produce competing products will find themselves under pressure to obtain access to the innovation, or to an imitation or to some other substitute. Industrialized countries, whose product lines overlap substantially and which sell a good deal in markets where foreign producers of similar items are also present, will find themselves constantly running in this Schumpeterian race, while those less developed countries which supply few products competing with those of the industrialized economies will not participate to the same degree.

There is reason to suspect that the pressures for rapidity in imitation of innovation in industrial countries have been growing. The explosion in exports reported in Table 10.1 has given them a considerably larger share of gross national product than they had in 1870. This suggests that more of each nation's output faces the direct competition of foreign rivals. Thus, the penalties for failure to keep abreast of innovations *in other countries* and to imitate them where appropriate have grown.

Second, the means required for successful imitations have improved and expanded enormously. World communications are now practically instantaneous, but required weeks and even months at the birth of the Industrial Revolution. While today meetings of scientists and technicians are widely encouraged, earlier mercantilist practices entailed measures by each country to prevent other nations from learning its industrial techniques, and the emigration of specialized workers was often forbidden. Though figures in this arena are difficult to interpret, much less substantiate, one estimate claims that employment in "information activities" in the United States has grown from less than 1 percent of the labor force in 1830 to some 45 percent today (James Beniger, forthcoming, p. 364, leaning heavily on Marc Porat, 1977). Presumably, growth of the information sector in other industrialized nations has been similar. This must surely facilitate and speed the innovative, counterinnovative, and imitative tasks of the entrepreneur. The combination of direct U.S. manufacturing investment in Europe, and the technology transfer activities of multinational corporations in the postwar era were also of great significance (see, for example, David Teece, 1976). All of this, incidentally, suggests that as the forces making for convergence were stronger in the postwar era than previously, the rate of convergence should have been higher. The evidence assembled by Abramovitz (1985) on the basis of Maddison's data indicates that this is in fact what has happened.

The process that has just been described, then, provides mutual benefits, but it inherently helps productivity laggards more than leaders. For the laggards have more to learn from the leaders, and that is why the process makes for convergence.

Like innovation, investment, generally considered the second main source of growth in labor productivity, may also exhibit international public good properties. Suppose two industrialized countries, A and B, each produce two traded products: say automobiles and shoes, with the former more capital intensive. If A's investment rate is greater than B's then, with time, A's output mix will shift toward the cars while B's will move toward shoes. The increased demand for auto workers in A will raise their real wages, while A's increased demand for imports of B's shoes will raise real wages in B, and will raise the *value* of gross domestic product per labor hour in that country. Thus, even investment in country A automatically tends to have a spillover effect on value productivity and real wages *in those other countries that produce and trade in a similar array of goods.*

While, strictly speaking, the factor-price equalization theorem is not applicable to my discussion because it assumes, among other things, that technology is identical in all the countries involved, it does suggest why (for the reasons just discussed) a high investment rate may fail to bring a relative wage advantage to the investing country. In practice, the conditions of the theorem are not satisfied precisely, so countries in which investment rates are relatively high do seem to obtain increased relative real wages. Yet the analysis suggests that the absolute benefits are contagious—that one country's successful investment policy will also raise productivity and living standards in other industrialized countries.[4]

Thus, effective growth policy does contribute to a nation's living standards, but it may also help other industrialized countries and to almost the same degree; meaning that relative deviations from the patterns indicated in Figure 10.1 will be fairly small, just as the diagram shows. (However, see Abramovitz, 1985, for a discussion of the counterhypothesis, that growth of a leader creates "backwash" effects inhibiting growth of the followers.)

All this raises an obvious policy issue. If productivity growth does indeed have such public good properties, what will induce each country to invest the socially optimal effort and other resources in productivity growth, when it can instead hope to be a free rider? In part, the answer is that in Western capitalistic economies, investment is decentralized and individual firms can gain little by free riding on the actions of investors in other economies, so that the problem does not appear to be a serious one at the national policy level.

IS CONVERGENCE UBIQUITOUS?

Does convergence of productivity levels extend beyond the free-market industrialized countries? Or is the convergence "club" a very exclusive organization? While century-long data are not available for any large number of countries, Summers and Heston provide pertinent figures for the 30-year period 1950–80 (data for more countries are available for briefer periods).[5] Instead of labor productivity figures, they give output per capita, whose trends can with considerable reservations be used as a rough proxy for those in productivity, as Maddison's figures confirm.

Figure 10.2 tells the story. Constructed just like Figure 10.1, it plots the 1950–80 real growth rate of GDP per capita for all 72 Summers–Heston countries against the initial (1950) level of this variable. The points form no tight relationship, and unlike those for the industrial countries, the dots show no negatively sloping pattern. Indeed, a regression yields a slightly positive slope. Thus, rather than sharing in convergence, some of the poorest countries have also been growing most slowly.

Figure 10.2 brings out the patterns more clearly by surrounding the set of points representing Maddison's 16 countries with a thin boundary and the centrally planned economy points[6] with a heavier boundary. We see that the Maddison country points lie near a sort of upper-right-hand boundary, meaning that most of them had the high incomes in 1950 (as was to be expected) and, for any given per capita income, the highest growth rates

Figure 10.2   Growth Rate, 1950–80, GDP/pc vs. 1950 Level 72 Countries

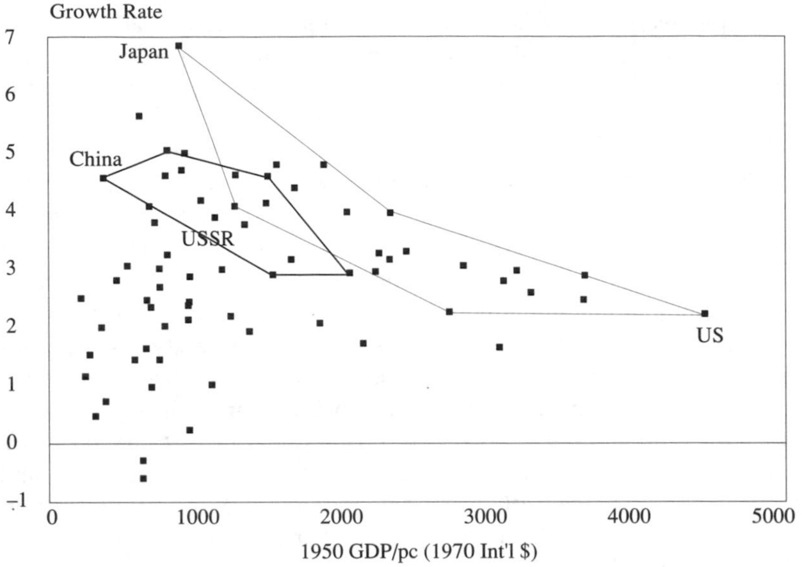

Growth Rate

1950 GDP/pc (1970 Int'l $)

Source: Summers and Heston, 1984.

between 1950 and 1980. This region is very long, narrow, and negatively sloped, with the absolute slope declining toward the right. As in the Figure 10.1, productivity data for a 110-year period, this is exactly the shape one expects with convergence. Second, we see that the centrally planned economies are members of a convergence club of their own, forming a negatively sloping region lying below and to the left of the Maddison countries. The relationship is less tight, so convergence within the group is less pronounced, but it is clearly there.

Finally, there is the region of remaining points (aside from the rightmost non-Maddison points in the graph) which lies close to the origin of the graph and occupies something like a distorted circle without any apparent slope. The points closest to the origin are less developed countries which were poor in 1950, and have grown relatively slowly since. They show no convergence among themselves, much less with other groups.

A few numbers suggest the difference in performance of various subgroups of the 72 countries. Using a four-set classification Summers, I. B. Kravis and Heston (1984, p. 254) provide Gini coefficients by decade from 1950 to 1980. For their set of industrialized countries, this coefficient falls precipitously from 0.302 in 1950 to 0.129 in 1980—a sharp drop in inequality. For the centrally planned economies the drop is much smaller—from 0.381 to 0.301. The middle-income group exhibits an even smaller decline, from 0.269 to 0.258. But the low-income countries underwent a small *rise* over the period, from 0.103 to 0.112, and the world as a whole experienced a tiny rise from 0.493 to 0.498.

There has also been little convergence among the groups. For the entire period, Summers et al. report (p. 245) an average annual growth rate in per capita real GDP of 3.1 percent for industrialized countries, 3.6 percent for centrally planned economies, 3.0 percent for middle-income market economies, and only 1.5 percent for the low-income group, with a world average group rate of 2.7 percent.

This suggests that there is more than one convergence club. Rather, there are perhaps three, with the centrally planned and the intermediate groups somewhat inferior in performance to that of the free-market industrialized countries. It is also clear that the poorer less developed countries are still largely barred from the homogenization processes. Since any search for "the causes" of a complex economic phenomenon of reality is likely to prove fruitless, no attempt will be made here to explain systematically why poorer less developed countries have benefited to a relatively small degree from the public good properties of the innovations and investments of other nations. But part of the explanation may well be related to product mix and education. A less developed country that produces no cars cannot benefit from the invention and adoption of a better car-producing robot in Japan (though it does benefit to a lesser degree from new textile and rice-growing technology), nor can it benefit from the factor-price equalization effect of the accompanying Japanese investments, since it cannot shift labor force out of its (nonexistent) auto industry as the theorem's logic requires. Lack of education and the associated skills prevent both the presence of high-tech industries and the effective imitation (adoption) of the Japanese innovation. Obviously, there is much more to any reasonably fuller explanation of the exclusion of many less developed countries from the convergence process, but that is not my purpose here. . . .

NOTES

1. This observation does not quite seem to square with Charles Feinstein's estimates (1972, pp. 82–94) which indicate that while output per worker in the United Kingdom increased 0.2 percent per year between 1761 and 1800, between 1801 and 1830 the growth rate leaped up to 1.4 percent per annum. He estimates that total factor productivity behaved similarly. However, between 1801 and 1810, total annual investment fell to 10 percent of gross domestic product, in comparison with its 14 percent rate in the immediately preceding and succeeding periods.

2. Space prevents extensive consideration of Paul Romer's (1985) objection to the evidence offered for the convergence hypothesis provided here and elsewhere, i.e., that the sample of countries studied is an *ex post* selection of successful economies. Successes, by definition, are those which have done best relative to the leader. However, the Summers-Heston 1950–80 data for 72 countries represented in

Figure 10.2 do permit an *ex ante* selection. Tests ranking countries both by 1950 and by 1960 GDP levels confirm that even an *ex ante* sample of the wealthiest countries yields a pattern of convergence which, while less pronounced than that calculated from an *ex post* group, is still unambiguous.

3. The high correlation should not be taken too seriously. Aside from the reasons why its explanation may be misunderstood that are presently discussed in the text, the tight fit of the data points is undoubtedly ascribable in good part to several biassing features of the underlying calculation. First, the 1870 figures were calculated by Maddison using backward extrapolation of growth rates, and hence their correlation is hardly surprising. Second, since growth rate, r, is calculated by solving $y_t = e^{rt} y_0$ for r, to obtain $r = (\ln y_t - \ln y_0)/t$, where $y_t = GDP$ per capita in period t, a regression equation $r = f(y_0)$ contains the same variable, y_0 on both sides of the equation, thus tending to produce a spurious appearance of close relationship. Indeed, if the convergence process were perfect, so that we would have $y_t = k$ with k the same for every country in the sample, every dot in the diagram would necessarily perfectly fit the curve $r = \ln k/t - \ln y_0/t$, and the r^2 would be unity, identically. The 72-country data depicted in Figure 10.2 hardly constitute a close fit (the R^2 is virtually zero), and do not even yield a negatively sloping regression line. Thus, a relationship such as that in Figure 10.1 is no tautology, nor even a foregone conclusion.

In addition, if the 1870 productivity levels are measured with considerable error, this must result in some significant downward bias in the regression coefficient on $\ln(GDP$ per $WorkHr$, 1870). This is a point distinct from the one concerning the size of the correlation coefficient, although the latter is affected by the fact that relatively large measurement errors in the 1870 productivity levels enter as inversely correlated measurement errors in the 1870–1979 growth rate. The argument that this bias is not sufficient to induce a negative correlation in the 72-country sample may not be wholly germane, as the relative seriousness of the measurement errors in the initial and terminal observations may be much the same for observations confined to the period 1950–80.

4. It must be conceded that the longer-run data do not seem to offer impressive support for the hypothesis that the forces of factor-price equalization have, albeit imperfectly, extended the benefits of exceptional rates of investment from those economies that carried out the successful investment programs to other industrialized economies. Since we have estimates of relative real wages, capital stock, and other pertinent variables for the United Kingdom and Germany, these have been compared below:

	Period	Ratio: German Increase to U.K. Increase[b]
Real Wages	1860–1980	4.25
GDP per Labor Hour	1870–1979	2.35
Capital Stock[a]	1870–1979	6.26
Capital Stock per Worker	1870–1979	3.8
Capital Stock per Capita	1870–1979	5.4

Sources: Real wages, same as in Note 6 [in original]; all other data from Maddison.

a. Net nonresidential fixed tangible capital stock.

b. (German 1979 figure/German 1870 figure)/(U.K. 1979 figure/U.K. 1987 figure) with appropriate modification of the dates for the wage figures.

If the public goods attribute hypothesis about the effects of investment in one country were valid and if factor-price equalization were an effective force, we would expect the relative rise in German real wages and in productivity to be small (on some criterion) in comparison with the relative increase in its capital stock. However, the figures do not seem to exhibit such a pattern.

5. There are at least two sources of such data: the World Bank and the University of Pennsylvania group. Here I report only data drawn from the latter, since their international comparisons have been carried out with unique sophistication and insight. Instead of translating the different currencies into one another using inadequate exchange rate comparisons, they use carefully constructed indices of relative purchasing power. I have also replicated my calculations using World Bank data and obtained exactly the same qualitative results.

6. The centrally planned economies are Bulgaria, China, Czechoslovakia, East Germany, Hungary, Poland, Romania, USSR, and Yugoslavia. The 5 countries with relatively high 1950 incomes included neither in Maddison's sample nor in the planned group are, in descending order of GDP per capita, Luxembourg, New Zealand, Iceland, Venezuela, and Argentina. The countries with negative growth rates are Uganda and Nigeria.

REFERENCES

Abramovitz, Moses. 1979. "Rapid Growth Potential and Its Realization: The Experience of the Capitalist Economies in the Postwar Period," in Edmond Malinvaud, ed., *Economic Growth and Resources, Proceedings of the Fifth World Congress of the International Economic Association*, Vol. 1, London: Macmillan.

———. 1985. "Catching Up and Falling Behind," delivered at the Economic History Association, September 20, 1985.

Ames, Edward and Rosenberg, Nathan. 1963. "Changing Technological Leadership and Industrial Growth," *Economic Journal* 73 (March): 13–31.

Beniger, James R. Forthcoming. *The Control Revolution: Technological and Economic Origins of the Information Society*. Cambridge: Harvard University Press.

Caves, Richard E. and Krause, Lawrence B. 1984. *The Australian Economy: A View from the North*. Washington: The Brookings Institution.

Cipolla, Carlo M. 1976. *Before the Industrial Revolution: European Society and Economy, 1000–1700*. New York: W. W. Norton.

Clark, Colin. 1957. *The Conditions of Economic Progress*, 3rd ed. London: Macmillan.

Darby, Michael. 1984. "The U.S. Productivity Slowdown: A Case of Statistical Myopia," *American Economic Review*, 74 (June): 301–322.

David, Paul A. 1977. "Invention and Accumulation in America's Economic Growth: A Nineteenth-Century Parable," in K. Brunner and A. H. Meltzer, eds., *International Organization, National Policies and Economic Development*, pp. 179–228. Amsterdam: North-Holland.

Deane, Phyllis and Cole, W. A. 1962. *British Economic Growth 1688–1959*. Cambridge: Cambridge University Press.

Feinstein, Charles. 1972. *National Income, Expenditure and Output of the United Kingdom, 1855–1965*. Cambridge: Cambridge University Press.

Gerschenkron, Alexander. 1952. "Economic Backwardness in Historical Perspective," in Bert F. Hoselitz, ed., *The Progress of Underdeveloped Areas*. Chicago: University of Chicago Press.

Landes, David S. 1969. *The Unbound Prometheus*. Cambridge: Cambridge University Press.
Lawrence, Robert Z. 1984. *Can America Compete?* Washington: The Brookings Institution.
McCloskey, D. N. 1981. *Enterprise and Trade in Victorian Britain*. London: Allen & Unwin.
Maddison, Angus. 1982. *Phases of Capitalist Development*. New York: Oxford University Press.
Marx, Karl and Engels, Friedrich. 1946. *Manifesto of the Communist Party* (1848). London: Lawrence and Wishart.
Matthews, R.C.O. 1982. *Slower Growth in the Western World*. London: Heinemann.
————, Feinstein, C. H. and Odling-Smee, J. C. 1982. *British Economic Growth, 1856–1973*. Stanford: Stanford University Press.
Mueller, Dennis C. 1983. *The Political Economy of Growth*. New Haven: Yale University Press.
Phelps Brown, E. H. and Hopkins, S. V. 1955. "Seven Centuries of Building Wages," *Economica*, 22 (August): 195–206.
————. 1956. "Seven Centuries of the Prices of Consumables," *Economica*, 23 (November): 296–314.
Porat, Marc Uri. 1977. "The Information Economy, Definitions and Measurement," Office of Telecommunications, Special Publication, 77-12(1), U.S. Department of Commerce, Washington.
Romer, Paul M. 1985. "Increasing Returns and Long Run Growth," Working Paper No. 27. University of Rochester, October.
Summers, Robert and Heston, Alan. 1984. "Improved International Comparisons of Real Product and Its Composition, 1950–1980," *Review of Income and Wealth*, 30 (June): 207–262.
Summers, Robert, Kravis, I. B., and Heston, Alan. 1986. "Changes in World Income Distribution," *Journal of Policy Modeling*, 6 (May): 237–269.
Teece, David J. 1976. *The Multinational Corporation and the Resources Cost of International Technology Transfer*. Cambridge: Ballinger.
U.S. Bureau of Census. 1973. *Long Term Economic Growth 1860–1970*. Washington, D.C., June.
Veblen, Thorstein. 1915. *Imperial Germany and the Industrial Revolution*. New York: Macmillan.
Viner, Jacob. 1958. *The Long View and the Short*. Glencoe: Free Press.
Williamson, Jeffrey G. 1983. "Why Was British Growth So Slow During the Industrial Revolution?" Unpublished, Harvard Institute of Economic Research.

11

. . . .

Productivity Growth, Convergence, and Welfare: Comment

. . . .

J. BRADFORD DE LONG

In the previous chapter, William Baumol confirmed the expectations of convergence theory by finding that between 1870 and 1979 productivity rates of poorer countries grew more rapidly than those of richer countries. In this chapter, J. Bradford De Long argues that because only countries that converged by 1979 were included in the data set used by Baumol, convergence was assured. When De Long corrects for this sample-selection bias, convergence disappears. De Long then analyzes other variables to determine if the pattern of growth that he found can be explained. He does not find an associa- tion between democracy in 1870 and subsequent growth. De Long did find a significant relationship between religion and growth: Protestant cultures grew faster. But the author notes that the correla- tions will not hold for long given the growth rates of countries such as Japan and Italy. (See Chapter 20 for further thoughts on the issue of religion and development.) The optimistic view that there is a process of economic homogenization, a closing of the gap between rich and poor, is not sustained by the data. As the author concludes, "It pushes us away from the belief that even the nations of the now industrial West will have roughly equal standards of living in 2090 or 2190."

Economists have always expected the "convergence" of national productiv- ity levels. The theoretical logic behind this belief is powerful. The per capi- ta income edge of the West is based on its application of the storehouse of industrial and administrative technology of the Industrial Revolution. This

Reprinted with permission from the *American Economic Review*, vol. 78, 5 (1986): 1038–1048.

storehouse is open: modern technology is a public good. The benefits of tapping this storehouse are great, and so nations will strain every nerve to assimilate modern technology and their incomes will converge to those of industrial nations.

William Baumol (1986) argues that convergence has shown itself strongly in the growth of industrial nations since 1870.[1] According to Baumol, those nations positioned to industrialize are much closer together in productivity now than a century ago. He bases this conclusion on a regression of growth since 1870 on 1870 productivity for sixteen countries covered by Angus Maddison (1982).[2]

Baumol's finding of convergence might—even though Baumol himself does not believe that it should—naturally be read to support two further conclusions. First, slow relative growth in the United States since World War II was inevitable: convergence implies that in the long run divergent national cultures, institutions, or policies cannot sustain significant productivity edges over the rest of the developed world. Second, one can be optimistic about future development. Maddison's sixteen all assimilated modern technology and converged; perhaps all developing nations will converge to Western living standards once they acquire a foundation of technological literacy.

But when properly interpreted Baumol's finding is less informative than one might think. For Baumol's regression uses an *ex post* sample of countries that are now rich and have successfully developed. By Maddison's choice, those nations that have not converged are excluded from his sample because of their resulting present relative poverty. Convergence is thus all but guaranteed in Baumol's regression, which tells us little about the strength of the forces making for convergence among nations that in 1870 belonged to what Baumol calls the "convergence club."

Only a regression run on an *ex ante* sample, a sample not of nations that have converged but of nations that seemed in 1870 likely to converge, can tell us whether growth since 1870 exhibits "convergence." The answer to this *ex ante* question—have those nations that a century ago appeared well placed to appropriate and utilize industrial technology converged?—is no. . . .

Maddison (1982) compiles long-run national income and aggregate productivity data for sixteen successful capitalist nations.[3] Because he focuses on nations which (a) have a rich data base for the construction of historical national accounts and (b) have successfully developed, the nations in Maddison's sixteen are among the richest nations in the world today. Baumol regresses the average rate of annual labor productivity growth over 1870–1979 on a constant and on the log of labor productivity in 1870 for this sample. He finds the inverse relationship of the first line of Table 11.1. The slope is large enough to erase by 1979 almost all initial income gaps, and the residual variance is small.

Table 11.1 Regressions Using Maddison's Sixteen

Independent Variable	Dependent Variable	Constant	Slope Coefficient	Standard Error of Estimate	R^2
Natural Log of 1870 Productivity	Annual Percent Productivity Growth	5.251	−0.749 .075	.14	.87
Natural Log of 1870 Income	Log Difference of 1979 and 1870 Income	8.457	−0.995 .094	.15	.88

Source: Data from Maddison (1982).

Regressing the log difference in per capita income between 1870 and 1979 on a constant and the log of per capita income in 1870 provides a slightly stronger case for convergence, as detailed in the second line of Table 11.1. The logarithmic income specification offers two advantages. The slope has the intuitive interpretation that a value of minus one means that 1979 and 1870 relative incomes are uncorrelated, and extension of the sample to include additional nations becomes easier.

Baumol's regression line tells us little about the strength of forces making for convergence since 1870 among industrial nations. The sample suffers from selection bias, and the independent variable is unavoidably measured with error. Both of these create the appearance of convergence whether or not it exists in reality. Sample selection bias arises because any nations relatively rich in 1870 that have not converged fail to make it into Maddison's sixteen. Maddison's sixteen thus include Norway but not Spain, Canada but not Argentina, and Italy but not Ireland. . . .

The unbiased sample used here meets three criteria. First, it is made up of nations that had high potential for economic growth as of 1870, in which modern economic growth had begun to take hold by the middle of the nineteenth century. Second, inclusion in the sample is not conditional on subsequent rapid growth. Third, the sample matches Baumol's as closely as possible, both because the best data exist for Maddison's sixteen and because analyzing an unbiased sample close to Baumol's shows that different conclusions arise not from different estimates but from removing sample selection and errors in variables' biases.

Per capita income in 1870 is an obvious measure of whether a nation was sufficiently technologically literate and integrated into world trade in 1870 to be counted among the potential convergers. . . .

. . . The choice of cutoff level itself requires balancing three goals: including only nations which really did in 1870 possess the social capability for rapid industrialization; including as many nations in Baumol's sample as possible; and building as large a sample as possible. . . .

If the convergence club membership cutoff is set low enough to include all Maddison's sixteen, then nations with 1870 incomes above 300 1975 dollars are included. This sample covers half the world. All Europe including Russia, all of South America, and perhaps others (Mexico and Cuba?) were richer than Japan in 1870. This sample does not provide a fair test of convergence. The Japanese miracle is a miracle largely because there was little sign in 1870 that Japan—or any nation as poor as Japan—was a candidate for rapid industrialization.

The second poorest of Maddison's sixteen in 1870 was Finland. Taking Finland's 1870 income as a cutoff leads to a sample in which Japan is removed, while Argentina, Chile, East Germany,[4] Ireland, New Zealand, Portugal, and Spain are added. . . .

All the additional nations have strong claims to belong to the 1870 convergence club. All were well integrated into the Europe-based international economy. All had bright development prospects as of 1870. . . . Argentina, Chile, and New Zealand were grouped in the nineteenth century with Australia and Canada as countries with temperate climates, richly endowed with natural resources, attracting large-scale immigration and investment, and exporting large quantities of raw and processed agricultural commodities. They were all seen as natural candidates for the next wave of industrialization.

Ireland's economy was closely integrated with the most industrialized economy in the world. Spain and Portugal had been the technological leaders of Europe during the initial centuries of overseas expansion—their per capita incomes were still above the European mean in the 1830s (Paul Bairoch, 1981)—and had retained close trading links with the heart of industrial Europe. Coke was used to smelt iron in Asturias in the 1850s, and by 1877 3,950 miles of railroad had been built in Spain. It is difficult to see how one could exclude Portugal and Spain from the convergence club without also excluding nations like Sweden and Finland.

Baumol's sample failed to include those nations that should have belonged to any hypothetical convergence club but that nevertheless did not converge. The enlarged sample might include nations not in the 1870 convergence club. Consider Kuwait today: Kuwait is rich, yet few would take its failure to maintain its relative standard of living over the next fifty years as evidence against convergence. For Kuwait's present wealth does not necessarily carry with it the institutional capability to turn oil wealth into next generation's industrial wealth. . . .

The volume of overseas investment poured into the additional nations by investors from London and Paris between 1870 and 1913 tells us that investors thought these nations' development prospects good. Herbert Feis' (1930) standard estimates of French and British overseas investment [the interested reader should refer to Table 2, p. 1143 of the original article—*Eds.*] show the six non-European nations among the top ten[5] recipients of investment per capita from France and Britain, and four of the five top recipients of investment belong to the once-rich twenty-two.[6] Every pound or franc invested is an explicit bet that the recipient country's rate of profit will remain high and an implicit bet that its rate of economic growth will be rapid. The coincidence of the nations added on a per capita income basis and the nations that would have been added on a foreign investment basis is powerful evidence that these nations do belong in the potential convergence club.

Errors in estimating 1870 income are unavoidable and produce equal and opposite errors in 1870–1979 growth. These errors therefore create the appearance of convergence where it does not exist in reality. . . .[7]

From one point of view, the relatively poor quality of much of the nineteenth century data is not a severe liability for this chapter. Only if there is less measurement error than allowed for will the results be biased against convergence. A more direct check on the importance of measurement error can be performed by examining convergence starting at some later date for which income estimates are based on a firmer foundation. A natural such date is 1913.[8] The relationship between initial income and subsequent growth is examined for the period 1913–1979 in Table 11.2.

The longer 1870–1979 sample of Table 11.3 . . . is slightly more hospitable to convergence than is the 1913–1979 sample, but for neither sample do the regression lines reveal a significant inverse relationship between initial income and subsequent growth. When it is assumed that there is no measurement error in 1870 income, there is a large negative slope to the regression line. But even in this case the residual disturbance term is large. When measurement error variance is assumed equal to half disturbance variance, the slope is slightly but not significantly negative.

For the central case of equal variances growth since 1870 is unrelated to income in 1870. There is no convergence. Those countries with income edges have on average maintained them. If measurement error is assumed

Table 11.2   Maximum Likelihood Estimation for the Once-Rich Twenty-Two, 1913–1979

p	Slope Coefficient B	Standard Error of Slope	Standard Error of Regression	Standard Error in 1870 PCI
0.0	−.333	.116	.171	.000
0.5	−.140	.136	.151	.107
1.0	0.021	.158	.133	.133
2.0	0.206	.191	.106	.150
infinity	0.444	.238	.000	.167

Source: Data from Maddison (1982).

Table 11.3   Maximum Likelihood Estimation for the Once-Rich Twenty-Two, 1870–1979

p	Slope Coefficient B	Standard Error of Slope	Standard Error of Regression	Standard Error in 1870 PCI
0.0	−.566	.144	.207	.000
0.5	−.292	.192	.192	.136
1.0	0.110	.283	.170	.170
2.0	0.669	.463	.134	.190
infinity	1.381	.760	.000	.196

Source: Data from Maddison (1982).

larger than the regression disturbance there is not convergence but divergence. Nations rich in 1870 or 1913 have subsequently widened relative income gaps. The evidence can be presented in other ways. The standard deviations of log income are given in Table 11.4. Maddison's sixteen do converge: the standard deviation of log income in 1979 is only 35 percent of its 1870 value. But the appearance of convergence is due to selection bias: the once-rich twenty-two have as wide a spread of relative incomes today as in 1870.

The failure of convergence to emerge for nations rich in 1870 is due to the nations—Chile, Argentina, Spain, and Portugal. In the early 1970s none of these was a democracy. Perhaps only industrial nations with democratic political systems converge. A dummy variable for democracy over 1950–80 is significant in the central ($p = 1$) case in the once-rich twenty-two regression in a at the 1 percent level, as detailed in Table 11.5.

But whether a nation is a democracy over 1950–80 is not exogenous but is partly determined by growth over the preceding century. As of 1870 it was not at all clear which nations would become stable democracies. Of the once-rich twenty-two, France, Austria (including Czechoslovakia), and Germany were empires; Britain had a restricted franchise; Spain and Portugal were semiconstitutional monarchies; the United States had just undergone a civil war; and Ireland was under foreign occupation. That all

Table 11.4   Standard Deviations of Log Output for Maddison's Sixteen and the Once-Rich Twenty-Two

Sample	1870	1913	1979
Maddison's 16	.411	.355	.145
Once-Rich 22	.315	.324	.329

Source: Data from Maddison (1982).

Table 11.5   Democracy over 1950–1980 and Long-Run Growth for the Once-Rich Twenty-Two, 1870–1979

p	Slope Coefficient B	Standard Error of Slope	Coefficient on Democracy Variable	Standard Error	Standard Error in 1870 PCI	Standard Error of Regression
0.0	−.817	.277	.495	.085	.155	.000
0.5	−.744	.203	.476	.084	.154	.109
1.0	−.599	.208	.437	.090	.150	.150
2.0	0.104	.227	.248	.071	.131	.185
Infinity	1.137	.019	.044	.003	.000	.198

Source: Data from Maddison (1982).

of these countries would be stable democracies by 1950 seems *ex ante* unlikely. Table 11.6 shows that shifting to an *ex ante* measure of democracy[9] removes the correlation. Whether a nation's politics are democratic in 1870 has little to do with growth since. The elective affinity of democracy and opulence is not one way with democracy as cause and opulence as effect.

There is one striking *ex ante* association between growth over 1870–1979 and a predetermined variable: a nation's dominant religious establishment. As Table 11.7 shows, a religious establishment variable that is one for Protestant, one-half for mixed, and zero for Catholic nations is significantly correlated with growth as long as measurement error variance is not too high.[10]

This regression is very difficult to interpret.[11] It does serve as an example of how culture may be associated with substantial divergence in growth performance. But "Protestantism" is correlated with many things—early specialization in manufacturing (for a given level of income), a high invest-

Table 11.6   Democracy in 1870 and Long-Run Growth for the Once-Rich Twenty-Two, 1870–1979

p	Slope Coefficient B	Standard Error of Slope	Coefficient on Democracy Variable	Standard Error	Standard Error in 1870 PCI	Standard Error of Regression
0.0	−.567	.342	.001	.091	.207	.000
0.5	−.272	.322	−.038	.094	.192	.136
1.0	0.164	.454	−.095	.115	.169	.169
2.0	0.742	.976	−.170	.180	.131	.155
Infinity	1.231	.167	−.195	.022	.000	.194

Source: Data from Maddison (1982).

Table 11.7   Dominant Religion in 1870 and Long-Run Growth for the Once-Rich Twenty-
Two, 1870–1979

p	Slope Coefficient B	Standard Error of Slope	Coefficient on Democracy Variable	Standard Error	Standard Error in 1870 PCI	Standard Error of Regression
0.0	−.789	.252	.429	.088	.166	.000
0.5	−.688	.225	.403	.088	.164	.116
1.0	−.470	.248	.347	.098	.158	.158
2.0	0.375	.232	.132	.061	.132	.187
Infinity	1.199	.021	−.003	.004	.000	.197

Source: Data from Maddison (1982).

ment ratio, and a northern latitude, to name three. Almost any view—
except a belief in convergence—of what determines long-run growth is
consistent with this correlation between growth and religious establishment. Moreover, this correlation will not last: neither fast grower Japan nor
fast grower Italy owes anything to the Protestant ethic. The main message
of Table 11.7 is that, for the once-rich twenty-two, a country's religious
establishment has been a surprisingly good proxy for the social capability
to assimilate modern technology.

The long-run data do not show convergence on any but the most optimistic reading. They do not support the claim that those nations that should
have been able to rapidly assimilate industrial technology have all converged. Nations rich among the once-rich twenty-two in 1870 have not
grown more slowly than the average of the sample. And of the nations outside this sample, only Japan has joined the industrial leaders.

This is not to say that there are no forces pushing for convergence.
Convergence does sometimes happen. Technology is a public good.
Western Europe (except Iberia) and the British settlement colonies of
Australia, Canada, and the United States are now all developed. Even Italy,
which seemed outside the sphere of advanced capitalism two generations
ago, is near the present income frontier reached by the richest nations. The
convergence of Japan and Western Europe toward U.S. standards of productivity in the years after World War II is an amazing achievement, and
this does suggest that those present at the creation of the post–World War II
international order did a very good job. But others—Spain, Portugal,
Ireland, Argentina, and Chile—that one would in 1870 have thought capable of equally sharing this prosperity have not done so.[12] The capability to
assimilate industrial technology appears to be surprisingly hard to acquire,
and it may be distressingly easy to lose.

The forces making for "convergence" even among industrial nations
appear little stronger than the forces making for "divergence." The absence

of convergence pushes us away from a belief that in the long run technology transfer both is inevitable and is the key factor in economic growth. It pushes us away from the belief that even the nations of the now industrial West will have roughly equal standards of living in 2090 or 2190. And the absence of convergence even among nations relatively rich in 1870 forces us to take seriously arguments like Romer's (1986) that the relative income gap between rich and poor may tend to widen.

NOTES

1. Consider Baumol (1986): "Among the main observations . . . is the remarkable convergence. . . . [T]here is a strong inverse correlation between a country's productivity . . . in 1870 and its . . . productivity growth since then," and Baumol (1987): "Even more remarkable . . . is the convergence in . . . living standards of the leading industrial countries. . . . In 1870 . . . productivity in Australia, the leader, was 8 times . . . Japan's (the laggard). By 1979, the ratio . . . had fallen to about two."

2. Moses Abramovitz (1986) follows the behavior of these sixteen over time and notes that even among these nations "convergence" is almost entirely a post World War II phenomenon. Abramovitz' remarks on how the absence of the "social capability" to grasp the benefits of the Industrial Revolution may prevent even nations that could benefit greatly from industrializing are well worth reading. Also very good on the possible determinants of the social capability to assimilate technology are Irma Adelman and Cynthia Taft Morris (1980), Gregory Clark (1987), and Richard Easterlin (1981).

3. Maddison's focus on nations that have been economically successful is deliberate; his aim in (1964), (1982), and (1987) is to investigate the features of successful capitalist development. In works like Maddison (1970, 1983) he has analyzed the long-run growth and development of less successful nations.

4. Perhaps only nations that have remained capitalist should be included in the sample, for occupation by the Red Army and subsequent relative economic stagnation have no bearing on whether the forces making for convergence among industrial capitalist economies are strong. There is only one centrally planned economy in the unbiased sample, and its removal has negligible quantitative effects on the estimated degree of convergence.

5. The foreign investment figures do provide a powerful argument for adding other Latin American nations—Mexico, Brazil, and Cuba—to the sample of those that ought to have been in the convergence club. Inclusion of these nations would weigh heavily against convergence.

6. Japan would not merit inclusion in the 1870 convergence club on the basis of foreign investment before World War I, for Japanese industrialization was not financed by British capital. Foreign investors' taste for Japan was much less, investment being equal to about one pound sterling per head and far below investment in such nations as Venezuela, Russia, Turkey, and Egypt. Admittedly, Japan was far away and not well known, but who would have predicted that Japan would have five times the measured per capita GNP of Argentina by 1979?

7. By contrast, errors in measuring 1979 per capita income induce no systematic bias in the relationship between standard of living in 1870 and growth since, although they do diminish the precision of coefficient estimates.

8. The data for 1913 are much more plentiful and solid than for other years in

the early years of the twentieth century because of the concentration of historians' efforts on obtaining a pre–World War I benchmark. Beginning the sample at 1913 does mean that changes in country's "social capability" for development as a result of World War I appear in the error term in the regression. If those nations that suffered most badly in World War I were nations relatively poor in World War I, there would be cause for alarm that the choice of 1913 had biased the sample against finding convergence when it was really present. But the major battlefields of World War I lay in and the largest proportional casualties were suffered by relatively rich nations at the core of industrial Europe.

9. Defined as inclusion of the electorate of more than half the adult male population.

10. The once-rich twenty-two are split into nations that had Protestant religious establishments in 1870 (Australia, Denmark, Finland, E. Germany, Netherlands, New Zealand, Norway, Sweden, U.K., and United States), intermediate nations—nations that either were split in established religion in 1870 or that had undergone violent and prolonged religious wars between Protestant and Catholics in the centuries after the Protestant Reformation—(Belgium, Canada, France, West Germany, and Switzerland), and nations that had solid Catholic religious establishments in 1870 (Argentina, Austria, Chile, Ireland, Italy, Portugal, and Spain). This classification is judgmental and a matter of taste: are the Netherlands one of the heartlands of the Protestant Ethic or are they one of the few nations tolerant and pluralistic on matters of religion in the seventeenth century?

11. The easy explanation would begin with the medieval maxim *homo mercato vix aut numquam placere potest Deo:* the merchant's business can never please God. Medieval religious discipline was hostile to market capitalism, and the Protestant Reformation broke this discipline down in some places, and capitalism flourished most and modern democratic growth took hold strongest where this breakdown of medieval discipline had been most complete.

But this easy explanation is at best incomplete. Initially the Reformation did not see a relaxation of religious control. Strong Protestantism—Calvin's Geneva or Cromwell's Republic of the Saints—saw theology and economy closely linked in a manner not unlike the Ayatollah's Iran. And religious fanaticism is not often thought of as a source of economic growth.

Nevertheless the disapproval of self-interested profit seeking by radical Protestantism went hand-in-hand with seventeenth century economic development. And by 1800 profit seeking and accumulation for accumulation's sake had become morally praiseworthy activities in many nations with Protestant religious establishments. How was the original Protestant disapproval for the market transformed? Accounting for the evolution of the economic ethic of the Protestant West from Jean Calvin to Cotton Mather to Benjamin Franklin to Andrew Carnegie is a deep puzzle in economic history. The best analysis may still be the psychological account given by Max Weber (1958). Originally published in 1905.

12. One can find good reasons—ranging from the Red Army to landlord political dominance to the legacy of imperialism—for the failure of each of the additional nations to have reached the world's achieved per capita income frontier in 1979. But the fact that there are good reasons for the relative economic failure of each of these seven nations casts substantial doubt on the claim that the future will see convergence, for "good reasons" for economic failure will always be widespread. It is a safe bet that in 2090 one will be able *ex post* to identify similar "good reasons" lying behind the relative economic decline of those nations that will have fallen out of the industrial core.

REFERENCES

Abramovitz, M. 1986. "Catching Up, Forging Ahead, and Falling Behind," *Journal of Economic History*, June, 46: 385–406.

Adelman, I. and C. T. Morris. 1980. "Patterns of Industrialization in the Nineteenth and Early Twentieth Centuries," in Paul Uselding, ed., *Research in Economic History*, Vol. 5, Greenwich: JAI Press, 217–46.

Bairoch, P. 1981. "The Main Trends in National Economic Disparities Since the Industrial Revolution," in P. Bairoch and M. Lévy-Leboyer, eds., *Disparities in Economic Development Since the Industrial Revolution*, New York: St. Martin's Press.

Baumol, W. 1987. "America's Productivity 'Crisis'," *The New York Times*, February 15, 3:2.

———. 1986. "Productivity Growth, Convergence, and Welfare," *American Economic Review*, December, 76: 1072–85.

Clark, G. 1987. "Why Isn't the Whole World Developed? Lessons from the Cotton Mills," *Journal of Economic History*, March, 47: 141–74.

Easterlin, R. 1981. "Why Isn't the Whole World Developed?," *Journal of Economic History*, March, 41: 1–19.

Feis, H. 1930. *Europe, The World's Banker*, New Haven: Yale.

Maddison, A. 1987. "Growth and Slowdown in Advanced Capitalist Economies," *Journal of Economic Literature*, June, 25: 649–98.

———. 1983. "A Comparison of Levels of GDP per Capita in Developed and Developing Countries, 1700–1980," *Journal of Economic History*, March, 43: 27–41.

———. 1982. *Phases of Capitalist Development*, Oxford: Oxford University Press.

———. 1970. *Economic Progress and Policy in Developing Countries*, London: Allen & Unwin.

———. 1964. *Economic Growth in the West*, New York: The Twentieth Century Fund.

Romer, P. 1986. "Increasing Returns and Long Run Growth," *Journal of Political Economy*, October, 94: 1002–37.

Weber, M. 1958. *The Protestant Ethic and the Spirit of Capitalism*, New York: Scribner's. Originally published in 1905.

12

· · · · · · ·

Could It Be That the
Whole World Is Already Rich?
A Comparison of RGDP/pc
and GNP/pc Measures

· · · · · · ·

John T Passé-Smith

Measuring growth is not an easy task. Although poverty and wealth are eas-ily discernible to anyone traveling across the frontiers of rich and poor countries, they are not easy to quantify. Visitors to foreign lands are con-fronted with the "traveler's dilemma": After conversion from U.S. coin into foreign currency, one dollar does not necessarily yield the same buying power in India as it does in the United States, or Botswana, or France. The amount of cash it took to buy a feast in one country might purchase only a partial loaf of bread in the next. This dilemma alerted scholars to the need to replace exchange rates with a conversion factor that would better reflect purchasing power.

Few people argue over the existence of a gap between rich and poor countries, but the extent of the gap is often disputed, in part because of a lack of confidence in the accuracy of exchange rate conversions. Com-paring the general conditions in Burkina Faso to those in Switzerland, one may be satisfied that the GNP/pc accurately reflects the difference in stan-dards of living; however, some have argued that this is not the case. Many scholars (Ward 1985; Summers and Heston 1984, Morris 1979, Kravis et al. 1975; Heston 1973; Kuznets 1972) have suggested that converting GNPs to a common currency utilizing official exchange rates overstates the poverty of poor countries.

Exchange rate conversions are said to distort the actual purchasing power of currencies because they fluctuate away from a hypothesized equi-librium value. The fluctuations may occur rapidly—because of inflation, changes in production techniques, import and export barriers (or perhaps the quick removal of present barriers), price shocks originating domestical-ly or internationally, etc.—but the restoration of equilibrium occurs much more slowly. Thus, exchange rate fluctuations represent malalignments of currency prices that will ultimately move back toward a relative unity value

(Katseli-Papaefstratiou 1979:4). Morris (1979:10) pointed out that it is not uncommon for exchange rates to oscillate rather wildly in a relatively short time. For example, Brazil's official exchange rate during the first quarter of 1981 was 70.8 *cruzeiros* per U.S. dollar; the midyear rate climbed to 91.8; and by the end of the year the official rate stood at 118, a 60 percent shift.[1]

Some contend that the exchange rate/PPP difference involves more than a lag time for correction of an equilibrium-tending exchange rate. Simon Kuznets, for example, asserts that

> even if exchange rates are assumed to reflect purchasing power parities of goods entering foreign trade, the price structures of the latter do not fully represent the prices of the wider range of goods entering countrywide output and comprising gross domestic product; and more important, the degree of non-representation differs among countries at different levels of development and hence of per capita product . . . the overstatement . . . is apparently smaller for the country with the lower per capita product (Kuznets 1972:8–9).[2]

The United Nations commissioned a series of related projects, beginning in 1968 and continuing today, dubbed the International Comparison Project (ICP).[3] The purpose of the ICP is to produce PPP conversion factors so that cross-national comparisons of national account statistics can be made. In 1984 Robert Summers and Alan Heston reported that the project had "develop[ed] a structural relationship between purchasing power parities and exchange rates . . . [that took] account of the variability for exchange rates" (1984:207–208). Using extensive research in thirty-four "benchmark" countries, this relationship was to be extrapolated to the remaining "nonbenchmark" countries of similar size, economic structure, and so on. In 1988 the sample of countries and the years of coverage were expanded to include 130 countries covering the period 1950–1985.

The following sections offer some simple comparisons of World Bank– and International Monetary Fund–produced GNP/pcs (*World Tables 1992;* IMF 1984) and the data produced by the ICP group. Only those countries present in both data sets and in every year are used. The merged sample includes 107 countries for the years 1962–1985. At least two questions are raised: First, how different are the data for individual countries? Second, how has the change in data altered the extent of the gap between rich and poor as illustrated in Chapter 4?

GNP/PC AND RGDP/PCS COMPARED

The gross national product of a country is equal to the gross domestic product less factor payments abroad, so in comparing the two one should expect a difference even if the GDPs are not "real" GDPs (RGDPs) produced with a purchasing power parity index. Although factor payments most often represent a negative flow, they are sometimes positive, so it cannot be readily assumed that the GNP will be smaller than the GDP. A quick glance at the International Monetary Fund's *International Financial Statistics, 1980 Yearbook* (IMF 1980) seems to show that the industrialized countries of Europe and the United States are more likely to experience an inflow of factor payments than developing countries, but this is impressionistic, not systematic, evidence.

The left-hand side of Table 12.1 lists RGDP/pcs (the ICP data) for 1962 and 1985, the rankings for both years, and the annual average growth rate.[4] The right-hand side of the table includes comparable GNP/pc data (World Bank/IMF data set). The countries are also broken down by geographic regions as defined by the International Monetary Fund (IMF 1984). The IMF classifications include one nonregionally defined group, the "developed countries"; the less developed countries were divided into geographic regions: Africa, Asia, East Asia/Pacific,[5] the Western Hemisphere, and Europe/Middle East.[6] Finally, the column running down the center offers the difference between RGDP/pc ranking and GNP/pc ranking for the year 1985.

Among the developed countries, only five differed by five or more places in the RGDP-GNP comparison, and only Canada (+5) ranked higher in RGDP/pc than it did in GNP/pc. The other four countries—Australia (–8), Iceland (–7), Luxembourg (–6), and Sweden (–5)—all moved downward in the RGDP rankings. Canada was also one of only five countries in the developed category whose GNP/pc ($12,173) was smaller—albeit very slightly—than its RGDP/pc ($12,196).

Proponents of PPPs have argued that exchange rate conversions overstate the poverty of poor countries. As might be expected, only three nondeveloped countries have exchange rate–converted GNP/pcs larger than their purchasing power–converted RGDP/pcs: Algeria, Côte D'Ivoire, and Mauritania. On average, however, a developed country's RGDP/pc was $1,878 *less* than its GNP/pc. Both Switzerland's and Luxembourg's RGDP/pcs were over $6,000 less than their GNP/pcs. If these figures are accurate, then the ICP project is demonstrating not only that the poverty of the developing countries is exaggerated but also that the wealth of the rich is at least partially an illusion.

As for the regional groupings, the Asian countries—Bangladesh, India, Pakistan, Nepal, and Sri Lanka—experienced the largest apparent increase between GNP/pc and RGDP/pc. The mean GNP/pc for this region was $262 in 1985—ranging from $141 for Bangladesh to $398 for Pakistan—increasing to an RGDP/pc of $923. Here the GNP/pc is but 28 percent of the RGDP/pc. For every country in this group the change was very large. Indeed, Sri Lanka had a GNP/pc of $335 in 1985 but a purchasing power equivalence of $1,539. This disparity is either indicative of the type of

Table 12.1 Comparison of RGDP/pc and GNP/pc: Levels, Rank, and Growth Rates by Region

	Real Gross Domestic Product per Capita					Difference Between RGDP/pc and GNP/pc 1985	Gross National Product per Capita (1980 U.S. dollars)				
	1962	1985	Rank 1962	Rank 1985	Annual Growth 1962–85		1962	1985	Rank 1962	Rank 1985	Annual Growth 1962–85
					Developed Countries						
Norway	5,416	12,623	11	1	3.66	2	7,154	15,916	5	3	3.42
United States	7,726	12,532	1	2	1.88	3	8,475	13,348	3	5	1.89
Canada	6,411	12,196	3	3	2.78	5	6,471	12,173	10	8	2.70
Denmark	6,057	10,884	5	4	2.41	2	7,482	12,967	4	6	2.21
Germany	5,529	10,708	10	5	2.91	2	6,734	12,773	8	7	2.89
Switzerland	7,342	10,640	2	6	1.38	-4	11,292	17,200	1	2	1.63
Luxembourg	6,234	10,540	4	7	2.37	-6	7,077	17,724	6	1	4.26
France	4,881	9,918	15	8	3.35	3	5,763	11,315	14	11	3.15
Sweden	5,654	9,904	8	9	2.22	-5	8,600	14,455	2	4	2.08
Belgium	4,827	9,717	17	11	3.25	3	5,468	10,657	15	14	3.11
Japan	2,687	9,447	29	12	5.38	3	3,043	10,507	20	15	5.20
Finland	4,405	9,232	18	13	3.36	-1	5,310	11,305	16	12	3.39
Netherlands	4,896	9,092	14	15	2.89	-2	6,281	10,996	11	13	2.45
Iceland	4,877	9,037	16	16	2.82	-7	6,575	11,876	9	9	2.66
Austria	4,189	8,929	19	17	3.48	-1	4,570	9,982	17	16	3.62
Australia	5,336	8,850	12	18	1.95	-8	6,943	11,563	7	10	1.99
United Kingdom	5,104	8,665	13	19	2.32	-2	6,276	9,912	12	17	1.85
New Zealand	5,669	8,000	7	20	1.38	-2	5,764	7,828	13	18	1.12
Italy	3,660	7,425	20	21	3.32	-2	3,514	6,940	18	19	3.00
Spain	2,893	6,437	26	23	3.42	-1	2,571	5,284	23	22	3.13
Ireland	2,752	5,205	28	29	2.97	-4	2,981	4,701	22	25	2.34
Mean	5,074	9,523	13	12	2.83	-1	6,112	11,401	11	11	2.77

					Africa						
South Africa	2,754	3,885	27	33	1.65	1	1,862	2,332	29	34	1.20
Gabon	996	3,103	61	42	5.58	−10	2,284	2,376	25	32	1.44
Algeria	1,086	2,142	57	51	2.81	−18	977	2,334	44	33	3.56
Tunisia	825	2,050	65	53	4.41	−6	562	1,396	63	47	4.51
Mauritius	1,088	1,869	56	57	2.65	−4	834	1,270	49	53	2.23
Botswana	541	1,762	81	58	5.24	−1	263	1,201	88	57	7.95
Congo	773	1,338	67	65	1.26	−11	649	1,246	61	54	3.22
Morocco	740	1,221	71	68	2.23	−2	550	830	66	66	2.19
Swaziland	529	1,187	86	71	3.67	−11	430	1,008	76	60	3.23
Cameroon	560	1,095	80	73	2.51	−10	425	898	77	63	3.37
Zimbabwe	634	948	76	75	1.57	−11	680	844	60	64	1.09
Côte D'Ivoire	748	920	70	76	0.57	−14	715	956	56	62	1.17
Lesotho	277	771	104	78	4.58	−2	159	493	103	76	6.03
Senegal	777	754	66	79	−0.06	−1	457	442	75	78	−0.08
Kenya	429	598	94	83	1.13	1	225	349	92	84	2.23
Zambia	721	584	73	84	−0.02	−5	555	425	64	79	−1.41
Nigeria	532	581	84	85	1.55	−16	570	740	62	69	2.21
Mauritania	446	550	92	86	1.02	−3	319	379	81	83	0.67
Sudan	754	540	69	87	−0.83	−5	398	391	78	82	0.70
Mozambique	845	528	64	88	−2.45	10	482	249	71	98	−2.61
Gambia, The	402	526	97	90	1.53	−3	254	297	90	87	1.28
Benin	586	525	78	91	−0.69	1	239	272	91	92	0.46
Madagascar	660	497	75	92	−1.00	−2	382	282	79	90	−1.13
Liberia	406	491	96	93	0.38	−12	462	395	73	81	0.08
Togo	427	489	95	94	0.32	−5	217	291	93	89	1.06
Sierra Leone	334	443	101	95	1.24	−4	275	279	87	91	0.16
Central Africa	474	434	91	96	−0.4	−8	297	296	83	88	0.02
Niger	317	429	102	97	1.5	3	350	214	80	100	−1.90
Malawi	243	387	105	98	2.52	3	132	212	105	101	2.37
Tanzania	209	355	107	100	1.31	−4	206	255	95	96	1.03
Mali	381	355	98	99	0.0	5	135	158	104	104	0.96

(continues)

Table 12.1 *(continued)*

	Real Gross Domestic Product per Capita					Difference Between RGDP/pc and GNP/pc 1985	Gross National Product per Capita (1980 U.S. dollars)				
	1962	1985	Rank 1962	Rank 1985	Annual Growth 1962–85		1962	1985	Rank 1962	Rank 1985	Annual Growth 1962–85
Africa (continued)											
Ghana	534	349	83	101	-1.89	-16	490	345	70	85	-1.76
Somalia	506	348	88	102	-0.64	-5	297	254	84	97	-0.16
Burundi	334	345	100	103	0.91	-10	163	269	101	93	2.22
Rwanda	211	341	106	104	3.53	-5	200	227	96	99	1.78
Ethiopia	294	310	103	105	0.06	2	103	120	107	107	0.93
Chad	539	254	82	106	-2.98	0	191	128	98	106	-2.63
Zaire	336	210	99	107	-2.20	-4	212	165	94	103	-1.28
Mean	612	882	83	83	1.18	-5	474	648	78	79	1.22
Asia and East Asia/Pacific											
Sri Lanka	1,029	1,539	60	62	1.61	24	177	335	100	86	2.81
Pakistan	584	1,153	79	72	2.33	8	199	398	97	80	2.73
India	530	750	85	80	1.11	15	182	268	99	95	1.60
Bangladesh	444	647	93	81	1.08	24	117	141	106	105	0.67
Nepal	485	526	90	89	0.15	13	161	165	102	102	-0.22
Mean	614	923	81	77	1.25	17	167	262	101	94	1.52
Singapore	1,670	9,834	39	10	8.01	10	1,421	6,791	31	20	7.67
Hong Kong	1,984	9,093	33	14	6.81	7	1,337	5,694	33	21	6.75
Malaysia	1,194	3,415	52	40	5.56	5	758	1,789	53	45	4.28
Korea	704	3,056	74	43	7.14	-3	491	2,134	69	40	6.78

Fiji	1,795	2,893	37	46	2.72	0	1,122	1,656	37	46	2.53
Thailand	729	1,900	72	56	4.42	9	318	841	82	65	4.36
Papua New Guinea	1,168	1,374	54	63	0.59	4	550	765	65	67	1.30
Philippines	941	1,361	52	64	2.54	9	465	616	72	73	2.26
Indonesia	494	1,255	89	67	5.29	5	259	617	89	72	4.57
Mean	972	1,973	65	57	4.77	4	534	1,105	69	61	4.50

Western Hemisphere

Trinidad and Tobago	5,548	6,384	9	22	0.58	1	3,484	5,079	19	23	2.00
Barbados	1,996	5,212	32	28	4.14	1	1,352	2,889	32	29	3.85
Mexico	2,212	3,985	30	32	2.89	11	1,063	2,017	39	43	3.04
Venezuela	5,878	3,548	6	35	-2.63	-5	2,306	2,649	24	30	1.12
Suriname	1,605	3,522	41	36	3.99	1	1,193	2,256	34	37	3.91
Chile	3,128	3,486	25	38	0.49	4	2,020	2,092	27	42	0.07
Argentina	3,130	3,486	24	37	0.77	-1	2,021	2,269	26	36	0.82
Uruguay	3,221	3,462	22	39	1.3	2	1,986	2,118	28	41	1.17
Brazil	1,421	3,282	46	41	4.78	-3	1,002	2,180	41	38	4.40
Panama	1,432	2,912	45	44	3.25	0	1,030	1,990	40	44	2.96
Costa Rica	1,726	2,650	38	47	2.5	5	919	1,276	45	52	1.80
Colombia	1,402	2,599	47	48	3.32	2	808	1,359	51	50	2.95
Ecuador	1,134	2,387	55	50	4.12	8	702	1,119	58	58	2.96
Peru	1,940	2,114	34	52	0.58	7	1,011	1,014	42	59	0.19
Paraguay	1,039	1,996	59	54	3.54	-3	754	1,306	54	51	3.58
Nicaragua	1,804	1,989	36	55	-0.24	13	918	747	46	68	-1.17
Dominican Rep	1,069	1,753	58	59	3.04	-3	762	1,216	52	56	2.92
Jamaica	1,556	1,725	43	60	0.15	-5	1,172	1,224	36	55	-0.09
Guatemala	1,297	1,608	48	61	1.57	0	737	962	55	61	1.70
Guyana	1,284	1,259	49	66	0.51	9	537	515	67	75	0.48
El Salvador	1,182	1,198	53	69	0.35	1	701	716	59	70	0.07
Bolivia	926	1,089	63	74	1.40	3	458	480	74	77	0.59
Honduras	755	911	68	77	1.07	-3	533	596	68	74	0.59

(continues)

Table 12.1 *(continued)*

	Real Gross Domestic Product per Capita					Difference Between RGDP/pc and GNP/pc	Gross National Product per Capita (1980 U.S. dollars)				
	1962	1985	Rank 1962	Rank 1985	Annual Growth 1962–85	1985	1962	1985	Rank 1962	Rank 1985	Annual Growth 1962–85
Western Hemisphere (continued)											
Haiti	598	631	77	82	0.77	12	277	268	86	94	0.54
Mean	1,970	2,654	42	50	1.72	2	1,157	1,597	46	53	1.69
Europe and Middle East											
Israel	3,203	6,270	23	24	3.12	0	2,998	4,803	21	24	2.19
Hungary	3,485	5,765	21	25	2.18	14	888	2,174	47	39	4.36
Malta	1,214	5,319	51	26	7.71	2	812	3,619	50	28	7.99
Cyprus	2,089	5,310	31	27	3.93	−1	1,185	4,225	35	26	5.89
Yugoslavia	1,901	5,063	35	30	4.58	1	1,119	2,544	38	31	4.10
Greece	1,644	4,464	40	31	4.43	−4	1,616	4,151	30	27	4.20
Portugal	1,592	3,729	42	34	4.11	1	993	2,323	43	35	3.95
Syria	1,548	2,900	44	45	4.31	3	849	1,386	48	48	3.45
Turkey	1,255	2,533	50	49	3.16	0	708	1,382	57	49	2.99
Egypt	525	1,188	87	70	3.52	1	295	703	85	71	3.98
Mean	1,846	4,254	42	36	4.10	2	1,146	2,731	45	38	4.31

Sources: Calculated from data in *The World Tables 1992* (World Bank); *International Financial Statistics: Supplement on Output Statistics*, No. 8, 1984 (International Monetary Fund); Summers and Heston, 1988; and *Human Development Report*, 1990 (United Nations).

overestimation of poverty that PPP proponents were speaking of or an overstatement of the wealth of Sri Lanka. With these changes, the Asian countries ranked on average seventeen places higher than they did in GNP/pc.

For other regions the changes were less dramatic. In Africa, for instance, GNP/pc was about 73 percent of RGDP/pc, and the mean RGDP/pc rank (83) was four places lower than GNP/pc rank (79). The average RGDP/pc for Africa was only $234 higher than GNP/pc. The other regions, ranked by 1985 RGDP/pc and, in parentheses, the difference between RGDP/pc and GNP/pc, were: Europe/Middle East, $4,254 ($1,523); Westen Hemisphere, $2,654 ($1,057); East Asia/Pacific, $1,973 ($868); Asia, $923 ($661); and Africa, $882 ($234). Every group other than the developed countries had a significantly higher mean RGDP/pc than GNP/pc.

Proponents of PPPs have therefore argued that the gap between rich and poor countries is swollen by exchange rate conversions. If this is the case, then a PPP conversion must either increase the apparent wealth of the poor, decrease the apparent wealth of the rich, or a combination of both. Both effects have been found using the ICP data: The developed countries' RGDP/pcs average $1,878 less than their exchange rate-converted GNP/pcs, whereas the non-developed countries' RGDP/pcs are approximately $870 dollars higher on the average.

Table 12.2 isolates the countries with the largest disparities between RGDP/pc and GNP/pc. The table also includes the income level designated by the World Bank in the *World Development Report 1990*. The most dramatic differences occur among the countries in the lower income group. For instance, Sri Lanka and Bangladesh move from GNP/pcs of $283 and $129 to RGDP/pcs of $1,199 and $540, respectively. Again, these differences either reflect that actual purchasing power in these two countries is greater than it seems or exaggerate their "wealth." At the very least, this ambiguity points to the need for further study.

Although this chapter does not address the issue of distribution of income or the provision of basic goods, Table 12.2 lists the human development index (HDI) to determine if the countries experiencing the greatest change from GNP/pc to RGDP/pc appear to more closely approximate the conditions of countries with similar RGDP/pcs or similar GNP/pcs. The countries with GNP/pcs similar to Sri Lanka's ($200–300) in Table 12.2— Benin, Haiti, India, Kenya, Madagascar, Mozambique, Pakistan, Sierra Leone, and Togo—score significantly lower on the HDI index (.343) than Sri Lanka (.789). In addition, many of the countries with significantly higher RGDP/pcs than Sri Lanka in Table 12.2 have HDI scores only slightly larger. For all 107 countries in the sample, the human development index varies (positively) with the RGDP/pc (.76) and GNP/pc (.68) and is statistically significant.

Table 12.2 The Most Severe Changes in the Conversion from GNP/pc to RGDP/pc

Country	World Development Report 1990 Grouping	Real GDP/pc 1980	GNP/pc 1980	Difference (RGDP/pc −GNP/pc)	GNP/pc as a Percentage of RGDP/pc	Human Development Index
Mexico	Lower-Middle	4,333	2,133	2,200	49.23	.876
Chile	Lower-Middle	4,271	2,512	1,759	58.82	.931
Hungary	Upper-Middle	5,508	2,048	3,460	37.19	.915
Yugoslavia	Upper-Middle	4,733	2,703	2,030	57.11	.913
Uruguay	Upper-Middle	4,502	2,886	1,616	64.10	.916
Venezuela	Upper-Middle	4,424	3,306	1,118	74.73	.861
Argentina	Upper-Middle	4,342	2,823	1,519	65.02	.910
South Africa	Upper-Middle	4,286	2,558	1,728	59.68	.731
Sri Lanka	Low Income	1,199	283	916	23.64	.789
Pakistan	Low Income	989	341	648	34.49	.423
Senegal	Low Income	744	452	292	60.75	.273
Haiti	Low Income	696	308	388	44.31	.356
Lesotho	Low Income	694	453	241	65.27	.580
Kenya	Low Income	662	379	283	57.25	.481
Sudan	Low Income	652	415	237	63.65	.255
Mozambique	Low Income	637	366	271	57.46	.239
Togo	Low Income	625	339	286	54.24	.337
India	Low Income	614	234	380	38.14	.439
Madagascar	Low Income	589	366	223	62.14	.440
Mauritania	Low Income	576	409	167	71.01	.208
Bangladesh	Low Income	540	129	257	23.89	.318
Benin	Low Income	534	288	246	53.93	.224
Sierra Leone	Low Income	512	325	187	63.48	.150

Sources: Calculated from data in *The World Tables 1992*; *International Financial Statistics*, 1984; Summers and Heston, 1988; and *Human Development Report*, 1990.

THE GAP BETWEEN RICH, MIDDLE-INCOME, AND POOR

If the income groups used in Chapter 4 were used here to analyze RGDP/pcs, the results would in many ways be quite different. These categories, similar to those defined by the World Bank in the *World Development Report 1990,* define low-income countries as those with per capita incomes of less than $500; $500 to $3,999, middle-income; and greater than $4,000, high-income. The most striking contrast is displayed in Table 12.3. Of the 107 countries, only 19 are considered low-income in 1962 using RGDP/pc. This figure further declines to 13 countries in 1970 before climbing back up to 16 by 1985. Among the countries in the sample, the portion of the population living in countries with an RGDP/pc of less than $500 never surpasses 13 percent and declines to only 5.7 percent by 1985 (40.5 percent using the GNP/pc figures). According to the ICP data, only 177 million people lived in impoverished countries in 1985, as opposed to 1.265 *billion* in the World Bank/IMF data.

Although RGDP/pc appears to be indicating that exchange rate–converted GNP/pcs overstate poverty to some degree, it is doubtful that only sixteen countries are impoverished. A much more in-depth study or series of studies that include all of the elements of development (elements such as the level of growth, economic diversity, income distribution, and basic needs provision) must be conducted to adequately define the world's poverty level.

Still, even without defining income groups, it is possible to determine if the gap between rich and poor is widening or narrowing. A simple method of detecting such a trend is to examine annual standard deviations. If the gap is closing, then the standard deviations should grow smaller, meaning that countries are moving closer to the world average RGDP/pc.

Table 12.3   Income Groups' Percentage of World Population

Year	World Population[a] (billions)	Rich Percent	Rich Number of Countries	Middle-Income Percent	Middle-Income Number of Countries	Poor Percent	Poor Number of Countries
1962	1.980	22.3	19	64.9	69	12.8	19
1965	2.105	21.8	19	65.7	72	12.5	16
1970	2.322	30.7	25	62.2	69	7.1	13
1975	2.568	30.5	29	64.2	64	5.2	14
1980	2.830	33.0	37	61.6	57	5.4	13
1985	3.119	25.8	31	68.6	60	5.7	16

a. The world total reflects population data for the 107 countries for which there is also GNP/pc data. China is not included.
Source: The World Tables 1992.

Figure 12.1 shows the standard deviations of RGDP/pc and the GNP/pc for the world (N=107). The figure illustrates that both RGDP/pc and GNP/pc are growing larger over time. In fact, they move very similarly. In 1974 it appears that both measures point to a very slight closing—or at least slowing of the expansion of—the gap. The heavy line in Figure 12.1 shows the world mean RGDP/pc, and the lighter line is the average GNP/pc.[7] As might be expected, the standard deviation of the RGDP/pc is consistently smaller than that of the GNP/pc, yet still of considerable size.

The gap as illustrated in Figure 12.1, however, may be presenting a misleading picture. It would not be surprising that as the world grows richer, the increase in the standard deviation would also grow larger. The coefficient of variation adjusts the standard deviation for changing means; one can be relatively sure that an increase in the coefficient of variation is not merely a by-product of an increasing mean value.[8] Figure 12.2 displays the coefficient of variation for the RGDP/pc, the GNP/pc, presenting a slightly different picture of the world than appeared in the previous figure.

The coefficient of variation in both cases registers an increase from 1962 to 1985. However, after a brief rise, the measure for both the RGDP/pc and the GNP/pc slides downward until around 1977 and then begins to rise, accelerating in both cases in 1981. In terms of the gap, this pattern means that from around 1964 until 1977 countries were moving toward the world mean RGDP/pc and GNP/pc—the gap narrowed. This trend reversed, and the gap began to widen again in 1977. These movements may have been relatively small, but they were captured by both the RGDP/pc and GNP/pc measures. In fact, it is remarkable that with all the differences between the two measures, they show almost identical trends. The main difference between the two is that the RGDP/pc produces a slightly smaller gap. It would also appear that the difference between the two is slightly smaller in 1985 than it was in 1962.

Growth Rates

The world economy grew at an average annual rate of 2.21 percent as measured by both RGDP/pc and GNP/pc for the 107 countries in the sample (see Table 12.4). As explained in Chapter 4, this growth rate is quite impressive, yet the data from both methods of conversion showed an even faster rate for the 1962–1975 period. Both the RGDP/pc and the GNP/pc growth rates for the world slowed to under 1 percent between 1975 and 1985. Thus, both measures show very rapid growth in roughly the first half of the 1962–1985 period, slowing significantly in the second half. This pattern is replicated for all of the regions except Asia, which experienced slower first-half than second-half growth.

Except in a few instances, the RGDP/pc growth rates are very similar to the exchange rate–converted GNP/pc rates. The regions, however,

Figure 12.1   Standard Deviations and Means of World RGDP/pc and GNP/pc

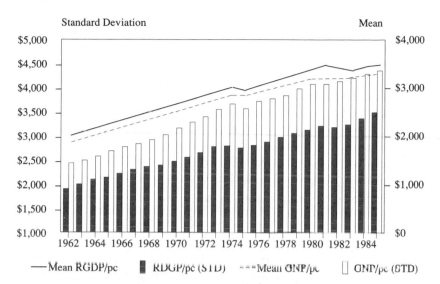

Sources: Calculated from data in *The World Tables 1992; International Financial Statistics,* 1984; Summers and Heston, 1988; and *Human Development Report, 1990.*

Figure 12.2   Variation from the World Mean RGDP/pc and GNP/pc

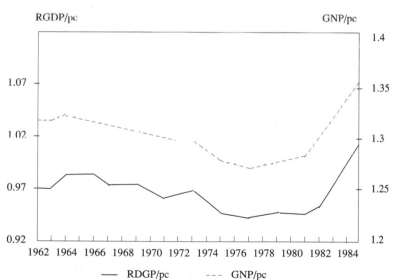

Note: Coefficient of variation is the standard deviation divided by the mean.
Sources: Calculated from data in *The World Tables 1992; International Financial Statistics,* 1984; Summers and Heston, 1988; and *Human Development Report,* 1990.

Table 12.4   Growth Rates by Geographic Region, 1962–1985, 1962–1975, 1975–1985

| | Annual Growth (percentages) RGDP/pc | | | GNP/pc | | |
Region	1962– 1985	1962– 1975	1975– 1985	1962– 1985	1962– 1975	1975– 1985
World	2.21	3.02	.85	2.21	3.11	.49
Developed	2.83	3.70	1.87	2.77	3.77	1.66
East Asia/Pacific	4.77	5.09	3.74	4.50	5.01	3.38
Europe	4.30	5.19	2.77	4.78	5.98	2.59
Middle East	3.65	3.76	2.30	3.20	3.14	1.65
Western Hemisphere	1.72	2.73	−.23	1.69	2.76	−.86
Asia	1.25	.44	2.40	1.52	1.03	2.20
Africa	1.18	2.22	−.38	1.22	2.27	−.70

Sources: Calculated from data in *The World Tables 1992; International Financial Statistics,* 1984; Summers and Heston, 1988; and *Human Development Report,* 1990.

change order when ranked by rate of growth. For the entire period, East Asia/Pacific grows the fastest in terms of RGDP/pc but is second on the GNP/pc list. Three of the regional groupings have RGDP/pc growth rates lower than their GNP/pc rates—Asia, Africa, and Europe.

This comparison makes some sense for the two poorer regions because of the way the purchasing power conversions work. Proponents of the PPP conversion index argue that the gap between rich and poor is overstated. They claim that exchange rates do not adjust quickly enough to reflect distortions more likely to be present in developing countries and that more economic activity goes on outside of the capitalist monied economy in these countries. For Africa and Asia, the PPP conversion would be likely to increase the apparent wealth of those countries when they were the poorest, i.e., 1962; as they grew, PPP could increase their apparent wealth less and less. Thus, their growth rate would slow. Because Europe was relatively rich to begin with, this explanation does not apply.

CONCLUSIONS

This chapter had two foci: (a) to outline the rationale for purchasing power parity; and (b) to compare the results of the ICP project (RGDP/pcs) and World Bank/IMF data (GNP/pcs). Fundamentally, the argument for PPP conversion factors is based on evidence demonstrating that exchange rate conversions of national account statistics may introduce distortions, especially in poor countries.

Although Tables 12.1 and 12.2 highlighted some extreme changes for individual countries, they did not have a visible impact on *trends* in the gap between rich and poor countries nor in annual average growth rates. When some of the larger changes were examined, as in the comparison of Sri Lanka with other countries at similar levels of growth, RGDP/pc appeared, at least tentatively, to be more reliable.

Second, although RGDP/pcs did raise the level of growth of the regional groups, as PPP proponents suggested would be the case, they also *lowered* the apparent level of growth of the developed nations from $11,401 (GNP/pc 1985) to $9,523 (RGDP/pc 1985). Thus, the conversion factor did not leave the developed countries virtually unchanged, as its proponents predicted.

Third, analysis of standard deviations and coefficients of variation indicated that both PPP conversion factors and exchange rates show that the gap between rich and poor countries is growing wider. Upon closer scrutiny, the coefficient of variation showed the gap narrowing slightly between 1962 and 1977 (although not consistently every year), then widening for the rest of the period under examination.

Fourth, overall growth rates were very similar for the ICP and World Bank data. Both pointed to the 1962 to 1975 period as one of very rapid growth, with all of the regions except Asia witnessing a severe reversal of fortunes over the remaining years. This agreement suggests the possibility that contradictory findings in studies attempting to explain growth may be due to the period under study. Depending upon the research question, it would probably be useful not only to specify the longest possible period but also to be sensitive to crossing periods of rapid and slow growth.

Finally, more research needs to be done to define a poverty level for the ICP data. What does it mean to have an RGDP/pc of $1,000 or $3,000 in terms of economic diversity, distribution of income, and provision of basic needs? In other words, what constitutes poverty and wealth?

NOTES

1. The example follows the logic of that used by Morris (1979:10–11).

2. Kuznets also noted that if the currency of a rich country is used as the *numeraire* currency, the PPP conversion for richer countries is not affected by the conversion, and the poorer the country, the more the PPP conversion inflates the resulting figure. This means the PPP-converted GNP/pcs make the gap between rich and poor countries look smaller (1972:9–10).

3. Other institutions making significant contributions to this work have been the University of Pennsylvania, the Ford Foundation, and the World Bank. For a more complete history of this project, see Irving Kravis, Zoltan Kenessey, Alan Heston, and Robert Summer, *A System of International Comparisons of Gross Product and Purchasing Power* (Baltimore and London: Johns Hopkins University Press, 1975).

4. The growth rates for both the RGDP/pcs and GNP/pcs are calculated by the regression method described in the *World Development Report 1988* (WDR

1988:288–289). The least squares method finds the growth rate by fitting a least squares trend line to the log of the gross national product per capita. This takes the equation form of X_t=a+bt+e_t, where x equals the log of the GNP/pc, t is time, and b is the parameter to be estimated. The growth rate, r, is the [antilog (b)]–1. For a discussion of different methods of computing growth rates see Robert Jackman, "A Note on the Measurement of Growth Rates in Cross-National Research," *American Journal of Sociology*, 86:604–610.

    5. This region actually comes from the World Bank's *World Tables*. I included this category because it places the so-called baby dragons and the proposed next generation of rapid industrializers in a group that is virtually their own (other than Papua New Guinea and Fiji).

    6. I merged these two categories because the Middle East only included three countries: Egypt, Israel, and Syria.

    7. The minimum RGDP/pc for all of the years is $152 and the maximum is $12,623. The minimum and maximum figures for the GNP/pc are $93 and $17,724, respectively.

    8. The coefficient of variation is the standard deviation divided by the mean.

REFERENCES

Bairoch, P. 1981. "The Main Trends in National Economic Disparities Since the Industrial Revolution." In P. Bairoch and M. Lévy-Leboyer, eds., *Disparities in Economic Development Since the Industrial Revolution*. London: Macmillan Press Ltd.

Beckerman, W. 1966. *International Comparisons of Real Income*. Paris: OECD Development Center.

Gilbert, M., and I. Kravis. 1954. *An International Comparison of National Products and the Purchasing Power of Currencies*. Paris: Organization for European Economic Cooperation.

————. 1958. *An International Comparison of Comparative National Products and Price Levels: A Study of Western Europe and the United States*. Paris: Organization for European Economic Cooperation.

Heston, A. 1973. "A Comparison of Some Short-Cut Methods of Estimating Real Product per Capita," *Review of Income and Wealth* (March):79–104.

International Money Fund. 1980. *International Financial Statistics: Yearbook 1980*. Washington, D.C.: IMF.

————. 1984. *International Financial Statistics: Supplement on Output Statistics*, No. 8. Washington, D.C.: IMF.

Jackman, R. W. 1980. "A Note on the Measurement of Growth Rates in Cross-National Research," *American Journal of Sociology*, 86:604–610.

Kravis, I. B., Z. Kenessey, A. Heston, and R. Summers. 1975. *A System of International Comparisons of Gross Product and Purchasing Power*. Baltimore and London: Johns Hopkins University Press.

Kuznets, S. 1972. "The Gap: Concept, Measurement, Trends." In G. Ranis, ed., *The Gap Between Rich and Poor Nations*. London: Macmillan Press, Ltd.

Morris, M. D. 1979. *Measuring the Condition of the World's Poor: The Physical Quality of Life Index*. New York: Pergamon Press.

Summers, R., and A. Heston. 1984. "Improved International Comparisons of Real Product and Its Composition: 1950–1980," *The Review of Income and Wealth* 3 (September):207–259.

Summers, R., and A. Heston. 1988. "A New Set of International Comparisons of Real Product and Prices: Estimates for 130 Countries, 1950–1985," *The Review of Income and Wealth* (March):1–25.

United Nations. 1990. *Human Development Report.* New York: Oxford University Press.

Ward, M. 1985. *Purchasing Power Parities and Real Expenditures in the OECD.* Paris: OECD Press.

World Bank. 1988. *World Development Report.* Oxford: Oxford University Press.

World Bank. 1992. *The World Tables of Economic and Social Indicators, 1960–86.* Washington, D.C.: The World Bank.

World Bank. 1992. *The World Tables 1992.* Washington, D.C.: The World Bank.

13

· · · · · · ·

Forget Convergence: Divergence Past, Present, and Future

· · · · · · ·

LANT PRITCHETT

In this chapter, Lant Pritchett looks at the international gap in national wealth in both the long term and the short term. The long-term investigation traces the width of the gap back to 1870, whereas the short term looks at the gap between 1960 and 1990. Pritchett shows that from 1870 to 1960, the absolute gap between the poorest and richest countries grew by more than eight times, whereas from 1960 to 1990 the ratio of the incomes of the richest to the poorest countries rose by 45 percent. This evidence seems to dash any hope that the incomes of the poor countries are likely to converge on those of the rich in the long or the short run. Pritchett explains the small number of cases of poor countries that have converged on the rich.

Convergence—the tendency for poorer countries to grow faster than richer ones and, hence, for their levels of income to converge—recently received a great deal of attention in the economics literature. Along with "globalization" and "competitiveness," the theme of "convergence" has spilled over into public discussions of policies and prospects for developing countries. Well, forget convergence—the overwhelming feature of modern economic history is a massive divergence in per capita incomes between rich and poor countries, a gap which is continuing to grow today. Moreover, unless the future is different in important ways from the recent past we can expect this gap to grow ever wider.

Reprinted with permission from *Finance and Development*, vol. 33, no. 2 (June 1996):40–43.

DIVERGENCE PAST

The very feature that marks the beginning of modern economic history also implies a major increase in the difference in per capita incomes across nations. Call it the industrial revolution, the emergence of modern capitalism, or the take-off into sustained growth, at some point in the late nineteenth century the annual growth rates of the now-rich industrial countries accelerated from historically low levels (0.5 percent or less), to 1–2 percent per year. The fact that this acceleration was not universal, or even widespread, implies that the gap between rich and poor countries' growth rates widened and the gulf between their per capita incomes—which was probably already wide—began to grow.

Given different exchange rates and different mixes of tradable and nontradable goods among countries, how can we compare income levels? We can compare them by using purchasing-power-adjusted measures of income. One important feature of this adjustment of incomes is to account for the relative cheapness of nontradables in poorer countries. Using a purchasing-power-parity measure substantially raises the estimate of income of poor countries relative to their income expressed in US dollars at official exchange rates—typically by a factor of 3 to 5, depending on particular countries' prices.

Measured in purchasing-power-parity terms at 1985 prices (P$), the ratio of the per capita income of the richest country (the United States) to the average per capita income of the poorest countries grew from around 9 (P$2,181 compared with P$250) in 1870 to over 50 (P$16,779 compared with P$325) in 1960. In absolute terms, the income gap between countries grew even more, expanding more than eightfold over this period. The average absolute difference between the income of the richest country and the incomes of all others was about P$1,500 in 1870 but, by 1960, this gap had grown to P$12,662.

Alert readers may wonder how the incomes of poor countries in 1870 can be estimated. Most of the industrial countries have roughly comparable estimates of GDP per capita extending back to 1870. In contrast, GDP estimates for most developing countries began only in 1950 or 1960. Moreover, most did not even exist as independent countries with their present boundaries in 1870. How then can we venture to guess what the evolution of income gaps from 1870 to 1960 might have been?

It can be done. Suppose that we only needed to estimate the change in the gap between the richest and the poorest country between 1870 and 1960. To do this we would need the income of today's richest country in 1870 and 1960 (P$2,181 and P$9,900, respectively), and the average income of today's poorest country—Ethiopia—for those years. The data for the United States are available, as is the income per capita of Ethiopia in 1960 (P$260). What is missing is Ethiopia's per capita income in 1870. But we are not stuck, because if we can make a sufficiently good guess at how low incomes could possibly have been in 1870, we can work backward by a process of deduction to estimate income divergence for all countries.

Since we know the growth rate of the United States over the entire period, we also know that the ratio of US income per capita in 1960 to its level in 1870 is about 4.5. If Ethiopia grew faster than the United States over this period, then the ratio of Ethiopia's per capita income in 1960 to its level in 1870 would have to be larger than 4.5. But, if the ratio between Ethiopia's 1960 income and the lowest it could plausibly have been in 1870 is smaller than 4.5, then we know that Ethiopia in fact grew more slowly than the United States and, hence, that there has been a divergence in per capita incomes between the world's richest country and the poorest countries. Moreover, applying this methodology to other countries, we can make rough guesses of the average magnitude of divergence in the cross-national distribution of income.

In "Divergence, Big Time," a background study for the World Bank's *World Development Report 1995*, five different methods were used to estimate the lower bound of incomes: the lowest recorded incomes in the data available for 1960–90; current estimates of poverty lines (the level of income that defines poverty in a given country); incomes required for nutritional adequacy; the relationship between income, mortality, and demographic sustainability; and known historical estimates of income. Using these five distinct approaches we arrived at a figure of P$250 as a reasonable guess at the lowest level that income could have reached in 1870.

But using this lower bound of P$250, we extrapolate incomes backward from per capita incomes observed today. For example, assume that every country grew at the same rate as the richest country (of course, to generate convergence, poorer countries would need to have grown even faster). But it is simply impossible for the countries considered poor today to have grown that fast on average since 1870, as the assumption of equal growth rates—or equivalently, of no divergence—implies impossibly low incomes for those countries in 1870. Therefore, for historical growth rates to be compatible with the current level of income in poor countries, growth must have been considerably slower for the poor countries than for the leaders. Even without historical data, we know that there has been massive divergence in income levels since 1870. . . .

DIVERGENCE PRESENT

Divergence is not confined to the past century. For relative income levels to converge, poor countries must grow faster than rich countries. Between 1960 and 1990, income grew, on average, 2.6 percent per year in the Organization for Economic Cooperation and Development (OECD) countries, and 1.8 percent in other countries. Among the poor countries, 43 percent have grown more slowly than the slowest-growing OECD country, and 70 percent have grown at a slower rate than the median for OECD countries. Since poor countries are growing more slowly on average, the dispersion in incomes among countries (as measured by the standard deviation—the dispersion of observations around an average measure—of the natural logarithm of per capita income) between 1960 and 1990 increased by 28 percent (from 0.86 to 1.1) and the ratio of the incomes of the richest to the poorest countries rose by 45 percent just since 1960.

Especially given the recent record of developing countries, it is very difficult to understand an upsurge of interest in convergence. During the Great Depression of the 1930s, income fell by 32 percent in the United States and by 19 percent in France, two of the hardest-hit industrial countries. Since 1960, more than 60 percent of the developing countries have experienced at least one episode during which incomes fell more than the decline recorded in France, and almost one-third of developing countries have suffered an episode of income reduction larger than that which occurred in the United States. Moreover, in many developing countries, the decline in income has not been reversed. Estimates of income in 1990 show that 72 percent of developing countries still fell short of their own peak income level and two-thirds were not within 5 percent of their peak. In discussions about developing countries, it is not surprising that the 1980s are often referred to as the "lost" decade, but never as the "convergence" decade.

DIVERGENCE FUTURE?

What would happen if current growth rates in developing and industrial countries were to persist? How quickly would developing countries overtake the United States in per capita income? Using the data for the 93 developing countries for which the *World Development Report 1995* reports income growth rates for 1980–93, we calculated how long it would take various countries to achieve three levels of income: their own peak income level; the current income level of high-income countries; and the average future income of high-income countries, assuming that high-income countries also continue to grow.

First, more than half of the developing countries had negative growth during 1980–93. These countries are not gaining on anything—their incomes are converging only on the floor of subsistence. Unless their growth rates accelerate, they will never reach even their previous peaks. (The reported data are, if anything, optimistic about the number of countries with negative growth, as many of the countries that do not report data fail to do so because of internal and external strife.)

Second, many developing countries had positive growth rates during 1980–93, but in more than four-fifths of these countries growth rates were still lower than the average (2.2 percent) registered by the high-income countries. Moreover, many developing countries grew slowly after suffering recessions during the 1980s. Against this admittedly pessimistic background and assuming unchanged growth rates, if Brazil, for example, were to grow annually only at its 1980–93 pace of 0.3 percent, it would take 33 years for the country to regain its own previous income peak, and 487 years before it achieved the current income level of the high-income countries.

Third, a few developing countries were actually "converging," that is, they were growing faster than the United States. When are these lucky "convergers" going to overtake the United States? India, for example, registered an annual average growth rate of 3 percent between 1980 and 1993. If India could sustain this pace for another 100 years, its income would reach the level of high-income countries today. And, if India can sustain this growth differential for 377 years, my great-great-great-great-great-great-great-great-great-great grandchildren will be alive to see India's income level "converge."

Fourth, since 1980 only 10 developing countries have had growth rates that were more than 1 percentage point higher than the average for high-income countries. These counties can be said to be converging rapidly to high-income country levels. If they can maintain this pace, these countries can look forward to attaining today's level of income in high-income countries within a couple of generations (50 years in the case of Indonesia), and they would actually reach the future income level of the high-income countries in less than a century.

DOES CONVERGENCE EVER OCCUR?

Of course, what will happen "if current trends persist" is not really a prediction of the future. First, the 1980s were an exceptionally bad decade and things may get somewhat better for poor countries because of improved global conditions. Second, the future will be determined by policy actions taken today, and there is no iron law that dictates divergence. Convergence can happen. There are several instances of absolute income convergence among deeply integrated economies and there are examples of very rapid growth among countries that were quite poor.

The best-documented examples of absolute convergence are those of economies that have achieved deep integration. This includes regions within nations (particularly in Europe, Japan, and the United States), the European Union countries—which have experienced absolute convergence—and, perhaps, all OECD countries, as the European countries as a group have made some gains on the United States in the postwar period.

Even where deep integration has been achieved, three points can be made. First, by any absolute standard, the rate of convergence within Europe, Japan, and the United States has been slow. Robert Barro and Xavier Sala-I-Martin (1995) have argued that within these countries, regional convergence occurs at a near-uniform rate of about 2 percent per year, meaning that only 2 percent of the income gap is eliminated each year. Second, the integration needed to achieve even that slow pace may well be very deep. In the United States, for instance, in any given five-year period, 10 percent of the population moves across state borders.

Some countries do not show regional convergence. For instance, the data presented in "Regional Economic Growth and Convergence in India," by Paul Cashin and Ratna Sahay, *Finance & Development,* March 1996, show substantial absolute divergence among the states of India, with the dispersion of the logarithm of incomes increasing from 0.29 to 0.33. In another example, China, the evidence for income convergence is mixed, but certainly does not show any uniform tendency toward absolute convergence over time.

Third, the mechanisms that lead to regional convergence may not be applicable to countries. In the United States, for example, from 1930 to 1970, there is evidence of convergence because states like California had high initial incomes and low per capita growth, while states like Mississippi had low initial incomes and high per capita growth. However, one should not ignore the fact that population growth in California was 10 times higher than in Mississippi and hence the growth of absolute (not per capita) output in California was substantially higher than in Mississippi. No one really thinks that California's economy was outperformed by Mississippi's.

A second type of absolute convergence obviously occurs when countries that start out behind experience truly rapid growth. That a country has to be behind to gain on the leader has led economists from Hume to Gershenkron to expect that poor countries would gain on the leaders. But can doesn't mean will.

What can we learn from the examples of Japan and Korea and, most recently, China? If anything, they demonstrate the possibility of "policy-conditional" conditional convergence. That is, if a country's initial income is low and its government pursues growth-oriented policies, then very rapid growth rates may be possible. Jeffrey Sachs and Andrew Warner (1995), for instance, have recently suggested that countries that adopted such policies did in fact exhibit very strong conditional convergence, while those poor countries that did not adopt them did not display any conditional convergence. However, it is important to note that only 12 developing countries, using their criteria, did adopt growth-oriented policies. This suggests that the likelihood of having good policies was lower the poorer a country might be, and that this strong "policy-conditional" conditional convergence is compatible with absolute divergence and very weak "unconditional" conditional convergence. . . .

CONCLUSION

There are three good reasons not to worry about convergence. First, it just hasn't happened, isn't happening, and isn't going to happen without serious changes in economic policies in developing countries. Second, casual talk of "convergence" conveys the wrong impression; there is nothing automatic or easy about economic development. Rapid growth is not the result of being poor—it is the result of creating a set of policies that facilitate rapid growth. The policy environment that developing countries need to establish rapid growth and development is difficult to achieve, as is evidenced by the fact that so few have done so, and there is no "advantage to backwardness" in this endeavor. Third, talk of convergence, especially in the industrial countries, implies that their real concern is to protect themselves from the "converging" poor countries when exactly the opposite is the case. Given the facts, more, not less, concern for the promotion of economic development and acceleration of growth in poor countries is in order.

REFERENCES

Barro, Robert, and Xavier Sala-I-Martin. 1995. *Economic Growth.* New York: McGraw-Hill.
Pritchett, Lant. 1995. "Divergence, Big Time," World Bank Policy Research Working Paper No. 1522 (Washington).
Sachs, Jeffrey, and Andrew Warner. 1995. "Economic Reform and the Process of Global Interpretation." Brookings Papers on Economic Activity: 1, pp. 1–118.

PART 4

. . . .

Culture, Modernization, and Development

. . . .

14

The Achievement Motive
in Economic Growth

DAVID C. McCLELLAND *The need for Achievement is a motive in a person's desire for economic growth*

In this chapter, David C. McClelland, a psychologist, expands upon ideas developed by Max Weber, who examined the relationship between the Protestant ethic and the rise of capitalism. McClelland posits a more generalized psychological attribute he calls the "need for Achievement," or n Achievement. In this discussion, which is a summary of a book on the subject, McClelland presents some very interesting historical data he believes help explain the rise and decline of Athenian civilization. Turning to the present century, he produces data that show a close association between national levels of n Achievement and rates of economic growth. In seeking to determine what produces this psychological characteristic, McClelland finds that it is not hereditary but rather is instilled in people. It is therefore possible, he claims, to teach people how to increase their need to achieve and by so doing stimulate economic growth in developing countries. McClelland has been responsible for establishing training and management programs in developing countries in hopes that a change in the psychological orientation of public officials will help speed economic growth.

From the beginning of recorded history, men have been fascinated by the fact that civilizations rise and fall. Culture growth, as A. L. Kroeber has demonstrated, is episodic, and sometimes occurs in quite different fields.[1] For example, the people living in the Italian peninsula at the time of ancient Rome produced a great civilization of law, politics, and military conquest;

Reprinted with permission of UNESCO from *Industrialization and Society,* edited by Bert F. Hoselitz and Wilbert E. Moore, pp. 74–95. © UNESCO, 1963.

and at another time, during the Renaissance, the inhabitants of Italy produced a great civilization of art, music, letters, and science. What can account for such cultural flowerings? In our time we have theorists like Ellsworth Huntington, who stresses the importance of climate, or Arnold J. Toynbee, who also feels the right amount of challenge from the environment is crucial though he conceives of the environment as including its psychic effects. Others, like Kroeber, have difficulty imagining any general explanation; they perforce must accept the notion that a particular culture happens to hit on a particularly happy mode of self-expression, which it then pursues until it becomes overspecialized and sterile.

My concern is not with all culture growth, but with economic growth. Some wealth or leisure may be essential to development in other fields— the arts, politics, science, or war—but we need not insist on it. However, the question of why some countries develop rapidly in the economic sphere at certain times and not at others is in itself of great interest, whatever its relation to other types of culture growth. Usually, rapid economic growth has been explained in terms of "external" factors—favorable opportunities for trade, unusual natural resources, or conquests that have opened up new markets or produced internal political stability. But I am interested in the *internal* factors—in the values and motives men have that lead them to exploit opportunities, to take advantage of favorable trade conditions; in short, to shape their own destiny. . . .

Whatever else one thinks of Freud and the other psychoanalysts, they performed one extremely important service for psychology: once and for all, they persuaded us, rightly or wrongly, that what people said about their motives was not a reliable basis for determining what those motives really were. In his analyses of the psychopathology of everyday life and of dreams and neurotic symptoms, Freud demonstrated repeatedly that the "obvious" motives—the motives that the people themselves thought they had or that a reasonable observer would attribute to them—were not, in fact, the real motives for their often strange behavior. By the same token, Freud also showed the way to a better method of learning what people's motives were. He analyzed dreams and free associations: in short, fantasy or imaginative behavior. Stripped of its air of mystery and the occult, psychoanalysis has taught us that one can learn a great deal about people's motives through observing the things about which they are spontaneously concerned in their dreams and waking fantasies. About ten or twelve years ago, the research group in America with which I was connected decided to take this insight quite seriously and to see what we could learn about human motivation by coding objectively what people spontaneously thought about in their waking fantasies.[2] Our method was to collect such free fantasy, in the form of brief stories written about pictures, and to count the frequency with which certain themes appeared—rather as a medical technician counts the frequency with which red or white corpuscles appear in a blood sample. We were able to demonstrate that the frequency with which certain "inner concerns" appeared in these fantasies varied systematically as a function of specific experimental conditions by which we aroused or induced motivational states in the subjects. Eventually we were able to isolate several of these inner concerns, or motives, which, if present in great frequency in the fantasies of a particular person, enabled us to know something about how he would behave in many other areas of life.

Chief among these motives was what we termed "the need for Achievement" (*n* Achievement)—a desire to do well, not so much for the sake of social recognition or prestige, but to attain an inner feeling of personal accomplishment. This motive is my particular concern in this chapter. Our early laboratory studies showed that people "high" in *n* Achievement tend to work harder at certain tasks; to learn faster; to do their best work when it counts for the record, and not when special incentives, like money prizes, are introduced; to choose experts over friends as working partners; etc. Obviously, we cannot here review the many, many studies in this area. About five years ago, we became especially interested in the problem of what would happen in a society if a large number of people with a high need for achievement should happen to be present in it at a particular time. In other words, we became interested in a social-psychological question: What effect would a concentration of people with high *n* Achievement have on a society?

It might be relevant to describe how we began wondering about this. I had always been greatly impressed by the very perceptive analysis of the connection between Protestantism and the spirit of capitalism made by the great German sociologist, Max Weber.[3] He argues that the distinguishing characteristic of Protestant business entrepreneurs and of workers, particularly from the pietistic sects, was not that they had in any sense invented the institutions of capitalism or good craftsmanship, but that they went about their jobs with a new perfectionist spirit. The Calvinistic doctrine of predestination had forced them to rationalize every aspect of their lives and to strive hard for perfection in the positions in this world to which they had been assigned by God. As I read Weber's description of the behavior of these people, I concluded that they must certainly have had a high level of *n* Achievement. Perhaps the new spirit of capitalism Weber describes was none other than a high need for achievement—if so, then *n* Achievement has been responsible, in part, for the extraordinary economic development of the West. Another factor served to confirm this hypothesis. A careful study by M. R. Winterbottom had shown that boys with high *n* Achievement usually came from families in which the mothers stressed early self-reliance and mastery.[4] The boys whose mothers did not encourage their early self-reliance, or did not set such high standards of excellence, tended to develop lower need for achievement. Obviously, one of the key characteristics of the Protestant Reformation was its emphasis on self-reliance. Luther stressed the "priesthood of all believers" and translated the Bible so that every man could have direct access to God and religious thought. Calvin accentuated a rationalized perfection in this life for everyone. Certainly, the character of the Reformation seems to have set the stage, historically, for parents to encourage their children to attain earlier self-reliance and achievement. If the parents did in fact do so, they very possibly unintentionally produced the higher level of *n* Achievement in their children that was, in turn, responsible for the new spirit of capitalism.

This was the hypothesis that initiated our research. It was, of course, only a promising idea; much work was necessary to determine its validity. Very early in our studies, we decided that the events Weber discusses were probably only a special case of a much more general phenomenon—that it was *n* Achievement as such that was connected with economic development, and that the Protestant Reformation was connected only indirectly in the extent to which it had influenced the average *n* Achievement level of its adherents. If this assumption is correct, then a high average level of *n* Achievement should be equally associated with economic development in ancient Greece, in modern Japan, or in a preliterate tribe being studied by anthropologists in the South Pacific. In other words, in its most general form, the hypothesis attempts to isolate one of the key factors in the economic development, at least, of all civilizations. What evidence do we have that this extremely broad generalization will obtain? By now, a great deal has been collected—far more than I can summarize here; but I shall try to give a few key examples of the different types of evidence.

First, we have made historical studies. To do so, we had to find a way to obtain a measure of *n* Achievement level during time periods other than our own, whose individuals can no longer be tested. We have done this—instead of coding the brief stories written by an individual for a test, we code imaginative literary documents: poetry, drama, funeral orations, letters written by sea captains, epics, etc. Ancient Greece, which we studied first, supplies a good illustration. We are able to find literary documents written during three different historical periods and dealing with similar themes: the period of economic growth, 900 B.C.–475 B.C. (largely Homer and Hesiod); the period of climax, 475 B.C.–362 B.C.; and the period of decline, 362 B.C.–100 B.C. Thus, Hesiod wrote on farm and estate management in the early period; Xenophon, in the middle period; and Aristotle, in the late period. We have defined the period of "climax" in economic, rather than in cultural, terms, because it would be presumptuous to claim, for example, that Aristotle in any sense represented a "decline" from Plato or Thales. The measure of economic growth was computed from information supplied by F. Heichelheim in his *Wirtschaftsgeschichte des Altertums*.[5] Heichelheim records in detail the locations throughout Europe where the remains of Greek vases from different centuries have been found. Of course, these vases were the principal instrument of Greek foreign trade, since they were the containers for olive oil and wine, which were the most important Greek exports. Knowing where the vase fragments have been found, we could compute the trade area of Athenian Greece for different time periods. We purposely omitted any consideration of the later expansion of Hellenistic Greece, because this represents another civilization; our concern was Athenian Greece.

When all the documents had been coded, they demonstrated—as predicted—that the level of *n* Achievement was highest during the period of growth prior to the climax of economic development in Athenian Greece. (See Figure 14.1.) In other words, the maximum *n* Achievement level preceded the maximum economic level by at least a century. Furthermore, that

Figure 14.1   Average *n* Achievement Level (plotted at midpoints of periods of growth, climax, and decline of Athenian civilization as reflected in the extent of her trade area)

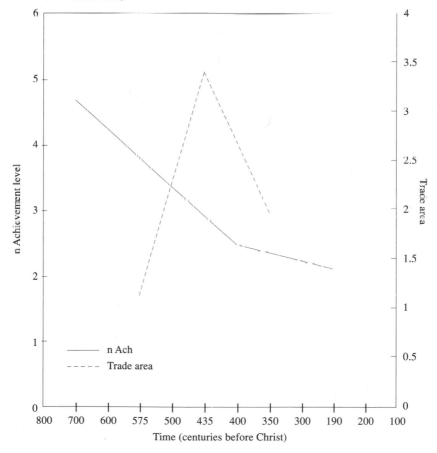

Note: Trade area measured for the sixth, fifth, and fourth centuries B.C. only.

high level had fallen off by the time of maximum prosperity, thus foreshadowing subsequent economic decline. A similar methodology was applied, with the same results, to the economic development of Spain in the sixteenth century[6] and to two waves of economic development in the history of England (one in the late sixteenth century and the other at the beginning of the industrial revolution, around 1800).[7] The *n* Achievement level in English history (as determined on the basis of dramas, sea captains' letters, and street ballads) rose, between 1400–1800, *twice,* a generation or two before waves of accelerated economic growth (incidentally, at times of Protestant revival). This point is significant because it shows that there is no "necessary" steady decline in a civilization's entrepreneurial energy from its earlier to its later periods. In the Spanish and English cases, as in the Greek, high levels of *n* Achievement preceded economic decline. Unfortunately, space limitations preclude more detailed discussion of these studies here.

We also tested the hypothesis by applying it to preliterate cultures of the sort that anthropologists investigate. At Yale University, an organized effort has been made to collect everything that is known about all the primitive tribes that have been studied and to classify the information systematically for comparative purposes. We utilized this cross-cultural file to obtain the two measures that we needed to test our general hypothesis. For over fifty of these cultures, collections of folk tales existed that I. L. Child and others had coded,[8] just as we coded literary documents and individual imaginative stories, for *n* Achievement and other motives. These folk tales have the character of fantasy that we believe to be so essential for getting at "inner concerns." In the meantime, we were searching for a method of classifying the economic development of these cultures, so that we could determine whether those evincing high *n* Achievement in their folk tales had developed further than those showing lower *n* Achievement. The respective modes of gaining a livelihood were naturally very different in these cultures, since they came from every continent in the world and every type of physical habitat; yet we had to find a measure for comparing them. We finally thought of trying to estimate the number of full-time "business entrepreneurs" there were among the adults in each culture. We defined "entrepreneur" as "anyone who exercises control over the means of production and produces more than he can consume in order to sell it for individual or household income." Thus an entrepreneur was anyone who derived at least 75 percent of his income from such exchange or market practices. The entrepreneurs were mostly traders, independent artisans, or operators of small firms like stores, inns, etc. Nineteen cultures were classified as high in *n* Achievement on the basis of their folk tales; 74 percent of them contained some entrepreneurs. On the other hand, only 35 percent of the twenty cultures that were classified as low in *n* Achievement contained any entrepreneurs (as we defined it) at all. The difference is highly significant statistically (Chi square = 5.97, p<.02). Hence data about primitive tribes seem to confirm the hypothesis that high n Achievement leads to a more advanced type of economic activity.

But what about modern nations? Can we estimate their level of n Achievement and relate it to their economic development? The question is obviously one of the greatest importance, but the technical problems of getting measures of our two variables proved to be really formidable. What type of literary document could we use that would be equally representative of the motivational levels of people in India, Japan, Portugal, Germany, the United States, and Italy? We had discovered in our historical studies that certain types of literature usually contain much more achievement imagery than others. This is not too serious as long as we are dealing with time changes within a given culture; but it is very serious if we want to compare two cultures, each of which may express its achievement motivation in a different literary form. At last, we decided to use children's stories, for several reasons. They exist in standard form in every modern nation, since all modern nations are involved in teaching their children to read and use brief stories for this purpose. Furthermore, the stories are imaginative; and, if selected from those used in the earliest grades, they are not often influenced by temporary political events. (We were most impressed by this when reading the stories that every Russian child reads. In general, they cannot be distinguished, in style and content, from the stories read in all the countries of the West.)

We collected children's readers for the second, third, and fourth grades from every country where they could be found for two time periods, which were roughly centered around 1925 and around 1950. We got some thirteen hundred stories, which were all translated into English. In all, we had twenty-one stories from each of twenty-three countries about 1925, and the same number from each of thirty-nine countries about 1950. Code was used on proper names, so that our scorers would not know the national origins of the stories. The tales were then mixed together, and coded for n Achievement (and certain other motives and values that I shall mention only briefly).

The next task was to find a measure of economic development. Again, the problem was to ensure comparability. Some countries have much greater natural resources; some have developed industrially sooner than others; some concentrate in one area of production and some in another. Economists consider national income figures in per capita terms to be the best measure available; but they are difficult to obtain for all countries, and it is hard to translate them into equal purchasing power. Ultimately, we came to rely chiefly on the measure of electricity produced: the units of measurement are the same all over the world; the figures are available from the 1920s on; and electricity is the *form* of energy (regardless of how it is produced) that is essential to modern economic development. In fact, electricity produced per capita correlates with estimates of income per capita in the 1950s around .90 anyway. To equate for differences in natural resources, such as the amount of water power available, etc., we studied *gains* in kilowatt hours produced per capita between 1925 and 1950. The level of electrical production in 1925 is, as one would expect, highly correlated with the size of the gain between then and 1950. So it was necessary to resort to a regression analysis; that is, to calculate, from the average regression of gain on level for all countries, how much gain a particular country should have shown between 1925 and 1950. The actual gain could then be compared with the expected gain, and the country could be classified as gaining more or less rapidly than would have been expected on the basis of its 1925 performance. The procedure is directly comparable to what we do when we predict, on the basis of some measure of I.Q., what grades a child can be expected to get in school, and then classify him as an "under-" or "over-achiever."

The correlation between the *n* Achievement level in the children's readers in 1925 and the growth in electrical output between 1925 and 1950, as compared with expectation, is a quite substantial .53, which is highly significant statistically. It could hardly have arisen by chance. Furthermore, the correlation is also substantial with a measure of gain over the expected in per capita income, equated for purchasing power by Colin Clark. To check this result more definitively with the sample of forty countries for which we had reader estimates of *n* Achievement levels in 1950, we computed the equation for gains in electrical output in 1952–58 as a function of level in 1952. It turned out to be remarkably linear when translated into logarithmic units, as is so often the case with simple growth functions. Table 14.1 presents the performance of each of the countries, as compared with predictions from initial level in 1952, in standard score units and classified by high and low *n* Achievement in 1950. Once again we found that *n* Achievement levels predicted significantly ($r = .43$) the countries which would perform more or less rapidly than expected in terms of the average for all countries. The finding is more striking than the earlier one, because many Communist and underdeveloped countries are included in the sample. Apparently, *n* Achievement is a precursor of economic growth—and not only in the Western style of capitalism based on the small entrepreneur, but also in economies controlled and fostered largely by the state.

For those who believe in economic determinism, it is especially interesting that *n* Achievement level in 1950 is *not* correlated either with *previous* economic growth between 1925 and 1950, or with the level of prosperity in 1950. This strongly suggests that *n* Achievement is a *causative* factor—a change in the minds of men which produces economic growth rather than being produced by it. In a century dominated by economic determinism, in both Communist and Western thought, it is startling to find concrete evidence for psychological determinism, for psychological developments as preceding and presumably causing economic changes.

Table 14.1   Rate of Growth in Electrical Output (1952-1958) and National *n* Achievement
Levels in 1950

Above Expectation Growth Rate			Below Expectation Growth Rate		
National *n* Achievement levels (1950)[a]	Country	Deviation from Expected Growth Rate[b]	National *n* Achievement Levels (1950)[a]	Country	Deviations from Expected Growth Rate[b]
High *n* Achievement Countries					
3.62	Turkey	+1.38			
2.71	India[c]	+1.12			
2.38	Australia	+0.42			
2.32	Israel	+1.18			
2.33	Spain	+0.01			
2.29	Pakistan[d]	+2.75			
2.29	Greece	+1.18	3.38	Argentina	−0.56
2.29	Canada	+0.08	2.71	Lebanon	−0.67
2.24	Bulgaria	+1.37	2.38	France	−0.24
2.24	U.S.A.	+0.47	2.33	South Africa	−0.06
2.14	West Germany	+0.53	2.29	Ireland	−0.41
2.10	U.S.S.R.	+1.61	2.14	Tunisia	−1.87
2.10	Portugal	+0.76	2.10	Syria	−0.25
Low *n* Achievement Countries					
1.95	Iraq	+0.29	2.05	New Zealand	−0.29
1.86	Austria	+0.38	1.86	Uruguay	−0.75
1.67	U.K.	+0.17	1.81	Hungary	−0.62
1.57	Mexico	+0.12	1.71	Norway	−0.77
0.86	Poland	+1.26	1.62	Sweden	−0.64
			1.32	Finland	−0.08
			1.48	Netherlands	−0.15
			1.33	Italy	−0.57
			1.29	Japan	−0.04
			1.20	Switzerland[e]	−1.92
			1.19	Chile	−1.81
			1.05	Denmark	−0.89
			0.57	Algeria	−0.83
			0.43	Belgium	−1.63

Note: Correlation of *n* Achievement level (1950) x deviations from expected growth rate = .43, $p < .01$.

a. Deviations in standard score units. The estimates are computed from the monthly average electrical production figures, in millions Kwh, for 1952 and 1958, from United Nations, *Monthly Bulletin of Statistics* (January, 1960), and *World Energy Supplies, 1951-1954* and *1955-1958* (Statistical Papers, Series 3). The correlation between log level 1952 and log gain 1952-1958 is .976. The regression equation based on these thirty-nine countries, plus four others from the same climatic zone on which data are available (China-Taiwan, Czechoslovakia, Rumania, Yugoslavia), is: log gain (1952-1958) = .9229 log level (1952) + .0480. Standard scores deviations from mean gain predicted by the regression formula (M = −.01831) divided by the standard deviation of the deviations from the mean predicted gain (SD = .159).

b. Based on twenty-one children's stories from second-, third-, and fourth-grade readers in each country.

c. Based on six Hindi, seven Telegu, and eight Tamil stories.

d. Based on twelve Urdu and eleven Bengali stories.

e. Based on twenty-one German Swiss stories, mean = .91; twenty-one French Swiss stories, mean = 1.71; overall mean obtained by weighting German mean double to give approximately proportionate representation of the two main ethnic populations.

The many interesting results which our study of children's stories yielded have succeeded in convincing me that we chose the right material to analyze. Apparently, adults unconsciously flavor their stories for young children with the attitudes, the aspirations, the values, and the motives that they hold to be most important.

I want to mention briefly two other findings, one concerned with economic development, the other with totalitarianism. When the more and less rapidly developing economies are compared on all the other variables for which we scored the children's stories, one fact stands out. In stories from those countries which had developed more rapidly in both the earlier and later periods, there was a discernible tendency to emphasize, in 1925 and in 1950, what David Riesman has called "other-directedness"—namely, reliance on the opinion of particular others, rather than on tradition, for guidance in social behavior.[9] *Public opinion* had, in these countries, become a major source of guidance for the individual. Those countries which had developed the mass media further and faster—the press, the radio, the public-address system—were also the ones who were developing more rapidly economically. I think that "other-directedness" helped these countries to develop more rapidly because public opinion is basically more flexible than institutionalized moral or social traditions. Authorities can utilize it to inform people widely about the need for new ways of doing things. However, traditional institutionalized values may insist that people go on behaving in ways that are no longer adaptive to a changed social and economic order.

The other finding is not directly relevant to economic development, but it perhaps involves the means of achieving it. Quite unexpectedly, we discovered that every major dictatorial regime which came to power between the 1920s and 1950s (with the possible exception of Portugal's) was foreshadowed by a particular motive pattern in its stories for children: namely, a low need for affiliation (little interest in friendly relationships with people) and a high need for power (a great concern over controlling and influencing other people).

The German readers showed this pattern before Hitler; the Japanese readers, before Tojo; the Argentine readers, before Perón; the Spanish readers, before Franco; the South African readers, before the present authoritarian government in South Africa; etc. On the other hand, very few countries which did not have dictatorships manifested this particular motive combination. The difference was highly significant statistically, since there was only one exception in the first instance and very few in the second. Apparently, we stumbled on a psychological index of ruthlessness—i.e., the need to influence other people (*n* Power), unchecked by sufficient concern for their welfare (*n* Affiliation). It is interesting, and a little disturbing, to discover that the German readers of today still evince this particular combination of motives, just as they did in 1925. Let us hope that this is one case where a social science generalization will not be confirmed by the appearance of a totalitarian regime in Germany in the next ten years.

To return to our main theme—let us discuss the precise ways that higher *n* Achievement leads to more rapid economic development, and why it should lead to economic development rather than, for example, to military or artistic development. We must consider in more detail the mechanism by which the concentration of a particular type of human motive in a population leads to a complex social phenomenon like economic growth. The link between the two social phenomena is, obviously, the business entrepreneur. I am not using the term "entrepreneur" in the sense of "capitalist": in fact, I should like to divorce "entrepreneur" entirely from any connotations of ownership. An entrepreneur is someone who exercises control over production that is not just for his personal consumption. According to my defini tion, for example, an executive in a steel production unit in Russia is an entrepreneur.

It was Joseph Schumpeter who drew the attention of economists to the importance that the activity of these entrepreneurs had in creating industrialization in the West. Their vigorous endeavors put together firms and created productive units where there had been none before. In the beginning, at least, the entrepreneurs often collected material resources, organized a production unit to combine the resources into a new product, and sold the product, Until recently, nearly all economists—including not only Marx, but also Western classical economists—assumed that these men were moved primarily by the "profit motive." We are all familiar with the Marxian argument that they were so driven by their desire for profits that they exploited the workingman and ultimately forced him to revolt. Recently, economic historians have been studying the actual lives of such entrepreneurs and finding—certainly to the surprise of some of the investigators—that many of them seemingly were not interested in making money as such. In psychological terms, at least, Marx's picture is slightly out of focus. Had these entrepreneurs been above all interested in money, many more of them would have quit working as soon as they had made all the money that they could possibly use. They would not have continued to risk their money in further entrepreneurial ventures. Many of them, in fact, came from pietistic sects, like the Quakers in England, that prohibited the enjoyment of wealth in any of the ways cultivated so successfully by some members of the European nobility. However, the entrepreneurs often seemed consciously to be greatly concerned with expanding their businesses, with getting a greater share of the market, with "conquering brute nature," or even with altruistic schemes for bettering the lot of mankind or bringing about the kingdom of God on earth more rapidly. Such desires have frequently enough been labeled as hypocritical. However, if we assume that these men were really motivated by a desire for achievement rather than by a desire for money as such, the label no longer fits. This assumption also simplifies further matters considerably. It provides an explanation for the fact that these entrepreneurs were interested in money without wanting it for its own sake, namely, that money served as a ready quantitative index of how well they were doing—e.g., of how much they had achieved by their efforts over the past year. The need to achieve can never be satisfied by money; but estimates of profitability in money terms can supply direct knowledge of how well one is doing one's job.

The brief consideration of the lives of business entrepreneurs of the past suggested that their chief motive may well have been a high n Achievement. What evidence have we found in support of this? We made two approaches to the problem. First, we attempted to determine whether individuals with high n Achievement behave like entrepreneurs; and second, we investigated to learn whether actual entrepreneurs, particularly the more successful ones, in a number of countries, have higher n Achievement than do other people of roughly the same status. Of course, we had to establish what we meant by "behave like entrepreneurs"—what precisely distinguishes the way an entrepreneur behaves from the way other people behave?

The adequate answers to these questions would entail a long discussion of the sociology of occupations, involving the distinction originally made by Max Weber between capitalists and bureaucrats. Since this cannot be done here, a very brief report on our extensive investigations in this area will have to suffice. First, one of the defining characteristics of an entrepreneur is *taking risks* and/or innovating. A person who adds up a column of figures is not an entrepreneur—however carefully, efficiently, or correctly he adds them. He is simply following established rules. However, a man who decides to add a new line to his business is an entrepreneur, in that he cannot know in advance whether this decision will be correct. Nevertheless, he does not feel that he is in the position of a gambler who places some money on the turn of a card. Knowledge, judgment, and skill enter into his decision making; and, if his choice is justified by future developments, he can certainly feel a sense of personal achievement from having made a successful move.

Therefore, if people with high n Achievement are to behave in an entrepreneurial way, they must seek out and perform in situations in which there is some moderate risk of failure—a risk which can, presumably, be reduced by increased effort or skill. They should not work harder than other people at routine tasks, or perform functions which they are certain to do well simply by doing what everyone accepts as the correct traditional thing to do. On the other hand, they should avoid gambling situations, because, even if they win, they can receive no sense of personal achievement, since it was not skill but luck that produced the results. (And, of course, most of the time they would lose, which would be highly unpleasant to them.) The data on this point are very clear-cut. We have repeatedly found, for example, that boys with high n Achievement choose to play games of skill that incorporate a moderate risk of failure. . . .

Another quality that the entrepreneur seeks in his work is that his job be a kind that ordinarily provides him with accurate knowledge of the results of his decisions. As a rule, growth in sales, in output, or in profit margins tells him very precisely whether he has made the correct choice under uncertainty or not. Thus, the concern for profit enters in—profit is a measure of success. We have repeatedly found that boys with a high n Achievement work more efficiently when they know how well they are doing. Also, they will not work harder for money rewards; but if they are asked, they state that greater money rewards should be awarded for accomplishing more difficult things in games of skill. In the ring-toss game, subjects were asked how much money they thought should be awarded for successful throws from different distances. Subjects with high n Achievement and those with low n Achievement agreed substantially about the amounts for throws made close to the peg. However, as the distance from the peg increased, the amounts awarded for successful throws by the subjects with high n Achievement rose more rapidly than did the rewards by those with low n Achievement. Here, as elsewhere, individuals with high n Achievement behaved as they must if they are to be the successful entrepreneurs of society. They believed that greater achievement should be recognized by quantitatively larger reward.

What produces high n Achievement? Why do some societies produce a large number of people with this motive, while other societies produce so many fewer? We conducted long series of researches into this question. I can present only a few here.

One very important finding is essentially a negative one: n Achievement cannot be hereditary. Popular psychology has long maintained that some races are more energetic than others. Our data clearly contradict this in connection with n Achievement. The changes in n Achievement level within a given population are too rapid to be attributed to heredity. For example, the correlation between respective n Achievement levels in the 1925 and 1950 samples of readers is substantially zero. Many of the countries that were high in n Achievement at one or both times may be low or moderate in n Achievement now, and vice versa. Germany was low in 1925 and is high now; and certainly the hereditary makeup of the German nation has not changed in a generation.

However, there is substantiating evidence that n Achievement is a motive which a child can acquire quite early in life, say, by the age of eight or ten, as a result of the way his parents have brought him up. . . . The principal results . . . indicate the differences between the parents of the "high n Achievement boys" and the parents of boys with low n Achievement. In general, the mothers and the fathers of the first group set higher levels of aspiration in a number of tasks for their sons. They were also much warmer, showing positive emotion in reacting to their sons' performances. In the area of authority or dominance, the data are quite interesting. The mothers of the "highs" were more domineering than the mothers of the "lows," but the *fathers* of the "highs" were significantly *less* domineering than the fathers of the "lows." In other words, the fathers of the "highs" set high standards and are warmly interested in their sons' performances, but they do not directly interfere. This gives the boys the chance to develop initiative and self-reliance.

What factors cause parents to behave in this way? Their behavior certainly is involved with their values and, possibly, ultimately with their religion or their general world view. At present, we cannot be sure that Protestant parents are more likely to behave this way than Catholic parents—there are too many subgroup variations within each religious portion of the community: the Lutheran father is probably as likely to be authoritarian as the Catholic father. However, there does seem to be one crucial variable discernible: the extent to which the religion of the family emphasizes individual, as contrasted with ritual, contact with God. The preliterate tribes that we studied in which the religion was the kind that stressed the individual contact had higher n Achievement; and in general, mystical sects in which this kind of religious self-reliance dominates have had higher n Achievement.

The extent to which the authoritarian father is away from the home while the boy is growing up may prove to be another crucial variable. If so, then one incidental consequence of prolonged wars may be an increase in n Achievement, because the fathers are away too much to interfere with their sons' development of it. And in Turkey, N. M. Bradburn found that those boys tended to have higher n Achievement who had left home early or whose fathers had died before they were eighteen.[10] Slavery was another factor which played an important role in the past. It probably lowered n Achievement—in the slaves, for whom obedience and responsibility, but not achievement, were obvious virtues; and in the slave-owners, because household slaves were often disposed to spoil the owner's children as a means for improving their own positions. This is both a plausible and a probable reason for the drop in n Achievement level in ancient Greece that occurred at about the time the middle-class entrepreneur was first able to afford, and obtain by conquest, as many as two slaves for each child. The idea also clarifies the slow economic development of the South in the United States by attributing its dilatoriness to a lack of n Achievement in its elite; and it also indicates why lower-class American Negroes, who are closest to the slave tradition, possess very low n Achievement.[11]

I have outlined our research findings. Do they indicate ways of accelerating economic development? Increasing the level of n Achievement in a country suggests itself as an obvious first possibility. If n Achievement is so important, so specifically adapted to the business role, then it certainly should be raised in level, so that more young men have an "entrepreneurial drive." The difficulty in this excellent plan is that our studies of how *n* Achievement originates indicate that the family is the key formative influence; and it is very hard to change on a really large scale. To be sure, major historical events like wars have taken authoritarian fathers out of the home; and religious reform movements have sometimes converted the parents to a new achievement-oriented ideology. However, such matters are not ordinarily within the policymaking province of the agencies charged with speeding economic development.

Such agencies can, perhaps, effect the general acceptance of an achievement-oriented ideology as an absolute *sine qua non* of economic development. Furthermore, this ideology should be diffused not only in business and governmental circles, but throughout the nation, and in ways that will influence the thinking of all parents as they bring up their children. As B. C. Rosen and R. G. D'Andrade found, parents must, above all, set high standards for their children. The campaign to spread achievement-oriented ideology, if possible, could also incorporate an attack on the extreme authoritarianism in fathers that impedes or prevents the development of self-reliance in their sons. This is, however, a more delicate point, and attacking this, in many countries, would be to threaten values at the very center of social life. I believe that a more indirect approach would be more successful. One approach would be to take the boys out of the home and to camps. A more significant method would be to promote the rights of women, both legally and socially—one of the ways to undermine the absolute dominance of the male is to strengthen the rights of the female! Another reason for concentrating particularly on women is that they play the leading role in rearing the next generation. Yet, while men in underdeveloped countries come in contact with new achievement-oriented values and standards through their work, women may be left almost untouched by such influences. But if the sons are to have high *n* Achievement, the mothers must first be reached.

It may seem strange that a chapter on economic development should discuss the importance of feminism and the way children are reared; but this is precisely where a psychological analysis leads. If the motives of men are the agents that influence the speed with which the economic machine operates, then the speed can be increased only through affecting the factors that create the motives. Furthermore—to state this point less theoretically—I cannot think of evinced substantial, rapid long-term economic development where women have not been somewhat freed from their traditional setting of "Kinder, Küche und Kirche" and allowed to play a more powerful role in society, specifically as part of the working force. This generalization applies not only to the Western democracies like the United States, Sweden, or England, but also to the USSR, Japan, and now China.

In the present state of our knowledge, we can conceive of trying to raise *n* Achievement levels only in the next generation—although new research findings may soon indicate *n* Achievement in adults can be increased. Most economic planners, while accepting the long-range desirability of raising *n* Achievement in future generations, want to know what can be done during the next five to ten years. This immediacy inevitably focuses attention on the process or processes by which executives or entrepreneurs are selected. Foreigners with proved entrepreneurial drive can be hired, but at best this is a temporary and unsatisfactory solution. In most underdeveloped countries where government is playing a leading role in promoting economic development, it is clearly necessary for the government to adopt rigid achievement-oriented standards of performance like those in the USSR.[12] A government manager or, for that matter, a private entrepreneur, should have to produce "or else." Production targets must be set, as they are in most economic plans; and individuals must be held responsible for achieving them, even at the plant level. The philosophy should be one of "no excuses accepted." It is common for government officials or economic theorists in underdeveloped countries to be weighed down by all the difficulties which face the economy and render its rapid development difficult or impossible. They note that there is too rapid population growth, too little capital, too few technically competent people, etc. Such obstacles to growth are prevalent, and in many cases they are immensely hard to overcome; but talking about them can provide merely a comfortable rationalization for mediocre performance. It is difficult to fire an administrator, no matter how poor his performance, if so many objective reasons exist for his doing badly. Even worse, such rationalization permits, in the private sector, the continued employment of incompetent family members as executives. If these private firms were afraid of being penalized for poor performance, they might be impelled to find more able professional managers a little more quickly. I am not an expert in the field, and the mechanisms I am suggesting may be far from appropriate. Still, they may serve to illustrate my main point: if a country short in entrepreneurial talent wants to advance rapidly, it must find ways and means of ensuring that only the most competent retain positions of responsibility. One of the obvious methods of doing so is to judge people in terms of their *performance*—and not according to their family or political connections, their skill in explaining why their unit failed to produce as expected, or their conscientiousness in following the rules. I would suggest the use of psychological tests as a means of selecting people with high *n* Achievement; but, to be perfectly frank, I think this approach is at present somewhat impractical on a large enough scale in most underdeveloped countries.

Finally, there is another approach which I think is promising for recruiting and developing more competent business leadership. It is the one called, in some circles, the "professionalization of management." Frederick Harbison and Charles A. Myers have recently completed a worldwide survey of the efforts made to develop professional schools of high-level management. They have concluded that, in most countries, progress in this direction is slow.[13] Professional management is important for three reasons: (1) It may endow a business career with higher prestige (as a kind of profession), so that business will attract more of the young men with high *n* Achievement from the elite groups in backward countries; (2) It stresses *performance* criteria of excellence in the management area—i.e., what a man can do and not what he is; (3) Advanced management schools can themselves be so achievement-oriented in their instruction that they are able to raise the *n* Achievement of those who attend them.

Applied toward explaining historical events, the results of our researches clearly shift attention away from external factors and to man—in particular, to his motives and values. That about which he thinks and dreams determines what will happen. The emphasis is quite different from the Darwinian or Marxist view of man as a creature who *adapts* to his environment. It is even different from the Freudian view of civilization as the sublimation of man's primitive urges. Civilization, at least in its economic aspects, is neither adaptation nor sublimation; it is a positive creation by a people made dynamic by a high level of *n* Achievement. Nor can we agree with Toynbee, who recognizes the importance of psychological factors as "the very forces which actually decide the issue when an encounter takes place," when he states that these factors "inherently are impossible to weigh and measure, and therefore to estimate scientifically in advance."[14] It is a measure of the pace at which the behavioral sciences are developing that even within Toynbee's lifetime we can demonstrate that he was mistaken. The psychological factor responsible for a civilization's rising to a challenge is so far from being "inherently impossible to weigh and measure" that it has been weighed and measured and scientifically estimated in advance, and, so far as we can now tell, this factor is the achievement motive.

NOTES

1. A. L. Kroeber, *Configurations of Culture Growth* (Berkeley, Calif., 1944).

2. J. W. Atkinson (Ed.), *Motives in Fantasy, Action, and Society* (Princeton, N.J., 1958).

3. Max Weber, *The Protestant Ethic and the Spirit of Capitalism,* trans. Talcott Parsons (New York, 1930).

4. M. R. Winterbottom, "The Relation of Need for Achievement to Learning and Experiences in Independence and Mastery," in Atkinson, *op. cit.,* pp. 453–478.

5. F. Heichelheim, *Wirtschaftsgeschichte des Altertums* (Leiden, 1938).

6. J. B. Cortés, "The Achievement Motive in the Spanish Economy Between the Thirteenth and the Eighteenth Centuries," *Economic Development and Cultural Change,* IX (1960), 144–163.

7. N. M. Bradburn and D. E. Berlew, "Need for Achievement and English Economic Growth," *Economic Development and Cultural Change,* 1961.

8. I. L. Child, T. Storm, and J. Veroff, "Achievement Themes in Folk Tales Related to Socialization Practices," in Atkinson, *op. cit.,* pp. 479–492.

9. David Riesman, with the assistance of Nathan Glazer and Reuel Denney, *The Lonely Crowd* (New Haven, Conn., 1950).

10. N. M. Bradburn, "The Managerial Role in Turkey" (unpublished Ph.D. dissertation, Harvard University, 1960).

11. B. C. Rosen, "Race, Ethnicity, and Achievement Syndrome," *American Sociological Review,* XXIV (1959), 47–60.

12. David Granick, *The Red Executive* (New York, 1960).

13. Frederick Harbison and Charles A. Myers, *Management in the Industrial World* (New York, 1959).

14. Arnold J. Toynbee, *A Study of History* (abridgment by D. C. Somervell; Vol. I; New York, 1947).

15

. . . .

Reevaluating the Effect of
N-Ach on Economic Growth

. . . .

Jeffrey Lewis

Lewis found no support for McClelland's n-Achievement theory of economic growth

This chapter represents a significant challenge to the findings presented in the previous chapter. Here Jeffrey Lewis reviews David McClelland's assertion that high levels of n-ach precede rapid economic growth. Lewis states that even though McClelland's methodological decisions seem to have been made post hoc, support is found for his hypothesis for the period 1929 to 1950. For the period 1950 to 1977, however, no support exists for McClelland's hypothesis. Lewis concludes that McClelland's findings were based on the chance results of data mining.

INTRODUCTION

David McClelland's psychological theory of economic growth has received considerable attention over the last 25 years. When McClelland introduced the theory in 1960, it was hailed as a breakthrough in the understanding of economic development.[1] Although much of its luster has worn off in the eyes of development economists, McClelland's theory is still a mainstay of interventionist development policy.[2] His n-achievement measure has been employed not only in analyses of economic growth but in more generic production functions and welfare comparisons.[3]

While many agree that psychological factors similar to the "need for achievement" may explain some aspects of entrepreneurial activity and economic growth, questions have been raised about both the validity and

Reprinted with permission from Elsevier Science Ltd., Oxford, England, from *World Development,* vol. 19, no. 9 (1991):1269–1274.

the reliability of the empirical evidence McClelland used to support his theory.[4] Some, such as Hagen (1975, 272–273), have questioned his statistical methods and wondered how they may have affected the outcome of his original analysis. In this paper, we seek to explore these issues through an investigation of McClelland's methods and a replication of his analysis using new data.

McClelland lays the groundwork for his theory of entrepreneurial supply in *The Achieving Society* (1961). He holds that certain individuals are more willing to play entrepreneurial roles because they have a particular ordering of psychological needs. Psychological needs are defined (Davidoff 1980, 311) as "deficiencies which may be based on specific bodily or learned requirements." The ability to learn these needs, even in later life (as McClelland has come to believe is possible), forms the basis of entrepreneurial development policies. McClelland presents three basic learned needs: the need for power (n-pow), the need for affiliation (n-aff) and the need for achievement (n-ach).

N-pow is manifest in the "concern with the control of means of influencing a person" (McClelland 1961, 167). N-aff regards "establishing, maintaining or restoring an affective relationship with another person" or, in a word, "friendship" (McClelland 1961, 160). Finally, n-ach can be considered as the need for challenge and success. In experimental situations where subjects could choose the level of difficulty of their task, those with high levels of n-ach consistently chose tasks that were the most difficult that they could reasonably expect to complete. Those subjects with low n-ach showed no particular propensity toward any level of difficulty. This sort of risk-bearing behavior is very similar to that which Knight and others have ascribed to the entrepreneur.[5] McClelland feels that n-ach motivates entrepreneurial activity.

To measure individuals' psychological needs, McClelland could not apply objective testing techniques. These spontaneous inner concerns are fundamentally unconscious. Answers that subjects would give to an objective test are typically biased by societal norms of how one "should" respond to such a question. Therefore, all measures of need strength must be taken indirectly by such methods as content analysis of writing samples, folk tales, art work and dreams. In *The Achieving Society*, McClelland uses each of these measures in various parts of his analysis of the achievement motive over 3000 years of history.

McCLELLAND'S TEST

In setting up what is undoubtedly the most critical test of this hypothesis, McClelland chooses to compare not individuals but countries. This sort of aggregation poses many problems, but does have the advantage of allowing more cultures to be represented and removing possible sampling errors.

Additionally, the move to the nation as the unit of analysis allows McClelland to measure entrepreneurial activity in easily comparable terms of economic growth. In so doing, McClelland makes the common assumption that economic growth is significantly related to the quantity and quality of entrepreneurial activity.

The basic causal relationship that McClelland wants to test is:

$$\text{n-ach} \rightarrow \text{entrepreneurship} \rightarrow \text{economic growth}$$

There is a methodological problem in the assumption that the distribution of n-ach is the same in all countries. If the variance and skew of the distribution are not the same in all countries, measuring a sort of national average amount of achievement motive is not an accurate way to test this hypothesis. McClelland assumes that n-ach has the same distribution around its central tendency in all countries. Because we know that only a certain percentage of the population is involved in entrepreneurial activity, even in vibrant economies, it is logical to assume that a country with a bimodal distribution of n-ach would have a higher degree of entrepreneurial activity than a country with the same mean level and a unimodal distribution.[6]

McClelland excludes tropical countries from the study because he feels they have uniformly slow growth which he attributes to factors beyond the scope of his study (McClelland 1961, 71). N-ach is measured for 1925 and economic growth from 1929 to 1950.

Measuring the Need for Achievement

In order to measure the need for achievement in a wide variety of countries without drawing samples of individuals (which would have been too costly and demographically complicated) McClelland looks for writing from each country from which he can easily and reasonably score n-ach levels and which he can consider representative of the country as a whole. To achieve these ends, he settles on samples of 21 grade school readers from each country because they may be taken as representative of "popular culture," do not deal with factual, historical events, and are universal in that they are read "by second- to fourth-grade children of all lands" (McClelland 1961, 71–72).

The readers do not prove to be very a reliable measure. The split half correlation coefficient for the measure was only 0.43.[7] As McClelland points out, this level of measurement error in the independent variable makes it very difficult to gain significant results.

Measuring Economic Growth

McClelland, somewhat surprisingly, rejects conventional measures of economic growth for his study. He argues that simple GDP in dollar terms is too contaminated by exchange rate distortions and other deviations in purchasing power parity to be a reliable measure of economic growth. It might be noted that this problem is of less concern in comparing growth in GDP insofar as any such distortions remain more or less constant. Rather than using dollar denominated GDP at official exchange rates, McClelland would like to use a properly adjusted GDP figure; unfortunately, such a measure was not well developed at that time.

McClelland selects electrical power output as a better proxy for economic growth. He argues this is a good measure because "in our time the production and use of electricity is highly diagnostic of the level of technology in a country" (1961, 85). Moreover, electrical output is uniformly measured everywhere in the world and data are thus easily comparable and available from the United Nations for almost any country.

In measuring growth in electrical output in this manner, McClelland (1961, 88) decides, following Kuznets, that percentage changes should not be used because their "statistical properties are simply not very well known." Instead he takes as a measure of relative growth the standardized residual from a regression which fits the equation:

Gain in output =
$$\beta_0 + \beta_1[\text{base year output}] + e_1 \qquad (1)$$

He considers this to be a useful process because base year output has a high positive correlation with subsequent gain in output. This high correlation implies that much of the variation in electrical power growth stems from the initial level of output, not from factors of entrepreneurial activity. The residual is then, in some sense, a measure of whether a country is over- or under-performing with respect to the growth of an average country with a given base year electrical reduction. We might note that McClelland had in the past used percentage change based measures of growth and that if he had used them here his results would have been significantly lower (Shatz 1971). This raises the question whether McClelland makes these methodological decisions on some basis other than *a priori*. . . .

APPLYING NEW DATA

As we have seen, McClelland's test provides reasonably strong and accurate evidence for his hypothesis despite the fact that his methods are a bit convoluted. We may then ask whether his findings reflect a real world relationship or are merely the result of considerable data mining. McClelland has afforded us the opportunity to make just such a test. Taking the data on n-ach for 1950 published in *The Achieving Society*, we can refit the model using new and improved data on economic growth for the period 1950–77.

The new data on economic growth are based on estimates of real GDP originally calculated by Kravis, Summers and Heston (1978) for the World Bank.[8] These GDP data are just the sort that McClelland wanted for his own test. They adjust for price levels and exchange rates in a comprehensive manner. Having the measure of growth that McClelland desired, we can make a more definitive test.

In order to avoid the problems encountered by McClelland in using the two-step process and still have comparable results, the relationship is modeled in two different ways. In the two-step model, the regression of base on gain is estimated as:

$$\text{Gain in Real GDP} = 917.3 + 0.478 \text{ [RGDP in 1950]}$$
$$(0.17)$$
$$R^2 = 0.19$$

The R^2 of regression is considerably less than in McClelland's study using electrical power; at a level of 0.19 versus 0.88. The standardized predicted gain is then fit in a regression in the second step of the procedure yielding:

$$\text{Standardized predicted gain} = -0.02 - 0.17 \text{ [n-ach]}$$
$$(0.182)$$
$$R^2 = 0.015$$

Here the results are insignificant. The R^2 is a negligible 0.015. The results of the one-step procedure are equally insignificant. McClelland's hypothesis does not stand up to the new data. Not only is the relationship insignificant but it is not even in the predicted direction.

We now want to suggest a few modifications in the model specification that might lend more support to McClelland. First, following the work of Teikner (1979, 293–320), we would like to propose that economic growth is a function not only of n-ach but also of n-aff and n-pow. McClelland feels that effects of these other needs are minor and indirect. However, given the nature of markets and institutional structures since WWII other needs might effect growth. For example, high n-aff could block a country from implementing an incomes policy necessary to promote growth. Since we have no preconceived notion of effects of n-aff and n-pow, we simply enter them into the equation additively. For the dependent variable, we decided to use a more conventional compound rate of gain. The regression fit the equation as follows:

$$\%\text{RGDP} = 3.171 - 0.2745 \text{ (n-ach)}$$
$$(0.2639)$$

$$-0.2586 \text{ (n-aff)} - 0.2748 \text{ (n-pow)}$$
$$(0.2256) \qquad (0.2376)$$
$$R^2 = 0.067$$

This modification in the equation does not have the impact we might have expected. The adjusted $R^2 = -0.0152$, and none of the variables are significant.

As a final attempt to confirm McClelland's operational hypothesis, we propose that the 1925 data for n-ach be used in the estimation of the 1950–77 period. It may be that the mass adoption of Freudian theory after 1925 had changed school readers by 1950. If that were the case, we might expect that they were no longer a valid measure of n-ach, because what McClelland believed were subconscious themes in the readers may have been, as Kilby argues, deliberate attempts to mold children's beliefs. To test this hypothesis, we fit the equation:

$$\%RGDP = 4.034 - 0.775 \text{ [n-ach in 1925]}$$
$$(0.31)$$
$$R^2 = 0.26$$

For this equation, n-ach is significant and $R^2 = 0.23$. The problem of course is that the sign of the n-ach parameter is not in the predicted direction. We are at a loss to explain this. We felt it might have been due to an increasing number of centrally planned economies that may not require the same level of entrepreneurship to achieve economic growth. However, dummy weights to control for the effects of centrally planned economies did not result in any change in the sign of the n-ach parameter.

CONCLUSION

We have answered two questions posed by McClelland's critics. On the question of statistical method, we have shown that while his techniques may not have been arrived at *a priori*, McClelland actually underestimated the effect of n-ach in his original study. On the question of whether McClelland's results would be confirmed with new data, the results were more discouraging. The later data showed little support for his hypothesis. We attempted to improve the model and make *post hoc* suggestions as to why it failed. These assertions also proved false. In one case the effect of n-ach was actually significant in the opposite direction than that predicted.

The failure of n-ach to explain economic growth in the 1950–77 period leads us to question the validity of McClelland's use of electrical power as a proxy for economic growth in his original study. Regressing electrical power growth on the adjusted GNP data for the period of 1950–77, we find that electrical power growth explains about 42% of the variance in adjusted GNP growth.[9] Moreover, electrical power growth is statistically unrelated to n-ach for the 1950–77 period. While electrical power is not a good proxy for GNP, there does not appear to be any special enduring relationship between electricity and n-ach. Thus, we conclude that n-ach, at least as measured in this test, has little ability to explain the economic growth of nations.

NOTES

1. For a more complete discussion of McClelland's reception see Shatz (1971):184.

2. See V. V. Blatt (1986).

3. Freeman (1976 and 1984).

4. In a critique, Shatz (1971) pointed to various statistical difficulties with McClelland's use of a modified index of electrical production as a principal dependent variable in a model fitted to 20th century data.

In his 1968 treatment of McClelland's work, Higgins provides a probing assessment of each of the numerous measures of need for achievement employed by McClelland (Higgins 1968, 241–249).

In "Hunting the Heffalump," Peter Kilby contends that on the basis of McClelland's own findings (McClelland 1961, 78–79), McClelland's scoring of achievement imagery in school textbooks is not measuring a spontaneous inner psychic drive, but rather is measuring a normative sociological variable (Kilby 1971, 19–20).

5. Knight (1985):245. To Knight, in the economy the task "of uncertainty bearing [is] in the hands of the entrepreneur."

6. Assume country A is populated entirely by people with a moderate level of n-ach, while country B's population is 90% low n-ach and 10% high n-ach. We show that even in advanced economies very few people play entrepreneurial roles. Thus, while country A would have a higher level of n-ach, country B would have a higher level of entrepreneurial activity.

7. McClelland (1961):161. The split half correlation takes half of the readers used for a given country and correlates their n-ach scores with those of the other half.

8. The revised and updated data used in this analysis are from Summers et al. (1980). Data for centrally planned economies from Summers and Heston (1984).

9. Data on electrical power production for the original 22 countries from the United Nations (1955, 1979, 1980). Electrical power measured for 1950 and 1977.

REFERENCES

Bhatt, V.V. 1986. "Entrepreneurship and Development: India's Experience," *Finance and Development* (March).

Davidoff, Linda. 1980. *Introduction to Psychology*. New York: McGraw Hill Book Co.

Freeman, Katherine. 1984. "The Significance of Motivational Variables in International Public Welfare Expenditures." *Economic Development and Cultural Change*, Vol. 32 (July).

Freeman, Katherine. 1976. "The Significance of McClelland's Achievement Variable in the Aggregate Production Function," *Economic Development and Cultural Change*, Vol. 24 (July).

Goldberger, Arthur S. 1964. *Econometric Theory*. New York: John Wiley & Sons, Inc.

Hagen, Everett. 1975. *The Economics of Development*, 2nd edition. Homewood, IL: R. D. Irwin.

Higgins, Benjamin. 1968. *Economic Development*. New York: Norton.

Kilby, Peter (Ed.). 1971. *Entrepreneurship and Economic Development*. New York: The Free Press.

Knight, Frank. 1985. *Risk, Uncertainty, and Profit*. Chicago: University of Chicago Press.

Kravis, Irving B., Alan W. Heston, and Robert Summers. 1978. *International Comparisons of Real Product and Purchasing Power*. Baltimore, MD: Johns Hopkins University Press.

LeVine, Robert. 1965. *Dreams and Deeds: Achievement Motivation in Nigeria*. Chicago: University of Chicago Press.

Maddison, Angus. 1970. *Economic Progress and Policy in Developing Countries*. New York: W. W. Norton and Co., Inc.

McClelland, David. 1984. *Motives, Personality and Society Selected Papers*. New York: Praeger Publishers.

McClelland, David. 1961. *The Achieving Society*. Princeton: D. Van Nostrand and Co.

Pindyck, Robert S., and Daniel Rubinfeld. 1981. *Econometric Models and Economic Forecasts*. New York: McGraw Hill Book Co.

Statz, Sayre. 1971. "N-achievement and Economic Growth: A Critical Appraisal," in P. Kilby (Ed.), *Entrepreneurship and Economic Growth*. New York: The Free Press.

Summers, Robert, and Alan Heston. 1984. "Improved International Comparisons of Real Product and Its Composition: 1950–1980," *Review of Income and Wealth* Series 30.

Summers, Robert, Irving Kravis, and Alan Heston. 1980. "International Comparisons of Real Product and Composition." *Review of Income and Wealth*, 26. No. 1 (March).

Teikner, Ahmet. 1979–80. "Need for Achievement and International Differences in Income Growth," *Economic Development and Cultural Change*, Vol. 28.

United Nations. 1955, 1979 and 1980. *Statistical Yearbook*. New York: United Nations.

16

. . . .

The Effect of Cultural Values on Economic Development: Theory, Hypotheses, and Some Empirical Tests

. . . .

Jim Granato, Ronald Inglehart, & David Leblang

In Chapter 15, Jeffrey Lewis attacked McClelland's cultural explanation of economic growth using an improved methodology. In this chapter, the authors reexamine this issue by presenting Max Weber's argument for the importance of cultural values for economic growth. They utilize the "achievement motive" thesis developed by McClelland as a specific empirical point of reference. The authors test the theory using the World Values Survey, a database of interviews collected in many countries around the world. In this study data are used for twenty-five countries, and strong evidence indicates that certain cultural values help to spur economic growth. In the same journal from which this chapter was drawn, however, the findings are disputed by other authors. The jury still seems to be out on this fascinating debate.

Do cultural factors influence economic development? If so, can they be measured and their effect compared with that of standard economic factors such as savings and investment? This article examines the explanatory power of the standard endogenous growth model and compares it with that of two types of cultural variables capturing motivational factors—achievement motivation and postmaterialist values. We believe that it is not an either/or proposition: cultural and economic factors play complementary roles. This belief is borne out empirically; we use recently developed econometric techniques to assess the relative merits of these alternative explanations.

Reprinted by permission of the University of Wisconsin Press from *American Journal of Political Science*, vol. 40, no. 3 (August 1996):607–631.

Cultural factors alone do not explain all of the cross-national variation in economic growth rates. Every economy experiences significant fluctuations in growth rates from year to year as a result of short-term factors such as technological shocks or unforeseen circumstances that affect output. These could not be attributed to cultural factors, which change gradually. A society's economic and political institutions also make a difference. For example, prior to 1945, North Korea and South Korea had a common culture, but South Korea's economic performance has been far superior.

On the other hand, the evidence suggests that cultural differences are an important part of the story. Over the past five decades, the Confucian-influenced economies of East Asia outperformed the rest of the world by a wide margin. This holds true despite the fact that they are shaped by a wide variety of economic and political institutions. Conversely, during the same period most African economies experienced low growth rates. Both societal-level and individual-level evidence suggests that a society's economic and political institutions are not the only factors determining economic development; cultural factors are also important.

Traditionally, the literature presents culture and economic determinants of growth as distinct. Political economists and political sociologists view their respective approaches as mutually exclusive. One reason lies in the level of analysis employed and with this the underlying assumptions about human behavior. Another reason is that we have had inadequate measures of cultural factors. Previous attempts to establish the role of culture either infer culture from economic performance or estimate cultural factors from impressionistic historical evidence. Both factors could be important, but until cultural factors are entered into a quantitative analysis, this possibility could not be tested.

By *culture*, we refer to a system of basic common values that help shape the behavior of the people in a given society. In most preindustrial societies, this value system takes the form of a religion and changes very slowly; but with industrialization and accompanying processes of modernization, these worldviews tend to become more secular, rational, and open to change.

For reasons discussed below, the cultures of virtually all preindustrial societies are hostile to social mobility and individual economic accumulation. Thus, both medieval Christianity and traditional Confucian culture stigmatized profit-making and entrepreneurship. But (as Weber argues), a Protestant version of Christianity played a key role in the rise of capitalism—and much later—a modernized version of Confucian society encourages economic growth, through its support of education and achievement.

The theory and evidence presented in this paper are organized as follows: section one discusses theories that deal with the effect of culture on economic development. This literature emphasizes the importance of motivational factors in the growth process. Section two introduces the data. This data, based on representative national surveys of basic values, enable us to construct two measures of cultures—achievement motivation and postmaterialist values. Section three discusses the baseline endogenous growth model. We draw upon a recent paper by Levine and Renelt (1992) to specify this model, and we augment it with cultural variables. Section four is the multivariate analysis. Economic and cultural variables each explain unique aspects of the cross-national variation in economic growth. Using the *encompassing* principles we find that an improved and parsimonious explanation for economic growth comes from a model that includes both economic and cultural variables. Section four also examines the robustness of this economic-cultural model and finds that the specification is robust to alterations in the conditioning set of information, the elimination of influential cases, and variations in estimation procedure. Section five concludes.

CULTURE, MOTIVATIONAL FACTORS, AND ECONOMIC GROWTH

We first discuss the literature that views achievement motivation as an essential component in the process of economic development, and then we explore how cultural measures from the World Values Survey can be used to examine the effect of motivation on growth.

The motivational literature stresses the role of cultural emphasis on economic achievement. It grows out of Weber's (1904–1905) Protestant Ethic thesis. This school of thought gave rise to the historical research of Tawney (1926, 1955), case studies by Harrison (1992), and empirical work by McClelland et al. (1953) and McClelland (1961) on achievement motivation. Inglehart (1971, 1977, 1990) extends this work by examining the shift from materialist to postmaterialist value priorities. Although previous work mainly focuses on the political consequences of these values, their emergence represents a shift away from emphasis on economic accumulation and growth. These "new" values could be viewed as the erosion of Protestant Ethic among populations that experience high levels of economic security.

We suggest that Weber is correct in arguing that the rise of Protestantism is a crucial event in modernizing Europe. He emphasizes that the Calvinist version of Protestantism encourages norms favorable to economic achievement. But we view the rise of Protestantism as one case of a more general phenomenon. It is important, not only because of the specific content of early Protestant beliefs, but because this belief system undermines a set of religious norms that inhibit economic achievement and are common to most preindustrial societies.

Preindustrial economies are zero-sum systems: they are characterized by little or no economic growth which implies that upward social mobility only comes at the expense of someone else. A society's cultural system generally reflects this fact. Social status is hereditary rather than achieved, and social norms encourage one to accept one's social position in this life. Aspirations toward social mobility are sternly repressed. Such value systems help to maintain social solidarity but discourage economic accumulation.

Weber's emphasis on the role of Protestantism seems to capture an important part of reality. The Protestant Reformation combined with the emergence of scientific logic broke the grip of the medieval Christian Worldview on a significant part of Europe. Prior to the Reformation, Southern Europe was economically more advanced than Northern Europe. During the three centuries after the Reformation, capitalism emerged, mainly among the Protestant regions of Europe and the Protestant minorities in Catholic countries. Within this cultural context, individual economic accumulation was no longer rejected.

Protestant Europe manifested a subsequent economic dynamism that moved it far ahead of Catholic Europe. Shifting trade patterns, declining food production in Southern Europe and other factors also contributed to this shift, but the evidence suggests that cultural factors played a major role. Throughout the first 150 years of the Industrial Revolution, industrial development took place almost entirely within Protestant regions of Europe, and the Protestant portions of the New World. It was only during the second half of the twentieth century that an entrepreneurial outlook emerged in Catholic Europe and in the Far East. Both now show higher rates of economic growth than Protestant Europe. In short, the concept of the Protestant Ethic would be outdated if we take it to mean something that exists in historically Protestant countries. But Weber's more general concept, that certain cultural factors influence economic growth, is an important and valid insight.

McClelland et al. (1953) and McClelland's (1961) work on achievement motivation builds on the Weberian thesis but focuses on the values that were encouraged in children by their parents, schools, and other agencies of socialization. He hypothesizes that some societies emphasize economic achievement as a positive goal while others give it little emphasis. Since it was not feasible for him to measure directly the values emphasized in given societies through representative national surveys, McClelland attempts to measure them indirectly, through content analysis of the stories and school books used to educate children. He finds that some cultures emphasize achievement in their school books more heavily than others— and that the former showed considerably higher rates of economic growth than did the latter.

McClelland's work is criticized on various grounds. It is questioned whether his approach really measures the values taught to children, or simply those of textbook writers. Subsequently, writers of the dependency school argue that any attempt to trace differences in economic growth rates to factors within a given culture, rather than to global capitalist exploitation, is simply a means of justifying exploitation of the peripheral economies. Such criticism tends to discredit this type of research but is hardly an empirical refutation.

Survey research by Lenski (1963) and Alwin (1986) finds that Catholics and Protestants in the United States show significant differences in the values they emphasize as the most important things to teach children. These differences are more or less along the lines of the Protestant Ethic thesis. Alwin also demonstrates that these differences erode over time, with Protestants and Catholics gradually converging toward a common belief system.

THE DATA

The World Values Survey asks representative national samples of the publics in a number of societies, "Here is a list of qualities which children can be encouraged to learn at home. Which, if any, do you consider to be especially important?" This list includes qualities that reflect emphasis on autonomy and economic achievement, such as "thrift," "saving money and things," and "determination." Other items on the list reflect emphasis on conformity to traditional social norms, such as "obedience" and "religious faith."

We construct an index of achievement motivation that sums up the percentage in each country emphasizing the first two goals minus the percentage emphasizing the latter two goals. This method of index construction controls for the tendency of respondents in some societies to place relatively heavy emphasis on all of these goals, while respondents in other countries mention relatively few of them.

Figure 16.1 shows the simple bivariate relationship between this index and rates of per capita economic growth between 1960 and 1989. The zero-point on the achievement motivation index reflects the point where exactly as many people emphasize obedience and religion, as emphasize thrift and determination. As we move to the right, the latter values are given increasing emphasis. A given society's emphasis on thrift and determination *over* obedience and religious faith has a strong bivariate linkage with its rate of economic growth over the past three decades (r = .66; p = .001).

Though often stereotyped as having authoritarian cultures, Japan, China, and South Korea emerge near the pole that emphasizes thrift more heavily than obedience. The three East Asian societies rank highest on that dimension, while the two African societies included in this survey rank near the opposite end of the continuum, emphasizing obedience and religious faith.

Figure 16.1 Economic Growth Rate by Achievement Motivation Scores of Public

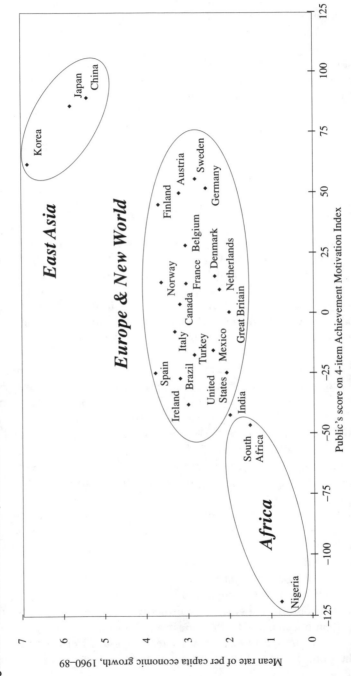

Note: Achievement Motivation Index is based on the percentage in each society who emphasized "Thrift" and "Determination" as important things for a child to learn *minus* the percentage emphasizing "Obedience" and "Religious Faith."

The publics of India and the United States also fall toward the latter end of the scale. This is *not* an authoritarianism dimension. It reflects the balance between emphasis on two types of values. One set of values—thrift and determination—support economic achievement; while the other—obedience and religious faith—tend to discourage it, emphasizing conformity to traditional authority and group norms. These two types of values are not necessarily incompatible: some societies rank relatively high on both, while others rank relatively low on both. But, the relative *priority* given to them is strongly related to its growth rate.

Do cultural factors lead to economic growth, or does economic growth lead to cultural change? We believe that the causal flow can work in both directions. For example, there is strong evidence that postmaterialist values emerge when a society attains relatively high levels of economic security. In this case, economic change reshapes culture. On the other hand, once these values become widespread, they are linked with relatively low subsequent rates of economic growth. Here, culture seems to be shaping economics—a parallel to the Weberian thesis, except that what is happening here is, in a sense, the rise of the Protestant Ethic in reverse.

Demonstrating causal connections is always difficult. In connection with our achievement motivation index, the obvious interpretation would be that emphasis on thrift and hard work, rather than on obedience and respect, is conducive to economic growth. The two most sensitive indicators of this dimension are thrift, on the one hand, and obedience on the other. For some time, economists have been aware that a nation's rate of gross domestic investment is a major influence on its long term growth rate. Investment, in turn, depends on savings. Thus, a society that emphasizes thrift produces savings, which leads to investment, and later to economic growth. We provide evidence below that this is probably the case. This does not rule out the possibility that economic growth might be conducive to thrift but this linkage is less obvious.

Emphasis on obedience is negatively linked with economic growth, for a converse reason. In preindustrial societies, obedience means conformity to traditional norms, which de-emphasize and even stigmatize economic accumulation. Obedience, respect for others, and religious faith all emphasize obligations to share with and support one's relatives, friends and neighbors. Such communal obligations are strongly felt in preindustrial societies. But from the perspective of a bureaucratized rational-legal society, these norms are antithetical to capital accumulation and conducive to nepotism. Furthermore, conformity to authority inhibits innovation and entrepreneurship.

The motivational component is also tapped by materialist/postmaterialist values, with postmaterialism having a negative relationship with economic growth. The achievement motivation variable is only modestly correlated with the materialist/postmaterialist dimension ($r = -.39$; $p = .0581$).

Though both dimensions have significant linkages with economic growth, they affect it in different ways. The achievement motivation dimension seems to tap the transition from preindustrial to industrial values systems, linked with the modernization process.

The materialist/postmaterialist dimension reflects the transition to post-industrial society, linked with a shift away from emphasis on economic growth, toward increasing emphasis on protection of the environment and on the quality of life more generally. Previous research demonstrates that: (1) a gradual shift from materialist toward postmaterialist goals has been taking place throughout advanced industrial society; (2) that this shift is strongly related to the emergence of democracy (r = .71); but (3) that it has a tendency to be negatively linked with economic growth (Abramson and Inglehart 1995).

MULTIVARIATE ANALYSIS

Our empirical approach is straightforward: we begin by estimating (via OLS) a baseline endogenous growth model that includes variables identified by Levine and Renelt (1992) as having robust partial correlations with economic growth. Using data for 25 countries[1] we first test the endogenous growth specification (Model 1 in Table 16.1). Following Equation [1], a nation's rate of per capita economic growth is regressed on its initial level of per capita income and human capital investment (education spending) as well as on its rate of physical capital accumulation. As expected, the results are quite compatible with the expectations of endogenous growth theory. The results of Model 1 are summarized as follows: (1) the significant negative coefficient on the initial level of per capita income indicates that there is evidence of "conditional convergence." That is, controlling for human and physical capital investment, poorer nations grow faster than richer nations; (2) investment in human capital (education spending) has a positive and statistically significant effect on subsequent economic growth; and (3) increasing the rate of physical capital accumulation increases a nation's rate of economic growth.

Overall this baseline economic model performs well: it accounts for 55% of the variation in cross-national growth rates and is consistent with prior cross-national tests of the conditional convergence hypothesis (e.g., Barro 1991; Mankiw, Romer, and Weil 1992). Model 1 also passes all diagnostic tests, indicating that the residuals are not serially correlated[2] (LM test), are normally distributed (Jarque-Bera test), and homoskedastic (White test).

Model 2 in Table 16.1 regresses the rate of per capita economic growth on a constant and the two cultural variables. As expected, both achievement motivation and postmaterialism are significant predictors of economic

Table 16.1   OLS Estimation of Economic Growth Models Dependent Variable: Mean Rate of per Capita Economic Growth (1960–1989)

Model Variable	Model 1	Model 2	Model 3	Model 4
Constant	−0.70	7.29*	3.16	2.40*
	(1.08)	(1.49)	(1.94)	(0.77)
Per Capita GDP in 1960	−0.63*		−0.42*	−0.43*
	(0.14)		(0.14)	(0.10)
Primary Education in 1960	2.69*		2.19*	2.09*
	(1.22)		(1.06)	(0.96)
Secondary Education	3.27*		1.21	
	(1.01)		(1.08)	
Investment	8.69*		3.09	
	(4.90)		(4.40)	
Achievement Motivation		2.07*	1.44*	1.88*
		(0.37)	(0.48)	(0.35)
Postmaterialism		−2.24*	−1.07	
		(0.77)	(1.03)	
R^2 Adjusted	.55	.59	.69	.70
SEE	.86	.83	.72	.71
$LM (x^2(1))$	.42	.65	.68	.87
Jarque-Bera $(x^2(2))$	.05	.30	.18	.57
White $(x^2(1))$	.28	.24	.31	.18
SC	.119	−.117	−.095	−.352

Notes: Mean of dependent variable: 3.04; N is 25 for all models; standard errors in parentheses.

*t test: $p < .05$

growth and have the expected sign. Thus, the arguments of both Protestant Ethic and postmaterialist type theories cannot be rejected by this evidence. In addition, these variables, taken by themselves, do fairly well, accounting for 59% of the variance in growth rates. A glance at the diagnostics also indicates that the residuals are well behaved.

Comparing Competing Empirical Models: Encompassing Results

Both the economic and cultural models give similar goodness-of-fit performance. Each model's regressors are statistically significant. Yet, which model is superior? Or do both models possess explanatory factors that are missing in the other? . . .

In short, both models explain aspects of growth that the rival cannot. The implication is straightforward: growth rates are best understood as a consequence of both economic and cultural factors.

What happens when we combine the economic model with the cultural model? The results of this experiment are contained in Model 3. Beginning with the endogenous growth variables, adding the variables from Model 2 significantly alters the parameter estimates and standard errors on secondary education spending and physical capital investment. In fact, the coefficient on the physical capital investment variable changes dramatically. It decreases from 8.69 in Model 1 to 3.09 in Model 3. While this coefficient still has the expected sign, it is now far from significant.

Why is physical capital investment, a variable "robustly" correlated with economic growth in a number of other studies, now insignificant? Achievement motivation quite possibly is conducive to economic growth at least partly because it encourages relatively high rates of investment. Achievement motivation also has an important direct effect on economic growth rates, quite apart from its tendency to increase investment. Presumably the direct path from culture to economic growth reflects the effect of motivational factors on entrepreneurship and effort.

Returning to the analysis of Model 3 in Table 16.1, we now examine the direct effect of cultural values, particularly achievement motivation, on economic growth. As in Model 2, achievement motivation is positively and significantly related to economic growth. Combining Model 2 and Model 3 results in postmaterialism now being insignificant, however. This is probably due to the fact that countries with postmaterialist values are already fairly rich; the bivariate correlation between the initial level of wealth and postmaterialism is .75 and is significant at the .0000 level. Combining the regressors of these models (Model 3) we again have a model that does not violate any diagnostic test. In addition, the fit is more accurate (SEE).

SENSITIVITY ANALYSIS

Table 16.1 contains an additional specification. In Model 4 we eliminate the three insignificant variables from Model 3—those for postmaterialism, investment, and secondary school enrollment—to check the stability of the remaining parameters. Model 4 is the most parsimonious and efficient model, explaining 70 percent of the variance in per capita growth rates with only three variables. . . .

CONCLUSION

The idea that economic growth is partly shaped by cultural factors has encountered considerable resistance. One reason for this resistance is because cultural values have been widely perceived as diffuse and permanent features of given societies: if cultural values determine economic growth, then the outlook for economic development seems hopeless, because culture cannot be changed. Another reason for opposition is that standard economic arguments supposedly suffice for international differences in savings and growth rates. For example, the standard life cycle model and not cultural arguments explains the difference in savings rates and growth rates between, say, Germany, Japan, and the United States.[3]

When we approach culture as something to be measured on a quantitative empirical basis, the illusion of diffuseness and permanence disappears. We no longer deal with gross stereotypes, such as the idea that "Germans have always been militaristic," or "Hispanic culture is unfavorable to development." We can move to the analysis of specific components of a given culture at a given time and place. Thus, we find that, from 1945 to 1975, West German political culture underwent a striking transformation from being relatively authoritarian to becoming increasingly democratic and participant (Baker, Dalton, and Hildebrandt 1981). And we find that, from 1970 to 1993, the United States and a number of West European societies experienced a gradual intergenerational shift from having predominantly materialist toward increasingly postmaterialist value priorities (Abramson and Inglehart 1995). Though these changes have been gradual, they demonstrate that central elements of culture can and do change.

Furthermore, empirical research can help identify specific components of culture that are relevant to economic development. One need not seek to change a society's entire way of life. The present findings suggest that one specific dimension—achievement motivation—is highly relevant to economic growth rates. In the short run, to change even a relatively narrow and well-defined cultural component such as this is not easy, but it should be far easier than attempting to change an entire culture. Furthermore, empirical research demonstrates that culture can and does change. Simply making parents, schools and other organizations aware of the potentially relevant factors may be a step in the right direction.

We find that economic theory already is augmented with "social norms" and "cultural" factors (Cole, Malaith, and Postlewaite 1992; Elster 1989; Fershtman and Weiss 1993). Where would cultural values fit theoretically in growth models? The economics literature is replete with models of savings behavior that focus on the "life cycle" and, more specifically, the bequest motive. Cultural variables matter here. Since savings and investment behavior holds an important place in growth models, a determination of how cultural and motivational factors can be used to augment these existing economic models, it seems to us, is the next step to uncovering a better understanding of economic growth.[4]

In the end, however, these arguments can only be resolved on the empirical battlefield. We use ordinary least squares regression to test economic and cultural models of growth on a cross section of 25 countries. We find that economic and cultural factors affect growth. . . .

The results in this article demonstrate that *both* cultural and economic arguments matter. Neither supplants the other. Future theoretical and empirical work is better served by treating these "separate" explanations as complementary.

NOTES

1. The nations included in the multivariate analysis are: Austria, Belgium, Brazil, Canada, China, Denmark, Finland, France, Germany, Great Britain, India, Ireland, Italy, Japan, Korea, Mexico, Netherlands, Nigeria, Norway, South Africa, Spain, Sweden, Switzerland, Turkey, United States.

2. This is a check for spatial correlation between the errors of the cases.

3. In the post–World War II period, the life cycle model argues that since Japan and Germany had a substantial portion of their capital stock destroyed, the "permanent income" of the population was going to be less than was expected at the onset of the war. The lower capital-labor ratio contributes to lower real wages and higher interest rates. In response the public raised its savings rate to "smooth" its postretirement income. The United States, on the other hand, saw a significant increase in its capital stock as a result of the war. This had the opposite effect since the higher capital-labor ratio depresses interest rates and raises real wages. The public's savings rate falls in this case since "permanent income" increases, while current consumption rises.

4. Institutional factors such as regime type and property rights have also been suggested as important determinants of economic growth (Helliwell 1994; Leblang 1996).

REFERENCES

Abramson, Paul, and Ronald Inglehart. 1995. *Value Change in Global Perspective.* Ann Arbor: University of Michigan Press.

Achen, Christopher. 1982. *Interpreting and Using Regression.* Beverly Hills: Sage.

Alwin, Duane F. 1986. "Religion and Parental Child-Rearing Orientations: Evidence of a Catholic-Protestant Convergence." *American Journal of Sociology* 92:412–40.

Baker, Kendall L., Russell Dalton, and Kai Hildebrandt. 1981. *Germany Transformed* Cambridge: Harvard University Press.

Barro, Robert. 1991. "Economic Growth in a Cross Section of Countries." *Quarterly Journal of Economics* 106:407–44.

Bollen, Kenneth, and Robert Jackman. 1985. "Regression Diagnostics. An Expository Treatment of Outliers and Influential Cases." *Sociological Methods and Research* 13:510–42.

Chatterjee, S., and A. S. Hadi. 1988. *Sensitivity Analysis in Linear Regression.* New York: John Wiley.

Cole, Harold, George Malaith, and Andrew Postlewaite. 1992. "Social Norms, Savings Behavior, and Growth." *Journal of Political Economy* 100:1092–125.

Cook, R. D., and S. Weisberg. 1982. *Residuals* and *Influence in Regression.* London: Chapman and Hall.

Davidson, Ronald, and James MacKinnon. 1991. "Several Tests for Model Specification in the Presence of Alternative Hypotheses." *Econometrica* 49:781–93.

Elster, Jon. 1989. "Social Norms and Economic Theory." *Journal of Economic Perspectives* 3:99–117.

Fershtman, Chaim, and Yoram Weiss. 1993. "Social Status, Culture, and Economic Performance." *The Economic Journal* 103:946–59.

Fox, John. 1991. *Regression Diagnostics: An Introduction.* Sage University Paper on Quantitative Applications in the Social Sciences, 07-079. Newbury Park, CA: Sage.

Godfrey, Leslie. 1984. "On the Uses of Misspecification Checks and Tests of Non-nested Hypotheses in Empirical Econometrics." *Economic Journal* Supplement 96:69–81.

Granato, Jim, and Motoshi Suzuki. N.d. "The Use of the Encompassing Principle to Resolve Empirical Controversies in Voting Behavior: An Application to Voter Rationality in Congressional Elections." *Electoral Studies.* Forthcoming.

Hamilton, Lawrence. 1992. *Regression with Graphics: A Second Course in Applied Statistics.* Pacific Grove, CA: Brooks/Cole Publishing.

Harrison, Lawrence E. 1992. *Who Prospers? How Cultural Values Shape Economic and Political Success.* New York: Basic Books.

Helliwell, J. F. 1994. "Empirical Linkages Between Democracy and Growth." *British Journal of Political Science* 24:225–48.

Hendry, David, and Jean-Francois Richard. 1989. "Recent Developments in the Theory of Encompassing." In *Contributions to Operations Research and Econometrics: The XXth Anniversary of CORE,* ed. B. Cornet and H. Tulkens. Boston: MIT Press.

Inglehart, Ronald. 1971. "The Silent Revolution in Europe." *American Political Science Review* 4:991–1017.

Inglehart, Ronald. 1977. *The Silent Revolution: Changing Values and Political Styles.* Princeton: Princeton University Press.

Inglehart, Ronald. 1990. *Culture Shift in Advanced Industrial Society.* Princeton: Princeton University Press.

Jackman, Robert. 1987. "The Politics of Economic Growth in Industrialized Democracies, 1974–1980." *Journal of Politics* 49:242–56.

Leamer, Edward. 1983. "Let's Take the 'Con' Out of Econometrics." *American Economic Review* 73:31–43.

Leblang, David. 1996. "Property Rights, Democracy, and Economic Growth." *Political Research Quarterly* 49:5–26.

Lenski, Gerhard. 1963. *The Religious Factor.* New York: Anchor-Doubleday.

Levine, Ross, and David Renelt. 1992. "A Sensitivity Analysis of Cross-Country Growth Regressions." *American Economic Review* 82:942–63.

Lucas, Robert. 1988. "On the Mechanics of Economic Development." *Journal of Monetary Economics* 1:3–32.

Mankiw, N. Gregory, David Romer, and David Weil. 1992. "A Contribution to the Empirics of Economic Growth." *Quarterly Journal of Economics* 152:407–37.

McClelland, David. 1961. *The Achieving Society.* Princeton: Van Nostrand.

McClelland, David, et al. 1953. *The Achievement Motive.* New York: Appleton-Century-Crofts.

Mizon, Grayham, and Jean-Francois Richard. 1986. "The Encompassing Principle and Its Application to Non-nested Hypothesis Tests." *Econometrica* 54:657–78.

Mooney, Christopher, and Robert Duval. 1993. *Bootstrapping: A Nonparametric Approach to Statistical Inference.* Sage University Paper Series on Quantitative Applications in the Social Sciences, 07-095. Newbury Park, CA: Sage.

Romer, Paul. 1990. "Endogenous Technological Change." *Journal of Political Economy* 98:71–102.

Solow, Robert. 1956. "A Contribution to the Theory of Economic Growth." *Quarterly Journal of Economics* 70:65–94.

Stine, Robert. 1990. "An Introduction to Bootstrap Methods." *Sociological Methods and Research* 18:243–91.

Swan, Trevor. 1956. "Economic Growth and Capital Accumulation." *Economic Record* 22:334–61.

Tawney, Richard. 1926. *Religion and the Rise of Capitalism: A History.* Gloucester, MA: P. Smith.

Tawney, Richard. [1922] 1955. *The Acquisitive Society.* Reprint. New York: Harcourt Brace.

Welsch, Roy. 1980. "Regression Sensitivity Analysis and Bounded-Influence Estimation." In *Evaluation of Econometric Models*, ed. Jan Kmenta and James Ramsey. New York: Academic Press.

17

· · · · · · ·

Becoming Modern

· · · · · · ·

ALEX INKELES & DAVID H. SMITH

*This chapter reports on what is perhaps the most extensive investiga
tion ever undertaken to explore the psychocultural factors influencing
development. Using interview data from some 6,000 young men in six
developing countries (Argentina, Chile, India, Israel, Nigeria, and East
Pakistan), the authors and their fellow researchers devised an overall
measure of modernization they call their "OM scale." The characteristics of the "modern man" are described in the portions of their work
that follow; the interested reader may consult the original book for
the methodological details of the study. The authors discuss the
developmental implications of the presence or absence of such
modern men in a given society and argue that modern attitudes produce modern behaviors that are essential to development.
Moreover, without modern men, modern institutions are bound to fail.
In sum, for these researchers "underdevelopment is a state of mind."
The reader should compare the qualities of n Achievement discussed
by McClelland (Chapter 14) with the qualities of OM discussed in this
chapter. In what ways are they similar, and how persuasive is the
argument that attitudes are, as Inkeles and Smith state, "the essence
of national development itself"?*

The main purpose of economic development is to permit the achievement
of a decent level of living for all people, everywhere. But almost no one

Reprinted by permission of the publishers from Becoming *Modern: Individual
Change in Six Developing Countries* by Alex Inkeles and David H. Smith
(Cambridge, MA: Harvard University Press). Copyright © 1974 by the President
and Fellows of Harvard College.

will argue that the progress of a nation and a people should be measured solely in terms of gross national product and per capita income. Development assumes, as well, a high degree of political maturation, as expressed in stable and orderly processes of government resting on the expressed will of the people. And it also includes the attainment of popular education, the burgeoning of the arts, the efflorescence of architecture, the growth of the means of communication, and the enrichment of leisure. Indeed, in the end, development requires a transformation in the very nature of man, a transformation that is both a means to yet greater growth and at the same time one of the great ends of the development process.

We have described this transformation as the shift from traditionalism to individual modernity. The object of our research was to delineate the elements of such personal change, to measure its degree, to explain its causes, and to throw some light on its observed and probable future consequences. It is time for us to sum up the progress we made in that task, taking the opportunity, in so doing, to deal briefly with some of the issues we earlier may have left unresolved.

DEFINING AND MEASURING INDIVIDUAL MODERNITY

One who sets out to define and to measure individual modernity is like the animal trainer whose new act requires he learn to ride on the back of his tiger. He may emerge alive, but the chances are very great he will have been knocked about quite a bit in the process. Nevertheless, we accepted as a critical element in the structure of our whole intellectual and scientific enterprise the construction of a reliable, cross-national measure of individual modernity.

We do not claim to have invented the idea of the modern man. The concept was already there when we began our work, even though its content was vague. Inventing types of men has, after all, always been a fundamental preoccupation of sociologists: Karl Marx described the consciousness of the bourgeoisie and the proletariat; Robert Redfield defined the contrasting attributes of the folk and urban types; Everett V. Stonequist gave us the marginal man; David Riesman the inner-, outer-, and other-directed man. These "ideal types" people the pages of almost every well-known sociologist's work. Yet it has been the rare instance, indeed, in which any systematic attempt has been undertaken to measure whether there are real people in the world who, in their own persons, actually incorporate the qualities identified by these ideal types.[1] We were determined to break with this sociological tradition, and firmly committed ourselves to testing how far the set of qualities by which we defined the modern man actually cohered as a psychosocial syndrome in real men.

Our results provide definitive evidence that living individuals do indeed conform to our model of the modern man, that they do so in substantial numbers, and that essentially the same basic qualities which define a man as modern in one country and culture also delineate the modern man in other places. The modern man is not just a construct in the mind of sociological theorists. He exists and can be identified with fair reliability within any population where our test can be applied.

The modern man's character, as it emerges from our study, may be summed up under four major headings. He is an informed participant citizen; he has a marked sense of personal efficacy; he is highly independent and autonomous in his relations to traditional sources of influence, especially when he is making basic decisions about how to conduct his personal affairs; and he is ready for new experiences and ideas, that is, he is relatively open-minded and cognitively flexible.

As an informed participant citizen, the modern man identifies with the newer, larger entities of region and state, takes an interest in public affairs, national and international as well as local, joins organizations, keeps himself informed about major events in the news, and votes or otherwise takes some part in the political process. The modern man's sense of efficacy is reflected in his belief that, either alone or in concert with others, he may take actions which can affect the course of his life and that of his community; in his active efforts to improve his own condition and that of his family; and in his rejection of passivity, resignation, and fatalism toward the course of life's events. His independence of traditional sources of authority is manifested in public issues by his following the advice of public officials or trade-union leaders rather than priests and village elders, and in personal matters by his choosing the job and the bride he prefers even if his parents prefer some other position or some other person. The modern man's openness to new experience is reflected in his interest in technical innovation, his support of scientific exploration of hitherto sacred or taboo subjects, his readiness to meet strangers, and his willingness to allow women to take advantage of opportunities outside the confines of the household.

These *main* elements of individual modernity seem to have in common a thrust toward more instrumental kinds of attitudes and behavior. The more expressive and interpersonal aspects of overall modernization or OM syndrome tended to be less important, by and large, although still significantly involved in the syndrome. This fits well with the relative emphasis on new and more effective ways of doing things as central to the modernization process, with changes in ways of relating to other people coming largely as side effects. The Japanese case is a good example of how the instrumental aspects of OM can be present with, we would judge, many fewer of the expressive elements.

Although these are the principal components, they by no means exhaust the list of qualities which cohere as part of the modernity syndrome. The modern man is also different in his approach to time, to personal and social planning, to the rights of persons dependent on or subordinate to him, and to the use of formal rules as a basis for running things. In other words, psychological modernity emerges as a quite complex, multifaceted, and multidimensional syndrome. . . .

Considering that the modernization process seems to work so consistently in so many different cultural settings, is there then no choice? Must everyone become modern, and to the same degree?

This issue seems to generate the greatest misunderstanding, and satisfying people with regard to it is most difficult. Dispassionate discussion becomes overshadowed by lurid images of modern science turning out a race of automatons, machine-produced golems who are as uniform and unfeeling as are the products of Detroit's massive assembly lines.

Our image of man's nature is not that of a sponge which must soak up everything with which it comes in contact. In our view individual change toward modernization is a process of interaction between the individual and his social setting. Quite contrary to the conception of men as putty passively taking on whatever shape their environment imposes on them, we see the process of individual modernization as one requiring a basic personal engagement between the individual and his milieu. In this engagement the individual must first selectively perceive the lessons the environment has to teach, and then must willingly undertake to learn them, before any personal change can come about.

If the qualities of industrial organization are truly alien to a man, he will not incorporate them. Moreover, even if he finds an organization to be unthreatening or, better, congenial, a man will not necessarily learn new ways unless he personally has the readiness and the capacity to learn. And even if the environment is benign and the individuals are ready to learn, the process will not work if the environment itself is confusing and the messages it conveys are unclear or even contradictory.

In brief, if the process of modernization were at all like the situation described in Aldous Huxley's *Brave New World,* the outcome of our study should have yielded a perfect correlation rather than the much more modest figure it attained. Moreover, *all* the men in our samples should have changed, and all should have become completely modern in short order. Instead, as we know, many did not change at all and most only changed to some degree, so that after years of exposure to the modernizing influences only a modest proportion qualified as truly modern. And these, like all others, became modern with some degree of selectivity, changing fully in some respects but holding to divergent and even traditional views in others.
. . .

THE SOCIAL SIGNIFICANCE
OF INDIVIDUAL MODERNIZATION

To a social psychologist, it is gratifying, indeed it is an activity sufficient unto itself, to be able to measure individual modernity, and to show how far and in what ways schooling and jobs bring about increased modernity scores. But the more pragmatic among our readers, and not only those from the developing countries, are likely to ask: "Is this purely an academic exercise? In particular, does it have any practical contribution to make to national development?: Are not attitude and value changes rather ephemeral and peripheral? Can you give us any evidence that all this has much to do with the real problem of underdevelopment?"

In response, we affirm that our research has produced ample evidence that the attitude and value changes defining individual modernity are accompanied by changes in behavior precisely of the sort which we believe give meaning to, and support, those changes in political and economic institutions which lead to the modernization of nations.

We were able to document most extensively those behavioral changes accompanying attitudinal modernization in the realm of political and civic action. The modern man more often took an interest in political affairs, he kept informed and could identify important political events and personalities, he often contacted governmental and political agencies, more often joined organizations, more often voted—and all these by large margins. He was in every way a more active participant citizen of his society.[2]

It seems obvious to us that these are precisely the qualities one needs in the citizen of a modern polity. The introduction of modern political institutions imported from outside, or imposed from above by elites, tends to be an empty gesture unless there are active, interested, informed citizens who can make the institutions really work. And, as we have seen, such citizens are the more modern men shaped by the modernizing institutions we have identified, namely, the school, the newspaper, and the factory.

Beyond politics, the modern man showed himself to perform differently from the more traditional man in many realms of action having practical bearing on the process of societal modernization. The more modern man is quicker to adopt technical innovation, and more ready to implement birth-control measures; he urges his son to go as far as he can in school, and, if it pays better, encourages him to accept industrial work rather than to follow the more traditional penchant for office jobs; he informs himself about the goods produced in the more modern sector of the economy, and makes an effort to acquire them; and he permits his wife and daughter to leave the home for more active participation in economic life. In these and a host of other ways, only some of which we have documented, the man who is more modern in attitude and values acts to support modern institutions and to facilitate the general modernization of society.

While it was important to show that men who were more modern in attitude and value also acted in more modern ways, we feel it even more important to challenge the assumption that a "mere" change in attitudes and values cannot in itself be a truly important factor in the process of national development.

In saying this we are not espousing some form of naive psychological determinism. We are not unaware that a modern psychology cannot alone make a nation modern. We fully understand that to be modern a nation must have modern institutions, effective government, efficient production, and adequate social services. And we recognize full well that there may be structural obstacles to such development stemming not only from nature, but from social, political, and economic causes as well. Narrow class interests, colonial oppression, rapacious great powers, international cartels, domestic monopolies, archaic and corrupted governments, tribal antagonisms, and religious and ethnic prejudices, to name but a few, are among the many objective forces which we know may act to impede modernization.

Nevertheless, we believe a change in attitudes and values to be one of the most essential preconditions for substantial and effective functioning of those modern institutions which most of the more "practical" programs of development hope to establish. Our experience leads us to agree with many of the intellectual leaders of the Third World who argue that, in good part, underdevelopment is a state of mind.[3] It is admittedly difficult with presently available techniques and information to establish the case scientifically, but we are convinced that mental barriers and psychic factors are key obstacles to more effective economic and social development in many countries.

The technology which is, perhaps, the most distinctive ingredient of modernity can be borrowed by and established in developing countries with relative ease. Machinery is influenced by temperature and humidity, but it is otherwise immune to culture shock. Although they travel less well, political, economic, and cultural institutions can also be relatively easily imitated in their totality. Systems of taxation and of voter registration, and even political party systems, are regularly copied from the more advanced countries by those in the earlier stages of development. Patterns of factory management, forms of administration for business and government, new faculties, research institutions, indeed whole universities are being created every day in the developing countries as copies of institutions and procedures originating in the more developed countries.

How many of these transplanted institutions actually take root and bear fruit in their new setting is not precisely known. But the experience of almost everyone who has worked extensively on problems of development is replete with examples of the failure of such transplantation. The disappointment of high hopes and aspirations is endemic among those who have attempted such transplanting, and the hollow shells of the institutions, sometimes transformed into grotesque caricatures of their original design, sometimes barely functioning, often standing altogether abandoned, can be found strewn about in almost any developing country in which one chooses to travel.

In the explanations which are offered for this situation, one hears again and again the echo of one basic refrain: "The people were not ready for it yet." When one probes this generalization, it quickly becomes apparent that the material resources, the manuals for repair and maintenance, the charts and tables for organization, and the guidelines for administration which accompanied the transplanted institutions were meaningless without the support of an underlying and widespread pattern of culture and personality which could breathe life into the otherwise sterile forms and give human meaning and continuity to their activity.

In the last analysis, the successful functioning of these institutions was critically dependent on the availability of individuals who could bring to the job certain special personal qualities. These new institutions required people who could accept and discharge responsibility without constant close supervision, could manifest mutual trust and confidence in co-workers which extended beyond the situations in which one could keep them under direct surveillance, could subordinate the special interests of one's clique or parochial group to the goals of the larger organization, could be flexible and imaginative in the interpretation of rules, could show sympathetic consideration for the feelings of subordinates and openness to their ideas and other potential contributions. These, and a host of other personal qualities requisite to running a complex modern institution effectively, are not in excess supply in any society. In many of the developing countries, moreover, people possessed of the requisite qualities are actually scarce. And in some cases, the small set of individuals who possess the qualities necessary for effectively running the new institutions are either not called upon, or may even be socially ineligible, for service in those roles in which they could be most useful.

Such conditions in the institutions of national standing have their precise analogue in the more commonplace situation of individuals engaged in very modest pursuits, within purely local and parochial settings. In such settings we find most widely diffused the qualities our research has identified as characteristic of the traditional man: passive acceptance of fate and a general lack of efficacy; fear of innovation and distrust of the new; isolation from the outside world and lack of interest in what goes on in it; dependence on traditional authority and the received wisdom of elders and religious and customary leaders; preoccupation with personal and especially family affairs to the exclusion of community concerns; exclusive identification with purely local and parochial primary groups, coupled to feelings of isolation from and fear of larger regional and national entities; the shaping and damping of ambition to fit narrow goals, and the cultivation of humble sentiments of gratitude for what little one has; rigid, hierarchical relations with subordinates and others of low social status; and undervaluing of education, learning, research, and other concerns not obviously related to the practical business of earning one's daily bread.

Of course, not all these qualities are prevalent in all traditional settings, and they are unequally distributed among the men in them. Yet they are extremely common in individuals, and exceptionally pervasive across cultures and settings, in the countries of the less-developed world.

We must acknowledge that some of these qualities of the traditional man facilitate his adaptation to life. Such qualities help men to make a successful adjustment to the real conditions which exist in, and indeed pervade, their life space. But those qualities also tend to freeze people into the situations and positions in which they find themselves, and this, in turn, serves to preserve the outmoded, indeed archaic, and often oppressive institutions which hold the people in their grip. To break out of that iron grip requires, among other things, that people become modern in spirit, that they adopt and incorporate into their personalities the attitudes, values, and modes of acting which we have identified with the modern man. Without this ingredient neither foreign aid nor domestic revolution can hope successfully to bring an underdeveloped nation into the ranks of those capable of self-sustained growth.

Economists define modernity in terms of gross national product per capita, and political scientists in terms of effective institutions for governance. We are of the opinion that neither rapid economic growth nor effective government can develop, or, if introduced, will be long sustained, without the widespread diffusion in the rank and file of the population of those qualities we have identified as those of the modern man. In the conditions of the contemporary world, the qualities of individual modernity are not a luxury, they are a necessity. They are not a marginal gain, derived from the process of institutional modernization, but are rather a precondition for the long-term success of those institutions. Diffusion through the population of the qualities of the modern man is not incidental to the process of social development; it is the essence of national development itself.

NOTES

1. There are, of course, some notable exceptions. The most important early example was the effort by Gordon Allport to test Spranger's belief that men could be classified according to the predominance in their personality of "theoretical," "religious," "social," or "economic-and-political" values. See Gordon Allport, Philip Vernon, and Gardner Lindzey, *Study of Values: A Scale for Measuring the Dominant Interests in Personality*, 3rd ed. (Boston: Houghton-Mifflin, 1959). Probably the best-known and most widely studied syndrome is that first proposed by Erich Fromm under the rubric "the authoritarian personality" in *Escape from Freedom* (New York: Farrar and Rinehart, 1941) and later built into the famous "F scale." See Theodor W. Adorno et al., *The Authoritarian Personality* (New York: Harper, 1950).

2. The evidence concerning these differences in political behavior is built into the OM scale, and may be observed by checking the list of questions in Appendix

A. [Not reproduced here—*Ed.*] A full account of the 39 items dealing with political orientations and behavior covered by our questionnaire, the scales those items yielded, and their relation to the independent variables is given in Alex Inkeles, "Participant Citizenship in Six Developing Countries," *American Political Science Review,* 63 (December 1969):1120–1141.

    3. In his unpublished contribution to the conference on Alternatives in Development sponsored by the Vienna Institute of Development in June 1971, Dr. Salazar Bondy, a leading intellectual of Peru, wrote as follows: "Underdevelopment is not just a collection of statistical indices which enable a socio-economic picture to be drawn. It is also a state of mind, a way of expression, a form of outlook and a collective personality marked by chronic infirmities and forms of maladjustment."

18

· · · · · · ·

The Confucian Ethic
and Economic Growth

· · · · · · ·

HERMAN KAHN

The most recent theory on the cultural origins of economic growth derives from the observation that a group of countries that have made spectacular strides since World War II (e.g., Japan, South Korea, Taiwan) are Confucian societies. Until his recent death, Herman Kahn was director of the Hudson Institute think tank and was well known as a futurist. In this contribution, Kahn says that much of the success of these nations can be attributed directly to their cultures. It is interesting to compare the attributes of Confucianism that Kahn suggests are important for development with the attributes of n Achievement and OM discussed in Chapters 14 and 17. It is also worth considering the implication of Kahn's argument for those nations in Latin America, Africa, and elsewhere that have dramatically different traditions. Has the absence of a "Confucian ethic" held back the development of these nations? If so, is it likely to make closing the gap between them and the developed nations an impossible dream?

Most readers of this book are familiar with the argument of Max Weber that the Protestant ethic was extremely useful in promoting the rise and spread of modernization.[1] Most readers, however, will be much less familiar with the notion that has gradually emerged in the last two decades that societies based upon the Confucian ethic may in many ways be superior to the West in the pursuit of industrialization, affluence, and modernization. Let us see what some of the strengths of the Confucian ethic are in the modern world.

Reprinted with permission from Mrs. Jane Kahn. *World Economic Development: 1979 and Beyond,* by Herman Kahn (Boulder, CO: Westview Press, 1979).

THE CONFUCIAN ETHIC

The Confucian ethic includes two quite different but connected sets of issues. First and perhaps foremost, Confucian societies uniformly promote in the individual and the family sobriety, a high value on education, a desire for accomplishment in various skills (particularly academic and cultural), and seriousness about tasks, job, family, and obligations. A properly trained member of a Confucian culture will be hard working, responsible, skillful, and (within the assigned or understood limits) ambitious and creative in helping the group (extended family, community, or company). There is much less emphasis on advancing individual (selfish) interests.

In some ways, the capacity for purposive and efficient communal and organizational activities and efforts is even more important in the modern world than the personal qualities, although both are important. Smoothly fitting, harmonious human relations in an organization are greatly encouraged in most neo-Confucian societies. This is partly because of a sense of hierarchy but even more because of a sense of complementarity of relations that is much stronger in Confucian than in Western societies.

The anthropologist Chie Nakane has pointed out that in Western societies there is a great tendency for "like to join like" in unions, student federations, women's groups, men's clubs, youth movements, economic classes, and so on.[2] This tends to set one group in society against another: students against teachers, employees against employers, youths against parents, and so on. In the Confucian hierarchic society, the emphasis is on cooperation among complementary elements, much as in the family (which is in fact the usual paradigm or model in a Confucian culture). The husband and wife work together and cooperate in raising the children; each has different assigned duties and responsibilities, as do the older and younger siblings and the grandparents. There is emphasis on fairness and equity, but it is fairness and equity in the institutional context, not for the individual as an individual. Synergism—complementarity and cooperation among parts of a whole—are emphasized, not equality and interchangeability. The major identification is with one's role in the organization or other institutional structure, whether it be the family, the business firm, or a bureau in the government.

Since the crucial issues in a modern society increasingly revolve around these equity issues and on making organizations work well, the neo-Confucian cultures have great advantages. As opposed to the earlier Protestant ethic, the modern Confucian ethic is superbly designed to create and foster loyalty, dedication, responsibility, and commitment and to intensify identification with the organization and one's role in the organization. All this makes the economy and society operate much more smoothly than one whose principles of identification and association tend to lead to egalitarianism, to disunity, to confrontation, and to excessive compensation or repression.

A society that emphasizes a like-to-like type of identification works out reasonably well as long as there is enough hierarchy, discipline, control, or motivation within the society to restrain excessive tendencies to egalitarianism, anarchy, self-indulgence, and so on. But as the society becomes more affluent and secular, there is less motivation, reduced commitment, more privatization, and increasingly impersonal and automatic welfare. Interest in group politics, group and individual selfishness, egoism, intergroup antagonisms, and perhaps even intergroup warfare all tend to increase. It becomes the old versus the young, insiders versus outsiders, men versus women, students versus teachers, and—most important of all—employees against employers. The tendencies toward anarchy, rivalry, and payoffs to the politically powerful or the organized militants become excessive and out of control.

For all these reasons we believe that both aspects of the Confucian ethic—the creation of dedicated, motivated, responsible, and educated individuals and the enhanced sense of commitment, organizational identity, and loyalty to various institutions—will result in all the neo-Confucian societies having at least potentially higher growth rates than other cultures. . . .

Whether or not one accepts our analysis of *why* neo-Confucian cultures are so competent in industrialization, the impressive data that support the final thesis are overwhelming. The performance of the People's Republic of China; of both North and South Korea; of Japan, Taiwan, Hong Kong, and Singapore; and of the various Chinese ethnic groups in Malaysia, Thailand, Indonesia, and the Philippines, discloses extraordinary talent (at least in the last twenty-five years) for economic development and for learning about and using modern technology. For example, the North Vietnamese operated one of the most complicated air defense networks in history more or less by themselves (once instructed by the Soviets), and the American army found that the South Vietnamese, if properly motivated, often went through training school in about half the time required by Americans. We do not gloss over the enormous differences among these neo-Confucian cultures. They vary almost as much as do European cultures. But all of them seem amenable to modernization under current conditions.

NOTES

1. Max Weber, *The Protestant Ethic and the Spirit of Capitalism,* translated by Talcott Parsons (New York: Charles Scribner's Sons, 1930).
2. Chie Nakane, *Japanese Society* (Berkeley, Calif.: University of California Press, 1970).

19

·······

The Culture of Poverty

·······

OSCAR LEWIS

The work of anthropologist Oscar Lewis has been distinctive in development literature. His studies tell fascinating stories of individual and family life in places like Cuba, Mexico, and Puerto Rico. So interesting have been Lewis's descriptions of the lives of families in the developing world struggling against the odds that filmmakers put The Children of Sanchez *on the big screen. From these tales Oscar Lewis not only drew a picture of life among the poor but began to describe what he called the culture of poverty. The culture of poverty involves more than economic deprivation; it is a subculture with its own way of life, structure, and rules. According to Lewis, the culture of poverty is passed down from one generation to the next as a set of adaptive mechanisms to provide solutions to problems not resolved by the existing institutions of society. In this chapter, Lewis discusses the conditions that give rise to the culture of poverty and the impact it has on individuals and on the societies in which they live.*

Although a great deal has been written about poverty and the poor, . . . I first suggested [the concept of a culture of poverty] in 1959 in my book *Five Families: Mexican Case Studies in the Culture of Poverty. . . .*

Throughout recorded history, in literature, in proverbs, and in popular sayings, we find two opposite evaluations of the nature of the poor. Some characterize the poor as blessed, virtuous, upright, serene, independent, honest, kind, and happy. Others characterize them as evil, mean, violent, sordid, and criminal. These contradictory and confusing evaluations are also reflected in the in-fighting that is going on in the current war against poverty. Some stress the great potential of the poor for self-help, leadership, and community organization, while others point to the sometimes irreversible destructive effect of poverty upon individual character, and therefore emphasize the need for guidance and control to remain in the hands of the middle class, which presumably has better mental health.

These opposing views reflect a political power struggle between competing groups. However, some of the confusion results from the failure to distinguish between poverty *per se* and the culture of poverty, and from the tendency to focus upon the individual personality rather than upon the group—that is, the family and the slum community.

As an anthropologist I have tried to understand poverty and its associated traits as a culture or, more accurately, as a subculture[1] with its own structure and rationale, as a way of life which is passed down from generation to generation along family lines. This view directs attention to the fact that the culture of poverty in modern nations is not only a matter of economic deprivation, of disorganization, or of the absence of something. It is also something positive and provides some rewards without which the poor could hardly carry on.

Elsewhere I have suggested that the culture of poverty transcends regional, rural-urban, and national differences and shows remarkable similarities in family structure, interpersonal relations, time orientation, value systems, and spending patterns.[2] These cross-national similarities are examples of independent invention and convergence. They are common adaptations to common problems.

The culture of poverty can come into being in a variety of historical contexts. However, it tends to grow and flourish in societies with the following set of conditions: (1) a cash economy, wage labor, and production for profit; (2) a persistently high rate of unemployment and underemployment for unskilled labor; (3) low wages; (4) the failure to provide social, political, and economic organization, either on a voluntary basis or by government imposition, for the low-income population; (5) the existence of a bilateral kinship system rather than a unilateral one; and finally, (6) the existence of a set of values in the dominant class which stresses the accumulation of wealth and property, the possibility of upward mobility, and thrift, and explains low economic status as the result of personal inadequacy or inferiority.

The way of life which develops among some of the poor under these conditions is the culture of poverty. It can best be studied in urban or rural slums and can be described in terms of some seventy interrelated social, economic, and psychological traits. However, the number of traits and the relationships between them may vary from society to society and from family to family. For example, in a highly literate society, illiteracy may be more diagnostic of the culture of poverty than in a society where illiteracy is widespread and where even the well-to-do may be illiterate, as in some Mexican peasant villages before the Revolution.

The culture of poverty is both an adaptation and a reaction of the poor to their marginal position in a class-stratified, highly individuated, capitalistic society. It represents an effort to cope with feelings of hopelessness and despair which develop from the realization of the improbability of achieving success in terms of the values and goals of the larger society. Indeed, many of the traits of the culture of poverty can be viewed as attempts at local solutions for problems not met by existing institutions and agencies because the people are not eligible for them, cannot afford them, or are ignorant or suspicious of them. For example, unable to obtain credit from banks, they are thrown upon their own resources and organize informal credit devices without interest.

The culture of poverty, however, is not only an adaptation to a set objective conditions of the larger society. Once it comes into existence, it tends to perpetuate itself from generation to generation because of its effect on the children. By the time slum children are six or seven years old, they usually have absorbed the basic values and attitudes of their subculture and are not psychologically geared to take full advantage of changing conditions or increased opportunities which may occur in their lifetime.

Most frequently the culture of poverty develops when a stratified social and economic system is breaking down or is being replaced by another as in the case of the transition from feudalism to capitalism or during periods of rapid technological change. Often it results from imperial conquest in which the native social and economic structure is smashed and the natives are maintained in a servile colonial status, sometimes for many generations. It can also occur in the process of detribalization such as that now going on in Africa.

The most likely candidates for the culture of poverty are the people who come from the lower strata of a rapidly changing society and are already partially alienated from it. Thus, landless rural workers who migrate to the cities can be expected to develop a culture of poverty much more readily than migrants from stable peasant villages with a well-organized traditional culture. In this connection there is a striking contrast between Latin America, where the rural population long ago made the transition from a tribal to a peasant society, and Africa, which is still close to its tribal heritage. The more corporate nature of many of the African tribal societies, in contrast to Latin American rural communities, and the persistence of village ties tend to inhibit or delay the formation of a full-blown culture of poverty in many of the African towns and cities. The special conditions of apartheid in South Africa, where the migrants are segregated into separate "locations" and do not enjoy freedom of movement, create special problems. Here, the institutionalization of repression and discrimination tends to develop a greater sense of identity and group consciousness.

The culture of poverty is studied from various points of view: the relationship between the subculture and the larger society; the nature of the slum community; the nature of the family; and the attitudes, values, and character structure of the individual.

1. The lack of effective participation and integration of the poor in the major institutions of the larger society is one of the crucial characteristics of the culture of poverty. This is a complex matter and results from a variety of factors which may include lack of economic resources, segregation and discrimination, fear, suspicion, or apathy, and the development of local solutions for problems. However, participation in some of the institutions of the larger society—for example, in the jails, the army, and the public-relief system—does not *per se* eliminate the traits of the culture of poverty. In the case of a relief system which barely keeps people alive, both the basic poverty and the sense of hopelessness are perpetuated rather than eliminated.

Low wages, chronic unemployment, and underemployment lead to low income, lack of property ownership, absence of savings, absence of food reserves in the home, and a chronic shortage of cash. These conditions reduce the possibility of effective participation in the larger economic system. And as a response to these conditions, we find in the culture of poverty a high incidence of pawning of personal goods, borrowing from local money lenders at usurious rates of interest, spontaneous informal credit devices organized by neighbors, the use of second-hand clothing and furniture, and the pattern of frequent buying of small quantities of food many times a day as the need arises.

People with a culture of poverty produce very little wealth and receive little in return. They have a low level of literacy and education, do not belong to labor unions, are not members of political parties, generally do not participate in the national welfare agencies, and make very little use of banks, hospitals, department stores, museums, or art galleries. They have a critical attitude toward some of the basic institutions of the dominant classes, hatred of the police, mistrust of government and those in high position, and a cynicism which extends even to the church. This gives the culture of poverty a high potential for protest and for being used in political movements aimed against the existing social order.

People with a culture of poverty are aware of middle-class values, talk about them, and even claim some of them as their own; but on the whole, they do not live by them.[3] Thus it is important to distinguish between what they say and what they do. For example, many will tell you that marriage by law, by the church, or by both, is the ideal form of marriage; but few will marry. For men who have no steady jobs or other source of income, who do not own property and have no wealth to pass on to their children, who are present-time oriented and who want to avoid the expense and legal difficulties involved in formal marriage and divorce, free union or consensual marriage makes a lot of sense. Women will often turn down offers of marriage because they feel that marriage ties them down to men who are immature, punishing, and generally unreliable. Women feel that consensual union gives them a better break; it gives them some of the freedom and flexibility that men have. By not giving the fathers of their children legal status as husbands, the women have a stronger claim on their children if they decide to leave their men. It also gives women exclusive rights to a house or any other property they may own.

2. In describing the culture of poverty on the local community level, we find poor housing conditions, crowding, gregariousness, but above all, a minimum of organization beyond the level of the nuclear and extended family. Occasionally there are informal temporary groupings or voluntary associations within slums. The existence of neighborhood gangs which cut across slum settlements represents a considerable advance beyond the zero point of the continuum that I have in mind. Indeed, it is the low level of organization which gives the culture of poverty its marginal and anachronistic quality in our highly complex, specialized, organized society. Most primitive peoples have achieved a higher level of socio-cultural organization than our modern urban slum dwellers. . . .

3. On the family level the major traits of the culture of poverty are the absence of childhood as a specially prolonged and protected stage in the life cycle, early initiation into sex, free unions or consensual marriages, a relatively high incidence of the abandonment of wives and children, a trend toward female- or mother-centered families and consequently a much greater knowledge of maternal relatives, a strong predisposition to authoritarianism, lack of privacy, verbal emphasis upon family solidarity, which is only rarely achieved because of sibling rivalry, and competition for limited goods and maternal affection.

4. On the level of the individual, the major characteristics are a strong feeling of marginality, of helplessness, of dependence, and of inferiority. I found this to be true of slum dwellers in Mexico City and San Juan among families that do not constitute a distinct ethnic or racial group and that do not suffer from racial discrimination. In the United States, of course, the culture of poverty of the Negroes has the additional disadvantage of racial discrimination; but as I have already suggested, this additional disadvantage contains a great potential for revolutionary protest and organization which seems to be absent in the slums of Mexico City or among the poor whites in the South.

Other traits include a high incidence of maternal deprivation, orality, weak ego structure, confusion of sexual identification, a lack of impulse control, a strong present-time orientation with relatively little ability to defer gratification and to plan for the future, a sense of resignation and fatalism, a widespread belief in male superiority, and a high tolerance for psychological pathology of all sorts.

People with a culture of poverty are provincial and locally oriented and have very little sense of history. They know only their own troubles, their own local conditions, their own neighborhood, their own way of life. Usually they do not have the knowledge, the vision, or the ideology to see the similarities between their problems and those of their counterparts elsewhere in the world. They are not class conscious although they are very sensitive indeed to status distinctions. . . .

I have not yet worked out a system of weighing each of the traits, but this could probably be done and a scale could be set up for many of the traits. Traits that reflect lack of participation in the institutions of the larger society or an outright rejection—in practice, if not in theory—would be the crucial traits; for example, illiteracy, provincialism, free unions, abandonment of women and children, lack of membership in voluntary associations beyond the extended family.

When the poor become class conscious or active members of trade-union organizations or when they adopt an internationalist outlook on the world, they are no longer part of the culture of poverty although they may still be desperately poor. Any movement, be it religious, pacifist, or revolutionary, which organizes and gives hope to the poor and which effectively promotes solidarity and a sense of identification with larger groups, destroys the psychological and social core of the culture of poverty. In this connection, I suspect that the civil-rights movement among the Negroes in the United States has done more to improve their self-image and self-respect than have their economic advances although, without a doubt, the two are mutually reinforcing.

The distinction between poverty and the culture of poverty is basic to the model described here. There are degrees of poverty and many kinds of poor people. The culture of poverty refers to one way of life shared by poor people in given historical and social contexts. The economic traits which I have listed for the culture of poverty are necessary but not sufficient to define the phenomena I have in mind. There are a number of historical examples of very poor segments of the population which do not have a way of life that I would describe as a subculture of poverty. Here I should like to give four examples:

a) Many of the primitive or preliterate peoples studied by anthropologists suffer from dire poverty which is the result of poor technology and/or poor natural resources or both, but they do not have the traits of the subculture of poverty. Indeed, they do not constitute a subculture because their societies are not highly stratified. In spite of their poverty, they have a relatively integrated, satisfying, and self-sufficient culture. Even the simplest food-gathering and hunting tribes have a considerable amount of organization—bands and band chiefs, tribal councils, and local self-government—elements which are not found in the culture of poverty.

b) In India the lower castes (the *Camars* or leatherworkers, and the *Bhangis* or sweepers) may be desperately poor both in the villages and in the cities, but most of them are integrated into the larger society and have their own *panchayat* organizations which cut across village lines and give them a considerable amount of power.[4] In addition to the caste system, which gives individuals a sense of identity and belonging, there is still another factor, the clan system. Wherever there are unilateral kinship systems or clans, one would not expect to find the culture of poverty because a clan system gives people a sense of belonging to a corporate body which has a history and a life of its own and therefore provides a sense of continuity, a sense of a past and of a future.

c) The Jews of Eastern Europe were very poor but they did not have many of the traits of the culture of poverty because of their tradition of literacy, the great value placed upon learning, the organization of the community around the rabbi, the proliferation of local voluntary associations, and their religion, which taught that they were the chosen people.

d) My fourth example is speculative and relates to socialism. On the basis of my limited experience in one socialist country—Cuba— and on the basis of my reading, I am inclined to believe that the culture of poverty does not exist in the socialist countries. I first went to Cuba in 1947 as a visiting professor for the State Department. At that time I began a study of a sugar plantation in Melena del Sur and of a slum in Havana. After the Castro Revolution I made my second trip to Cuba as a correspondent for a major magazine, and I revisited the same slum and some of the same families. The physical aspect of the slum had changed very little, except for a beautiful new nursery school. It was clear that the people were still desperately poor, but I found much less of the feelings of despair, apathy, and hopelessness which are so diagnostic of urban slums in the culture of poverty. They expressed great confidence in their leaders and hope for a better life in the future. The slum itself was now highly organized, with block committees, educational committees, party committees. The people had a new sense of power and importance. They were armed and were given a doctrine which glorified the lower class as the hope of humanity. (I was told by one Cuban official that they had practically eliminated delinquency by giving arms to the delinquents!)

It is my impression that the Castro regime, unlike Marx and Engels, did not write off the so-called lumpen proletariat as an inherently reactionary and anti-revolutionary force, but rather saw their revolutionary potential and tried to utilize it. In this connection, Frantz Fanon makes a similar evaluation of the role of the lumpen proletariat based upon his experience in the Algerian struggle for independence. In *The Wretched of the Earth* he writes:

> It is within this mass of humanity, this people of the shanty towns, at the core of the lumpen proletariat, that the rebellion will find its urban spearhead. For the lumpen-proletariat, that horde of starving men, uprooted from their tribe and from their clan, constitutes one of the most spontaneous and most radically revolutionary forces of a colonized people.[5]

My own studies of the urban poor in the slums of San Juan do not support the generalizations of Fanon. I have found little revolutionary spirit or radical ideology among low-income Puerto Ricans. On the contrary, most of the families I studied were quite conservative politically and about half of them were in favor of the Statehood Republican Party. It seems to me that the revolutionary potential of people with a culture of poverty will vary considerably according to the national context and the particular historical circumstances. In a country like Algeria, which was fighting for its independence, the lumpen proletariat were drawn into the struggle and became a vital force. However, in countries like Puerto Rico, in which the movement for independence has very little mass support, and in countries like Mexico, which have achieved their independence a long time ago and are now in their post-Revolutionary period, the lumpen proletariat is not a leading source of rebellion or of revolutionary spirit.

In effect, we find that in primitive societies, and in caste societies, the culture of poverty does not develop. In socialist, fascist, and highly developed capitalist societies with a welfare state, the culture of poverty tends to decline. I suspect that the culture of poverty flourishes in, and is generic to, the early free enterprise stage of capitalism and that it is also endemic in colonialism. . . .

NOTES

1. Although the term "subculture of poverty" is technically more accurate, I sometimes use "culture of poverty" as a shorter form.
2. Oscar Lewis, *Five Families: Mexican Case Studies in the Culture of Poverty* (New York: Basic Books, 1959).
3. In terms of Hyman Rodman's concept of "The Lower-Class Value Stretch" (*Social Forces,* vol. 42, No. 2 [December 1963], pp. 205–15), I would say that the culture of poverty exists where this value stretch is at a minimum, that is, where the belief in middle-class values is at a minimum.
4. It may be that in the slums of Calcutta and Bombay an incipient culture of poverty is developing. It would be highly desirable to do family studies there as a crucial test of the culture-of-poverty hypothesis.
5. New York: Grove, 1965, p. 103.

20

·······

Underdevelopment Is a
State of Mind

·······

LAWRENCE E. HARRISON

After twenty years of working for the United States Agency for International Development (USAID), Lawrence Harrison has concluded that Latin America's culture explains its lack of development. As should be clear by now, the cultural approach blames the poor for their poverty. According to Harrison, Latin Americans have become so preoccupied with a belief in the self-defeating "myths" of dependency and imperialism that they are paralyzed to the point that they do not use the resources they have to develop. At its heart, the process of development is one of human creative capacity, the ability to imagine, conceptualize, and so on. If a country is to tap the creative energy of its people, the government must establish an environment that encourages and uses all of its people's abilities.

WHAT MAKES DEVELOPMENT HAPPEN?

Development, most simply, is improvement in human well-being.[1] Most people today aspire to higher standards of living, longer lives, and fewer health problems; education for themselves and their children that will increase their earning capacity and leave them more in control of their lives; a measure of stability and tranquility; and the opportunity to do the

Table 20.1   (Gap in Well-Being, Low-Income and Industrialized Countries)

	Low-Income Countries	Industrialized Countries
Total population (mid-1980)	2.2 billion	671 million
Annual average population growth rate (1970–80)	2.1 percent	.8 percent
Average per capita gross national product (1980)	$260	$10,320
Average life expectancy at birth (1980)	57 years	74 years
Average adult literacy (1977)	50 percent	99 percent

things that give them pleasure and satisfaction. A small minority will take exception to one or more of these aspirations. Some others may wish to add one or more. For the purposes of this chapter, however, I think the list is adequate.

The enormous gap in well-being between the low-income and the industrialized countries is apparent from the above summary table, the source of which is the World Bank's *World Development Report* 1982. . . .

What explains the gap? What have the industrialized countries done that the low-income countries have not? Why was the Marshall Plan a monumental success, the Alliance for Progress much less successful? What makes development happen or not happen?

There are those who will say that what the industrialized countries have done that the low-income countries have not is to exploit the low-income countries; that development is a zero-sum game; that the rich countries are rich because the poor countries are poor. This is doctrine for Marxist-Leninists and it has wide currency throughout the Third World. To be sure, colonial powers often did derive great economic advantage from their colonies, and U.S. companies have made a lot of money in Latin America and elsewhere in the Third World, particularly during the first half of this century. But the almost exclusive focus on "imperialism" and "dependency" to explain underdevelopment has encouraged the evolution of a paralyzing and self-defeating mythology. The thesis of this chapter is in diametrical contrast. It looks inward rather than outward to explain a society's condition.

I believe that the creative capacity of human beings is at the heart of the development process. What makes development happen is our ability to imagine, theorize, conceptualize, experiment, invent, articulate, organize, manage, solve problems, and do a hundred other things with our minds and hands that contribute to the progress of the individual and of human-kind. Natural resources, climate, geography, history, market size, governmental policies, and many other factors influence the direction and pace of progress. But the engine is human creative capacity.

The economist Joseph Schumpeter (1883–1950) singled out the entrepreneurial geniuses—the Henry Fords of the world—as the real creators of wealth and progress, as indeed they must have appeared in the early years of Schumpeter's life. Economist and political scientist Everett Hagen was less elitist: "The discussion of creativity refers . . . not merely to the limiting case of genius but to the quality of creativity in general, in whatever degree it may be found in a given individual."[2]

My *own* belief is that the society that is most successful at helping its people—*all* its people—realize their creative potential is the society that will progress the fastest.

It is not just the entrepreneur who creates progress, even if we are talking narrowly about material—economic—progress. The inventor of the machine employed by the entrepreneur; the scientist who conceived the theory that the inventor turned to practical use; the engineer who designed the system to mass-produce the machine; the farmer who uses special care in producing a uniform raw material to be processed by the machine; the machine operator who suggests some helpful modifications to the machine on the basis of long experience in operating it—all are contributing to growth. So is the salesman who expands demand for the product by conceiving a new use for it. So, too, are the teachers who got the scientist, the inventor, and the engineer interested in their professions and who taught the farmer agronomy.[3]

Production takes place within a broader society, and the way that society functions affects the productive process. Good government can assure stability and continuity, without which investment and production will falter. Good government can provide a variety of services that facilitate production. And the policies government pursues, e.g., with respect to taxation, interest rates, support prices for agricultural products, will importantly affect producer decisions. Thus, the creativity and skill of government officials play a key role in economic development. It can be argued, in fact, that an effective government policymaker—e.g., a Treasury Secretary—is worth many Henry Fords.[4] W. Arthur Lewis observes, "The behaviour of government plays as important a role in stimulating or discouraging economic activity as does the behaviour of entrepreneurs, or parents, or scientists, or priests."[5]

But our definition of development is far broader than just the productive dimension of human existence. It also embraces the social dimension, particularly health, education, and welfare. It is government that bears the principal responsibility for progress in these sectors, and, as with economic progress, innovation and creativity are at the root of social progress. The people who conceive the policies that expand and improve social services are thus comparable in their developmental impact to industrial entrepreneurs, as are public-sector planners, administrators, technicians, and blue-collar workers to their private-sector counterparts.

It is not difficult to see how this view of what makes development happen can be extended to virtually all forms of work, intellectual and physical, performed within a society. While it is obvious that the contribution of some will be greater than that of others, and while the role of gifted people can be enormously important, all can contribute. It is thus probably more accurate, at least in the contemporary world, to think of development as a process of millions of small breakthroughs than as a few monumental innovations, the work of geniuses. A society that smooths the way for these breakthroughs is a society that will progress.

How does a society encourage the expression of human creative capacity? Basically, in seven ways:

1. Through creation of an environment in which people expect and receive fair treatment.
2. Through an effective and accessible education system: one that provides basic intellectual and vocational tools; nurtures inquisitiveness, critical faculties, dissent, and creativity; and equips people to solve problems.
3. Through a health system that protects people from diseases that debilitate and kill.
4. Through creation of an environment that encourages experimentation and criticism (which is often at the root of experimentation).
5. Through creation of an environment that helps people both discover their talents and interests and mesh them with the right jobs.
6. Through a system of incentives that rewards merit and achievement (and, conversely, discourages nepotism and "pull").
7. Through creation of the stability and continuity that make it possible to plan ahead with confidence. Progress is made enormously more difficult by instability and discontinuity.

TWO EXAMPLES IN NICARAGUA

My recent experience in Nicaragua provides two examples that symbolize what societies can do to nurture or frustrate human creative capacity.

The United States ambassador to Nicaragua during my two years there was Lawrence A. Pezzullo. Larry Pezzullo grew up in the Bronx, the son of an immigrant Italian butcher. His mother, also an immigrant, was illiterate. He attended public schools in New York City, served in the U.S. Army in Europe during World War II, and returned to New York to attend Columbia University under the GI bill. Following graduation, he taught in a public high school on Long Island for six years, then joined the Foreign Service. He rose steadily through the ranks, served as deputy assistant secretary of state for congressional affairs from 1975 to 1977, and was named ambassador to Uruguay in 1977. He became ambassador to Nicaragua in July

1979, simultaneous with the installation of the revolutionary Government of National Reconstruction.

Larry Pezzullo is a person of extraordinary talent. He has great capacity for understanding complicated political processes. But he also has a flair for conceiving and orchestrating responses to the circumstances he faces, and an unerring sense of timing. He is a diplomatic entrepreneur who, in Nicaragua, was the right man in the right place at the right time. (He has since become executive director of Catholic Relief Services.)

Rosa Carballo was born into similar humble circumstances, but in Nicaragua. She is a woman in her sixties, highly intelligent, dignified, and self-disciplined. She has a profound understanding of human nature and sees well below the surface of the political process in her country. With those qualities, she might well have been a successful professional in another society. In Nicaragua she is a domestic servant. She is effectively illiterate.

I want to note in passing that, today, there are few countries that could not virtually eradicate illiteracy within a generation if the will to do so existed.

VALUES AND ATTITUDES THAT FOSTER PROGRESS

We now have to ask what values and attitudes foster the conditions that facilitate the expression of human creative capacity—and development. . . .

The society's world view is the source of its value and attitude systems. The world view is formed by a complex of influences, including geography, economic organization, and the vagaries of history. The world view and its related value and attitude systems are constantly changing, but usually at a very slow pace, measurable in decades or generations. The world view is expressed at least in part through religion.

Of crucial importance for development are: (1) the world view's time focus—past, present, or future; (2) the extent to which the world view encourages rationality; and (3) the concepts of equality and authority it propagates.

If a society's major focus is on the past—on the glory of earlier times or in reverence of ancestors—or if it is absorbed with today's problems of survival, the planning, organizing, saving, and investment that are the warp and woof of development are not likely to be encouraged. Orientation toward the future implies the possibility of change and progress. And that possibility, as Max Weber stressed in his landmark work *The Protestant Ethic and the Spirit of Capitalism,* must be realizable in this life. The Calvinist concepts of "calling" and "election" force the eyes of the faithful toward the future. So do the basic tenets of Judaism: "Judaism clings to the idea of Progress. The Golden Age of Humanity is not in the past, but in the future."[6]

If the society's world view encourages the belief that humans have the capacity to know and understand the world around them, that the universe operates according to a largely decipherable pattern of laws, and that the scientific method can unlock many secrets of the unknown, it is clearly imparting a set of attitudes tightly linked to the ideas of progress and change. If the world view explains worldly phenomena by supernatural forces, often in the form of numerous capricious gods and goddesses who demand obeisance from humans, there is little room for reason, education, planning, or progress.

Many world views propagate the idea of human equality, particularly in the theme of the Golden Rule and its variations. The idea is stressed more in some ethical systems than in others. It is obviously present in both the Protestant and Catholic ethical systems. But Weber argues that the traditional Catholic focus on the afterlife, in contrast to the Protestant (and Jewish) focus on life in this world, vitiates the force of the ethical system, particularly when that focus is accompanied by the cycle of transgression/confession/absolution.[7] One possible consequence may be a relatively stronger Protestant orientation toward equality and the community, and a relatively stronger Catholic orientation toward hierarchy and the individual.

Directly related to the idea of equality is the concept of authority. Subsequent chapters [in the original book—*Eds.*] observe repeatedly the negative consequences of authoritarianism for growth of individuals and societies. There may well be truth in the belief of Weber and others that traditional Catholicism, with its focus on the afterlife and the crucial role of the church hierarchy and the priest, encouraged a dependency mindset among its adherents that was an obstacle to entrepreneurial activity. Martin Luther, by contrast, preached "the priesthood of all believers;"[8] "every Christian had to be a monk all his life."[9]

But there are also some religions—including, to be sure, some Protestant denominations—whose basic tenets embrace the idea of inequality. Traditional Hinduism comes immediately to mind, as do Gunnar Myrdal's comments on South Asia:

> . . . Social and economic stratification is accorded the sanction of religion. . . . The inherited stratification implies low social and spatial mobility, little free competition in its wider sense, and great inequalities.[10]
> It should be an hypothesis for further study that people in this region are not inherently different from people elsewhere, but that they live and have lived for a long time under conditions very different from those in the Western world, and that this has left its mark upon their bodies and minds. Religion has, then, become the emotional container of this whole way of life and work and by its sanction has rendered it rigid and resistant to change.[11]

The fundamental questions of future versus past orientation, encouragement or discouragement of rationality, and emphasis on equality versus emphasis on authority strongly influence three other cultural factors that play an important role in the way a society develops: (1) the extent of identification with others, (2) the rigor of the ethical system, and (3) attitudes about work.

Several of the people whose works are discussed . . . (e.g., Weber, Myrdal, David McClelland) have emphasized the importance for progress of a radius of identification and trust that embraces an entire society. There is evidence that the extended family is an effective institution for survival but an obstacle to development.[12] Weber observes, "The great achievement of ethical religions, above all of the ethical and ascetistic sects of Protestantism, was to shatter the fetters of the sib [i.e., the extended family]."[13]

The social consequences of widespread mistrust can be grave. Samuel Huntington makes the point:

> . . . the absence of trust in the culture of the society provides formidable obstacles to the creation of public institutions. Those societies deficient in stable and effective government are also deficient in mutual trust among their citizens, in national and public loyalties, and in organization skills and capacity. Their political cultures are often said to be marked by suspicion, jealousy, and latent or actual hostility toward everyone who is not a member of the family, the village, or, perhaps, the tribe. These characteristics are found in many cultures, their most extensive manifestation perhaps being in the Arab world and in Latin America. . . . In Latin America . . . traditions of self-centered individualism and of distrust and hatred for other groups in society have prevailed.[14]

A whole set of possibilities opens up when trust is extended beyond the family, possibilities that are likely to be reflected in both economic and social development. Myrdal observes, ". . . a more inclusive nationalism then becomes a force for progress . . . a vehicle for rationalism and for the ideals of planning, equality, social welfare, and perhaps democracy."[15] In such an environment, the idea of cooperation will be strengthened, with all that implies for modern production techniques, community problem-solving, and political stability. The idea of compromise, which is central to the working of a pluralistic system, is also reinforced.[16] When the idea of compromise—i.e., that a relationship is important enough to warrant seeking to avoid confrontation, even if some concession is necessary—is weak, the likelihood of confrontation is increased. Constant confrontation undermines stability and continuity, which, as noted earlier, are crucial to development.

There is a gap in all societies between the stated ethical system and the extent to which that system is honored in practice. Religions' treatment of ethical issues obviously has something to do with the size of the gap. Broad identification among the members of a society will strengthen the impact of the ethical system. Where the radius of identification and trust is small, there may effectively be no operative ethical system.

The rigor of the effective ethical system will shape attitudes about justice, which are central to several major development issues. If the members of a society expect injustice, the ideas of cooperation, compromise, stability, and continuity will be undermined. Corruption and nepotism will be encouraged. And the self-discipline necessary to keep a society working well (e.g., payment of taxes, resistance to the temptation to steal) will be weakened. The system of criminal and civil jurisprudence will be politicized and corrupted and will not be taken seriously by the citizenry. The idea of justice is also central to crucial social issues: the fairness of income distribution, availability of educational opportunities and health services, and promotion by merit.

Another link to these questions of radius of identification, rigor of the effective ethical system, and justice is the idea of dissent.[17] Its acceptance is fundamental to a functioning pluralistic political system, and it is clearly related to the idea of compromise. But it is also an important idea for creativity: what the inventor and the entrepreneur do is a kind of creative dissent.

Attitudes about work link back to several of these ideas, but particularly to future orientation. If the idea of progress is well established in the culture, there is a presumption that planning and hard work will be rewarded by increased income and improved living conditions. When the focus is on the present, on day-to-day survival, the ceiling on work may be the amount necessary to survive.

This brings us back to the seven conditions that encourage the expression of human creative capacity:

1. The expectation of fair play
2. Availability of educational opportunities
3. Availability of health services
4. Encouragement of experimentation and criticism
5. Matching of skills and jobs
6. Rewards for merit and achievement
7. Stability and continuity

Taken together, the seven conditions describe a functional modern democratic capitalist society. The extent to which countries realize their potential is determined, I believe, by the extent to which these conditions exist . . . [T]he seven conditions substantially exist in the fifteen countries whose per-capita gross national product (GNP) is the highest in the world (excluding four oil-rich Arab countries). These same fifteen countries accounted for 83 percent of the Nobel Prize winners from 1945 to 1981. . . .

NOTES

1. "Development" and "progress" are used synonymously in this chapter.
2. Everett E. Hagen, *On the Theory of Social Change: How Economic Growth Begins,* p. 88.
3. Hagen makes similar points on p. 11 of *On the Theory of Social Change.*
4. This point is elaborated in Lawrence E. Harrison, "Some Hidden Costs of the Public Investment Fixation," pp. 20–23.
5. W. Arthur Lewis, *The Theory of Economic Growth,* p. 376.
6. The words of a former Chief Rabbi of Great Britain in J. H. Hertz (ed.), *The Pentateuch and Haftorahs,* p. 196.
7. Clearly, contemporary Catholicism is moving toward the Protestant and Jewish focus on this life, particularly since Pope John XXIII.
8. Quoted in David C. McClelland, *The Achieving Society,* p. 48.
9. Max Weber, *The Protestant Ethic and the Spirit of Capitalism,* p. 121.
10. Gunnar Myrdal, *Asian Drama: An Inquiry into the Poverty of Nations,* p. 104.
11. *Ibid.,* p. 112.
12. The conditions for human progress and happiness are still worse where trust extends no further than the nuclear family, as in Banfield's "Montegrano." In that case, both development and survival are threatened.
13. Max Weber, *The Religion of China,* p. 237.
14. Samuel P. Huntington, *Political Order in Changing Societies,* p. 28.
15. Myrdal, *Asian Drama,* p. 122.
16. It is, I believe, significant that there is no truly apt Spanish word for "compromise."
17. It also seems significant that there is no truly apt Spanish word for "dissent."

REFERENCES

Hagen, E. E. 1962. *On the Theory of Social Change: How Economic Growth Begins.* Homewood, IL: Dorsey Press.

Harrison, L. E. 1970. "Some Hidden Costs of the Public Investment Fixation." *International Development Review* 12.

Hertz, J. H. (ed.). 1961. *The Pentateuch and Haftorahs.* London: Soncino Press.

Huntington, S. P. 1968. *Political Order in Changing Societies.* New York and London: Yale University Press.

Lewis, W. A. 1955. *The Theory of Economic Growth.* Homewood, IL: Richard D. Irwin, Inc.

McClelland, D. C. 1961. *The Achieving Society.* Princeton: D. Van Nostrand Co., Inc.

Myrdal, G. 1968. *Asian Drama: An Inquiry into the Poverty of Nations.* New York: Pantheon.

Weber, M. 1950. *The Protestant Ethic and the Spirit of Capitalism.* New York: Charles Scribner's Sons.

Weber, M. 1951. *The Religion of China.* New York: Macmillan.

World Bank. 1982. *World Development Report.* 1982.

21

· · · · · · ·

On the Sociology of National Development: Theories and Issues

· · · · · · ·

ALEJANDRO PORTES

In this chapter, sociologist Alejandro Portes calls into question the value of the cultural explanations of development and underdevelopment. He begins by criticizing the proponents of this view for having misunderstood Max Weber's explanation of the importance of the Protestant ethic for the rise of capitalism. Portes then enumerates three major flaws in the logic of the culturalists: (1) the failure to consider the importance of structural constraints on development; (2) the antidevelopmental role that so-called modern values can have; and (3) the "historical fiction" of development. Structural constraints will be elaborated on in greater detail in later chapters of this book dealing with dependency and the world system.

Myron Weiner (1966) notes that, for many scholars, the starting point of any definition of development is not the character of the society but the character of individuals. The same author observes that "although there are differences among social scientists as to how values and attitudes can be changed, it is possible to speak of one school of thought that believes that attitudinal and value changes are prerequisites to creating a modern society, economy, and political system" (Weiner 1966, p. 9).

For Szymon Chodak (1973, p. 11), writers of this school do not ask, "What is development?" or "What happens in its course?" but rather why it happened and what specifically caused the breakthrough from traditional into modern societies. Where such factors were present, development

Reprinted by permission from the University of Chicago Press from the *American Journal of Sociology,* vol. 82 (July 1976):68–74.

happens; where they are absent, stagnation prevails. The distinctive factor is then sought in the sphere of value orientation. . . .

The search in this case is for those "mental viruses" (McClelland 1967) changing the "spirit" (Inkeles 1969) of men so that they come to adapt and promote a modern society. This perspective derives its impetus from the general emphasis in United States sociology on value-normative complexes (Parsons 1964a) as opposed to the structure of material interests in society (Mills 1956). More specifically, the value approach to the problem of development lays claim to, and often labels itself as a direct continuation of, the thesis Max Weber developed in *The Protestant Ethic and the Spirit of Capitalism* (1958).

Weber's argument was, however, securely embedded in a body of research which clearly brought forth the importance of structural forms and the politico-economic interests of groups and classes. Emergence of an urban burgher class out of the feudal "oikos" and the relative vulnerability of feudalism, as opposed for example to the "prebendary" system of China, are subjects examined at length in his work (Weber 1951). The combined effects of the political assault by the central state and the economic assault by rising urban classes on the weakened feudal order meant an increasingly "open" structure for capitalist expansion (Weber 1958; Bendix 1962). Only because of the growing predicament of a lordly class incapable of defending its position by enforcing old prerogatives could the Protestant "spirit" of capitalism, or any other spirit for that matter, transform the economic order to its own advantage (Wallerstein 1974).

Psychological theories of development, such as those proposed by David G. McClelland (1967) and Everett E. Hagen (1962), have chosen to ignore the Weberian treatment of historico-structural issues and concentrate on the primacy of ideas in society: "This is just one more piece of evidence to support the growing conviction among social scientists that it is values, motives, or psychological forces that determine ultimately the rate of economic and social development. . . . *The Achieving Society* suggests that ideas are in fact more important in shaping history than purely materialistic arrangements" (McClelland 1963, p. 17).

Since ideas inhere in individuals, these theories result in an "additive" image of societal development in which the larger the number of people "infected" by the strategic psychological ingredient, the greater the economic growth of the country. This arithmetic approach is concerned neither with differences in positions in the stratification system nor with existing arrangements of economic and political power. Theorists of this persuasion subscribe to the proverb "Where there is a will, there is a way"; their voluntarism is, in turn, predicated on the creation of sufficiently high levels of motivation. In the best known of these theories, the factor responsible for this result is labeled "*n* Achievement": "The mental virus received the odd name of *n*-Ach (short for 'need for Achievement') because it was identified in a sample of a person's thoughts by whether the thoughts had to do with 'doing something well' or 'doing something better' than it had been done before: more efficiently, more quickly, with less labor, with a better result and so on" (McClelland 1966, p. 29). Extrapolating the result to national development, McClelland (1966, p. 30) reports: ". . . a country that was high in n-Ach level in its children's texts around 1925 was more likely to develop rapidly from 1929 to 1950 than one that was low in n-Ach in 1925. The same result was obtained when 1950 n-Ach levels were related to rates of economic development in the late nineteen-fifties." Apart from "n-Ach," McClelland prescribes a series of additional psychological ingredients making for societal development. Sense of collective responsibility and feelings of superiority over others are the most important ones.

Hagen's (1962) theory of "withdrawal of status respect" is more complex, in a psychoanalytic sense, than McClelland's. It comes, however, to the same formal conclusion. Again, a psychological motor, present in sufficiently large numbers of people, provides the strategic impulse for economic development. In this case, however, the "virus" is not transmitted by children's texts but instead has a gestation period of several generations. Humiliations resulting from status withdrawal among parents have certain psychic consequences for their sons who, in turn, transmit them to their own children. After a complicated evolution of complexes and stages, the "virus" finally matures and is ready to do its work in society. Whether the society is ready for the actions of the new entrepreneurial group is not of major importance to the theory.

More recent, and perhaps more accepted among sociologists, is the theory of "modernity" as a psychosocial complex of values. "Modern man" is characterized, internally, by a certain mental flexibility in dealing with new situations and, externally, by similarity to the value orientations dominant in industrial Western societies (see Lerner 1965). The spirit of modernity is regarded by these writers both as a precondition for societal modernization and as a major consequence of it: "Indeed, in the end, the ideal of development requires the transformation of the nature of man—a transformation that is both a *means* to the end of yet greater growth and at the same time one of the great *ends* itself of the development process" (Inkeles 1966, p. 138).

Alex Inkeles identifies nine major attitudes and values distinguishing modern man: (1) readiness for new experience and openness to innovation, (2) disposition to form and hold opinions, (3) democratic orientation, (4) planning habits, (5) belief in human and personal efficacy, (6) belief that the world is calculable, (7) stress on personal and human dignity, (8) faith in science and technology, and (9) belief in distributive justice.

This list is not complemented by a similar description of "traditional man." The latter tends to be defined by default: whatever is not properly modern must be traditional. It is difficult to understand, however, why "traditional man" does not stress "personal and human dignity" or believe in distributive justice.

The list of what goes on to make "modern man" tends to vary from author to author. This is not surprising, since much of what enters into the definition appears to come from introspection. Theorists of this persuasion vie with each other in developing ever more elaborate descriptions of what modern man is like. In doing so, they tend to contradict one another. While, for some, individualism and self-reliance are clearly modern traits, for others the ability to subordinate personal goals to the welfare of the collectivity and the ability to work with others toward its common pursuits constitute the mark of modernity (see Kahl 1968). As seen above, dichotomies between "traditional" and "modern" man are then built by extrapolation, through attributing to the former the reverse of characteristics assigned to the latter (Gusfield 1967).

In addition to the dimensions quoted above, the following are frequently encountered in characterizations of modern man: (1) participation: motivation and ability to take part in organizations and electoral processes; (2) ambition: high mobility aspirations for self and children and willingness to take risks; (3) secularism: limited religious attachments and low receptivity to religious and ideological appeals; (4) information: frequent contact with news media and knowledge of national and international affairs; (5) consumption orientation: desire to own new goods and technologically advanced recreation and labor-saving appliances; (6) urban preference: desire to move to or remain in urban areas; (7) geographic mobility: experience of moving and or willingness to move from original residence in search of better opportunities (Lerner 1965; Kahl 1968; Schnaiberg 1970; Horowitz 1970; Portes 1974). . . .

DISCUSSION

Discussion of this . . . sociology of development must consider, however, several important aspects. A systematic presentation of these will cover three major points: structural constraints, consumption-oriented values, and historical fiction.

Structural Constraints

No matter how compelling the image of highly motivated entrepreneurs racing to break the barriers of stagnation, the fact remains that individual action is highly conditioned by external social arrangements. Despite the frequent application of "tribal" imagery to underdeveloped nations, the reality of such societies is not one of an open frontier awaiting conquest by an entrepreneurial elite. Indeed, a complex structure of economic and political interests penetrates every aspect of them. To think that more modernity, achievement motivation, or status withdrawal will automatically transform these structures is, at best, naive. Regardless of what psychologists may think, societies are not the simple "additive" sum of individual members.

An active set of individuals, motivated by whatever psychological mechanism one may wish to posit, must still cope with existing economic and political arrangements. One way of doing so is to attempt to transform them, in which case "entrepreneurs" must organize themselves and enter the political arena in conflict with entrenched interest groups. The transformation of "modernity" or "*n* Achievement" into potential rebellion and ideologically committed elites is a possibility seldom contemplated in these theories.

A second alternative is that "entrepreneurs" may attempt to work through established channels. This alternative, the most likely one in view of the costs involved, may explain the embracement by established power groups of this perspective as their sociology of development. Highly motivated modern individuals may be extremely functional for maintenance of existing power structures. They may be hired, for example, as highly paid managers of foreign corporations, as has been increasingly the practice of multinational companies (see Blair 1974). They may also be brought into preexisting civilian and military bureaucracies. There are indeed many opportunities for entrepreneurial fulfillment within the existing social order. Altruistic motivations of "moderns" may even be employed in melioristic welfare activities, irrelevant for the structural task of development but functional for legitimizing the existing politico-economic system.

Individual motivations for achievement can be absorbed, fulfilled, and utilized without changing a basic situation of economic subordination and social maldistribution. The issue is not how much individual motivation there is, or what its sources are, but rather to what goals it is directed. The fundamental individualism apparent in theories of achievement and entrepreneurial motivation may be either irrelevant or inimical to struggles for national transformation. Elites committed to the task of development are not formed by "moderns" but by "modernizers"—individuals committed to achievement of collective economic and social change (Kerr et al. 1960).

Consumption-Oriented Values

A second, related aspect has to do with some of the values defined as "modern." That most modern of traits, "empathy," is usually described as ability to comprehend and place oneself symbolically in the midst of urban-industrial life (see Lerner 1965). This, in turn, is directly linked with a "demonstration effect" which raises demands for consumption beyond what a poor country can realistically afford. Excessive, media-promoted demand is a problem faced by both status quo and development-oriented governments in the Third World. For the latter, however, it presents a major difficulty, for it exercises pressure on scarce resources required for long-term investment. The dilemma of choosing between "political" and "economic" strategies (immediate consumption and resulting mass political loyalty versus consumption restrictions and long-term planning) emerges here as a major developmental issue (Malloy 1971).

Communications experts agree that modern values are diffused through the mass media. Some argue that advertisements in the commercial media are effective carriers of the "modern" message: "Advertising itself may also be a powerful instrument of development. It is a way of facilitating the distribution of commodities, broadening the market, and making people aware of possibilities with which they would not otherwise be familiar" (Pool 1966, p. 108).

The market is certainly broadened, often for the benefit of multinational enterprises, strains are placed on the country's capacity to import, and new "possibilities" are taught which often bear no relationship to local conditions. Such modern values—premature wants, imported needs and tastes, excessive consumption—are not the values of development. Historical experiences of national development in this century show consistently the necessity for restriction of consumption and for an orientation which places as much emphasis on achievement of national goals as on personal gratification. "Mobilization systems" in the Third World have evolved precisely as attempts to diffuse these "nonmodern" values (Apter 1967).

Finally, much-derided "traditional" cultures have often furnished value legitimations necessary in periods of rapid national change. Secular modernity lacks sufficient cultural depth to match the force of great national traditions. Japanese ideology during the Meiji period furnishes perhaps the best known, but not the only, example of the uses of tradition for development (Bellah 1965; Gusfield 1967; Walton 1976).

Historical Fiction

Theories of modernity share with those of evolutionary differentiation the belief that development proceeds from an early traditional stage toward a terminal "advanced" one. It is proper at this time to complete analysis of the character of this analogy.

As seen above, tradition is described in terms which are only logical counterparts to those embodied in modernity. There is no existing nation in the Third World which can be labeled "traditional" in this sense. The fictional character of the initial stage of the process is due to the fact that it is not based on observation of actual societies but on reflection on the features of the "terminal" stage. Modernity creates tradition very much as in Owen Lattimore's (1962) words, "Civilization gave birth to barbarism."

At the other extreme, as seen above, the current stage of development in industrial societies is unlikely to be replicated in underdeveloped countries. While providing points of reference for developmental efforts, features of currently industrialized nations are products of unique historical processes which already belong to mankind's past. The concrete features of advanced societies of today cannot be reproduced exactly in the future, nor is this the goal of most Third World nations (Illich 1969).

Sociologies of development dominant in the West thus come to posit a transition from a fictional stage to an impossible one. By concentrating on current characteristics of industrial societies, they neglect the fact that these traits, as well as those of underdeveloped societies, are themselves evolving and that social change in each type of society occurs in interaction with the other type. As a contemporary Latin American sociologist states: "A science of development is only science when it abandons the assumption of a formal goal to be reached and attempts instead to comprehend development as a historical process. . . . The object of [such] a theory cannot be to describe the passage from a society that is not really known to one that is not going to exist" (Dos Santos 1970a, p. 174).

REFERENCES

Apter, D. 1967. *The Politics of Modernization.* Chicago: University of Chicago Press.
Bellah, R. N. 1965. *Religion and Progress in Modern Asia.* New York: Free Press.
Bendix, R. 1962. *Max Weber: An Intellectual Portrait.* Garden City, N.Y.: Doubleday.
———. 1967. "Tradition and Modernity Reconsidered." *Comparative Studies in Society and History* 9 (April):292–346.
Blair, C. P. 1974. "Las Empresas multinacionales en el comercio Latino-americano: Una Mirada hacia el futuro." Mimeographed. Austin: University of Texas.
Chodak, S. 1973. *Societal Development.* New York: Oxford University Press.
Dos Santos, T. 1970a. "La Crisis de la teoria del desarrollo y las relaciones de dependencia en America Latina." Pp. 147–87 in *La Dependencia politico-economica de America Latina.* Mexico, D.F.: Siglo Veintiuno.
———. 1970b. "The Structure of Dependence." *American Economic Review* 60 (May):231–36.
Gusfield, J. R. 1967. "Tradition and Modernity: Misplaced Polarities in the Study of Social Change." *American Journal of Sociology* 72 (January):351–62.
Hagen, E. E. 1962. *On the Theory of Social Change.* Homewood, Ill.: Dorsey.
Horowitz, I. L. 1966. *Three Worlds of Development.* New York: Oxford University Press.
———. 1970. "Personality and Structural Dimensions in Comparative International Development." *Social Science Quarterly* 51 (December):494–513.
Illich, I. 1969. *Celebration of Awareness.* New York: Doubleday.
Inkeles, A. 1966. "The Modernization of Man." Pp. 138–50 in *Modernization: The Dynamics of Growth,* edited by Myron Weiner. New York: Basic.

————. 1969. "Making Men Modern: On the Causes and Consequences of Individual Change in Six Countries." *American Journal of Sociology* 75 (September):208–25.

Kahl, J. A. 1968. *The Measurement of Modernism.* Austin: University of Texas Press.

Kerr, C., J. T. Dunlop, F. Harbison, and C. A. Myers. 1960. *Industrialism and Industrial Man: The Problems of Labor and Management in Economic Growth.* New York: Oxford University Press.

Lattimore, O. 1962. "La Civilisation, mère de barbarie." *Annales* E.S.C. 17 (January–February):99.

Lerner, D. 1965. *The Passing of Traditional Society: Modernizing the Middle East.* New York: Free Press.

McClelland, D. G. 1963. "Motivational Patterns in Southeast Asia with Special Reference to the Chinese Case." *Journal of Social Issues* 29 (January):17.

————. 1966. "The Impulse of Modernization." Pp. 28–39 in *Modernization: The Dynamics of Growth,* edited by Myron Weiner. New York: Basic.

————. 1967. *The Achieving Society.* New York: Free Press.

Malloy, J. M. 1971. "Generation of Political Support and Allocation of Costs." Pp. 23–42 in *Revolutionary Change in Cuba,* edited by C. Mesa-Lago. Pittsburgh: University of Pittsburgh Press.

Mills, C. W. 1956. *The Power Elite.* New York: Oxford University Press.

Parsons, T. 1964a. *The Social System.* New York: Free Press.

————. 1964b. "Evolutionary Universals in Society." *American Sociological Review* 29 (June):339–57.

Pool, I. S. 1966. "Communications and Development." Pp. 98–109 in *Modernization: The Dynamics of Growth,* edited by Myron Weiner. New York: Basic.

Portes, A. 1974. "Modernity and Development: A Critique." *Studies in Comparative International Development* 9 (Spring):247–79.

Schnaiberg, A. 1970. "Measuring Modernism: Theoretical and Empirical Explorations." *American Journal of Sociology* 76 (December):399–425.

Wallerstein, I. 1974. *The Modern World-System—Capitalist Agriculture and the Origins of the European World-Economy in the Sixteenth Century.* New York: Academic Press.

Walton, J. 1974. "Urban Hierarchies and Patterns of Dependence in Latin America." Paper presented at the May 1974 Seminar on New Directions of Urban Research in Latin America, Institute of Latin American Studies, University of Texas at Austin.

————. 1976. "Elites and the Politics of Urban Development." In *Urban Latin America: The Political Condition from Above and Below,* by A. Portes and J. Walton. Austin: University of Texas Press.

Weber, M. 1951. *The Religion of China.* New York: Free Press.

————. 1958. *The City.* New York: Free Press.

Weiner, M. 1966. "Introduction." Pp. 1–14 in *Modernization: The Dynamics of Growth,* edited by Myron Weiner. New York: Basic.

PART 5

. . . .

Dependency and World-System Theory

. . . .

22

The Structure of Dependence

Theotonio dos Santos

In Part 4 of this book we examined internal causes of slow growth among the poor countries. In Part 5 we examine external causes, starting with dependency. In this chapter, Theotonio dos Santos, a Brazilian economist, provides a classical definition of dependency. Dos Santos is a member of what has been called the "dependentista school" of development thinkers, the great majority of whom are Latin American intellectuals. Dependency theory comes in many varieties; indeed, some argue that there is no such thing as dependency "theory." Nonetheless, there is a body of thinking common to many of those in the dependista school, and in this chapter dos Santos presents a concise statement of some of its fundamental tenets. He defines dependence and shows its linkages to Marxian theory, then goes on to elaborate three basic forms of dependence: (1) colonial, (2) financial-industrial, and (3) multinational. This latter form, arising out of the power of the large multinational corporations that maintain operations in developing countries, is of greatest concern to dos Santos because he sees it as limiting the developmental potential of newly industrializing nations. This new form of dependence restricts the size of the local market and thus contributes to income inequality in developing nations. Ultimately, according to dos Santos, dependent development must culminate in revolutionary movements of the left or right.

This chapter attempts to demonstrate that the dependence of Latin American countries on other countries cannot be overcome without a qualitative

Reprinted with permission from *The American Economic Review*, vol. 60 (May 1970):231–236.

change in their internal structures and external relations. We shall attempt to show that the relations of dependence to which these countries are subjected conform to a type of international and internal structure which leads them to underdevelopment or more precisely to a dependent structure that deepens and aggravates the fundamental problems of their peoples.

I. WHAT IS DEPENDENCE?

By dependence we mean a situation in which the economy of certain countries is conditioned by the development and expansion of another economy to which the former is subjected. The relation of interdependence between two or more economies, and between these and world trade, assumes the form of dependence when some countries (the dominant ones) can expand and can be self-sustaining, while other countries (the dependent ones) can do this only as a reflection of that expansion, which can have either a positive or a negative effect on their immediate development [see reference no. 7, p. 6].

The concept of dependence permits us to see the internal situation of these countries as part of world economy. In the Marxian tradition, the theory of imperialism has been developed as a study of the process of expansion of the imperialist centers and of their world domination. In the epoch of the revolutionary movement of the Third World, we have to develop the theory of laws of internal development in those countries that are the object of such expansion and are governed by them. This theoretical step transcends the theory of development which seeks to explain the situation of the underdeveloped countries as a product of their slowness or failure to adopt the patterns of efficiency characteristic of developed countries (or to "modernize" or "develop" themselves). Although capitalist development theory admits the existence of an "external" dependence, it is unable to perceive underdevelopment in the way our present theory perceives it, as a consequence and part of the process of the world expansion of capitalism— a part that is necessary to and integrally linked with it.

In analyzing the process of constituting a world economy that integrates the so-called "national economies" in a world market of commodities, capital, and even of labor power, we see that the relations produced by this market are unequal and combined—unequal because development of parts of the system occurs at the expense of other parts. Trade relations are based on monopolistic control of the market, which leads to the transfer of surplus generated in the dependent countries to the dominant countries; financial relations are, from the viewpoint of the dominant powers, based on loans and the export of capital, which permit them to receive interest and profits, thus increasing their domestic surplus and strengthening their control over the economies of the other countries. For the dependent countries these relations represent an export of profits and interest which carries off part of the surplus generated domestically and leads to a loss of control over their productive resources. In order to permit these disadvantageous relations, the dependent countries must generate large surpluses, not in such a way as to create higher levels of technology but rather creating superexploited manpower. The result is to limit the development of their internal market and their technical and cultural capacity, as well as the moral and physical health of their people. We call this combined development because it is the combination of these inequalities and the transfer of resources from the most backward and dependent sectors to the most advanced and dominant ones which explains the inequality, deepens it, and transforms it into a necessary and structural element of the world economy.

II. HISTORIC FORMS OF DEPENDENCE

Historic forms of dependence are conditioned by: (1) the basic forms of this world economy which has its own laws of development; (2) the type of economic relations dominant in the capitalist centers and the ways in which the latter expand outward; and (3) the types of economic relations existing inside the peripheral countries which are incorporated into the situation of dependence within the network of international economic relations generated by capitalist expansion. It is not within the purview of this chapter to study these forms in detail but only to distinguish broad characteristics of development.

Drawing on an earlier study, we may distinguish: (1) Colonial dependence, trade export in nature, in which commercial and financial capital in alliance with the colonialist state dominated the economic relations of the Europeans and the colonies by means of a trade monopoly, complemented by a colonial monopoly of land, mines, and manpower (self or slave) in the colonized countries. (2) Financial-industrial dependence, which consolidated itself at the end of the nineteenth century, characterized by the domination of big capital in the hegemonic centers, and its expansion abroad through investment in the production of raw materials and agricultural products for consumption in the hegemonic centers. A productive structure grew up in the dependent countries devoted to the export of these products (which I. V. Lenin labeled export economies [11]; other analysis in other regions [12] [13]), producing what the Economic Commission for Latin America (ECLA) has called "foreign-oriented development" (*desarrollo hacia afuera*) [4]. (3) In the postwar period a new type of dependence has been consolidated, based on multinational corporations which began to invest in industries geared to the internal market of underdeveloped countries. This form of dependence is basically technological-industrial dependence [6].

Each of these forms of dependence corresponds to a situation which conditioned not only the international relations of these countries but also their internal structures: the orientation of production, the forms of capital accumulation, the reproduction of the economy, and, simultaneously, their social and political structure.

III. THE EXPORT ECONOMIES

In forms (1) and (2) of dependence, production is geared to those products destined for export (gold, silver, and tropical products in the colonial epoch; raw materials and agricultural products in the epoch of industrial-financial dependence); i.e., production is determined by demand from the hegemonic centers. The internal productive structure is characterized by rigid specialization and monoculture in entire regions (the Caribbean, the Brazilian Northeast, etc.). Alongside these export sectors there grew up certain complementary economic activities (cattle-raising and some manufacturing, for example) which were dependent, in general, on the export sector to which they sell their products. There was a third, subsistence economy which provided manpower for the export sector under favorable conditions and toward which excess population shifted during periods unfavorable to international trade.

Under these conditions, the existing internal market was restricted by four factors: (1) Most of the national income was derived from export, which was used to purchase the inputs required by export production (slaves, for example) or luxury goods consumed by the hacienda- and mine-owners, and by the more prosperous employees. (2) The available manpower was subject to very arduous forms of superexploitation, which limited its consumption. (3) Part of the consumption of these workers was provided by the subsistence economy, which served as a complement to their income and as a refuge during periods of depression. (4) A fourth factor was to be found in those countries in which land and mines were in the hands of foreigners (cases of an enclave economy): a great part of the accumulated surplus was destined to be sent abroad in the form of profits, limiting not only internal consumption but also possibilities of reinvestment [1]. In the case of enclave economies the relations of the foreign companies with the hegemonic center were even more exploitative and were complemented by the fact that purchases by the enclave were made directly abroad.

IV. THE NEW DEPENDENCE

The new form of dependence, (3) above, is in process of developing and is conditioned by the exigencies of the international commodity and capital markets. The possibility of generating new investments depends on the existence of financial resources in foreign currency for the purchase of machinery and processed raw materials not produced domestically. Such purchases are subject to two limitations: the limit of resources generated by the export sector (reflected in the balance of payments, which includes not only trade but also service relations); and the limitations of monopoly on patents which leads monopolistic firms to prefer to transfer their machines in the form of capital rather than as commodities for sale. It is necessary to analyze these relations of dependence if we are to understand the fundamental structural limits they place on the development of these economies.

1. Industrial development is dependent on an export sector for the foreign currency to buy the inputs utilized by the industrial sector. The first consequence of this dependence is the need to preserve the traditional export sector, which limits economically the development of the internal market by the conservation of backward relations of production and signifies, politically, the maintenance of power by traditional decadent oligarchies. In the countries where these sectors are controlled by foreign capital, it signifies the remittance abroad of high profits, and political dependence on those interests. Only in rare instances does foreign capital not control at least the marketing of these products. In response to these limitations, dependent countries in the 1930s and 1940s developed a policy of exchange restrictions and taxes on the national and foreign export sector; today they tend toward the gradual nationalization of production and toward the imposition of certain timid limitations on foreign control of the marketing of exported products. Furthermore, they seek, still somewhat timidly, to obtain better terms for the sale of their products. In recent decades, they have created mechanisms for international price agreements, and today the United Nations Conference on Trade and Development (UNCTAD) and ECLA press to obtain more favorable tariff conditions for these products on the part of the hegemonic centers. It is important to point out that the industrial development of these countries is dependent on the situation of the export sector, the continued existence of which they are obliged to accept.

2. Industrial development is, then, strongly conditioned by fluctuations in the balance of payments. This leads toward deficit due to the relations of dependence themselves. The causes of the deficit are three:

a. Trade relations take place in a highly monopolized international market, which tends to lower the price of raw materials and to raise the prices of industrial products, particularly inputs. In the second place, there is a tendency in modern technology to replace various primary products with synthetic raw materials. Consequently, the balance of trade in these countries tends to be less favorable (even though they show a general surplus). The overall Latin American balance of trade from 1946 to 1968 shows a surplus for each of those years. The same thing happens in almost every underdeveloped country. However, the losses due to deterioration of the terms of trade (on the basis of data from ECLA and the International Monetary Fund), excluding Cuba, were $26,383 million for the 1951–66 period, taking 1950 prices as a base. If Cuba and Venezuela are excluded, the total is $15,925 million.

b. For the reasons already given, foreign capital retains control over the most dynamic sectors of the economy and repatriates a high volume of profit; consequently, capital accounts are highly unfavorable to dependent countries. The data show that the amount of capital leaving the country is much greater than the amount entering; this produces an enslaving deficit in capital accounts. To this must be added the deficit in certain services which are virtually under total foreign control—such as freight transport, royalty payments, technical aid, etc. Consequently, an important deficit is produced in the total balance of payments; thus limiting the possibility of importation of inputs for industrialization.

c. The result is that "foreign financing" becomes necessary, in two forms: to cover the existing deficit, and to "finance" development by means of loans for the stimulation of investments and to "supply" an internal economic surplus which was decapitalized to a large extent by the remittance of part of the surplus generated domestically and sent abroad as profits.

Foreign capital and foreign "aid" thus fill up the holes that they themselves created. The real value of this aid, however, is doubtful. If overcharges resulting from the restrictive terms of the aid are subtracted from the total amount of the grants, the average net flow, according to calculations of the Inter-American Economic and Social Council, is approximately 54 percent of the gross flow [5].

If we take account of certain further facts—that a high proportion of aid is paid in local currencies, that Latin American countries make contributions to international financial institutions, and that credits are often "tied"—we find a "real component of foreign aid" of 42.2 percent on a very favorable hypothesis and of 38.3 percent on a more realistic one [5, II, p. 33]. The gravity of the situation becomes even clearer if we consider that these credits are used in large part to finance North American investments, to subsidize foreign imports which compete with national products, to introduce technology not adapted to the needs of underdeveloped countries, and to invest in low-priority sectors of the national economies. The hard truth is that the underdeveloped countries have to pay for all of the "aid" they receive. This situation is generating an enormous protest movement by Latin American governments seeking at least partial relief from such negative relations.

3. Finally, industrial development is strongly conditioned by the technological monopoly exercised by imperialist centers. We have seen that the underdeveloped countries depend on the importation of machinery and raw materials for the development of their industries. However, these goods are

not freely available in the international market; they are patented and usually belong to the big companies. The big companies do not sell machinery
and processed raw materials as simple merchandise: they demand either the
payment of royalties, etc., for their utilization or, in most cases, they convert these goods into capital and introduce them in the form of their own
investments. This is how machinery which is replaced in the hegemonic
centers by more advanced technology is sent to dependent countries as capital for the installation of affiliates. Let us pause and examine these relations in order to understand their oppressive and exploitative character.

The dependent countries do not have sufficient foreign currency, for
the reasons given. Local businessmen have financing difficulties, and they
must pay for the utilization of certain patented techniques. These factors
oblige the national bourgeois governments to facilitate the entry of foreign
capital in order to supply the restricted national market, which is strongly
protected by high tariffs in order to promote industrialization. Thus, foreign
capital enters with all the advantages: in many cases, it is given exemption
from exchange controls for the importation of machinery; financing of sites
for installation of industries is provided; government financing agencies
facilitate industrialization; loans are available from foreign and domestic
banks, which prefer such clients; foreign aid often subsidizes such investments and finances complementary public investments; after installation,
high profits obtained in such favorable circumstances can be reinvested
freely. Thus it is not surprising that the data of the U.S. Department of
Commerce reveal that the percentage of capital brought in from abroad by
these companies is but a part of the total amount of invested capital. These
data show that in the period from 1946 to 1967 the new entries of capital
into Latin America for direct investment amounted to $5,415 million, while
the sum of reinvested profits was $4,424 million. On the other hand, the
transfers of profits from Latin America to the United States amounted to
$14,775 million. If we estimate total profits as approximately equal to
transfers plus reinvestments we have the sum of $18,983 million. In spite
of enormous transfers of profits to the United States, the book value of the
United States' direct investment in Latin America went from $3,045 million
in 1946 to $10,213 million in 1967. From these data it is clear that: (1) Of
the new investments made by U.S. companies in Latin America for the
period 1946–67, 55 percent corresponds to new entries of capital and 45
percent to reinvestment of profits; in recent years, the trend is more
marked, with reinvestments between 1960 and 1966 representing more than
60 percent of new investments. (2) Remittances remained at about 10 percent of book value throughout the period. (3) The ratio of remitted capital
to new flow is around 2.7 for the period 1946–67; that is, for each dollar
that enters $2.70 leaves. In the 1960s this ratio roughly doubled, and in
some years was considerably higher.

The *Survey of Current Business* data on sources and uses of funds for direct North American investment in Latin America in the period 1957–64 show that, of the total sources of direct investment in Latin America, only 11.8 percent came from the United States. The remainder is, in large part, the result of the activities of North American firms in Latin America (46.4 percent net income, 27.7 percent under the heading of depreciation), and from "sources located abroad" (14.1 percent). It is significant that the funds obtained abroad that are external to the companies are greater than the funds originating in the United States.

V. EFFECTS ON THE PRODUCTIVE STRUCTURE

It is easy to grasp, even if only superficially, the effects that this dependent structure has on the productive system itself in these countries and the role of this structure in determining a specified type of development, characterized by its dependent nature.

The productive system in the underdeveloped countries is essentially determined by these international relations. In the first place, the need to conserve the agrarian or mining export structure generates a combination between more advanced economic centers that extract surplus value from the more backward sectors and internal "metropolitan" centers on the one hand, and internal interdependent "colonial" centers on the other [10]. The unequal and combined character of capitalist development at the international level is reproduced internally in an acute form. In the second place the industrial and technological structure responds more closely to the interests of the multinational corporations than to internal developmental needs (conceived of not only in terms of the overall interests of the population, but also from the point of view of the interests of a national capitalist development). In the third place, the same technological and economic-financial concentration of the hegemonic economies is transferred without substantial alteration to very different economies and societies, giving rise to a highly unequal productive structure, a high concentration of incomes, underutilization of installed capacity, intensive exploitation of existing markets concentrated in large cities, etc.

The accumulation of capital in such circumstances assumes its own characteristics. In the first place, it is characterized by profound differences among domestic wage-levels, in the context of a local cheap labor market, combined with a capital-intensive technology. The result, from the point of view of relative surplus value, is a high rate of exploitation of labor power. (On measurements of forms of exploitation, see [3].)

This exploitation is further aggravated by the high prices of industrial products enforced by protectionism, exemptions and subsidies given by the national governments, and "aid" from hegemonic centers. Furthermore, since dependent accumulation is necessarily tied into the international economy, it is profoundly conditioned by the unequal and combined character of international capitalist economic relations, by the technological and financial control of the imperialist centers by the realities of the balance of payments, by the economic policies of the state, etc. The role of the state in the growth of national and foreign capital merits a much fuller analysis than can be made here.

Using the analysis offered here as a point of departure, it is possible to understand the limits that this productive system imposes on the growth of the internal markets of these countries. The survival of traditional relations in the countryside is a serious limitation on the size of the market, since industrialization does not offer hopeful prospects. The productive structure created by dependent industrialization limits the growth of the internal market.

First, it subjects the labor force to highly exploitative relations which limit its purchasing power. Second, in adopting a technology of intensive capital use, it creates very few jobs in comparison with population growth, and limits the generation of new sources of income. These two limitations affect the growth of the consumer goods market. Third, the remittance abroad of profits carries away part of the economic surplus generated within the country. In all these ways limits are put on the possible creation of basic national industries which could provide a market for the capital goods this surplus would make possible if it were not remitted abroad.

From this cursory analysis we see that the alleged backwardness of these economies is not due to a lack of integration with capitalism but that, to the contrary, the most powerful obstacles to their full development come from the way in which they are joined to this international system and its laws of development.

VI. SOME CONCLUSIONS: DEPENDENT REPRODUCTION

In order to understand the system of dependent reproduction and the socio-economic institutions created by it, we must see it as part of a system of world economic relations based on monopolistic control of large-scale capital, on control of certain economic and financial centers over others, on a monopoly of complex technology that leads to unequal and combined development at a national and international level. Attempts to analyze backwardness as a failure to assimilate more advanced models of production or to modernize are nothing more than ideology disguised as science. The same is true of the attempts to analyze this international economy in terms of relations among elements in free competition, such as the theory of comparative costs which seeks to justify the inequalities of the world economic system and to conceal the relations of exploitation on which it is based [14].

In reality we can understand what is happening in the underdeveloped countries only when we see that they develop within the framework of a process of dependent production and reproduction. This system is a dependent one because it reproduces a productive system whose development is limited by those world relations which necessarily lead to: the development of only certain economic sectors, to trade under unequal conditions [9], to domestic competition with international capital under unequal conditions, to the imposition of relations of superexploitation of the domestic labor force with a view to dividing the economic surplus thus generated between internal and external forces of domination. (On economic surplus and its utilization in the dependent countries, see [1].)

In reproducing such a productive system and such international relations, the development of dependent capitalism reproduces the factors that prevent it from reaching a nationally and internationally advantageous situation; and it thus reproduces backwardness, misery, and social marginalization within its borders. The development that it produces benefits very narrow sectors, encounters unyielding domestic obstacles to its continued economic growth (with respect to both internal and foreign markets), and leads to the progressive accumulation of balance-of-payments deficits, which in turn generate more dependence and more superexploitation.

The political measures proposed by the developmentalists of ECLA, UNCTAD, Inter-American Development Bank (BID), etc., do not appear to permit destruction of these terrible chains imposed by dependent development. We have examined the alternative forms of development presented for Latin America and the dependent countries under such conditions elsewhere [8]. Everything now indicates that what can be expected is a long process of sharp political and military confrontations and of profound social radicalization which will lead these countries to a dilemma: governments of force, which open the way to fascism, or popular revolutionary governments, which open the way to socialism. Intermediate solutions have proved to be, in such a contradictory reality, empty and utopian.

REFERENCES

1. Paul Baran, *Political Economy of Growth* (Monthly Review Press, 1967).
2. Thomas Balogh, *Unequal Partners* (Basil Blackwell, 1963).
3. Pablo Gonzalez Casanova, *Sociología de la explotación, Siglo XXI* (México, 1969).
4. Cepal, *La CEPAL y el análisis del desarrollo Latinoamericano* (Santiago, Chile, 1968).
5. Consejo Interamericano Economico Social (CIES) O.A.S., Interamerican Economic and Social Council, External Financing for Development in L.A. *El Financiamiento externo para el desarrollo de América Latina* (Pan-American Union, Washington, 1969).

6. Theotonio dos Santos, *El nuevo carácter de la dependencia,* CESO (Santiago de Chile, 1968).

7. ———, *La crisis de la teoría del desarrollo y las relaciones de dependencia en América Latina,* Boletin del CESO, 3 (Santiago, Chile, 1968).

8. ———, *La dependencia económica y las alternotivas de cambio en América Latina,* Ponencia al IX Congreso Latinoamericano de Sociología (México, Nov. 1969).

9. A. Emmanuel, *L'Echange Inégal* (Maspero, Paris, 1969).

10. Andre G. Frank, *Development and Underdevelopment in Latin America* (Monthly Review Press, 1968).

11. I. V. Levin, *The Export Economies* (Harvard Univ. Press, 1964).

12. Gunnar Myrdal, *Asian Drama* (Pantheon, 1968).

13. K. Nkrumah, *Neocolonialismo, última etapa del imperialismo* (Siglo XXI, México, 1966).

14. Cristian Palloix, *Problèmes de la Croissance en Economie Ouverte* (Maspero, Paris, 1969).

23
. . . .

Modernization and Dependency: Alternative Perspectives in the Study of Latin American Underdevelopment
. . . .

J. Samuel Valenzuela & Arturo Valenzuela

This chapter contrasts the modernization and dependency perspectives. Because the main notions of modernization theory have been covered in the previous chapters, only those portions of the Valenzuelas' discussion that elaborate on dependency theory are included here. The Valenzuelas enumerate the principal assumptions held by dependency thinkers and present some of the supporting evidence for the theory's validity, drawing upon the Latin American experience. After evaluating the relative merits of the two perspectives, they conclude that dependency is the superior framework primarily because it is firmly grounded in historical reality.

THE DEPENDENCY PERSPECTIVE

Like the modernization perspective, the dependency perspective resulted from the work of many different scholars in different branches of the social sciences. Much of the work proceeded in an inductive fashion. This was the case with economists working in the Economic Commission for Latin America (ECLA) who first sought to explain the underdevelopment of Latin America by focusing on the unequal terms of trade between exporters of raw materials and exporters of manufactured goods. ECLA "doctrine" called for a concerted effort to diversify the export base of Latin American

Reprinted with permission from *Comparative Politics*, vol. 10 (July 1978), pp. 543–557.

countries and accelerate industrialization efforts through import substitution. However, the continued difficulties with that model of development soon led to a focus on the internal constraints to industrialization, with an emphasis on factors such as the distorting effects of unequal land tenure patterns and the corrosive results of an inflation best explained by structural rather than monetary variables. Soon these two trends came together when scholars, such as Osvaldo Sunkel, combined the early emphasis on external variables with the internal constraints to development.[1]

But this dependency perspective was anticipated by Latin American historians who had been working for years on various aspects of economic history. Studies such as those of Sergio Bagú stressed the close interrelation of domestic developments in Latin America and developments in metropolitan countries. And in Brazil, sociologists such as Florestan Fernandes, Octávio Ianni, Fernando Henrique Cardoso, and Theotonio dos Santos also turned to broad structural analyses of the factors of underdevelopment. The fact that many of these scholars found themselves in Santiago in the 1960s only contributed to further development of the perspective.

In its emphasis on the expansive nature of capitalism and in its structural analysis of society, the dependency literature draws on Marxist insights and is related to the Marxist theory of imperialism. However, its examination of processes in Latin America implies important revisions in classical Leninist formulations, both historically and in light of recent trends. The focus is on explaining Latin American underdevelopment, and not on the functioning of capitalism, though some authors argue that their efforts will contribute to an understanding of capitalism and its contradictions.

Assumptions

The dependency perspective rejects the assumption made by modernization writers that the unit of analysis in studying underdevelopment is the national society. The domestic cultural and institutional features of Latin America are in themselves simply not the key variables accounting for the relative backwardness of the area, though, as will be seen below, domestic structures are certainly critical intervening factors. The relative presence of traditional and modern features may, or may not, help to differentiate societies; but it does not in itself explain the origins of modernity in some contexts and the lack of modernity in others. As such, the tradition-modernity polarity is of little value as a fundamental working concept. The dependency perspective assumes that the development of a national or regional unit can only be understood in connection with its historical insertion into the worldwide political-economic system which emerged with the wave of European colonizations of the world. This global system is thought to be characterized by the unequal but combined development of its different components. As Sunkel and Pedro Paz put it:

Both underdevelopment and development are aspects of the same phenomenon, both are historically simultaneous, both are linked functionally
and, therefore, interact and condition each other mutually. This results . . .
in the division of the world between industrial, advanced or "central"
countries, and underdeveloped, backward or "peripheral" countries. . . .[2]

The center is viewed as capable of dynamic development responsive to
internal needs, and as the main beneficiary of the global links. On the other
hand, the periphery is seen as having a reflex type of development; one
which is both constrained by its incorporation into the global system and
which results from its adaptation to the requirements of the expansion of
the center. As dos Santos indicates:

Dependency is a situation in which a certain number of countries have
their economy conditioned by the development and expansion of another
. . . placing the dependent countries in a backward position exploited by
the dominant countries.[3]

It is important to stress that the process can be understood only by reference to its historical dimension and by focusing on the total network of
social relations as they evolve in different contexts over time. For this reason dependence is characterized as "structural, historical and totalizing" or
an "integral analysis of development."[4] It is meaningless to develop, as
some social scientists have, a series of synchronic statistical indicators to
establish relative levels of dependence or independence among different
national units to test the "validity" of the model.[5] The unequal development
of the world goes back to the sixteenth century with the formation of a capitalist world economy in which some countries in the center were able to
specialize in industrial production of manufactured goods because the
peripheral areas of the world which they colonized provided the necessary
primary goods, agricultural and mineral, for consumption in the center.
Contrary to some assumptions in economic theory, the international division of labor did not lead to parallel development through comparative
advantage. The center states gained at the expense of the periphery. But,
just as significantly, the different functions of center and peripheral societies had a profound effect on the evolution of internal social and political
structures. Those which evolved in the periphery reinforced economies
with a narrow range of primary exports. The interdependent nature of the
world capitalist system and the qualitative transformations in that system
over time make it inconceivable to think that individual nations on the
periphery could somehow replicate the evolutionary experience of the now
developed nations.[6]

It follows from an emphasis on global structural processes and variations in internal structural arrangements that contextual variables, at least in
the long run, shape and guide the behavior of groups and individuals. It is
not inappropriate attitudes which contribute to the absence of entrepreneur-

ial behavior or to institutional arrangements reinforcing underdevelopment. Dependent, peripheral development produces an opportunity structure such that personal gain for dominant groups and entrepreneurial elements is not conducive to the collective gain of balanced development. This is a fundamental difference with much of the modernization literature. It implies that dependence analysts, though they do not articulate the point explicitly, share the classical economic theorists' view of human nature. They assume that individuals in widely different societies are capable of pursuing rational patterns of behavior; able to assess information objectively in the pursuit of utilitarian goals. What varies is not the degree of rationality, but the structural foundations of the incentive systems which, in turn, produce different forms of behavior given the same process of rational calculus. It was not attitudinal transformations which generated the rapid industrialization which developed after the Great Depression, but the need to replace imports with domestic products. Or, as Cardoso points out in his studies of entrepreneurs, it is not values which condition their behavior as much as technological dependence, state intervention in the economy, and their political weakness vis-à-vis domestic and foreign actors.[7] What appear as anomalies in the modernization literature can be accounted for by a focus on contextual processes in the dependence literature.

It is necessary to underscore the fact that dependency writers stress the importance of the "way internal and external structural components are connected" in elaborating the structural context of underdevelopment. As such, underdevelopment is not simply the result of "external constraints" on peripheral societies, nor can dependency be operationalized solely with reference to clusters of external variables.[8] Dependency in any given society is a complex set of associations in which the external dimensions are determinative in varying degrees and, indeed, internal variables may very well reinforce the pattern of external linkages. Historically, it has been rare for local interests to develop on the periphery which are capable of charting a successful policy of self-sustained development. Dominant local interests, given the nature of class arrangements emerging from the characteristics of peripheral economies, have tended to favor the preservation of rearticulation of patterns of dependency in their interests.

It is also important to note that while relations of dependency viewed historically help to explain underdevelopment, it does not follow that dependent relations today necessarily perpetuate across the board underdevelopment. With the evolution of the world system, the impact of dependent relations can change in particular contexts. This is why Cardoso, in studying contemporary Brazil, stresses the possibility of "associated-dependent development," and Sunkel and Edmundo Fuenzalida are able to envision sharp economic growth among countries most tied into the contemporary transnational system.[9] Because external-internal relations are complex, and because changes in the world system over time introduce new realities, it is indispensable to study comparatively concrete national and historical situations. As Aníbal Quijano says, "The relationships of dependency . . . take on many forms. The national societies in Latin America are dependent, as is the case with the majority of the Asian, African and some European countries. However, each case does not present identical dependency relations."[10] The dependency perspective has thus concentrated on a careful historical evaluation of the similarities and differences in the "situations of dependency" of the various Latin American countries over time implying careful attention to "preexisting conditions" in different contexts.[11]

The description of various phases in the world system and differing configurations of external-internal linkages follow from this insistence on diachronic analysis and its application to concrete cases. The dependency perspective is primarily a historical model with no claim to "universal validity." This is why it has paid less attention to the formulation of precise theoretical constructs, such as those found in the modernization literature, and more attention to the specification of historical phases which are an integral part of the framework.

The dependency literature distinguishes between the "mercantilistic" colonial period (1500–1750), the period of "outward growth" dependent on primary exports (1750–1914), the period of the crisis of the "liberal model" (1914–1950), and the current period of "transnational capitalism."

As already noted, because of the need for raw materials and foodstuffs for the growing industrialization of England, Germany, the United States, and France, Latin American productive structures were aimed from the outset at the export market. During the colonial period, the economic specialization was imposed by the Iberian monarchies. As Bagú notes in his classic study, "Colonial production was not directed by the needs of national consumers, and not even by the interests of local producers. The lines of production were structured and transformed to conform to an order determined by the imperial metropolis. The colonial economy was consequently shaped by its complementary character. The products that did not compete with those of Spain or Portugal in the metropolitan, international or colonial markets, found tolerance or stimulus. . . ."[12] During the nineteenth century, exports were actively pursued by the politically dominant groups. The independence movement did not attempt to transform internal productive structures; it was aimed at eliminating Iberian interference in the commercialization of products to and from England and northern Europe. The logic of the productive system in this period of "outwardly directed development," in ECLA's terms, was not conducive to the creation of a large industrial sector. Economic rationality, not only of individual entrepreneurs but also of the system, dictated payments in kind and/or extremely low wages and/or the use of slavery, thus markedly limiting the internal market. At the same time, the accumulation of foreign exchange made relatively easy the acquisition of imported industrial products. Any expansion of exports was due more to political than economic factors and depended on a saleable export commodity, and plenty of land and labor, for its success.

There were, however, important differences among regions and countries. During the colonial period these are attributable to differences in colonial administrations, natural resources, and types of production. During the nineteenth century a key difference was the degree of local elite control over productive activities for export. Though in all countries elites controlled export production initially (external commercialization was mainly under foreign control), toward the end of the century in some countries control was largely relinquished to foreign exploitation. Where this occurred, the economic role of local elites was reduced considerably, though the importance of this reduction varied depending both on the degree to which the foreign enclave displaced the local elite from the export sector and the extent to which its economic activities were diversified. Concurrently, the state bureaucracy expanded and acquired increasing importance through regulations and taxation of the enclave sector. The state thus became the principal intermediary between the local economy and the enclave, which generally had little *direct* internal secondary impact. Other differences, especially at the turn of the century, are the varying importance of incipient industrialization, the size and importance of middle- and working-class groups, variations in export products, natural resources, and so on.[13]

The world wars and the depression produced a crisis in the export-oriented economies through the collapse of external demand, and therefore of the capacity to import. The adoption of fiscal and monetary policies aimed at supporting the internal market and avoiding the negative effects of the external disequilibrium produced a favorable climate for the growth of an industrial sector under national auspices. The available foreign exchange was employed to acquire capital goods to substitute imports of consumer articles.[14] The early successes of the transition to what ECLA calls "inwardly directed development" depended to a large extent on the different political alliances which emerged in the various national settings, and on the characteristics of the social and political structures inherited from the precrisis period.

Thus, in the enclave situations the earliest developments were attained in Mexico and Chile, where middle- and lower-class groups allied in supporting state development policies, ultimately strengthening the urban bourgeoisie. The alliance was successful in Chile because of the importance of middle-class parties which emerged during the final period of export-oriented development, and the early consolidation of a trade union movement. The antecedents of the Mexican situation are to be found in the destruction of agricultural elites during the revolution. Such structural conditions were absent in other enclave situations (Bolivia, Perú, Venezuela, and Central America) where the internal development phase began later under new conditions of dependence, though in some cases with similar political alliances (Bolivia, Venezuela, Guatemala, Costa Rica). Throughout the crisis period agrarian-based and largely nonexporting groups were able to remain in power, appealing in some cases to military governments, and preserving the political scheme that characterized the export-oriented period.

In the nonenclave situations, considerable industrial growth was attained in Argentina and Brazil. In the former, export-oriented entrepreneurs had invested considerably in production for the internal market and the contraction of the export sector only accentuated this trend. In Brazil the export-oriented agrarian groups collapsed with the crisis and the state, as in Chile and Mexico, assumed a major developmental role with the support of a complex alliance of urban entrepreneurs, nonexport agrarian elites, popular sectors, and middle-class groups. In Colombia the export-oriented agrarian elites remained in power and did not foster significant internal industrialization until the fifties.[15]

The import substituting industrialization attained greatest growth in Argentina, Brazil, and Mexico. It soon, however, reached its limits, given the parameters under which it was realized. Since capital goods for the establishment of industrial parks were acquired in the central nations, the success of the policy ultimately depended on adequate foreign exchange supplies. After reaching maximum growth through the accumulation of foreign exchange during World War II, the industrialization programs could only continue—given the available political options—on the basis of an increased external debt and further reliance on foreign investments. This accumulation of foreign reserves permitted the success of the national-populist alliances in Argentina and Brazil which gave the workers greater welfare while maintaining investments. The downfall of Perón and the suicide of Vargas symbolized the end of this easy period of import substitution.

But the final blow to "import substitution" industrialization came not from difficulties in the periphery but further transformations in the center which have led, in Sunkel's term, to the creation of a new "transnational" system. With rapid economic recovery the growing multinational corporations sought new markets and cheaper production sites for their increasingly technological manufacturing process. Dependency consequently acquired a "new character" as dos Santos noted, which would have a profound effect on Latin America. Several processes were involved resulting in (1) the investment of centrally based corporations in manufactures within the periphery for sales in its internal market or, as Cardoso and Enzo Faletto note, the "internationalisation of the internal market"; (2) a new international division of labor in which the periphery acquires capital goods, technology, and raw materials from the central nations, and export profits, along with its traditional raw materials and a few manufactured items produced by multinational subsidiaries; and (3) a denationalization of the older import substituting industries established originally.[16] Although the "new dependence" is in evidence throughout the continent, the process has asserted itself more clearly in the largest internal markets such as Brazil, where the weakness of the trade-union movement (the comparison with Argentina in this respect is instructive) coupled with authoritarian political structures has created a singularly favorable investment climate.

In subsequent and more recent works writers in the dependency framework have pursued different strategies of research. Generally speaking, the early phases of the historical process have received less attention, though the contribution of Immanuel Wallerstein to an understanding of the origins of the world system is a major addition to the literature.[17] Most writers have preferred to focus on the current "new situation" of dependence. Some have devoted more attention to an effort at elaborating the place of dependent capitalism as a contribution to the Marxist analysis of capitalist society. Scholars in this vein tend to argue more forcefully than others that dependent capitalism is impossible and that socialism provides the only historically viable alternative.[18] Others have focused more on the analysis of concrete cases of dependence, elaborating in some detail the various interconnections between domestic and foreign forces, and noting the possibility of different kinds of dependent development.[19] Still others have turned their attention to characterizing the nature of the new capitalist system, with particular emphasis on the emergence of a "transnational system" which is rendering more complex and problematic the old distinctions of center and periphery.[20] Particularly for the last two tendencies, the emphasis is on the design of new empirical studies while attempting to systematize further some of the propositions implicit in the conceptual framework.

SUMMARY AND CONCLUSIONS

Modernization and dependency are two different perspectives each claiming to provide conceptual and analytical tools capable of explaining the relative underdevelopment of Latin America. The object of inquiry is practically the only thing that these two competing "visions" have in common, as they differ substantially not only on fundamental assumptions, but also on methodological implications and strategies for research.

Though there are variations in the literature, the *level of analysis* of a substantial tradition in the modernization perspective, and the one which informs most reflections on Latin America, is behavioral or microsociological. The primary focus is on individuals or aggregates of individuals, their values, attitudes, and beliefs. The dependency perspective, by contrast, is structural or macrosociological. Its focus is on the mode of production, patterns of international trade, political and economic linkages between elites in peripheral and central countries, group and class alliances and conflicts, and so on. Both perspectives are concerned with the process of development in national societies. However, for the modernization writer the national society is the basic *unit of analysis,* while the writer in a dependence framework considers the global system and its various forms of interaction with national societies as the primary object of inquiry.

For the dependency perspective, the *time dimension* is a crucial aspect of what is fundamentally a historical model. Individual societies cannot be presumed to be able to replicate the evolution of other societies because the very transformation of an interrelated world system may preclude such an option. The modernization potential of individual societies must be seen in light of changes over time in the interactions between external and internal variables. The modernization perspective is obviously concerned about the origins of traditional and modern values; but, the time dimension is not fundamental to the explanatory pretensions of a model which claims "universal validity." Without knowing the source of modernity-inhibiting characteristics, it is still possible to identify them by reference to their counterparts in developing contexts.

At the root of the differences between the two perspectives is a fundamentally different *perception of human nature.* Dependency assumes that human behavior in economic matters is a "constant." Individuals will behave differently in different contexts not because they are different but because the contexts are different. The insistence on structures and, in the final analysis, on the broadest structural category of all, the world system, follows logically from the view that opportunity structures condition human behavior. Modernizationists, on the other hand, attribute the lack of certain behavioral patterns to the "relativity" of human behavior; to the fact that cultural values and beliefs, regardless of opportunity structures, underlie the patterns of economic action. Thus, the *conception of change* in the modernization perspective is a product of innovations which result from the adoption of modern attitudes among elites, and eventually followers. Though some modernization theorists are now more pessimistic about the development potential of such changes, modernizing beliefs are a prerequisite for development. For dependency analysts the conception of change is different. Change results from the realignment of dependency relations over time. Whether or not development occurs and how it occurs are subject to controversy. Given the rapid evolution of the world system, dependent development is possible in certain contexts, not in others. Autonomy, through a break in relations of dependency, may not lead to development of the kind already arrived at in the developed countries because of the inability to re-create the same historical conditions, but it might lead to a different kind of development stressing different values. Thus, the *prescription for change* varies substantially in the dependency perspective depending on the ideological outlook of particular authors. It is not a logical consequence of the historical model. In the modernization perspective the prescription for change follows more automatically from the assumptions of the model, implying greater consensus.

From a methodological point of view the modernization perspective is much more parsimonious than its counterpart. And the focus of much of the literature on the microsociological level makes it amenable to the elaboration of precise explanatory propositions such as those of David McClelland or Everett Hagen. Dependency, by contrast, is more descriptive and its macrosociological formulations are much less subject to translation into a simple set of explanatory propositions. Many aspects of dependency, and particularly the linkages between external phenomena and internal class and power relations, are unclear and need to be studied with more precision and care. For this reason the dependency perspective is an "approach" to the study of underdevelopment rather than a "theory." And yet, precisely because modernization theory relies on a simple conceptual framework and a reductionist approach, it is far less useful for the study of a complex phenomenon such as development or underdevelopment.

But the strengths of the dependency perspective lie not only in its consideration of a richer body of evidence and a broader range of phenomena, it is also more promising from a methodological point of view. The modernization perspective has fundamental flaws which make it difficult to provide for a fair test of its own assumptions. It will be recalled that the modernization perspective draws on a model with "universal validity" which assumes that traditional values are not conducive to modern behavioral patterns of action. Given that underdevelopment, on the basis of various economic and social indicators, is an objective datum, the research task becomes one of identifying modernizing values and searching for their opposites in underdeveloped contexts.

In actual research efforts, the modernity-inhibiting characteristics are often "deduced" from impressionistic observation. This is the case with much of the political science literature on Latin America. However, more "rigorous" methods, such as survey research, have also been employed, particularly in studies of entrepreneurial activity. Invariably, whether through deduction or survey research, less appropriate values for modernization such as "arielismo" (a concern for transcendental as opposed to material values) or "low-achievement" (lack of risk-taking attitudes) have been identified thus "confirming" the hypothesis that traditional values contribute to underdevelopment. If by chance the use of control groups should establish little or no difference in attitudes in a developed and underdeveloped context, the research instrument can be considered to be either faulty or the characteristics tapped not the appropriate ones for identifying traditional attitudes. The latter alternative might lead to the "discovery" of a new "modernity of tradition" literature or of greater flexibility than anticipated in traditional norms or of traditional residuals in the developed country.

The problem with the model and its behavioral level of analysis is that the explanation for underdevelopment is part of the preestablished conceptual framework. It is already "known" that in backward areas the modernity-inhibiting characteristics play the dominant role, otherwise the areas would not be backward. As such, the test of the hypothesis involves a priori acceptance of the very hypothesis up for verification, with empirical evidence gathered solely in an illustrative manner. The focus on individuals simply does not permit consideration of a broader range of contextual variables which might lead to invalidating the assumptions. Indeed, the modernity of tradition literature, which has pointed to anomalies in the use of the tradition-modernity "polarities," is evidence of how such a perspective can fall victim to the "and so" fallacy. Discrepancies are accounted for not by a reformulation, but by adding a new definition or a new corollary to the preexisting conceptual framework.

Much work needs to be done within a dependency perspective to clarify its concepts and causal interrelationships, as well as to assess its capacity to explain social processes in various parts of peripheral societies. And yet the dependency approach appears to have a fundamental advantage over the modernization perspective: It is open to historically grounded conceptualization in underdeveloped contexts, while modernization is locked into an illustrative methodological style by virtue of its very assumptions.

NOTES

1. See Osvaldo Sunkel, "Política nacional de desarrollo y dependencia externa," *Estudios Internacionales*, I (April 1967). For reviews of the dependency literature see Norman Girvan, "The Development of Dependency Economics in the Caribbean and Latin America: Review and Comparison," *Social and Economic Studies*, XXII (March 1973); Ronald H. Chilcote, "A Critical Synthesis of the Dependency Literature," *Latin American Perspectives*, I (Spring 1974); and Phillip O'Brien, "A Critique of Latin American Theories of Dependence," in I. Oxaal et al., eds. *Beyond the Sociology of Development* (London, 1975).

2. Osvaldo Sunkel and Pedro Paz, *El subdesarrollo latinoamericano y la teoría del desarrollo* (Mexico, 1970), p. 6.

3. Theotonio dos Santos, "La crisis del desarrollo y las relaciones de dependencia en América Latina," in H. Jaguaribe et al., eds. *La dependencia político-económica de América Latina* (Mexico, 1970), p. 180. See also his *Dependencia y cambio social* (Santiago, 1970) and *Socialismo o Fascismo: El nuevo carácter de la dependencia y el dilema latinoamericano* (Buenos Aires, 1972).

4. Sunkel and Paz, p. 39; Fernando Henrique Cardoso and Enzo Faletto, *Dependencia y desarrollo en América Latina* (Mexico, 1969).

5. This is the problem with the studies by Robert Kaufman et al., "A Preliminary Test of the Theory of Dependency," *Comparative Politics*, VII (April

1975), 303–30, and C. Chase-Dunn, "The Effects of International Economic Dependence on Development and Inequality: A Cross National Study," *American Sociological Review,* XL (December 1975). It is interesting to note that Marxist scholars make the same mistake. They point to features in the dependency literature such as unemployment, marginalization, etc., noting that they are not peculiar to peripheral countries but characterize capitalist countries in general. Thus "dependence" is said to have no explanatory value beyond a Marxist theory of capitalist society. See Sanyaya Lall, "Is Dependence a Useful Concept in Analyzing Underdevelopment?," *World Development,* III (November 1975) and Theodore Weisscopf, "Dependence as an Explanation of Underdevelopment: A Critique" (paper presented at the Sixth Annual Latin American Studies Association Meeting, Atlanta, Georgia, 1976). The point of dependency analysis is not the relative mix at one point in time of certain identifiable factors but the evolution over time of structural relations which help to explain the differential development of capitalism in different parts of the world. As a historical model it cannot be tested with cross national data. For an attempt to differentiate conceptually contemporary capitalism of the core and peripheral countries, and thus more amenable to such criticism, see Samir Amin, *Accumulation on a World Scale* (New York, 1974).

6. Some authors have criticized the focus of the literature on the evolution of the world capitalist system. David Ray, for example, has argued that "soviet satellites" are also in a dependent and unequal relationship vis-à-vis the Soviet Union and that the key variable should not be capitalism but "political power." Robert Packenham has also argued that the most important critique of the dependency literature is that it does not consider the implications of "power." See Ray, "The Dependency Model of Latin American Underdevelopment: Three Basic Fallacies," *Journal of Interamerican Studies and World Affairs,* XV (February 1973) and Packenham, "Latin American Dependency Theories: Strengths and Weaknesses" (paper presented to the Harvard-MIT Joint Seminar on Political Development, February 1974), especially pp. 16–17, 54. This criticism misses the point completely. It is not power relations today which cause underdevelopment, but the historical evolution of a world economic system which led to economic specialization more favorable to some than others. It is precisely this concern with the evolution of world capitalism which has led to the preoccupation in the dependency literature with rejecting interpretations stressing the "feudal" rather than "capitalist" nature of colonial and postcolonial Latin American agriculture. On this point see Sergio Bagú, *Económia de la Sociedad Colonial* (Buenos Aires, 1949); Luis Vitale, "América Latina: Feudal o Capitalista?," *Revista Estrategia,* III (1966) and *Interpretación Marxista de la historia de Chile* (Santiago, 1967); and E. Laclau, "Feudalism and Capitalism in Latin America," *New Left Review,* LXVII (May–July 1971). A brilliant recent exposition of the importance of studying the evolution of the capitalist world system in order to understand underdevelopment which focuses more on the center states than on the periphery is Immanuel Wallerstein, *The Modern World System: Capitalist Agriculture and the Origins of the European World Economy in the Sixteenth Century* (New York, 1974).

7. Cardoso, *Empresário industrial e desenvolvimento económico no Brazil* (São Paulo, 1964) and *Ideologías de la burguesia industrial en sociedades dependientes* (Mexico, 1971).

8. Cardoso and Faletto, *Dependencia y desarrollo,* p. 20. Indeed, Cardoso argues that the distinction between external and internal is "metaphysical." See his "Teoría de la dependencia o análisis de situaciones concretas de dependencia?," *Revista Latinoamericana de Ciencia Política,* I (December 1970), 404. The ontology implicit in such an analysis is the one of "internal relations." See Bertell

Ollman, *Alienation: Marx's Conception of Man in Capitalist Society* (London, 1971). This point is important because both André Gunder Frank and the early ECLA literature were criticized for their almost mechanistic relationship between external and internal variables. Frank acknowledges this problem and tries to answer his critics in *Lumpenbourgeoisie and Lumpendevelopment* (New York, 1967). "Tests" of dependency theory also attribute an excessively mechanical dimension to the relationship. See Kaufman et al., "A Preliminary Test of the Theory of Dependency."

9. Cardoso, "Associated Dependent Development: Theoretical Implications," in Alfred Stepan, ed. *Authoritarian Brazil* (New Haven, 1973), and Sunkel and Edmundo Fuenzalida, "Transnational Capitalism and National Development," in José J. Villamil, ed. *Transnational Capitalism and National Development* (London, forthcoming). It is thus incorrect to argue that dependency analysts ignore the evidence of certain kinds of economic growth. For fallacies in the dependency literature see Cardoso, "Las contradicciones del desarrollo asociado," *Desarrollo Económico*, IV (April–June 1974).

10. Aníbal Quijano, "Dependencia, Cambio Social y Urbanización en América Latina," in Cardoso and F. Weffort, eds. *América Latina: Ensayos de interpretación sociológico político* (Santiago, 1970).

11. Cardoso and Faletto, *Dependencia y desarrollo, pp. 19–20;* Sunkel and Paz, *El subdesarrollo latinoamericano,* pp. 5, 9.

12. Bagú, *Economía de la Sociedad Colonial,* pp. 122–23.

13. On industrialization see A. Dorfman, *La industrialisación en América Latina y las políticas de fomento* (Mexico, 1967).

14. See M. de C. Tavares, "El proceso de sustitución de importaciones como modelo de desarrollo reciente en América Latina," in Andres Bianchi, ed. *América Latina: Ensayos de interpretación económica* (Santiago, 1969).

15. For detailed discussions of nonenclave versus enclave situations see Cardoso and Faletto, and Sunkel and Paz.

16. Sunkel, "Capitalismo transnacional y desintegración nacional en América Latina," *Estudios Internacionales,* IV (January–March 1971) and "Big Business and Dependencia: A Latin American View," *Foreign Affairs,* L (April 1972); Cardoso and Faletto; dos Santos, *El nuevo carácter de la dependencia* (Santiago, 1966).

17. Wallerstein, *The Modern World System.*

18. V. Bambirra, *Capitalismo dependient latinoamericano* (Santiago, 1973); R. M. Marini, *Subdesarrollo y revolución* (Mexico, 1969); F. Hinkelammert, *El subdesarrollo latinoamericano: un caso de desarrollo capitalista* (Santiago, 1970).

19. Cardoso, "Teoría de la dependencia." A recent trend in dependency writings attempts to explain the current wave of authoritarianism in Latin America as a result of economic difficulties created by the exhaustion of the easy import substituting industrialization. The new situation leads to a process of development led by the state and the multinational corporations which concentrates income toward the top, increases the levels of capital accumulation, and expands heavy industry; the old populist alliances can therefore no longer be maintained. See dos Santos, *Socialismo o fascismo: el nuevo carácter de la dependencia y el dilema latinoamericano* (Buenos Aires, 1972); Guillermo O'Donnell, *Modernization and Bureaucratic Authoritarianism: Studies in Latin American Politics* (Berkeley, 1973); Atilio Borón, "El fascismo como categoría histórica: en torno al problema de las dictaduras en América Latina," *Revista Mexicana de Sociología,* XXXIV (April–June 1977); the effects of this situation on labor are explored in Kenneth P. Erickson and Patrick Peppe, "Dependent Capitalist Development, U.S. Foreign Policy, and Repression of the Working Class in Chile and Brazil," *Latin American Perspectives,*

III (Winter 1976). However, in the postscript to their 1968 book, Cardoso and Faletto caution against adopting an excessively mechanistic view on this point, against letting "economism kill history": Cardoso and Faletto, "Estado y proceso político en América Latina," *Revista Mexicana de Sociología,* XXXIV (April–June 1977), 383. Articles with dependency perspective appear frequently in the *Revista Mexicana de Sociología* as well as in *Latin American Perspectives.*

20. Sunkel, "Capitalismo transnacional y desintegración nacional en América Latina," and Sunkel and Fuenzalida, "Transnational Capitalism and National Development."

24

· · · · · · ·

The Present State of the Debate on World Inequality

· · · · · · ·

IMMANUEL WALLERSTEIN

Immanuel Wallerstein is generally considered the driving intellectual force behind the "world-system" school of thought. He has articulated his view of development in a series of books and articles, perhaps the best known of which is The Modern World-System: Capitalist Agriculture and the Origins of the European World-Economy in the Sixteenth Century *(Academic Press, 1974). Wallerstein sees dependency theory as a subset of his broader world-system perspective. In this chapter, he argues that all states form part of a capitalist world economy in which the existence of differences in wealth is not an anomaly but rather a natural outcome of the fundamental processes driving that economy. According to this perspective, the gap between rich and poor ultimately will disappear, but only when the capitalist world system that has been in place since the sixteenth century itself disappears.*

It has never been a secret from anyone that some have more than others. And in the modern world at least, it is no secret that some countries have more than other countries. In short, world inequality is a phenomenon about which most men and most groups are quite conscious.

I do not believe that there has ever been a time when these inequalities were unquestioned. That is to say, people or groups who have more have always felt the need to justify this fact, if for no other reason than to try to convince those who have less that they should accept this fact with relative

Reprinted with permission from *World Inequality: Origins and Perspectives on the World System,* edited by Immanuel Wallerstein (Montreal: Black Rose Books, 1975).

docility. These ideologies of the advantaged have had varying degrees of success over time. The history of the world is one of a constant series of revolts against inequality—whether that of one people or nation vis-à-vis another or of one class within a geographical area against another.

This statement is probably true of all of recorded history, indeed of all historical events, at least since the Neolithic Revolution. What has changed with the advent of the modern world in the sixteenth century is neither the existence of inequalities nor of the felt need to justify them by means of ideological constructs. What has changed is that even those who defend the "inevitability" of inequalities in the present feel the need to argue that eventually, over time, these inequalities will disappear, or at the very least diminish considerably in scope. Another way of saying this is that of the three dominant ideological currents of the modern world—conservatism, liberalism, and Marxism—two at least (liberalism and Marxism) are committed in theory and the abstract to egalitarianism as a principle. The third, conservatism, is not, but conservatism is an ideology that has been very much on the defensive ever since the French Revolution. The proof of this is that most conservatives decline to fly the banner openly but hide their conservative ideas under the mantle of liberalism or occasionally even Marxism.

Surely it is true that in the universities of the world in the twentieth century, and in other expressions of intellectuals, the contending ideologies have been one variant or another of liberalism and Marxism. (Remember at this point we are talking of ideologies and not of political movements. Both "liberal" parties and social democratic parties in the twentieth century have drawn on liberal ideologies.)

One of the most powerful thrusts of the eighteenth-century Enlightenment, picked up by most nineteenth- and twentieth-century thought-systems, was the assumption of progress, reformulated later as evolution. In the context of the question of equality, evolution was interpreted as the process of moving from an imperfect, unequal allocation of privileges and resources to some version of equality. There was considerable argument about how to define equality. (Reflect on the different meanings of "equality of opportunity" and "to each according to his needs.") There was considerable disagreement about who or what were the obstacles to this desired state of equality. And there was fundamental discord about how to transform the world from its present imperfection to the desired future, primarily between the advocates of gradualism based on education and advocates of revolution based on the use at some point in time of violence.

I review this well-known history of modern ideas to underline where I think our current debates are simply the latest variant of now classic debates and where I think some new issues have been raised which make these older formulations outdated.

If one takes the period 1945–1960, both politically and intellectually, we have in many ways the apogee of the liberal-Marxist debate. The world was politically polarized in the so-called cold war. There were two camps. One called itself the "free world" and argued that it and it alone upheld the first part of the French Revolution's trilogy, that of "liberty." It argued that its economic system offered the hope over time of approximating "equality" through a path which it came to call "economic development" or sometimes just "development." It argued too that it was gradually achieving "fraternity" by means of education and political reform (such as the 1954 Supreme Court decision in the United States, ending the legality of segregation).

The other camp called itself the "socialist world" and argued that it and it alone represented the three objectives of the French Revolution and hence the interests of the people of the world. It argued that when movements inspired by these ideas would come to power in all non-"socialist" countries (and however they came to power), each would enact legislation along the same lines and by this process the whole world would become "socialist" and the objective would be achieved.

These somewhat simplistic ideological statements were of course developed in much more elaborate form by the intellectuals. It has become almost traditional (but I think nonetheless just) to cite W. W. Rostow's *The Stages of Economic Growth* as a succinct, sophisticated, and relatively pure expression of the dominant liberal ideology which informed the thinking of the political leadership of the United States and its Western allies. Rostow showed no modesty in his subtitle, which was "a non-Communist Manifesto."

His basic thesis is no doubt familiar to most persons interested in these problems. Rostow saw the process of change as a series of stages through which each national unit had to go. They were the stages through which Rostow felt Great Britain had gone, and Great Britain was the crucial example since it was defined as being the first state to embark on the evolutionary path of the modern industrial world. The inference, quite overtly drawn, was that this path was a model, to be copied by other states. One could then analyze what it took to move from one stage to another, why some nations took longer than others, and could prescribe (like a physician) what a nation must do to hurry along its process of "growth." I will not review what ideological function such a formulation served. This has been done repeatedly and well. Nonetheless, this viewpoint, somewhat retouched, still informs the developmentalist ideas of the major Western governments as well as that of international agencies. I consider Lester Pearson's "Partners in Progress" report in the direct line of this analytic framework.

In the socialist world in this period there was no book quite the match of Rostow's. What there was instead was an encrusted version of evolutionary Marxism which also saw rigid stages through which every state or geographical entity had to go. The differences were that the stages covered longer historical time and the model country was the USSR. These are the stages known as slavery-feudalism-capitalism-socialism. The absurdities of the rigid formulation which dates from the 1930s and the inappropriateness of applying this on a *national* level have been well argued recently by an Indian Marxist intellectual, Irfan Habib, who argues not only the meaningfulness of the concept of the "Asiatic mode of production" but also the illogic of insisting that the various historical modes of extracting a surplus must each, necessarily, occur in all countries and follow in a specific order. Habib argues:

> The materialist conception of history need not necessarily prescribe a set universal periodisation, since what it essentially does is to formulate an analytic method for the development of class societies, and any periodisation, theoretically, serves as no more than the illustration of the application of such a method. . . . The crucial thing is the definition of principal contradiction (i.e., class-contradictions) in a society, the marking out of factors responsible for intensifying them, and the delineation of the shaping of the social order, when a particular contradiction is resolved. It is possible that release from the set P-S-F-C pattern [primitive communism-slavery-feudalism-capitalism] may lead Marxists to apply themselves better to this task, since they would no longer be obliged to look for the same "fundamental laws of the epoch" (a favorite Soviet term), or "prime mover," as premised for the supposedly corresponding European epoch.[1]

I give this excerpt from Habib because I very much agree with his fundamental point that this version of Marxist thought, so prevalent between 1945 and 1965, is a sort of "mechanical copying" of liberal views. Basically, the analysis is the same as that represented by Rostow except that the names of the stages are changed and the model country has shifted from Great Britain to the USSR. I will call this approach the developmentalist perspective, as espoused either by liberals or Marxists.

There is another perspective that has slowly pushed its way into public view during the 1960s. It has no commonly accepted name, in part because the early formulations of this point of view have often been confused, partial, or unclear. It was first widely noticed in the thinking of the Latin American structuralists (such as Raúl Prebisch and Celso Furtado) and those allied to them elsewhere (such as Dudley Sears). It later took the form of arguments such as the "development of underdevelopment" (A. G. Frank, in the heritage of Paul Baran's *The Political Economy of Growth*), the "structure of dependence" (Theotonio dos Santos), "unequal exchange" (Arghiri Emmanuel), "accumulation of world capital" (Samir Amin), "subimperialism" (Ruy Mauro Marini). It also surfaced in the Chinese Cultural Revolution as Mao's concept of the continuity of the class struggle under socialist regimes in single countries.[2]

What all these concepts have in common is a critique of the developmentalist perspective. Usually they make it from a Marxist tradition but it should be noted that some of the critics, such as Furtado, come from a liberal heritage. It is no accident that this point of view has been expressed largely by persons from Asia, Africa and Latin America or by those others particularly interested in these regions (such as Umberto Melotti of *Terzo Mondo*).[3]

I would like to designate this point of view the "world-system perspective." I mean by that term that it is based on the assumption, explicitly or implicitly, that the modern world comprises a single capitalist world-economy, which has emerged historically since the sixteenth century and which still exists today. It follows from such a premise that national states are *not* societies that have separate, parallel histories, but parts of a whole reflecting that whole. To the extent that stages exist, they exist for the system as a whole. To be sure, since different parts of the world play and have played differing roles in the capitalist world-economy, they have dramatically different internal socio-economic profiles and hence distinctive politics. But to understand the internal class contradictions and political struggles of a particular state, we must first situate it in the world-economy. We can then understand the ways in which various political and cultural thrusts may be efforts to alter or preserve a position within this world-economy which is to the advantage or disadvantage of particular groups located within a particular state.[4]

What thus distinguishes the developmentalists and the world-system perspective is not liberalism versus Marxism nor evolutionism vs. something else (since both are essentially evolutionary). Rather I would locate the distinction in two places. One is in mode of thought. To put it in Hegelian terms, the developmentalist perspective is mechanical, whereas the world-system perspective is dialectical. I mean by the latter term that at every point in the analysis, one asks not what is the formal structure but what is the consequence for both the whole and the parts of maintaining or changing a certain structure at that particular point in time, given the totality of particular positions at that moment in time. Intelligent analysis demands knowledge of the complex texture of social reality (historical concreteness) within a long-range perspective that observes trends and forces of the world-system, which can explain what underlies and informs the diverse historically concrete phenomena. If synchronic comparisons and abstracted generalizations are utilized, it is only as heuristic devices in search of a truth that is ever contemporary and hence ever-changing.

This distinction of scientific methodology is matched by a distinction of praxis, of the politics of the real world. For what comes through as the second great difference between the two perspectives (the developmentalist and the world-system) is the prognosis for action. This is the reason why the latter perspective has emerged primarily from the intellectuals of the Third World. The developmentalist perspective not only insists that the model is to be found in the old developed countries (whether Great Britain, USA, or USSR) but also that the fundamental international political issues revolve around the relations among the hegemonic powers of the world. From a world-system perspective, there are no "models" (a mechanical notion) and the relations of the hegemonic powers are only one of many issues that confront the world-system.

The emergence of the world-system perspective is a consequence of the dramatic challenge to European political domination of the world which has called into question all Europo-centric constructions of social reality. But intellectual evolution itself is seldom dramatic. The restructuring of the allocation of power in the world has made itself felt in the realm of ideas, particularly in the hegemonic areas of the world, via a growing malaise that intellectuals in Europe (including of course North America) have increasingly felt about the validity of their answers to a series of "smaller" questions—smaller, that is, than the nature of the world-system as such.

Let us review successively six knotty questions to which answers from a developmentalist perspective have increasingly seemed inadequate.

Why have certain world-historical events of the last two centuries taken place where and when they have? The most striking "surprise," at the moment it occurred and ever since, is the Russian Revolution. As we all know, neither Marx nor Lenin nor anyone else thought that a "socialist revolution" would occur in Russia earlier than anywhere else. Marx had more or less predicted Great Britain as the likely candidate, and after Marx's death, the consensus of expectation in the international socialist movement was that it would occur in Germany. We know that even after 1917 almost all the leading figures of the Communist Party of the Soviet Union (CPSU) expected that the "revolution" would have to occur quickly in Germany if the Soviet regime was to survive. There was however no socialist revolution in Germany and nonetheless the Soviet regime did survive.

We do not want for explanations of this phenomenon, but we do lack convincing answers. Of course, there exists an explanation that turns Marx on his head and argues that socialist revolutions occur not in the so-called "advanced capitalist" countries but precisely in "backward" countries. But this is in such blatant contradiction with other parts of the developmentalist perspective that its proponents are seldom willing to state it baldly, even less defend it openly.

Nor is the Russian Revolution the only anomaly. There is a long-standing debate about the "exceptionalism" of the United States. How can we explain that the USA replaced Great Britain as the hegemonic industrial power of the world, and in the process managed to avoid giving birth to a serious internal socialist movement? And if the USA could avoid socialism, why could not Brazil or Russia or Canada? Seen from the perspective of 1800, it would have been a bold social scientist who would have predicted the particular success of the USA.

Again there have been many explanations. There is the "frontier" theory. There is the theory that underlines the absence of a previously entrenched "feudal" class. There is the theory of the USA as Britain's "junior partner" who overtook the senior. But all of these theories are precisely "exceptionalist" theories, contradicting the developmentalist paradigm. And furthermore, some of these variables apply to other countries where they did not seem to have the same consequences.

We could go on. I will mention two more briefly. For a long time, Great Britain's primacy (the "first" industrial power) has been unquestioned. But was Britain the "first" and if so why was she? This is a question that only recently has been seriously adumbrated. In April 1974 at an international colloquium held here in Montreal on the theme of "Failed Transitions to Industrialism: The Case of 17th Century Netherlands and Renaissance Italy," one view put forward quite strongly was that neither Italy nor the Netherlands was the locus of the Industrial Revolution precisely because they were too far *advanced* economically. What a striking blow to a developmentalist paradigm.

And lastly one should mention the anomaly of Canada: a country which economically falls into a category below that of the world's leading industrial producers in structural terms, yet nonetheless is near the very top of the list in per capita income. This cannot be plausibly explained from a developmentalist perspective.

If the world has been "developing" or "progressing" over the past few centuries, how do we explain the fact that in many areas things seem to have gotten worse, not better? Worse in many ways, ranging from standard of living, to the physical environment, to the quality of life. And more to the point, worse in some places but better in others. I refer not merely to such contemporary phenomena as the so called "growing gap" between the industrialized countries and the Third World, but also to such earlier phenomena as the deindustrialization of many areas of the world (starting with the widely known example of the Indian textile industry in the late eighteenth and early nineteenth century).

You may say that this contradicts the liberal version of the developmentalist perspective but not its Marxist version, since "polarization" was seen as part of the process of change. True enough, except that "polarization" was presumably within countries and not between them. Furthermore, it is not clear that it is "polarization" that has occurred. While the rich have gotten richer and the poor have gotten poorer, there is surely a fairly large group of countries now somewhere in between on many economic criteria, to cite such politically diverse examples as Mexico, Italy, Czechoslovakia, Iran, and South Africa.

Furthermore, we witness in the 1970s a dramatic shift in the distribution of the profit and the international terms of trade of oil (and possibly other raw materials). You may say it is because of the increased political sophistication and strength of the Arab world. No doubt this has occurred, but is this an explanation? I remind this group that the last moment of time in which there was a dramatic amelioration of world terms of trade of primary products was in the period 1897–1913, a moment which represented in political terms the apogee of European colonial control of the world.

Once again it is not that there are not a large number of explanations for the rise in oil prices. It is rather that I find these explanations, for what they're worth, in contradiction with a developmentalist perspective.

Why are there "regressions"? In 1964, S. N. Eisenstadt published an article entitled "Breakdowns of Modernization," in which he discussed the fact that there seemed to be cases of "reversal" of regimes to "a lower, less flexible level of political and social differentiation. . . ."[5]

In seeking to explain the origins of such "reversals," Eisenstadt restricted himself to hesitant hypotheses:

> The problem of why in Turkey, Japan, Mexico, and Russia there emerge in the initial stages of modernization elites with orientations to change and ability to implement relatively effective policies, while they did not develop in these initial phases in Indonesia, Pakistan, or Burma, or why elites with similar differences tended to develop also in later stages of modernization, is an extremely difficult one and constitutes one of the most baffling problems in comparative sociological analysis. There are but four available indications to deal with this problem. Very tentatively, it may perhaps be suggested that to some extent it has to do with the placement of these elites in the preceding social structure, with the extent of their internal cohesiveness, and of the internal transformation of their own value orientation.[6]

As is clear, Eisenstadt's tentative explanation is to be found in anterior factors operating internally in the state. This calls into question the concept of stages through which all not only must pass but all *can* pass, but it leaves intact the state framework as the focus of analysis and explanation. This of course leads us logically to ask how these anterior factors developed. Are they pure historical accident?

Similarly, after the political rebellion of Tito's Yugoslavia against the USSR, the latter began to accuse Yugoslavia of "revisionism" and of returning to capitalism. Later, China took up the same theme against the USSR.

But how can we explain how this happens? There are really two varieties of explanation from a developmentalist perspective. One is to say that "regression" seems to have occurred, but that in fact "progress" had never taken place. The leader of a movement, whether a nationalist movement or a socialist movement, only pretended to favor change. In fact they were really always "neocolonialist" stooges or "revisionists" at heart. Such an explanation has partial truth, but it seems to me to place too much on "false consciousness" and to fail to analyze movements in their immediate and continuing historical contexts.

The second explanation of "regression" is a change of heart—"betrayal." Yes, but once again, how come sometimes, but not always? Are we to explain large-scale social phenomena on the basis of the accident of the biographic histories of the particular leaders involved? I cannot accept this, for leaders remain leaders in the long run only if their personal choices reflect wider social pressures.

If the fundamental paradigm of modern history is a series of parallel national processes, how do we explain the persistence of nationalism, indeed quite often its primacy, as a political force in the modern world? Developmentalists who are liberals deplore nationalism or explain it away as a transitional "integrating" phenomenon. Marxists who are developmentalists are even more embarrassed. If the class struggle is primary—that is, implicitly the intra-national class struggle—how do we explain the fact that the slogan of the Cuban revolution is "Patria o muerte—venceremos?" And how could we explain this even more astonishing quotation from Kim Il Sung, the leader of the Democratic People's Republic of Korea:

> The homeland is a veritable mother for everyone. We cannot live nor be happy outside of our homeland. Only the flourishing and prosperity of our homeland will permit us to go down the path to happiness. The best sons and daughters of our people, all without exception, were first of all ardent patriots. It was to recover their homeland that Korean Communists struggled, before the Liberation, against Japanese imperialism despite every difficulty and obstacle.[7]

And if internal processes are so fundamental, why has not the reality of international workers' solidarity been greater? Remember World War I.

As before, there are many explanations for the persistence of nationalism. I merely observe that all these explanations have to *explain away* the primacy of internal national processes. Or to put it another way, for developmentalists nationalism is sometimes good, sometimes bad. But when it is the one or the other, it is ultimately explained by developmentalists in an ad hoc manner, adverting to its meaning for the world-system.

An even more difficult problem for the developmentalists has been the recrudescence of nationalist movements in areas smaller than that of existing states. And it is not Biafra or Bangladesh that is an intellectual problem, because the usual manner of accounting for secessionist movements in Third World countries has been the failure to attain the stage of "national integration."

No, the surprise has been in the industrialized world: Blacks in the USA, Québec in Canada, Occitania in France, the Celts in Great Britain, and lurking in the background the nationalities question in the USSR. It is not that any of these "nationalisms" is new. They are all long-standing themes of political and cultural conflict in all these countries. The surprise has been that, as of say 1945 or even 1960, most persons in these countries, using a developmentalist paradigm, regarded these movements or claims as remnants of a dying past, destined to diminish still further in vitality. And lo, a phoenix reborn.

The explanations are there. Some cry, anachronism—but if so, then the question remains, how come such a flourishing anachronism? Some say, loud shouting but little substance, a last bubble of national integration. Perhaps, but the intellectual and organizational development of these ethno-national movements seems to have moved rapidly and ever more firmly in a direction quite opposite to national integration. In any case, what in the developmentalist paradigm explains this phenomenon?

One last question, which is perhaps only a reformulation of the previous five. How is it that the "ideal types" of the different versions of the developmentalist perspective all seem so far from empirical reality? Who has not had the experience of not being quite certain which party represents the "industrial proletariat" or the "modernizing elite" in Nigeria, or in France of the Second Empire for that matter? Let us be honest. Each of us, to the extent that he has ever used a developmentalist paradigm, has stretched empirical reality to a very Procrustean bed indeed.

Can the world-system perspective answer these questions better? We cannot yet be sure. This point of view has not yet been fully thought through. But let me indicate some possible lines of argument.

If the world-system is the focus of analysis, and if in particular we are talking of the capitalist world-economy, then divergent historical patterns are precisely to be expected. They are not an anomaly but the essence of the system. If the world-economy is the basic economic entity comprising a single division of labor, then it is natural that different areas perform different economic tasks. Anyway, it is natural under capitalism, and we may talk of the core, the periphery and the semiperiphery of the world-economy. Since, however, political boundaries (states) are smaller than the economic whole, they will each reflect different groupings of economic tasks and strengths in the world-market. Over time, some of these differences may be accentuated rather than diminished—the basic inequalities which are our theme of discussion.

It is also clear that over time the loci of economic activities keep changing. This is due to many factors—ecological exhaustion, the impact of new technology, climate changes, and the socio-economic consequences of these "natural" phenomena. Hence, some areas "progress" and others "regress." But the fact that particular states change their position in the world-economy, from semi-periphery to core say, or vice versa, does not in itself change the nature of the system. These shifts will be registered for individual states as "development" or "regression." The key factor to note is that within a capitalist world-economy, all states cannot "develop" simultaneously *by definition,* since the system functions by virtue of having unequal core and peripheral regions.[8]

Within a world-economy, the state structures function as ways for particular groups to affect and distort the functioning of the market. The stronger the state machinery, the more its ability to distort the world-market in favor of the interests it represents. Core states have stronger state machineries than peripheral states.

This role of the state machineries in a capitalist world-economy explains the persistence of nationalism, since the primary social conflicts are quite often between groups located in different states rather than between groups located within the same state boundaries. Furthermore, this explains the ambiguity of class as a concept, since class refers to the economy which is worldwide, but class consciousness is a political, hence primarily national, phenomenon. Within this context, one can see the recrudescence of ethno-nationalisms in industrialized states as an expression of class consciousness of lower caste-class groups in societies where the class terminology has been preempted by nationwide middle strata organized around the dominant ethnic group.

If then the world-system is the focus of analysis rather than the individual states, it is the natural history of this system at which we must look. Like all systems, the capitalist world-economy has both cyclical and secular trends, and it is important to distinguish them.

On the one hand, the capitalist world-economy seems to go through long cycles of "expansion" and "contraction." I cannot at this point go into the long discussion this would require. I will limit myself to the very brief suggestion that "expansion" occurs when the totality of world production is less than world effective demand, as permitted by the existing social distribution of world purchasing power, and that "contraction" occurs when total world production exceeds world effective demand. These are cycles of 75–100 years in length in my view and the downward cycle is only resolved by a political reallocation of world income that effectively expands world demand. I believe we have just ended an expansionary cycle and we are in the beginning of a contractual one.

These cycles occur within a secular trend that has involved the physical expansion and politico-structural consolidation of the capitalist world-economy as such, but has also given birth to forces and movements which are eating away at these same structural supports of the existing world-system. In particular, these forces which we call revolutionary forces are calling into question the phenomenon of inequality so intrinsic to the existing world-system.

The trend toward structural consolidation of the system over the past four centuries has included three basic developments:

The first has been the capitalization of world agriculture, meaning the ever more efficient use of the world's land and sea resources in large productive units with larger and larger components of fixed capital. Over time, this has encompassed more and more of the earth's surface, and at the present we are probably about to witness the last major physical expansion, the elimination of all remaining plots restricted to small-scale, so-called "subsistence" production. The counterpart of this process has been the steady concentration of the world's population as salaried workers in small, dense pockets—that is, proletarianization and urbanization. The initial impact of this entire process has been to render large populations more exploitable and controllable.

The second major structural change has been the development of technology that maximizes the ability to transform the resources of the earth into usable commodities at "reasonable" cost levels. This is what we call industrialization, and the story is far from over. The next century should see the spread of industrial activity from the temperate core areas in which it has hitherto been largely concentrated to the tropical and semi-tropical peripheral areas. Industrialization too has hitherto tended to consolidate the system in providing a large part of the profit that makes the system worth the while of those who are on top of it, with a large enough surplus to sustain and appease the world's middle strata. Mere extension of industrial activity will not change a peripheral area into a core area, for the core areas will concentrate on ever newer, specialized activities.

The third major development, at once technological and social, has been the strengthening of all organizational structures—the states, the economic corporate structures, and even the cultural institutions—vis-à-vis both individuals and groups. This is the process of bureaucratization, and while it has been uneven (the core states are still stronger than the peripheral states, for example), all structures are stronger today than previously. Prime ministers of contemporary states have the power today that Louis XIV sought in vain to achieve. This too has been stabilizing because the ability of these bureaucracies physically to repress opposition is far greater than in the past.

But there is the other side of each of these coins. The displacement of the world's population into urban areas has made it easier ultimately to organize forces against the power structures. This is all the more so since the ever-expanding market-dependent, property-less groups are simultaneously more educated, more in communication with each other, and hence *potentially* more politically conscious.

The steady industrialization of the world has eaten away at the political and hence economic justifications for differentials in rewards. The technological advances, while still unevenly distributed, have created a new military equality of destructive potential. It is true that one nation may have 1000 times the fire power of another, but if the weaker one has sufficient to incur grievous damage, of how much good is it for the stronger to have 1000 times as much strength? Consider not merely the power of a weaker state with a few nuclear rockets but the military power of urban guerrillas. It is the kind of problem Louis XIV precisely did *not* need to worry about.

Finally, the growth of bureaucracies in the long run has created the weakness of top-heaviness. The ability of the presumed decision makers to control not the populace but the bureaucracies has effectively diminished, which again creates a weakness in the ability to enforce politico-economic will.

Where then in this picture do the forces of change, the movements of liberation, come in? They come in precisely as not totally coherent pressures of groups which arise out of the structural contradictions of the capitalist world-economy. These groups seem to take organizational form as movements, as parties, and sometimes as regimes. But when the movements become regimes, they are caught in the dilemma of becoming part of the machinery of the capitalist world-economy they are presuming to change. Hence the so-called "betrayals." It is important neither to adulate blindly these regimes, for inevitably they "betray" in part their stated goals, nor to be cynical and despairing, for the movements which give birth to such regimes represent real forces, and the creation of such regimes is part of a long run process of social transformation.

What we need to put in the forefront of our consciousness is that both the party of order and the party of movement are currently strong. We have not yet reached the peak of the political consolidation of the capitalist world-economy. We are already in the phase of its political decline. If your outlook is developmentalist and mechanical, this pair of statements is an absurdity. From a world-system perspective, and using a dialectical mode of analysis, it is quite precise and intelligible.

This struggle takes place on all fronts—political, economic, and cultural—and in all arenas of the world, in the core states, in the periphery (largely in the Third World), and in the semi-periphery (many but not all of which states have collective ownership of basic property and are hence often called "socialist" states).

Take a struggle like that of Vietnam, or Algeria, or Angola. They were wars of national liberation. They united peoples in these areas. Ultimately, the forces of national liberation won or are winning political change. How may we evaluate its effect? On the one hand, these colonial wars fundamentally weakened the internal supports of the regimes of the USA, France and Portugal. They sapped the dominant forces of world capitalism. These wars made many changes possible in the countries of struggle, the metropolises, and in third countries. And yet, and yet—one can ask if the net result has not been in part further to integrate these countries, even their regimes, into the capitalist world-economy. It did both of course. We gain nothing by hiding this from ourselves. On the other hand, we gain nothing by showing Olympian neutrality in the form of equal disdain for unequal combatants.

The process of analysis and the process of social transformation are not separate. They are obverse sides of one coin. Our praxis informs, indeed makes possible, our analytic frameworks. But the work of analysis is itself a central part of the praxis of change. The perspectives for the future of inequality in the world-system are fairly clear in the long run. In the long run the inequalities will disappear as the result of a fundamental transformation of the world-system. But we all live in the short run, not in the long run. And in the short run, within the constraints of our respective social locations and our social heritages, we labor in the vineyards as we wish, toward what ends we choose. . . .

NOTES

1. Irfan Habib, "Problems of Marxist Historical Analysis in India," *Enquiry,* Monsoon, 1969, reprinted in S. A. Shah, ed., *Towards National Liberation: Essays on the Political Economy of India* (Montreal: n.p., 1973), 8–9.

2. See my "Class Struggle in China?" *Monthly Review,* XXV, 4, Sept. 1973, 55–58.

3. See U. Melotti, "Marx e il Terzo Mondo," *Terzo Mondo,* No. 13–14, sett. dict. 1971. Melotti subtitles the work: "towards a multilinear schema of the Marxist conception of historical development."

4. I have developed this argument at length elsewhere. See *The Modern World-System: Capitalist Agriculture and the Origins of the European World-Economy* (New York and London: Academic Press, 1974) and "The Rise and Future Demise of the World Capitalist System: Concepts for Comparative Analysis," *Comparative Studies in Society and History,* XVI, Oct. 1974, 387–415.

5. S. N. Eisenstadt, "Breakdowns of Modernization," *Economic Development and Cultural Change,* XII, 4, July 1964, 367.

6. Ibid., pp. 365–366.

7. *Activité Révolutionnaire du Camarade Kim Il Sung* (Pyongyang: Ed. en langues étrangères, 1970). Livre illustré, 52nd page (edition unpaginated). Translation mine—I. W.

8. As to how particular states can change their position, I have tried to furnish an explanation in "Dependence in an Interdependent World: The Limited Possibilities of Transformation Within the Capitalist World-Economy," *African Studies Review,* XVII, 1, April 1974, 1–26.

25

· · · · · · ·

Transnational Penetration
and Economic Growth

· · · · · · ·

VOLKER BORNSCHIER & CHRISTOPHER CHASE-DUNN

*Volker Bornschier and Christopher Chase-Dunn are notable among
world-system theorists in that they have broken with proponents of
world-system/dependency theory who deny the applicability of quantitative analysis of hypotheses generated by the approach. They have
also made great strides in identifying, defining, and measuring pertinent variables. In this chapter, Bornschier and Chase-Dunn explain the
impact of transnational corporations (TNCs) on economic growth. They
find support for their contention that TNCs have a positive short-term
impact on economic growth but that over the long term the inflow of
investment reverses, slowing growth. Earlier in their book, the authors
seemed to make a concession to those criticizing world-system theory
for minimizing, if not denying, the importance of the state in devising
development policy. State officials can make mistakes that undermine
growth, the authors said, but in the concluding sections of this chapter
Bornschier and Chase-Dunn see little hope that the state can overcome the negative impact of TNCs. Nevertheless, their concession
could open the way for new research on the role of the state in development policy within world-system theory.*

. . . The question at issue here is, what are the effects of transnational corporate penetration on economic growth? We are only concerned here with
the observed overall relationships and not with mediating variables. This
chapter examines the consequences of overall transnational penetration;

Reprinted with permission from *Transnational Corporations and Underdevelopment* by Volker Bornschier and Christopher Chase-Dunn, pp. 80–101. Copyright ©
1985 by Praeger Publishers. Praeger Publishers, an imprint of Greenwood
Publishing Group, Inc., Westport, Conn.

that is, the level of national dependence on foreign capital in all economic sectors combined. . . .

ECONOMIC THEORY AND LONG-RUN
CONSEQUENCES OF TRANSNATIONAL INVESTMENT

. . . Economic theory maintains that investment results in income growth. This is not at all at variance with our theory. Rather, we have specified the long-term consequences that take into account institutional and structural features of the world-system. These crucial elements, which are indispensable for reaching sound long-term predictions, are neglected by neo-classical economies.

The potential for investment by transnational corporations results from high profits due to their monopolistic or oligopolistic advantages. These advantages are based on sheer market power and on technological and organizational knowledge (Hymer 1960; Bornschier 1976). This investment potential need not logically result in an average social loss for the host country. It *could* allow a higher accumulation rate and therefore a higher economic growth rate, since national income growth is dependent on capital formation. This neglects, however, the capacity aspect as well as the "realization problem" in a capitalist economy. And it neglects the transnational corporation seen as an institution.

Considering the transnational firm as a substantive institution, a predictable social loss seems inevitable in the long run for peripheral countries. Since the capital and knowledge of transnational corporations are sector specific, there is a reluctance to move to other sectors within the same country. This is because such sectors do not offer monopolistic advantages and higher profitability. Thus, the continuous reinvestment of the comparatively high profits of transnational firms in their own sectors would result in overcapacity and/or overproduction relative to market demand—the realization problem. This is especially the case for manufacturing investment for the domestic market in peripheral countries, since the unequal distribution of income prevents mass consumption. In order to avoid overcapacities transnational corporations are unlikely to make investments in a particular country that will severely affect the accumulation process of higher profits within that country. The transnational corporation, as a private growth and profit-seeking institution, will look for new investment opportunities within its worldwide operations. The investment of these resources in less penetrated countries and in research and development in core countries can postpone the realization problem on the level of the world-economy as a whole.

Transnational corporations, after facing potential or actual overcapacities, start to take surplus out of the penetrated country. This means that their efforts to generate higher income for themselves affect the growth potential of the penetrated country adversely. As can be shown, such behavior results in disturbances with respect to steady growth conditions, analyzed by the Domar model in the post-Keynesian tradition. Domar's model (1946, 1948) is an abstract analysis of the *conditions* of steady growth.[1]

We deduce from the above argument that the penetration of a modern sector of a national economy generally starts with large increases of net-investment by transnational corporations and that the relative increase of net-investment slows down in the course of time and may even become negative (capital repatriation). This is because transnational corporations have expanded their activities within a particular country to a point where (1) market saturation is approached and/or (2) political risks increase due to high penetration and visibility. It follows from these considerations that from a certain point the transnational corporation is likely to start taking more money out of the penetrated country than it has ever brought into the country due to its investments. If this is true, the host country would lose money that is not compensated by prior inflows. More specifically, it loses resources for accumulation, which implies a negative investment multiplier (since "autonomous" investment is negative).

Let us assume, furthermore, that transnational corporations generally operate under monopolistic conditions and these are even more pronounced in peripheral countries. This allows for higher than "normal" profits, and also lowers the "normal" profit of other local enterprises or local competitors. Then it is, on the average, *unlikely* that the long-term decrease in transnational net-investment and the outflow of money can be compensated by indigenous capital formation. This is because indigenous capital has a lower profitability and thus a lower investment potential. And, for an abstract deduction, if we ignore imports and exports for a while (a closed system), then the long-term investment cycle of transnational corporations results in a distortion with respect to the equilibrium conditions of steady growth in Domar's model.

In an extension of Keynes, Domar analyzes not only the income, but also the capacity effect of investment. Distortions, according to his approach, can only be avoided if the additional production capacity, which is a function of net-investment of one period, is fully employed. And this can only be the case if the whole demand (income) expands by the same amount. Given a certain marginal propensity to consume, additional income is generated according to the investment multiplier and it is a function of the *relative increase* of net-investment. If it should hold that the increase in production (capacity) is equal to the increase in income, then the *relative* increase in net-investment must be equal to the coefficient of capital productivity times the investment multiplier (share of savings in total income).[2] This is the equilibrium condition for steady growth along the so-called "growth trajectory."[3] On the basis of the simplifying model assumptions (linear-homogeneous relationships) all variables grow, then, at the same constant growth rate.[4]

From a slowing down in the *relative* increase of net investment due to the long-term investment cycle of transnational corporations it follows that a new "equilibrium" has to be found on a lower growth rate level. Either the propensity to save has to decrease, or capital productivity, or both at the same time.[5] The first means that consumption as a share of total income has to increase, but this is limited by high income inequality. And a reduced capital coefficient, in reality, means that the degree of capital utilization becomes smaller, implying underemployment.

The conclusion of this digression into the formal economic model is that income growth is adversely affected by transnational corporations *in the long run*. Such a long-term distortion with regard to steady growth will be greater the more net investment relies on foreign capital inputs (i.e., the higher the penetration by transnational corporations, *and* the more these corporations slow down their relative increase in net investment in the course of time).[6] Given the assumptions of increasing monopoly and the threat of overcapacity, and thus reduction of profitability, this is unavoidable. Following this line of argument we can make different predictions for short- and long-term consequences of transnational penetration.

SHORT-TERM CONSEQUENCES

In a first phase, when there is a large increase in net investment of transnational corporations, the average growth of income should be affected positively. This effect is the stronger the higher the net investment of the transnational firms. At the same time, already in this phase, growth is expected to be uneven:

- with respect to sectors (modern versus traditional and, within the modern, monopolistic versus competitive sector)
- with respect to regions (enclaves where transnationals invest versus the others)
- with respect to labor income, which is higher in the monopolistic and foreign-dominated sectors than in the competitive and traditional sectors

LONG-TERM CONSEQUENCES

In a second phase, when the increase of the net investment slows down, or tends to stagnate, or even becomes negative, the average income growth is adversely affected. Again this will be more the case as more total investment depends on foreign corporations which slow down their investment (i.e., the higher the penetration). In this second phase the strains already produced by uneven growth in the first phase will add to the adverse growth effects. However, the growth-reducing consequence of high penetration is mitigated or compensated if net investment of the corporations remains very high.

The results in Table 25.1 suggest support for the hypotheses with regard to short- and long-term consequences of transnational penetration. The table lists the studies according to whether they find positive or negative associations with economic growth and whether they measure the short-term effect (flow of investments) or the long-term effect (accumulated stock of capital). With only one exception the studies with flow measures find positive effects, and of the 25 studies using a stock measure, 16 find a negative association. The exceptions will be discussed below.

Table 25.1   **Studies of the Effect of Transnational Corporations on Economic Growth Using Stock or Flow Measures, and Direction of Effects**

Measurement of Foreign Capital Dependency	Direction of Effects	
	Positive	Negative
Stocks	Kaufman et al. (1975)	Alschuler (1976)
	McGowan and Smith (1978)	*Berweger and Hoby (1978)
	Ray and Webster (1978)	*Bornschier (1975, 1980, 1981)
	Szymanski (1976)	*Bornschier and Ballmer-Cao
	*Jackman (1982)	(1978)
		Chase-Dunn (1975a)
		Delacroix and Ragin (1981)
		*Dolan and Tomlin (1980)
		Evans (1972)
		Gobalet and Diamond (1979)
		*Meyer-Fehr (1978, 1979)
		Rubinson (1977)
		*Stoneman (1975)
		Timberlake and Kentor (1983)
		*van Puijenbroek (1984)
		Weede (1981a, 1981b)
		Weede and Tiefenbach (1981b)
Flows	*Berweger and Hoby (1978)	Stevenson (1972)
	*Bornschier (1975, 1980, 1981)	
	*Dolan and Tomlin (1979)	
	*Jackman (1982)	
	Kaufman et al. (1975)	
	*Meyer-Fehr (1978, 1979)	
	Papanek (1973)	
	Ray and Webster (1978)	
	*Stoneman (1975)	
	*van Puijenbroek (1984)	

*Studies which test for the effect of transnational penetration (stocks) and which control for new investment by transnational corporations (flows) in the same analysis. Bornschier and Ballmer-Cao control for the ratio of later and earlier stocks instead of flows.

With one exception, discussed below, the studies using both flow and stock measures in the same analysis report that high transnational penetration has the consequence of lowering the economic growth rate of the host country. And high flows of new foreign investment have a positive consequence for growth, even when penetration is high. This means that new investment of transnational corporations can mitigate and compensate the effect of penetration. This is supported by the fact that most of these studies report stronger negative effects of penetration once new investment is controlled. Such a compensation is, however, on the average not very relevant since the empirical association between transnational penetration and new investment is only moderate.[7] This supports our argument about the investment cycle of transnational corporations.

There is also other evidence in these studies that indicates the importance of the long- versus short-term distinction. Stoneman (1975) reports that lagging the stock measure (using a penetration indicator measured earlier than the dependent variable) increases the significance of the negative effect. Chase-Dunn (1975b) reports a series of panel analyses that show that stock measures tend to have zero effects on growth over short time lags but increasingly negative ones over longer and longer lag periods. That is, the immediate effect of stocks tends to be zero, but the longer-term effect is negative.

The same result is shown by Bornschier (1975) with a different measure for transnational penetration. He also shows a similar result in analyses that include both the level of penetration and change in the level of penetration. He finds that increases in penetration, which are due to inflows of new investment, have positive effects on growth but become zero and then negative as the lag period is lengthened.

The above results in a good overall support for our hypotheses. But there are a few studies in Table 25.1 that report results that seem to contradict what we have said. Stevenson's (1972) study is the only one that does not find positive effects due to a flow measure. His finding is not an important contradiction because he uses a poor measure of economic growth. He analyzes simple rank correlations of yearly GNP per capita figures that are pooled over a seven year period, and his analyses include only seven Latin American countries. Thus, this one exception does not strongly contradict the mass of other evidence, and we can conclude that flows of new foreign investment do indeed cause economic growth.

Of the 25 studies employing capital stock measures, however, five find positive associations with economic growth. Three of these (Kaufman et al., Ray and Webster, and Szymanski) study countries in Latin America and one (McGowan and Smith) studies only African countries. A common element of these studies is that they investigate only countries of a specific geographical region. There are, however, two studies in Table 25.1 which analyze only Latin American countries and which report negative associations (Alschuler, Evans). Furthermore, there are studies which present their results separately for geographical subsamples, namely the studies of Stoneman, and Dolan and Tomlin. They find negative associations for Latin America, positive associations for Africa, and a positive and negative one for Asian countries. In the following we discuss the contradictory findings that appear in studies of separate geographic regions.

Table 25.2 shows those studies which use stock measures by the countries they include and their findings. We note first that 16 of the 17 studies which include countries unrestricted by geographic region find negative effects. These studies investigate either all countries for which data are available or all peripheral countries. They report stronger negative effects for peripheral countries when they exclude core countries from the analyses, and no or only small and insignificant effects for core countries analyzed separately.

The only study which fails to find a negative effect of penetration while studying a larger number of countries from all continents is that by Jackman (1980). Jackman's finding is negative but statistically insignificant. The study by Jackman uses both stock and flow measures similar to

Table 25.2   Studies of the Effect of Transnational Corporate Penetration (Stocks) on Economic Growth by Country Composition and Direction of Effects

Country Composition	Effect of Transnational Penetration	
	Positive	Negative
Unrestricted		Berweger and Hoby (1978)
		Bornschier (1975, 1980, 1981)
		Bornschier and Ballmer-Cao (1978)
		Chase-Dunn (1975a)
		Delacroix and Ragin (1981)
		Dolan and Tomlin (1980)
		Gobalet and Diamond (1979)
		Jackman (1982)
		Meyer-Fehr (1978, 1979)
		Rubinson (1977)
		Stoneman (1975)
		van Puijenbroek (1984)
		Weede (1981a, 1981b)
		Weede and Tiefenbach (1981b)
America, peripheral countries	Kaufman et al. (1975)	Alschuler (1976)
	Ray and Webster (1978)	Dolan and Tomlin (1980)
	Szymanski (1976)	Evans (1972)
		Stoneman (1975)
Asia	Stoneman (1975)	Dolan and Tomlin (1980
Africa	Dolan and Tomlin (1980)	
	McGowan and Smith (1978)	
	Stoneman (1975)	

the ones we employ in our reanalysis. This study, unlike the five other studies in Table 25.1 that use both flow and stock measures, finds no effects of transnational penetration in a sample of 72 "Third World" countries. This is inconsistent with our reanalysis below and we suspect the inconsistency is due to one or a combination of the following three factors:

1. Jackman's measure of stocks may be extremely skewed, and thus not appropriate for linear regression analysis. Most studies either recode the extreme outliers or log the measure to normalize distribution.

2. Jackman does not effectively control the earlier relationship between the level of economic development and the degree of transnational penetration. Since higher levels of development attract greater amounts of foreign investment, this confuses the effect of penetration on growth.

3. Jackman's use of the time dimension is sloppy. He looks at the effect of penetration in 1967 on growth from 1960 to 1978. Obviously penetration in 1967 could not have effected growth between 1960 and 1967. In many cases this misuse of the time dimension would not be crucial, but in this case it is. Fresh foreign investment is associated with growth and it adds to foreign capital stocks. Thus, the inaccurate use of the time dimensions suppresses the negative effect of accumulated stocks of transnational capital.

Also Weede (1981a, 1981b) and Weede and Tiefenbach report, for some of their tests, insignificant negative effects of penetration in 1967 on growth from 1960 to 1977. They vary the penetration measure, the treatment of outliers on that measure, and the control variables in order to estimate the robustness of the earlier findings. These studies report that:

1. The negative effect on GDP growth is smaller than the one on GNP per capita growth (Weede 1981a). Unfortunately the two growth measures do not cover the same period.

2. Some weights for the stock of foreign capital (used in the penetration measure) produce more significant effects than others (Weede 1981a).

3. A log transformation in order to solve the problem of outliers on the penetration variable results in negative, but insignificant effects (Weede 1981b).

4. The effect is only significant for the world sample but not for a sample of less developed countries (Weede and Tiefenbach 1981b). This is clearly opposite to the bulk of other findings which either find the same effect or a somewhat more negative effect in a sample of less developed countries.

Weede and Tiefenbach conclude from the various reanalyses that the reported finding of a negative effect of penetration on growth lacks robustness and that the capital dependency approach "fails to explain why some LDCs do so much better or worse than others" (Weede and Tiefenbach 1981b, 391). Following these reanalyses a controversy has evolved that includes a dispute over many technical details.[8] Beside these details we would like to stress the following points:

1. The reanalyses by Weede and Tiefenbach have generally revealed negative effects which in some cases do not reach statistical significance.
2. Unlike Jackman, these researchers do not try to test different effects of stocks of foreign investment and flows of foreign direct investment.
3. They have an inappropriate specification of the time dimension (as does Jackman) since they are analyzing the effect of penetration in 1967 on growth from 1960 to 1977.

Thus, studies unrestricted by geographic region unanimously find negative effects of penetration on growth. In those discrepant cases where the effect does not reach statistical significance there are shortcomings in the test design which are the likely reasons for failing to obtain significant results.

Contrary to the nearly unanimous results of studies including countries unrestricted by geographical region, those that study particular regions are inconsistent. Of the seven studies of peripheral countries in the Americas, four report a negative association and three find a positive one. One study of Asia finds a positive and one a negative association. All three studies of African countries report positive associations.

In comparing the three studies of peripheral countries in Latin America and the Caribbean that find positive effects with the four that find negative ones, it is not easy to discover any systematic reason that could explain the discrepant results. The studies include basically the same countries, with the exclusion or inclusion of Venezuela being the main difference. Ray and Webster (1978) show, however, that this has little effect on estimates. The measurement of transnational penetration, however, suffers from shortcomings in all studies except the ones by Stoneman, and Dolan and Tomlin. Evans, Kaufman et al., Ray and Webster, and Szymanski use figures for the stock of United States capital as a proxy for the total foreign stock. This is a problematic proxy.[9]

We should point out, however, that none of the findings is very large in a statistical sense.[10] Also, the number of countries analyzed ranges from 17 to 19 cases, the 22 cases in the Dolan and Tomlin analysis being an exception. Such small numbers of observations are rather problematic for correlation and regression analysis, since differences in one or two cases can affect the magnitude and direction of estimates. It should be noted that the two studies without shortcomings in the measurement of penetration and with larger samples (i.e., Dolan and Tomlin, and the study of Stoneman [who pools observations]), find consistently negative effects.

Thus, our comparison of the different studies reveals no systematic explanation of the different findings in the studies of peripheral countries in the Americas. Similarly, the positive effects found in the studies of the African and Asian subsamples are problematic. McGowan and Smith's findings of a positive effect of transnational penetration on growth may be due to the fact that they use a very short time lag. As noted above, it is the longer-term effects that are negative. Stoneman's as well as Dolan and Tomlin's findings do not suffer to the same extent from this drawback. The problem, then, is to explain why the findings in separate geographic regions diverge from those with larger numbers of countries unrestricted by region.

Thinking about the pattern in Table 25.2, we can offer five hypotheses to explain these different findings from the study of geographic regions.

Hypothesis 1. The discrepant results in geographical regions might indicate that the relationship between transnational penetration and economic growth actually varies by geographic region. Although the researchers who use only regional subsamples of countries do not offer any theoretical reason why it should vary by region, the possibility still exists.

Hypothesis 2. Another explanation may be that variables that should be controlled on theoretical grounds are not associated with foreign capital penetration in world comparisons, but are in regional subsamples. Therefore, a more specified, but spurious "geographical-region effect" may be operating. To test such a hypothesis requires that the same set of variables be used in each equation that tests the effects of foreign capital penetration in regional subsamples.

Hypothesis 3. The discrepant findings in subsamples could mean that the relationship between foreign capital penetration and economic growth varies with the size of the market (or the modernized segment of the economy) or with the level of economic development. Most of the African countries are very small with respect to market size and are the poorest in the world. This applies also to several countries in Asia, whereas market size, as well as per capita income, in peripheral America is, on the average, much greater. The hypothesis that the effect might vary with level of development is suggested by McGowan and Smith, as well as by Stoneman; Bornschier and Ballmer-Cao (1978) argue that the effect is less strong in smaller peripheral countries.

Hypothesis 4. Another explanation is suggested by the fact that in regional subsamples there is an accumulation of *special cases* that affect the relationship. Such theoretically suggested special cases for the analysis of economic growth are war regions, city-states, and countries that are extremely specialized in the export of petroleum. Asia is especially characterized by an accumulation of such special cases.

Hypothesis 5. The last hypothesis assumes that the results may be a "statistical artifact" produced by the limited range of variation and small sample sizes that naturally characterize any such subsample analysis. Since all the studies that use larger numbers of countries with greater variations find negative effects, it is possible that the studies that use smaller samples with limited variation are subject to greater sampling error. That is, if we imagine that the true regression line relating foreign capital penetration to economic growth is negative, it is possible that any limited subset of points along that line shows a smaller or even different relationship among the variables under study than the entire set of points. Stoneman suggests this explanation to account for why African and Asian subsamples differ from his much larger sample of all peripheral countries. This hypothesis can be tested by employing an analysis of covariance that analyzes all cases simultaneously and looks for statistical interaction effects for subsamples.

The method of comparing and contrasting existing studies does not allow us to choose among the five alternative hypotheses. The effect of level of development, market size, geographical region, and limited varia tion are all confounded in those studies that use only countries from a single region. Therefore, we have done new analyses in order to resolve the contradictory findings of earlier research.

NEW ANALYSES

The new analyses that we present in this section are intended to reconcile the discrepant findings in some of the earlier research, and incorporate a number of improvements over results presented earlier. The breadth of countries studied has been extended by the inclusion of cases formerly left out either because of missing data or sampling criteria. Our 103 cases include all nations with a population greater than one million, except that most centrally planned countries are not included.[11] In line with our discussion of the world-economy as a whole we have included all possible countries, even those formerly excluded because of special circumstances such as current involvement in war, exceptional oil producers, or city-states.

We have also improved our measures, added data for more recent years and included control variables that increase the amount of variance explained by the overall model to better specify the effects of penetration by transnational corporations. Our measure of penetration is the total book value of the stock of foreign direct investment at the end of 1967 (the first year for which these data are available), weighted by the amount of domestic capital stock of the country and the size of the population. The measure of penetration has been improved over that used in earlier studies

(Bornschier et al. 1978) by weighting it by an improved estimate of the total stock of capital. The estimation procedure for the weight used is described in Ballmer-Cao and Scheidegger (1979). There, all data can be found that are employed in the analyses, except for income growth (see below). The measure of transnational penetration we now use weights the total stock of FDI in million U.S. dollars as follows:

$$ PEN = \frac{Total\ Stock\ FDI_{67}}{\sqrt{Capital\ Stock\ *\ Labor\ Force}} $$

We take total population as a proxy for the labor force. The estimated total stock of capital in billion U.S. dollars is multiplied by the country's population in millions (and the square root taken) in order to correct for differences in average capital intensity. We consider a country to be highly penetrated if the stock of foreign capital is high relative to both major productive forces, capital and labor. . . .[12]

The dependent variable in our new analyses is the average annual real growth rate of GNP per capital (in percentage units) for the period between 1965 and 1977. The source is the World Bank.[13] This differs from earlier analyses (Bornschier et al. 1978) by including data for 1976 and 1977.

As in earlier analyses we control for flows of foreign direct investment in order to separate the effects of recent flows from the effects of accumulated stocks. The flow variable (FDI) is measured by the difference between the stock of foreign direct investment in 1973 and in 1967 divided by the average total Gross Domestic Product for the years 1965 to 1970. We use the flows only for the first part of the time studied because we do not want to confuse the effects of the new flows with those of accumulated stocks. Cumulating over a long period comes eventually to the point of equivalence with stocks because of the depreciation of capital.[14]

We also control the level of domestic capital formation because this is thought to be related to both prior flows of foreign direct investment and economic growth. Our measure is the Gross Domestic Investment divided by Gross Domestic Product, averaged for 1965, 1970, and 1973 (GDI).

In addition we control for the logged level of economic development (YN) in 1965 and the square of this $(YN)^2$. The squared term, which has only been included in two earlier analyses, is necessary to take into account the nonlinear shape of the relationship between level of development and penetration. Penetration is not evenly distributed among countries at different levels of development, but rather is more pronounced in those at middle levels. The squared term takes this into account and controls for the "ceiling effect" which produced smaller percentage increases in growth for countries at high levels of development—a situation in which socially determined processes of saturation are likely to be at work (Bornschier 1980).

We also control for the relative level of exports in order to separate out the effects of penetration on exports from its effects on income growth. Exports are positively related both to natural resources and overall penetration by foreign capital.[15] In a growing world-economy access to the world market has, in general, favorable consequences for economic growth due to returns for scarce mineral resources and/or due to enlarging the scale of the market and the scale of production for industrial products. Therefore, to the extent that penetration by transnational corporations goes together with exports, it should have a smaller adverse effect on growth.[16]

Controlling for the level of exports shows the income growth effect of penetration independently of the access to the world market.[17] Our measure of EXPORT is the total value of exports divided by the Gross Domestic Product, averaged for the years 1965, 1970, and 1973.

The size of the domestic market is also included as a variable in our complete model. Size indicates a growth potential which is allowed to develop more independently from the international market. Since this variable is empirically not linearly related either to penetration by transnational corporations, exports or relative importance of raw materials, it does not affect the other variables in linear regression. It is introduced in order to reach at a more complete specification of potential growth factors. Size can, however, be thought of as interacting with penetration in the following way. The fact that size of the domestic market is not linearly related to penetration can be seen to result from its contradictory implications for development. Market size can be either a resource for independent national development, or a factor that attracts more foreign industrial capital because of the larger domestic markets. In either case it is a resource which may help a country attain semiperipheral status and upward mobility within the core/periphery division of labor. We propose that political action is more crucial for countries with larger size in order to further either of the two development paths. Moreover, state strength is also likely to be greater in these countries so that the economic policy options mentioned are more feasible than in smaller peripheral countries.

We measure SIZE with the logged total energy consumption in 1967 in thousand tons of coal equivalent. This measure is preferred to total GDP or GNP because it estimates the absolute size of the monetized part of the economy, not the subsistence sector, which contributes only minimally to domestic market demand.

The results which will allow us to choose among the five hypotheses listed above are presented in the following way. First, following the form of the earlier studies cited in Table 25.2, we present analyses separately by the different regions, levels of development, and market sizes. In a next step we perform more detailed tests with regard to the effect of penetration by transnational corporations in countries with different market sizes and different levels of economic development. Finally, we use the whole sample

Table 25.3 Regression of Average Annual Real Growth of Income per Capita 1965–1977 (unstandardized regression estimates, F values in parentheses)

Equation	Sample	PEN	FDI	YN	$(YN)^2$	GDI	Export	Size	Constant	R^2 (adjusted)
1) $N=103$	World sample	−.0262‡ (16.15)	.0076† (9.27)	13.81† (14.48)	−2.49† (16.68)	.0664* (3.92)	.0444* (8.17)	.8856† (11.00)	−20.48	.39
2) $N=15$	Rich countries	.0012 (0.00)	−.0055 (0.11)	259.9 (2.94)	−35.37 (2.97)	.1773 (1.97)	.0538 (0.46)	1.1739 (0.85)	−485.64	.45
3) $N=88$	Less developed countries (LDCs)	−.0310 (15.61)	.0082† (9.10)	9.92 (2.56)	−1.69 (2.56)	.0606 (8.23)	.0510† (0.46)	.9137† (8.77)	−15.76	.40
4) $N=37$	LDCs in Africa	−.0065 (0.28)	.0067 (3.76)	−1.20 (0.01)	.13 (0.01)	.1211 (3.51)	−.0097 (0.14)	.2146 (0.16)	0.96	.05
5) $N=21$	LDCs in the Americas	−.0104 (0.45)	.0054 (2.15)	5.40 (0.03)	−1.32 (0.10)	.1782 (2.39)	−.0785 (1.66)	.1977 (0.00)	−3.68	.18
6) $N=23$	LDCs in Asia	−.0182 (0.74)	.0162 (3.26)	4.01 (0.10)	−0.32 (0.02)	−.0200 (0.06)	.0518 (1.03)	1.2546* (5.77)	−9.94	.60
7) $N=23$	LDCs in Asia (w/o special cases)	−.0421* (3.96)	.0180 (3.39)	20.50 (1.38)	−3.23 (0.96)	.0129 (0.03)	.0338 (0.34)	.7353 (1.88)	−30.22	.65
8) $N=41$	Larger LDCs (above 1.5 million t)	−.0447 (18.70)	.0072* (3.97)	26.88 (3.61)	−4.73 (3.42)	.0454 (0.58)	.0885† (10.92)	1.6433* (4.47)	−41.72	.37
9) $N=47$	Small LDCs (below 1.5 million t)	−.0103 (0.68)	.0102* (4.84)	3.50 (0.25)	−0.57 (0.19)	−.0378 (0.53)	.0156 (0.33)	.5361 (0.88)	−5.99	.17
10) $N=46$	Wealthier LDCs (above $400)	−.0413† (15.80)	.0075* (4.57)	17.29 (0.52)	−3.16 (0.65)	.0624 (1.12)	.0899† (13.86)	1.4706* (6.67)	−26.99	.36
11) $N=42$	Poor LDCs (below $400)	−.0222 (3.80)	.0167* (13.82)	−78.87* (6.66)	17.87* (6.95)	.0033 (0.01)	.0041 (0.02)	.9157* (7.77)	85.52	.41

Notes: Figures that are two, three, or four times as large as the standard error of the estimate are indicated by *, †, and ‡, respectively. Figures are given for data collected on penetration by transnational corporations in 1967 (PEN), flows of foreign direct investment (FDI), logged income per capita 1965 (YN), gross domestic investment (GDI), exports, and size of the internal market for a world sample of 103 countries and subsamples.

of 103 countries in an analysis of covariance model which allows us to test for interactions between regions and penetration. This analysis of a large number of countries allows us to overcome the problems of small sample size and restricted variation that occur in the separate analyses by region. Tables 25.3, 25.4, and 25.5 report the results of our new analyses.

Table 25.3 presents the regression estimates and F statistics for our basic model estimated for all the countries and also for subsamples. First, a subsample of the 15 richest countries is analyzed separately. These are the countries which have been, since World War II and before 1965, a stable group at the top of the world stratification structure. There has been a natural break in the distribution of income values between these 15 and the other countries. Most of the richest countries, 10 of the 15, are important headquarter countries of transnational corporations, both in absolute and relative terms.[18] We expect no significant negative impact of penetration by transnational corporations in these countries since the relations among them are relatively symmetrical, and they are all core states in the world economy.

The remaining 88 peripheral and semiperipheral countries are also analyzed separately. It should be kept in mind that this group, which is called "less developed," is rather heterogeneous with regard to wealth and size. It covers, on the one hand, countries like, for example, Burundi and India (both poor but different in size) and, on the other hand, countries like Ireland and Argentina (both wealthier, but different in size).

Earlier research (Bornschier et al. 1978, Gobalet and Diamond, and Dolan and Tomlin) has reported different magnitudes of the effect of penetration by transnational corporations for countries at different levels of development and different sizes of the internal market. In our research we have split the subsample of less developed countries in a number of different ways in order to evaluate the idea that penetration effects interact with size and level of development. In Table 25.3 we present the results of separately analyzing very small and very poor countries. The very small countries are those with less than 1.5 million tons of coal equivalent of total energy consumption in 1967. The very poor countries are those with less than $400 per capita GNP in 1965.

We also divide the sample of less developed countries into regional subsamples in order to reanalyze the contradictory findings for such regional subsamples in earlier research. We use, within the 88 less developed countries, regional samples for Africa, Asia and America. The Asian subsample is also analyzed excluding six countries that are thought to be special cases.[19]

Equation 1 in Table 25.3 shows the estimates of the variables in our basic model for the 103 countries of the world. This equation shows that penetration by transnational corporations (PEN) has an overall negative effect on economic growth which is statistically extremely unlikely to be by chance. This replicates the findings of previous research using large numbers of countries unrestricted by geographical region. The effect of flows of foreign direct investments (FDI) is in the predicted positive direction and also is statistically significant. This is further evidence of the conclusion drawn from our comparison of earlier studies that stocks and flows have opposite effects on economic growth.[20] The effect of the level of development is curvilinear. The term YN is positive and the effect of squared GNP per capita $(YN)^2$ is negative, showing the ceiling and/or saturation process discussed above. The turning point of the curvilinear function is at $600 per capita GNP.

The level of gross domestic capital formation (GDI) is positive and significant, as all economic theories would predict. The effects of exports is also positive and significant.[21] The effect of the world market position with regard to important raw commodities has been tested but this variable is not included in the model since its initial positive effect on growth vanishes once the level of exports is controlled. Equation 1 strongly supports our theory of development in the capitalist world-economy and the conclusions we have drawn from comparisons of earlier studies.

Equation 2 shows that penetration by transnational corporations does not have negative effects on the economic development of the 15 richest countries. This supports our contention that penetration of core countries by the corporations of other core countries results in a different process of development than asymmetrical penetration of the periphery by the core.

Equation 3, excluding the richest countries, shows the same basic patterns of effects as Equation 1 except that the estimated effect of penetration is larger because it is not diluted by the inclusion of the richer countries.[22] The penetration by transnational corporations is the most significant single predictor of the economic growth of the peripheral countries.[23] The other growth predictors have the same direction of influence as in the whole sample, but only market size and exports are significant, whereas capital formation is not.

This suggests that capital formation is of less importance for peripheral countries than it is generally assumed. This indirectly supports the proposition that many of the problems of the peripheral countries are due to lack of *effective* demand, which is a long-term consequence of the unequal distribution of income. This puts into question some conventional "wisdoms" in development theory that advocate more transfers of investment capital from rich to poor countries. The share of capital formation in total product, in general, does not seem to be a crucial variable for economic growth within peripheral countries in the world-economy, and more specifically, while fresh capital formation by transnational corporations (PDI) has a positive effect, accumulated prior capital formation (PEN) has clearly disadvantageous consequences for economic growth.

The effects in regional subsamples (Equation 4–7 of Table 25.3) are consistently negative, but small. This is consistent with earlier studies of regional subsamples, and as we have hypothesized above could be due to a number of different possibilities: sample size, restricted variation, interaction with size and level of economic development, or real regional differences in the operation of dependency processes.

The effect for the Asian subsample is small until the six special case nations (*see* note 19) are excluded from the subsample. Then, as shown in Equation 7, the estimated effect of penetration is large and statistically significant. Thus, we can support Hypothesis 4 as an explanation of the small or inconsistent effects of transnational corporate penetration on economic growth found in studies that do not control for special case countries in Asia. However, special cases (defined in the same way as for Asia) do not play an important role in the other regions.[24] Before examining the other hypotheses in order to find an explanation for the small negative effects in American and African subsamples, we shall first discuss the interaction with size and wealth.

Equations 8 and 9 show the consequences of splitting the less developed sample to separate those countries with a small internal market from the rest of peripheral countries. In Equation 8 the estimated effect of penetration is larger and more significant than in the whole sample of peripheral countries analyzed in Equation 3. In Equation 9, including only the small countries, the effect of penetration is much smaller. This supports the idea that the effects of penetration are different for countries depending on market size. Similarly, Equations 10 and 11 show the results of separating the very poor from the rest of the less developed countries. Among the countries with higher and middle levels of economic development the effects of penetration remain large, but among the poor countries the effects are clearly smaller.

These results, by splitting the sample according to the size and wealth, are similar to those of earlier research.[25] [26] Our empirical research for the true shape of the interaction between penetration, market size and level of development led us to split the subsamples in several different ways.[27] We performed more analyses (1) in order to try to locate a natural breaking point or step-function in the interaction effect, and (2) in order to discover whether both interaction effects are of the same importance or whether one is spurious, since market size and level of economic development are substantially correlated for less developed countries. This detailed analysis leads to new insights with regard to the shape of the interaction. The results will be reported in Table 25.4 before we try to explain the smaller effect for African countries on the basis of many small countries in that region (Hypothesis 3).

Table 25.4 shows that by employing various splitting points for internal market size the relationship between penetration and economic growth is of similar strength and negative for all less developed countries in the

Table 25.4   Regressions for Peripheral and Semiperipheral Countries in Different Ranges of Internal Market Size and GNP per Capita

Market Size in Million Tons
(ranges schematically)

0.03	0.2	0.5	1.5	2.5	5	20	226	N	PEN	(F)
							———	88	−.0310†	(15.61)
						———		11	−.0347	(1.03)
					———————		27	−.0438†	(10.07)
				———————			30	−.0369†	(9.82)
			———————				35	−.0274	(3.30)
		———————					28	−.0342*	(4.67)
					———————————————	34	−.0457‡	(16.10)
				———————————————————	41	−.0447‡	(18.70)
			———————————————————————	62	−.0401‡	(20.63)
		———————————————————————————	72	−.0359‡	(20.17)
	———————						47	−.0103	(0.68)
———————							26	.0045	(0.11)
———								16	.0262	(1.46)

GNP per Capita in U.S. Dollars
(ranges schematically)

88	150	200	300	400	2,450	N	PEN	(F)
				———————	46	−.0413†	(15.80)
			———————————	52	−.0384‡	(17.27)
		———————————————	65	−.0341‡	(16.04)
———————————————————————	42	−.0222	(3.80)
———————————————————		36	−.0154	(0.91)
———————————————			23	−.0138	(0.72)
———————————				14	−.0217	(0.15)

Note: For explanations of significance levels, see Table 25.3. The same control variables have been used in Table 25.3. Total energy consumption figured in million tons of coal equivalent.

range between 0.5 and 226 million tons of coal equivalent, the latter being the maximum value among less developed countries. In this broad range the association is therefore practically independent of size. In the range between 0.03 and 0.5 million tons a discontinuity can be detected. The relationship, which is independent of size above this range, changes direction from negative to positive for countries below 0.5, and especially below 0.2, million tons. Below 0.5 million tons there are 26 countries, 19 of which are located in Africa. We refer to these 26 countries as very small with regard to internal market size. And below 0.2 million tons there are 16 countries, which we call extremely small countries, Of these, 13 are located in Africa.

A similar detailed subsample analysis is performed in Table 25.4 according to various ranges of income per capita of less developed countries. It is revealed that the effect of penetration on growth becomes smaller in samples below $300 per capita GNP, but also for countries below this limit the association is always negative, even for the 14 very poor countries with a per capita of GNP of below $150. The explanation for this different pattern is that poorer peripheral countries are frequently very or extremely small, and this is the reason that they show smaller effects. For example, among the 23 countries below $200 GNP per capita there are 11 which are extremely small and another three are very small.

According to these new results the interaction effect of wealth with penetration is spurious. It is thus not the level of economic development that acts as a decisive variable, but the size of the internal market. This interaction with size occurs, however, only in the sense of a threshold variable. Very poor countries, for example India and Indonesia, are well above this threshold size due to their vast population. This means that a monetized sector, although it might be small in relative terms, is still considerable in absolute terms. Such large poor countries can be heavily integrated into the world-economy, whereas extremely small, poor countries like Rwanda and Mali do not have a similar potential for integration into the world-economy. They can be considered, therefore, as territories which are on the edge of the periphery of the world-economy.

Even though the very or extremely small countries do not stand completely outside the world-economy, their average level of penetration by transnational corporations is far below the average for all less developed countries. We assume that for these countries on the edge of the periphery every contact with the world-economy increases money circulation and thus the relative size of the monetized sector. Statistically, this could well lead to a spurious association between intensity of contact with the world-economy and economic growth expressed in money terms. The empirical finding that penetration by transnational corporations has a small positive effect on economic growth (not statistically significant) within this special group of countries may thus be explained.

The findings in Table 25.4 provide an explanation for the smaller negative effect of penetration found for African countries in Table 25.3. Out of 16 extremely small countries, 13 are located in Africa. The African sample is large enough to repeat the analysis excluding the 13 extremely small countries (below 0.2 million tons). Table 25.5 shows a substantial and statistically significant negative association between penetration by transnational corporations and economic growth for other than extremely small African countries. Also the positive effect of fresh foreign direct investment becomes more significant if the extremely small countries are excluded.

Thus, we can conclude that the small negative effect for the sample in Africa can be explained with Hypothesis 3. This hypothesis about threshold size cannot be used for the explanation of the small effect found for the Americas sample since only one out of 21 countries in the Americas, Haiti, falls into the extremely small category. Even if Haiti is excluded, the effect

Table 25.5   Effects of Penetration and Flows of Foreign Investment in Larger and Smaller African Countries

	N	PEN (F-value)	FDI (F-value)	R^2 (adjusted)
Without extremely small countries	24	−.0318 (5.29)	.0086 (5.81)	.28
Results for all African countries	37	−.0065 (0.28)	.0067 (3.76)	.05

of penetration does not become stronger. In the case of the Asian sample the exclusion of the six special case countries (Hypothesis 4) demonstrates significant results (see Table 25.3, Equation 7). The additional exclusion of the two extremely small countries in Asia does not make the relationship larger.

For an explanation of the small effect in the Americas sample, Hypothesis 5 should be considered. Before exploring this possibility, we shall test for Hypothesis 1 in Table 25.6. Hypothesis 1 proposes that there are different effects of penetration in subsamples.

The analysis of covariance in Table 25.6 tests for statistical interaction with region by using the world sample of 103 cases. Therefore, the problem of analyzing small samples is removed. The equations contain, besides the statistical interactions, the same control variables as in Table 25.3. The

Table 25.6   Analysis of the Statistical Interactions Between Transnational Penetration and Dummy Variables for Core Countries and Countries Located in Africa, America, and Asia

Equations	PEN	PEN Core Country Dummy	PEN Africa Dummy	PEN America Dummy	PEN Asia Dummy	R^2 (adjusted)
(1)	−.0262‡ (16.15)					.39
(2)	−.0301‡ (17.81)	.0205 (1.52)				.39
(3)	−.0259† (10.56)	.0172 (1.07)	−.0025 (0.06)			.43
(4)	−.0267† (10.50)	.0170 (0.97)		−.0098 (0.42)		.38
(5)	−.0282† (13.97)	.0186 (1.22)			.0023 (0.02)	.40

Notes: For the estimation of the regression the same control variables as in Table 25.3 have been used (results not shown). The main effect of the various dummy variables has been included in the equations (results not shown in order to simplify presentation). Number of Cases = 103 in all equations.

dummy variables used for the interactions take values one (1) or zero (0). The interactions with regional dummy variables (for example PEN times AFRICA) take either the value of penetration for those countries which are located in that region or the value zero for countries outside the region.

Equation 1 in Table 25.6 is the same as Equation 1 in Table 25.3 and is included for purposes of comparison with the other equations. The effects of FDI and the other variables in the model are similar to those shown in Table 25.3 and so they are not presented in the analysis of covariance results in Table 25.6, although they were included in each equation. Equation 2 adds to the model for the interaction between PEN and the richest countries to control for the different consequences of the operations of transnational corporations in the richest countries of the world-economy. As can be seen, this interaction term is positive although not statistically significant, and its inclusion results in an increase in the estimated negative direct effect of PEN. This is consistent with the subsample analysis presented in Table 25.3.[28]

Equations 3 through 5 show the effects of interaction between geographical regions and penetration. It can be seen that all the regional interactions are extremely small and insignificant while the main effects remain large. This can be interpreted to mean that there are no interactions between geographical location and penetration which are independent of the other variables included in our model. Therefore, we can dismiss Hypothesis 1 which suggests such interactions. The rather more negative estimate for the interaction between PEN and location in the Americas is evidence against the possibility that the small effect in less developed America can be attributed to different relationships in these countries.

Hypothesis 5 remains a plausible explanation for the small effect of penetration in less developed American countries. Among all the regional subsamples, the Americas have the highest average value of penetration and the lowest coefficient of variation (i.e., all American countries in our sample of peripheral countries tend to be penetrated rather substantially).[29] Without being able to compare situations of higher and lower degrees of penetration in this subsample, the effects of penetration are not revealed. The absence of a significant positive interaction between penetration and location in America (Table 25.6) indicates that these countries lie on the line within the overall pattern, but have too small a variation among them to detect the effect in the regional subsample. This is support for Hypothesis 5.

We have thus found the explanation of our contradictory results from geographical regions in earlier studies. Our new analyses find only small effects of penetration by transnational corporations on economic growth in regional subsamples (Table 25.3). Detailed analyses show that this is, however, a spurious finding. Out of the five hypotheses which were proposed, the first one can be dismissed on the basis of the results of Table 25.6. Also, the second hypothesis is disproven since we use the same control variables for all subsamples in Table 25.3. The third hypothesis is supported in the sense that there exists a significant negative effect of penetration on economic growth only for countries above a threshold level of the size of the international market. This accounts for the results of studies of Africa. The larger African countries show the same significant association as all less developed countries. The fourth hypothesis is applicable to Asia; here special cases dilute the pattern. Without these special cases the negative effect for Asia is as strong as for all peripheral countries. The fifth hypothesis explains earlier findings based on studies of countries in the Americas. The peripheral American countries fit into the overall negative pattern which holds for all peripheral countries, but they have among them too low a variation, which hinders the detection of a substantial association when this region is analyzed separately.

NOTES

1. Contrary to neoclassical analysis, Domar's model does not assume that the growth trajectory is inherently stable. In this it is similar to Harrod's knife-edge theorem.

2. The formal deduction is as follows:

$$\Delta P = \sigma I$$

the increase in production is a function of social average capital productivity and net investment.

$$\Delta Y = \frac{1}{dS / dy} \, \Delta I,$$

the increase in national income, is a function of the "investment multiplier" and *increase* of net investment. With regard to the multiplier theory, Domar (1946, 140) states that it is "too familiar to need any comment, except for an emphasis on the obvious but often forgotten fact that with any given marginal propensity to save, dy/dt is a function not of I, but of dI/dt." If it should hold that $\Delta P = \sigma Y$, then $\Delta I / I = \sigma dS / dy$.

3. The growth trajectory is $Y_t = Y_0 E^s \sigma^t$, income as a function of time, where s denotes the propensity to save, (dS/dY) and E the base of the natural logarithm.

4. This growth rate would be: $g = s\sigma$. The maintenance of full employment requires investment to grow at a constant compound-growth rate.

5. Cross-national evidence seems to support this deduction. There is empirical support for the proposition that foreign capital inflows are inversely related to domestic savings (Weisskopf 1971; Papanek 1972; Stoneman 1975).

6. $\Delta I / I$, see above, note 2, can be split up in: $\Delta I^d + \Delta I^f / I^d + I^f$, where d denotes domestic and f foreign.

7. According to our own results the correlation in the world sample of 103 cases is $r = .40$. For 15 core countries the correlation is somewhat higher than in

larger peripheral countries since the limits to growth are less important due to comparatively low income inequality which allows high mass consumption ($r = .43$).

In the larger peripheral countries the correlation is very low ($r = .19$). Here a large part of the foreign capital can be assumed to be producing for the domestic market. The great income inequality in these countries limits the size of the market and thus they suffer from unfavorable long-term investment opportunities.

In smaller peripheral countries, where most of the foreign capital produces for export to the international market, internal growth constraints are less important and, consistent with this, the correlation is higher ($r = .65$).

8. For replies and rejoinders in that controversy see Bornschier (1981b, 1982c).

9. This can be shown with the following figures. According to the Organization for Economic Cooperation and Development (OECD-DAC 1972) estimates of the book value of the stock of foreign direct investment in 1967 in peripheral countries, $17.4 billion was controlled by U.S. companies and $17.7 by companies in other D.A.C. (core) countries. The U.S. share was not the same across regions. For example, in Africa the U.S. share was $1.4 billion and the non-U.S. share $5.2 billion. In peripheral America the U.S. share was $7.4 billion and the non-U.S. share $4.7 billion. Nor are the relative shares of U.S. and non-U.S. stocks the same across countries within regions. Within peripheral America, for example, the U.S. share in Argentina was 56 percent in 1967, in Brazil 35 percent, in Colombia 86 percent, and in Venezuela 73 percent. These figures strongly suggest that the U.S. stocks of foreign direct investment are not good proxies for the total stocks.

10. Only Ray and Webster, using data on U.S. investment, find large and significant positive effects of foreign capital stocks on economic growth in Latin America. But in reanalyses of their results and those of the other Latin American studies, we found their unusually large effects resulted from their use of the GNP per capita figures compiled by the United States Agency for International Development (USAID). The use of the GNP per capita data compiled by either the World Bank or the United Nations produces small positive effects similar to the findings of Kaufman et al. and Szymanski. Given the extreme care with which the World Bank compiles GNP data, we suspect that its data are superior to those provided by USAID.

11. We include only Yugoslavia and Romania in our comparison because the World Bank presents growth data for these countries. We would want to include the other "socialist" countries in our analysis because of the contention that they are part of the larger capitalist world-economy, but growth data for these countries are contradictory between United Nations and World Bank sources. These countries have no penetration by transnational corporations during the time period studied, and their growth rates are relatively high. This would produce even larger negative results if these countries were included in our analyses.

12. This variable is fairly evenly distributed except for 18 outliers. These we have recoded, maintaining the rank order of the recorded cases . . . to make the variable useful for linear regression. Other researchers have employed log scores or rank scores to obtain a more even distribution, but recoding the outliers preserves the metric of the measure for the great majority of cases.

13. The measure is constructed in the following way:

$$[(\sqrt[12]{YN_{1977}/YN_{1965}} - 1)*100]$$

The data are from a series of GNP per capita (YN) figures in constant market prices and U.S. dollars of the base period 1975–1977 provided by the Economic Analysis and Projections Department of the World Bank, computer run April 12, 1977, Washington (D.C.), mimeo. All the income per capita data used in the new analyses are from this source.

14. For our estimate of the total stock of capital we argue that cumulated domestic investment over a period of 18 years (times a correction factor for partial depreciation or loss of capital) is equivalent to total stock (Ballmer-Cao and Scheidegger 1979). This is to assume that the average time in which capital stock depreciates is 18 years or less. With regard to FDI we should note, in addition, that 12 outliers have been recoded maintaining their rank order. As with the penetration measure, this is done to normalize the distribution, a requirement of linear regression.

15. This is somewhat similar to earlier studies (Chase-Dunn 1975; Gobalet and Diamond 1979) that controlled for specialization in production of mineral resources (percentage of GDP in mining and petroleum production) to separate the effects of penetration from the effects of endowment with natural resources. Developing nations with high levels of exports are most often those that have natural resources that attract foreign capital. We want to know the effect of penetration by transnational corporations net of the effect of having these natural resources.

16. Stepwise regression substantiates this expectation. Without controlling for exports, penetration by transnational corporations has a significant negative effect on economic growth which becomes even more substantial after controlling for exports.

17. Albert Szymanski (1983) argues that controlling for the level of exports is misleading because one of the ways foreign investment positively affects economic development is by increasing exports. Our response to his criticism demonstrates that transnational penetration does not cause the growth of exports and thus exports are not an intervening variable between investment dependence and growth (Bornschier and Chase-Dunn 1983).

18. Absolute and relative criteria that make sense are based on data reported by the Kommission der Europaeischen Gemeinschaften (1976, 43) for 1973. Important headquarter countries (Belgium, Denmark, France, West Germany, Netherlands, Norway, Sweden, Switzerland, United Kingdom, United States) are those having more than 100 transnational corporations and those having more than 100 foreign links (subsidiaries and direct or indirect participation abroad) per million inhabitants. We should remark that Japan, which is often thought of as a core country, is not in the group of 15 richest countries before 1965 and it does not qualify for being an important headquarter country according to the above criteria. In 1973 Japan had 211 transnational corporations (as compared to an average of 799 for the ten important headquarter countries) and had only 11 subsidiaries abroad per million inhabitants (the range for the ten important headquarter countries varies from 119 for the U.S. to 645 for Switzerland). The other countries belonging to the group of 15 richest countries before 1965 which do not qualify as important transnational headquarters are: Australia, Austria, Canada, Finland, and New Zealand.

19. The six cases excluded from the Asian subsample are Hong Kong, Singapore, Israel, Jordan, Syria, and Saudi Arabia. These were all excluded from earlier analyses because they were considered special cases outside the scope conditions of the theoretical model (Bornschier and Ballmer-Cao 1978). Hong Kong and Singapore are city-states playing a specialized entrepôt role in the world-economy. As such they are unlikely to have the same type of development processes as countries that include hinterland regions within their political boundaries. Israel, Jordan and Syria composed a war zone during the period we are studying. Vietnam and

Cambodia are not in our world sample because of missing data. While we do not wish to exclude warfare as a "normal" process for restructuring political relations in the evolution of the world-economy, it does disrupt the economic growth processes we are studying in this book. Saudi Arabia is a special case due to its extreme specialization in the export of oil. This commodity is not only a natural resource, but in the period under study it exhibits incredible price inelasticity combined with rising prices due to cartelization. The exclusion of these six cases from the Asian subsample changes the estimate of the effect of penetration on growth from a small and insignificant negative one to a large and significant negative estimate (Table 25.3). This illustrates the dangers inherent in small sample analyses such as those employed by studies focusing on a single geographical region. The six cases are included in the world sample and the larger subsamples but in these the less restricted variance does not allow them to mask the overall pattern of effects.

20. In order to make sure that the results are not affected by the recodings for PEN and FDI, the same equation has been estimated *excluding* the 23 cases where either PEN and/or FDI has been recoded. The coefficients for the remaining eighty cases are as follows. PEN: $b = -.0245$ ($F = 8.07$), FDI: $b = .0097$ ($F = 8.12$). It is noteworthy that the exclusion of 18 countries with the highest values for penetration does not change the coefficient for PEN substantially. This means that the unfavorable impact of penetration on growth is a continuous one that does not rely on extreme cases.

21. Note that this measure for the level of exports does not consider the trade composition. Measures of trade composition like the one proposed by Galtung (1971) which are interpreted as trade dependency have been found by various researchers to affect economic growth in the following way. An unfavorable position with regard to "vertical trade" is negatively related to growth. The same is reported in the literature for trade commodity and trade partner concentration. However, the detailed reanalysis of most of the trade dependency studies by Bornschier and Hartlieb (1981) does not find support for earlier findings regarding trade effects on long-term economic growth (1965 to 1977) within large samples (up to 100 cases).

22. We have also tested whether the strong negative effect of penetration is mainly due to including Romania and Yugoslavia, which did not show any penetration in 1967 and which were growing rapidly during the period under study. The results without these two countries (i.e., with the remaining 78 LDCs) are much the same: PEN: $b = -.0285$ ($F = 12.82$), FDI: $b = .0084$ ($F = 9.99$), $R^2 = .37$.

23. Stepwise regression shows that the control of FDI (flows) increases the negative weight of PEN (stocks). Such an increase also occurs when the level of income is controlled and applies both to the linear and the squared term. Furthermore, the already significant negative effect of PEN gets more substantial when level of exports is controlled. Exports, however, enter as a positive predictor into the equation only after penetration is controlled. For a discussion of trade variables, see Bornschier and Hartlieb (1981).

24. In peripheral America there is no country which could be excluded due to the same criteria. Venezuela, although being highly specialized in oil exports, is not comparable to the extreme specialization exhibited by Saudi Arabia. And in Africa, there are only two cases, namely Egypt (war region) and Libya (oil exports), which could be excluded. These two cases are, however, unlikely to affect the result of the large African sample which contains 37 countries.

25. The cutting point was in both cases the mean of the logged values for SIZE and *YN*.

26. Bornschier et al. (1978), Bornschier and Ballmer-Cao (1978) and Dolan

and Tomlin (1980) report similar findings, whereas the findings of Gobalet and Diamond (1979) are inconsistent.

27. This led us also to consider the possibility that penetration effects may be relatively greatest among the semiperipheral countries. We identified 15 countries from our sample of less developed countries that are deemed to be semiperipheral in the contemporary world-economy (Wallerstein 1979) and performed a separate analysis with these, most of which were relatively large in terms of internal market size. The comparison between this subsample and the sample of remaining less developed countries revealed that there is a somewhat larger estimated effect for semiperipheral countries. This larger effect is, however, very similar to the one which results if only small countries are excluded. Thus, we conclude that there is no special interaction effect for semiperipheral countries.

28. We have also tested the interaction between SIZE and PEN but the results are not presented here. This analysis shows a negative effect of the interaction term, indicating support for the subsample results in Tables 25.3 and 25.4, but the interaction effect is not statistically significant, indicating that, in the range of the world sample, this interaction between level of development and penetration reveals a similar small effect in the analysis of the whole sample. In order to further substantiate the conclusion in Table 25.4 that the interaction effect is with SIZE and not with level of development (YN), we entered both of them in the same analysis. This supports the earlier conclusion: the far more important interaction effect is with the size of the domestic market rather than the level of income. The latter interaction becomes zero when the interaction with SIZE is controlled.

29. Here are the mean values for penetration by transnational corporations in the whole sample of less developed countries and in the regional subsamples, and also the coefficients of variation. As can be seen the mean value for the American subsample is the highest and the coefficient of variation is the lowest.

Sample	N	Mean for PEN	Coefficient of Variation
All less developed	88	49.04	.72
Africa	37	50.00	.72
Asia	23	34.89	1.04
Asia without special cases	17	26.61	1.16
Europe	7	36.25	.90
America	21	67.24	.42

REFERENCES

Alschuler, L. R. 1976. "Satellization and Stagnation in Latin America." *International Studies Quarterly* 20 (1):39–82.

Ballmer-Cao, T.-H. and J. Scheidegger. 1979. Compendium Data for World System Analysis. *Bulletin of the Sociological Institute of the University of Zurich*, March.

Berweger, G. and J.-P. Hoby. 1978. Wirtschaftspolitik gegenüber Auslandskapital. *Bulletin des Soziologischen Instituts der Universität Zurich* Nr. 35:1–136.

Bornschier, V. 1975. "Abhaengige Industrialisierung und Einkommensentwicklung." *Schweizerische Zeitschrift für Soziologie* 1(1):67–105.

———. 1976. *Wachstum, Konzentration und Multinationalisierung von Industrieunternehmen*. Frauenfeld and Stuttgart: Verlag Huber.

————. 1980. "Multinational Corporations and Economic Growth: A Cross-National Test of the Decapitalization Thesis." *Journal of Development Economics* 7 (June):191–210.

————. 1981a. "Dependent Industrialization in the World Economy: Some Comments and Results Concerning a Recent Debate." *Journal of Conflict Resolution* 25 (3):371–400.

————. 1981b. "Weltwirtschaft, Wachstum und Verteilung: Eine Replik zur Arbeit von Erich Weede." *Schweizerische Zeitschrift für Soziologie* 7 (1):129–136.

————. 1982c. "Dependence on Foreign Capital and Economic Growth: A Reply to Weede and Tiefenbach's Critique." *European Journal of Political Research* 10 (4):445–450.

Bornschier, V., C. Chase-Dunn, and R. Rubinson. 1978. "Cross-National Evidence of the Effects of Foreign Investment and Aid on Economic Growth and Inequality: A Survey of Findings and a Reanalysis." *American Journal of Sociology* 84 (3):651–683.

Bornschier, V. and T.-H. Ballmer-Cao. 1978. "Multinational Corporations in the World Economy and National Development. An Empirical Study of Income per Capita Growth 1960–1975." *Bulletin of the Sociological Institute of the University of Zurich* no. 32:1–169.

Bornschier, V. and O. Hartlieb. 1981. "Weltmarktabhaengigkeit und Entwicklung: Uebersich ueber die Evidenzen und Reanalyse" [Structure and Income Distribution]. *Bulletin of the Sociological Institute of the University of Zurich* no. 39.

Bornschier, V. and C. Chase-Dunn. 1983. "Reply to Szymanski." *American Journal of Sociology* 89 (3):694–699.

Chase-Dunn, C. 1975a. "The Effects of International Economic Dependence on Development and Inequality: A Cross-National Study." *American Sociological Review* 40 (6):720–738.

———— 1975b. *International Economic Dependence in the World-System.* Dissertation, Department of Sociology, Stanford University.

Delacroix, J. and C. C. Ragin. 1981. "Structural Blockage: A Cross-national Study of Economic Dependency, State Efficiency, and Underdevelopment." *American Journal of Sociology* 86:1311–1347.

Dolan, M. B. and B. W. Tomlin. 1980. "First World–Third World Linkages: External Relations and Economic Development." *International Organization* 34 (1):41–63.

Domar, E. D. 1946. "Capital Expansion, Rate of Growth, and Employment." *Econometrica* 14:137–147.

————. 1948. "The Problem of Capital Accumulation." *American Economic Review* 38 (5):777–794.

Evans, P. 1980. "The Developmental Effects of Direct Investment." Paper read at the Annual Meeting of the American Sociological Association, New Orleans, August.

Galtung, J. 1971. "A Structural Theory of Imperialism." *Journal of Peace Research* 8 (2):81–117.

Gobalet, J. G. and L. J. Diamond. 1979. "Effects of Investment Dependence on Economic Growth: The Role of Internal Structural Characteristics and Periods in the World Economy," *International Studies Quarterly* 23:412–444.

Hymer, S. H. 1972. "The Multinational Corporation and the Law of Uneven Development." In J. N. Bhagwati (ed.), *Economics and the World Order.* New York: Macmillan.

Jackman, R. W. 1982. "Dependence on Foreign Investment and Economic Growth in the Third World." *World Politics* 34:175–196.

Kaufman, R. R., H. I. Chernotsky, and D. S. Geller. 1975. "A Preliminary Test of the Theory of Dependency." *Comparative Politics* 7:303–330.

McGowan, P. and D. Smith. 1978. "Economic Dependency in Black Africa: A Causal Analysis of Competing Theories." *International Organization* 32 (Winter):179–235.

Meyer-Fehr, P. 1978. "Bestimmungsfaktoren des Wirtschaftswachstums von Nationen. Komparative Analyse unter Berücksichtigung Multinationaler Konzerne." *Bulletin des Soziologischen Instituts der Universität Zurich* Nr. 34:1–105.

―――. 1980. "Technologische Kontrolle durch Multinationale Konzerne und Wirtschaftswachstum." In V. Bornschier (ed.), *Multinationale Konzerne, Wirtschaftspolitik und Nationale Entwicklung im Weltsystem*, pp. 106–128. Frankfurt: Campus Verlag.

OECD (Organization for Economic Cooperation and Development). 1972. *Stock of Private Direct Investments by D.A.C. Countries in Developing Countries, End 1967*. Paris: Development Assistance Directorate.

Papanek, G. 1972. "The Effect of Aid and Other Resource Transfers on Savings and Growth in Less Developed Countries." *Economic Journal* 82 (September):934–950.

Ray, J. L. and T. Webster. 1978. "Dependency and Economic Growth in Latin America." *International Studies Quarterly* 22:409–434.

Rubinson, R. 1976. "Reply to Bach and Irwin." *American Sociological Review* 42 (5):817–821.

Stevenson, P. 1972. "External Economic Variables Influencing the Economic Growth Rate of Seven Major Latin American Nations." *Canadian Review of Sociology and Anthropology* 9:347–356.

Stoneman, C. 1975. "Foreign Capital and Economic Growth." *World Development* 3 (1):11–26.

Szymanski, A. 1976. "Dependence, Exploitation, and Development." *Journal of Military and Political Sociology* 4 (Spring):53–65.

―――. 1983. "Comment on Bornschier, Chase-Dunn, and Rubinson." *American Journal of Sociology* 89 (3):690–694.

Timberlake, M. and J. Kentor. 1983. "Economic Dependence, Overurbanization, and Economic Growth: A Study of Less Developed Countries." *Sociological Quarterly* 24 (4):489–508.

van Puijenbroek, R.A.G. 1984. "Enkele politieke en economische determinanten van economische groei." Doctoral thesis, Katholieke Universiteit, Nijmegen (Netherlands).

Wallerstein, I. 1979. *The Capitalist World Economy*. Cambridge: Cambridge University Press.

Weede, E. 1981a. "Militär, Multis und Wirtschaft. Eine international vergleichende Studie unter besonderer Berücksichtigung der Entwicklungsländer. *Schweizerische Zeitschrift für Soziologie* 7:113–127.

―――. 1981. "Dependenztheorie und Wirtschaftswachstum." *Kölner Zeitschrift für Soziologie und Sozialpsychologie* 33 (4):690–707.

Weede, E. and H. Tiefenbach. 1981a. "Some Recent Explanations of Income Inequality." *International Studies Quarterly* 25 (2):255–282.

―――. 1981b. "Three Dependency Explanations of Economic Growth." *European Journal of Political Research* 9:391–406.

Weisskopf, T. E. 1971. "The Impact of Foreign Capital Inflow on Domestic Savings in Underdeveloped Countries." Summary in *Econometrica* 39 (Appendix of abstracts of the papers presented at the Second World Congress of the Econometric Society, Cambridge, England): 109.

26

· · · · · · ·

Growth Effects of Foreign
and Domestic Investment

· · · · · · ·

GLENN FIREBAUGH

*In Chapters 22–25, a strong case has been made for the argument
that dependency explains the gap between rich and poor countries
by slowing the growth of the poor. One of the ways it does so is by
using foreign rather than domestic investment. The Bornschier and
Chase-Dunn approach presented in Chapter 25 is part of an extensive body of quantitative evidence that supports the thesis that
dependency slows growth over the long run. In this chapter,
Firebaugh argues that the quantitative evidence has been seriously
misinterpreted and that although domestic investment is better for
growth than foreign investment, both spur growth in the short and
long terms. This chapter, therefore, helps to undermine the dependency perspective.*

Among the most fundamental principles in economics is the principle that
economic growth requires capital investment. Indeed, capital is generally
thought to constitute one of the three basic categories of the factors of production (the other two categories being land and labor). A long and hal-
lowed tradition in economics assumes positive effects for all three. Other
endowments being equal, the more land, the more output; the more labor,
the more output; and the more capital, the more output.

Recent work in sociology breaks sharply with this tradition by arguing
that a particular type of capital—foreign investment stock—retards and distorts development in the Third World (Bornschier and Chase-Dunn 1983,
1985; Bornschier, Chase-Dunn, and Rubinson 1978; Boswell and Dixon

Reprinted by permission of the University of Chicago Press from *American Journal
of Sociology,* vol. 98, no. 1 (July 1992): 105–130.

1990; London 1987, 1988; London and Robinson 1989; London and Smith 1988; London and Williams 1988, 1990; Wimberley 1990, 1991). The claim is that capital-poor Third World nations actually tend to be better-off in the long run if they eschew foreign capital. To quote Boswell and Dixon (1990, 554), "Previous research has documented the negative effects of economic dependency [foreign investment] on domestic growth." Such claims are legion in sociology.[1]

In this four-part article, I test the adverse-effects claim. . . .

THE SOURCE OF CAPITAL: DOES IT MATTER?

In the antiseptic world of some economic theories, capital and labor are completely mobile, political leaders are all wise and altruistic, and class interests do not exist. In such a world capital is capital; its source is irrelevant. However, in the real world of structural barriers, ineffective and corrupt governments, and class interests, the source of capital could matter—plenty (e.g., Amin 1974, 1976; Barnet and Mueller 1974; Bornschier and Chase-Dunn 1985; Hymer 1979).

There are certainly compelling reasons for expecting Third World countries to benefit less from foreign investment than from the indigenous kind. Compared with domestic investment, foreign investment is (1) less likely to contribute to public revenues, as transnational corporations are often able to avoid taxes through mechanisms such as "transfer pricing" (e.g., Streeten 1973), (2) less likely to encourage the development of indigenous entrepreneurship, (3) more likely to use inappropriate capital-intensive technology (though this is controversial; see White 1978), (4) less likely to reinvest profits in the host country, and (5) more likely to be "linkage weak" (Hirschman 1977).

These last two reasons are especially important. Foreign investment may be "outward looking" in two respects. Not only does the profit flow outward, but the products often do as well. In such cases output "can slip out of a country without leaving much trace in the rest of the economy," as Hirschman (1958, 110) so aptly puts it. Domestic industries, in contrast, are more likely to form links with other industries in the domestic economy. According to Hirschman (1977, 80–81), such linkages are the stuff of economic development: "A linkage exists whenever an ongoing activity gives rise to economic or other pressures to lead to the taking up of a new activity," and "development is essentially the record of how one thing leads to another, and the linkages are that record." In a similar vein, Amin (1974, 1976) argues that poor nations tend to remain poor because their internal economic sectors are "disarticulated," and—like Hirschman—he believes that an outward-looking economy is more likely to be disarticulated. If these arguments are correct, then surely the growth effects of foreign investment fall well short of those of domestic investment.

CAPITAL DEPENDENCY RESEARCH

It is one thing to claim that foreign investment is *not as good* as the home-grown variety. It is quite another matter to claim that foreign investment is bad. To actually retard growth, foreign investment must impede domestic enterprises. There are several possibilities. Transnational corporations could destroy nascent or even well-established local businesses (e.g., Amin 1976, chap. 4). Or they could co-opt local entrepreneurial talent. Or they could stimulate inappropriate consumption patterns, thereby lowering domestic savings rates. The result would be "investment decapitalization"—long-run decline in investment—if the shortfall due to lower savings exceeded the capital pumped into the economy from the outside.

Capital dependency or PEN research—so called because it is based on the PEN (foreign capital penetration) measure of Bornschier and Chase-Dunn (1985)—does claim that foreign investment is pernicious for Third-World nations. Indeed, recent cross-national research in sociology appears to be preoccupied with demonstrating how foreign investment is a full-fledged menace in the Third World. how it reduces economic growth, increases inequality, impedes fertility reduction, promotes mortality, incites rebellion, fuels urban bias, and, in general, makes life miserable for residents. Lest there be any doubt as to whether PEN researchers really mean to say that foreign investment is bad (and not just "less good"), consider these conclusions culled from studies that use the PEN variable to measure investment dependence or "multinational corporation (MNC) penetration":

> [Foreign] capital formation (PEN) has clearly disadvantageous consequences for economic growth [in LDCS]. [Bornschier and Chase-Dunn 1985, 96]

> [PEN] clearly distorts development in ways that impede fertility decline. [London 1988, 615]

> This analysis shows that MNC penetration [PEN] promotes high mortality levels in the Third World. [Wimberley 1990, 87]

> Taken together, the findings above lead to the conclusion that it is multinational corporate penetration [PEN], not income inequality, that directly accounts for increased levels of collective political violence experienced by nations. [London and Robinson 1989, 307]

> Our overall conclusion is that dependency [PEN and military dependence] in the world economy and international state system gives rise to rebellion. [Boswell and Dixon 1990, 555]

> The results . . . reveal a significant positive relationship between penetration [PEN] and urban bias. [London and Smith 1988, 461]

> There is a significant negative relation between multinational corporate penetration [PEN] and basic needs provision. [London and Williams 1988, 761]

This study adds strong empirical support to the world-system and dependency perspectives' claim that economic ties between the core and noncore harm the majority of noncore inhabitants. [Wimberley 1991, 427]

Transnational corporate investment [TNC] dependence has an exceptionally strong harmful effect on [food] consumption.... [TNCs] promote immiseration in the non-core. [Wimberley and Bello, in press]

Unless they are used vacuously, "harm," "immiserate," and similar words must mean that foreign investment actually is bad for the Third World—and not just that it is "less good" than domestic investment. Yet what precisely do PEN researchers mean when they say foreign capital "immiserates"? Dependency writers of the 1960s "stagnationist" school appear to claim that dependency precludes growth (see Gereffi 1983, chap. 1). The growth of many LDCs since then has deflated that claim, so the revised claim is that dependency tends to reduce—not preclude—economic growth. Hence by "immiseration" PEN researchers appear not to mean that capital penetration renders LDCs incapable of growth; rather, their claim is only that capital-penetrated LDCs are poorer than they would have been without the foreign investment.

There are, then, three viable positions regarding foreign investment's effect on economic growth. (1) Capital is capital. Foreign investment's effect is positive and the same size as that of domestic investment. (2) Foreign investment on balance tends to promote growth, albeit its effect is often not as large as that of domestic investment. This middle-of-the-road position is popular in development economics (see Gillis et al. 1983, chap. 14). (3) Foreign investment reduces growth. This is the conclusion of PEN research. Distinguishing between numbers 2 and 3—growth-promoting and growth-reducing investment—clearly is not hairsplitting. Naturally, LDCs try to encourage growth-promoting investment and avoid the other kind. So it is important to know which of these three positions characterizes foreign investment.

DATA AND MEASURES

The three positions can be tested using existing data. To avoid the accusation that the results are stacked against dependency theory, I use the PEN data set (from Ballmer-Cao and Scheidegger [1979], supplemented by data in Bornschier and Chase-Dunn [1985]). As in Bornschier and Chase-Dunn, the dependent variable is economic growth rate. In the PEN data set economic growth rate is measured by rate of growth of per capita GNP over the period 1965–77, expressed as an annual percentage.

Investment rate (I_τ) is the crucial independent variable. Here "rate" refers of course to change relative to initial level, so investment rate is change in capital relative to initial stock of capital. The PEN studies are based on foreign capital stock as of 1967 and 1973. To ensure that my results do not depend on the way I calculate investment rate, I do it three ways. The first is simply the percentage increase from 1967 to 1973:

$$\%I_\gamma = [(1973K - 1967K)/1967K] \times 100, \tag{1}$$

where K is capital stock. The second is annual rate of change, expressed as a percentage:

$$\text{ann}I_\gamma = [\sqrt[6]{(1973K/1967K)} - 1] \times 100, \tag{2}$$

where $\sqrt[6]{(1973K/1967K)}$ denotes sixth root of $1973K/1967K$. The third measure is the continuous-time analogue to annual I_γ. To distinguish it from (2), I refer to the continuous-time annual rate as "annualized I_γ," (annzI_γ). It is calculated as follows:

$$\text{annz}I_\gamma = \{[\ln(1973K/1967K)]/6\} \times 100, \tag{3}$$

where ln is the natural logarithm.

From the PEN data, foreign and domestic investment rates can be calculated for 76 LDCs and 15 wealthy nations for a total of 91 nations (see App. A). To be consistent with earlier research, I include the conventional PEN control variables in my analysis, using the measures and data given in Bornschier and Chase-Dunn (1985). These measures are: (1) the logarithm of total energy consumption in 1967, to control for the effect of domestic market demand or "size"; (2) the average value of exports as a percentage of gross domestic product for the years 1965, 1970, and 1973, to control for the effect of export activity; (3) the logarithm of gross national product per capita (GNP/c) in 1965, to control for the effect of 1965 GNP/c on 1965–77 growth rate of GNP/c. Again, to be consistent with PEN research, I include this third variable as both log(GNP/c) and [log(GNP/c)]², so that I can model the presumed quadratic effect of initial GNP on subsequent GNP growth (Bornschier and Chase-Dunn 1985, 92). . . .

RESULTS FOR GROWTH RATE

What do we find? There is strong support for the view that foreign is *not as good* as domestic investment (Table 26.1). Other things constant, annual economic growth is boosted by an estimated .23% for every 1% annual increase in domestic investment, but only by .08% for every 1% annual increase in foreign investment (see Table 26.1, col. 3). The difference between the slopes (domestic vs. foreign I_γ) is significant ($P < .05$) in every

Table 26.1   Estimated Economic Effects of Foreign and Domestic Investment: Growth Rate Models

| | Investment Rate Measure[a] | | | | | |
| | $\%I_\tau$ | | $AnnI_\gamma$ | | $AnnzI_\gamma$ | |
Independent Variable	(1)	(2)	(3)	(4)	(5)	(6)
Foreign investment rate:						
Metric b	.005**	.005**	.077**	.076**	.084**	.083**
t-value	3.1	3.1	3.6	3.6	3.6	3.6
Standardized b	.29	.29	.33	.33	.33	.33
Domestic investment rate:						
Metric b	.029**	.029**	.233**	.233**	.253**	.254**
t-value	4.0	4.0	3.8	3.9	3.9	4.0
Standardized b	.39	.38	.36	.36	.36	.37
PEN control variables:						
Market demand:						
Metric b	.50	.50	.56*	.56*	.57*	.57*
t-value	1.9	2.0	2.2	2.2	2.2	2.3
Standardized b	.23	.23	.25	.25	.26	.26
Exports:						
Metric b	.004	.004	.004	.004	.004	.005
t-value	.3	.3	.3	.3	.3	.3
Standardized b	.02	.02	.03	.03	.03	.03
1965 GNP/c (log):[b]						
Metric b	−.35	.76	.87	.63	1.2	.61
t-value	−.1	1.3	.2	1.1	.2	1.1
Standardized b	−.07	.15	.17	.12	.22	.12
$[Log(1965)\ GNP/c)]^2$:						
Metric b	.21		−.05		−.10	
t-value	.2		−.04		−.1	
Standardized b	.22		−.05		−.11	
Adjusted R^2	.50	.51	.51	.52	.51	.42
Adjusted R^2 without						
control variables	.42		.42		.42	

Note: In order to be consistent with PEN research, coefficients are reported for the model in which both log (1965 GNP/c) and its square are included (see cols. 1, 3, and 5). Because the two variables correlate +.997, results are also reported for the model without the squared term (see cols. 2, 4, and 6). Partial regression plots and diagnostic statistics indicate that results are not due to outliers. $N = 76$ LDCs.

a. See eqq. (1)–(3) in text for definitions of the three rates.
b. GNP/c denotes GNP per capita.
* $P < .05$ (two-tailed)
** $P < .01$ (two-tailed)

instance (significance tests not shown). Regardless of measure—invest-ment rate as percentage increase or annual rate or annualized rate—domes-tic investment is better.

Hence the results contradict the view that "capital is capital." But they also contradict the PEN view that foreign investment impedes growth. In every instance the slope for foreign investment is *positive* ($P < .01$). This holds whether investment is measured as percentage increase (Table 26.1, cols. 1 and 2), as annual rate (cols. 3 and 4), or as annualized rate (cols. 5 and 6); it holds when *per capita* investment rates are used (results not shown in Table 26.1), it holds when collinearity is reduced by dropping $[\log(\text{GNP}/c)]^2$ (cols. 2, 4, 6); and it holds when the PEN controls are dropped altogether (results not shown in Table 26.1). The robustness of the foreign-investment effect is in sharp contrast to the usual instability of cross-national research. The positive investment effects reported in Table 26.1 are typical of what I found in estimating literally dozens of models.

In contrast to the investment slopes, the slopes for the PEN controls tend to be small and nonsignificant. Aside from market demand, the coefficients for the PEN control variables all fall well short of statistical significance. Using the PEN data set, I find that LDCs with greater rates of foreign investment tend to exhibit faster rates of economic growth, independent of the effects of domestic investment, export activity, and so on (Table 26.1). Nevertheless, PEN researchers conclude that LDCs tend to be richer if they eschew foreign investment. The argument is based on a sharp distinction between foreign investment's short-run and long-run effects (Bornschier and Chase-Dunn 1985, xi): "We find that, while flows of foreign investment have short-run positive effects on economic growth, accumulated stock of foreign capital (indicating a high degree of penetration and control by transnational corporations) has a long-run retardant effect on economic growth."

The claim then is that, other endowments equal, LDCs with higher accumulations of foreign capital are worse off in the long run than those with lower accumulations of foreign capital. Growth rate per se is not the concern here, since rates reflect short-run effects; rather, I want to determine the *cumulative* economic effect of foreign investment. Will LDCs eventually prosper more—enjoy higher levels of income per capita—with or without foreign investment? To answer that question I must determine foreign investment's total (direct + indirect) long-run effects on GNP/c.

Without wishing to belabor the obvious, it is important to stress that a long-run effect is a cumulation of short-run effects. So if PEN researchers are right about the positive short-run effects of foreign investment—and Table 26.1 certainly supports their view—then one wonders how positive short-run effects "add up" to a negative long-run effect.

The dependency answer lies in the notion of "decapitalization." Though decapitalization stories can be complex (Vernon 1971, chap. 5)—involving trade, balance of payments, and so forth—the PEN version is based on Bornschier's thesis that foreign capital harms LDCs by severely depressing their domestic investment. Lest there be any doubt, Bornschier (1980, fig. 1) formalizes his thesis by ordering the variables as follows: foreign capital $\rightarrow$ domestic capital $\rightarrow$ GNP growth. The critical test of decapitalization, then, is whether the path coefficient from cumulated foreign capital to cumulated domestic capital is negative (since all agree that domestic investment has a positive effect on GNP).[2]

Development economists most often tell a very different story. The famous Harrod-Domar capital theory, for example, assumes augmentation, not decapitalization (Gillis et al. 1983): "In a Harrod-Domar world . . . the role of foreign saving of all kinds is to *augment* domestic saving to increase investment and thus accelerate growth" (374; emphasis added). Thus Harrod-Domar theory claims that foreign investment boosts total investment: foreign investment → total investment → economic performance. . . . Contrary to what one might infer from PEN studies, the augmentation view is not bereft of empirical support. Indeed, Salvatore (1983) claims that "It has been conclusively confirmed empirically that foreign capital inflows . . . make a positive net contribution to the rate of foreign formation" (69– 70; see Sprout and Weaver [1990] for recent evidence supporting augmentation).

Because it contains *cumulated* data on foreign and domestic investment, the PEN data set is especially well suited for testing the long-run effects of capital. Stock in 1967 refers to cumulated investment *as of* 1967. Domestic stock goes back 18 years; hence 1967 domestic stock reflects investment cumulated from 1950 to 1967 (see Ballmer-Cao and Scheidegger [1979, 73] for the depreciation formula used). The foreign stock measure goes back even further: it refers to the net book value of foreign holdings. So the PEN data on foreign stock are ideal for determining foreign investment's long-run effects, since, in principle, book value reflects investment from day 1. Moreover, "day 1" for foreign investment is well before 1950 for many LDCs, so there is a built-in lag for the foreign stock relative to the domestic stock. This is a critical point in view of the claim that foreign investment reduces domestic investment over the long run. If that claim is true, the reduction certainly should be evident in the PEN data.

Table 26.2 summarizes the PEN-data results for decapitalization and augmentation. In the 1967 models, accumulated capital as of 1967 (domestic capital in the case of decapitalization, total capital in the case of augmentation) is regressed on accumulated foreign capital as of 1967. To repeat, foreign capital is exogenous in PEN decapitalization models (Bornschier 1980), so it is exogenous here. Capital is in dollars per capita (logged to reduce skew; see Jackman 1980). Results are given for regressions with and without the PEN controls.[3] The 1973 models use accumulated capital as of 1973, rather than as of 1967. If, perchance, book value of foreign holdings from day 1 fails to capture all time-delay dependency effects, the PEN data permit an additional six-year lag by regressing 1973 domestic cumulation on 1967 foreign cumulation.

The results are unambiguous: augmentation, not decapitalization. The coefficient for cumulated foreign investment is always positive, and always statistically significant at $P < .0001$ or better (see Table 26.2).

Table 26.2   Estimated Effect of Accumulated Foreign Capital on Accumulated Domestic Capital and Accumulated Total Capital[a]

Model	Dependent Variable	
	Accumulated Domestic K (Decapitalization Test)	Accumulated Domestic K (Augmentation Test)
Accumulation as of 1967:		
No controls:		
Standardized b	.74	.78
t-value	9.5	10.9
PEN controls:		
Standardized b	.66	.71
t-value	10.0	11.5
Accumulation as of 1973:		
No controls:		
Standardized b	.76	.80
t-value	10.1	11.7
PEN controls:		
Standardized b	.65	.70
t-value	10.3	12.0
Accumulation as of 1973, with additional lag:		
No controls:		
Standardized b	.73	.77
t-value	9.1	10.3
PEN controls:		
Standardized b	.63	.67
t-value	9.5	10.7

Note: Standardized coefficients are used because they are handier here for calculating indirect and total effects (see Table 26.3). Partial regression plots and diagnostic statistics indicate that results are not due to outliers.

a. Accumulated total capital = total foreign stock plus an 18-year accumulation of domestic stock.

b. Demand and exports, as in Table 26.1. GNP/c is not controlled for, because both decapitalization and augmentation assume that GNP is endogenous with respect to accumulated capital.

c. 1973 accumulation is regressed on 1967 accumulation, allowing an additional six years for foreign investment effects to appear.

What about the long-run *economic* effect of foreign investment? As just observed (Table 26.2), cumulated foreign investment boosts cumulated total investment. Of course, countries with more cumulated total investment tend to be richer than those with lower cumulations, so some of the long-run economic effect of foreign investment is indirect, through its positive effect on total investment. By contrast, the unmediated effect of foreign investment should be negative, reflecting the earlier finding that foreign investment is *not as good* as domestic investment.[4]

The dependent variable—logged GNP/c—is not cumulated output, but rather output for a single year. Unless vacuous, the claim that foreign investment has a long-run retardant economic effect must mean that at some point in time accumulated foreign capital demonstrably lowers output.

The estimates are given in Table 26.3. By boosting accumulated total capital, accumulated foreign capital boosts economic level in the long run. This indirect effect is large. The unmediated long-run effect of foreign capital—reflecting the earlier finding that foreign investment is less beneficial than domestic investment—is negative, but much smaller (and statistically insignificant when the PEN controls are added). As a result, the total effect of foreign investment is positive; the estimates range from +0.56 to +0.67. In short, *according to the PEN data,* foreign investment has a *positive* long-run economic effect in the Third World. This conclusion holds whether I use capital cumulation as of 1967 or as of 1973; it holds whether or not the PEN control variables are included; and it holds when I allow an additional six-year lag.

ACCOUNTING FOR THE CONTRARY
CONCLUSIONS OF EARLIER RESEARCH

If the PEN data in fact show that foreign investment has a beneficial long-run effect, why do PEN studies conclude otherwise? The problem lies not in wrong coefficients but in wrong interpretations of coefficients. The PEN

Table 26.3   Estimated Long-Run Economic Effect on Foreign Investment[a]

Model	Even Through Total Investment[b]	Direct Investment[c]	Total Effect[d]
Accumulation as of 1967:			
No controls	.83**	−.16*	.67**
PEN controls	.67**	−.06	.61**
Accumulation as of 1973:			
No controls	.88**	−.21*	.67**
PEN controls	.68**	−.11	.57**
Accumulation as of 1973 with additional lag:			
No controls	.81**	−.17*	.64**
PEN controls	.62**	−.06	.56**

Note: Partial regression plots and diagnostic statistics indicate that results are not due to outliers. $N = 76$ LDCs.

a. Total accumulation of foreign stock; 18-year accumulation of domestic stock.

b. Product of standardized regression coefficients for foreign accumulation→total accumulation→GNP.

c. Expressed as a standardized regression coefficient. A negative coefficient is consistent with the view that foreign investment is *not as good* as domestic investment.

d. Direct effect plus indirect effect through total investment.

* $P < .05$ (two-tailed)

** $P < .01$ (two-tailed)

researchers arrive at conclusions that are at odds with their results. To understand how this has happened, we must first understand the importance these studies attach to the distinction between capital stock and capital flow.

CAPITAL STOCK VERSUS CAPITAL FLOW

The long-standing economic distinction between capital flow and capital stock was popularized in sociology in an early dependency study by Bornschier et al. (1978). By distinguishing foreign capital stock—"total cumulated value of foreign-owned capital in a country"—from foreign capital flow—"current account inflows of foreign capital for some time period" (661)—Bornschier et al. try to account for an interesting pattern in cross-national studies of foreign capital and economic growth. Studies using capital flow to measure the effect of foreign capital (e.g., Papanek 1973) typically find beneficial investment effects, whereas those using capital stock with flow controlled for (e.g., Stoneman 1975) typically find the opposite. "What this pattern suggests is that the immediate effect of inflows of foreign capital . . . is to increase the rate of economic growth, while the long-run cumulative effects operate to reduce the rate of economic growth" (Bornschier et al. 1978, 667).

The Bornschier et al. thesis about stock and flow effects spawned the PEN research that still dominates cross-national work in sociology. From 1987 to 1990 in the *American Sociological Review* alone there were eight studies that used PEN or its log. Such interest is understandable: the capital dependency issue is timely, the theory controversial, the studies often painstaking. Unfortunately, though, this line of research is based on a faulty premise. A negative coefficient for stock, controlling for flow, does *not* mean that investment has a long-run adverse effect.

This point is easy to demonstrate by using the formula for investment rate as percentage increase (eq. [1]). The numerator is change in capital stock, 1967–73; PEN researchers call this *flow*. The denominator is capital accumulation as of 1967, that is, *stock*. So, in the stock and flow terminology, investment rate is simply flow divided by stock:

$$\%I_\gamma = (\text{flow/stock}) \times 100. \tag{4}$$

Observe that equation (4) still holds when flow and stock are each expressed as a percentage of GDP—that is, when total flow and total stock both are divided by GDP—as is typical in PEN research.

From equation (4) it is immediately apparent that, with stock constant, the faster the flow the *greater* the investment rate; and with flow constant, the larger the stock the *smaller* the investment rate. So when stock and flow are entered as separate variables in a regression equation it follows logically that

1. a positive flow coefficient and a negative stock coefficient indicate a beneficial investment effect;
2. a negative flow coefficient and a positive stock coefficient indicate an adverse investment effect.

These principles hold whether investment rate is measured as percentage increase (eq. [1]), as annual rate (eq. [2]), or as annualized rate (eq. [3]).

Now we see why PEN researchers get the results they do. When the flow coefficient (controlling for stock) is positive, and the stock coefficient (controlling for flow) is negative—precisely what PEN researchers find—investment has a beneficial effect. . . . Because domestic investment is *better* than foreign investment, the ratio of foreign to domestic stock . . . will have a negative slope. Because investment rate has a beneficial effect, stock per capita . . . will also have a negative slope. The latter factor dominates. . . . The overriding point, however, is that either way—whether PEN is capturing the denominator effect, or the effect of foreign investment relative to that of domestic investment—PEN researchers have misinterpreted their results.

PEN RESEARCH ON THE *NONECONOMIC* EFFECTS OF FOREIGN INVESTMENT

The PEN studies of the noneconomic effects of foreign investment likewise routinely reach conclusions that are at odds with their findings.

A recent study well illustrates the point. In a painstaking analysis of the effect of foreign investment on Third World mortality, Wimberley (1990, 89) concludes that "in the long run, the greater the penetration of non-core areas by the capitalist world economy, the greater the privation of the majority in those areas." His findings indicate just the opposite, however. Using the three-components PEN model, he consistently finds a positive flow coefficient and a negative stock (PEN) coefficient for life expectancy.

Still other PEN studies of the noneconomic effects of foreign investment use *one*-component (PEN only) models. Because such one-component models have no defensible interpretation, conclusions from those studies remain suspect until they can be confirmed using sensible models of investment's effect.

SUMMING UP

Piqued by dependency and world-system theory, sociologists have begun to study a subject previously thought to be the stuff of development economics; that is, foreign investment's economic and welfare effects in the Third World.[5] The sociological studies draw on published estimates of cumulated capital as of 1967 and 1973—the "PEN data." Analyses of this data set are not altogether satisfactory, however, because the analysts' findings and conclusions are antipodal.

Dependency theory is too important to be ignored (as it is, by and large, in economics). Regrettably, its study in sociology has used illogic. A fresh start is needed. Reanalysis of the PEN data provides such a start. The reanalysis yields three major conclusions.

1. From the host country's perspective, all capital is not equal; the source *does* matter. Homegrown capital outperforms imported capital. This is true whether investment rate is measured as percentage increase, annual rate, or annualized rate.

2. If the PEN data are reliable, foreign investment benefits LDCs. The coefficients for foreign investment rate are always positive and statistically significant. Contrary to the earlier conclusions of sociologists, foreign investment apparently promotes growth over the long run as well as over the short run. This is not to deny that particular nations at particular times for particular reasons are hurt by foreign investment (see O'Hearn 1989; contrast Barrett and Whyte [1982], and Bradshaw [1988]). There is nonetheless no evidence in the PEN data of a general tendency for foreign investment to retard growth.

3. The capital dependency tradition that has recently dominated cross-national research in sociology is based on an error. Although the error has methodological implications, it is more aptly described as an error in logic. The PEN researchers employ growth rate or panel models, that is, models based on change in the dependent variable over the short run. In those models, salutary investment effects have paraded as negative stock coefficients. This is just as it should be since—flow constant—the greater the stock the *lower* the investment rate. Researchers have overlooked that mathematical fact, however, and have concluded that negative stock (PEN) slopes somehow reflect harmful "long-run" effects.

I close on a more upbeat note. Sociological models of Third World development can be improved by a quantum leap merely by adding appropriate measures of investment. Investment rate should be included routinely in panel and rate models. In this study I use data from capital dependency researchers—a conservative strategy, since such researchers would hardly want to choose data that exaggerate the benefits of investment—yet in that data investment is by far the *most important determinant* of economic growth in the Third World. In efforts to show how our perspectives add to those of "mere economics" then, we sociologists must not eschew all things economic. Foreign and domestic investment have important effects, albeit not necessarily of the sort described in recent sociological research.

APPENDIX A

Nations in Study[6]

Seventy-six less developed countries. Burundi, Cameroon, Central African Republic, Chad, Dahomey (Benin) Ethiopia, Ghana, Guinea, Ivory Coast, Kenya, Liberia, Madagascar, Malawi, Mali, Mauritania, Niger, Nigeria, Rwanda, Senegal, Sierra Leone, Somalia, South Africa, Zimbabwe, (South Rhodesia), Tanzania, Togo, Uganda, Upper Volta, Zaire, Zambia, Algeria, Egypt, Morocco, Sudan, Tunisia, Costa Rica, Dominican Republic, El Salvador, Guatemala, Honduras, Jamaica, Mexico, Nicaragua, Panama, Argentina, Bolivia, Brazil, Chile, Colombia, Ecuador, Paraguay, Peru, Uruguay, Venezuela, Iran, Iraq, Turkey, Afghanistan, Burma, Hong Kong, India, Indonesia, Japan, South Korea, Malaysia, Pakistan, Philippines, Sri Lanka, Thailand, Greece, Ireland, Italy, Portugal, Spain, Papua New Guinea, Taiwan, and Trinidad and Tobago.

Fifteen rich nations. Canada, United States, Austria, Belgium, Denmark, Finland, France, Germany (West), Netherlands, Norway, Sweden, Switzerland, United Kingdom, Australia, and New Zealand.

NOTES

1. By "Previous research" Boswell and Dixon (1990) refer to research in sociology, not economics. Economists most often find that foreign investment augments domestic investment (see below), thus spurring growth.

2. Research in the PEN tradition keys on the Bornschier (1980) "depressed investment" model, so that is the decapitalization model I test here. The PEN data do not permit tests of trade- or remittance-based decapitalization stories.

3. I do not control for GNP/c because it is the criterion variable in both the decapitalization and augmentation models. Bornschier and Chase-Dunn fault Jackman (1982) for failing to control for the effect of "the level of economic development . . . [on] the degree of transnational penetration" (Bornschier and Chase-Dunn 1985, 86). Here, however, level of economic development is measured by GNP/c at time *t*, and transnational penetration is measured by *accumulated* foreign capital *as of t*. And GNP/c obviously does not work backward in time to determine earlier investment.

4. When total investment is constant, the more foreign investment there is, the higher the ratio of foreign investment to domestic investment. Hence if foreign investment is not as good as domestic investment, the coefficient for foreign investment, total investment controlled, should be negative.

5. A common misperception is that most foreign investment goes to LDCs. Multinational corporations are much more likely to invest in rich nations, especially in recent years. From 1985–89, new foreign investment in *all* LDCs totaled $78 billion; in the United States alone the total was $231 billion (Turner 1991, tables 12 and 13). The United States in fact is the leading recipient of foreign direct investment by far, accounting for over 40% of the world total since 1985. While foreign investment in the United States exploded during the 1980s, such investment in LDCs stagnated, giving rise to a new worry about the adverse global effect of "reconcentration of industrial capital in core areas" (Sassen 1988, 188).

6. The 76 LDCs and the 15 rich nations are defined as such in Bornschier and Chase-Dunn (1985).

REFERENCES

Amin, Samir. 1974. *Accumulation on a World Scale: A Critique of the Theory of Underdevelopment*, 2 vols. New York: Monthly Review.
———. 1976. *Unequal Development: An Essay on the Social Formations of Peripheral Capitalism*. New York: Monthly Review.
Ballmer-Cao, Thanh Huyen, and Juerg Scheidegger. 1979. *Compendium of Data for World-System Analysis: Bulletin of the Sociological Institute of the University of Zurich*. March.
Barnet, Richard, and Ronald Mueller. 1974. *Global Reach: The Power of Multinational Corporations*. New York: Simon & Schuster.
Barrett, Richard E., and Martin K. Whyte. 1982. "Dependency Theory and Taiwan: Analysis of a Deviant Case." *American Journal of Sociology* 82:1064–89.
Bornschier, Volker. 1980. "Multinational Corporations and Economic Growth: A Cross-national Test of the Decapitalization Thesis." *Journal of Development Economics* 7:191–210.
Bornschier, Volker, and Christopher Chase-Dunn. 1985. "Reply to Szymanski." *American Journal of Sociology* 89:694–99.
———. 1985. *Transnational Corporations and Underdevelopment*. New York: Praeger.
Bornschier, Volker, Christopher Chase-Dunn, and Richard Robinson. 1978. "Cross-national Evidence of the Effects of Foreign Investment and Aid on Economic Growth and Inequality: A Survey of Findings and a Reanalysis. *American Journal of Sociology* 84:651–83.
Boswell, Terry, and William J. Dixon. 1990. "Dependency and Rebellion: A Cross-national Analysis." *American Sociological Review* 55:540–59.
Bradshaw, York W. 1988. "Reassessing Economic Dependency and Uneven Development: The Kenyan Experience." *American Sociological Review* 53:693–708.
Crenshaw, Edward. 1991. "Foreign Investment as a Dependent Variable: Determinants of Foreign Investment and Capital Penetration in Developing Nations, 1967–1978." *Social Forces* 69:1169–82.
Domar, Evsey. 1946. "Capital Expansion, Rate of Growth and Employment." *Econometrica* 14:137–47.

———. 1947. "Expansion and Employment." *American Economic Review* 37:34–55.

Firebaugh, Glenn, and Jack P. Gibbs. 1985. "User's Guide to Ratio Variables." *American Sociological Review* 50:713–22.

Gereffi, Gary. 1983. *The Pharmaceutical Industry and Dependency in the Third World*. Princeton, N.J.: Princeton University Press.

Gillis, Malcolm, Dwight H. Perkins, Michael Roemer, and Donald Snodgrass. 1983. *Economics of Development*. New York: Norton.

Harrod, Roy F. 1939. "An Essay in Dynamic Theory." *Economic Journal* 49:14–33.

Hirschman, Albert O. 1958. *The Strategy of Economic Development*. New Haven, Conn.: Yale University Press.

———. 1977. "A Generalized Linkage Approach to Development, with Special Reference to Staples." 67–98 in *Essays on Economic Development and Cultural Change in Honor of B. F. Hoselitz*, edited by Manning Nash. Chicago: University of Chicago Press.

Hymer, Stephen H. 1979. *The Multinational Corporation: A Radical Approach*. Cambridge: Cambridge University Press.

Jackman, Robert W. 1980. "A Note on the Measurement of Growth Rates in Cross-national Research." *American Journal of Sociology* 86:604–17.

———. 1982. "Dependence on Foreign Investment and Economic Growth in the Third World." *World Politics* 34:175–96.

London, Bruce. 1987. "Structural Determinants of Third World Urban Change: An Ecological and Political Economic Analysis." *American Sociological Review* 52:28–43.

———. 1988. "Dependence, Distorted Development, and Fertility Trends in Noncore Nations: A Structural Analysis of Cross-national Data." *American Sociological Review* 53:606–18.

London, Bruce, and Thomas D. Robinson. 1989. "The Effect of International Dependence on Income Inequality and Political Violence." *American Sociological Review* 54:305–8.

London, Bruce, and David A. Smith. 1988. "Urban Bias, Dependence, and Economic Stagnation in Noncore Nations." *American Sociological Review* 53:454–63.

London, Bruce, and Bruce A. Williams. 1988. "Multinational Corporate Penetration, Protest, and Basic Needs Provision in Non-core Nations: A Cross-national Analysis." *Social Forces* 66:747–73.

———. 1990. "National Politics, International Dependency, and Basic Needs Provision: A Cross-national Study." *Social Forces* 69:565–84.

O'Hearn, Denis. 1989. "The Irish Case of Dependency: An Exception to the Exceptions?" *American Sociological Review* 54:578–96.

Papanek, Gustav F. 1973. "Aid, Foreign Private Investment, Savings, and Growth in Less Developed Countries." *Journal of Political Economy* 81:120–30.

Salvatore, Dominick. 1983. "A Simultaneous Equations Model of Trade and Development with Dynamic Policy Simulations." *Kyklos* 36:66–90.

Sassen, Saskia. 1988. *The Mobility of Labor and Capital*. Cambridge: Cambridge University Press.

Sprout, Ronald V. A., and James H. Weaver. 1990. "Exports and Economic Growth: Neoclassical and Dependency Theory Contrasted." American University Department of Economics Working Paper no. 130. Washington, D.C.

Stoneman, Colin. 1975. "Foreign Capital and Economic Growth." *World Development* 3:11–26.

Streeten, Paul. 1973. "The Multinational Enterprise and the Theory of Development Policy." *World Development* 1:1–14.

Szymanski, Albert. 1983. "Comment on Bornschier, Chase-Dunn, and Rubinson." *American Journal of Sociology* 89:690–94.

Todaro, Michael P. 1981. *Economic Development in the Third World*, 2d ed. New York: Longman.

Turner, Philip. 1991. *Capital Flows in the 1980s: A Survey of Major Trends.* Economic Paper no. 30. Basel: Bank for International Settlements.

Vernon, Raymond W. 1971. *Sovereignty at Bay: The Multinational Spread of U.S. Enterprises.* New York: Basic.

White, Lawrence J. 1978. "The Evidence on Appropriate Factor Proportions for Manufacturing in Less Developed Countries: A Survey." *Economic Development and Cultural Change* 27:27–59.

Wimberley, Dale W. 1990. "Investment Dependence and Alternative Explanations of Third World Mortality: A Cross-national Study." *American Sociological Review* 55:75–91.

———. 1991. "Transnational Corporate Investment and Food Consumption in the Third World: A Cross-national Analysis." *Rural Sociology* 56:406–31.

Wimberley, Dale W., and Rosario Bello. 1992. "Effects of Foreign Investment, Exports, and Economic Growth on Third World Food Consumption." *Social Forces.* In press.

27

· · · · · · ·

American Penetration
and Canadian Development:
A Study of Mature Dependency

· · · · · · ·

Heather-Jo Hammer & John W. Gartrell

In Chapter 25, Volker Bornschier and Christopher Chase-Dunn find that extensive foreign capital penetration dampens long-term economic growth. In the previous edition of this volume, Edward N. Muller has suggested that up to that point, dependency theory was unable to explain how Canada—a country highly penetrated by foreign invest-ment—could be wealthy, fast growing, and experiencing relatively low levels of income inequality. In this chapter, Heather-Jo Hammer and John W. Gartrell argue that dependency theorists had failed to acknowledge that a country could be both a member of the core and a dependent country. After noting some similarities between mature dependency and Peter Evans's dependent development, the authors provide a model for Canada's mature dependence and offer evidence of a negative long-term effect of change in American direct investment on change in Canadian economic growth.

The dependency perspective on the sociology of development has had diffi-culties in coming to terms with the Canadian situation. Canada seems to fall between types of social formations, displaying the social relations of advanced capitalism and the economic structure of dependency (Drache 1983, 36). Indeed, the Innisian tradition of Canadian political economy[1] stems from a perceived need for both original theory and distinctive methodology in the explanation of Canadian development (Drache 1983, 38). There is little doubt within the dependency perspective that Canada is "profoundly dependent" in the critical sense that it is extensively penetrated

Reprinted with permission of the American Sociological Association and the authors from *American Sociological Review*, vol. 51, no. 2 (April 1986):201–213.

by American direct investment. Nevertheless, Canadian dependency is of a "different genre" than classic peripheral dependency (Portes 1976, 78). . . .

As a theory of development, dependency cannot adequately explain why core economies are not susceptible to the negative consequences of penetration as long as dependency is defined as a structural distortion that is evident exclusively in peripheral modes of development. We think that a demonstration of the negative structural effect of dependency is possible in the case of extensively penetrated core countries. The situation of "relative" core underdevelopment is described with the concept "mature dependency" (Hammer 1982, 1984a, 1984b). The differentiation of mature dependency from other forms of economic power dependency requires that the theory be liberated from its focus on the periphery and the semi-periphery, and the empirical studies be liberated from cross-national analysis. Our endeavour to specify a model of the structural effect of mature dependency on economic growth in Canada reflects Duvall's suggestion to merge dialectical analysis with time series methodology (Duvall 1978).

Mature Dependency and Canadian Development: Reformulating Dependency Theory

Dialectical analysis requires that each new situation of dependency be specified in a "search for differences and diversity" (Cardoso and Faletto 1979, xiii). Contrary to Caporaso and Zare (1981, 47) who state that "The questions of identification and measurement must be answered before theoretical ones can be raised," the dialectical method suggests that ". . . before measuring, previous elaboration of adequate theories and categories is required to give sense to the data" (Cardoso and Faletto 1979, xiii). In brief, Cardoso and Faletto's strategy is to establish the evidence on theoretical grounds and to interpret the data historically. Shifting to the language of empirical models, historical arguments must be interpreted in terms of the important context-defining variables that specify the form of dependency (Duvall 1978, 74).

The existing form of dependency that is most relevant to the Canadian case is Evans's (1979) statement of dependent development. There are some striking similarities between the Canadian and Brazilian developmental histories, particularly in relation to changes in the concentration of foreign capital. In both countries there is an historical shift from British portfolio to American direct investment, and from concentration in resources to concentration in industry. The key difference rests with the timing of the changes and the initial mode of incorporation into the world economy. During the period of Canada's initial industrialization at the end of the nineteenth century, American direct investment in Canadian manufacturing accounted for about 34 percent of total manufacturing investment, compared to less than 4 percent in Brazil. The proportion of American to total direct investment in Canadian manufacturing was 55.6 percent by 1924 (Lewis 1938); in Brazil, by 1929, American direct investment accounted for only 24 percent of total manufacturing investment (Evans 1979, 78). It was not until the 1950s that American direct investment in Brazilian manufacturing attained the concentration levels evident in Canada before the 1920s.

Most of the American MNEs that are currently dominant in Canada had already been established by the end of 1920 (Gonick 1970, 62). By 1897, Canada accounted for about 25 percent of total American direct investment abroad. By 1913, there were 450 American branch plants in Canada, including such giants as Singer, Bell, and Houston Electric (now General Electric) (Field 1914). When the American MNEs asserted their interests in Canadian manufacturing, Canada was the eighth largest manufacturing country in the world, not a peripheral country in transition (Maizels 1963). In 1870, manufacturing accounted for 19 percent of Canada's gross national product, with the production of iron and steel leading the composition.

"Production moves to the periphery only after the technology has become routinized" (Evans 1979, 28). Therefore, the comparative advantage of the periphery in the international market becomes the low cost of its labor (Evans 1979, 28). In addition to the economic disarticulation that results from the lack of integration between subsidiary firms,[2] there exists a disarticulation between technology and social structure. The problem is evident in the failure of imported technology to absorb the huge reserves of underemployed agricultural labor that have been excluded from urban industrialization (Evans 1979, 29). For the elite, disarticulation is an obstacle to self-sustained, autocentric accumulation (Evans 1979, 29). For the masses, economic exclusion is followed by political repression in order to prevent a rise in wages that would mean a loss in comparative advantage (Evans 1979, 48). Evans (1979, 29) describes both exclusion and disarticulation as the constant features of dependency, in the case of dependent development.[3]

Certainly, there is evidence of internal economic disarticulation in Canada. The establishment and protection of foreign technology and the control of the market by oligopolistic MNEs has resulted in a miniature replica effect. The Canadian goods market is fragmented due to an excess of buyers and sellers relative to size, and the concentration of MNEs in central Canada has resulted in regional disparity (Britton and Gilmour 1978, 93–96). However, the only way one can argue for the exclusion of the Canadian masses is in a relative sense, and only in comparison to the U.S. Historically, the wage levels of Canadian workers have been considerably higher than the wage levels of European workers. In fact, when American direct investment moved into Canadian industry at the end of the 1800s, Canada was at a comparative "disadvantage" because of its high wage levels. Where the wage differential does show up is in comparison to American industrial wages which were 60 percent higher than those in Canada during the period (Logan 1937, 90). Firestone's (1958) research suggests that real productivity in Canada outstripped real wages, but this relationship was reversed in the 1930s.

Canada had a reserve army of unskilled labor working in resources, construction and agriculture, whose wage rates were tied to the boom-bust cycle of export-led growth rather than to the import of technology (Drache 1983). This relation is accounted for by Canada's unique situation of being extensively penetrated by MNE investment simultaneously in resource extraction and manufacturing (Gherson 1980). In this sense the Canadian economy remains classically dependent, in that its export composition is predominated by primary resources.[4] In 1913, Canada was exporting an average of 31 percent less finished manufactures than the largest seven manufacturing countries (Maizels 1963). It was not the case that Canada lacked domestic savings for investment in the technology needed to further develop the manufacturing sector. Instead, Canadian funds were being directed into an elaborate banking and financial system to support the domestic transportation and utilities infrastructure needed for the export of wheat (Laxer 1984).

Technology was being imported at a much faster rate than manufactured goods were being exported. Consequently, foreign capital inflows were solicited to maintain the overall rate of economic growth (Ingram 1957). Gonick (1970, 70) argues that the import-substitution mentality implicit in the Canadian National Policy of 1897 was motivated by the commercial capitalists' concern with protecting their trade monopoly in staple exports. The policy of establishing a tariff barrier around Canadian manufacturing was intended to force the American MNEs to finance the Canadian industrial sector in order to penetrate the Canadian market. Apart from sidestepping the Canadian tariff, the opportunity to compete under the terms of British preference in export trade was a further attraction to American direct investment. In addition, the MNEs were able to take advantage of tax benefits and offers of free land that were a result of the regional competition within Canada to attract investment (Scheinberg 1973, 85).

The Canadian railway and financial capitalists were the same central Canadian capitalists who stood to gain from the protection of Canadian manufacturing and from government assistance to the Canadian Pacific Railway. Levitt (1970, 50–51) explains that Canadian private capital flowed freely from railway enterprises into the financial sector and manufacturing industries. In dependent development, the industrial bourgeoisie has no choice but to ally with the state and foreign capital (Evans 1979), whereas in mature dependency, the position and privileges of the commercial industrialists are not contingent upon the tripartite alliance. The alliance is formed by invitation, not necessity.

Innis (1956) argues that even though Canada had liberal democratic institutions, it lacked "strong" popular and democratic traditions. He suggests that this anomaly is linked to Canada's historical dependence and the way Canada was settled. The white settlers who colonized Canada were either fleeing revolution or were exiled when their revolution failed. "It was the presence of a deeply entrenched counter-revolutionary tradition which fundamentally altered not only the liberal democratic character and institutions of Canada but class relations as well" (Drache 1983, 44). Nevertheless, the history of democratic government in Canada can hardly be described as repressive, particularly in comparison to the history of Brazilian government. Thus, the two constant features of dependent development, exclusion of the masses and disarticulation, are evident in Canada, but to a relatively small degree. We suggest that the historical evidence does not support the argument that Canada has experienced dependent development. Rather, Canadian dependency is mature.

Mature dependency diverges from dependent development in the following respects:

1. The mature dependent's economy is functionally complete at the time when the tripartite alliance is formed. External capital inputs are invited, not essential.
2. The economic disarticulation associated with MNE investment is superimposed upon an intact economy that has demonstrated the capacity for self-sustained, autocentric accumulation. Mature dependency is a concrete historical alternative to classic autocentric development rather than an advanced phase of dependent development.
3. Mature dependency does not require economic exclusion of the masses, nor does it result in the associated conditions of political repression.
4. Mature dependency is the condition that causes rich, industrialized core countries to exhibit relative underdevelopment vis-à-vis some of the other core countries on some criteria. The variability in relative status is determined, to a large extent, by the effectiveness of a state's development policy.

In contrast to its non-core counterparts, the mature dependent has abundant social, economic, and political resources that can be mobilized to regulate the negative effects of dependency (Duvall 1978, 69; Bornschier 1980a, 166–67). The contemporary features of mature dependency reflect a slow, historical process that has extended over a period of at least 120 years.

Similar to dependent development, mature dependency emerged during the period of classic colonial dependence on staple-export growth. The continuity between Canada's early reliance on staple exports and contemporary mature dependency is a result of the continued interest of the Canadian state and the dominant capital interests in the encouragement of American MNE investment.

The difficulty in modeling mature dependency empirically is that we do not expect that the negative structural effects associated with MNE penetration will be evident in a rich, industrialized host until after the division of labor within the multinationals has come to dominate economic structure and growth. The actual effect, according to the decapitalization thesis, will appear only when inflows of fresh foreign capital slow down, or as we will demonstrate for the Canadian case, in combination with actual disinvestment. Although 80 percent of total direct investment in Canada has been American (Government of Canada 1981, 10), British portfolio investment was the primary source of foreign long-term investment capital until 1926.

Circa 1926, American portfolio investment split the market with the U.K., and by 1933, total American long-term investment came to exceed total British investment. Yet, at the onset of World War I, American direct investment accounted for only 13.5 percent of total foreign long-term investment in Canada. Fully 73.2 percent of all foreign long-term investment capital in Canada was in the form of British portfolio investment, imported by the sale of government-guaranteed railway bonds in order to subsidize Canadian investments.

American economic domination was not perceived as a threat to the Canadian state (Marshall et al. 1976, 15), because of its relatively small proportion and because it was complementary to British and Canadian investment (Behrman 1970). Moreover, for the period 1930–1946, portfolio investment (American and British) accounted for twice as much foreign long-term investment as did American direct investment. Flows of portfolio capital generally contribute to economic growth whereas the structural effects of foreign direct investment reduce growth (Behrman 1970, 19). Direct investments are those in which control lies with the foreign investor (Aitken 1961, 24). The organizational form of foreign direct investment is the multinational (Evans 1979, 38). In contrast, portfolio investments involve the acquisition of foreign securities by individuals or institutions with limited control over the companies concerned. In fact, there is considerable agreement that portfolio investment does not involve foreign control at all (Aitken 1961, 24; Hood and Young 1979, 9; Levitt 1970, 58; Gonick 1970, 50). As an economy expands, the foreign sector recedes (Gonick 1970, 50), whereas foreign direct investment may well expand faster than the general economy due to its concentration in the most dynamic and profitable sectors.

World War II changed the balance of foreign capital investments in

Canada. Prior to the war, foreign portfolio investment accounted for an average of 71 percent of total foreign capital investment. After World War II, the average dropped to 34.8 percent. American direct investment, which had accounted for only 19.3 percent of the pre-war average, increased to 42.9 percent of foreign long-term investment for the period after 1946. Although American direct exceeded British portfolio investment as a proportion of total foreign long-term investment for the first time in 1946, it took about six more years for American direct investment to emerge as the primary source of foreign capital investment in Canada. While World War II facilitated an important increase in Canadian-owned manufacturing, it also brought closer economic ties with the U.S. Prior to 1950, American direct investment was linked closely to changes in the Canadian economy, accelerating during periods of high tariffs and decelerating during periods of recession (Marshall et al. 1976, 21). Pope (1971, 24) and Aitken (1961, 104) suggest that by 1950, American direct investment had become so large that it not only exploited opportunities, it created them by molding the Canadian economic structure.

The acceleration of American direct investment in Canada during the post-war boom period (1946-1960) is related to both the loss of Canadian access to British portfolio investment and markets and the ascent of the American economy to world economic hegemony. However, the crucial years, according to Grant (1970, 8), were the early 1940s when it was decided that Canada would become a branch plant economy. Both the organization of the war and the postwar construction were carried out under the assumption that government supported business interests in all national economic decisions. World War II brought the Ogdensburg agreements of 1940 to establish a joint defense board, the Hyde Park Declaration on the specialization of munitions production in 1941, a Joint War Production Committee, and Article VII of the Lend-Lease Law, which provided for a reduction in trade barriers. At this point, states Scheinberg (1973), Canadian leaders did perceive a threat to sovereignty, but were not prepared to change course in a period of accelerated wartime production.

Levitt (1970) describes how American direct investment continued to flow into the Canadian economy after the recession of 1957–1958, despite rising rates of unemployment and a slowing of Canadian output. The most important feature of the post-recession expansion was that only a very small proportion of foreign investment actually involved the importation of foreign savings (Gonick 1970, 64). American direct investment was financed largely from corporate capital raised in Canada through the sale of Canadian resources extracted and processed by Canadian labor, or from the sale of branch plant manufactures back to Canadian consumers at tariff-protected prices (Levitt 1970, 63).

Levitt (1970, 63–64) estimates that between 1957 and 1964, American direct investment in manufacturing, petroleum and natural gas, and mining and smelting secured 73 percent of investment funds from retained earnings and depreciation reserves. The strongest cross-national evidence (Bornschier 1980a, 161) of the negative impact of MNE penetration on specific economic sectors is evident in two of the three areas of American concentration in Canada, manufacturing and mining and smelting.

Although the proportion of American direct investment declined in the late 1970s, Canada's liabilities to the U.S. continued to rise through the reinvestment of retained earnings. Since 1975, almost 90 percent of the net increase in the book value of the stock of foreign direct investment in Canada has been accounted for by this process (Government of Canada 1981, 10).

Within the post-war period, both Grant and Levitt select 1960 as an important turning point in Canadian economic history. Grant (1970, 8) argues that since 1960, Canada has developed as a "northern extension" of the continental economy. Levitt (1970, 65) divides the post-war period into a boom period followed by a period of stabilization and disinvestment that she dates precisely to 1960. Levitt describes the latter phase of Canadian economic history as the period of "American Corporate Imperialism." In our analysis, the specification of this structural break is critical in the demonstration of the long-term negative effect of American direct investment on Canadian economic growth. Bergesen (1982) emphasizes the importance of considering structural breaks in world economic development as parameters that delineate the time frame of analysis. World wars are structural breaks, and in the context of dependency analysis World War II takes on particular significance as the demarcation of the emergence of the MNEs as the basic organizational units of world production (Bergesen 1982, 33; Bornschier and Ballmer-Cao 1979, 488; Blake and Walters 1983, 87; Hood and Young 1979, 18), and the establishment of American direct investment as the dominant form of foreign investment capital in Canada. Our restriction of the time series analysis to the post–World War II period is consistent with the literature. . . .

RESULTS

The results of the time series regression analysis support our hypothesis. Change in American direct investment for the post-war period has a negative effect on change in Canadian GNP after a lag of nine years. This effect is evident after 1960. The equation is reported in Table 27.1.

According to the full equation with all the variables included, IL9USDI has a negative effect on GNP of −1.88. As indicated by the value of the Durbin-Watson statistic (2.14), the model is free of autocorrelation. The coefficient for the long-term negative effect, specified as an interaction, is significant at the .025 level. The main effect of the lagged change in

Table 27.1   Change in American Direct Investment and Change in Canadian Gross National Product: Ordinary Least Squares Time Series Estimates for the Period 1947–1978

Variable	Estimated Coefficient	Standard Error	T
DIFF	4709.16	882.282	5.33748
GFCF	.992951	.253596	3.91549
USDI	1.31187	.441842	2.96909
L9USDI	−.118747	.207940	−.571065
IUSDI	−.560369	.615555	−.910347
IL9USDI	−1.87526	.899004	−2.08593

Sum of the squared residuals = .321235E+08.
Standard error of the regression = −1111.54.
Mean of the dependent variable = −3066.78.
Standard deviation = 1893.11.
Log of the likelihood function = −266.516.
Number of observations = 32.
Sum of the residuals = 3486.96.
Durbin-Watson statistic = 2.1452.

American direct investment (L9USDI) is small, negative and not significant for the entire post-war period. There is no evidence of a negative effect for the boom period (this run is not reported). The difference between the pre- and post-1960 series is significant at the .005 level. This difference . . . is equal to $4,709 million. Also significant at this level are the coefficients for the short-term (synchronous) effect of GFCF and USDI. As predicted by dependency theory, these effects are positive, and the immediate effect of change in American direct investment on change in Canadian economic growth is .42 larger than the GFCF coefficient. The main effect of the interaction term (IUSDI) is negative and not significant.

Although the Durbin-Watson statistic does not call for reestimation of the full equation, the variables are taken as first differences; therefore, the time-series procedure does not calculate in R^2. For this reason, the Cochrane-Orcutt iterative procedure (see Pindyck and Rubinfeld 1981, 157) has been performed on the equation as a check on the amount of variance explained. The R^2 and the R^2 adjusted both exceed .90. Various specifications of this full model have been estimated, eliminating the nonsignificant variables. What is most remarkable about the restricted equations is the stability of the coefficients and reported statistics across the different models. In the equation that includes only the difference between the periods, GFCF, USDI and IL9USDI, the estimated long-term negative effect for the post-1960 period is −1.92, compared to −1.88 in the full model. The other statistics are comparably close (results are not reported).

The argument could be made that the negative effect of change in USDI is simply a reflection of an underlying business cycle of the Juglar type (7–10 years). If this were the case, it is likely that a similarly lagged GFCF would show a negative effect on change in GNP. In the equation which estimates both main and interaction effects, the Durbin-Watson statistic indicates a problem of autocorrelation (D.W. = 1.54). The Cochrane-Orcutt estimation indicates that the period difference and the short-term effect of change in GFCF are both significant at the .005 level. The coefficient for GFCF is 1.77. These are the only significant effects in the equation. The other coefficients are estimated with enormous standard errors. The R^2 and adjusted R^2 are reduced to .83 and .81 respectively.

American direct investment in Canada is part of the composite measure of total American long-term investment. If the structural effect of mature dependency is related to the organization of the multinationals, we would expect to see a similar structure in total American long-term investment, to the extent that direct investment is proportionally dominant. The other two components of total long-term investment, portfolio and miscellaneous investments, should not exhibit the dependency effect on growth when they are disaggregated from the composite. Because American miscellaneous investment in Canada has accounted for only about 2.7 percent of total American long-term investment since 1926 (Government of Canada 1978), we will elaborate on the total of investment and on portfolio investment disaggregated.

Again, the analyses support our hypotheses about the nature of mature dependency. Comparing the lagged effects of American long-term and American direct investment, there is a similarity in the magnitudes and relative size of the coefficients, although the lagged effect is not significant. The portfolio estimates exhibit very little similarity to the direct investment estimates, and the short-term effect of portfolio investment is not significant. In fact, there is no significant effect for any of the portfolio variables when the American direct investment model is used to structure the equation. The evidence suggests that foreign direct investment is the only component of foreign long-term capital investments that has a long-term negative effect on the growth of the host economy. Granted, the empirical demonstration of a structural economic effect of dependency is a narrow delineation of the complexity of the alliance of social forces whose coincidence of interests causes the internalization of MNE investment. In fact, Portes (1976, 77) describes the internal impact of the multinationals as a remolding of the domestic social structure. Although our demonstration is limited to the transformation of the domestic economic structure, the specificities of our model are clearly defined by the contextual specificity of the larger social structure.

The importance of the findings is enhanced by their application to Canada, a dependent and yet non-peripheral economy. In this sense the findings and the historical evidence upon which they are based, suggest that dependency theory requires some modification. According to economic theories of the internal markets of MNES, it is possible for core countries to experience MNE-based dependency. The implications for the social structure of the dependent mature economy are not as devastating as they are in the periphery and the semi-periphery, but the structural effect on long-term economic growth is precisely the same.

DISCUSSION AND CONCLUSIONS

For the researcher interested in the demonstration of dependency effects in non-peripheral countries, model specification is the key directive in research design. Duvall (1978, 74) argues that the design of dependency research must incorporate the notion that context affects causal relations. "To effectuate this requirement, it is necessary to interpret verbal historicist arguments in terms of the important context-defining variables that are implied in the contextually-specific analysis" (Duvall 1978, 74). The context of mature dependency is provided by both history and theory. The historical legacy of the process of incorporation into the world economy has resulted in a hierarchical division of labor that requires both the measurement of variation between different structural positions and the measurement of variations within positions.

The restriction of current empirical studies of dependency to comparative non–time series designs has meant that events which are major sources of variation in independent variables have been largely ignored (Esteb 1977, 13). In the case of Canada's mature dependency, a time series design is required to capture the structural break that occurs in 1960. Moreover, the cross-national analysis of core countries as a block has obscured the structural distinctions that differentiate Canada from other developed countries.

Dependency theory suggests that extensive foreign capital penetration will have a long-term negative effect on the host's economic growth. The critical importance of theory in the design of dependency research is evident in variable selection, specification of the functional form of the relationship between variables, and the identification of the structure of lagged effects. Dependency theory has integrated organizational economics to explain how the dominance of multinational enterprises has changed the structure of the postwar world economy (see Evans 1979; dos Santos 1970; Cardoso and Faletto 1979). However, dependency theory has not seriously considered the implications of cross-penetration within the core for the structure of developed economies.

New theories addressing the organizational economics of multinational enterprises suggest that the structural effect associated with dependency need not be confined to the peripheral economies of the world system. The couching of dependency arguments in terms of peripheral modes of development does not accommodate "deviant" case analyses without some modification to the theory. Although Wallerstein himself waivers between essays, he classifies Canada, Australia and New Zealand as members of the semi-periphery in order to deal with the "doubtful" economic structures of these countries (see Wallerstein 1974; 1976). Evans (1979, 293) does the same. On this point, we must disagree with both theorists.

The theoretical definition of what constitutes the semi-periphery is admittedly imprecise; however, the term is used as a catch-all category for those countries which cannot simply be considered "peripheral" and yet are structurally distinguishable from center countries (Evans 1979, 291; Wallerstein 1976). Wallerstein (1974) suggests that the coherence of the category is derived from the fact that the semi-periphery is formed by the more advanced exemplars of dependent development. According to Evans's (1979) theory or dependent development, Canada does not fit the category.

The resolution of the issue of Canada's status requires both theoretical and methodological innovation. We suggest that a country can be both a member of the core and dependent. The situation has been described by the concept "mature dependency." The demonstration of a negative long-term effect of change in American direct investment on change in Canadian economic growth provides strong evidence for the existence of mature dependency as a variation in core development. We suggest that future empirical research be directed into case-by-case analyses of core country dependency. Portes (1976) suggests that Australia may be a good candidate for analysis. The Canadian case was a good place to start, particularly because of the significance of retained earnings in Canada, a characteristic which sets Canada apart from other American dependencies (see Hood and Young 1979, 39). In conclusion, we may have inadvertently bridged the rift between the dialectical method of analysis and empirical dependency research. As we have demonstrated in this paper, theoretically and historically informed time series analysis is the appropriate design for modeling the contextual specificity of variations in dependency.

NOTES

1. The Innisian tradition began with the work of Harold Innis in the 1930s. He explained Canadian development in terms of its domination by staple-export-led growth. The tradition is a reformulation or Marxism tailored to Canada's mode of capitalist accumulation. It negates the liberal argument Canada's development has been principally autonomous, introverted and autocentric (Drache 1983, 27).

2. "Firms in dependent countries buy their equipment and other capital goods from outside. so that the 'multiplier effect' of new investments is transferred back to the center" (Evans 1979, 28).

3. Because the masses are effectively barred from economic participation, "to allow them political participation would be disruptive. Social and cultural exclusion follow from political and economic exclusion" (Evans 1979, 29).

4. See Richards and Pratt (1979) on "advanced resource capitalism."

REFERENCES

Aitken, Hugh G.J. 1961. *American Capital and Canadian Resources.* Cambridge, MA: Harvard University Press.

Behrman, Jack N. 1970. *National Interests and the Multinational Enterprise: Tensions Among the North Atlantic Countries.* Englewood Cliffs, NJ: Prentice-Hall.

Bergesen, Albert. 1982. "The Emerging Science of the World-System." *International Social Science Journal* 34:23–25.

Blake, David H. and Robert S. Walters. 1983. *The Politics of Global Economic Relations.* Englewood Cliffs, NJ: Prentice-Hall.

Bornschier, Volker. 1980a. "Multinational Corporations, Economic Policy and National Development in the World System." *International Social Sciences Journal* 32:158–72.

Bornschier, Volker and Thanh-Huyen Ballmer-Cao. 1979. "Income Inequality: A Cross-national Study of the Relationship Between MNC-Penetration, Dimensions of the Power Structure and Income Distribution." *American Sociological Review* 44:487–506.

Britton, John H. and James A. Gilmour. 1978. *The Weakest Link—A Technological Perspective on Canadian Industrial Underdevelopment.* Ottawa. Science Council of Canada.

Caporaso, James A. and Behrouz Zare. 1981. "An Interpretation and Evaluation of Dependency Theory." 43–56 in *From Dependency to Development: Strategies to Overcome Underdevelopment and Inequality,* edited by Herald Manoz. Boulder, CO: Westview Press.

Cardoso, Fernando Henrique and Enzo Faletto. 1979. *Dependency and Development in Latin America.* Berkeley, CA: University of California Press.

dos Santos, Theotonio. 1970. "The Structure of Dependence." *American Economic Review* 60:231–36

Drache, Daniel. 1983. "The Crisis of Canadian Political Economy Dependency Theory Versus the New Orthodoxy." *Canadian Journal of Political and Social Theory* 7:25–49.

Duvall, Raymond. 1978. "Dependency and Dependencia Theory: Notes Towards Precision of Concept and Argument." *International Organization* 32:51–78.

Duvall, Raymond and John Freeman. 1981. "The State and Dependent Capitalism." *International Studies Quarterly* 25:99–118.

Esteb, Nancy. 1977. "Methods for World System Analysis: A Critical Appraisal." Paper presented at the 72nd annual meetings of the American Sociological Association in Chicago, September 5–9.

Evans, Peter. 1979. *Dependent Development: The Alliance of Multinational, State, and Local Capital in Brazil.* Princeton, NJ: Princeton University Press.

Field, F. W. 1914. *Capital Investments in Canada.* Montreal: The Monetary Times of Canada.

Firestone, O. John. 1958. *Canada's Economic Development, 1867–1953.* London: Bowes and Bowes.

Gherson, Joan. 1980. "U.S. Investment in Canada." *Foreign Investment Review* 3:11–14.

Gonick, Cyril Wolfe. 1970. "Foreign Ownership and Political Decay." 44–73 in *Close the 49th Parallel etc.: The Americanization of Canada,* edited by Ian Lumsden. Toronto: University of Toronto Press.

Government of Canada. Statistics Canada. 1983. *National Income and Expenditure Accounts 1965–1982.* Ottawa: Minister of Supply and Services (catalogue no. 13-201) GNP CANSIM MATRIX 000531. GNP CANSIM MATRIX 000528.

————. 1978. Canada's International Investment Position 1978. Ottawa: Minister of Supply and Services (catalogue no. 67-202).

————. 1981. Canada's International Investment Position 1978. Ottawa: Minister of Supply and Services (catalogue no. 67-202).

Grant, George. 1970. *Lament for a Nation*. Toronto: McClelland and Stewart.

Hammer, Heather-Jo. 1982. "Multinational Corporations and National Development: American Direct Investment in Canada." Paper presented at the 10th annual congress meetings of the International Sociological Association in Mexico City, August 16–21.

————. 1984a. Comment on "Dependency Theory and Taiwan: Analysis of a Deviant Case." *American Journal of Sociology* 89:932–36.

————. 1984b. "Mature Dependency: The Effects of American Direct Investment on Canadian Economic Growth." Unpublished Ph.D. dissertation. Department of Sociology, University of Alberta, Edmonton, Canada.

Hood, Neil and Stephen Young. 1979. *The Economics of Multinational Enterprise*. London: Longman Group Limited.

Ingram, James C. 1957. "Growth in Capacity in Canada's Balance of Payments." *American Economic Review* 47:93–104.

Innis, Harold. 1956. *Essays in Canadian Economic History*. Toronto: Toronto University Press.

Laxer, Gordon. 1984. "Foreign Ownership and Myths About Canadian Development." *Review of Canadian Sociology and Anthropology* 22:311–45.

Levitt, Kari. 1970. *Silent Surrender: The Multinational Corporation in Canada*. Toronto: Macmillan.

Lewis. Cleona. 1938. *America's Stake in International Investments*. Washington, DC: Brookings Institute.

Logan, Harold. 1937. "Labour Costs and Labour Standards." 63–97 in *Labour in Canadian-American Relations*, edited by H. Innis. Toronto: University of Toronto Press.

Maizels, Alfred. 1963. *Industrial Growth and World Trade*. London: Cambridge University Press.

Marshall, Herbert, Frank A. Southard Jr. and Kenneth W. Taylor. 1976. *Canadian-American Industry: A Study in International Investment*. New Haven: Yale University Press.

Pindyck, Robert S. and Daniel Rubinfeld. 1981. *Econometric Methods and Economic Forecasting*. New York: McGraw-Hill.

Pope, William H. 1971. *The Elephant and the Mouse*. Toronto: McClelland and Stewart.

Portes, Alejandro. 1976. "On the Sociology of National Development: Theories and Issues." *American Journal of Sociology* 82:55–85.

Richards, John and Larry Pratt. 1979. *Prairie Capitalism: Power and Influence in the New West*. Toronto: McClelland and Stewart.

Scheinberg, Stephen. 1973. "Invitation to Empire: Tariffs and American Economic Expansion in Canada." 80–100 in *Enterprise and National Development: Essays on Canadian Business and Economic History*, edited by Glenn Porter and Robert D. Cuff. Toronto: Hakkert.

Stoneman, Colin. 1975. "Foreign Capital and Economic Growth." *World Development* 3:11–26.

Wallerstein, Immanuel. 1974. "Dependence in an Interdependent World: The Limited Possibilities of Transformation Within the Capitalist World Economy." *African Studies Review* 17:1–26.

————. 1976. "Semi-Peripheral Countries and the Contemporary World Crisis." *Theory and Society* 3:461–83.

PART 6

· · · · · · · · · · · · · ·

The State, Growth, and Inequality

· · · · · · · · · · · · · ·

28

· · · · · · ·

Governments and
Agricultural Markets in Africa

· · · · · · ·

ROBERT H. BATES

*The focus of Part 6 of this book shifts from external causes of the gaps
to domestic causes. Flawed policies of governments in the Third
World are viewed as being largely responsible for slowed growth and
domestic inequality. The negative consequences of interference with
the market is a central theme in much of this research. In this chapter,
Robert Bates focuses on, among other things, the pernicious effect in
Africa of state-controlled "marketing boards" for export crops and
government monopsonies for the purchase of food crops. Given that
these programs are notorious failures, why do governments maintain
them? Bates describes farm and industrial policies and presents two
different explanations for why governments act as they do: They act
as agents of private interests and as agencies that seek to retain
power. In his analysis of government actions, the author attempts to
provide a theory of government that is so often lacking in economic
analysis.*

Governments in Africa intervene in agricultural markets in characteristic
ways: they tend to lower the prices offered for agricultural commodities, and
they tend to increase the prices that farmers must pay for the goods they buy
for consumption. And although African governments do subsidize the prices
farmers pay for the goods they use in farming, the benefits of these subsidies
are appropriated by the rich few: the small minority of large-scale farmers.

*DIFF
US?*

Other patterns, too, are characteristic of government market intervention. Insofar as African governments seek increased farm production, their policies are project-based rather than price-based. Insofar as they employ prices to strengthen production incentives, they tend to encourage production by lowering the prices of inputs (that is, by lowering costs) rather than by increasing the prices of products (that is, by increasing revenues). A last characteristic is that governments intervene in ways that promote economic inefficiency: they alter market prices, reduce market competition, and invest in poorly conceived agricultural projects. In all of these actions, it should be stressed, the conduct of African governments resembles the conduct of governments in other parts of the developing world.

One purpose of this paper is to describe more fully these patterns of government intervention. A second is to examine a variety of explanations for this behavior.

THE REGULATION OF COMMODITY MARKETS

It is useful to distinguish between two kinds of agricultural commodities: food crops, many of which can be directly consumed on the farm, and cash crops, few of which are directly consumable and which are instead marketed as a source of cash income. Many cash crops are in fact exported; they provide not only cash incomes for farm families but also foreign exchange for the national economies of Africa.

Export Crops

An important feature of the African economies is the nature of the marketing systems employed for the purchase and export of cash crops. The crops are grown by private farm families, but they are then sold through official, state-controlled marketing channels. At the local level, these channels may take the form of licensed agents or registered private buyers; they may also take the form of cooperative societies or farmers' associations. But the regulated nature of the marketing system is clearly revealed in the fact that these primary purchasing agencies can in most cases only sell to one purchaser: a state-owned body, commonly known as the marketing board. . . .

Government Taxation. Initially, the revenues accumulated by the marketing boards were to be used for the benefit of the farmers, in the form of price assistance funds. At times of low international prices, these funds were to be employed to support domestic prices and so to shelter the farmers from the vagaries of the world market. For example, 70 percent of the western Nigerian marketing board's revenues were to be retained for such purposes. But commitments to employ the funds for the benefit of the farmers proved short-lived. They were overborne by ambitions to implement development programs and by political pressures on governments from nonagricultural sectors of the economy. . . .

Food Crops

African governments also intervene in the market for food crops. And, once again, they tend to do so in ways that lower the prices of agricultural commodities.

One way African governments attempt to secure food cheaply is by constructing bureaucracies to purchase food crops at government-mandated prices. A recent study by the United States Department of Agriculture examined the marketing systems for food crops in Africa and discovered a high incidence of government market intervention. In the case of three of the food crops studied, in over 50 percent of the countries in which the crop was grown the government had imposed a system of producer price controls, and in over 20 percent the government maintained an official monopsony for the purchase of that food crop; in these instances, the government was by law the sole buyer of the crop.

Regulation of food markets entails policing the purchase and movement of food stocks and controlling the storage, processing, and retail marketing of food. An illustration is offered by the maize industry of Kenya; according to subsection 1 of section 15 of the Maize Marketing Act, "All maize grown in Kenya shall, subject to the provision of this Act, be purchased by and sold to the Board, and shall, without prejudice to the Board's liability for the price payable in accordance with section 18 of this Act, rest in the Board as soon as it has been harvested. . . ."

More directly relevant to the concerns of this chapter, however, is the impact of food marketing controls on food prices. For insight into this subject we can turn to Doris Jansen Dodge's study of NAMBoard, the food marketing bureaucracy in Zambia. Over the years studied by Dodge (1966–1967 to 1974–1975) NAMBoard depressed the price of maize by as much as 85 percent; that is, in the absence of government controls over maize movements, the farmers could have gotten up to 85 percent higher prices for their maize than they were able to secure under the market controls imposed by NAMBoard. Gerrard extends Dodge's finding for Zambia to Kenya, Tanzania, and Malawi; Dodge herself extends them to eight other African countries.[1] The result is a weakening of incentives to produce food.

Projects. In order to keep food prices low, governments take additional measures. In particular, they attempt to increase food supplies. This can be done either by importing food or by investing in food production projects. Foreign exchange, however, is scarce; especially since the rise of petroleum prices, the cost of imports is high. So as to conserve foreign exchange, then, African governments attempt to become self-sufficient in food. To keep prices low, they invest in projects that will yield increased food production.

In some cases, governments turn public institutions into food production units: youth-league farms and prison farms provide illustrative cases. In other instances, they attempt to provide factors of production. In Africa, water is commonly scarce and governments invest heavily in river-basin development schemes and irrigation projects. Capital equipment is also scarce; by purchasing and operating farm machinery, governments attempt to promote farm production. Some governments invest in projects to provide particular crops: rice in Kenya, for example, or wheat in Tanzania. In other instances, governments divert large portions of their capital budgets to the financing of food production schemes. Western Nigeria, for example, spent over 50 percent of the Ministry of Agriculture's capital budget on state farms over the period of the 1962–1968 development program.[2]

Nonbureaucratic Forms of Intervention

Thus far I have emphasized direct forms of government intervention. But there is an equally important, less direct form of intervention: the overvaluation of the domestic currency.

Most governments in Africa maintain an overvalued currency.[3] Foreign money therefore exchanges for fewer units of local currency. A result is to lower the prices received by the exporters of cash crops. For a given sum earned abroad, the exporters of cash crops receive fewer units of the domestic currency. In part, overvaluation inflicts losses on governments; deriving a portion of their revenues from taxes levied by the marketing boards, the governments command less domestic purchasing power as a result of overvaluation. But because their instruments of taxation are monopolistic agencies, African governments are able to transfer much of the burden of overvaluation: they pass it on to farmers, in the form of lower prices.

In addition to lowering the earnings of export agriculture, overvaluation lowers the prices paid for foreign imports. This is, of course, part of the rationale for a policy of overvaluation: it cheapens the costs of importing plant, machinery, and other capital equipment needed to build an industrial sector. But items other than plant and equipment can be imported, and among these other commodities is food. As a consequence of overvaluation, African food producers face higher levels of competition from foreign foodstuffs. And in search of low-price food, African governments do little to protect their domestic food markets from foreign products—products whose prices have artificially been lowered as a consequence of public policies.

Industrial Goods

In the markets for the crops they produce, African farmers face a variety of government policies that serve to lower farm prices. In the markets for the goods that they consume, however, they face a highly contrasting situation: they confront prices for consumers that are supported by government policy.

In promoting industrial development, African governments adopt commercial policies that shelter local industries from foreign competition. To some degree they impose tariff barriers between the local and the international markets. To an even greater extent, they employ quantitative restrictions. Quotas, import licenses, and permits to acquire and use foreign exchange are all employed to conserve foreign exchange, on the one hand, while, on the other, protecting the domestic market for local industries. In connection with the maintenance of overvalued currencies, these trade barriers create incentives for investors to import capital equipment and to manufacture domestically goods that formerly had been imported from abroad.[4]

Not only do government policies shelter industries from low cost foreign competition, they shelter them from domestic competition as well. In part, protection from domestic competition is a by-product of protection from foreign competition. The policy of allocating licenses to import in conformity with historic market shares provides an example of such a measure. The limitation of competition results from other policies as well. In exchange for commitments to invest, governments guarantee periods of freedom from competition. Moreover, governments tend to favor larger projects; seeking infusions of scarce capital, they tend to back the proposals that promise the largest capital investments. With the small markets typical of most African nations, the result is that investors create plants whose output represents a very large fraction of the domestic market; a small number of firms thus come to dominate the market. Finally, particularly where state enterprises are concerned, governments sometimes confer virtual monopoly rights upon particular enterprises. The consequence of all these measures is to shelter industries from domestic competition.

One result is that inefficient firms survive. Estimates of the use of industrial capacity range as low as one-fifth of the single-shift capacity of installed plant.[5] Another consequence is that prices rise. Protected from foreign competition and operating in noncompetitive market settings, firms are able to charge prices that enable them to survive despite operating at very high levels of cost.

Farm Inputs

By depressing the prices offered farmers for the goods they sell, government policies lower the revenues of farmers. By raising the prices that consumers—including farmers—must pay, governments reduce the real value of farm revenues still further. As a consequence of these interventions by governments, then, African farmers are taxed. Oddly enough, while taxing farmers in the market for products, governments subsidize them in the market for farm outputs.

Attempts to lower input prices take various forms. Governments provide subsidies for seeds and fertilizers, the level of the latter running from 30 percent, in Kenya, to 80 percent, in Nigeria. They provide tractor-hire services at subsidized rates—up to 50 percent of the real costs in Ghana in the mid-1970s.[6] They provide loans at subsidized rates of interest for the purchase and rental of inputs. And they provide highly favorable tax treatment for major investors in commercial farming ventures.[7] Moreover, through their power over property rights African governments have released land and water to commercial farmers at costs that lie below the value they would generate in alternative uses. The diversion of land to large-scale farmers and of water to private tenants on government irrigation schemes, without paying compensation to those who had employed these resources in subsistence farming, pastoral production, fishing or other ventures, represents the conferring of a subsidy on the commercial farmer—and one that is paid at the expense of the small-scale, traditional producer. . . .

In the case of land and water use, then, a major effect of government intervention in the market for inputs is to augment the fortunes of large-scale farmers at the expense of small-scale farmers. . . . Because the large farmers have the same social background as those who staff the public services, the public servants feel they can work most congenially and productively with these people.[8] Moreover, to favor the large farmer is politically productive. I will elaborate this argument below.

DISCUSSION

Governments intervene in the market for products in an effort to lower prices. They adopt policies which tend to raise the price of the goods farmers buy. And while they attempt to lower the costs of farm inputs, the benefits of this policy are reaped only by a small minority of the richer farmers. Agricultural policies in Africa thus tend to be adverse to the interests of most producers.

Studies in other areas suggest that this configuration of pricing decisions is common in the developing nations.[9] Indeed, it is argued by some that the principal problems bedeviling agriculture in the developing areas originate from bad public policies. . . . In the remaining sections, I will advance several explanations for their choices. . . .

GOVERNMENTS AS AGENTS OF PRIVATE INTERESTS

Put bluntly, food policy in Africa appears to represent a form of political settlement, one designed to bring about peaceful relations between African governments and their urban constituents. And it is a settlement in which the costs tend to be borne by the mass of the unorganized: the small-scale farmers. . . .

Urban consumers in Africa constitute a vigilant and potent pressure group demanding low-priced food. Because they are poor, much of their income goes for food; some studies suggest that urban consumers in Africa spend between 50 and 60 percent of their incomes on food.[10] Since changes in the price of food have a major impact on the economic well-being of urban dwellers in Africa, they pay close attention to the issue of food prices.

Urban consumers are potent because they are geographically concentrated and strategically located. Because of their geographic concentration, they can be organized quickly; and because they control transport, communications, and other public services, they can impose deprivations on others. They are therefore influential. Urban unrest frequently heralds a change of government in Africa, and the cost and availability of food supplies are major factors promoting urban unrest.

It should be noted that it is not only the workers who care about food prices. It is also the employers. Employers care about food prices because food is a wage good; with higher food prices, wages rise and, all else being equal, profits fall. Governments care about food prices not only because they are employers in their own right but also because as owners of industries and promoters of industrial development programs they seek to protect industrial profits. Indicative of the significance of these interests is that the unit that sets agricultural prices often resides not in the Ministry of Agriculture but in the Ministry of Commerce or of Finance.

When urban unrest begins among food consumers, the political discontent often spreads rapidly to upper echelons of the polity: to those whose incomes come from profits, not wages, and to those in charge of major bureaucracies. Political regimes that are unable to supply low-cost food are seen as dangerously incompetent and as failing to protect the interests of key elements of the social order. At times of high prices, influential elites are likely to ally with the urban masses, to shift their political loyalties and replace those in power. Thus it was that protests over food shortages and rising prices formed a critical prelude to the coups and coup attempts in Ghana, Liberia, Kenya, and Guinea.

It is ironic but true that among those governments most committed to low-cost food are the "radical" governments in Africa. Despite their stress on economic equality, they impose lower prices on the commodity from which the poorest of the poor, the peasant farmers, derive their income. A major reason for their behavior is that they are deeply committed to rapid industrialization; moreover, they are deeply committed to higher real wages for urban workers and have deep institutional ties to organized labor.

We can thus understand the demand for low-cost food. Its origins lie in

IMPT FOOD

the urban areas. It is supported by governments, both out of political necessity and, on the part of more radical ones, out of ideological preference. Food is a major staple and higher prices for such staples threaten the real value of wages *and* profits. . . .

There are thus fundamental political reasons for governments to seek to lower the prices of food. There are also real limitations on their ability to do so. One limitation is political: insofar as farmers themselves are powerful, they are likely to resist the efforts of governments to lower agricultural prices. Only occasionally, however, are farmers powerful. In West Africa, urban/bureaucratic elites have entered rice farming; and where they have done so, they have won protected commodity prices and subsidized prices for farm inputs.[11] In East Africa, similar elites maintain large-scale wheat farms; they too have employed their political influence to avoid adverse pricing policies. But most farms are owned by members of the peasantry, not the elite; they are small-scale, not large-scale; and the farmers are politically weak, not strong. Rarely, then, are farmers powerful; and most often they are taxed.

Political power on the part of farmers thus occasionally influences the pricing decisions of governments. A more common influence is the limitation of governmental resources. When lower price levels are imposed on farmers, consumers may face shortages; indeed, food production tends to be highly price-elastic. A necessary corollary to low-food-price policies in Africa is thus the use of public resources to produce or to import food. But most African governments are poor and have little foreign exchange. Governments therefore lack the resources with which to make up the shortfalls resulting from their pricing policies, and this places a major limitation on the degree to which they can lower agricultural prices. . . .

Pressure groups form only one component of a pluralist model of politics.[12] A second is competitive elections. Clearly, were competitive elections contested by rival parties in Africa, agricultural policy could not be so strongly biased against rural dwellers. With less than 10 percent of their population in cities, most nations would contain electoral majorities composed of farm families; and electoral incentives would almost inevitably lead politicians to advocate pro-agrarian platforms in their efforts to secure votes and to win power.

Evidence of the significance of electoral incentives is to be found in Zambia. From 1964 to 1972, the government of Zambia devoted on average over 70 percent of its capital budget to expenditures in the urban areas. In the years prior to national elections, however, the government reallocated its capital program: over 40 percent of the capital budget was then spent in the rural districts. Moreover, it was in the years prior to elections that major rural development programs were announced: the creation of zones of intensive rural development, new credit programs, mechanization schemes, the decentralization of rural administration. The commitment to rural development was thus tied to the electoral cycle. Having periodically to face a rural constituency, the government periodically recommitted itself to the enhancement of their fortunes.[13]

There is thus a tension between the two components of the pluralist model. In the African context, the impact of organized interest groups works to the detriment of agrarian interests, whereas competitive elections work to their advantage. In recent years the frequency of the return to democratic forms of government among the African states has been more than matched by the frequency of the demise of competitive party systems. Electoral incentives have little opportunity to counter the biases produced by interest-group politics.

GOVERNMENTS AS AGENCIES
THAT SEEK TO RETAIN POWER

The interest-group model thus accounts for major elements of the food policies maintained by African governments. It explains the political pressures for low food prices and thus helps to explain why, when governments want more food, they prefer to secure it by building more projects rather than offering higher prices. By the same token, it helps to account for the governments' preference for production subsidies rather than higher food prices as incentives for food production.

Nonetheless, an interest-group explanation too is incomplete. Its primary virtue is that it helps to account for the essentially draconian pricing policies adopted by African governments. Its primary limitation is that it fails to explain how governments get away with such policies. How, in nations where the majority of the population are farmers and the majority of the resources are held in agriculture, are governments able to succeed in implementing policies that violate the interests of most farmers? In search of answers to this question, a third approach is needed, one that looks at agricultural programs as part of a repertoire of devices employed by African governments in their efforts to secure political control over their rural populations and thus to remain in power.

Organizing a Rural Constituency

We have already seen that adopting policies in support of higher prices for agricultural commodities would be politically costly to African governments. It is also important to note that such a stance would generate few political benefits. From a political point of view, conferring higher prices offers few attractions for politicians, for the benefits of the measure could be enjoyed by rural opponents and supporters alike. The benefits could not be restricted to the faithful or withheld from the politically disloyal. Pricing policies therefore cannot be employed by politicians to organize political followings.

Project-based policies suffer less from this liability. Officials can exercise discretion in locating projects; they can also exercise discretion in staffing them. Such discretion allows them to bestow benefits selectively on those whose political support they desire. Politicians are therefore more likely to be attracted to project-based policies as a measure of rural development.

The relative political utility of projects explains several otherwise puzzling features of government agricultural investments. One is the tendency to construct too many projects, given the budgetary resources available. A reason for this proliferation is that governments often wish to ensure that officials in each administrative district or electoral constituency have access to resources with which to secure a political backing.[14] Another tendency is to hire too large a staff or a staff that is technically untrained, thus undercutting the viability of the projects. A reason for this is that jobs on projects—and jobs in many of the bureaucracies involved with agricultural programs, for that matter—represent political plums, given by those in charge of the programs to their political followers. State farms in Ghana were staffed by the youth brigade of the ruling Convention People's Party, and the cooperative societies in Zambia were formed and operated by the local and constituency level units of the governing party, to offer just two examples of the link between staffing and political organization. . . .

Disorganizing the Rural Opposition

We have seen that government policies are often aimed at establishing low prices for agricultural products. Particularly in the market for cash crops, governments maintain monopsonistic agencies and use their market power to lower product prices. They therefore impose deprivations on all producers. What is interesting, however, is that they return to selected members of the farm community a portion of the resources which they thus exact. Some of the earnings taxed from farmers are returned to a privileged few, in the form of subsidies for farm inputs. While imposing collective deprivations, governments thus confer selective benefits.

These benefits serve as side-payments: they compensate selected members of the rural sector for the losses they sustain as a consequence of the government's programs. They thereby make it in the private interests of particular members of the rural sector to abide by policies that are harmful to rural dwellers as a whole. By so doing, they secure the defection of favored farmers from a potential rural opposition and their adherence to the governing coalition, which implements agricultural programs that are harmful to farming as a whole. . . .

It should be noted, incidentally, that the bestowal of privileged access to farm inputs was a technique employed by the colonial governments as well. And the exchange of political loyalty for access to these inputs was widely recognized to be part of the bargain. In Northern and Southern Rhodesia, for example, the colonial governments used revenues secured by their monopsonistic maize marketing agency to subsidize the costs of inputs, which they then lavished upon a relatively small number of so-called improved or progressive farmers. The nationalist movements presciently labeled these farmers stooges of the colonial regimes. They saw that the apportionment of the inputs had been employed to separate the interests of these privileged farmers from the interests of the mass of rural producers and to detach their political loyalties from those of their fellow Africans.

By conferring selective benefits in the markets for farm inputs while imposing collective deprivations in the markets for products, governments secure the deference of a privileged few to programs that are harmful to the interests of most farmers. By politicizing farm-input programs and making access to their benefits contingent upon political loyalty, the governments secure acquiescence to those in power and compliance with their policies. The political efficacy of these measures is underscored by the fact that they are targeted to the large producers, who have the most to gain from a change in pricing policy and who might otherwise provide the leadership for efforts on the part of farmers to alter the agricultural policies of their governments. . . .

CONCLUSION

Governments in Africa, like governments elsewhere in the developing world, intervene in agricultural markets in ways that violate the interests of most farmers. They tend to adopt low-price policies for farm products; they tend to increase the prices farmers must pay for the goods they consume. And while they subsidize the prices of goods that farmers use in production, the benefits of these subsidies are appropriated by the richer few. In addition, the farm policies of African governments are characterized by a stress on projects rather than prices; when price policies are used, by a preference for lowering farm costs rather than increasing farm revenues; and by widespread economic inefficiency.

I have examined several political explanations for this configuration of agricultural policies. I conclude by commenting on their durability.

The pattern of price interventions, I have argued, represents the terms of a political pact among organized political interests, the costs of which are transferred to unorganized interests who are excluded from the price-setting coalition. Members of the pact are labor, industry, and government; small-scale farmers constitute its victims; and large-scale farmers stand as passive allies, politically neutralized through subsidy programs.

No member of the winning coalition possesses an incentive to alter its political demands unilaterally. Organized labor, for example, will not unilaterally alter its demand for cheap food. Nor will industry call for reforms that raise food prices, and thus wages, unless other members of the coalition make credible commitments to offsetting concessions. In the short term, then, the coalition and the price structure that supports it appear stable.

Over the longer run, however, the structure of the payoffs achieved by the coalition changes. Farmers adjust; in response to pricing policies, they produce less. The result in food markets is lower supplies at higher prices. The result in export markets is fewer exports and less foreign exchange. The costs which once were externalized upon the unorganized agrarian sector are now internalized, through the operation of markets, onto the dominant coalition. The farmers have transferred the costs of the political settlement to the intended beneficiaries. And as these costs mount, the pact among them becomes less stable.

As the payoffs from this basis for governance in Africa erode, opportunities arise for the introduction of new pricing policies. And as the costs of the present policies are disproportionately borne by one of the more influential of the coalition partners, the governments themselves, the likelihood of policy changes is enhanced. To support low food prices, governments must provide additional supplies, either by subsidizing local production or by financing imports from abroad. But, throughout Africa, states are undergoing a fiscal crisis; they lack both revenues and foreign exchange. One consequence is that governments are less willing or able to bear the costs of current agricultural policies. Another is the reallocation of political power. At moments of fiscal crisis, finance ministers and directors of the central banks gain greater influence over public policy. Moreover, they find allies among foreign donors and international creditors, who pressure governments to make adjustments that will lessen their burden of debt. In league with international agencies, these figures have assumed greater influence over public policy.

The set of public policies described in this paper have thus formed the basis for a political pact among organized interests. But they have set in motion economic forces which erode their economic and political value. Moreover, the fiscal crisis in contemporary Africa has restructured power relations within African governments and has brought new players into the policymaking process. The result is that the commitment to these policies may not be stable and they may in fact be subject to change.

NOTES

1. See Doris J. Jansen, "Agricultural Pricing Policy in Sub-Saharan Africa of the 1970s," unpublished paper, 1980 (mimeo.); Christopher David Gerrard,

"Economic Development, Government Controlled Markets, and External Trade in Food Grains: The Case of Four Countries in East Africa," Ph.D. dissertation, University of Minnesota, 1981; and Doris Jansen Dodge, *Agricultural Policy and Performance in Zambia* (Berkeley: Institute of International Studies, 1977).

2. Frances Hill, "Experiments with a Public Sector Peasantry," *African Studies Review* 20 (1977):25–41; and Werner Roider, *Farm Settlements for Socio-Economic Development: The Western Nigerian Case* (Munich: Weltforum, 1971).

3. International Bank for Reconstruction and Development, *Accelerated Development in Sub-Saharan Africa: An Agenda for Action* (Washington, D.C.: IBRD, 1981); and Franz Pick, *Pick's Currency Yearbook, 1976–1977* (New York: Pick Publishing, 1978).

4. J. Dirck Stryker, "Ghana Agriculture," paper for the West African Regional Project, 1975 (mimeo.); Scott R. Pearson, Gerald C. Nelson, and J. Dirck Stryker, "Incentives and Comparative Advantage in Ghanaian Industry and Agriculture," paper for the West African Regional Project, 1976 (mimeo.); International Bank for Reconstruction and Development, *Kenya: Into the Second Decade* (Washington, D.C.: IBRD, 1975); and International Bank for Reconstruction and Development, *Ivory Coast: The Challenge of Success* (Washington, D.C.: IBRD, 1978).

5. Ghana, *Report of the Commission of Enquiry into the Local Purchasing of Cocoa* (Accra: Government Printer, 1967); and Tony Killick, *Development Economics in Action: A Study of Economic Policies in Ghana* (New York: St. Martin's Press, 1978), p. 171.

6. Stryker, "Ghana Agriculture"; G. K. Kline, D. A. G. Green, Roy L. Donahue, and B. A. Stout, *Industrialization in an Open Economy: Nigeria 1945–1966* (Cambridge, England: Cambridge University Press).

7. See, for example, David Onaburekhale Ekhomu, "National Food Policies and Bureaucracies in Nigeria: Legitimization, Implementation, and Evaluation," paper presented at the African Studies Association Convention, Baltimore, Maryland, 1978 (mimeo.).

8. See David M. Leonard, *Reaching the Peasant Farmer: Organization Theory and Practice in Kenya* (Chicago: University of Chicago Press, 1977); and H. U. E. Van Velzen, "Staff, Kulaks and Peasants" in Lionel Cliffe and John Saul, eds., *Socialism in Africa,* vol. 2 (Dar es Salaam: East African Publishing House, 1973).

9. Raj Krishna, "Agricultural Price Policy and Economic Development" in M. Southworth and Bruce F. Johnston, eds., *Agricultural Development and Economic Growth* (Ithaca: Cornell University Press); U.S. General Accounting Office, *Disincentives to Agricultural Production in Developing Countries* (Washington, D.C.: Government Printer, 1975); Carl Gotsch and Gilbert Brow, "Prices, Taxes and Subsidies in Pakistan Agriculture, 1960–1976," World Bank Staff Working Paper no. 387 (Washington, D.C.: World Bank, 1980); Keith Griffin, *The Green Revolution: An Economic Analysis* (Geneva: United Nations Research Institute, 1972); Michael Lipton, *Why Poor People Stay Poor: Urban Bias in World Development* (Cambridge, Mass.: Harvard University Press, 1977).

10. Hiromitsu Kaneda and Bruce F. Johnston, "Urban Food Expenditure Patterns in Tropical Africa," *Food Research Institute Studies* 2 (1961):229–75.

11. Scott R. Pearson, J. Dirck Stryker, and Charles P. Humphreys, *Rice in West Africa* (Stanford: Stanford University Press, 1981).

12. A more systematic analysis of pressure-group politics, based on more rigorous microeconomic foundations, is contained in Robert H. Bates and William P. Rogerson, "Agriculture in Development: A Coalition Analysis," *Public Choice* 35

(1980): 513–27; and Bates, *Markets and States*. The first deals primarily with the demand for price intervention; the second, with the supply. Both attempt to explain the relative inefficacy of farmers in pressure-group politics in the developing areas. A major source of relevant theorizing for this portion of the analysis is the capture-theory approach to industrial regulation. See George Stigler, "The Theory of Economic Regulation," *Bell Journal of Economics and Management Science* 3 (1971):3–21; Sam Peltzman, "Toward a More General Theory of Regulation," *Journal of Law and Economics* 19 (1976):211–40.

13. See Robert H. Bates, *Rural Responses to Industrialization: A Study of Village Zambia* (New Haven: Yale University Press, 1978).

14. See Bates, *Rural Responses;* Jerome C. Wells, *Agricultural Policy and Economic Growth in Nigeria, 1962–1968* (Ibadan: Oxford University Press for the Nigerian Institute of Social Science and Economic Research, 1974); Alfred John Dadson, "Socialized Agriculture in Ghana, 1962–1965," Ph.D. dissertation, Harvard University, 1970.

29

. . . .

Why People
Stay Poor Elsewhere

. . . .

ERICH WEEDE

GAMBA, TED

Erich Weede is one of the leading scholars in the field of conducting empirical tests of dependency and world-system theory. In this chapter, drawn from his book on the subject, Weede reviews the arguments against dependency theory while suggesting that rent seeking, another explanation of Third World poverty, is more persuasive. He agrees with dependency theorists that the rich create the conditions in which poverty thrives, but he believes the blame for that situation should be placed on the rich within the Third World rather than on the rich countries. He concludes this chapter by offering some policy suggestions.

1. IS DEPENDENCY THE ANSWER?

For a long time dependency theorists have suggested that the persistence of Third World poverty is not accidental, that somebody makes or keeps poor people poor, and that Northern affluence and Southern poverty are just two sides of a single coin. While dependency theorists disagree among themselves on exactly which mechanisms maintain Third World poverty, they tend to shift responsibility for poverty from the poor to the privileged. Since the general idea that the privileged make or keep poor people poor is so plausible, criticism of dependency theories—all of which (like dependency theory) comes from more or less privileged persons—sounds implausible, self-serving, and even immoral. That is why I cannot imagine that dependency theories will lose their grip on the minds of people because of anomalies, falsification, or destructive criticism. Pointing to

Reprinted with permission from *Economic Development, Social Order, and World Politics,* Chapter 5 (Boulder: Lynne Rienner Publishers, 1996); with notes deleted.

evidence that is incompatible with dependency theories is important because it forces dependency theorists to withdraw on this or on that intellectual front, but it does not suffice to overcome the paradigm. Only a competing paradigm can do so. The theory of the rent-seeking society offers such a competing paradigm, which will be discussed in detail in Sections 2 and 3 of this chapter.

Adherents of rent-seeking and dependency theories do agree on the general notion that the privileged make or keep poor people poor. Therefore, the rent-seeking approach looks as plausible as the dependency paradigm. Of course, dependency theories and the rent-seeking approach do differ in many important respects. At best, dependency theorists demonstrate "benign neglect" for microeconomic theory and the rational choice approach—despite the fact that economists find it easier to agree on microeconomic theory than on macroeconomic theory (see Bell and Kristol, 1981) and despite the widespread feeling that economics is the "queen of the social sciences." By contrast, the rent-seeking approach is not only compatible with microeconomic theory but should be conceived of as a broadening and deepening of the theory.

The issues to be discussed are what dependency and rent-seeking theories do assert, what evidence is available for a preliminary evaluation of these theories, what the policy implications of these theories are, and why I believe rent-seeking theory to be superior to dependency theories. Wherever possible, I shall give special attention to cross-national analyses of economic growth rates or income distribution. Given the scope and urgency of the global poverty problem, there is little hope of reducing it without more economic growth in poor countries (Ahluwalia, Carter, and Chenery, 1979) or without equalizing the distribution of income in many or most of them. Since I compare an older and—albeit only outside the discipline of economics!—more established paradigm, dependency, with a younger or even still nascent one, rent-seeking, the reader should not be surprised that there is more quantitative and cross-national evidence on dependency theories than on rent-seeking and that dependency theories tend to suffer from anomalies whereas the rent-seeking approach tends to suffer from a dearth of quantitative evidence. Such a state of affairs is typical when a new paradigm aspires to replace an older one (see Kuhn, 1962).

Dependency theorists agree with one another that poor people stay poor because privileged people contribute to and maintain their poverty and because privileged nations somehow benefit from the international economic order at the expense of poor nations. But they disagree with each other on exactly how worldwide inequity is created and maintained. I shall restrict myself to a discussion of those three dependency theories that so far have received the most scrutiny in quantitative and cross-national research on economic growth and income inequality: Galtung's (1971) "structural theory of imperialism"; Wallerstein's (1974; 1979; 1980) world-system approach, which has been translated into quantitative research designs by an adherent of the theory (Rubinson, 1976; 1977); and Bornschier's (1980a; 1980b; Bornschier and Ballmer-Cao, 1979; Bornschier and Chase-Dunn, 1985) view that investment dependence and penetration of LDCs by multinational corporations contribute to stagnation and inequality.

According to Galtung (1971), developing countries suffer from vertical trade and feudal interaction patterns. Vertical trade refers to the fact that most rich, industrialized, and powerful countries tend to import raw materials but to export processed goods, while LDCs demonstrate the reverse pattern. In Galtung's (1971) view, the production of raw materials in LDCs creates few positive spin-offs; sometimes the eventual exhaustion of mineral deposits will leave nothing behind but a hole in the ground. But production of sophisticated processed goods in industrial societies necessarily contributes to human capital formation. Workers and managers learn new skills that tend to remain useful even when production is shifted from one good to another. In essence, the worldwide division of labor that concentrates manufacturing and processing, and in particular sophisticated processing, in some nations and extraction and agricultural raw material production in others is the root cause of more privileged circumstances of life in wealthy industrial societies and of deprivation in LDCs. The need for a broad human-capital base in sophisticated industrial economies exerts some equalizing pressure in these countries. Since raw-material extraction or production favors landed property owners, the global division of labor permits a highly unequal distribution of income in LDCs.

Galtung's (1971) mechanism of vertical trade is supplemented by feudal interaction patterns. By and large, the export earnings of many LDCs derive from a very small number of products; sometimes a single product accounts for most export earnings. Moreover, commodity concentration is often accompanied by partner concentration. For example, some Central American "banana republics" not only depend on the export of bananas but also suffer from exporting most of them to the U.S. market, where those countries also buy most of their imports. Comparable degrees of dependency characterize the relationship between France and some former French colonies in Africa. Even where the pattern is less obvious, commodity concentration and partner concentration create opportunities for privileged nations to keep poor nations poor.

This crude sketch of Galtung's theory suffices to raise a number of questions. Countries like Australia or Canada and, most importantly, the United States do not really fit the theory. Australia, Canada, and even the United States do too well by exporting raw materials or agrarian products, as do some sparsely populated Organization of Petroleum Exporting Countries (OPEC) nations, which even enjoy (close to) tax-free welfare states. Moreover, the theory looks somewhat dated and ever less appealing the more the pattern of North-South trade shifts from the exchange of industrial goods for raw materials or agricultural goods toward trade in industrial goods produced by more or less skilled workers. While manufactures amounted to merely 5 percent of all Southern exports to the North in 1955 and only 15.2 percent in 1980, they had jumped to 53.5 percent by 1989 (Wood, 1994, 2). But I do not want to evaluate Galtung's "structural theory of imperialism" by pointing to a couple of anomalies and its declining relevance over time. After all, "all theories are born refuted" (Lakatos, 1968–1969, 163; see also Kuhn, 1962). More important than the existence of anomalies is whether the independent variables of this theory, which Galtung already operationalized, do or do not contribute to the explanation of cross-national patterns of economic growth or income inequality. Do the import of (sophisticated) processed goods and the export of raw materials reduce the growth prospects of LDCs and simultaneously contribute to income inequality? Do export commodity concentration and partner concentration in trade decrease economic growth rates but increase income inequality?

Before I attempt to summarize the empirical evidence on Galtung's theory, I want to continue my sketch of various lines of reasoning within the dependency paradigm. According to Wallerstein (1974, 406), "the functioning of a capitalist world economy requires that groups pursue their economic interests within a single world-market while seeking to distort this market for their benefit by organizing to exert influence on states, some of which are more powerful than others but none of which controls the market in its entirety." In this view, some groups and nations succeed in distorting markets and rigging prices to their own benefit and at the expense of other groups and nations.

In his effort to translate this general idea into quantitative research designs, Rubinson (1977, 7) argued that a strong state "is able to control the activities of the population within its boundaries . . . one indicator of state strength is the government revenues of a state as a proportion of GNP. . . . This indicator measures the degree to which the total economic resources of the country are available to the state." In addition to a domestic dimension of state strength, there is an international dimension. While Rubinson (1976; 1977) discusses and applies a variety of indicators, some of the most potent ones are trade, i.e., import and/or export, and shares of gross national product (GNP). To summarize the Wallerstein-Rubinson perspective: States are most likely and able to promote economic growth and income equalization if they exercise much control of economic activities within their borders, as indicated by the proportion of government revenue to gross domestic product (GDP) or GNP, and if they depend little on the vicissitudes of the world market, as indicated by low trade to GNP shares.

Finally, there is a third perspective. According to Bornschier (1980a; 1980b; Bornschier and Ballmer-Cao, 1979; Bornschier and Chase-Dunn, 1985), multinational corporations (MNCs) are the main culprits in Third

World poverty. LDCs depend heavily on foreign investment, most of which is supplied by MNCs. In the short run, the inflow of MNC capital contributes to investment and growth. In the long run, however, MNCs succeed in getting more out of LDCs than they put in, i.e., in decapitalizing Third World economies. Rigging the terms of trade in *intra*-MNC, but simultaneously *inter*national, trade is one of the mechanisms whereby such decapitalization can be achieved. Moreover, given the strength of MNCs vis-à-vis LDCs, such corporations contribute to early market concentration and often enjoy monopoly power and monopoly profits. The more powerful MNCs are in a less developed economy, the worse that economy's growth prospects become. But MNCs do even more harm in LDCs. Since MNCs apply capital-intensive production technologies that do not need much local and unskilled labor input and since they tend to produce only for the more privileged classes in LDCs and ally themselves politically with those classes, MNC penetration reinforces income inequality as well.

This crude sketch of three dependency explanations of why poor people stay poor has yielded a list of six independent variables: vertical trade (or export of raw materials and import of processed goods), export commodity concentration, trade partner concentration, low government revenues as a proportion of GDP, high trade-to-GNP proportions, and strong MNC penetration. According to these dependency theories, all six variables should simultaneously reduce growth rates and increase inequality and thereby hurt the poor. Do they?

Adherents and opponents of dependency theories have done a lot of cross-national and cross-sectional work. So there is some evidence that LDCs that are extraordinarily dependent on exporting raw materials and importing processed goods or that suffer from severe export commodity concentration and trade partner concentration do indeed demonstrate greater income inequality and/or grow more slowly than other nations (Alschuler, 1976; Galtung, 1971; Rubinson, 1977; Stokes and Jaffee, 1982; Walleri, 1978a; 1978b). But there are also studies that cast a much less favorable light on Galtung's "structural theory of imperialism" (Bradshaw, 1985a; Delacroix, 1977; Delacroix and Ragin, 1978; 1981; Kaufmann, Chernotsky, and Geller, 1975; Pampel and Williamson, 1989, chapter 5; Ray and Webster, 1978; Weede and Tiefenbach, 1981a; 1981b). Similarly, there is some evidence of a relationship between low government-revenue/GDP or high-trade/GNP ratios on the one hand and less economic growth and more income inequality on the other hand (Bornschier, 1980a; Bornschier, Chase-Dunn, and Rubinson, 1978; Meyer and Hannan, 1979; Rubinson, 1976; 1977; Rubinson and Quinlan, 1977). But there are also other studies that call these findings, and thereby the Wallerstein-Rubinson line of reasoning, into question (Landau, 1983; Levine and Renelt, 1992; Marsden, 1983; Weede, 1980a; Weede and Tiefenbach, 1981a; 1981b; Wood, 1994, 223). Finally, there is some evidence for the negative impact of investment dependence, or MNC penetration, on economic growth and income equality (Bornschier, 1980a; 1980b; 1981a; 1982; Bornschier and Ballmer-Cao, 1979; Bornschier and Chase-Dunn, 1985; Chase-Dunn, 1975; Gobalet and Diamond, 1979). But again, there are studies that do not support these contentions (Bradshaw, 1985a, 202; 1985b, 93–94; Delacroix and Ragin, 1981; Jackman, 1982; Muller, 1984; Pampel and Williamson, 1989, chapter 5; Weede and Tiefenbach, 1981a; 1981b). Even a study by Bornschier (1985) himself conceded that the negative effects of MNC penetration on economic growth were no longer significant in the late 1970s.

Since these studies differ in sample size, period of observation, operationalization of variables, and specification of regression equations, it is difficult to explain their inconsistent findings. In my view, it is not essential to do so for the purposes of this chapter. The mere fact of contradictory findings instead of robust support in favor of dependency theories justifies some doubt. One route of criticism starts with the observation that most studies neglect competing explanations of cross-national differences of growth rates or income inequality and thereby risk some specification error. If one takes into account that income inequality and economic growth demonstrate curvilinear and nonmonotonic relationships with the level of economic development; that human-capital formation (as assessed by literacy, school enrollment ratios, or even military participation ratios) contributes to growth and equality; and that investment contributes to growth, then empirical support for dependency theories tends to wither away (Weede and Tiefenbach, 1981a; 1981b). The list of control variables . . . is similar to the one used and confirmed recently by Levine and Renelt (1992). While the research strategy I have outlined suffices to call dependency theories into question, it is not necessary to employ it in order to arrive at similar conclusions (see Delacroix, 1977; Muller, 1984; Ray and Webster, 1978).

Firebaugh [this volume—*Eds.*] (1992; Firebaugh and Beck, 1994) staged an even more devastating attack on dependency research and its preferred research designs than empirically minded critics who by the nature of their approach could do little more than detect a lack of robustness in claimed dependency effects. According to Firebaugh and Beck (1994, 639) the single-equation stock and flow models used by Bornschier and Chase-Dunn (1985) "do not separate the long-run effects from short-run effects of dependence. A single equation has only one dependent variable, not one reflecting short-run effects and one reflecting long-run effects." Worse than attempting the impossible, the observable foreign-investment effects have been misinterpreted. According to Firebaugh and Beck (1994, 635) the negative effects of foreign-investment stocks on economic growth do not support the MNC or investment variant of dependency theory but instead call its validity into question:

Investment rate is, in effect, the ratio of capital flow to capital stock. . . . With flow held constant, the greater the stock, the *lower* the ratio of capital flow to stock. So if investment boosts economic growth, then the greater the stock (holding flow constant) the *slower* the investment and therefore the *slower* the growth. In short, a negative coefficient for foreign stock indicates a *beneficial* effect of foreign investment in the dependency model. Researchers have simply misconstrued the effect of the denominator as a "dependence effect."

Firebaugh and Beck's (1994, 645) sophisticated study of caloric consumption, infant survival probability, and life expectancy rejected Wimberley and Bello's (1992) earlier claims concerning foreign investment and food consumption and arrived at the following conclusion: "There is no credible cross-national evidence that foreign investment is the leading cause of the 'immiseration' of the world's poor" (Firebaugh and Beck, 1994, 645). But they did find "some tantalizing support for the weak version of the theory," according to which the quality-of-life benefits of foreign investment are somewhat less than those of domestic investment (Firebaugh and Beck, 1994, 647). In my view, the contrast between capital returns accruing to citizens versus foreigners and the differential degrees of monopolization often coming with foreign versus domestic investment are plausible candidates for the interpretation of this finding.

To sum up: The dependency approach provides no reliable and valid answer to the question: Why do poor people stay poor? Although it is always conceivable that a research program in trouble—as dependency theory currently is—may recover and score better and more lasting explanatory success in the future than it has in the past, the search for alternative and possibly better explanations of why poor people stay poor seems justified.

2. KLEPTOCRACY AND RENT-SEEKING AT HOME

Rents are profits above opportunity costs. In a truly competitive market in which everyone is a price-taker, rents do not exist. Therefore, rent-seeking is an attempt to distort markets and to evade competition. Where rent-seeking is prevalent we refer to rent-seeking societies. The fundamental problem of rent-seeking societies is that they suffer from a serious distortion of incentives. There are strong incentives to engage in distributional struggles and to seek contrived transfers but comparatively weak incentives to engage in productive and growth-promoting activities. While rent-seeking decreases growth, there is no reason to expect the poor to be particularly successful in distributional struggles.

Rent-seeking aims at escaping from competition by monopolization, cartels, and barriers to entry. . . . Cartels are little better than monopolies. Their purpose is the same: to maximize profits by selling lower quantities at higher prices. In general, the regressive transfer from poorer buyers or consumers to richer cartel members still exists. The consumer surplus of those who are ready to pay competitive prices, but not cartel prices, still disappears. In particular where it is illegal, cartelization requires resources. But in contrast to monopolies, cartels require collective action. Seen from the perspective of a group of producers of some good, a cartel provides a collective good. If higher prices can be imposed on consumers, every producer receives some rent. For simplicity's sake, let us assume that cartelization is illegal and requires bribing politicians and bureaucrats to look the other way. In that case, there is a freeriding tendency. Every producer would like to benefit from the cartel but to make other producers pay for it. According to Olson (1965; 1982), the prospects for the provision of collective goods and for overcoming freeriding tendencies are much better in small groups than in large groups, which is why oligopolists should find cartelization easier than a multitude of small and scattered producers. Elitist interests always enjoy a head start in the cartelization game. Equalization by cartelization is extremely unlikely. Since cartelization consumes resources and interferes with efficient allocation and growth, it is a collective bad for society as a whole.

So far the discussion of rent-seeking has been rather abstract and removed from the problems of LDCs. This need not be so. Although not all of the quoted authors use the term *rent-seeking,* Lipton (1977) in his seminal book *Why Poor People Stay Poor,* Olson (1985; 1987), Bates (1988b), and Krueger (1992) analyze the phenomenon. In their view, there is a conflict of interest between urban and rural populations in LDCs that urban dwellers tend to decide in their own favor. In a conflict of interest between groups, the recipe for successful collective action and overcoming resistance is to generate concentrated gains for a relatively small group and diffused and preferably invisible losses for a much larger group (Olson, 1965). In most LDCs, by far the largest group is the rural population tilling the land. In general, this rural agrarian population is poorer than the urban population. If the smaller, relatively more privileged urban population can succeed in rigging the urban-rural terms of trade, the recipe of concentrated gains and diffused losses is realized, which is why an incentive exists for urban exploitation of the rural population.

It is much easier for urban people to organize themselves for the promotion of their collective interests than for scattered rural agrarian people. Karl Marx (1852/1966) knew this fact, and Olson (1985) recently reaffirmed it. Urban interests are concentrated in small but densely populated areas. Rural interests in LDCs are widely scattered and often suffer from poor transportation and communication facilities. The higher cost of collective action in the underdeveloped countryside makes a rural defense of agrarian interest less likely. While Lipton (1977, 13) does not hesitate to refer to class struggle, he rejects traditional Marxist theories and neo-Marxist dependency and world-system theories alike:

> The most important class conflict in the poor countries of the world today is not between labour and capital. Nor is it between foreign and national interest. It is between the rural and urban classes. The rural sector contains most of the poverty, and most of the low-cost sources of potential advance; but the urban sector contains most of the articulateness, organisation and power. So the urban classes have been able to "win" most rounds of the struggle with the countryside; but in so doing they have made the development process needlessly slow and unfair.

A comparatively small number of urban producers in LDCs finds little difficulty in establishing an informal cartel where the law does not permit a formal one. It is much easier for urban factory workers to unionize than for scattered rural people, some of whom may be tenants or sharecroppers. Nevertheless, these rural people do share an interest in obtaining high prices for whatever they sell. Finally, the largely urban public sector with its bureaucratic structure tends to be born organized for collective action. Aggregation of these somewhat organized urban interests is relatively easy. Urban employers and manufacturers, urban workers, and largely urban civil servants and politicians do share an interest in cheap food to be supplied from the rural hinterland to the cities. Obviously, distorted urban-rural terms of trade—i.e., artificially low prices for food and artificially high prices for urban products—depend on governmental policies and some degree of state interference with international trade. If farmers were free to sell their products to the highest-bidding buyers from inside or outside the country, then food prices could not be distorted downward. But prohibition of exports or official monopsonies (marketing boards) may prevent such harmful interference with urban interests. Differing degrees of unionization and corresponding urban-rural terms of trade simultaneously decrease the labor-absorption capacity of unionized, urban sectors.

Why should ruling politicians contribute to, or at least tolerate, some distortion of urban-rural terms of trade in LDCs? There are a number of reasons. First, but possibly least important, such a distortion benefits them personally by reducing their cost of living. Second, it is much easier for a political entrepreneur to build a power base from better-organized groups than from amorphous groups. The costs of resource mobilization for political action can be dramatically cut by assembling a coalition of previously existing interest groups or organizations, compared with calling them into existence in the first place (Hechter, 1987; Oberschall, 1973). Third, most rulers prefer poverty, disorder, and violence to occur out of sight if they cannot prevent it. They prefer starvation in remote villages to an urban riot in front of the presidential palace. Fourth, since unorganized rural agrarian groups in remote parts of the country cannot effectively fight back (short of guerrilla warfare, which probably requires some foreign help; see Gurr, 1968; Gurr and Duvall, 1973), it may even be politically stabilizing to redistribute from the rural poor to somewhat better-off urban dwellers.

The size of urban bias, or the burden imposed on agriculture, can be very large. For five Latin American economies, Krueger et al. (1992, 3) report that "on average, the relative price of agricultural goods would have been 42 percent higher in the absence of government price intervention." Much of the distortion (about two-thirds) arises because of *indirect* intervention, i.e., as the result of high levels of protection of nonagricultural importables or of exchange-rate misalignment. Agricultural interest groups in less developed countries find it very hard to fight against the indirect interventions that put such heavy burdens on them. Krueger et al. (1992, 33) suspect "that the producer organizations of agriculture realize that the removal of indirect interventions would require an alignment of forces that goes far beyond their particular sectoral interests." In effect, they would have to attack most urban vested interests at the same time.

Sometimes low food prices and government action to achieve them are rationalized by state support for agriculture, such as subsidizing pesticides or fertilizers. In Latin America, such benefits compensate, at best, for about half of the burden (Krueger et al., 1992, 4–5). Moreover, subsidization makes inputs appear cheaper than they are, so demand is bound to increase. In LDCs it usually cannot be met. Then somebody has to decide which farmers obtain the subsidized inputs and which ones do not. This somebody is likely to be a bureaucrat or a local politician. Even if the decisionmaker is honest—and that is a big if—allocation is likely to be discriminatory. Bureaucrats want to be properly approached. They like written applications or might even be legally required to insist on them. The smallest and poorest farmers in the remotest areas are least likely to pass this obstacle. Richer farmers are more likely to find somebody in their family or among their personal friends who is able to write an application or to fill out a form. Since Third World bureaucrats or local politicians rarely enjoy affluence, even though their incomes are much higher than those of ordinary peasants, tenants, or sharecroppers, there is a strong temptation to accept gifts or bribes for allocations of subsidized fertilizers or pesticides. If worst comes to worst, what has been intended as a subsidy for agriculture turns into a subsidy for bureaucrats and/or politicians and into an incentive for corruption. At best, when subsidy programs are competently and honestly administered, they still focus on "progressive farmers" and thereby deprive peasants of their natural leaders in the fight against harmful regulation by official marketing boards.

Urban bias in the economic policies of LDCs is married to a more general inclination in many such countries not to face the fact of their comparative disadvantage (relative to Western industrial societies) in large-scale organization, administration, and planning. Olson (1987, 86, 91) points out that "the skills, attitudes and expectations of most people in these societies [are] . . . derived from and geared to small institutions rather than large ones" and that "in poor and truly underdeveloped areas the government must usually be either very small (as were medieval governments of individual manors or the governments of various primitive tribes) or else relatively ineffective, corrupt, or even merely nominal as many governments in underdeveloped regions now appear to be." Based on these considerations, one may conclude with Olson (1987, 96) but in contrast to many ambitious but unsuccessful Third World governments, that "whatever the optimal role of government may be in developed nations, it is smaller in developing countries."

Although subsidies are often justified by the need to serve the poor, they rarely do so. World Bank (1994, 81) officials have recently observed: "Price subsidies to infrastructure almost always benefit the nonpoor disproportionately. In developing countries, the poor use kerosene or candles rather than electricity for lighting, they rely on private vendors or public standpipes rather than inhouse connections for water supply, and they are infrequently served by sewerage systems." Of course, infrastructure availability and use are correlated not only with income but also with urban or rural residence. By and large, urban areas are better served than rural areas.

Overvaluation of the domestic currency is a useful tool for rigging urban-rural terms of trade. It automatically reduces farmers' export prospects and simultaneously benefits mostly urban consumers of imported goods. Since overvaluation necessarily reduces the competitiveness of urban industries and tends to suck in imports, a poor country with an overvalued currency is likely to experience some balance-of-payments problems. To handle the problem and to protect domestic industry, what an Indian newspaper once termed "permit, license, quota Raj" is created. Such regulations boost bureaucratic employment and promotion opportunities, to the benefit of some urban people. They provide gratifying rents for those who obtain them. Take an import license, for example. Even after illegal payments to bureaucrats or politicians, such a license may still be a source of nice profits. The licensed importer and bureaucrats or politicians in regulatory agencies share the rent that has been created by the regulation of foreign trade.

As Lipton (1977; 1984) has pointed out, the distortion of urban-rural terms of trade in LDCs is closely related to inefficient development strategies. Investment is often characterized by an urban bias that neglects factor scarcities in LDCs. Except for capital-surplus oil exporters, most LDCs suffer from a scarcity of capital but command an ample supply of unskilled or even semiskilled labor. Urban investments often outperform rural investments in raising labor productivity, but rural investments generally outperform urban ones in capital productivity. Where capital is scarce and labor is not, it is more important to maximize productivity per unit of capital than per unit of labor. Nevertheless, many LDCs prefer urban investments as a matter of principle and neglect rural ones. Therefore, they get lower rates of growth than they could. While a capital-intensive strategy of industrialization retards development, it pleases some industrialists and unionized urban labor aristocracies that succeed in obtaining higher wages. At the same time, such higher wages slow down the labor-absorption capacity of the modern industrial sector and thereby condemn those not yet employed there to remain in the agricultural or in the urban informal sector, both of which contain the bulk of absolutely poor people in LDCs.

Although de Soto (1989) does not use the term *rent-seeking,* his *mercantilism* refers to the same facts. In the Peruvian rent-seeking society, many people are simply pushed out of the legal economy. According to de Soto (1989, 12) the informal sector employed 48 percent of the working population of Peru and contributed 61 percent of the hours worked and 39 percent to the GDP in the early 1980s. Since the informal sector grows rapidly, it might contribute as much as 61 percent to the Peruvian GDP by the year 2000. Estimates of the informal sector, or the shadow economy, imply that productivity in this sector is lower than in the formal sector, but people simply have no choice.

The weight of the informal sector in Peru can be explained by the shortcomings of government, administration, and the legal system. Many activities can be pursued legally not at all, or at best at a snail's pace. De Soto's (1989, 134–135) associates needed 289 days to legalize a small textile factory in the Lima metropolitan area. The cost was thirty-two local minimum wages. Public officials attempted to extort bribes ten times. Twice the bribes had to be paid in order to continue the experiment. Obviously, this kind of legal barrier shuts many Peruvians out of the formal economy.

Housing in Lima faces similar problems. In principle, poor families might get legal access to urban wasteland for settlement purposes, but the bureaucratic process takes—according to de Soto (1989, 136–137)—more than six years and consists of more than two hundred bureaucratic steps by forty-eight different offices. Given this bureaucratic nightmare, only illegal seizures of land and illegal housing can satisfy the urgent needs of 47 percent of the population. Even municipal housing projects involve illegal seizures of land. The informal sector provides housing and jobs and dominates local transport with buses, minibuses, and cabs. About 90,000 street vendors and about 40,000 additional traders in informal markets supply much of Lima's poor population and support the lives of about half a million inhabitants (de Soto, 1989, 60–61). . . .

Informality is bad for business and for the national economy. First, informal businesses have to be small and hardly visible in order to evade punishment and repression. They have to remain small and to forgo economies of scale, whether or not it is efficient. They must not be capital intensive. They must not advertise. Second, informal business depends on cash payments and is severely affected by inflation, which tends to be high or exorbitant in Latin America and which results from the fiscal and monetary policies of the state. Third, informal possessions cannot easily be sold and bought. This limitation must interfere with the efficient allocation of resources. Fourth, informal businesspeople have to invest much time and effort in the defense of their possessions—primarily by belonging to political associations and making contact with politicians in order to persuade the authorities to "overlook" their activities. Fifth, the lack of safe property rights increases transaction costs and thereby reduces gains from trade.

According to de Soto (1989, 191) the main problem with the Peruvian administrative, political, and legal system is its redistributive orientation: "A legal system whose sole purpose is redistribution thus benefits neither rich nor poor, but only those best organized to establish close ties with the people in power. It ensures that the businesses that remain in the market are those which are most efficient politically, not economically."

Rent-seeking is bad for society and growth since it distorts incentives and interferes with efficient resource allocation. In LDCs most rents benefit urban groups and harm rural agrarian ones because the latter find it hard to organize themselves for collective action and to become included in prevailing distributional coalitions. In rent seeking societies there is a protracted distributional struggle in which the poorest rural groups are destined to become losers. Equity is lost alongside efficiency.

The basic cross-nationally testable proposition advanced by Lipton (1977) holds that urban bias reduces growth rates. Lipton (1977, 435–437) has himself published some data on the urban-rural disparity in output per person, i.e., incomes per person in the urban and rural sectors of the economy. Since Lipton's own data set covers only sixty-three LDCs ca. 1970, other researchers have operationalized urban bias or the disparity as a ratio of ratios from widely available data. . . .

With this kind of measure, Bradshaw (1985a; 1985b; 1987), Weede (1987b), and London and Smith (1988) could demonstrate that urban bias, or income disparities between the nonagricultural and agricultural sectors of the economy, does significantly reduce growth rates. In this context, it may be noted that earlier interpretations of English economic history, according to which discrimination against agriculture contributed to early industrialization, are now refuted (Bates, 1988a, 512). Of course, this insight into the negative effects of urban bias does little to reduce the political attractiveness of this type of rent-seeking in LDCs (see Bates, 1983).

In my view, all societies are to some degree afflicted by rent-seeking. After all, the generation and distribution of rents is what makes politics and government attractive for many (or most?) active participants. But societies differ in the degree to which they tolerate or encourage rent-seeking. Is there any quantitative evidence beyond urban bias effects that those LDCs that permit more rent-seeking grow more slowly than others without at least generating a more equal distribution of income? While there is not much evidence, the existing evidence is fairly strong.

There is no rent-seeking without price distortion. Therefore, an index of price distortion is simultaneously an index of rent-seeking. For the 1970s and thirty-one LDCs, the World Bank (1983, 57–63) provides such an index. The Bank's price distortion index "concentrates on distortions in the prices of foreign exchange, capital, labor, and infrastructural services (particularly power)." If the trade-weighted exchange rate of an LDC currency appreciates or does not depreciate despite higher inflation at home than abroad, if competitiveness is thereby eroded, this is simultaneously a cue to the presence of price distortions and a cause for protectionist interference with international trade, which is another cue to the existence of price distortions. Distortion of capital prices is assumed to exist wherever real interest rates are negative. Minimum-wage laws, high social security taxes, and cheap provision of infrastructural services by state agencies are further indications of price distortions and rent-seeking. The World Bank's (1983, 57–63) price distortion index alone explained about one-third of the variance in GDP growth rates in the 1970s. Recently, the World Bank (1993b, 5) attributed the extraordinary economic performance of some East Asian economies to the fact that they "kept price distortions within reasonable bounds." But price distortion is not significantly correlated with income inequality. While certainly in need of replication in larger samples and for different periods of observation, the reported correlation between price distortion and reduced growth rates is much stronger than what dependency theory can offer. Moreover, if one introduces those control variables that make effects hypothesized by dependency theorists wither away, then the negative impact of price distortions on growth remains essentially as it was in bivariate analysis, and the relationship between price distortions and equality remains close to zero and insignificant (Weede, 1986a). . . .

3. RENT-SEEKING AND INTERNATIONAL RELATIONS

Even when a discussion of rent-seeking focuses on the domestic context, reference to the world economy as a whole is unavoidable. The deadliest blow to the rent-seeking society that I can imagine is to throw the doors wide open to foreign competition. In essence, rent-seeking requires barriers to entry in order to avoid competition. While international borders are not the only conceivable barriers to entry, they constitute probably the most powerful and persistent ones that actually exist. International borders enable some domestic distributional coalitions to capture rents not only at the expense of other groups at home but also at the expense of other groups abroad. Moreover, the winning group at home may be fairly inclusive, whereas the losers or losses may be scattered worldwide, or nearly so. . . .

One may improve one's understanding of worldwide rent-seeking if one applies a line of reasoning similar to Emmanuel's (1972) major observations, as Becker (1971) did in his work on the economics of discrimination or as Krauss (1983) did more recently. From a global perspective the most efficient solution would be to overlook the Northern (or Organization for Economic Cooperation and Development [OECD]) or Southern (or Third World) origin of capital and labor; i.e., no nation-state would interfere with movements of capital or labor, and newly arrived laborers could compete on an equal footing with others. Capital and labor would move to places where the outlook for high returns is best. Obviously, much Southern labor would move to the North and some Northern capital would move to the South. These movements of capital and labor would exert globally equalizing pressures on capital and labor returns. In this scenario, some people would gain and others would lose, compared with the status quo. By and large, unskilled and semiskilled Northern labor would suffer great losses and Southern labor would score major gains. Just imagine the pain in Chicago or Paris and the joy in Calcutta or Lagos if the gap in wages for, say, garbage collection began to close, since no one would prevent garbage collectors from poor countries from threatening the job security of garbage collectors in rich countries.

Whether Southern capital would lose and Northern capital would win depends on one's assessment of the effectiveness of current restrictions on international capital movements. I am inclined to accept Emmanuel's (1972) belief that current restrictions on capital movements are by and large ineffective—even more so now than at the time of his writing. Dismantling such restrictions would not make much of a difference. So, it is evident that the overriding effect of abolishing all state interference with capital and labor movements would be beneficial for Southern labor (or parts of it) and harmful for unskilled Northern labor.

This scenario, if it ever came true, would do much more to fight absolute poverty on a global scale than do welfare states in industrialized democracies. As Tullock (1983, 64) and Krauss (1983) observed, Northern welfare states cater to or redistribute within the most privileged decile or quintile of mankind; at the same time, their redistributive efforts depend on keeping the less fortunate majority of mankind out. But the scenario I have just sketched is unlikely ever to become true, for the obvious reason that relatively well-organized and unionized workers in the North will prevent it from happening. They are likely to succeed in protecting their rents. . . .

International organizations such as the World Health Organization (WHO) spend their money in ways that cannot be justified on humanitarian grounds. According to Tollison and Wagner (1993, 16), the WHO spends on the inhabitants of poor Ethiopia only a quarter of the amount that it spends on the inhabitants of Kuwait, which enjoys more than a hundred times the per capita income of Ethiopia. On top of this misallocation of aid, one may even argue with Krauss (1983) that OECD welfare states slow down LDC growth rates *by being welfare states*. First, the welfare state distorts incentives and reduces allocative efficiency and growth (Bernholz, 1982; 1986; Pampel and Williamson, 1989; Weede, 1984a; 1986c; 1991). Less growth in rich countries simultaneously hurts the growth prospects of poor countries. Second, the transformation of a capitalist country into a welfare state affects the structure of demand as public demand partially replaces private demand. Public demand is less likely than private demand to improve the export prospects of LDCs. American and Japanese hesitation to become full welfare states according to the Scandinavian model may help LDCs more than generous Scandinavian aid does.

The very existence of a multitude of states on the globe and state interference with the world economy is closely related to the problem of why poor people stay poor. State-supported or -tolerated price distortions within domestic economies are supplemented by state-generated price distortions within the world economy. Both kinds of distortions keep poor people poor. Now I find myself in partial agreement with a dependency theorist whom I critically evaluated above. Therefore, I quote Wallerstein (1974, 406) once more: "The functioning of the capitalist world economy requires that groups pursue their economic interests within a single world-market while seeking to distort this market for their benefit by organizing to exert influence on states, some of which are more powerful than others but none of which controls the market in its entirety." I agree with Wallerstein on the harmful impact of price distortions and on the state's role in generating these distortions, although I do not regard these observable aberrations as functional requisites of a capitalist world economy. Nor can I conceive of avoiding the negative effects of price distortions by manipulating these distortions to the benefit of the poor, as Wallerstein (1974; 1979; 1980) seems to imagine.

Olson (1982, 175) deplored the fact that "in these days it takes an enormous amount of stupid policies or bad or unstable institutions to prevent economic development. Unfortunately, growth-retarding regimes, policies, and institutions are the rule rather than the exception, and the majority of the world's population lives in poverty." From a global perspective, rent-seeking at the expense of other groups at home or abroad is indeed incredibly wasteful and—if one wants to call it so—stupid. Losers always lose much more than winners gain. Still, the game looks gratifying to those who win it. The "stupidity" of the game serves winners well. Privileged people keep poor people poor, and must do so if they want to protect their rental incomes, because rents rest on barriers to entry. Of course, inequality and poverty would persist even without rent-seeking, but there would probably be less inequality and almost certainly less poverty. . . .

While I do not know how to overcome the rent-seeking society, or how to achieve the equivalent of general disarmament in distributional struggles, I do think that one obvious strategy does not work. The poor cannot as easily unite, exert political pressure, or compel revolutionary change and obtain a better deal as more privileged groups. Meanwhile, the predicament of the poor facilitates rent-seeking by some privileged persons. As Bauer (1981, 13) has observed, "Most beneficiaries of redistribution include its advocates, organizers and administrators, notably politicians and civil servants, who are not among the poor." Politics and the price distortions thereby created are related at least as much, if not more closely, to the causes of poverty than to their cure. If the poor only unite, they have no chance to prevail. If some poor groups receive an offer to participate in a winning coalition, they will accept it. The winning coalition will aim at concentrated gains for its members, including previously poor ones, and dispersed and preferably invisible losses for others who cannot fight back—for example, because they are yet not organized and still poor.

It is possible that the true heroes of human history and improvement are those who aim for minor but useful reforms, who never get tired in the uphill struggle against rent-seeking. But to ask for this kind of work is to ask for a kind of altruism, and the trouble with altruism is that it is so rare that we should not trust one self-confident group to enforce it in others. Most guardians of morality are likely to defect and to look for rents in the end.

NO END OF POLITICS

BIBLIOGRAPHY

Ahluwalia, Montek S., Nicholas G. Carter, and Hollis B. Chenery. 1979. "Growth and Poverty in Developing Countries." *Journal of Development Economics* 6: 299–341.

Allais, Maurice. 1994. *Combats pour L'Europe 1992–1994.* Paris: Clément Juglar.

Alschuler, Lawrence R. 1976. "Satellization and Stagnation in Latin America." *International Studies Quarterly* 20(1): 39–82.

Amsden, Alice H. 1985. "The State and Taiwan's Economic Development." In Peter B. Evans, Dietrich Rueschemeyer, and Theda Skocpol (eds.), *Bringing the State Back In,* pp. 78–106. Cambridge: Cambridge University Press.

Andreski, Stanislav. 1969. *Parasitism and Subversion: The Case of Latin America.* New York: Schocken.

Balassa, Bela. 1981. *The Newly Industrialized Countries in the World Economy.* New York: Pergamon.

Bates, Robert H. 1983. *Essays on the Political Economy of Rural Africa.* Berkeley: University of California Press.

———. 1988a. "Lessons from History, or the Perfidy of English Exceptionalism and the Significance of Historical France." *World Politics* 40(4): 498–516.

———. 1988b. *Toward a Political Economy of Development.* Berkeley: University of California Press.

Bauer, Peter T. 1981. *Equality, the Third World and Economic Delusion.* London: Weidenfeld and Nicholson.

Bell, Daniel, and Irving Kristol (eds.). 1981. *The Crisis in Economic Theory.* New York: Basic Books.

Bernholz, Peter. 1982. "Expanding Welfare State, Democracy and Free Market Economy: Are They Compatible?" *Zeitschrift für die gesamte Staatswissenschaft* 138: 583–598.

————. 1986. "Growth of Government, Economic Growth and Individual Freedom." *Journal of Institutional and Theoretical Economics* 142: 661–683.

Bornschier, Volker. 1980a. *Multinationale Konzerne, Wirtschaftspolitik und nationale Entwicklung im Weltsystem.* Frankfurt/Main: Campus.

————. 1980b. "Multinational Corporations and Economic Growth." *Journal of Development Economics* 7: 191–210.

————. 1981a. "Dependent Industrialization in the World Economy." *Journal of Conflict Resolution* 25(3): 371–400.

————. 1981b. "Comment" (on Weede and Tiefenbach, 1981a). *International Studies Quarterly* 25: 283–288.

————. 1982. "Dependence on Foreign Capital and Economic Growth." *European Journal of Political Research* 10(4): 445–450.

————. 1985. "World Social Structure in the Long Economic Wave." Paper delivered at the 26th Annual Meeting of the International Studies Association, Washington, DC, March 5–9.

Bornschier, Volker, and Thanh-Huyen Ballmer-Cao. 1979. "Income Inequality: A Cross National Study of the Relationships Between MNC-Penetration, Dimensions of the Power Structure and Income Distribution." *American Sociological Review* 44: 487–506.

Bornschier, Volker, and Christopher Chase-Dunn. 1985. *Transnational Corporations and Underdevelopment.* New York: Praeger.

Bornschier, Volker, Christopher Chase-Dunn, and Richard Rubinson. 1978. "Cross-National Evidence of the Effects of Foreign Investment and Aid on Economic Growth and Inequality: A Survey of Findings and a Reanalysis." *American Journal of Sociology* 84: 651–683.

Bradshaw, York W. 1985a. "Dependent Development in Black Africa." *American Sociological Review* 50: 195–207.

————. 1985b. "Overurbanization and Underdevelopment in Sub-Saharan Africa." *Studies in Comparative International Development* 20(3): 74–101.

————. 1987. "Urbanization and Underdevelopment." *American Sociological Review* 52(2): 224–223.

Chan, Steve. 1993. *East Asian Dynamism: Growth, Order, and Security in the Pacific Region.* 2d ed. Boulder, CO: Westview Press.

Chan, Steve, and Alex Mintz (eds.). 1992. *Defense, Welfare, and Growth.* London: Routledge.

Chase-Dunn, Christopher. 1975. "The Effects of International Economic Dependence on Development and Inequality." *American Sociological Review* 40: 720–738.

Chirot, Daniel. 1986. *Social Change in the Modern Era.* San Diego: Harcourt Brace Jovanovich.

Delacroix, Jacques. 1977. "Export of Raw Materials and Economic Growth." *American Sociological Review* 42: 795–808.

Delacroix, Jacques, and Charles C. Ragin. 1978. "Modernizing Institutions, Mobilization, and Third World Development: A Cross-National Study." *American Journal of Sociology* 84: 123–150.

————. 1981. "Structural Blockage: A Cross-National Study of Economic Dependency, State Efficiency, and Underdevelopment." *American Journal of Sociology* 86: 1311–1347.

Dollar, David. 1992. "Outward-Oriented Developing Economies Really Do Grow More Rapidly: Evidence from 95 LDCs." *Economic Development and Cultural Change* 40(3): 523–544.

Economist, The. 1994c. "Survey: The Global Economy." *The Economist,* vol. 333, no. 7883, October 1.

Firebaugh, Glenn. 1992. "Growth Effects of Foreign and Domestic Investment." *American Journal of Sociology* 98: 105–130.

Firebaugh, Glenn, and Frank D. Beck. 1994. "Does Economic Growth Benefit the Masses? Growth, Dependence, and Welfare in the Third World." *American Sociological Review* 59(5): 631–653.

Galtung, Johan. 1971. "A Structural Theory of Imperialism." *Journal of Peace Research* 8: 81–117.

Gobalet, Jeanne G., and Larry J. Diamond. 1979. "Effects of Investment Dependence on Economic Growth: The Role of Internal Structural Characteristics and Periods in the World Economy." *International Studies Quarterly* 23: 412–444.

Greenaway, David, and Chong Hyun Nam. 1988. "Industrialization and Macroeconomic Performance in Developing Countries Under Alternative Trade Strategies." *Kyklos* 41(3): 419–435.

Gurr, Ted Robert. 1968. "A Causal Model of Civil Strife." *American Political Science Review* 62(4): 1104–1124.

———. 1993. "Why Minorities Rebel: A Global Analysis of Communal Mobilization and Conflict Since 1945." *International Political Science Review* 14(2): 157–197.

Gurr, Ted Robert, and Raymond Duvall. 1973. "Civil Conflict in the 1960s." *Comparative Political Studies* 6: 135–169.

Gurr, Ted Robert, Keith Jaggers, and Will H. Moore. 1990. "The Transformation of the Western State: The Growth of Democracy, Autocracy, and State Power Since 1800." *Studies in Comparative International Development* 25(1): 73–108.

Hechter, Michael. 1987. *Principles of Group Solidarity.* Berkeley: University of California Press.

Jackman, Robert W. 1982. "Dependence on Foreign Investment and Economic Growth in the Third World." *World Politics* 34: 175–196.

Kaufmann, Robert R., Harry I. Chernotsky, and Daniel S. Geller. 1975. "A Preliminary Test of the Theory of Dependency." *Comparative Politics* 7: 303–330.

Krauss, Melvyn B. 1983. *Development Without Aid: Growth, Poverty and Government.* New York: New Press (McGraw-Hill).

Krueger, Anne O. 1992. *The Political Economy of Agricultural Pricing.* Baltimore: The Johns Hopkins University Press.

Kuhn, Thomas S. 1962. *The Structure of Scientific Revolutions.* Chicago: The University of Chicago Press.

Lakatos, Imre. 1968–1969. "Criticism and the Methodology of Scientific Research Programmes." *Proceedings of the Aristotelian Society* 69: 149–186.

Landau, Daniel. 1983. "Government Expenditure and Economic Growth." *Southern Economic Journal* 49: 783–792.

Levine, Ross, and David Renelt. 1992. "A Sensitivity Analysis of Cross-Country Growth Regressions." *American Economic Review* 82: 942–963.

Lipton, Michael. 1977. *Why Poor People Stay Poor.* London: Temple Smith.

———. 1984. "Urban Bias Revisited." *Journal of Development Studies* 20(3): 139–166.

London, Bruce, and David A. Smith. 1988. "Urban Bias, Dependence, and Economic Stagnation." *American Sociological Review* 53(3): 454–463.

Marsden, Keith. 1983. "Steuern und Wachstum." *Finanzierung und Entwicklung* (HWWA-Institut für Wirtschaftsforschung, Hamburg) 20(3): 40–43.

Marx, Karl. 1852/1966. "Der achtzehnte Brumaire des Louis Bonaparte." *Marx-Engels-Studienausgabe*. Vol. 4, pp. 34–121. Frankfurt/Main: Fischer.

Meyer, John W., and Michael T. Hannan (eds.). 1979. *National Development and the World System: Educational, Economic and Political Change*. Chicago: University of Chicago Press.

Moon, Bruce E. 1991. *The Political Economy of Basic Human Needs*. Ithaca, NY: Cornell University Press.

Morris, M. David. 1979. *Measuring the Condition of the World's Poor: The Physical Quality of Life Index*. New York: Pergamon.

Mosley, Paul. 1987. *Overseas Aid: Its Defence and Reform*. Brighton, U.K.: Wheatsheaf.

Muller, Edward N. 1984. "Financial Dependence in the Capitalist World Economy and Distribution of Income Within Nations." In Mitchell A. Seligson (ed.), *The Gap Between Rich and Poor*, pp. 256–282. Boulder, CO: Westview Press.

Nielson, François. 1994. "Income Inequality and Industrial Development." *American Sociological Review* 59(5): 654–677.

Oberschall, Anthony. 1973. *Social Conflict and Social Movements*. Englewood Cliffs, NJ: Prentice Hall.

OECD. 1993. *Employment Outlook*. Paris: Organization for Economic Co-operation and Development.

Olson, Mancur. 1965. *The Logic of Collective Action*. Cambridge, MA: Harvard University Press.

———. 1982. *The Rise and Decline of Nations: Economic Growth, Stagflation and Social Rigidities*. New Haven: Yale University Press.

———. 1985. "Space, Agriculture, and Organization." *American Journal of Agricultural Economics* 67(5): 928–937.

———. 1987. "Diseconomies of Scale and Development." *Cato Journal* 7(1): 77–97.

Olson, Mancur, and Richard Zeckhauser. 1966. "An Economic Theory of Alliances." *Review of Economics and Statistics*.

Pampel, Fred C., and John B. Williamson. 1989. *Age, Class, Politics, and the Welfare State*. Cambridge: Cambridge University Press.

Porter, Bruce D. 1994. *War and the Rise of the State*. New York: Free Press.

Porter, Michael E. 1990. *The Competitive Advantage of Nations*. New York: Free Press.

Ray, James Lee, and Thomas Webster. 1978. "Dependency and Economic Growth in Latin America." *International Studies Quarterly* 22: 409–434.

Rubinson, Richard. 1976. "The World Economy and the Distribution of Income Within States." *American Sociological Review* 41: 638–659.

———. 1977. "Dependence, Government Revenue, and Economic Growth, 1955–1970." *Studies in Comparative International Development* 12: 3–28.

Rubinson, Richard, and Dan Quinlan. 1977. "Democracy and Social Inequality." *American Sociological Review* 42: 611–623.

Schumpeter, Joseph A. 1942. *Capitalism, Socialism and Democracy*. New York: Harper and Brothers.

Singh, Ram D. 1985. "State Intervention, Foreign Economic Aid, Savings and Growth in LDCs." *Kyklos* 38(2): 216–232.

Soto, Hernando de. 1989. *The Other Path*. New York: Harper and Row.

Stokes, Randall, and David Jaffee. 1982. "The Export of Raw Materials and Economic Growth." *American Sociological Review* 47(3): 402–407.

Tamas, G. M. 1993. "Socialism, Capitalism, and Modernity." In Larry Diamond and Marc F. Plattner (eds.), *Capitalism, Socialism, and Democracy Revisited,* pp. 54–68. Baltimore: The Johns Hopkins University Press.

Tollison, Robert D., and Richard E. Wagner. 1993. *Who Benefits from WHO? The Decline of the World Health Organization.* London: The Social Affairs Unit.

Tullock, Gordon. 1974. *The Social Dilemma: The Economics of War and Revolution.* Blacksburg, VA: University Publications.

———. 1980a. "Rent-Seeking as a Negative-Sum Game." In James B. Buchanan, Robert D. Tollison, and Gordon Tullock (eds.), *Toward a Theory of the Rent-Seeking Society,* pp. 16–36. College Station: Texas A&M University Press.

———. 1983. *Economics of Income Redistribution.* Boston, The Hague, and London: Kluwer-Nijhoff.

Wade, Robert. 1990. *Governing the Market.* Princeton: Princeton University Press.

———. 1992. "East Asia's Economic Success." *World Politics* 44: 270–320.

Walleri, R. Dan. 1978a. "The Political Economy Literature on North-South Relations: Alternative Approaches and Empirical Evidence." *International Studies Quarterly* 22: 587–624.

———. 1978b. "Trade Dependence and Underdevelopment." *Comparative Political Studies* 11: 94–127.

Wallerstein, Immanuel. 1974. *The Modern World System: Capitalist Agriculture and the Origins of the European World Economy in the Sixteenth Century.* New York: Academic Press.

———. 1979. *The Capitalist World-Economy (Essays).* Cambridge: Cambridge University Press.

———. 1980. *The Modern World System II: Mercantilism and the Consolidation of the European World-Economy, 1600–1750.* New York: Academic Press.

Weede, Erich. 1980a. "Beyond Misspecification in Sociological Analyses of Income Inequality." *American Sociological Review* 45: 497–501.

———. 1983b. "Military Participation Ratios, Human Capital Formation, and Economic Growth." *Journal of Political and Military Sociology* 11: 11–19.

———. 1984a. "Democracy, Creeping Socialism, and Ideological Socialism in Rent-Seeking Societies." *Public Choice* 44(2): 349–366.

———. 1986a. "Rent Seeking, Military Participation and Economic Performance in LDCs." *Journal of Conflict Resolution* 30(2): 291–324.

———. 1986c. "Sectoral Reallocation, Distributional Coalitions and the Welfare State as Determinants of Economic Growth Rates in Industrial Democracies." *European Journal of Political Research* 14: 501–519.

———. 1986d. "Rent-Seeking or Dependency as Explanations of Why Poor People Stay Poor." *International Sociology* 1(4): 421–441.

———. 1987b. "Urban Bias and Economic Growth in Cross-National Perspective." *International Journal of Comparative Sociology* 28(1–2): 30–42.

———. 1991. "The Impact of State Power on Economic Growth Rates in OECD Countries." *Quality and Quantity* 25: 421–438.

———. 1992a. *Mensch und Gesellschaft.* Tübingen: Mohr.

———. 1993b. "The Impact of Military Participation on Economic Growth and Income Inequality." *Journal of Political and Military Sociology* 21(2): 241–258.

Weede, Erich, and Horst Tiefenbach. 1981a. "Some Recent Explanations of Income Inequality." *International Studies Quarterly* 25: 255–282, 289–293.

———. 1981b. "Three Dependency Explanations of Economic Growth." *European Journal of Political Research* 9(4): 391–406.

———. 1982. "A Reply to Volker Bornschier." *European Journal of Political Research* 10(4): 451–454.

Wimberley, Dale W., and Rosario Bello. 1992. "Effects of Foreign Investment, Exports, and Economic Growth on Third World Food Consumption." *Social Forces* 70: 895–921.

Wood, Adrian. 1994. *North-South Trade, Employment and Inequality.* Oxford: Oxford University Press (Clarendon).

World Bank. 1981. *World Development Report 1981. 1983.* 1994. New York: Oxford University Press.

———. 1993b. *The East Asian Miracle.* New York: Oxford University Press.

30

Urban Bias and Inequality

MICHAEL LIPTON

Michael Lipton is the principal advocate of the thesis that the primary explanation for the internal gap between rich and poor is "urban bias." He argues that even though leaders of developing countries sympathize with the plight of the rural poor, they consistently concentrate scarce development resources in the urban sector. The result is that the urban sectors, which are already well-off in a comparative sense, get an increasing share of national income, which exacerbates the inequalities. In the book from which this chapter is drawn, Lipton tries to show that it is in the interests of the elites of developing countries to maintain this urban bias because they benefit directly from it. Critics of Lipton's thesis claim that historically there has been a rural bias in development and that much political power continues to reside in the hands of the rural elite. One might also ask if there is anything about the cultures found in developing nations that encourages policies favoring one sector over another; rural or urban biases (if they truly exist) might be a function of conditions established by the international environment.

The most important class conflict in the poor countries of the world today is not between labor and capital. Nor is it between foreign and national interests. It is between the rural classes and the urban classes. The rural

Reprinted by permission of the publishers from *Why Poor People Stay Poor: A Study of Urban Bias in World Development,* by Michael Lipton. Cambridge, MA: Harvard University Press, Copyright © 1976 by the President and Fellows of Harvard College. [References made by the author to other sections of the book from which this selection was drawn have been deleted.—*Eds.*]

sector contains most of the poverty, and most of the low-cost sources of potential advance; but the urban sector contains most of the articulateness, organization, and power. So the urban classes have been able to "win" most of the rounds of the struggle with the countryside; but in so doing they have made the development process needlessly slow and unfair. Scarce land, which might grow millets and beansprouts for hungry villagers, instead produces a trickle of costly calories from meat and milk, which few except the urban rich (who have ample protein anyway) can afford. Scarce investment, instead of going into water-pumps to grow rice, is wasted on urban motorways. Scarce human skills design and administer, not village wells and agricultural extension services, but world boxing championships in showpiece stadia. Resource allocations, within the city and the village as well as between them, reflect urban priorities rather than equity or efficiency. The damage has been increased by misguided ideological imports, liberal and Marxian, and by the town's success in buying off part of the rural elite, thus transferring most of the costs of the process to the rural poor.

But is this urban bias really damaging? After all, since 1945 output per person in the poor countries has doubled; and this unprecedented growth has brought genuine development. Production has been made more scientific: in agriculture, by the irrigation of large areas, and more recently by the increasing adoption of fertilizers and of high-yield varieties of wheat and rice; in industry, by the replacement of fatiguing and repetitive effort by rising levels of technology, specialization and skills. Consumption has also developed, in ways that at once use and underpin the development of production; poor countries now consume enormously expanded provisions of health and education, roads and electricity, radios and bicycles. Why, then, are so many of those involved in the development of the Third World— politicians and administrators, planners and scholars—miserable about the past and gloomy about the future? Why is the United Nations' "Development Decade" of the 1960s, in which poor countries as a whole exceeded the growth target,[1] generally written off as a failure? Why is aid, which demonstrably contributes to a development effort apparently so promising in global terms, in accelerating decline and threatened by a "crisis of will" in donor countries?[2]

The reason is that since 1945 growth and development, in most countries, have done so little to raise the living standards of the poorest people. It is scant comfort that today's mass-consumption economies, in Europe and North America, also featured near-stagnant mass welfare in the early phases of their economic modernization. Unlike today's poor countries, they carried in their early development the seeds of mass consumption later on. They were massively installling extra capacity to supply their people with simple goods: bread, cloth, and coal, not just luxury housing, poultry, and airports. Also the nineteenth-century "developing countries," including Russia, were developing not just market requirements but class structures that practically guaranteed subsequent "trickling down" of benefits. The workers even proved able to raise their share of political power and economic welfare. The very preconditions of such trends are absent in most of today's developing countries. The sincere egalitarian rhetoric of, say, Mrs. Indira Gandhi or Julius Nyerere was—allowing for differences of style and ideology—closely paralleled in Europe during early industrial development: in Britain, for example, by Henry Brougham and Lord Durham in the 1830s.[3] But the rural masses of India and Tanzania, unlike the urban masses of Melbourne's Britain, lack the power to organize the pressure that alone turns such rhetoric into distributive action against the pressure of the elite.

Some rather surprising people have taken alarm at the persistently unequal nature of recent development. Aid donors are substantially motivated by foreign-policy concerns for the stability of recipient governments; development banks, by the need to repay depositors and hence to ensure a good return on the projects they support. Both concerns coalesce in the World Bank, which raises and distributes some £3,000 million of aid each year. As a bank it has advocated—and financed—mostly "bankable" (that is, commercially profitable) projects. As a channel for aid donors, it has concentrated on poor countries that are relatively "open" to investment, trade and economic advice from those donors. Yet the effect of stagnant mass welfare in poor countries, on the well-intentioned and perceptive people who administer World Bank aid, has gradually overborne these traditional biases. Since 1971 the president of the World Bank, Robert McNamara, has in a series of speeches focused attention on the stagnant or worsening lives of the bottom 40 percent of people in poor countries.[4] Recently this has begun to affect the World Bank's projects, though its incomplete engagement with the problem of urban bias restricts the impact. For instance, an urban-biased government will prepare rural projects less well than urban projects, will manipulate prices to render rural projects less apparently profitable (and hence less "bankable"), and will tend to cut down its own effort if donors step up theirs. Nevertheless, the World Bank's new concern with the "bottom 40 percent" is significant.

These people—between one-quarter and one-fifth of the people of the world—are overwhelmingly rural: landless laborers, or farmers with no more than an acre or two, who must supplement their incomes by wage labor. Most of these countryfolk rely, as hitherto, on agriculture lacking irrigation or fertilizers or even iron tools. Hence they are so badly fed that they cannot work efficiently, and in many cases are unable to feed their infants well enough to prevent physical stunting and perhaps even brain damage. Apart from the rote-learning of religious texts, few of them receive any schooling. One of four dies before the age of ten. The rest live the same overworked, underfed, ignorant, and disease-ridden lives as thirty, or three hundred, or three thousand years ago. Often they borrow (at 40 percent or more yearly interest) from the same moneylender families as their ancestors, and surrender half their crops to the same families of landlords. Yet the last thirty years have been the age of unprecedented, accelerating growth and development! Naturally men of goodwill are puzzled and alarmed.

How can accelerated growth and development, in an era of rapidly improving communications and of "mass politics," produce so little for poor people? It is too simple to blame familiar scapegoats—foreign exploiters and domestic capitalists. Poor countries where they are relatively unimportant have experienced the paradox just as much as others. Nor, apparently, do the poorest families cause their own difficulties, whether by rapid population growth or by lack of drive. Poor families do tend to have more children than rich families, but principally because their higher death rates require it, if the aging parents are to be reasonably sure that a son will grow up, to support them if need be. And it is the structure of rewards and opportunities within poor countries that extracts, as if by force, the young man of ability and energy from his chronically stagnant rural background and lures him to serve, or even to join, the booming urban elite.

The disparity between urban and rural welfare is much greater in poor countries now than it was in rich countries during their early development. This huge welfare gap is demonstrably inefficient, as well as inequitable. It persists mainly because less than 20 percent of investment for development has gone to the agricultural sector (the situation has not changed much since 1965), although over 65 percent of the people of less-developed countries (LDCs), and over 80 percent of the really poor who live on $1 per week each or less, depend for a living on agriculture. The proportion of skilled people who support development—doctors, bankers, engineers—going to rural areas has been lower still; and the rural-urban imbalances have in general been even greater than those between agriculture and industry. Moreover, in most LDCs, governments have taken numerous measures with the unhappy side-effect of accentuating rural-urban disparities: their own allocation of public expenditure and taxation; measures raising the price of industrial production relative to farm production, thus encouraging private rural saving to flow into industrial investment because the value of industrial output has been artificially boosted; and educational facilities encouraging bright villagers to train in cities for urban jobs.

Such processes have been extremely inefficient. For instance, the impact on output of $1 of carefully selected investment is in most countries two to three times as high in agriculture as elsewhere, yet public policy and private market power have combined to push domestic savings and foreign aid into nonagricultural uses. The process has also been inequitable. Agriculture starts with about one-third the income per head as the rest of the economy, so that the people who depend on it should in equity receive special attention not special mulcting. Finally, the misallocation between sectors has created a needless and acute conflict between efficiency and equity. In agriculture the poor farmer with little land is usually efficient in his use of both land and capital, whereas power, construction, and industry often do best in big, capital-intensive units; and rural income and power, while far from equal, are less unequal than in the cities. So concentration on urban development and neglect of agriculture have pushed resources away from activities where they can help growth and benefit the poor, *and* toward activities where they do either of these, if at all, at the expense of the other.

Urban bias also increases inefficiency and inequity within the sectors. Poor farmers have little land and much underused family labor. Hence they tend to complement any extra developmental resources received—pumpsets, fertilizers, virgin land—with much more extra labor than do large farmers. Poor farmers thus tend to get most output from such extra resources (as well as needing the extra income most). But rich farmers (because they sell their extra output to the cities instead of eating it themselves, and because they are likely to use much of their extra income to support urban investment) are naturally favored by urban-biased policies; it is they, not the efficient small farmers, who get the cheap loans and the fertilizer subsidies. The patterns of allocation and distribution within the cities are damaged too. Farm inputs are produced inefficiently, instead of imported, and the farmer has to pay, even if the price is nominally "subsidized." The processing of farm outputs, notably grain milling, is shifted into big urban units and the profits are no longer reinvested in agriculture. And equalization between classes inside the cities becomes more risky, because the investment-starved farm sector might prove unable to deliver the food that a better-off urban mass would seek to buy.

Moreover, income in poor countries is usually more equally distributed within the rural sector than within the urban sector.[5] Since income creates the power to distribute extra income, therefore, a policy that concentrates on raising income in the urban sector will worsen inequalities in two ways: by transferring not only from poor to rich, but also from more equal to less equal. Concentration on urban enrichment is triply inequitable: because countryfolk start poorer; because such concentration allots rural resources largely to the rural rich (who sell food to the cities); and because the great inequality of power *within* the towns renders urban resources especially likely to go to the resident elites.

But am I not hammering at an open door? Certainly the persiflage of allocation has changed recently, under the impact of patently damaging deficiencies in rural output. Development plans are nowadays full of "top priority for agriculture."[6] This is reminiscent of the pseudo-egalitarian school where, at mealtimes, Class B children get priority, while Class A children get food.[7] We can see that the new agricultural priority is dubious from the abuse of the "green revolution" and of the oil crisis (despite its much greater impact on *industrial* costs) as pretexts for lack of emphasis on agriculture: "We don't need it," and "We can't afford it," respectively. And the 60 to 80 percent of people dependent on agriculture are still allocated barely 20 percent of public resources; even these small shares are seldom achieved; and they have, if anything, tended to diminish. So long as the elite's interests, background and sympathies remain predominantly urban, the countryside may get the "priority" but the city will get the resources. The farm sector will continue to be squeezed, both by transfers of resources from it by prices that are turned against it. Bogus justifications of urban bias will continue to earn the sincere, prestige-conferring, but misguided support of visiting "experts" from industrialized countries and international agencies. And development will be needlessly painful, inequitable and slow.

NOTES

1. The UN target was a 5 percent yearly rate of "real" growth (that is, allowing for inflation) of total output. The actual rate was slightly higher.

2. Net aid from the donor countries comprising the Development Assistance Committee (DAC) of the Organization for Economic Cooperation and Development (OECD) comprises over 95 percent of all net aid to less-developing countries (LDCs). It fell steadily from 0.54 percent of donors' GNP in 1961 to 0.30 percent in 1973. The real value of aid per person in recipient countries fell by over 20 percent over the period. M. Lipton, "Aid Allocation When Aid is Inadequate," in T. Byres, ed., *Foreign Resources and Economic Development,* Cass, 1972, p. 158; OECD (DAC), *Development Cooperation* (1974 Review), p. 116.

3. L. Cooper, *Radical Jack,* Cresset, 1969, esp. pp. 183–97; C. New, *Life of Henry Brougham to 1830,* Clarendon, 1961, Preface.

4. See the mounting emphasis in his *Addresses to the Board of Governors,* all published by the International Bank for Reconstruction and Development, Washington; at Copenhagen in 1970, p. 20; at Washington in 1971, pp. 6–19, and 1972, pp. 8–15; and at Nairobi in 1973, pp. 10–14, 19.

5. M. Ahluwalia, "The Dimensions of the Problem," in H. Chenery et al., *Redistribution with Growth,* Oxford, 1974.

6. See K. Rafferty, *Financial Times,* 10 April 1974, p. 35, col. 5; M. Lipton, "Urban Bias and Rural Planning," in P. Streeten and M. Lipton, eds., *The Crisis of Indian Planning,* Oxford, 1968, p. 85.

7. F. Muir and D. Norden, "Comonon Entrance," in P. Sellers, *Songs for Swinging Sellers,* Parlophone PMC 111, 1958.

31

· · · · · · ·

Political Regimes
and Economic Growth

· · · · · · ·

ADAM PRZEWORSKI & FERNANDO LIMONGI

In this chapter, Adam Przeworski and Fernando Limongi review the findings of eighteen articles that assess the relationship between regime type and economic growth. The authors show that the results have been inconclusive. According to Przeworski and Limongi, the confusion stems from the need for a more complex research design. Whereas the authors demonstrate that previous studies mistakenly attribute regime type as a cause of growth, they do not attempt to resolve the debate empirically. They state that ample evidence suggests that politics does affect growth, but they do not believe the debate over regime types captures the relevant differences between regimes that may be under investigation.

ARGUMENTS: HOW DEMOCRACY
MIGHT AFFECT GROWTH

Arguments that relate regimes to growth focus on property rights, pressures for immediate consumption, and the autonomy of dictators. While everyone seems to agree that secure property rights foster growth, it is controversial whether democracies or dictatorships better secure these rights. The main mechanism by which democracy is thought to hinder growth is pressures for immediate consumption, which reduce investment. Only states that are institutionally insulated from such pressures can resist them, and democratic states are not. The main argument against dictatorships is that authoritarian rulers have no interest in maximizing total output. . . .

Reprinted by permission of the American Economics Association from *Journal of Economic Perspective,* vol. 7, no. 3 (Summer 1993).

THE STATISTICAL EVIDENCE

In one way, the critics and defenders of democracy talk past each other. The critics argue that dictatorships are better at mobilizing savings; the defenders that democracies are better at allocating investment. Both arguments can be true but, as we shall see, the statistical evidence is inconclusive and the studies that produced it are all seriously flawed.

Table 31.1 summarizes the 18 studies we examined. These generated 21 findings, since some distinguished areas or periods. Among them, eight found in favor of democracy, eight in favor of authoritarianism, and five discovered no difference. What is even more puzzling is that among the 11 results published before 1988, eight found that authoritarian regimes grew faster, while none of the nine results published after 1987 supported this finding. And since this difference does not seem attributable to samples or periods, one can only wonder about the relation between statistics and ideology.[1]

For reasons discussed below, we hesitate to attach much significance to these results one way or another. Hence, we still do not know what the facts are.

INFERENCES BASED ON
STANDARD REGRESSION MODELS ARE INVALID

The reason social scientists have little robust statistical knowledge about the impact of regimes on growth is that the research design required to generate such knowledge is complex. This complexity is due to three sources: simultaneity, attrition, and selection.

Following the seminal work of Lipset (1960), there is an enormous body of theoretical and statistical literature to the effect that democracy is a product of economic development. This literature suffers from ambiguities of its own. While the belief is widespread that democracy requires as a "prerequisite" some level of economic development, there is much less agreement which aspects of development matter and why. Some think that a certain level of development is required for a stable democracy because affluence reduces the intensity of distributional conflicts; others because development generates the education or the communication networks required to support democratic institutions; still others because it swells the ranks of the middle class, facilitates the formation of a competent bureaucracy, and so on. Statistical results are somewhat mixed (Lipset 1960; Cutright 1963; Neubauer 1967; Smith 1969; Hannan and Carroll 1981; Bollen and Jackman 1985; Soares 1987; Arat 1988; Helliwell 1992). They suggest that the level of development, measured by a variety of indicators, is positively related to the incidence of democratic regimes in the

Table 31.1   Studies of Democracy, Autocracy, Bureaucracy, and Growth

Author	Sample	Time Frame	Finding
Przeworksi (1966)	57 countries	1949–1963	dictatorships at medium development level grew fastest
Adelman and Morris (1967)	74 underdeveloped countries (including communist bloc)	1950–1968	authoritarianism helped less and medium developed countries
Dick (1974)	59 underdeveloped countries	1959–1968	democracies develop slightly faster
Huntington and Dominguez (1975)	35 poor nations	the 1950s	authoritarian grew faster
Marsh (1979)	98 countries	1955–1970	authoritarian grew faster
Weede (1983)	124 countries	1960–1974	authoritarian grew faster
Kormendi and Meguire (1985)	47 countries	1950–1977	democracies grew faster
Kohli (1986)	10 underdeveloped countries	1960–1982	no difference in 1960s; authoritarian slightly better in 1970s
Landau (1986)	65 countries	1960–1980	authoritarian grew faster
Sloan and Tedin (1987)	20 Latin American countries	1960–1979	bureaucratic-authoritarian regimes do better than democracy; traditional dictatorships do worse
Marsh (1988)	47 countries	1965–1984	no difference between regimes
Pourgerami (1988)	92 countries	1965–1984	democracies grew faster
Scully (1988, 1992)	115 countries	1960–1980	democracies grew faster
Barro (1989)	72 countries	1960–1985	democracies grew faster
Grier and Tullock (1989)	59 countries	1961–1980	democracy better in Africa and Latin America; no regime difference in Asia
Remmer (1990)	11 Latin American countries	1982–1988 1982 and 1988	democracy faster, but result statistically insignificant
Pourgerami (1991)	106 less developed countries	1986	democracies grow slower
Helliwell (1992)	90 countries	1960–1985	democracy has a negative, but statistically insignificant effect on growth

population of world countries, but not necessarily within particular regions. Moreover, the exact form of the relationship and its relation to regime stability are left open to debate. Yet the prima facie evidence in support of this hypothesis is overwhelming: all developed countries in the world constitute stable democracies while stable democracies in the less developed countries remain exceptional.

Attrition is a more complicated issue. Following Lipset again, everyone seems to believe that durability of any regime depends on its economic performance. Economic crises are a threat to democracies as well as to dictatorships. The probability that a regime survives a crisis need not be the same, however, for democracies and dictatorships: one reason is that under democracy it is easier to change a government without changing the regime, another is that democracies derive legitimacy from more than their economic performance. We also have the argument by Olson (1963; also Huntington 1968) that rapid growth is destabilizing for democracies but not for dictatorships.

This evidence suffices to render suspect any study that does not treat regimes as endogenous. If democratic regimes are more likely to occur at a higher level of development or if democracies and dictatorships have a different chance of survival under various economic conditions, then regimes are endogenously selected. Since this is the heart of the statistical difficulties, we spell out the nature of this problem in some detail. (The following discussion draws on Przeworski and Limongi 1992.)

We want to know the impact of regimes on growth. Observing Brazil in 1988, we discover that it was a democracy which declined at the rate of 2.06 percent. Would it have grown had it been a dictatorship? The information we have, the observation of Brazil in 1988, does not answer this question. But unless we know what would have been the growth of Brazil in 1988 had it been a dictatorship, how can we tell if it would have grown faster or slower than under democracy?

Had we observed in 1988 a Brazil that was simultaneously a democracy and a dictatorship, we would have the answer. But this is not possible. There is still a way out: if the fact that Brazil was a democracy in 1988 had nothing to do with economic growth, we could look for some country that was exactly like Brazil in all respects other than its regime and, perhaps, its rate of growth, and we could match this country with Brazil. But if the selection of regimes shares some determinants with economic growth, an observation that matches Brazil in all respects other than the regime and the rate of growth will be hard to find. And then the comparative inferences will be biased: Whenever observations are not generated randomly, quasi-experimental approaches yield inconsistent and biased estimates of the effect of being in a particular state on outcomes. Indeed, this much is now standard statistical wisdom, as evidenced in the vast literature reviewed by Heckman (1990), Maddala (1983), and Greene (1990). Yet the implications of this failure are profound: we can no longer use the standard regression models to make valid inferences from the observed to the unobserved cases. Hence, we cannot compare.

The pitfalls involved in the studies summarized above can be demonstrated as follows. Averaging the rates of growth of ten South American countries between 1946 and 1988, one discovers that authoritarian regimes grew at the average rate of 2.15 percent per annum while democratic regimes grew at 1.31 percent. Hence, one is inclined to conclude that authoritarianism is better for growth than democracy. But suppose that in fact regimes have no effect on growth. However, regimes do differ in their probabilities of surviving various economic conditions: authoritarian regimes are less likely than democracies to survive when they perform badly. In addition, suppose that the probability of survival of both regimes depends on the number of other democracies in the region at each moment. These probabilities jointly describe how regimes are selected: the dependence of survival on growth constitutes endogenous selection, the diffusion effect represents exogenous selection.

In Przeworski and Limongi (1992), we used the observed regime-specific conditional survival probabilities to generate 5,000 (500 per country) 43-year histories obeying these assumptions, each beginning with the level and the regime observed in 1945. As one would expect, authoritarian regimes grew faster than democracies—indeed, we reproduced exactly the observed difference in growth rates—despite the fact that these data were generated under the assumption that regimes have no effect on growth. It is the difference in the way regimes are selected—the probabilities of survival conditional on growth—that generate the observed difference in growth rates. Hence, this difference is due entirely to selection bias.[2]

If one applies ordinary least squares to data generated in this way, with a dummy variable set to 1 for Authoritarianism and 0 for Democracy, the regime coefficient turns out to be positive and highly significant. Thus standard regression fails the same way as the comparison of means, even with controls. To correct for the effect of selection, we followed the procedure developed by Heckman (1978) and Lee (1978). Once we corrected the effects of selection, we generated the unbiased means for the two regimes and these, not surprisingly, reproduced the assumptions under which the data were generated: no difference in growth between the two regimes.

These methodological comments should end with a warning. Selection models turn out to be exceedingly sensitive: minor modifications of the equation that specifies how regimes survive can affect the signs in the equations that explain growth. Standard regression techniques yield biased (and inconsistent) inferences, but selection models are not robust (Greene 1990, 750; Stolzenberg and Relles 1990). While reverting to simulation provides at least the assurance that one does not attribute to regimes the effects they do not have, it may still fail to capture the effects they do exert.

CONCLUSIONS

The simple answer to the question with which we began is that we do not know whether democracy fosters or hinders economic growth.[3] All we can offer at this moment are some educated guesses.

First, it is worth noting that we know little about determinants of growth in general. The standard neoclassical theory of growth was intuitively unpersuasive and it implied that levels of development should converge: a prediction not born by the facts. The endogenous growth models are intuitively more appealing but empirically difficult to test since the "engine of growth" in these models consists, in Romer's (1992, 100) own words, of "ephemeral externalities." Statistical studies of growth notoriously explain little variance and are very sensitive to specification (Levine and Renelt 1991). And without a good economic model of growth, it is not surprising that the partial effect of politics is difficult to assess.

Secondly, there are lots of bits and pieces of evidence to the effect that politics in general does affect growth. At least everyone, governments and international lending institutions included, believes that policies affect growth and, in turn, scholars tend to think that politics affect policies. Reynolds (1983), having reviewed the historical experience of several countries, concluded that spurts of growth are often associated with major political transformations. Studies examining the impact of government spending on growth tend to find that the size of government is negatively related to growth, but the increase of government expenditures has a positive effect (Ram 1986; Lindauer and Velenchik 1992). Studies comparing the Far East with Latin America argue that there is something about the political institutions of the Asian countries which makes them propitious for growth. But while suggestive stories abound, there is little hard evidence.

Our own hunch is that politics does matter, but "regimes" do not capture the relevant differences. Postwar economic miracles include countries that had parliaments, parties, unions, and competitive elections, as well as countries run by military dictatorships. In turn, while Latin American democracies suffered economic disasters during the 1980s, the world is replete with authoritarian regimes that are dismal failures from the economic point of view.[4] Hence, it does not seem to be democracy or authoritarianism per se that makes the difference but something else.

What that something else might be is far from clear. "State autonomy" is one candidate, if we think that the state can be autonomous under democracy as well as under authoritarianism, as do Bardhan (1988, 1990) and Rodrik (1992). But this solution meets the horns of a dilemma: an autonomous state must be both effective at what it wants to do and insulated from pressures to do what it does not want to do. The heart of the neo-liberal research program is to find institutions that enable the state to do what it should but disable it from doing what it should not.

In our view, there are no such institutions to be found. In a Walrasian economy, the state has no positive role to play, so that the constitutional rule is simple: the less state, the better. But if the state has something to do, we would need institutions which enable the state to respond optimally to all contingent states of nature and yet prevent it from exercising discretion in the face of group pressures. Moreover, as Cui (1992) has argued, if markets are incomplete and information imperfect, the economy can function only if the state insures investors (limited liability), firms (bankruptcy), and depositors (two-tier banking system). But this kind of state involvement inevitably induces a soft-budget constraint. The state cannot simultaneously insure private agents and not pay the claims, even if they result from moral hazard.

Even if optimal rules do exist, pre-commitment is not a logically coherent solution. The reason is that just any commitment is not good enough: it must be a commitment to an optimal program. And advocates of commitment (like Shepsle 1989) do not consider the political process by which such commitments are established. After all, the same forces that push the state to suboptimal discretionary interventions also push the state to a suboptimal commitment. Assume that the government wants to follow an optimal program and it self-commits itself. At the present it does not want to respond to private pressures but it knows that in the future it would want to do so; hence, it disables its capacity to do it. The model underlying this argument is Elster's (1979) Ulysses.[5] But the analogy does not hold since Ulysses makes his decision *before* he hears the Sirens. Suppose that he has already heard them: why does he not respond to their song now and is afraid that he would respond later? If governments do bind themselves, it is already in response to the song of the Sirens and their pre-commitment will not be optimal.

Clearly, the impact of political regimes on growth is wide open for reflection and research.

NOTES

1. Indeed, it is sufficient to read Scully (1992, xiii–xiv) to stop wondering. "The Anglo-American paradigm of free men and free markets unleashed human potential to an extent unparalled in history. . . . One needs evidence to persuade those who see promise in extensive government intervention in the economy. I have found such evidence, and the evidence is overwhelmingly in favor of the paradigm of classical liberalism." The evidence on the effect of democracy on growth consists of cross-sectional OLS regressions in which investment is controlled for, so that political effects measure efficiency but not the capacity to mobilize savings.

2. We could have gotten the same result in a different way. Suppose that (1) levels converge, that is, growth is a negative function of income, and (2) dictatorships occur at low levels while democracies are more frequent at high levels. Then we will observe fast growing dictatorships (at low levels) and slowly growing democracies (at high levels).

3. Note that we considered only indirect impacts of regimes on growth via investment and the size of the public sector, but we did not consider the impacts via income equality, technological change, human capital, or population growth.

4. As Sah (1991) has argued, authoritarian regimes exhibit a higher variance in economic performance than democracies: President Park of South Korea is now seen as a developmentalist leader, while President Mobutu of Zaire is seen as

nothing but a thief (Evans 1989). But we have no theory that would tell us in advance which we are going to get. We do know, in turn, that until the early 1980s the democratic regimes which had encompassing, centralized unions combined with left-wing partisan control performed better on most economic variables than systems with either decentralized unions or right-wing partisan dominance.

5. Note that Elster (1989, 196) himself argues against the analogy of individual and collective commitment.

REFERENCES

Adelman, Irma, and Cynthia Morris. 1967. *Society, Politics and Economic Development.* Baltimore: Johns Hopkins University Press.

Alesina, Alberto, and Dani Rodrik. 1991. "Distributive Politics and Economic Growth," National Bureau of Economic Research, Working Paper No. 3668.

Amsden, Alice H. 1989. *Asia's Next Giant: South Korea and Late Industrialization.* New York: Oxford University Press.

Arat, Zehra F. 1988. "Democracy and Economic Development: Modernization Theory Revisited," *Comparative Politics,* October, 21:1, 21–36.

Bardhan, Pranab. 1988. "Comment on Gustav Ranis' and John C. H. Fei's 'Development Economics: What Next?'" In Ranis, Gustav, and T. Paul Schultz, eds., *The State of Development Economics: Progress and Perspectives.* Oxford: Basil Blackwell, pp. 137–38.

Bardhan, Pranab. 1990. "Symposium on the State and Economic Development." *Journal of Economic Perspectives,* Summer, 4:3, 3–9.

Barro, Robert J. 1989. "A Cross-country Study of Growth, Saving, and Government," NBER Working Paper No. 2855.

Barro, Robert J. 1990. "Government Spending in a Simple Model of Endogenous Growth," *Journal of Political Economy,* October, 98:5, S103–S125.

Becker, Gary S. 1983. "A Theory of Competition Among Pressure Groups for Political Influence," *Quarterly Journal of Economics,* August, 98:3, 371–400.

Bollen, K. A., and R. W. Jackman. 1985. "Economic and Noneconomic Determinants of Political Democracy in the 1960s," *Research in Political Sociology,* 1, 27–48.

Collini, Stefan, Donald Winch, and John Burrow. 1983. *That Noble Science of Politics.* Cambridge: Cambridge University Press.

Crain, W. Mark. 1977. "On the Structure and Stability of Political Markets." *Journal of Political Economy,* August, 85:4, 829–42.

Cui, Zhiyuan. 1992. "Incomplete Markets and Constitutional Democracy," manuscript, University of Chicago.

Cutright, Philips. 1963. "National Political Development: Measurement and Analysis," *American Sociological Review,* 28, 253–64.

de Schweinitz, Karl Jr. 1959. "Industrialization, Labor Controls and Democracy," *Economic Development and Cultural Change,* July, 385–404.

de Schweinitz, Karl Jr. 1964. *Industrialization and Democracy.* New York: Free Press.

Dick, William G. 1974. "Authoritarian Versus Nonauthoritarian Approaches to Economic Development," *Journal of Political Economy,* July/August, 82:4, 817–27.

Dore, Ronald. 1978. "Scholars and Preachers." *IDS Bulletin.* Sussex, U.K.: International Development Studies, June.

Downs, Anthony. 1957. *An Economic Theory of Democracy.* New York: Harper and Row.

Elster, Jon. 1979. *Ulysses and the Sirens: Studies in Rationality and Irrationality.* Cambridge: Cambridge University Press.

Elster, Jon. 1989. *Solomanic Judgements. Studies in the Limitations of Rationality.* Cambridge: Cambridge University Press.

Elster, Jon, and Karl Ove Moene, eds. 1989. "Introduction." In *Alternatives to Capitalism.* Cambridge: Cambridge University Press, 1–38.

Evans, Peter B. 1989. "Predatory, Developmental, and Other Apparatuses: A Comparative Political Economy Perspective on the Third World State." *Sociological Forum*, December, 4:4, 561–87.

Fernandez, Raquel, and Dani Rodrick. 1991, "Resistance to Reform; Status Quo Bias in the Presence of Individual-Specific Uncertainty," *American Economic Review*, December, 81:5, 1146–55.

Findlay, Ronald. 1990. "The New Political Economy: Its Explanatory Power for the LDCS," *Economics and Politics*, July, 2:2, 193–221.

Galenson, Walter. 1959. "Introduction" to Galenson, W., ed. *Labor and Economic Development.* New York: Wiley.

Galenson, Walter, and Harvey Leibenstein. 1955. "Investment Criteria, Productivity and Economic Development," *Quarterly Journal of Economics,* August, 69, 343–70.

Gereffi, Gary, and Donald I. Wyman, eds. 1990. *Manufacturing Miracles: Paths of Industrialization in Africa and East Asia.* Princeton: Princeton University Press.

Greene, William H. 1990. *Econometric Analysis.* New York: Macmillan.

Grier, Kevin B., and Gordon Tullock. 1989. "An Empirical Analysis of Cross-national Economic Growth, 1951–80," *Journal of Monetary Economics*, September 1989, 24:2, 259–76.

Haggard, Stephan. 1990. *Pathways from Periphery: The Politics of Growth in the Newly Industrializing Countries.* Ithaca: Cornell University Press.

Hannan, M. T., and G. R. Carroll. 1981. "Dynamics of Formal Political Structure: An Event History Analysis," *American Sociological Review,* February, 46:1, 19–35.

Heckman, James J. 1978. "Dummy Endogenous Variables in a Simultaneous Equation System," *Econometrica*, July, 46:4, 931–59.

Heckman, James J. 1990. "Selection Bias and Self-selection." In Eatwell, John, Murray Milgate, and Peter Newman, eds., *The New Palgrave Econometrics.* New York: W. W. Norton, 287–97.

Helliwell, John F. 1992. "Empirical Linkages Between Democracy and Economic Growth," NBER Working Paper #4066. Cambridge: National Bureau of Economic Research.

Huntington, Samuel P. 1968. *Political Order in Changing Societies.* New Haven: Yale University Press.

Huntington, Samuel P., and Jorge I. Dominguez. 1975. "Political Development." In Greenstein, F. I., and N. W. Polsby, eds. *Handbook of Political Science,* 3. Reading: Addison-Wesley, 1–114.

Kaldor, Nicolas. 1956. "Alternative Theories of Distribution," *Review of Economic Studies*, 23:2, 83–100.

Kohli, Atul. 1986. "Democracy and Development." In Lewis, John P., and Valeriana Kallab, eds. *Development Strategies Reconsidered.* New Brunswick: Transaction Books, 153–82.

Kormendi, Roger C., and Philip G. Meguire. 1983. "Macroeconomic Determinants of Growth: Cross-Country Evidence," *Journal of Monetary Economics*, September, 162: 141–63.

Landau, Daniel. 1986. "Government and Economic Growth in the Less Developed Countries: An Empirical Study for 1960–1980," *Economic Development and Cultural Change*, October, 35:1, 35–75.

Lee, L. F. 1978. "Unionism and Wage Rates: A Simultaneous Equations Model with Qualitative and Limited Dependent Variables," *International Economic Review*, June, 19:2, 415–33.
Levine, Ross, and David Renelt. 1991. "A Sensitivity Analysis of Cross-country Growth Regressions," World Bank Working Paper WPS 609.
Lindauer, David L., and Ann D. Velenchik. 1992. "Government Spending in Developing Countries: Trends, Causes, and Consequences," *World Bank Research Observer*, January, 7:1. Washington, D.C.: The World Bank, 59–78.
Lipset, Seymour M. 1960. *Political Man*. Garden City: Doubleday, 1960.
Macaulay, Thomas B. 1900. *Complete Writings, 17*. Boston and New York: Houghton-Mifflin.
Maddala, G. S. 1983. *Limited-Dependent and Qualitative Variables in Econometrics*. Cambridge: Cambridge University Press.
Marsh, Robert M. 1979. "Does Democracy Hinder Economic Development in the Latecomer Developing Nations?" *Comparative Social Research*, 2:2, 215–48.
Marsh, Robert M. 1988. "Sociological Explanations of Economic Growth," *Studies in Comparative International Development*, Winter, 23:4, 41–76.
Marx, Karl. 1934. *The Eighteenth Brumaire of Louis Bonaparte*. Moscow: Progress Publishers.
Marx, Karl. 1952. *The Class Struggle in France, 1848 to 1850*. Moscow: Progress Publishers.
Marx, Karl. 1971. *Writings on the Paris Commune*. Edited by H. Draper. New York: International Publishers.
Neubauer, Deane E. 1967. "Some Conditions of Democracy," *American Political Science Review*, December, 61:4, 1002–9.
North, Douglass C. 1990. *Institutions, Institutional Change and Economic Performance*. Cambridge, U.K.: Cambridge University Press.
North, Douglass C., and Robert Paul Thomas. 1973. *The Rise of the Western World: A New Economic History*. Cambridge, U.K.: Cambridge University Press.
North, Douglass C., and Barry R. Weingast. 1989. "Constitutions and Commitment: The Evolution of Institutions Governing Public Choice in Seventeenth-Century England," *Journal of Economic History*, December, 49:4, 803–32.
O'Donnell, Guillermo. 1973. *Modernization and Bureaucratic-Authoritarianism*. Berkeley: UC Berkeley Press.
Olson, Mancur, Jr. 1963. "Rapid Growth as a Destabilizing Force," *Journal of Economic History*, December, 23, 529–52.
Olson, Mancur, Jr. 1991. "Autocracy, Democracy and Prosperity." In Zeckhauser, Richard J., ed., *Strategy and Choice*. Cambridge: MIT Press, 131–57.
Pasinetti, Luigi. 1961-62. "Rate of Profit and Income Distribution in Relation to the Race of Economic Growth," *Review of Economic Studies*, October, 29:81, 267–79.
Persson, Torsten, and Guido Tabellini. 19. "Is Inequality Harmful for Growth? Theory and Evidence." Working paper No. 91-155, Department of Economics, University of California, Berkeley, 1991.
Pourgerami, Abbas. 1988. "The Political Economy of Development: A Cross-national Causality Test of Development-Democracy-Growth Hypothesis," *Public Choice*, August, 58:2, 123–41.
Pourgerami, Abbas. 1991. "The Political Economy of Development: An Empirical Investigation of the Wealth Theory of Democracy," *Journal of Theoretical Politics*, April, 3:2, 189–211.
Przeworski, Adam. 1966. *Party Systems and Economic Development*. Ph.D. dissertation. Northwestern University.

Przeworski, Adam. 1990. *The State and the Economy Under Capitalism: Fundamentals of Pure and Applied Economics*, 40. Chur, Switzerland: Harwood Academic Publishers.

Przeworski, Adam, and Fernando Limongi. 1992. "Selection, Counterfactuals and Comparisons," manuscript, Department of Political Science, University of Chicago.

Przeworski, Adam, and Michael Wallerstein. 1988. "Structural Dependence of the State on Capital," *American Political Science Review*, March, 82:1, 11–29.

Ram, Rati. 1986. "Government Size and Economic Growth: A New Framework and Some Evidence from Cross-Section and Time-Series Data," *American Economic Review*, March, 76:1, 191–203.

Rao, Vaman. 1984. "Democracy and Economic Development," *Studies in Comparative International Development*, Winter 1984, 19:4, 67–81.

Remmer, Karen. 1990. "Democracy and Economic Crisis: The Latin American Experience," *World Politics*, April, 42:3, 315–35.

Reynolds, Lloyd G. 1983. "The Spread of Economic Growth to the Third World: 1850-1980," *Journal of Economic Literature*, September, 21:3, 941–80.

Rodrik, Dani. 1992. "Political Economy and Development Policy." *European Economic Review*, April, 36:2/3, 329–36.

Romer, Paul. 1992. "Increasing Returns and New Developments in the Theory of Growth." In Barnett, W. A., ed. *Equilibrium Theory and Applications*. New York: Cambridge University Press, 83–110.

Sah, Raaj K. 1991. "Fallibility in Human Organizations and Political Systems," *Journal of Economic Perspectives*, Spring 1991, 5:2, 67–88.

Schepsle, Kenneth. 1989. "Studying Institutions: Some Lessons from the Rational Choice Approach," *Journal of Theoretical Politics*, April, 1:2, 131–49.

Scully, Gerald W. 1988. "The Institutional Framework and Economic Development," *Journal of Political Economy*, June, 96:3, 652–62.

Scully, Gerald W. 1992. *Constitutional Environments and Economic Growth*. Princeton: Princeton University Press.

Sloan, John, and Kent L. Tedin. 1987. "The Consequences of Regimes Type for Public-Policy Outputs," *Comparative Political Studies*, April, 20:1, 98–124.

Smith, Arthur K. Jr. 1969. "Socio-economic Development and Political Democracy: A Causal Analysis," *Midwest Journal of Political Science*, 13: 95–125.

Soares, G. A. D. 1987. "Desenvolvimento Economico e Democracia na America Latina," *Dados*, 30:3, 253–74.

Stolzenberg, Ross M., and Daniel A. Relles. 1990. "Theory Testing in a World of Constrained Research Design," *Sociological Methods and Research*, May, 18:4, 395–415.

Wade, Robert. 1990. *Governing the Market: Economic Theory and the Role of Government in West Asian Industrialization*. Princeton: Princeton University Press, 1990.

Weede, Erich. 1983. "The Impact of Democracy on Economic Growth: Some Evidence from Cross-National Analysis," *Kyklos*, 36:1, 21–39.

Westphal, Larry E. 1990. "Industrial Policy in an Export-Propelled Economy: Lessons from South Korea's Experience," *Journal of Economic Perspectives*, Summer, 4:3, 41–60.

Wittman, Donald. 1989. "Why Democracies Produce Efficient Results," *Journal of Political Economy*, December, 97:6, 1395–1424.

World Bank. 1987. *World Development Report*. Washington, DC: The World Bank.

28, 29, 32, 34

32

· · · · · · ·

Growth in East Asia:
What We Can and
What We Cannot Infer

· · · · · · ·

MICHAEL SAREL

This chapter takes a hard and critical look at the theories that have attempted to explain rapid growth in East Asia. Increases in productivity have often been declared to be the central explanatory factor; therefore, as Sarel writes, we can conclude two things: "First, economic growth in the Four Tigers is hardly miraculous: it is just the expected outcome of a massive accumulation of labor and capital. Second, the progress of these economies along this growth path for the past thirty years cannot continue." Yet, the evidence for these assertions is very weak, as Sarel shows. Furthermore, the evidence that argues that export-led growth or "correct" government macroeconomic policies are the causes of the Asian "miracle" is similarly tenuous. In contrast, Sarel finds that when the "initial conditions" that existed prior to the growth explosion are examined, some explanatory factors do stand out. Foremost among those conditions are a strong investment in education and health and reductions in inequality brought on by land reform. These findings suggest again the key importance of equality in stimulating or inhibiting growth and serve as an appropriate background to the next chapter by Birdsall and Sabot.

The spectacular growth of many economies in East Asia over the past 30 years has amazed the economics profession and has evoked a torrent of books and articles attempting to explain the phenomenon. Articles on why the most successful economies of the region—Hong Kong, Korea,

Reprinted with permission from the International Monetary Fund, *Growth in East Asia: What We Can and What We Cannot Infer,* Economic Issues, no. 1 (1996): 1–7, 11–22.

Singapore, and Taiwan Province of China—have grown, to say the least, robustly invariably refer to the phenomenon as "miraculous." When practitioners of the Dismal Science have recourse to a Higher Power, the reader knows that he is in trouble. Confusion is compounded when he discovers that ideological debate has multiplied even further the analyses of this phenomenon. Rather than swelling the torrent of interpretations, this paper sets for itself the modest agenda of reviewing the weightiest arguments in the literature that attempt to identify the reasons for the extraordinary economic growth in East Asia and trying to decide which arguments make sense. The exercise has value because finding the right explanation might suggest how to replicate this success elsewhere and, as a bonus, might also satisfy the reader's urge to solve an engaging intellectual puzzle. It is best if we start with the facts.

Since 1960, Asia, the largest and most populous of the continents, has become richer faster than any other region of the world. Of course, this growth has not occurred at the same pace all over the continent. The western part of Asia grew during this period at about the same rate as the rest of the world, but, as a whole, the eastern half (ten countries: China, Hong Kong, Indonesia, Japan, Korea, Malaysia, the Philippines, Singapore, Taiwan Province of China, and Thailand) turned in a superior performance, although variations in achievement can be observed here too. The worst performer was the Philippines, which grew at about 2 percent a year (in per capita terms), about equal to the average of non-Asian countries. China, Indonesia, Japan, Malaysia, and Thailand did better, achieving growth rates of 3–5 percent. This impressive achievement is, however, still modest compared with the phenomenal growth of Hong Kong, Korea, Singapore, and Taiwan Province of China, known as the "Four Tigers" because of their powerful and intimidating economic performance. The Tigers have had annual growth rates of output per person well in excess of 6 percent. These growth rates, sustained over a 30-year period, are simply amazing. While the average resident of a non-Asian country in 1990 was 72 percent richer than his parents were in 1960, the corresponding figure for the average Korean is no less than 638 percent.

This paper begins by looking at the long-running debate over the nature of growth. Is growth the result for the most part of an accumulation of manpower and machinery, or is it the result of employing the latest technology? The paper then looks at the growth record of the four countries from three other angles: the influence of government intervention, the extent to which investments and exports can be considered the main engines of growth, and the significance for sustained growth of the economic conditions prevailing at the very beginning of the countries' period of extended growth. The paper concludes with a few minimalist observations on possible areas for future study.

THE NATURE OF GROWTH: FACTOR
ACCUMULATION OR TECHNOLOGICAL PROGRESS

Everyone agrees that the economies of East Asia, and particularly the Four Tigers, have grown spectacularly over the past generation, but nobody seems to agree on why. The debate over why they have grown so well in the past raises difficult questions about regional growth in the future and about the aspiration of countries elsewhere to replicate the East Asian success. The arguments at the center of the debate are based on theoretical notions of growth accounting.

This accounting method deals with three elements that contribute to the production of goods and services: labor, capital, and technology. Labor and capital, known collectively as the "factors of production," refer in this context to the workforce and to the capital goods (buildings, machines, vehicles) that the workforce uses in manufacturing some product or providing some service. Technology refers to all the methods employed by labor and capital to produce a good and depends on the development or acquisition of practical skills to get the job done more quickly and more efficiently. No one denies that all three elements must be present to some degree if an economy is to grow. What is subject to debate is the contribution of the factors of production relative to that of technology. Some believe that increased use of labor and capital explain all growth; others are persuaded that the answer to growth lies in the use of more efficient technology.

Within the growth accounting framework it is possible to describe mathematically, using a simple equation, the contributions of these three elements to the overall production of an economy. By dividing the equation by the number of people in the workforce, one can derive a dynamic equation that shows how output per person increases over time. Such an equation mathematically describes the contribution to higher output of the growth rate of labor participation, of capital employed per person, and of technology (the latter also known as the growth of "total factor productivity"). If applied empirically to specific economies this equation can give a good idea of what proportion of increased output is a result of higher labor participation and better use of capital and what proportion is the result of technological progress.

The traditional formulation of this equation suggests that a significant and sustained rate of technological progress is the only possible way, over the long run, for an economy to achieve a sustained rate of growth in output per person. Why? The labor participation rate can be increased for a while and will increase production, but obviously it cannot increase indefinitely (everybody will ultimately be employed). And more growth in capital than in labor ultimately leads to diminishing returns to capital, resulting in a fall in the growth of output even if capital continues to grow at a constant rate.

Therefore, in order to achieve permanent growth, an economy must continuously improve its technology. This kind of growth is called "intensive growth." In contrast to intensive growth, increasing output by increasing inputs of labor and capital (extensive growth) can work only for a limited period, but it cannot last too long.

In a famous study, Solow (1956) conducted a growth accounting exercise such as the one described above. He found that accumulation of capital and an increase in the labor participation rate had a relatively minor effect, while technological progress accounted for most of the growth in output per person. Further studies have reconfirmed the validity of these conclusions. Accordingly, the standard view about the success of the East Asian countries emphasizes the role of technology in their high growth rates and focuses on the fast technological catch-up in these economies. In this view, these economies have succeeded because they learned to use technology faster and more efficiently than their competitors did.

A CONTRARIAN VIEW

The collapse of the Soviet Union in about 1990, after years of apparent economic success, caught most people by surprise. This collapse seemed to lend credence to the "extensive growth hypothesis," which argues that the Soviet Union, after many decades of extensive growth, ran into the inevitable diminishing returns effect, just as predicted in the growth accounting framework, because it had relied for its economic growth on a massive accumulation of capital and labor and had been slow to accept innovative technology. These developments in the economy of the Soviet Union served to raise concerns about other economies, including some East Asian countries, that have invested primarily in labor and capital rather than in technology over the past few decades. Krugman (1994) makes the comparison specific: "The newly industrializing countries of Asia, like the Soviet Union of the 1950s, have achieved rapid growth in large part through an astonishing mobilization of resources. Once one accounts for the role of rapidly growing inputs in these countries' growth, one finds little left to explain. Asian growth, like that of the Soviet Union in its high-growth era, seems to be driven by extraordinary growth in inputs like labor and capital rather than by gains in efficiency" (Krugman 1994).

Likewise, in explaining the extraordinary postwar growth of the Four Tigers, Young (1994b) concludes that "one arrives at total factor productivity growth rates, both for the nonagricultural economy and for manufacturing in particular, which are well within the bounds of those experienced by the OECD and Latin American economies over equally long periods of time. While the growth of output and manufacturing exports in the newly industrializing countries of East Asia is virtually unprecedented, the growth of total factor productivity in these countries is not" (Young 1994b).

In the same vein, Kim and Lau (1994), comparing the sources of economic growth in these countries with those of Germany, France, Japan, the United Kingdom, and the United States, found that "by far the most important source of economic growth in these countries [the Four Tigers] is capital accumulation, accounting for between 48 and 72 percent of their economic growth, in contrast to the case of the Group of Five industrialized countries, in which technical progress has played the most important role, accounting for between 46 and 71 percent of their economic growth" (Kim and Lau 1994).

The results of these studies are not only strikingly different from the view presented earlier of the primacy of technological progress, but they also convey a very pessimistic message. First, economic growth in the Four Tigers is hardly miraculous: it is just the expected outcome of a massive accumulation of labor and capital. Second, the progress of these economies along this growth path for the past 30 years cannot continue. Sooner or later they will experience a dramatic decrease in growth. Third, the societies in these countries made enormous sacrifices of consumption and leisure to achieve these growth rates. Therefore, even if their so-called success can be replicated in other countries, it is probably not wise to do so.

But how conclusive are these results? In fact, conclusions based on these studies are not very robust in that they are sensitive to the specific assumptions of each study.

The main reason for this sensitivity is the difficulty of estimating the rate of growth of capital stock in the East Asian countries during the period under study. Especially in the case of the Four Tigers, for which there are no good data before 1960, it is extremely difficult to estimate the capital stock at that time. To estimate how much capital was available in 1960, dubious assumptions have to be made about the depreciation rate of capital stock and about how much investment flowed in during the years of explosive growth beginning in 1960. What, for example, are the depreciation rates of different types of capital (buildings, industrial machinery, computers)? Are they equal for all countries and for all industries, or are they higher in faster-growing economies? What method is being used to estimate investment flows in the past?

Additional interpretational problems come from trying to estimate the share of national income attributable to capital and the share attributable to labor. Does the same amount of capital produce equal income in all countries and in all industries? Can statistics about the labor participation rate be trusted? Is the amount of effective work proportional to the hours that people work, or do working extra hours lead to diminishing returns?

Should different types of labor (factory, office) be summed together? How should human capital be treated?

Because of these unanswered and perhaps unanswerable questions, the results of studies that emphasize the contribution to growth of capital and labor and depreciate that of technology should not be regarded as definitive. They should be viewed as interesting, but only suggestive. . . .

Although the Four Tigers accumulated capital and increased labor participation at a much faster rate than other economies, the increase in these two factors far from fully explains their exceptional growth rates; growth in productivity attributable to innovative technology also accounts for a significant fraction. In the case of Hong Kong, Korea, and Taiwan Province of China, their growth rates of total factor productivity are as outstanding as their output growth rates. Productivity growth in Singapore is less spectacular, but is still much above the world average. As a percentage of the growth rates of output per person, the productivity growth rates in these four economies are roughly similar to those in Japan and the United States.

ROLE OF PUBLIC POLICY

As the foregoing consideration suggests, the labor and capital accumulation versus total factor productivity debate remains inconclusive. Can other factors shed light on the mystery of growth? One suggestion is to look at the role of government.

Lucas (1988) asked, "Is there some action a government of India could take that would lead the Indian economy to grow like Indonesia's or Egypt's? If so, what, exactly?" The importance of this question can hardly be exaggerated. A usable answer would be the academic equivalent of alchemy, turning the dross of everyday economics into pure gold. Accordingly, the highest ambition of economists who examine the East Asian success is to identify a set of public policies that has promoted economic growth there and gives promise of doing so elsewhere.

It should come as no surprise that opinions vary considerably about the effect of public policy and selective government interventions on stimulating economic growth. Exponents of these opinions fall into three schools. The first emphasizes the primacy of free markets. This school requires only that the government "get the basics right" and opposes any other kind of government intervention. (Getting the basics right means creating an environment in which the economy will thrive by, for example, making sure that the exchange rate reflects the economic fundamentals, that interest rates yield a positive return, that inflation is kept under control, and that taxes are not so burdensome as to discourage economic activity.) The second also embraces the view that the government get the basics right, but in addition advocates selective interventionist policies, particularly in developing countries. The third, somewhat agnostic, school denies the possibility of coming to any conclusion about the effects of public policy or of selective interventions on economic growth. The whole debate, according to this school, gets you nowhere.

FREE MARKETS

The first school, basing its views on what is known as the neoclassical approach to economics in general and to economic growth in particular, espouses an underlying belief in classical liberalism. The production possibilities of any economy at any time are determined, according to this view, by the availability of physical resources and of innovative technology. The rate of economic growth in the long run is determined by the rate of technological progress, which is itself a natural outcome of fierce competition in the laissez-faire economic system. Since it regards markets as efficient, this school maintains that government should confine itself to providing public goods (roads and bridges, police protection) and to getting the basics right and should abstain from any further intervention in the market.

This school wishes to restrict the role of government in the economy, but it is not anarchistic. It would assign to government both a microeconomic and a macroeconomic function. In its microeconomic aspect, government should ensure property rights, law and order, and adequate provision of public goods. It should avoid high tax rates, price controls, and other distortions of relative prices. On the macroeconomic side, government should ensure stable and low inflation, avoid excessive budget deficits, promote the integrity of the financial and banking system, provide for open markets, and strive for stable and realistic exchange rates.

Advocates of this view see the success of East Asia as the natural outcome of these cautious policies.

SELECTIVE INTERVENTION

The revisionist view does not share the neoclassical belief in the efficiency of markets. It asserts that, especially in the poorer countries, markets work imperfectly. In poor countries, production creates externalities (unintended undesirable effects, such as pollution), credit is limited, and the market is a melee in which foreign and domestic firms savage one another and the public through unfair trade practices. Accordingly, the revisionists recommend an activist government that will moderate the excesses of the market and assist the orderly development of the economy by acquiring technology and by allocating funds for useful projects that promise a good rate of return. De Long and Summers (1991) sum up this view: "The government should jump-start the industrialization process by transforming economic structure faster than private entrepreneurs would." Advocates of this view see the success of East Asia as confirming their conviction.

The revisionist view recognizes that the government must often choose firm-specific, highly complex, and nonuniform interventions. In extreme contradiction to the neoclassical doctrine, it allows, and even recommends, the active use of tax policy to manipulate relative prices in the economy. Even the World Bank (1993) report, after emphasizing the necessity of neoclassical "getting the basics right" policies in East Asia, concedes that "these fundamental policies do not tell the entire story. In each of these economies the government also intervened to foster development, often systematically and through multiple channels. Policy interventions took many forms: targeted and subsidized credit to selected industries, low deposit rates and ceilings on borrowing rates to increase profits and retained earnings, protection of domestic import substitutes, subsidies to declining industries, the establishment and financial support of government banks, public investment in applied research, firm- and industry-specific export targets, development of export marketing institutions, and wide sharing of information between public and private sectors" (World Bank 1993).

AGNOSTICISM

A third school, rejecting the claims of both the neoclassicists and the revisionists, claims that we can say nothing meaningful about selective interventions because we cannot properly identify how such policies spur economic growth. There are four reasons for this skepticism.

First, in analyzing "successful" policies, there is clear selection bias. Success has a thousand fathers; failure is an orphan. We know from the outset that the East Asian economies have been successful and that therefore government intervention did not inhibit growth. Consequently interventions in these economies are widely studied. On the other hand, since economists find unsuccessful economies much less attractive to study, they rarely look at government intervention in economies of this type. The selection of interventions to be analyzed is therefore skewed and is not scientifically neutral.

Second, in most cases it is impossible to offer a realistic counterfactual scenario. Would the Hawaiians have invented innovative igloos if it snowed a lot in Honolulu? Would the U.S. economy have grown faster if, like the Soviet Union, its government had turned Communist in 1917? In other words, in analyzing specific interventions, we cannot address the most (and perhaps the only) relevant question, "How fast would these economies have grown if these policies had not been in place?"

Third, public policy in the successful East Asian economies is far from homogeneous. Variation is large in the specific sectors and industries targeted for selective intervention in different countries. The more one examines the policies individual East Asian economies have pursued, the more evident it becomes how different, and indeed contradictory, these policies have been. Rodrik (1994), for example, remarks that the East Asian model encompasses highly interventionist strategies (Japan and Korea), as well as noninterventionist ones (Hong Kong and Thailand); explicitly redistributive policies (Malaysia), as well as distributionally neutral ones (most of the rest); clientelism (Indonesia and Thailand), as well as strong, autonomous states (Japan, Korea, Singapore); emphasis on large conglomerates (Korea), as well as on small, entrepreneurial firms (Taiwan). This range of strategies, all followed more or less successfully, suggests that the search for a simple explanation of the East Asian miracle may well be futile.

Fourth, determining the correct direction of causality is tricky. For instance, in successful economies one usually finds policies that encourage low fiscal deficits and good educational systems. Are these policies responsible for the success of the economy, or is the success of the economy responsible for the policies? Observing that a specific variable is present along with growth does not necessarily constitute proof that the policy generates growth. It might be the other way around. For example, it is much easier for a government to maintain a healthy fiscal position when the economy is growing and tax revenues are on the increase than when the economy is stagnant and demand is strong for deficit-creating social expenditures, such as unemployment compensation. Is a small deficit a result or is it a cause of economic growth? Conventional wisdom relates education to wealth. But which causes which? When an economy is booming, a government can afford generous subsidies for education. Moreover, the demand for education increases when an economy is growing and the population is becoming richer (it is unnecessary for children to start working at age 12). Furthermore, when an economy experiences rapid technological change, the advantage of educated over uneducated workers will be greater than when the economy is stagnant. Therefore there will be an increase in the demand for education by individuals who want a better job in the dynamic economy. In this case, by the way, further education constitutes an advantage for the specific individual relative to other individuals but does not necessarily improve the macroeconomic prospects of the economy.

These examples are presented not to prove that government policies are unimportant, but to make the modest point that we still understand very little about the relationship between public policy and the extraordinary growth rates of the East Asian economies. Other countries should be careful in trying to imitate the East Asian policies. Not understanding the causality between growth and industrialization, in particular, has proved to be a costly mistake for many poor countries that pushed for rapid industrialization in a futile effort to boost economic growth.

INVESTMENT AND EXPORTS: THE ENGINES OF GROWTH?

Among the many reasons suggested to account for the East Asian success, the investment rate and the export orientation of these economies enjoy enthusiastic support. These are often called "engines of growth" because their strength seems to be pulling the whole economy forward. Moreover, they appear to generate beneficial spillover effects for the rest of the economy. The policy implication of this view is obvious. If the hypothesis is valid, the government should jump start the engines of growth, and if certain sectors continue to contribute to economic progress, while others do not, then government should assist the economy's forward motion by promoting the "good" sectors. Therefore, it should encourage investments and exports, using such policy instruments as direct subsidies or preferential allocation of credit to promote these activities.

Main Arguments

The view that investments and exports are engines of growth is based on one empirical and one theoretical argument. The empirical argument is that most East Asian countries that experience phenomenal growth rates also enjoy impressive rates of investment and are successful exporters. The theoretical argument as regards investment is that a high investment rate increases the capital stock (things used to create wealth) and that this can permanently increase the growth rate through economies of scale (e.g., bigger, more efficient factories, larger markets) and other beneficial side effects. In the case of exports, the theoretical argument is that export orientation increases the openness of the economy and, by exposing it to foreign technology and foreign competition, provokes a rapid rate of technological progress.

What Is the Direction of Causality?

As stated above, a positive correlation between two variables (where one is found, the other is found) does not prove that one causes the other. In all the East Asian economies one can find export orientation and rapid technological progress. How are export orientation and technological progress related? The theoretical argument suggests that because a country is oriented to exporting, it becomes exposed to foreign technology: export orientation is the cause of technological advance. But the opposite might also be true, that technological advances cause export orientation. Suppose that some industries improve their technology and others do not. It is natural that industries with more advanced technology can compete in international markets and increase the quantity of their exports. In this case, the data will reveal a strong correlation between export performance and the rate of technological progress across industries. Likewise, developing countries that are better in learning and applying advanced foreign technology will enjoy an advantage in world markets and be able to sell their products abroad.

Investment rates (or equivalently, saving rates) appear to have a causal relationship to growth rates (i.e., saving causes growth). Nevertheless, a strong argument of reversed causality can be made even in this case. A study by Carroll and Weil (1994), examining data on savings and investment within households in various countries, found, in fact, that growth causes saving, but saving does not cause growth. Using these data, they discovered that households whose income is on the rise save more than households that experience little or no growth in income, a finding that represents a powerful reinterpretation of the growth-saving relationship. The study also offers from its findings a theoretical explanation that recognizes savers as creatures of habit. Although their incomes may be growing, households will respond slowly to their expanding wealth and will increase their consumption only gradually, with the effect that they save more. In this case, increased saving rates are caused by increased growth rates, and not vice versa.

Initial Conditions

The main empirical argument that a high rate of investment and a concentration on exporting have caused economic growth is the strong positive correlation between these two variables and the rates of growth found in the East Asian economies. In particular, the Four Tigers, the best performing economies in the region, display exceptional investment rates and an extremely high degree of openness (that is, they have a lot of exports and imports relative to the size of the economy). The section above stressed the problem of possible reverse causality between growth and these variables. A further problem is that of averages. Most studies observe a correlation between investment and exporting that are averaged over a period and a rate of growth that is averaged over the same period. Using averages over a period obscures the relation between the variables. A simple partial solution to disentangling the skein of causality is to observe the values of the explanatory variables at the beginning of the period rather than to take their average values over the period. Finding, for example, that economies with high growth rates during the 1960–90 period had very high investment rates or a significant export orientation around 1960 would go a long way toward solving the problem of reverse causality.

An examination of the dynamics of the investment rate and the openness of the economies of Hong Kong, Korea, Singapore, and Taiwan Province of China that compares the 1960 levels of these variables in the Four Tigers with those in other countries does not offer much support for the view that export orientation and investment have been engines of growth. The comparison of the 1960 investment rates of the four economies with the investment rates of 100 other economies clearly rejects the view that investment rates were high in the Four Tigers in 1960. Not only were the investment rates in these economies low in absolute values, but they were very modest even when compared with rates in other countries with a comparable level of income.

The same comparative exercise can be performed to test for openness (imports and exports as a percentage of GDP), taking into consideration such factors as the geographical size of the country, an important variable in determining the degree of openness of an economy. Small countries need to trade more than large countries with big internal markets. Reflecting this, Hong Kong and Singapore show a high degree of openness both during 1960–90 and at the beginning of the same period. On the other hand, Korea and Taiwan Province of China, which are geographically much larger, were not particularly open in 1960, either in absolute terms or relative to other countries of comparable size.

This analysis demonstrates that high investment rates and a large degree of openness were certainly not a general feature of the Four Tigers in 1960. The high investment rates (Korea, Singapore, and Taiwan Province of China) and the high degree of openness (Korea and Taiwan Province of China) were economic features that evolved in these economies only gradually, accompanying rather than preceding the process of economic growth. The conclusion is that the view of these activities as engines of growth does not find much support in the data.

Some Positive Evidence Regarding Initial Conditions

Were there other variables that characterized the initial conditions in the East Asian countries and, if so, what contribution might they have made to the subsequent growth of these economies? A study by Rodrik in 1994 examined precisely this question. It was inspired by the view that "In searching for the secrets of the East Asian miracle, the obvious place to look is the set of initial conditions that precede economic take-off." Examining the initial conditions, the study finds that, in certain important respects, they were very different from what one would expect, given the income level of these economies.

Tracing average growth of income per person in 41 countries during 1960–85 back to initial conditions in 1960, Rodrik shows that countries that were poorer, but that had good primary education systems and less inequality of income and land distribution around 1960, grew faster than the others during the following period. The study compares actual data on education and demographics (fertility rate and mortality rate) in eight East Asian countries with the predicted values we would expect, given their initial income, and compared inequality of income and land ownership around 1960 with the same characteristics of other developing countries at a comparable income level. The results show strong evidence that in terms of initial conditions (equality of land and income, school enrollment, high life expectancy and low fertility rates), the eight East Asian countries were significantly better off than countries with similar levels of income. These findings raise the possibility (but do not prove) that these initial conditions may help explain the phenomenal growth rates we observed in East Asia after 1960.   *NON-ECON*

The empirical evidence presented by Rodrik regarding the possible influence of initial conditions in explaining the East Asian miracle is impressive but should be accepted with caution because of the small number of observations. Data on initial conditions in 1960, especially for developing countries, are rare and are of questionable quality. While Rodrik's results suggest a possible explanation for the East Asian success, they are not robust enough to rule out other possibilities. Furthermore, it is not clear what the normative implications of these findings are. For example, suppose that land equality is indeed beneficial for economic growth. Does that mean that land redistribution is a good policy to promote growth? Not necessarily. The redistribution may be extremely damaging by weakening property rights or disrupting political stability, which are obviously essential to growth. Likewise, lowering fertility rates by government decree may be bad for growth, even if low fertility rates are found to be good for growth.

CONCLUDING REMARKS

The recent literature on the East Asian growth experience has sparked an intense intellectual debate. This study has attempted to review critically the main arguments in this debate, covering some of its most important dimensions. Inevitably, other important dimensions did not receive fair representation, such as theories about nonmonotonic dynamics of growth (in which middle-income countries can take off and grow faster than either rich or poor countries) and about the importance of the geographical concentration of growth successes (why is East Asia the habitat of all Four Tigers?).   *culture*

The study does not offer clear and conclusive results nor does it make clear policy recommendations. Its main judgment is that, from a positive point of view, a promising avenue for the explanation of growth performance is the examination of initial conditions. Nevertheless, from a normative point of view, it is far from clear what specific policies governments should pursue, beyond the standard set of policies aimed at getting the basics right.

REFERENCES

Carroll, Christopher D., and David N. Weil, "Saving and Growth: A Reinterpretation," Carnegie-Rochester Conference Series on Public Policy, Vol. 40 (1994), pp. 133–92.

De Long, J. Bradford, and Lawrence H. Summers, "Equipment Investment and Economic Growth," *Quarterly Journal of Economics,* No. 106 (May 1991), pp. 445–502.

Kim, Jong-Il, and Lawrence J. Lau, "The Sources of Economic Growth of the East Asian Newly Industrialized Countries," *Journal of the Japanese and International Economies,* Vol. 8 (1994), pp. 235–71.

Krugman, Paul, "The Myth of Asia's Miracle," *Foreign Affairs,* Vol. 73 (November–December 1994), pp. 62–78.

Lucas, Robert E., Jr., "On the Mechanics of Economic Development," *Journal of Monetary Economics,* No. 22 (July 1988), pp. 3–42.

Rodrik, Dani, "King Kong Meets Godzilla: The World Bank and the East Asian Miracle," Chapter 1 in *Miracle or Design? Lessons from the East Experience,* ed. by Albert Fishlow and others (Washington: Overseas Development Council, 1994).

Solow, Robert M., "A Contribution to the Theory of Economic Growth," *Quarterly Journal of Economics,* No. 70 (1956), pp. 65–94.

World Bank, *The East Asian Miracle: Economic Growth and Public Policy,* Summary (New York: Oxford University Press, 1993).

Young, Alwyn, "Tale of Two Cities: Factor Accumulation and Technical Change in Hong Kong and Singapore," *NBER Economics Annual* (1992), pp. 13–54.

———, "Lessons from the East Asian NICs: A Contrarian View," *European Economic Review,* No. 38 (April 1994a), pp. 964–73.

———, "Tyranny of Numbers: Confronting the Statistical Realities of the East Asian Growth Experience," *NBER Working Paper,* No. 4680 (March 1994b).

33

·······

Inequality as a Constraint
on Growth in Latin America

·······

NANCY BIRDSALL & RICHARD SABOT

This chapter presents strong evidence that inequality and slow growth in the Third World are not inevitable but are the direct outcome of choices made by governments. The chapter contrasts Latin America, where growth has been slow and inequality high, with East Asia, where growth has been extremely rapid and inequality very low. The empirical research on which the chapter is based demonstrates that large investments in education in East Asia help to explain a "virtuous circle" that leads to both higher growth and greater equality, whereas the low and stagnating investment in education in Latin America creates an opposite "vicious circle." Human capital investment is what sets East Asia apart from Latin America, a lesson many developing countries need to learn.

The conventional wisdom has been that there is a tradeoff between augmenting growth and reducing inequality, so that an unequal distribution of income is necessary for, or the likely consequence of, rapid economic growth. If this is so, however, why do we find in Latin America relatively low rates of economic growth and high inequality, and in East Asia low inequality and rapid growth? Figure 33.1 shows rates of GNP growth for the period 1965 to 1989 and levels of income inequality in the mid-1980s (measured by the ratio of the income shares of the top and bottom quintiles) for Latin American and East Asian countries. The difference between the two regions is striking: Latin American countries, concentrated in the

Reprinted from *Development Policy,* Inter-American Development Bank, vol. 3, no. 3 (September 1994):1–5.

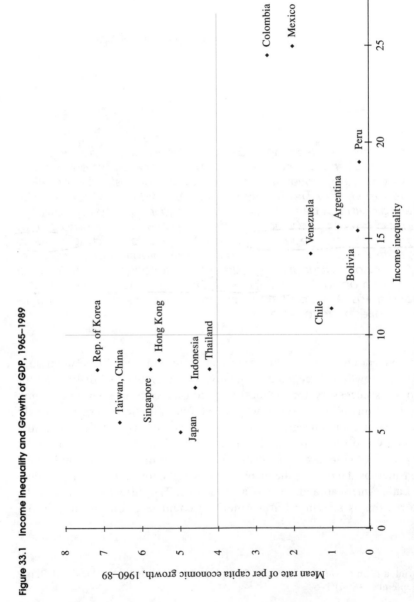

Figure 33.1 Income Inequality and Growth of GDP, 1965-1989

Mean rate of per capita economic growth, 1960-89

Income inequality

Source: World Bank, 1993. *The East Asian Miracle: Econmic Growth and Public Policy.*

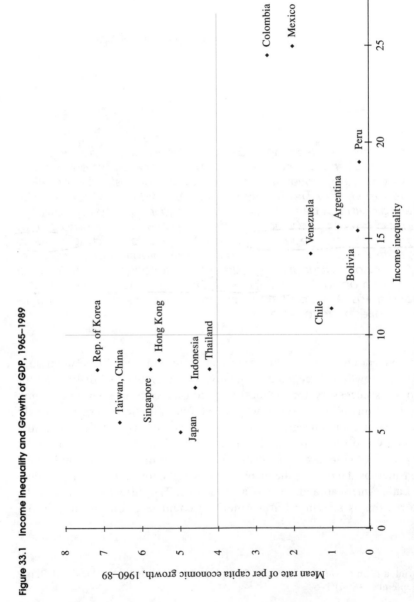

southeast corner, experienced slow or negative growth with high inequality, while East Asian countries, concentrated in the northwest corner, achieved rapid growth with low inequality.

Differences in the political economy of the two regions may be part of the explanation. In the postwar period, governing elites in East Asia, their legitimacy threatened by domestic communist insurgents, sought to widen the base of their political support via policies such as land reform, public housing, investment in rural infrastructure, and, most common, widespread high-quality basic education. In Latin America governing elites appear to have believed they could thrive irrespective of what happened to those with the lowest incomes since tax, expenditure, and trade policies benefitted the poor relatively little. For example, East Asia's export oriented, labor-demanding development strategy contributed to rapid growth of output and, by increasing employment opportunities and wages, ensured that the benefits of that growth were widely shared. In contrast, Latin America's strategy tended to be biased against both agriculture and exports, resulting in relatively slow growth in the demand for labor. . . .

The association of slow growth and high inequality in Latin America could in part be due to the fact that high inequality itself may be a constraint on growth. Conversely, East Asia's low level of inequality may have been a significant stimulus to economic growth. If so, investment in education is a key to a sustained growth not only because it contributes directly through productivity effects, but also because it reduces income inequality.

ECONOMETRIC RESULTS

To assess the impact of the distribution of income on subsequent economic growth we regressed the growth rate of real per capita income of 74 developing countries over the period 1960–85 on determinants of growth such as per capita GDP and education enrollments at the start of the period and on a measure of income inequality, the ratio of the income shares of the top 40 percent and the bottom 20 percent. We found that inequality and growth are in fact inversely related: countries with higher inequality tend to have lower growth.

How big a constraint on growth is high inequality? It is substantial. The results suggest that ceteris paribus, after 25 years, GDP per capita would be 8.2 percent higher in a country with low inequality than in a country with inequality one standard deviation higher. How big was the constraint of high inequality in Latin America? The ratio of the income shares of the top 20 percent to the bottom 20 percent is 26 in Brazil and 8 in Korea. Simulations suggest that if, in 1960, Brazil had had Korea's lower level of inequality Brazil's predicted growth rate over the following 25 years would have been 0.66 percentage points higher each year. This implies that after 25 years GDP per capita in Brazil would have been 17.2 percent higher.

POOR EDUCATIONAL PERFORMANCE, SLOW GROWTH, AND HIGH INEQUALITY IN LATIN AMERICA

Differences in educational performance help to explain why Latin America experienced relatively low rates of growth and high inequality while East Asia experienced high rates of growth and low inequality. Most countries in East Asia have significantly higher primary and secondary enrollment rates than predicted based on their per capita income; most Latin American countries have rates at or below those predicted. Moreover, where enrollment rates are low, as in Brazil and Guatemala, children of the poor are the least likely to be enrolled, perpetuating high income inequality.

Furthermore, in contrast to East Asia, where increases in quantity were associated with improvements in the quality of education, expansion of enrollments in many Latin American countries has resulted in the erosion of quality. In Brazil, the expansion of primary school coverage has been associated with declines in completion rates—probably a sign of failure to raise quality. By contrast, in East Asian countries, as quantity increased completion rates remained high. Declines in quality also tend to hurt the poor most, since they are least able to use private schools or change residence.

EDUCATION AND GROWTH

Human capital theory says that education augments cognitive and other skills of individuals which, in turn, augment their productivity as workers. Our growth rate functions show that this accumulation of skills at the individual level translates into higher economic growth at the country level. Our statistical work also shows that increasing primary-school enrollments for girls, though they are less likely to become formal workers, is just as effective in stimulating growth as increasing primary enrollments for boys.

The reason: the economic payoff to educating girls is not confined to increases in the productivity of wage labor. It works through changes in behavior within households. For example, educated mothers have fewer children. Closing a virtuous circle, the fertility decline in East Asia that started in the mid-1960s resulted in a marked slowing of the growth of the school-age population in the 1970s. This made it easier to increase public expenditures on basic education per child, permitting rapid increases in the quantity of schooling as well as improvements in the quality of schools. . . .

Although fertility rates in Latin America have declined during the past two decades, they remain high relative to East Asian rates, particularly in the poorer countries. High fertility has placed added stress on already strained resources for education; per child spending on books, equipment, and teacher training in Latin America has declined. Declines in per-child spending in the region (from an estimated $164 per primary school child in 1980 to $118 in 1989) have probably contributed to declines in school quality and continued high repetition—the highest in the world—and high dropout rates. Between 1970 and 1990 expenditure on basic education per eligible child increased by 350 percent in Korea and 64 percent in Mexico. During the same period, the number of eligible children increased by 59 percent in Mexico, in Korea the number of eligible children actually declined by 27 percent. . . .

In addition, Latin America missed out on the positive feedback between rapid growth and household behavior with respect to human-capital accumulation. Investment in human capital by households is greater in East Asia than in Latin America in part because the demand for educated workers is greater, and consequently the returns to the household of invest-ment in schooling are higher. In other words, stronger demand for educated workers elicits a greater supply. Furthermore, rapid economic growth in East Asia increased the numerator, while declining fertility reduced the denominator, of the ratio of public expenditures on basic education per school-age child. Neither in 1960 nor in 1989 was public expenditure on education as a percentage of GNP much higher in East Asia than in Latin America. However, it is obvious that the more rapid the growth of aggregate output, the more rapid the growth of the constant share of GDP that goes to education.

EDUCATION AND INEQUALITY

In Korea the proportion of high school and postsecondary graduates in the wage-labor force sharply increased between the mid-1970s and the mid-1980s, and the proportion of workers with elementary schooling or less declined to just 8 percent. As a consequence, the wage premium earned by educated workers in Korea declined. In Brazil the increment to the labor force of relatively well-educated workers was so small that it did not take much of an increase in the demand for educated workers to offset any wage compression effect of the increase in supply. As a result, the educational structure of wages barely changed in Brazil. What would the inequality of pay in Brazil have been had educational policy resulted in educational attainment comparable to that in Korea in the mid-1980s? Simulations indi-cate that Brazil would have had a log variance of wages in the mid-1980s some 17 percent lower than the actual. This 17 percent reduction represents over one-quarter of the gap between Brazil and Korea in the log variance of wages.

In Latin America there has also been a feedback effect, one that closed a vicious circle from high inequality to low enrollment rates. High income inequality limits household demand for education among the poor. Poor families may want to keep children in school, but they cannot afford to do so because they do not have money for school clothes or books or because they need children to work. Unable to borrow, poor households thus do not invest in their children's education even if they know that the benefits would be great. The pressing need to use income simply to subsist crowds out this high-return investment and reduces society's demand for education. High inequality makes this problem worse. For example, while the per capita income of Brazil (in 1983) slightly exceeded average income in Malaysia (in 1987) the bottom quintile received 4.6 percent of total income in Malaysia but only 2.4 percent of total income in Brazil. The per capita income of the poorest households in Brazil was thus only half the income of the poorest in Malaysia. Given an income elasticity of demand for basic education of 0.50 if the distribution of income were as equal in Brazil as in Malaysia, enrollments among poor Brazilian children would be more than 40 percent higher.

THE DIRECT EFFECT OF INEQUALITY ON GROWTH

Our results indicate that low inequality stimulates growth independent of its effects through education. However, using income transfers to reduce income inequality is unlikely to be good for growth: transfers often result in the diversion of scarce savings from investment to the subsidization of consumption; the targeted group is often not the one to benefit from transfers, reducing their effectiveness as a means of raising the standard of living, and hence the savings and investment rates, of the poor; transfers tend to distort incentives and reduce both allocative efficiency and X efficiency. But policies that increase the productivity and earning capacity of the poor may be quite a different matter.

Consider four ways in which low inequality can be a stimulus to growth:

- by inducing large increases in the savings and investments of the poor
- by contributing to political and macroeconomic stability—for example by reducing the tendency for fiscal prudence to be sacrificed to political expediency, by discouraging inappropriate exchange rate valuation, and by accelerating the adjustment to macroeconomic

- by increasing the "X-efficiency" of low-income workers, and
- by raising rural incomes, which limits intersectoral income gaps and the rent seeking associated with them, while increasing the domestic multiplier effects of a given increase in per capita income.

CONCLUSION

The contrasting experiences of Latin America and East Asia suggest that, contrary to conventional wisdom, inequalities in the distribution of both education and income may have a significant and negative impact on the rate of economic growth. The unequal distribution of education in Latin America, in terms of both quantity and quality, constrained economic growth in the region by forestalling opportunities to increase labor productivity and change household behavior. At the same time, the relatively small size of the educated labor force and high scarcity rents of the more educated contributed to high inequality in the distribution of income. Closing a vicious circle, slower growth and high income inequality, in turn, further limited the supply of, and demand for, education.

Education policy alone, however, does not explain the marked differences in equity and growth between Latin America and East Asia. Macroeconomic and sectoral policies in the former, which favored capital-intensive production and were biased against the agricultural sector, almost certainly exacerbated the inequality problem and have hindered growth as well. The East Asian development strategy promoted instead a dynamic agricultural sector and a labor-demanding, export-oriented growth path, thereby reducing inequality and stimulating growth. In East Asia low inequality not only contributes to growth indirectly, for example, by increasing investment in education, but appears to have had a direct positive effect on the growth rate.

The experience of the two regions is sufficient to reject the conventional wisdom of a necessary link between high income inequality and rapid growth. While our analysis has not been sufficient to confirm the opposite, we hope others will now seriously consider the hypothesis that high inequality, and policies that ignore or even exacerbate inequality, constrain growth in the long run. The challenge in Latin America is to find ways to reduce inequality, not by transfers, but by eliminating consumption subsidies for the rich and increasing the productivity of the poor.

34

· · · · · · ·

Growth and the Environment: Allies or Foes?

· · · · · · ·

Vinod Thomas & Tamara Belt

In this chapter, Vinod Thomas and Tamara Belt note the successes of East Asian countries in their rates of economic expansion and relatively low levels of income inequality. The countries, however, have emphasized economic expansion at the expense of severe environmental losses. Thomas and Belt note that nine of the world's fifteen most polluted cities are in East Asia. Although economic growth is not the lone culprit in environmental destruction—witness Central America's environmental devastation without economic growth comparable to that of East Asia's—it does appear to worsen environmental problems. Citing the higher costs of cleaning up pollution once it has occurred, the potential for permanent losses in terrestrial and aquatic biodiversity, and increased health costs, the authors suggest that preliminary environmental experiments in environmentally sensitive economic growth initiatives should be conducted.

Over the past quarter of a century, economic growth per capita in the southeast part of East Asia—Indonesia, Malaysia, Singapore, and Thailand—averaged 5 percent a year. Socioeconomic well-being improved enormously. In Indonesia, Malaysia, and Thailand, the percentage of the population living below the poverty line is estimated to have declined by some 50–70 percent. Starting from even earlier periods, Hong Kong, Japan, Korea, Singapore, and Taiwan Province of China made dramatic economic gains. Over the past decade and a half China experienced very high growth rates and a sharp reduction in poverty.

At the same time, environmental losses in East Asia have surpassed in

Reprinted with permission from *Finance and Development*, June 1997.

many respects those of other regions. For example, 9 of the world's 15 cities with the highest levels of particulate air pollution are in this region. About 20 percent of land covered by vegetation suffers from soil degradation owing to waterlogging, erosion, and overgrazing at levels above world averages. Fifty to 75 percent of coastlines and marine protected areas are classified as areas with highly threatened biodiversity, and the region has witnessed some of the highest deforestation rates in the world.

One lesson is that rapid growth can be a great ally of poverty reduction when supported by certain policy fundamentals. In East Asia these have included substantial and efficient investments in education, a relatively good income and asset distribution, a labor-intensive export orientation, and an emphasis on agricultural development. A second lesson, however, is that rapid growth has come at the expense of the environment. Rapid growth does not automatically improve the environment—environmental policies must also be put in place.

To be sure, many growth-inducing policies, such as clarifying property rights, investing in sanitation, improving education (especially for girls), and sound economic policies, help to improve resource use and contribute to a better environment. But in crucial areas, such as the control of pollution or sustainable forest use, environmental actions such as imposing taxes and standards, investing in technology, improving production methods, and recycling are necessary. Rapidly growing economies are learning this lesson the hard way and some are now taking corrective actions.

It is also interesting to focus on Central America. For a variety of economic and sociopolitical reasons, the Central American economies have grown slowly in recent decades, although their potential for sustainable development remains high. An exception is Costa Rica, a country with a strong record in promoting human development. But, more generally, the economies of Central America have been dominated by traditional exports, which have faced declining terms of trade; by a highly unequal income distribution; and by inadequate educational investments—all exacerbated by political instability. Costa Rica remains a notable exception. Because growth rates have been low, poverty levels have remained stubbornly high—as in other regions with slow growth. Environmental quality has deteriorated—there are large deforested areas, soil degradation, overfishing, and polluted water in coastal zones.

The experiences of East Asia and Central America show that both slow- and fast-growing economies can suffer from severe environmental degradation. The question then is whether, with the right priorities and policies, the environment can be protected irrespective of the pace of growth.

Growth per se is not to be blamed for environmental degradation, but, in some respects, rapid growth appears to make the problem worse. When the sources of environmental problems—underpriced resources (forests, water, or air), weak institutions, and unclear property rights—are not addressed adequately, rapid growth seems to aggravate them. However, growth and high incomes can mitigate environmental degradation and improve resource use if accompanied by timely environmental actions.

GROW FIRST AND CLEAN UP LATER?

The human and ecological costs of environmental deterioration have been widely studied. In many instances, convincing evidence is available of the large social gains from environmental actions. And yet, environmental actions have been inadequate. The literature has emphasized a basic reason: the divergence between what is beneficial to society and what is beneficial for the private individual. When coupled with the lack of resources at low income levels, the pattern worldwide has been to grow first and clean up later.

Experience that calls this approach into question is accumulating. For one thing, it is a costly strategy socially and ecologically, and might threaten the sustainability of growth itself. Furthermore, new institutional arrangements, technologies, production methods, and targeted investments are beginning to offer opportunities to address growth and environmental protection in ways that are good for government finances as well as for private business.

The Higher Costs of Cleaning Up Later

Ecological damage is often irreversible. Cleaning up later is not an option, when terrestrial and aquatic biodiversity has been lost because of habitat destruction. For example, pollution and destructive fishing techniques have damaged a large proportion of coral reefs in some areas. As up to one-fourth of all marine species and one-fifth of known marine fish species live in coral reef ecosystems, the loss of reef habitats disproportionately threatens a high percentage of the ocean's plant and animal life. Complete reversal of this damage is unlikely; therefore, efforts need to focus on preserving global biological resources before they are damaged.

Environmental pollution causes considerable health costs, which are compounded when pollution control is postponed. Some of the evidence comes from widely publicized episodes—for example, mercury poisoning from a manufacturing firm in Minamata, Japan, resulting in severe neurological afflictions ("Minamata Disease") for people in the area since the mid-1950s, or exposure to toxic materials causing acute illness or death as in the Bhopal, India, tragedy of 1984. Other evidence, even if less visible, is widely prevalent, such as the steady health losses to children and adults from air pollution.

The cost is usually far less than the benefits to society of investing in pollution control. In this regard, an ounce of prevention is worth a pound of cure. It is usually cheaper to control pollution at its source through policy reforms, especially by removing subsidies, than by investing in pollution control later.

Better Use of Resources

With proper concern for the environment, scarce resources can be put to high-return and sustainable uses. For example, in parts of Southeast Asia, uplands can be used for sustainable planting of fruit trees or other perennials rather than for planting maize or cassava for a few years and then abandoning cultivation as yields decline. Similarly, in areas of Latin America, forests can be protected for their higher social value rather than converted to ranches that generate negative returns. And in many cases, putting a resource to multiple uses generates a large net benefit. For example, management of tropical forests for multiple uses that include nontimber goods, water and soil conservation, biological diversity, and other environmental services, as well as timber, could generate higher social returns as well as revenue.

Bringing in Revenue

Applying pollution taxes, in addition to inducing lower emissions and better conservation of resources, can raise revenues that allow governments to scale back more distortionary forms of taxation. In Thailand, for example, a 10 percent tax on the coal and lignite used in manufacturing could yield a return of 1 to 2 percent of government revenue. The cost of such a tax is usually a fraction of the estimated health benefits it helps to produce.

It's Good Business

Finally, there is the economy-wide link between a country's competitiveness and the environment. In one direction, trade liberalization without environmental policies makes the environment more vulnerable. The higher prices for forest resources resulting from trade liberalization can lead to excessive deforestation if property rights are unclear and logging rights fail to incorporate the resource costs. In the other direction, trade liberalization can increase the profitability of industries that have environmental safeguards in place.

HOW CAN IT BE DONE?

Although the record is limited, innovative approaches in East Asia and Latin America offer the promise of growth with sustainable resource use.

To take one example, a coalition of conservation and research organizations in El Salvador developed an ecolabeling initiative, ECO-OK, to give coffee farmers the incentives and information to produce coffee in an eco-friendly way. The program simultaneously raises awareness and motivates consumers to seek products from socially and environmentally responsible farms. ECO-OK products meet environmental standards that protect rainforests, workers, and wildlife.

User Charges and Tradable Resource Rights

Experience with market-based instruments and regulations, notwithstanding the obstacles to their enforcement, illustrates the range of policies that are possible and widens the debate on options. In East Asia, considerable progress has been made in removing subsidies on gasoline, diesel, and kerosene. In Latin America, there are several examples of the application of market-based instruments (see Table 34.1). Some have been ineffective in achieving their full objectives as a result of institutional weaknesses such as under-funding, unclear jurisdiction, monitoring requirements, and legal design requirements. Nevertheless, there are some promising examples:

- *Resource user charges.* Brazil, Colombia, and Venezuela charge a forestry tax when tree harvesting is not compensated by equivalent reforestation. So far the taxes have been set at too low a level, and enforcement has been weak; nonetheless, the principle is sound
- *Joint Implementation agreements.* Central America is relatively advanced in the creation of agreements for carbon sequestration through forest protection under Joint Implementation programs. Costa Rica has just initiated such an agreement with Norway. The development of such agreements will depend in part on an emerging international consensus, but initial activities are promising.

Participation and Community Involvement

Where institutions are weak or enforcement is expensive, public participation and community involvement can be effective in enforcing sustainable resource use and adapting local conditions to development needs. Traditional communities have known and used this approach for ages. It could be strengthened for today's market economy, as evidenced in Japan. The local government and resident groups in Japan negotiate with firms to arrive at a detailed written agreement on emissions levels. Between 1971 and 1991, the number of agreements increased from approximately 2,000 to 37,000. Once standards were agreed upon, they were effectively implemented. This consensual approach benefits local governments, residents, and companies alike.

Table 34.1 Protecting the Environment: Application of Market-Based Instruments in Latin America

	Credit Subsidies	Tax/Tariff Relief	Deposit-Refund Schemes	Waste Fees and Levies	Forestry Taxation	Pollution Charges	Earmarked Renewable Resource Taxes	Earmarked Conventional Tax Levy	Tradable Permits	Eco-labeling	Liability Insurance
Barbados	✔		✔	✔							✔
Bolivia	✔	✔	✔	✔	✔					✔	✔
Brazil	✔	✔	✔	✔	✔	✔	✔	✔	*	✔	
Chile	✔	✔	✔	✔	✔	✔	✔	✔		✔	✔
Colombia		✔	✔	✔							
Ecuador	✔	✔	✔	✔		✔	✔			✔	
Jamaica			✔	✔		*	✔				
Mexico	✔		✔	✔		✔		✔	*	✔	✔
Peru			✔								
Trinidad & Tobago	✔	✔	✔	✔	✔						
Venezuela		✔	✔								

✔ in place
* under introduction

Source: Richard M. Huber, Jack Rultenbeak, and Ronaldo Saron de Motta, 1996, "Market Based Instruments for Environmental Policymaking in Latin America and the Caribbean," World Bank, Washington.

Mainstreaming Environmental Concerns

A crucial approach involves mainstreaming environmental concerns in national plans and policies. This means that the environmental consequences of actions pursued by finance and planning, as well as environmental, ministries are made explicit within core economic policies. In some countries innovative approaches to confront environmental problems are beginning to be applied. Mainstreaming them would mean that these options are put on the table at the time key fiscal, trade, and industrial policies are discussed. Their benefits and costs would be revealed, providing the basis to pursue the best approaches.

Inserting the environment into policymaking can produce much stronger results for economic growth and environmental sustainability than responding to individual environmental concerns along the way. Practical ways to do this are beginning to emerge, and there would be great benefit from disseminating them. More generally, integrating environmental awareness in education programs, especially at the early stages, and influencing values and behavior would be a fundamental step in mainstreaming environmental concerns.

UNCERTAINTIES

Tough questions remain with respect to both policy choices and the implementation of environmental actions. Win-win policy choices (for example, reducing energy subsidies to benefit both economic performance and the environment) should be relatively easy for the policymaker to make. Pushing ahead with them should therefore be a high priority. But even in this case, there will be winners and losers from the changes, requiring the policymaker to manage the political economy of reforms.

Policy choices involving trade-offs to the policymaker are more difficult to make, even if society would benefit on balance (for example, financial investments for pollution control that produce net gains in health and welfare). This difficulty is compounded if the benefits accrue later and especially if future benefits involve uncertainty, or if some of the benefits accrue to the rest of the world (for example, part of the gains from biodiversity from the protection of forests). Financial constraints make the decision hard to take even if it is socially beneficial.

Higher incomes eventually contribute to the demand for a more sustainable environment, especially in the so-called "brown" areas such as urban pollution. Higher incomes also provide the resources to help address the problem. However, this chain of events is particularly delayed in the case of the "green" dimensions of the environment, which faces severe deterioration in the early phases of rapid growth. And they also involve unacceptable thresholds of degradation, and irreversible losses, such as bio-diversity. Protecting the "green" aspects during rapid growth remains a tough challenge.

Countries' institutional capacity to make, implement, and enforce difficult decisions is a key consideration. Even the best solutions require the support of well-functioning markets and property rights. Where trade-offs are involved, additional measures to align the social and private benefits (through taxes, quotas, investments, etc.) are needed. When the benefits go beyond individual countries, financial and institutional arrangements across borders might be called for.

These dilemmas need to be reorganized. Clearly, priorities have to be set, resource limits acknowledged, and systemic processes put in place to help make tough choices. There is a growing body of experience on how innovative approaches can help address trade-offs and institutional rigidities. Meanwhile, the evidence on the high costs of not taking these measures is mounting.

CONCLUSION

In the main, the experience of rapidly growing countries has been to grow first and clean up later. However, this neglect of the environment has resulted in irreversible losses and high cleanup costs. Current experiences and policies, even if limited, demonstrate that it is possible to protect the environment, promote growth, and enhance competitiveness at the same time. Most developing countries can benefit from both the positive and the negative lessons of rapid growth elsewhere. If they can take economic and environmental actions now, they could become the "green tigers" of the future.

REFERENCES

Esty, Daniel. 1997. "Environmental Protection During the Transition to a Market Economy," in Wing Woo, Steven Parker, and Jeffrey Sachs, eds., *Economies in Transition, Asia and Europe*. Cambridge, Massachusetts: MIT Press.

Hammer, Jeffrey S., and Sudhir Shetty. 1995. "East Asia's Environment," *World Bank Discussion Paper No. 287*. Washington, D.C.

Steer, Andrew. 1996. "Ten Principles of New Environmentalism," *Finance and Development*. December.

World Resources Institute. UNEP, UNDP, and World Bank. 1996. *World Resources, 1996–97*. New York: Oxford University Press.

PART 7

. . . .

Conclusion

. . . .

35

. . . .

Inequality in a Global Perspective: Directions for Further Research

. . . .

MITCHELL A. SELIGSON

The fact that a vast gap exists between the world's rich and its poor is beyond dispute. The causes and dynamics of the gap, however, are the subject of considerable debate, as the reader of this book now knows. Fortunately, the debate over the gap between rich and poor differs considerably from the pattern normally encountered in the social sciences—debates that rarely lead to the development of a cumulative body of knowledge. Indeed, research in this area represents one of the best illustrations of a cumulative social science continually deepening its understanding of a complex problem. In this concluding chapter, I suggest some directions for future research so continued rapid progress can be made in our understanding of the problem.

EVOLUTION OF RESEARCH ON THE GAPS

Once it became clear that the post–World War II hopes for rapid, universal development in the Third World were not going to be fulfilled, social scientists set to determining why that was the case. It was obvious, then as now, that unless development in the Third World were to surge ahead, the gap between these economies and those of the increasingly prosperous developed countries would inevitably widen. The serious implications of this situation for world peace are too great to ignore.

Early thinking focused on the cultural distinctiveness of the Third World. The observation that these cultures were indeed different from those found in the First World of industrial, capitalist development was enough to convince a generation of social scientists to view cultural barriers as the principal explanation for underdevelopment. Many of those explanations were extraordinarily intriguing, showed creative scholarship, and, moreover, seemed to make a good deal of sense.

As research proceeded, however, disenchantment with this perspective began to grow. The more that was known about the Third World, the less that cultural factors seemed to explain its underdevelopment. Many researchers found the explanation ethnocentric at best and insulting at worst. Studies also revealed many instances of a single "underdeveloped culture" producing vastly different developmental outcomes; wide variation was observed within supposedly monolithic cultures. In addition, people proved highly capable of tailoring their cultures to conform to more "modern" ways of doing things. Cultures proved to be far more malleable and responsive than had originally been believed. Finally, despite putative cultural limitations, some Third World nations made rapid strides in economic growth; in recent years some middle-income countries, for example, have achieved higher growth rates than many industrialized countries.

The debate on the impact of culture on development continues to be lively, as the reviews of the L. E. Harrison book, excerpted in Chapter 20, have shown. Indeed, Harrison (1992) has published a newer book entitled *Who Prospers? How Cultural Values Shape Economic and Political Success,* and, more recently, Francis Fukuyama (1995a, 1995b) has argued for the importance of trust in development. The debate has become more technical as a series of quantitative studies have attempted to reinvigorate the study of culture (Inglehart 1988, 1990) and other studies have challenged that approach (Booth and Seligson 1984; Seligson and Booth 1993). A recent empirical study on the subject is included in this volume in Chapter 16. That article by Ronald Inglehart and collaborators was strongly refuted, however, by Robert Jackman and Ross Miller in a 1996 article on the subject.

Whatever their explanatory power, cultural explanations no longer dominate the field; as a result, other theories have emerged. Increasingly, thinking about development has become "globalized." The very nature of the gap problem probably forced such thinking to emerge. After all, to study the gap one must first specify the frame of reference in some sort of comparative perspective. Studies can focus on the absolute or on the relative gap, but those terms have no meaning unless they are situated within a comparative framework: Poor people are poor only with respect to rich people.

In this book, extensive consideration has been given to the "inverted U-curve" of development. In global terms, according to Kuznets (Chapter 5) and other proponents of this thesis, developing nations are likely to experience a widening internal gap before they see the gap narrow in the later phases of industrialization. Dependency and world-system thinkers agree that the gaps are widening but do not believe they will ultimately narrow as industrialization matures because the widening internal and external gaps between rich and poor are seen as a function of the world capitalist economic system.

The studies by Maddison (Chapter 3) and Passé-Smith (Chapter 4) suggest strongly that the gaps are very wide and are widening further with each passing decade. Yet, the controversy presented in Part 3 of this book between those who argue that the world economies are on a path toward convergence and those who argue that the gaps are widening shows that the issue has not been resolved.

This disagreement has led some scholars to examine more closely key cases of dependency and development. Heather-Jo Hammer and John W. Gartrell (Chapter 27) show that dependency is not confined to poor nations but seems to affect Canada as well. Yet, the masterful analysis by Glenn Firebaugh (Chapter 26) shows that much of the slowed growth reportedly caused by dependency (as argued by Volker Bornschier and Christopher Chase-Dunn, Chapter 25) comes from a serious misreading of the data. Like the culture paradigm before it, dependency and world-system thinking no longer seems to offer *the* explanation for the gaps between rich and poor.

Current attention is focused on the role of the state, and some of the key thinking in that area is contained in the contributions in Part 6 of this volume. Rent-seeking behavior within states enables privileged groups to benefit from state policies while producing an overall negative impact on the national level of economic development. The contributions by Erich Weede (Chapter 29) and Michael Lipton (Chapter 30) show how rent seeking has a pernicious impact on development. Rent-seeking states, therefore, seem bad for economic growth. At the same time, however, the democratic versus authoritarian nature of the state seems to make little difference in its growth. It was long thought that dictatorships do better than democracies, which allowed such highly regarded scholars as Samuel P. Huntington to suggest that to get development one had to pass through a protected period of strongman rule. Yet, as Adam Przeworski and Fernando Limongi show in Chapter 31, dictatorships seem no better than democracies at stimulating economic development. For a time it appeared the Asian NICs were demonstrating that interventionist, export-oriented states that promoted state capitalism were more successful in both growth and distribution, but the evidence presented by Michael Sarel in Chapter 32 shows that is probably not the case. What does seem to be true, however, is that investment in human capital in the form of education and health really does spur growth and stem inequality (see Nancy Birdsall and Richard Sabot, Chapter 33).

Considerable data have been brought to bear on the various theories seeking to explain these dual gaps. It is in the analysis and interpretation of these data that we see the clearest example of cumulative social science in the making. This book presents some of the best examples of rigorous testing of theory with data. Although it is too early to predict a definitive resolution of the debates, and it may even be too early to say which side seems to have the edge, it is possible to look ahead and suggest some directions for future research. A pessimistic interpretation of the present state of the debate is that each side is locked into its own position, and future research will thus be stalemated. The vital importance of the problem, not only to the world's poor but also to those responsible for helping to secure peace, requires that such a stalemate be avoided. It is therefore appropriate at this juncture to assess where research has taken us and where it ought to go. The contributions in this volume trace the intellectual history of the debate over the gaps; the remainder of this chapter outlines the directions in which fruitful further research might proceed.

THE INTERNATIONAL GAP

By the early 1980s, in GNP per capita terms, a small group of oil-exporting nations enjoyed incomes higher than the average found among industrial market economies. In 1981, Saudi Arabia had a GNP per capita of $12,600; Kuwait, $20,900; and the United Arab Emirates, $24,660; whereas the mean income of the industrial market economies was $11,120. None of the industrialized countries came close to exceeding the incomes of Kuwait and the United Arab Emirates; Switzerland, at $17,430, had the highest GNP per capita of the industrial countries. The United States, traditionally the world's GNP per capita leader, was far behind, at $12,820. Oil-rich Libya was moving up rapidly, with its per capita GNP reaching $8,450, only slightly behind that of the United Kingdom ($9,110).[1]

Yet, we now know that much of the dramatic increase in the GNPs of the oil states was a short-term phenomenon resulting from the sharp petroleum price increases in the 1970s. By 1995, the World Bank (1997:214–215) was reporting that Saudi Arabia had a GNP per capita of only $7,040, compared with the United States, $26,980. Kuwait, still recovering from the Gulf War, had declined to a GNP/pc of $17,390, and the United Arab Emirates had declined to $17,400.

The rapid growth and equally rapid decline of the oil states, however, are the exception to the rule. As John Passé-Smith has shown in Chapter 4, very little movement occurs over the long term from rich to poor and vice versa. Although South Korea, Taiwan, and Malaysia, for example, are rapidly growing, their incomes are only a fraction of those of the industrialized countries. In GNP per capita terms, a near-universal gap is widening between rich and poor.

This conclusion, however, is based on a single indicator—namely GNP per capita. The use of a single indicator of any social phenomenon has long been in disrepute in the social sciences. Why, then, base conclusions about such an important subject entirely on GNP per capita data? The response to this query is that GNP/pc is by far the most widely accepted indicator. The principal problem emerges not because of the unreliability of the data collected on each nation but because of validity problems associated with converting local currency values into dollars using exchange rates, the standard currency normally employed by those who compare such data.

To convert the multitude of currencies used around the world into a single standard, it has long been common practice to use the exchange rate of the foreign currency in U.S. dollars, which appeared to be the only reasonable way to compare the value of different currencies. In fact, however, it is now known that such comparisons introduce considerable distortion into the data. Exchange rate comparisons do not accurately measure differences in the relative domestic purchasing power of currencies. The net result is that exchange rate GNP measures *can* greatly exaggerate the gap between rich and poor countries, in part because international exchange rates are susceptible to fluctuations from equilibrium value. In addition, according to the "law of one price," the cost of goods and services that are traded among countries tends to equalize. For a developing country in which little production enters the world trade market, the exchange rate–converted GNP figures will be an underestimate of true income.

To correct for this bias, the United Nations has undertaken the International Comparisons Project, which has provided some revealing findings.[2] Using purchasing power rather than exchange rates, Passé-Smith (Chapter 12) finds that the gap is less expansive than when measured with exchange rate–converted GNPs but is still considerable. For some countries the change is large; for example, Sri Lanka exhibits nearly four times the gap using the traditional measure than that produced by the new purchasing power index. Countries such as Colombia and Mexico also reveal considerable differences, although those differences are not as great as the case of Sri Lanka.

It seems appropriate to suggest that future research on the international gap should employ the purchasing power index rather than the exchange rate–based comparison to obtain a truer picture of income comparisons. When purchasing power–converted GNPs are used, the gap remains, although it is slightly smaller. Hence, despite the dramatic narrowing of the international gap in the case of Sri Lanka, as noted earlier, even using the purchasing power index, that country's income per capita in 1995 was only 12.1 percent of that of the United States. Kenya, in which the GNP per capita is more than quadrupled with the new index, still confronts income levels that are only 5.1 percent of those of the United States (World Bank 1997:214). The revised measure, therefore, does not eliminate the gap between rich and poor but does provide what appears to be a more appropriate standard of comparison. The mere fact that the gap narrows with the use of the new index does not necessarily imply an overall trend toward a narrowing of the international gap. Fortunately, the World Bank annually reports these purchasing power parity measures in its annual *World Development Report*.

Another way of looking at the gap problem is to shift the focus away from per capita income measures to human needs and human development. Using this criterion, one obtains a rather different perspective of the international gap. According to studies conducted by the World Bank (1980:32–45), major strides have been made in reducing absolute poverty since the end of World War II, and the proportion of people around the world living in absolute poverty has declined. In addition, worldwide literacy levels have increased such that since World War II, literacy in developing countries has risen from 30 percent to over 50 percent of the population. Even more dramatic improvements have been experienced in the area of health. Infant mortality rates have dropped considerably, and life expectancy has been extended. For example, in 1950 citizens of low-income countries had a life expectancy of only 35.2 years, whereas by 1995 that figure had risen to 63.0 years (World Bank 1980:34, 1997:214). The World Bank (1980:35) stated that "the gaps in education and health have narrowed—by 15 percentage points in adult literacy and five years in life expectancy" between industrial and middle-income countries.

Research on the international gap more consciously directed at the indicators of basic human needs may provide a clearer picture of the impact of the gap than that presented by income figures alone. But before one leaps to the conclusion that the human needs approach can demonstrate that the gap is narrowing, some additional context is needed. The *proportion* of people who are experiencing improved education, health, and life expectancy has increased, but the absolute number of poor people in the world has increased dramatically because of high birth rates in the developing world. Hence, in 1980 the World Bank (1980:35) estimated that despite increases in the level of literacy, the number of illiterate people had grown by around 100 million since 1950. And by 1995, in the low-income countries of the world alone, the number of illiterate adults had grown to 1.1 billion compared with 800 million in 1980 (World Bank 1980:110, 1995:214). Moreover, increasing evidence reveals that the quality of education in much of the developing world outside of East Asia lags far behind that found in the industrialized countries. The quality gap is especially acute in secondary and higher education, where technical advances are very rapid and modern training equipment is increasingly expensive. It is increasingly difficult for developing countries to train young people adequately to compete in today's high technology world.

The education gap has two particularly pernicious implications. First, the increasing frustration that the brightest youngsters in developing countries face as a result of antiquated equipment and poorly prepared teachers leads them increasingly to migrate to industrialized nations. Hence, the problem of the brain drain promises to continue to adversely affect poor nations' ability to develop as they steadily lose the sector of their population with the greatest intellectual potential.

Second, the high technology nature of contemporary society seems to be creating a greater and more impenetrable barrier between rich and poor countries. The efficiency of modern manufacturing techniques, along with the requirement of exceptional precision, makes it more and more difficult for developing nations to compete with industrialized nations. Developing nations' price advantage as a result of their considerably lower labor costs remains an advantage only for those items that require relatively low technical inputs. Hence, the proliferation of in-bond industries in the Far East and Latin America, where consumer goods are assembled for reexport, only highlights the gap in technology, since nearly all of the machinery and much of the managerial skill used in those factories are imported from the industrialized nations. Even without tariff barriers, the Third World faces a growing gap in technology that is serving to reinforce the income gap.

In sum, the use of improved income measures and basic needs data provides an important avenue of research for those who wish to study the international income gap. A look at some of these data gives reason for optimism that conditions in poor countries are improving. At the same time, however, there is little reason to believe the international income gap is narrowing. In fact, it appears that each day the world is inhabited by a larger *number* of people who live in absolute poverty, even though the *proportion* of the population in absolute poverty may be declining. This gap, then, seems to remain the most serious problem confronting the family of nations and is one that cries out for the attention of policymakers.

THE INTERNAL GAP

However problematic the reliability, validity, and availability of data on the international gap may be, they present an even more formidable barrier to the study of the internal gap. The empirical testing of dependency and world-system explanations for the internal gap has produced widely varying results. Any reader of the major social science journals today is rightly confused by the varied findings reported in the ever more frequent articles on the subject. In reviewing this growing body of research, Edward N. Muller (1993) has pointed out a number of the weaknesses and goes a long way toward correcting many of them. The data set presented in this volume by Klaus Deininger and Lyn Squire (Chapter 7) gives us the best measure to date. Nonetheless, at least four chronic problems beset macrolevel empirical tests of internal gap theories, and they may ultimately lead down a blind alley of inconclusive findings even after the "best" methodology has been applied.

The first difficulty plaguing these macroanalytic investigations concerns sample skewing. Inequality data are difficult to obtain because many nations do not collect them (or at least do not publicly acknowledge doing so), a problem noted in several of the chapters in this volume. In spite of the availability problem, researchers have proceeded with the data that *are* available, following the time-honored tradition in the social sciences of making do with what one finds rather than postponing research indefinitely.

Although such a procedure is justifiable in many research situations, one wonders if it is in this one. The principal reason for this cautionary note is that the countries reporting income distribution data are probably not a random sample of all nations. Rather, one suspects that at least two factors tend to skew the sample. First, the poorest, least developed nations often lack the resources (financial and technical) to conduct such studies; indeed, the need may not even arise to collect such data in some of these nations. For example, whereas all of the countries in the 1997 *World Development Report* with GNPs at least as high as that of the United Kingdom reported income distribution data, six of the ten poorest countries in the world did not (World Bank 1997:222–223). Second, nations in which income distributions are badly skewed are probably reluctant to authorize the collection of such data; even if the data are collected, governments may not make them publicly available. Hence, the data we do have may reflect a sample that has fewer cases of the poorest nations and of highly unequal distribution than one might expect if the sample were random.

The second major problem with macroanalytic investigations is a direct outgrowth of the first. I call this problem the "Mauritania effect," that is, the dramatic differences in regression results produced by the inclusion or exclusion of as few as one or two countries. In one investigation, for example, the inclusion of Mauritania, with a population of only 2.3 million people, had a major impact on the results of a key regression equation (Muller 1993). The findings tend not to be robust when minor variations in sample design occur; one's confidence in the results is therefore shaken: "It seems impossible to predict with any confidence what would happen if inequality data on all or about twice as many countries were to become available" (Weede and Tiefenbach 1981 as cited in Seligson 1984, 238).

The third problem concerns the general lack of cross-time data. However limited the sample of countries for the present period, even less reliable information exists on developing countries for the pre–World War II period. This problem is particularly serious since both dependency/world-system analysis and the traditional developmental approach propose longitudinal hypotheses, whereas data limitations generally impose cross-sectional designs. Although such designs can sometimes be a useful surrogate for longitudinal studies, the problem of skewed samples reduces the value of those studies.

One serious manifestation of the lack of longitudinal data emerges in studies that include Latin American cases. As a region, Latin America is more developed than most Third World nations, and not surprisingly, some-what more income distribution data are available than is true of other Third World regions. Latin American nations have also been found to exhibit comparatively high levels of both dependency and income inequality. One might conclude, as some have, that this proves inequality is a function of dependency. Another, equally appealing thesis, however, suggests that inequality in Latin America is part of a corporatist bureaucratic-authoritarian political culture considered characteristic of the region. One does not know, therefore, if Latin America's comparatively high level of inequality is a function of its intermediate level of development (as Kuznets [Chapter 5] suggests), its dependency (as the dependency/world-system proponents suggest [Chapters 22–27]), or its political culture (Chapter 20). To determine which of these hypotheses is correct would require longitudinal data to explore the dynamics of dependency, development, and inequality.

A final difficulty with macroanalytic research is that no meeting of the minds exists about what constitutes suitable standards of verifiability. For example, a wide gulf separates many dependency/world-system theorists and researchers who seek to test their hypotheses with quantitative data. Cardoso and Faletto (1979), whose book on dependency theory is among the most influential and highly respected works on the subject (see Pakenham 1982:131–132), argue that empirical tests of dependency theory have largely missed the target. Cardoso (1977:23, n. 12) explains that this is so because the tests have been "ahistorical." In addition, although Cardoso does not reject empirical verification as useful, he questions the validity of many of these studies, even those that sustain the dependency approach. Finally, in the preface to the English edition of their book, Cardoso and Faletto argue that "statistical information and demonstrations are useful and necessary. But the crucial questions for demonstration are of a different nature" (Cardoso and Faletto 1979.xiii). The demonstrations proposed are heavily grounded in historical detail and therefore highlight all the more the lack of longitudinal income distribution data. The chapter by J. Samuel Valenzuela and Arturo Valenzuela in this volume (Chapter 23) argues this point very clearly.

In the coming years, many more macroanalytic empirical investigations will likely be published and will continue to add to our understanding. It is difficult to imagine, however, how the four major problems enumerated here will be overcome entirely. Given the difficulties apparently inherent (to a greater or lesser degree) in the macroanalytic studies conducted to date, more attention needs to be paid to methodologies that will examine the origin of domestic inequality from a microanalytic perspective. In concluding an extensive review of the dependency/world-system literature, Palma (1981:413) argues for microstudies of "specific situations in concrete terms." And the study by Bornschier, Chase-Dunn, and Rubinson (1978 as cited in Seligson 1984, 205) concludes by arguing for microsociological studies that would "clarify the specific mechanisms by which these processes operate."

Problems of data availability need not lead to the abandonment of future studies of the internal gap. Rather, a series of microanalytic studies seems to be a promising alternative. Such investigations would make it possible to trace the ways in which inequality is stimulated in developing countries. The emphasis needs to be placed on drawing the explicit links, if they exist, between income distribution and factors such as culture, dependency, rent seeking, and urban bias. Indeed, it can be argued that even if the data problems were not as serious as they are and if macroanalytic empirical research were to demonstrate unequivocally the existence of a connection between, for example, culture and domestic inequality, one would still need to understand *how* one affects the other—something that cannot be known from the macrostudies. Without knowing how the process works, it is impossible to recommend policy "cures."

Some research has already opened the door to this type of analysis. Studies of transnational corporations in Colombia (Chudnowsky 1974) and Brazil (Evans 1979; Newfarmer 1980) reveal much about the internal dynamics of dependency. A more recent microstudy has demonstrated that imperialist penetration in one African state, Yorubaland, at the end of the nineteenth century produced a "vibrant and creative" reaction by Yoruba traders to new opportunities in the international market (Laitin 1982:702).

These microanalytic studies, helpful though they are in beginning to penetrate the "black box," reflect weaknesses that need to be overcome by those seeking to test the various explanations of income inequality proposed in this volume. First, these detailed case studies, although they provide a wealth of rich, descriptive material, betray all of the limitations of generalizability inherent in the case study method. It is hoped, of course, that the accumulation of these various cases will ultimately lead to a synthesis; but given the widely divergent methods, time periods, and databases employed in these studies, it is unclear at this juncture whether such optimism is warranted. What *is* clear is that if a cumulative social science is to continue to emerge in this field, future research will need to be not only microanalytic but self-consciously comparative as well. Only by applying the comparative method at the outset of a study of the internal causes of inequality will the data generated allow immediate comparisons and subsequent theory testing.

In sum, an appropriate study should be microanalytic, comparative, and capable of testing the relative merits of competing paradigms. That is a tall order for any researcher, but one way to achieve this goal and still plan a project of manageable proportions is to focus on key institutions through which dependency mechanisms are thought to operate. In an effort to accomplish this task, one study analyzed exchange rate policies as the "linchpin" that helps to "uncover the mechanisms through which these various [dependency] effects occur" (Moon 1982:716). A major advance of this study over previous work is the explicit linking of dependency effects to particular policies of Third World governments. Hence, the analysis goes far beyond most dependency literature, which typically makes frequent reference to the so-called internal colonialist comprador elite without revealing precisely how such elites affect income distribution. Studies such as Moon's, which examine the impact of other such crucial linchpins through which dependency is thought to operate, should be encouraged.

Two efforts, therefore, need to be made if one is to hope for the debate to advance beyond its present state. First, historians need to assist those working in this field to develop measures of income distribution for prior epochs. Creative use of historical records (e.g., tax roles, property registers, and census data) might permit the reconstruction of such information. Reconstruction, in turn, would provide the longitudinal data that are so sadly lacking. John H. Coatsworth (1993) has done this for Latin America, and the payoffs of his approach are evident, since he seems to have been able to refute dependency theory and make a case for the role of institutions in development and underdevelopment. William Glade (1996) recently extended this argument. Second, once the historical data have been gathered, social scientists must direct their attention to the various linchpins of the causes of growth and inequality and study them in a comparative context. Perhaps with these two efforts under way, significant advances can be made in a relatively short period.

CONCLUSION

The research presented in this volume was not written in a vacuum. Investigators study problems such as the gap between rich and poor because they are concerned, and the great majority hope their findings will ultimately be translated into public policy. Even though definitive findings are still far from our grasp, as has been made clear by the debate presented in this volume, many world leaders have sought to implement policies to correct the problem.

As the gaps between rich and poor grow wider throughout the world, the debate grows more heated. Discussions in international forums today are characterized by increasing intolerance. It is hoped that this collection of studies, along with the suggestions made in this concluding chapter, will help in some small way to moderate tempers and guide thinking and research toward more productive answers to this important question.

NOTES

1. The data are from World Bank (1983).
2. See Kravis et al. (1975, 1982). A summary explanation is provided in World Bank (1997:251).

REFERENCES

Booth, J. A., and M. A. Seligson. 1984. "The Political Culture of Authoritarianism in Mexico: A Reexamination." *Latin American Research Review* (no. 1): 106–124.

Bornschier, V., C. Chase-Dunn, and R. Rubinson. 1978. "Cross-National Evidence of the Effects of Foreign Investment and Aid on Economic Growth and Inequality: A Survey of Findings and a Reanalysis." *American Journal of Sociology* 84 (November): 651–685.

———. 1984. "Cross-national Evidence of the Effects of Foreign Investment and Aid on Economic Growth and Inequality: A Survey of Findings and a Reanalysis," in Mitchell A. Seligson, ed., *The Gap Between Rich and Poor: Contending Perspectives on the Political Economy of Development*. Boulder: Westview.

Cardoso, F. H. 1977. "The Consumption of Dependency Theory in the United States." *Latin American Research Review* 12 (3): 7–24.

Cardoso, F. H., and E. Faletto. 1979. *Dependency and Development in Latin America*. Berkeley: University of California Press.

Chudnowsky, D. 1974. *Empresas multinacionales y ganancias monopolicias en una economía latinoamericana*. Buenos Aires: Siglo XXI Editores.

Coatsworth, John H. 1993. "Notes on the Comparative Economic History of Latin America and the United States." In Walther L. Bernecker and Hans Werner Tobler (eds.), *Development and Underdevelopment in America: Contrasts of Economic Growth in North and Latin America in Historical Perspective*. New York: Walter de Gruyter.

Evans, P. 1979. *Dependent Development: The Alliance of Multinational, State and Local Capital in Brazil*. Princeton: Princeton University Press.

Fukuyama, Francis. 1995a. "Social Capital and the Global Economy." *Foreign Affairs* 74 (September–October): 89–103.

———. 1995b. *Trust: The Social Virtues and the Creation of Prosperity*. New York: Free Press.

Glade, William. 1996. "Institutions and Inequality in Latin America: Text and Subtext." *Journal of Interamerican Studies and World Affairs* 38 (Summer–Fall): 159–179.

Harrison, L. E. 1992. *Who Prospers? How Cultural Values Shape Economic and Political Success*. New York: Basic Books.

Inglehart, R. 1988. "The Renaissance of Political Culture." *American Political Science Review* 82 (December): 1203–1230.

———. 1990. *Culture Shift in Advanced Industrial Societies*. Princeton: Princeton University Press.

Jackman, R. W., and R. A. Miller. 1996. "The Poverty of Political Culture." *American Journal of Political Science* 40 (August): 697–717.

Kravis, Irving B., Zoltan Kenessey, Alan Heston, and Robert Summerrs. 1975. *A System of International Comparisons of Gross Product and Purchasing Power*. Baltimore: Johns Hopkins University Press.

———. 1982. *World Product and Income: International Comparisons of Real GDP*. Baltimore: Johns Hopkins University Press.

Laitin, D. D. 1982. "Capitalism and Hegemony: Yorubaland and the International Economy." *International Organization* 36 (Autumn): 687–714.

Moon, B. E. 1982. "Exchange Rate System, Policy Distortions, and the Maintenance of Trade Dependence." *International Organization* 36 (Autumn): 715–740.

Muller, Edward N. 1993. "Financial Dependence in the Capitalist World Economy and the Distribution of Income Within States." In Mitchell A. Seligson and John T Passé-Smith (eds.), *Development and Underdevelopment: The Political Economy of Inequality.* Boulder: Lynne Rienner.

Newfarmer, R. 1980. *Transnational Conglomerates and the Economics of Dependent Development: A Case Study of the International Electrical Oligopoly and Brazil's Electrical Industry.* Greenwich, Conn.: JAI.

Packenham, R. A. 1982. "Plus ça change . . . : The English Edition of Cardoso and Faletto's Dependencia y Desarrollo en América Latina." *Latin American Research Review* 17 (1): 131–151.

Palma, G. 1981. "Dependency: A Formal Theory of Underdevelopment or a Methodology for the Analysis of Concrete Situations." In Paul Streetin and Richard Jolly (eds.), *Recent Issues in World Development.* New York: Pergamon.

Ray, J. L., and T. Webster. 1978. "Dependency and Economic Growth in Latin America." *International Studies Quarterly* 22 (September): 409–434.

Seligson, M. A., and J. A. Booth. 1993. "Political Culture and Regime Type: Evidence from Nicaragua and Costa Rica." *Journal of Politics* 55 (August): 777–792.

Weede, E., and H. Tiefenbach. 1981. "Some Recent Explanations of Income Inequality." *International Studies Quarterly* 25 (June): 255–282.

———. 1984. "Some Recent Explanations of Income Inequality," in Mitchell A. Seligson, ed., *The Gap Between Rich and Poor: Contending Perspectives on the Political Economy of Development.* Boulder: Westview.

World Bank. 1980. *World Development Report 1980.* New York: Oxford University Press.

———. 1982. *World Development Report 1982.* New York: Oxford University Press.

———. 1992. *World Development Report 1992.* New York: Oxford University Press.

———. 1993. *World Development Report 1993.* New York: Oxford University Press.

———. 1995. *World Development Report 1995.* New York: Oxford University Press.

———. 1997. *World Development Report 1997.* New York: Oxford University Press.

Appendix:
Basic Indicators
of the Gaps Between
Rich and Poor for
133 Countries

Appendix
Basic Indicators of the Gaps Between Rich and Poor for 133 Countries

	GNP per capita[a]		PPP Estimates of GNP per Capita (current int'l $ estimates)[b]	Life Expectancy at Birth (years) 1995	Adult Illiteracy 1995		Percentage Share of Income or Consumption	
	Dollars 1995	Average Annual Growth (%) 1985–1995			Female	Male	Highest 20%	Year
Low-Income economies	430w	3.8w	—	63w	45w	24w	—	—
Excluding China and India	290w	-1.4w	—	56w	55w	37w	—	—
1. Mozambique	80	3.6	810[c]	47	77	42	—	—
2. Ethiopia[m]	100	-0.3	450	49	75	55	—	—
3. Tanzania[d]	120	1.0	640[c]	51	43	21	45.4	1993[eh]
4. Burundi	160	-1.3	630	49	78	51	—	—
5. Malawi	170	-0.7	750	43	58	28	—	—
6. Chad	180	0.6	700[c]	48	65	38	—	—
7. Rwanda	180	-5.4	540	46	48	30	39.1	1983–1985[eh]
8. Sierra Leone	180	-3.6	580	40	82	55	—	—
9. Nepal	200	2.4	1,170[c]	55	86	59	44.8	1995–1996[eh]
10. Niger	220	—	750[c]	47	93	79	44.1	1992[eh]
11. Burkina Faso	230	-0.2	780[c]	49	91	71	—	—
12. Madagascar	230	-2.2	640	52	74	51	50.0	1993[eh]
13. Bangladesh	240	2.1	1,380	58	50	26	37.9	1992[eh]
14. Uganda	240	2.7	1,470[c]	42	50	26	48.1	1992–1993[eh]
15. Vietnam	240	—	—	68	9	4	44.0	1993[eh]
16. Guinea-Bissau	250	2.0	790[c]	38	58	32	58.9	1991[eh]
17. Haiti	250	-5.2	910[c]	57	58	52	—	—
18. Mali	250	0.8	550	50	77	61	—	—
19. Nigeria	260	1.2	1,220	53	53	33	49.3	1992–1993[eh]
20. Yemen, Republic of	260	—	—	53	—	—	—	—
21. Cambodia	270	—	—	53	47	20	—	—
22. Kenya	280	0.1	1,380	58	30	14	62.1	1992[eh]
23. Mongolia	310	-3.8	1,950	65	—	—	—	—
24. Togo	310	-2.7	1,130[c]	56	63	33	—	—
25. Gambia, The	320	—	930[c]	46	75	47	—	—

26. Central African Republic	340	-2.4	1,070[c]	48	48	32	—	—
27. India	340	3.2	1,400	62	62	35	42.6	1992[eh]
28. Laos, PDR	350	2.7	—	52	56	31	40.2	1992[eh]
29. Benin	370	-0.3	1,760	50	74	51	—	1993[eh]
30. Nicaragua	380	-5.4	2,000[c]	68	33	35	55.2	1993[eh]
31. Ghana	390	1.4	1,990[c]	59	47	24	42.2	1992[eh]
32. Zambia	400	-0.8	930	46	29	14	50.4	1993[eh]
33. Angola	410	-6.1	1,310	47	—	—	—	—
34. Georgia[f]	440	-17.0	1,470	73	—	—	—	—
35. Pakistan	460	..2	2,230	60	76	50	39.7	1991[eh]
36. Mauritania	450	0.5	1,540[c]	51	74	50	46.5	1988[eh]
37. Azerbaijan	430	-10.3	1,460	70	—	—	—	—
38. Zimbabwe	540	-0.6	2,030	57	20	10	62.3	1990[eh]
39. Guinea	550	1.4	—	44	78	50	50.2	1991[eh]
40. Honduras	600	0.1	1,900	67	27	27	57.4	1992[ij]
41. Senegal	600	—	1,780	50	77	52	58.6	1991[eh]
42. China	620	8.3	2,920	69	27	10	47.5	1995[ij]
43. Cameroon	650	-6.6	2,110	57	48	25	—	—
44. Cote D'Ivoire	660	—	1,580	55	70	50	44.1	1988[eh]
45. Albania	670	—	—	73	—	—	—	—
46. Congo	680	-3.2	2,050	51	33	17	—	—
47. Kyrgyz Republic[f]	700	-6.9	1,300	68	—	—	—	—
48. Sri Lanka	700	2.5	3,250	72	13	—	39.3	1990[eh]
49. Armenia[f]	730	-15.1	2,260	71	—	—	—	—
Middle-income	2,390[w]	-0.7[w]	—	68[w]	23[w]	14[w]	—	—
Lower-middle-income	1,670[w]	-1.3[w]	—	67[w]	—	—	—	—
50. Lesotho	770	1.2	1,730[c]	51	38	19	60.1	1986–1987[eh]
51. Egypt, Arab Rep.	790	1.1	3,820	53	61	36	41.1	1991[eh]
52. Bolivia	800	1.8	2,540	60	24	10	48.2	1990[ij]
53. Macedonia, FYR	850	—	—	73	—	—	—	—
54. Moldova[f]	920	-3.5	2,370	69	—	—	41.5	1992[ij]
55. Uzbekistan	970	—	3,800	70	22	10	—	—
56. Indonesia	980	6.0	2,850	64	6	5	40.7	1993[eh]
57. Philippines	1,050	1.5	—	56	69	43	47.8	1988[eh]
58. Morocco	1,110	0.9	3,340	65	—	—	46.3	1990–1991[eh]

	GNP per capita[a]		PPP Estimates of GNP per Capita (current int'l $ estimates)[b]	Life Expectancy at Birth (years) 1995	Adult Illiteracy 1995		Percentage Share of Income or Consumption	
	Dollars 1995	Average Annual Growth (%) 1985–1995			Female	Male	Highest 20%	Year
59. Syrian Arab Republic	1,120	0.9	5,320	68	44	14	—	—
60. Papua New Guinea	1,160	2.3	2,420c	57	37	19	—	—
61. Bulgaria	1,330	-2.6	4,480	71	—	—	39.3	1992ij
62. Kazakstan[f]	1,330	-8.6	3,010	69	—	—	40.4	1993ij
63. Guatemala	1,340	0.3	3,340	66	51	38	63.0	1989ij
64. Ecuador	1,390	0.8	4,220	69	12	8	52.6	1994eh
65. Dominican Republic	1,460	2.1	3,870	69	18	18	55.7	1989ij
66. Romania	1,480	-3.8	4,360	71	—	—	34.8	1992ij
67. Jamaica	1,510	3.6	3,540	70	11	19	47.5	1991eh
68. Jordan	1,510	-4.5	4,060c	74	21	—	50.1	1991eh
69. Algeria	1,600	-2.4	5,300	70	51	26	46.1	1988eh
70. El Salvador	1,610	2.8	2,610	70	30	27	35.4	1992ij
71. Ukraine[f]	1,630	-9.2	2,400	67	—	—	—	
72. Paraguay	1,690	1.2	3,650	69	9	—	46.3	1990eh
73. Tunisia	1,820	1.9	5,000	68	45	21	42.1	1993ij
74. Lithuania[f]	1,900	11.7	4,120	69	—	—	55.8	1991ij
75. Colombia	1,910	2.6	6,130	69	9	9	—	
76. Namibia	2,000	2.9	4,150c	70	—	—	32.9	1993ij
77. Belarus[f]	2,070	-5.2	4,220	59	—	—	53.8	1993eh
78. Russian Federation[f]	2,240	-5.1	4,480	70	—	—	36.7	1993ij
79. Latvia[f]	2,270	-6.6	3,370	65	—	—	50.4	1994eh
80. Peru	2,310	-1.6	3,770	69	17	6	50.7	1989ij
81. Costa Rica	2,610	2.8	5,850	66	5	5	—	
82. Lebanon	2,660	—	—	77	10	5	—	
83. Thailand	2,740	8.4	7,540	68	8	4	52.7	1992eh
84. Panama	2,750	-0.4	5,980	69	10	9	59.8	1989ij
85. Turkey	2,780	2.2	5,580	73	28	8	—	
86. Poland	2,790	1.2	5,400	67	—	—	36.6	1992eh
87. Estonia	2,860	-4.3	4,220	70	—	—	46.3	1993ij
88. Slovak Republic	2,950	-2.8	3,610	72	—	—	31.4	1992ij

89. Botswana	3,020	6.1	5,580	68	40	20	—	—
90. Venezuela	3,020	0.5	7,900	71	10	8	58.4	1990[ij]
Upper-middle-income	4,260[w]	0.2[w]	—	69[w]	14[w]	12[w]	—	—
91. South Africa	3,160	-1.1	3,030[c]	64	18	18	63.3	1993[eh]
92. Croatia	3,250	—	—	74	—	—	—	—
93. Mexico	3,320	0.1	3,400	72	13	8	55.3	1992[eh]
94. Mauritius	3,380	5.4	13,210	71	21	13	—	—
95. Gabon	3,490	-8.2	—	55	47	26	—	—
96. Brazil	3,640	-0.8	5,400	67	17	17	67.8	1989
97. Trinidad and Tobago	3,770	-1.7	8,610[c]	72	3	1	—	—
98. Czech Republic	3,870	-1.8	9,770	73	—	—	—	—
99. Malaysia	3,890	5.7	9,020	71	22	11	37.4	1993[ij]
100. Hungary	4,120	-1.0	6,410	70	—	—	53.7	1989[ij]
101. Chile	4,160	6.1	9,520	72	5	5	36.6	1993[eh]
102. Oman	4,820	0.3	8,140[c]	70	—	—	61.0	1994[ij]
103. Uruguay	5,170	3.1	6,630	73	2	3	—	—
104. Saudi Arabia	7,040	-1.9	—	70	50	29	—	—
105. Argentina	8,030	1.8	8,310	73	4	4	—	—
106. Slovenia	8,200	—	—	74	—	—	37.9	1993[ij]
107. Greece	8,210	1.3	11,710	78	—	—	—	—
High-income	24,530[w]	1.9[w]	—	77[w]	—	—	—	—
108. Korea, Rep. of	9,700	7.7	11,450	72	n	n	—	—
109. Portugal	9,740	3.6	12,670	75	—	—	—	—
110. Spain	13,580	2.6	14,520	77	—	—	36.6	1988[kl]
111. New Zealand	14,340	0.8	16,360	76	n	n	44.7	1981-1982[kl]
112. Ireland	14,710	5.2	15,680	77	n	n	—	—
113. Israel[z]	15,920	2.5	16,490	77	—	—	39.6	1979[kl]
114. Kuwait[z]	17,390	1.1	23,790[c]	76	25	18	—	—
115. United Arab Emirates[z]	17,400	-2.8	16,470	75	20	21	—	—
116. United Kingdom	18,700	1.4	19,260	77	n	n	44.3	1988[kl]
117. Australia	18,720	1.4	18,940	77	n	n	42.2	1985[kl]
118. Italy	19,020	1.8	19,870	78	n	n	41.0	1986[kl]
119. Canada	19,380	0.4	21,130	78	n	n	40.2	1987[kl]

	GNP per capita[a]		PPP Estimates of GNP per Capita (current int'l $ estimates)[b]	Life Expectancy at Birth (years) 1995	Adult Illiteracy 1995		Percentage Share of Income or Consumption	
	Dollars 1995	Average Annual Growth (%) 1985–1995			Female	Male	Highest 20%	Year
120. Finland	20,580	0.2	17,760	76	n	n	37.6	1981[kl]
121. Hong Kong[z]	22,990	4.8	22,950[g]	79	12	4	47.0	1980[kl]
122. Sweden	23,750	-0.1	18,540	79	n	n	36.9	1981[kl]
123. Netherlands	24,000	1.9	19,950	78	n	n	36.9	1988[kl]
124. Belgium	24,710	2.2	21,660	77	n	n	36.0	1978–1979[kl]
125. France	24,990	1.5	21,030	78	n	n	41.9	1989[kl]
126. Singapore[z]	26,730	6.2	22,770[c]	76	14	4	48.9	1982–1983[kl]
127. Austria	26,890	1.9	21,250	77	n	n	—	—
128. United States	26,980	1.3	26,980	76	n	n	41.9	1985[kl]
129. Germany[o]	27,510	—	20,070	76	n	n	40.3	1988[kl]
130. Denmark	29,890	1.5	21,230	75	n	n	38.6	1981[kl]
131. Norway	31,250	1.7	21,940	78	n	n	36.7	1979[kl]
132. Japan	39,640	2.9	22,110	80	n	n	37.5	1979[kl]
133. Switzerland	40,630	0.2	25,860	78	n	n	44.6	1982[kl]
World	4,880w	0.8w	—	67w	—	—	—	—

Source: Data are from the *World Development Report, 1997* (tables 1, 5, and 7).

Notes: a. Atlas methods; see technical note [in the original text]. b. Purchasing Power Parity; see technical notes. c. Estimate is based on regression. d. GNP and GDP cover mainland Tanzania. e. Refers to expenditure shares by percentiles of persons. f. Estimates for economies of the former Soviet Union. g. Data refer to GDP. h. Ranked by per capita expenditure. i. Refers to income shares by percentiles of persons. j. Ranked by per capita income. k. Refers to income shares of households. l. Ranked by household income. m. Data for 1980 include Eritrea. n. According to UNESCO, illiteracy is less than 5 percent. o. Data before 1990 refer to the Federal Republic of Germany before unification. w. Weighted [see original text for methodology]. z. Economies classified by the United Nations or otherwise regarded by their authorities as developing.

Index

About the Book

This revised and expanded edition of *Development and Underdevelopment* retains many of the selections that made the first edition so popular for classroom use while adding new material to make it even more appealing. New material includes studies that enable readers to trace levels of national development back to the beginning of the nineteenth century and in some cases even earlier, income inequality data on more than twice the number of countries included in the first edition, coverage of important theoretical advances, and new work on the role of education in development. The book continues to feature short introductions to each reading, highlighting the significance of the selections.

Mitchell A. Seligson is Daniel H. Wallace Professor of Political Science at the University of Pittsburgh. His many publications include *Elections and Democracy in Central America, Revisited* (coedited) and *The Gap Between Rich and Poor: Contending Perspectives on the Political Economy of Development*. **John T Passé-Smith** is associate professor of political science at the University of Central Arkansas. He is coauthor of *The Unionization of the Maquiladora Industry: The Tamaulipan Case in National Context* and coeditor of *International Political Economy: State-Market Relations in the Changing Global Order*.